THE OPEN COURT
LIBRARY OF PHILOSOPHY
SERIES EDITOR
Eugene Freeman
SAN JOSE STATE COLLEGE

KANT
STUDIES
Today

KANT
STUDIES
Today

Edited by **LEWIS W. BECK**

OPEN COURT • LA SALLE, ILLINOIS

KANT STUDIES TODAY

Library of Congress Catalog Card Number: 68-57207

Printed in the United States of America

CONTENTS

PREFACE

The reputation of, and the interest in, a philosopher of the past rises and falls from decade to decade. Some will see in this only fads in intellectual history. But there is more to it than that. Philosophy uses its past. As philosophical questions change, it is natural that thinkers will give their attention to earlier philosophers who have dealt with the problems they themselves confront. Thus in the 'thirties and 'forties, Hume was the subject of perhaps the most intense historical inquiry and philosophical exploitation, since Anglo-Saxon philosophy at that time had most in common with Hume's situation. Upon the decline of logical positivism as a *Wissenschaftstheorie* with a too simple structure and a too ready dismissal of some intractable problems, it is natural that in the 'fifties and 'sixties Hume's successor Kant should be at the focus of attention of men looking for stimulus or guidance from the past. The decline of purely emotive theories and a new appreciation of the role of reason in ethics no doubt contributed to the same effect. There is, indeed, some intimation now that the history of philosophy may be recapitulated in the future course of interest in that history; if so, we may anticipate a markedly increased attention to post-Kantian speculative philosophy. But that time has not yet come, and now in 1968 it is still true that Kant is the pre-twentieth-century philosopher most in the minds of men moving forward on their own paths. He stands closest to the junctures of contemporary philosophical issues, either as a warning or as a guide.

When the editors of *The Monist* announced that we would devote an issue to papers under the general title "Kant Today," we desired and expected contributions by well-known students of Kant, and were gratified to receive them in good measure. What we did not anticipate was a kind of fraternal response from philosophers who had not hitherto make known, through extensive publication, how deep was their interest in Kant. We were surprised to learn how many of them had been reading, meditating upon, and learning from Kant, and how many of them still thought old Kant was still a figure alive enough to merit their critical attention. Together the two groups of writers show how much contemporary light can be thrown back upon Kant's problems and how much Kantian light can be thrown upon those of our own day. It was this meeting of interests from both quarters which occasioned the reflections in the previous paragraph.

It also forced the editors of *The Monist* to make two considerable changes in their plans. The number of papers we received in answer to our original announcement and invitation was so large that we decided to relieve the pain of having to reject papers that ought to be published by reserving not one but two issues of *The Monist* for papers on "Kant Today." Still the papers came in, and then it was decided to publish a book of them. Hence the present volume. Even so, we must express our thanks to many authors who submitted papers for which we still could not find room; and our regrets to our readers for making them await the publication of these papers elsewhere.

In a volume which grew from the spontaneous interests of the contributors and without the strong guiding hand of an editor assigning topics, it is natural that not all aspects of present concern with Kant would be equally represented. No German scholars offered us papers, and hence the ontological interpretation of Kant now so widespread among them is not present here except in one paper by an American student of the movement, Mr. Sherover. Most surprising is the fact that Kant's ethics, which is surely receiving as much attention and analysis and is the subject of as vigorous debate as his theory of knowledge, should have been taken up by so few contributors; only Mr. Murphy devotes his entire paper to this. Hardly less astonishing is the fact that the growing interest in Kant's aesthetic theory was not shown by any contributors, and that only Mr. Collins let us have a paper on the philosophy of religion. Fortunately Mr. Scott-Taggart rectifies the near one-sidedness by giving a comprehensive review of many different topics discussed in recent writings about Kant.

But how manifold are the contributions on the theory of knowledge! Messrs. Paton and Turbayne discuss Kant's relation to two of his forebears. The next papers are ordered roughly in the way in which their topics arise in the *Critique of Pure Reason:* Messrs. Hintikka, Vuillemin, Sellars, Gram, and Walsh are concerned with

space, time, intuition, and the philosophy of mathematics; Messrs.
Körner, Garver, and Barker deal with some basic problems Kant
discussed, or ought to have discussed, in the Analytic of Concepts;
Mr. Butts, Mrs. Milmed, and Messrs. Buchdahl and Suchting are
alike in their interest in the Analytic of Principles and especially
the Analogies; Messrs. French and Baumer (as well as Mr. Gram)
deal with problems arising in the Dialectic. While the isomorphism
of this arrangement of papers and the major divisions of the *Critique* is not perfect, only the papers by Messrs. Sherover and Michel
fail to fit quite neatly under any simple rubrics of topics in the
Critique.

The essays in this book were published in *The Monist,* Volume
51, numbers 3 and 4, with the exception of the following. Mr. Scott-
Taggart's paper was originally published, in a somewhat different
form, in the *American Philosophical Quarterly,* Volume III, (1966),
pp. 171-209. He has substantially revised it in order to take account
of still later publications. I am grateful to the editor of that journal,
Professor Nicholas Rescher, for permission to reprint it and to Mr.
Scott-Taggart for making revisions. Mr. Turbayne's paper first appeared in *The Philosophical Quarterly,* Volume V, (1955), pp. 225-
244 under the title, "Kant's Refutation of Dogmatic Idealism," and
appears here, slightly modified, with the kind permission of Professor G. P. Henderson, the editor of *The Philosophical Quarterly.* Mr.
Suchting's paper was published in *Kant-Studien,* vol. LVIII (1967),
pp. 355-69, and I am grateful to the editor, Professor Gottfried
Martin for permission to reprint it. M. Vuillemin's paper appeared
in French in *The Monist* and is here for the first time in English. The
papers by Messrs. Buchdahl, Butts, and Paton have not previously
been published.

I am grateful to my colleagues on the editorial board of *The
Monist,* especially Professors Eugene Freeman, Wilfrid Sellars, and
John E. Smith, for much helpful advice in choosing among the
papers. The final responsibility for the decisions reached, however,
is mine alone.

LEWIS WHITE BECK

UNIVERSITY OF ROCHESTER

RECENT WORK ON THE PHILOSOPHY OF KANT

1. *Introduction*

I have been able to limit the scope of this review because of the existence of two good surveys of the literature made by de Vlee-schauwer [2,3].[1] Presupposing acquaintance with these I have been able to deal only fleetingly with books previous to 1960, and hence to deal more fully with articles going back to the *Festschriften* of 1954. My treatment is necessarily selective, and reflects, besides my own interests, largely those areas where there is some unity of discussion.

Although for several decades there was a fair degree of commerce between the Continental and the English-speaking schools, the last twenty or thirty years have seen a considerable divergence of both interests and methods. About the English scene I shall say little at this stage. There has been a great deal of activity in connection with both the first two *Critiques,* and the last year has seen something essentially new in Kantian studies with the books of Bennett [3] and Strawson [3]. At the same time there have been a number of excellent translations of Kant's works (sometimes, to my view, marred by a failure to include the Akademie edition pagination). Beck's translations of the second *Critique* and the *Foundations* set the standard, and of the following translations those of the *Metaphysical Principles of Virtue* (Mary Gregor, and James Ellington's with a good introduction by W. A. Wick), the *Metaphysical Elements of Justice* (John Ladd), and selected writings on history (Beck, Anchor, Fackenheim), deserve special attention, while Cerf's translation of the *Analytic of the Beautiful* is distinguished by its

---

[1] Details of the works mentioned can be collected from the bibliography: "[3:121]" refers to p. 121 of the third work of the author mentioned; "[3]" refers either to the third work, or to p. 3 of the only work, of the author mentioned; "[Ak. II.273]" refers to vol. II, p. 273 of the Prussian Academy edition of Kant's work.

philosophical introduction, and Zweig's *Kant: Philosophical Correspondence 1759-99* is exemplary in its translation as in its scholarship, while providing material that will be useful to the most unscholarly.

If we turn to the Continent we find interest centered largely on the first *Critique*. While English commentary has tended to stem through Paton and Kemp Smith from the work of Adickes and Vaihinger, things happened in Germany in and around 1924 that have scarcely begun to influence the English scene—quite apart from the work of Husserl which, in its relation to Kant, has been the subject of an informed if somewhat uncritical inquiry by Kern. Most significant of these were the works of Max Wundt, Nicolai Hartmann, and Heimsoeth [cf. §§2-3] (and, in a somewhat different way, Heidegger) which provided a point of departure for a school which has come to be known as the ontological or historico-ontological school. While not all German authors can be reckoned as belonging to this school, most can be shown to be influenced by it, or, at least, to share features with it, and it is to these common features that I wish here to draw attention.

The first feature comes out well in de Vleeschauwer's revision of some of his earlier views. While still insisting that we must look at Kant through the question 'Is metaphysics possible?', he now points out that the historian must look at Kant in terms of both individuality and continuity. Previously we have looked to Kant for a revolutionary originality, but we must now look at him as the product of his time. We must notice, for example, how the *objectum materiale* of the *Critique*—i.e., metaphysics—corresponds exactly to the Wolffian scheme, with the Analytic corresponding to *metaphysica generalis,* and the Dialectic to *metaphysica specialis;* and, noticing this, we shall be led to renew our study of the *Critique* "not as a divided totality, but as a unity that comprehends within itself an entire tradition of thought and systematization" [4:356]. Such a suggestion, that we must confront Kant with the rationalist metaphysicians of his time—most notably Baumgarten, Wolff, and the early Kant—has been acted upon in the articles of Heimsoeth and Tonelli, as well as in the books by Martin and Delekat. It describes an approach to Kant that has produced three decades of historical studies of Kant's work that are informed by scholarship and illuminated by imagination.

There are signs that this approach is over-reaching itself, even though it does provide a necessary corrective to the Neo-Kantian bias. One of its most important results is to show that the contrast of "Precritical" and "Critical" views is an exegetical fiction—a polemical device for eliminating unwanted parts of the *Critique*. The continuity in Kant's thought is so great that it leads Heimsoeth to use, and not only to mention, the word 'Critical' within quotation marks. But while these studies show that an understanding of much of the *Critique* is contingent upon an understanding of Kant's earlier work (as ethical studies are showing how understanding of the *Foundations* is contingent upon an understanding of the later work), there is a danger of minimizing those features of Kant's thought that made the Neo-Kantian movement possible. These features may not have sprung into existence between 1770, or 1768, and 1781, but they came into existence during Kant's lifetime, and their isolation in a revisionary interpretation is a legitimate task. They must even find their place in an historical account of Kant's work, and we must not allow the historical approach of the ontological school to serve as a guarantee of the historical validity of their results.

A determining ground of this possible exaggeration of the metaphysical motives in Kant's development lies in the conscious reaction of recent commentary against Neo-Kantianism, and this on philosophical as well as upon historical grounds. This phenomenon appears in one of the manifestos that Martin has published for the German school:

> Neo-Kantianism restricted the systematic task of philosophy to theory of knowledge, and consequently extended this restriction to the philosophy of Kant and to its interpretation. The ontological school contests this restriction. It contests in general that philosophy exhausts itself in theory of knowledge, and it contests in particular that the philosophy of Kant exhausts itself in this way [2:105].

This claim is problematic. I shall not say anything about the general claim that philosophy is not reducible to epistemology, although it means that a lot of German commentary is being written by philosophers with an axe of their own to grind. This is also true in a straightforward sense of English commentary, but here the convictions to be saved are Neo-Kantian convictions. So far as Kantian exegesis is concerned, the approach to Kant is original in that it ceases to be obsessed (as the Neo-Kantians were) with the relations of Kant to Newton and Hume, while the leading interest of English authors is still centered on these relations. The approach declares Kant's interest in founding a "practical-dogmatic metaphysics," and not merely in laying a safe foundation for geometry and Newtonian physics. One English commentator who shares this view is Silber. He argues for the primacy of Kant's ethical views [4] and maintains:

> That Kant should direct metaphysics to the objects of freedom, God, and immortality, only to carry out the inquiry into these objects in terms of the ideas of the soul, the world, and God, clearly shows that Kant presents the inquiry into the moral ideas of reason as a genuinely metaphysical and speculative inquiry as well as a moral investigation [1:243].

As a feature of the work of the ontological school, this is not by any means as widely shared as the first, yet it combines with it to produce an interest in Kant that is not restricted to the Deduction and the Analogies. As a result parts of Kant's work that were previously of only incidental interest have moved closer to the middle of the stage, and these are studied in the context of all the material, unpublished in Kant's lifetime, that is now so readily available. As a further result, the question of Kant's view of things in themselves has again become the turning point against which different attitudes can be gauged.

2. Things in Themselves

I have said that the ontological school is distinguished from the Neo-Kantian movement by mutually complementary historical and philosophical interests. Commenting on previous commentary, Martin says that:

> the question was constantly posed of whether Kant was able to speak of things in themselves. Being answered negatively, the things in themselves were either excised altogether from the Critical philosophy, or else reinterpreted so that nothing but the word remained [2:82].

The ontological school is distinguished from this style of commentary by an absolute insistence on Kant's commitment to things in themselves. The later treatments are mostly developments of positions taken by Heimsoeth in his influential thesis on the *Metaphysische Motive in der Ausbildung des kritischen Idealismus* (1924), which is in many respects to be taken together with the equally important article on *Persönlichkeitsbewusstsein und Ding an sich in der kantischen Philosophie* (1924). In the first of these articles Heimsoeth exhibits the conscious reaction to the Neo-Kantian doctrines that I have mentioned, claiming to show that:

> the Critical limitation of knowledge (in particular the withdrawal of spatio-temporal experience from actual being in itself as a mere knowledge of appearance) is determined by certain basic metaphysical convictions [1:191].

He first of all argues that intellectual intuition is not an artificially constructed concept that emerges at the same time as the distinction between sensibility and understanding, but "it signifies for Kant the primary representation of knowledge: as a pure and spontaneous mental intuition" [1:192]. But a knowing subject intuits only what he himself "makes." Heimsoeth shows himself aware of the difficulties of the metaphor of making by using quotation marks, but whatever its difficulties it plays an undeniable part in Kant's thinking on intellectual intuition, which is often called "productive intuition," and which can be traced back to the writings of the middle fifties. Man, however, as a finite intelligence has spontaneity limited by receptivity: and all knowledge which one finite substance possesses of another is the product of both mental spontaneity and of a real affection through something beyond itself. If this is correct, then it would follow that Kant always maintained a contrast of things in themselves and things as they appear, and this is what Heimsoeth claims. It existed before 1770 as the contrast between internal and external properties. With the *Dissertation* the external properties acquire their own principle of unity and form the phenomenal world: but the things in themselves remain. Three characteristic quotations may illuminate this bare account:

> (1) finite beings cannot know other things out of themselves, for they are not their creators, so that it is only the mere appearances that they are able to know a priori, (2) man is the *principium*

originarium of the appearances, and (3) as the noumenon within ourselves is related to the appearances, so is the highest intelligence related to the *mundi intelligibilis*.[2]

The first two quotations date from later than 1781, and show the connection between apriority and spontaneity, while the last illustrates the contrast of Divine and human understanding, and dates from the silent decade. Occurring with these dates they leave untouched the problems of showing the role of spontaneity in the Precritical period, and of the role of receptivity in the Critical period, but they nevertheless give content to a vigorous and extremely suggestive article that breathes new life into the old problem of Kant's view of things in themselves. It has recently been made available in English by Gram, in a well-edited and well-chosen selection.

Some of the distinctive insights are developed by Herring. After giving an historical account of the different views on the role of things in themselves, Herring starts from the distinction between finite and infinite intelligences to which Heimsoeth draws attention, and goes on to develop a theory that involves both a double affection theory, and also a double aspect account known to us through Paton. Thus, for example, it is said that the distinction of things in themselves from appearances concerns:

> neither one and the same object of experience to which two contradictory predicates are applied, nor does it concern two ontologically distinct objects; it is, rather, one and the same object that is regarded under two different aspects, as object of experience and as object of pure thought [1:82].

There is a great deal to agree with in Herring's article, but I should like to single out one point for special consideration, and for comparison with the views of Bird. Both men maintain that there is a distinction to be drawn between the transcendental object and things in themselves.[3] Bird does so on the grounds that, by means of the transcendental object, Kant poses the problem that:

---

2 Reflexionen 6048, 6057, 5109; Ak. vol. 18, pp. 433, 440, 91.

3 Both Bird and Herring use A253 to sustain their case, but where Herring supports this with A358, Bird uses A493-6=B521-4, which is used by Herring rather differently.

the thought of an object in general is presupposed in all our empirical knowledge, and it is this thought that stimulates Kant's problem about the meaning of our notion of an object. This notion is precisely not the thought of any intelligible object, but only the idea of certain objective features of our knowledge and experience [3:80].

In maintaining such a view Bird fails to give an account of those passages where Kant uses the terms 'transcendental object' and 'thing in itself' as synonymous.[4] These passages have given rise to an orthodox view which is reported by Wolff:

using Kant's terminology more precisely than he was accustomed to do, we may say that he began with the concept of a transcendent object = x, and then shifted to the concept of a transcendental object = x. The former is merely the concept of the thing in itself, but the latter is the concept of the ground of the unity of a manifold of representation in one consciousness [2:314].

It is to be noticed, however, that Wolff is not altogether consistent about this, since strong support is also given to the alternative view that the terms are always used synonymously by Kant [cf. 2:136]. The 'orthodox' view to which I refer is that which accepts that there is equivocation between 'transcendent object' and 'transcendental object', and treats this as linked with a distinction between 'Precritical' and 'Critical' views: perhaps also in the strong sense of the patch-work theory.[5] It is the 'Critical' view that Bird is maintaining, revealing his to be essentially a revisionary interpretation of Kant. Herring, however, accepts that there is an equivocation in the term 'transcendental object', but thinks of this equivocation as essential to it. He concludes that the affecting object is the transcendental object, which has the two transcendental aspects of being either appearance or thing in itself.

---

4 Adickes, in *Kants Opus Postumum* (1920), gives the following list: A358, 361, 366, 372, 379, A46=B63m A180-1=B236, A277=B333, A288=B344, A478= B506, A538-40=B566-8, A565=B593, A698=B726. Compare Herring, p. 81 where the import of the list is obscured.

5 Classic expositions are those of Adickes, Vaihinger, and Paton. The distinction is not, in fact, paired with the patch-work theory, because Kemp Smith adopted the view that the terms were used synonymously, in which opinion he is joined by Aebi and Cassirer. The principal papers by Vaihinger and Paton are reprinted by Gram.

I find that I cannot fully agree with any of these opinions. I might mention the reason for this, since it does illustrate the usefulness of one of the features of modern European Kant exegesis. The question has never been asked: What is the origin of the concept of the transcendental object? If we ask this question, we find that the concept is used in the *Critique* in one of the ways that Kant used the concept of God in his earlier writings. Like Leibniz, Kant found difficulty in the idea of external relations, and it is this that is troubling him when, asking the question 'How is it possible that there should be outer intuition in a thinking subject?', he answers that no man can answer, because in order to answer it we should have to possess knowledge of the transcendental object [A392-3]. This passage quite clearly needs to be interpreted in the light of the passage in the Dissertation where he says that:

> the human mind . . . senses things external to it only through the presence of the one upholding common cause; and space, which is the universal and necessary condition, sensitively apprehended, of the co-presence of things, can therefore be entitled [the] *omnipraesentia phaenomenon* [*of the general cause*] [Ak.II.409-10].

Already we find Critical diffidence, for Kant speaks of this as "overstepping the limits of apodictic certainty befitting metaphysics," and as "pushing out into the open sea of mystical enquiries." From this passage, however, the issue can be traced farther back through the *Habilitationschrift* [Ak.I.413-5] to Kant's first published work [Ak.I.20-1], where it is held that only through God does our knowledge acquire relation to an object. In the *Critique* the ontological guarantee gives way to an epistemological problem; but the nature of the problem, and the call for the transcendental object, can be defined through consideration of the pre-critical role played by God. This is a topic which has been collecting attention in its own right, my favourite article in the field being by Schmucker [4] who provides an account of Kant's changing position in relation to the three main dogmatic arguments for God's existence. Here it is the implications of Kant's criticisms rather than their validity which is in question: I shall not attempt to touch the recent Anglo-American debate on the question of validity, beyond pointing to the articles by Dryer [1], Engel [2], and (with replies) Plantinga, who tie this debate to the Kantian background.

A second major problem about things in themselves has been whether we are entitled even to speak of them [sic], i.e. whether, denying that they can be known, we are asserting something meaningful, let alone true, if we say (or imply) that they exist. Traditional discussions show that advance is only likely to be made through an understanding of Kant's use of the modal concepts. Schneeberger's excellent monograph on these concepts is therefore to be welcomed. Of singular importance is the concept of possibility which, he reminds us, is built up out of the concept of agreement; and we may have different species of possibility depending upon the quantity of statements with which we require agreement. In the case of empirical possibility we may demand consistency with all the laws of an existing body of science, or with all the laws of an ideal science, or with either of these in conjunction with a set of factual conditions. In the case of real possibility we require consistency with the necessary conditions of experience, i.e., require that it be a possible experience. These are both questions of 'external possibility'. In the case of logical, or 'internal', possibility, we require no more than self-consistency, and, because this concept is less specific than that of real possibility, it licenses talk of objects which are not objects of a possible experience.

More work will have to be done before this line of approach can afford us an altogether acceptable introduction to things in themselves, but, quite apart from this Kantian context, Kant's views on possibility deserve development. The Humean 'test' for possibility in terms of imaginability is horribly circular, and our constant use of it blurs the Kantian distinction between internal and external consistency. It is because of my objections to the Humean account that I find Schneeberger's account more helpful than a distinction between 'imaginable' and 'conceivable' with which Stenius [1] moves into the same area. He is concerned with the move from 'the categories are a priori valid of appearances' to 'the categories are a priori valid no farther than appearances': the first of which summarizes Kant's critique of empiricism, while the second is the foundation of his critique of rationalism. Stenius holds that Kant makes the move in the *Critique* through the view that everything conceivable must also be imaginable. Although I find this contrast unrevealing, I would take it to be related to Kant's move from the insistence of the *Dissertation* that the categories must not be subject to sensible conditions to the position of the *Critique* where he insists that the a priori validity of the categories can only be established in relation to such sensible conditions. The 'real use' of the understanding gives way to the Critical understanding of 'real possibility', and the fallacy of subreption gives way to the doctrine of Schematism. Through an understanding of these historical moves I would expect progress to come, if not in our understanding of the Kantian position about things in themselves, then at least in our understanding of why he said those things that he did say.

3. *The Early Writings*

Erdmann at one time suggested that a decision about Kant's philosophical motivation in 1769 carried with it a decision about the foremost positions of the *Critique,* and the suggestion is well founded. The year 1769 is a crucial one in the Kantian development, and it is certainly and perhaps trivially true that philosophical and historical differences of opinion are always linked with one another. It is therefore significant that such writers as Heimsoeth, Martin, Delekat, and Tonelli call upon 17th and 18th century scenes that are much more richly populated than those familiar to less recent commentators. The point is worth emphasizing because there is a formal similarity between the position of the ontological school and the position adopted by Erdmann concerning the influences determining Kant in 1769: both emphasize the Antinomies.

Martin has shown the peculiar importance of the first two Antinomies for the ontological school [1:42ff.; cf.2], and, more recently, Heimsoeth has been devoting considerable attention to them. In the first of a group of three articles he cited the normal passages to show the influence of the Antinomies upon Kant's development [Ak.XII.254; Ak.XVIII.69; Ak.IV.338; etc.], but he argues beyond them, and against the position of Paulsen, that "the idea of an empirical-sceptical period determined by Hume and others in the development of Kant's thought has become untenable" [3:8]. He argues for this by taking the framework so often used by Neo-Kantian authors, but traces Kant's idea of a progression from dog-

matism through scepticism to criticism not to the middle term of
Humean scepticism, but instead to the scepticism of Bayle in his
famous article on Zeno. The merest glance at the *Reflexionen* is
sufficient to show the way in which Kant arranged his thought
within the framework of positions labeled by the names of Plato
and Leibniz, Aristotle and Epicurus, and it is by developing such
hints that Heimsoeth is able not only to show the defects of a naive
Neo-Kantian view, but also to throw new light on the Antinomies
by locating Kant in the main streams of Western Philosophy. One
of the particularly important results of his inquiry is the essential
connectedness of the Second Antinomy and the Second Paralogism
that it reveals. The following passage from Samuel Clarke gives an
idea of the way in which material simplicity and psychological
unity were connected in the eighteenth-century mind:

> . . . suppose three, or three hundred, particles of matter, at a
> mile or any given distance from one another, is it possible, that
> all those separate parts should in that state be one individual
> conscious being? Suppose, then, all these particles brought to-
> gether into one system, so as to touch one another, will they
> thereby or by any motion or composition whatsoever, become any
> whit less truly distinct beings than they were at the greatest dis-
> tance? How, then, can their being disposed in any possible sys-
> tem make them one individual conscious being?

The purely material question Heimsoeth deals with mainly in
connection with the *Monadologia Physica,* and the question of the
relation of soul to matter is treated through the *Traüme.* Granted
the importance of the Antinomies, and given the amount of work
that has now been done on their Kantian history,[6] this relating of
the two questions offers hope of important advance because, if we
cease looking for what is changing rather than for what is constant,
the question of how the soul is present to the world is revealed as
one of the questions most constantly in Kant's mind throughout his
life. Is it not so for any philosopher? But the eighteenth century
horizons of the problem were very different from those of today,

---

[6] Apart from Heimsoeth, see especially Carl Siegel, "Kants Antinomielehre
in Lichte der Inaugural-Dissertation," *Kant-Studien,* 30 (1925-6), pp. 67-86;
H. Feist, *Der Antinomiegedanke bei Kant* and *seine Entwicklung in den
vorkritischen Periode* (Borna-Leipzig, 1932); and Hinske (2).

and it is therefore fascinating to have not only Heimsoeth's latest and most explicit treatment of the paralogisms [9], but also Strawson's lofty but invigorating treatment of this portion of the *Critique* [cf. 3] to set beside it.

Another neglected Precritical work has always been the *Allgemeine Naturgeschichte,* and this has also been given an Heimsoeth treatment in his shorter article on the First Antinomy [cf. 4]. Kant's view of a definite origin combined with "Entwicklung in dem Abflusse der Ewigkeit" is related once more to traditional views and to its immediate ancestors in Baumgarten and Knutzen. This time I was less satisfied, perhaps because I have always wanted this view related to the writings of the same period where Kant, for example, says that although every contingent event has its determining reason, not every determining reason has, of necessity, its consequence [Ak.I.396, 408-9]. Paneth has provided a second, and very different sort of essay devoted to Kant's cosmological views. He shows the relationship between Kant's views on the Milky Way and those of Thomas Wright delineates the way in which Kant eliminated the Newtonian God that held the fixed stars apart, and argues that despite the frequent linking of their names, there is a great deal of difference between the position of Kant and Laplace.

Heimsoeth's example has been of considerable importance for shaping the structure of contemporary views of Kant, while his current work ensures that he will continue to exercise this influence. An introduction to his views may well be obtained through the reviews of it that have already been published: by Heidemann [2], Knittermeyer, Wagner, or the more specific review by Kaulbach [7], and the largely bibliographical exercise by Nicolin. One of the more important results has been that we are all now more inclined to view the transition from early to late in terms of continuity rather than discontinuity. In Heimsoeth's words:

> the conceptual world of the practical-dogmatic metaphysics, as projected and prepared by Kant in his later writings, stands in unbroken continuity with the conceptual world of the pre-critical period [1:164].

One could say that in the English-speaking world, where there is an increasingly ruthless philosophical examination which separates results in the Kantian spirit from mistakes in the Kantian text, there is implicitly involved the same view. But it would then also be true to ascribe the view to Fichte or Schopenhauer. The implicit view is not the same as the view explicitly held, when it leads to an historically imaginative rereading of Kant whose results are not always of a merely historical interest.

Another writer to whom attention needs to be paid is Tonelli. Perhaps because of the variety of tongues that he employs his total work remains neglected, although attention has been given to his two larger works by de Vleeschauwer [2:140-2; 3:78-81], and in his work on Kant's early theory of genius [15] the English reader has a good example of it. His views on the year 1769 are worth attention (although they are not yet fully available) in that he holds the decisive move made by Kant in 1769 was the separation of sensibility and understanding, and the explanation of space and time as pure forms of intuition is not the driving force leading to the separation, but a consequence of it [12:369]. Certainly, Kant saw his position most clearly distinguished from that of Leibniz in that he did make such a distinction, but philosophical appraisal tends to minimize its importance because it mediates such unacceptable inferences as: space and time are intuitions, and are therefore to be ascribed to sensibility, and being ascribed to sensibility are therefore representations only of how things appear and not of how they are. But it is wrong to let such illegitimate uses of the distinction divert attention solely onto the subordinate distinctions, and Tonelli's work promises to give it an accurately placed position which will lead to a more careful philosophical examination of it.

At the same time, the careful scholarship that results from Tonelli's intimate acquaintance with the eighteenth-century scene leads to results that are in other ways serviceable. I found myself without curiosity when Wolff recently, in a slight amplification of Kemp Smith's views, argued that although Kant knew Hume's *Essays* through the Sulzer translation of 1752-4, he was only acquainted with the *Treatise* through the extensive quotation from it in Beattie's *Essay on the Nature and Immutability of Truth*. One feels that Humean views must have been well known to Kant even if the words of the *Treatise* were not, and this Tonelli is able to demonstrate by showing how Hume indirectly influenced the *Traüme* through Basedow's *Philalethie*. I might at the same time mention a more dramatic piece of work by Turbayne, who upsets all our previous views on the relationship of Kant and Berkeley. It was, of course, allowed that Berkeleian and Cartesian idealism were simply positions created by Kant as contrasts to his own, but Turbayne argues to my complete persuasion that (1) Kant could have been acquainted with Berkeley's *Three Dialogues* and *De Motu*, (2) there is a point by point parallelism between Kant's and Berkeley's accounts of the external world, (3) Kant knew that there was, but (4) distinguished his position from that of Berkeley by his theory of the a priori nature of space. Turbayne's argument is a model of clarity throughout, and my only objection to it is a slight tendency to underestimate the force of (4); but, a more accurate estimation of its force, while slightly disturbing the parallelism, would endorse the general conclusion that Kant was fully aware of his general agreement with the Berkeleian position.

Further work by Tonelli may be exampled in the article examining the previous occurrences of some of the new terms that appeared with a systematic role in Kant's thought after 1769. Some of the earlier ones can be traced to Leibniz and Locke [*perceptio purus, intuitio*], others to Lambert (transcendental, transcendent), or Darjes (analytic, dialectic) [10;11]. Tonelli points to the way in which so many of these terms rarely occur in the eighteenth, but belong to the German Aristotelian tradition of the seventeenth century; and hence through them Kant could emphasize his difference from the Wolffian school while not introducing a technical vocabulary that was totally alien to his readers. This sort of work, while not overtly dramatic, is extremely useful. It can have its dramatic moments, however, and Kahl-Furthmann's investigation of the reversal of meaning that has occurred in the words 'subject' and 'object' since the Middle Ages is a fascinating example of this. His argument carries well to the conclusion that:

> in the transference of the term originally relating to the knowledge side to the side of the object, the insight into the contribution of the subject in the constitution of the object is implicitly expressed [334],

and, it is interesting that this index of the change from pre-Kantian to post-Kantian pictures of the world should be traceable to the early seventeenth century.

I have been relating this discussion to 1769 because today, even more than at earlier times, the *Dissertation* is seen as a Critical work, and the most decisive break in Kant's thought as that between 1768 and 1770. But this is in part illusory, since the break between 1766 and 1768, although not as extensive as that after 1768, laid the foundation for the conceptual apparatus that was developed in the *Dissertation*. It was in 1768 that Kant dropped his view that spatiality was a phenomenon dependent upon the *commercium substantiarum,* and so made possible its disengagement from the noumenal world. His argument for this is that from incongruent counterparts.

There have been several studies devoted to this phenomenon. The first, by Pears, has been developed by Mayo. These studies, although not explicitly concerned with the way in which Kant made use of incongruent counterparts to establish a theory of space, deal with many of the peculiarities of the phenomenon through outlining the number of contingent statements which lead us to say that we are reversed right to left when we look in a mirror. Mayo's article is mainly valuable for orientating ourselves within the Kantian problem, and seems to me to contain only one mistake, which may well be a simple slip. This is that, on Mayo's account, any three-dimensional object will be incongruent with its mirror image [109-10], whereas for Kant this is only true of three-dimensional objects which exhibit no plane of symmetry. Two objects are incongruent if they will not fit into the same spatial boundary. This is important in relation to a second article that deals specifically with the Kantian use of the phenomenon. Peter Remnant argues that the existence, or possibility, of incongruent counterparts does not entail an absolute space. His argument is not without difficulties. He supposes Kant's argument to be that if a single hand were created, then, if a handless human body were next created, the hand would either be a right or a left hand, and therefore would previously have been a right or a left hand. The 'previously' he believes to be a mistake. He implicitly points out that a handless body is virtually left-right symmetrical, and therefore he supposes the symmetry entirely disturbed by the right sides of our handless bodies being red, and the left sides being green. If, now, 'right' meant 'on the red side of the body', then God could make a single hand either right or left by next creating a red-on-the-introspectively-right-side body or creating the mirror image of this, i.e., a red-on-the-introspectively-left-side body. Instead of the body being coloured, we could just as easily suppose a handless body created that had been conditioned to report our right by 'left' and our left by 'right'. Thus Remnant concludes that "in a universe which contains nothing but a single hand, it would not just be empirically undecidable whether that hand were right or left; it would be strictly indeterminate" [2:399].

I am not sure that this supposed indeterminacy refutes Kant's claim that the existence of incongruous counterparts is impossible without the existence of an absolute space: I should think it could be construed as essential to Kant's argument rather than as a refutation of it. Perhaps Remnant plays into Kant's hands. For let us suppose that God begins his creation with a single hand: Remnant would surely not deny that he has performed a different act of creation from that which he would have performed if he had created its counterpart. But according to Remnant's argument this cannot mean 'He created a right instead of a left hand', since this remains indeterminate until God creates other things. But we can surely say categorically that whichever hand God created, it occupied a different region of space from that which its counterpart would have occupied: this must follow from the definition of incongruence, according to which incongruent figures are those which cannot occupy the same space. Therefore if God cannot choose between the two hands by asking "Which way round shall I place it?" but only by asking "Where shall I put it?" it seems that if the question is to be significant then space must exist antecedently to objects.

I do not think that if the question is to be significant it must entail the existence of space, nor, indeed, do I think that the question is significant. But if (1) Remnant allows that one hand will occupy a different space from that which its counterpart would have occupied—and how can this be denied?—(2) he also allows, as he does with some diffidence, that there is not any "intrinsic difference" between the two hands, and (3) he does not allow God to choose by means of the question 'Which way round?' then I do not see that he can avoid Kant's conclusion that God will have to ask "Where?" and thus, apparently, presuppose an absolute space. The solution to the problem lies in denying (2); i.e., maintaining that there is an intrinsic difference between a right and a left hand, and because of this God can choose by asking "Which?" Space must prevent me from dealing with this here, as also with the uses that Kant makes of incongruent counterparts in the *Dissertation* and the *Prolegomena*, although a recent article by Lange, replying on Kant's behalf to an older article by Reidemeister, throws a certain amount of light on this topic that has remained dormant since Vaihinger's synoptic treatment.

4. *The Aesthetic* (1)

One of the sources of difficulty in the Aesthetic lies with Kant's easy movement between the substantival terms 'Vorstellung' and 'Anschauung' and their verbal forms 'vorstellen' and 'anschauen'. But if we take the terms substantivally and noematically the main outlines are clear: intuition is a singular representation. Kant is often unclear about whether his contrast between singular and general is to be construed as the contrast between singular and plural, or as the contrast between particular and universal—Bennett [3] is one of the few to explicitly mark the difference. Without begging this question, it is undeniable that 'There can be no more than one space' and 'There can be no more than one time' are integral parts of Kant's position. They are integral parts in this way: they are necessary conditions for describing space and time as "forms of the sensible world." By this it is meant that space and time will, if these statements are true, provide a system of relations in which it is possible that every particular should be located, and, through this location, obtain a relation to every other particular. In order to say that space and time are forms of the sensible world, however, Kant needs to conclude not only that it is possible for every particular to be located in space and time, but also that this is necessary. This necessity is in part expressed and argued for in the first two space arguments, where Kant argues that space is a "condition of the possibility of appearances." These connections are exhibited in the following passage:

> Space, therefore, is an absolutely first formal principle of the sensible world, not only for the reason that the objects composing the universe cannot be phenomena save through the concept of space, but especially for the reason that by its essence space has

to be single, embracing absolutely all outer sensibles, and so it constitutes a principle of totality, i.e. of a world which cannot be part of another [Ak.II.405].

This is as much as I may do here towards indicating the importance to the Kantian theory of the statements (1) 'There is one space', (2) 'There is one time', and (3) 'Every object has a spatial location and a history'. They are conjunctively necessary and sufficient for the statement (4) 'There is one (phenomenal) world'.

The third statement is a central topic of Strawson's *Individuals*: a book that has grown out of his earlier objections to Russell's theory of descriptions, and which investigates the presuppositions of our being able to use referring expressions. The second chapter is of particular Kantian relevance. Firstly, it brings out the connection between the phrases 'is outside us' and 'is in space', and the value of a clear grasp of this connection needs no recommendation. Second, the chapter is mainly concerned with re-identification, and by showing that we could not have a use for 'A is qualitatively unlike B, although numerically identical with it' unless we also had a use for 'A is qualitatively like C and is numerically identical with it', and that we could not have a use for this last statement unless we had a use for 'A is qualitatively like D, but is numerically different from it', Strawson shows how many of the problems involved with re-identification are solved by means of answering questions about individuation. But since he also shows that the spatio-temporal conditions for identifying particulars are only realized through our ability to re-identify particulars, the circle involved can be used to show the mutual dependence of the Aesthetic and the Analytic. This becomes one of the themes of *The Bounds of Sense,* but, as Strawson tends to presuppose acquaintance with the earlier work, it is well to go to Bennett, by whom the argument is intelligently appropriated and developed in a way which makes these connections clear [3:33-43;219].

Strawson also deals with the necessity of the spatio-temporal system for identifying individuals: a topic also dealt with by several other philosophers.[7] The necessity of space and time for individuation was at least claimed by Kant:

---

[7] Cf. papers under the title "Identity of Indiscernibles" A. J. Ayer, *Philosophical Essays* (London, 1954); M. Black, *Mind,* 61 (1952), pp. 153-164;

all our intuition is bound to a certain formal principle under which alone anything can be apprehended by the mind immediately, that is, as singular, and not as conceived discursively through general concepts [Ak.II.396].

If, then, experience is to be experience of particulars, as it must be if we are to have synthetic judgments, we have good reason for saying that Kant was saying that space and time are necessary conditions of experience in that they are necessary for individuating particulars.

I am not sure that the significance of Kant's rejection of the identity of indiscernibles has yet been appreciated. I might hint at this importance by remarking that in its context the passage just quoted is an argument from the falsity of the identity of indiscernibles to the impossibility of intellectual intuition. The problem about the identity of indiscernibles is essentially a problem about external relations, and so to concentrate on it is to concentrate upon the distinction between things in themselves (the sum of the internal properties) and phenomena (which exhaust themselves in external relations), and through this upon Kant's distinction between transcendental realism and transcendental idealism. Some of these connections are dealt with by Herring in an article that may well be of use in showing how Strawson's arguments may be integrated, to the benefit of our understanding, into Kantian exegesis. I cannot agree, however, with his conclusion that Kant does not contest the identity of indiscernibles as such, "but solely its illegitimate use to argue by analogy from the subjective representation of an object to its constitution in itself" [2:399]. Kant's argument against the identity of indiscernibles in the Amphiboly is a dressed up version of an argument that long antedates *die kritische Wendung,* and the terminology of sensibility and understanding [Ak.I.409-10]. This earlier argument provides the basis for the Kantian discontent, and it cannot be described in the terms that Herring employs.

D. Pears, *Mind,* 64 (1955) , pp. 522-57, and N. Rescher, JP, 52 (1955) , pp. 152-155, as also G. Bergmann, "The Identity of Indiscernibles and the Formalist Definition of 'Identity'," *Mind,* 62 (1953) , pp. 75-79, and N. L. Wilson, "The Identity of Indiscernibles and the Symmetrical Universe," *Mind,* 62 (1953) , pp. 506-511.

I have suggested that Kant maintains that every particular must have a spatio-temporal location because without this it would not be a particular. But this is not Kant's only reason for saying that every sensible particular must be in space and time. For Kant an element A formed part of the world made up of further elements B . . .N if and only if A were related in some way to every other element of B . . .N. The systems of spatial and temporal relations, as systems in which every point of each system is uniquely related to every other point of that system, provide a means whereby every element, through occupying a position in those systems, can be related to every other element. The systems of spatial and temporal relations are means of conferring unity upon the world [cf. Ak.II.398]. This I believe, is Kant's main interest in the singleness of space and time, and he is only incidentally interested in the fact that through them we can uniquely identify any particular element: although for this latter feature we must also, it seems, presuppose the statement that every point of space and time is uniquely related to every other point of space and time.

The relationship of being spatially connected is ordinarily a transitive one, so that if A is connected with B, and B with C, then A will also be connected with C. But it seems that every object that I perceive will be spatially related to my body, and therefore this, through the terms of the Copernican revolution, will act as a conduit for spatially connecting all the particulars that I perceive. The most contingent feature of this situation is my association with one particular body, and it is through an implicit challenge to this feature that Quinton has recently thrown light upon the necessity of there being only one space. We might suppose, to start with, that a person is in perceptual relation with the world through two bodies, and so is perceiving the world from two different positions. It is only, of course, if the two bodies stand in spatial relation to one another that they will act as a conduit for connecting all perceived particulars, and Quinton considers a situation where this connection is broken. He supposes there to be a person who falls asleep in England, dreams of waking in the midst of a lakeside community where he spends a normal day before falling asleep there and, at that moment, wakes in England. He argues that if there were regular alteration, with waking in one world always coordinated with falling asleep in the other, we should have no reason to speak of the lakeside world as a fictitious world; and he takes the story far enough, to my mind, to establish its freedom from inconsistency. Under these conditions we should speak of 'two spaces', and the normal connection of spatial occupancy with spatial connectedness would have broken down.

I do not think that Quinton's conclusions affect the force of Strawson's arguments—although Strawson gives only small credence to these "familiar fantasies," and had earlier overlooked them altogether [1:22]—for they serve only to emphasize the importance of a present perceptual context for individuation. But although Quinton's argument shows the falsity of Kant's claim that "we can represent to ourselves only one space" [A25-B39], I think it does more than merely show the falsity of an isolated claim: it also serves to highlight the more correct and important aspects of his other claims. In his early work Kant was inclined to rule out the possibility of a plurality of worlds by means of two premises (1) there is only one God, (2) God always works through the Leibnizian principle of providing a maximum coherence for his handiwork [Ak.I.25]. If there were more than one God, then Kant concedes not only the possibility but also the necessity of there being more than one world [Ak.I.414-5]. In the *Critique,* however, man adopts the position in relation to world unity that had been the Precritical prerogative of God, and it is therefore important to note that it is only by disturbing our concept of a unitary person, as a complex of body and mind, that we have been able to create the possibility of there being more than one world; and this is therefore analogous to the Precritical consideration of the possibility of there being more than one God. To follow through the implications of this argument (which I cannot do here) is therefore to locate oneself in the essential Kantian framework of one space, one world, and one consciousness.

I have considered only unitary space, and not unitary time. Quinton considers it impossible that there should be more than one time, and although he is indubitably correct in holding that there must, in any story that we tell, be a single subjective temporal order, it is not the case that our concept of an objective temporal order would remain undisturbed. This is important in connection with the first Analogy and the Refutation, where Kant maintains that a unitary objective temporal series presupposes a unitary space, so that it is worth remarking that even in the story that Quinton tells, the temporal correlation of happenings in the two worlds would be relatively *ad hoc*, employing incidental rather than essential features of the methods used to establish whether A happened before, after, or at the same time as Swinburne has tried to construct a multi-temporal but unispatial myth in terms of tribes vanishing and then later reappearing to each other, but objections by Skillen, Ward, and Hollis convince me that the multi-temporal myth is really a multi-spatial myth; although I am inclined to add: and *therefore* multi-temporal.

5. *The Aesthetic* (II)

More orthodox debate on the Aesthetic remains inconclusive. Take, for example, Delekat's view that Kant's *Gemüt* is formally equivalent to Newton's *sensorium Dei,* and who argues for this by placing an eighteenth-century environment around the dispute. He suggests various analogies designed to make the translatability of these terms into one another more appealing. One of these is Shaftesbury's use of "sensus communis," which helps very little indeed, since Shaftesbury took his term from Juvenal, and uses it to point a contrast between 'the sense of the common people' and 'the sense for the common people', which has very little relevance to the perceptual context. More appealing is Augustine's use of the same phrase, which is made relevant by Delekat's interpretation of 'sensorium Dei', of which he says that:

> as there is a central part of the human brain in which, when we perceive, the sensations from the particular senses come together to produce a picture of the whole of what is perceived, and so provide the possibility of our being present to things independently of the place and time in which we found ourselves: so it is with God [3:33].

That is, just as I am present to, although not in, this typewriter when I perceive it, so God is present to space and time although not in them. God's *sensus communis* and my own resemble each other in everything except that His is not supplied with messages from various afferent nerves; i.e., God's intuition is *originarius* and not *derivatus.*

Having given this view of a *sensus communis,* Delekat is in a position (a) to formally identify Kant's *Gemüt* with a human, and Newton's *sensorium Dei* with a divine *sensus communis,* (b) to argue that the content of Kant's space is the same as the content of the Newtonian space, and (c) to say, therefore that "Kant changed nothing in the material determinations of the concepts of space and time, but he located them in the human mind rather than in the *sensorium Dei*" [3:62].

To contrast with Delekat we may consider Martin's views, which start from the more orthodox ascription to Newton of a space-as-attribute position. Contesting (a) he also contests (b), saying that "for Kant [like Leibniz] space is merely a complex of relations" [1:37]. In this conflict of views it is well nigh impossible to isolate the separate issues involved, even in so far as this merely involves the locating of the disagreement as one about the interpretation of Kant, or of Newton, or of Leibniz. There is no settled view on any of their positions: least of all on Kant, who would appear to adopt an 'absolute' view in the Aesthetic, and a 'relative' view in the Analytic.

Another confusion which it may be as well to ignore is introduced by Delekat, for one of the questions he puts to Kant is this:

> Are space and time forms of intuiting, or forms which can themselves be intuited? If we understand the concept of intuition in the sense of *intuitus originarius* . . . then space and time are forms of what is intuited. But how is it if we regard them as pure intuitions of mankind? In this case are they only forms of intuiting, or are they also forms of what is intuited? [3:62].

The question inevitably reminds one of the following famous description of Kant's argument in the Aesthetic:

> Space and time are a priori, because necessary and universal, and if a priori then subjective, and only subjective.

It was this description that led to the most acrimonious of all Kant-debates: the controversy between Adolf Trendelenburg and Kuno Fischer in the last century. Trendelenburg had held that:

> even if we concede the argument that space and time are demonstrated to be subjective conditions which, in us, precede percep-

tion and experience, there is still no word of proof to show that they cannot at the same time be objective forms [*Logische Untersuchungen* (1862) :163].

History has so far given the verdict to Trendelenburg. Despite Fischer's advocates including such men as Arnoldt and Caird, the final statements on the controversy have been those of Vaihinger and Kemp Smith, so that today Trendelenburg's position is almost that of an unquestionable truth. The position that he wished to maintain was that space and time could be transcendentally real as well as transcendentally ideal, and although this was disputed, common ground was found in the consistency of asserting that space was both empirically real and transcendentally ideal. Delekat is therefore going in the face of all received opinion when he says that Kant's attempts to reconcile 'form of intuiting' with 'form of what is intuited' simply cannot be carried through [3:64].

I believe that the whole of this controversy could well come up for reappraisal, if anyone had the patience for it, and with Delekat taking sides against both parties it is perhaps time that it did. There is further reason for this reappraisal. In apparent ignorance of the earlier controversy, Lotz has recently been arguing an extremely strong version of the Trendelenburg thesis. He believes that disputes have been based upon the unquestioned (!) assumption that the absolute reality of space is inconsistent with its transcendental ideality, and so he proposes to question this assumption. So far this would appear to be the same ground as the earlier dispute, but Lotz goes on to argue not only that the absolute reality of space is quite consistent with its transcendental ideality, but also that it is a presupposition of it. He proposes to give "a kind of transcendental deduction of the absolute reality of space from its transcendental ideality" [31]. Is there anyone with the time and persistence necessary to discover what is going on here?

It is with relief that one turns to the recent work of Strawson and Bennett, both of whom carefully separate what might be called the metaphysical and the geometrical interests of the Aesthetic. In detailed working out there is a great deal of difference between their views, but there is a common front, even though this becomes narrower as they traverse the Analytic. Both are clear that Kant's views on geometry provide the basis for an 'impositional' theory of space and time which is indubitably present in the Aesthetic, and which gets confused with those other elements of the Aesthetic that Kant requires to further his metaphysical interests in the Analytic. Both reject this theory. Bennett goes on to argue by a presumptively possible counter-example to Pythagoras' theorem for the analytic-or-synthetic nature of Euclidean geometry, and explains Kant's belief in its synthetic and a priori status as due to an excessive concern with sight rather than touch [3:29-32]. This seems to me a good explanation of something that does need explanation—and it is indicative of the Anglo-American awareness of what Heidegger is getting at with his talk of *Zu-* and *Vorhandensein.* The explanation is valuably supplemented by Strawson's tentative defence of the Kantian view using the idea of a visual-phenomenal space [3:277-292].

There is not, perhaps, much that is both substantial and novel in these views, as may be seen by comparing them with those of Schrader [2], which was for me one of the best previous treatments of the Aesthetic. But what is novel is a clarity and, particularly in Bennett's case, an attention to detail which ought to become exemplary. Should I ever again undertake to review work on Kant, it is my hope that it will have become so.

6. *The Analytic*

In this section I wish primarily to deal with the five important English studies of this area of the *Critique,* and to begin with Bird's book that, if retrograde from the point of view of recent Continental commentary, is often exciting and persuasive. Positively, (and it is only with this aspect that I shall be concerned) *Kant's Theory of Knowledge* is a study of Kant's word 'appearance' and of its relations to the categories and to the concept of a thing in itself. It deals first of all with the problem of how we might reconcile Kant's conflicting claims about appearances, for these are said to be "objects, spatial, and distinct from our ideas, and yet they are also representations, mere modifications of the mind, and in us" [16]. The problem is dealt with through a distinction between transcendental and empirical beliefs. The crucial point that Bird wishes to make is that our empirical beliefs are insulated from our transcendental ones [39]. Accepting this, Bird applies it to questions about perception, where he finds that two sorts of

answers might be given to the question 'What do you perceive?'
The first will be an answer of the kind 'A flash of light', or 'An
electric discharge', and the second will be of the kind 'An appearance', or 'A thing in itself'. These are clearly very different sorts of
answers, and it is not misleading to say that the first is an informa-
tive empirical answer and the second an uninformative transcendental answer. The transcendental answer imposes no limits on our
ordinary empirical descriptions, for it does not in any way discriminate between things, or even, in any ordinary sense, sorts of
things.

It is the failure of the transcendental answer to discriminate
between the items perceived that, in Bird's opinion, poses the
problem that the Analytic is designed to solve:

> by showing how the categories and their associated principles
> enable us to discriminate between the phenomenal objects in cer-
> tain allegedly basic ways [43].

Using this concept of discrimination, Bird is able to maintain
some interesting theses. It enables him, for example, to harden his
objection to the phenomenalist interpretation of Kant, since, he
says, Kant's construction of physical objects is now seen to be "not
'vertical', from low level to higher level descriptions, but 'hori-
zontal', from an indiscriminate manifold of sense to discriminated
items within it" [57]. It further enables him to give an interpretation of the distinction between sensibility and understanding as the
distinction between the indeterminate manifold (appearance) and
the discriminated categorized manifold (phenomenon). The revisionary nature of the interpretation is evident when, on this
basis, he can further say that the distinction between the faculties is
not strictly required, since:

> it is an indisputable truth that we are able to discriminate between
> items in our perception, and this is enough by itself to introduce
> a general problem about the ways in which we are enabled to
> do this [63].

The second part of the book deals with the explanation of how
Kant can say that (1) appearances are necessarily related to the
categories, and also (2) objects can appear to us without their
being under the necessity of being related to the categories. This is
the problem of showing how and why discriminations are necessary.

In answering it Bird takes us through the two Deductions and the Analogies focusing his interpretation on the Second Analogy. Here his position is unfortunately unclear. He is certainly right in saying that Kant is not interested

> in the inference from 'The event A—B appeared to take place' to 'The event A—B really took place', but in the prior inference from 'I perceived A and then perceived B' to 'I perceived the *event* A—B' [157].

The point at which there is difficulty is where Bird says that Kant was "right to say that the issue between himself and Hume over [causality] was not that of its usefulness or indispensability" [164], and also that Kant attempted to reinstate the distinction between objective claims and subjective associations of ideas, which is left closed at the end of the Deduction,

> by showing that the concept 'cause' was important. His additional step beyond Hume was to show what kind of importance, and what kind of necessity, can be said to belong to this concept [165].

And what kind of importance is it? It is an importance that is a

> reflection of the fundamental part which this concept plays in our experience, for without it the discrimination of an event, and of an objective time order, would not be possible. The central position of this law explains the importance of the concept 'cause' in our experience in a way in which Hume did not explain it [166].

But is this showing of the "central position" of the concept any more than showing its "usefulness or indispensability"? And is it not true that Hume did much the same job in the section of the *Treatise* called "Scepticism with Regard to the Senses."?8 I would be inclined to take these as merely *ad hominem* objections, because I do not think that Kant can do anything else than establish the concept of causality as conditionally necessary. But the point is worth dwelling on, for there is still great confusion over it, and work by Bennett, Beck, and Dryer may well help to make the discussion more coherent. First Bennett, who says we must distinguish the claims (1) that Kant shows in the Second Analogy that it is necessary that there should be causal laws and (2) that Kant

---

8 Cf. H. H. Price, *Hume's Theory of the External World* (London, 1940).

shows that it is necessary that there are necessary causal laws [2. The argument may also be found in 3:153-163]. To adopt (1) would be to adopt the view that Kant charges Hume with under-estimating the indispensability of causal laws, while to adopt (2) would be to adopt the view that Kant charges Hume with provid-ing a wrong analysis of causal laws. On (1) both Bennett and Strawson are rather hard on Kant's famous "irreversibility" argu-ment, while finding some support for Kant's contention: this I shall consider below. On (2), Bennett points out that we cannot show the wrongness of the empiricist programme for the analysis of causal laws, for

> if we know perfectly well that this whistle's blowing does not cause those workers to down tools, the empiricist has only to ask how we know this, and to amend his analysis in the light of the answer [109].

What sort of objection could be brought against Hume? Bennett argues that

> just because he thinks that the concept of causality can be analysed in purely empirical terms—and crucially in terms of regularity—Hume does not and cannot attach a fundamental importance to the difference between a rule which holds always and one which nearly always holds [113].

There could therefore be, and Bennett argues that there is, a dispute between Kant and Hume over whether the body of causal rules shown to be necessary by (1) has to consist of strongly quantified laws ("for all values of . . .") or whether it might consist of weakly quantified laws ("for most values of . . ."). It is further argued that Kant did not, because he could not, establish the former, since

> a preparedness to accept a weakly quantified science is not only permissible but is mandatory upon any scientist who wishes to be able to cope sensibly with a really well attested but unrepeatable experiment, if one should occur [119].

This article should help towards clearing the air, but conceding the validity of the argument, the question remains of what the statement or statements are for which the concept of causality is conditionally necessary. Before I deal with this, I shall first look at

Wolff's book on Kant, in which I think (1) and (2) are confused with one another, the most important sections of which are reproduced in Wolff [3]. His book is ambitious in its programme, which is to provide a strict deduction of the law of causation from the fact of self-consciousness. The sort of interpretation against which he is arguing can be seen in Janoska's examination of Aebi's argument in *Kants Begründing der "Deutschen Philosophie"* (Basel, 1947). She had unpacked Kant's argument in the Deduction into the following syllogism:

(1) Each (objective) unity of apperception is a unity according to a rule.
(2) What makes possible the givenness of a manifold is a (transcendental) unity of apperception.
(3) What makes possible the givenness of a manifold is a unity according to a rule.

Janoska discusses two possible types of equivocation, employing the distinctions (1) between 'subjective$_1$', or not necessarily true, and 'subjective$_2$', or stemming from the subject and (2) between 'unity of apperception$_1$' as the unity of what is perceived, and 'unity of apperception$_2$' as the unity of the act of perceiving an object. It is first argued that if the unity of apperception is to be described as 'transcendental', then it must also be described as 'objective$_1$', and this is both consistent with its being described as 'subjective$_2$', and with its not being a source of equivocation. It is then argued that if 'unity of apperception' is not to be a source of equivocation, then 'unity of apperception$_2$' must be shown to entail 'unity of apperception$_1$', so that the move can properly be made from the apodosis of (2) through the protasis of (1) to the conclusion (3): that is, "we can only oppose Aebi's interpretation . . . if the unity of the object is effected through the spontaneity of the transcendental subject." [145]. Janoska then argues that the move from apperception$_2$ to apperception$_1$ is made by Kant in the section of the first edition Deduction where Kant speaks of the transcendental object. The formal argument which Janoska discovers in this section, and which he sets out attractively, is described in the following way:

Under the presupposition that there are, in the Kantian sense, synthetic a priori judgments, it follows from the Kantian definition of knowledge that apperception$_2$ is a necessary condition of apperception$_1$ [208].

This, certainly, is to make Kant's argument a regressive one, i.e., one that fits the pattern of the *Prolegomena* rather than the pattern that we should expect to find in the *Critique*. This does not make it bad exegesis (in fact I think it correct), but in the Deduction as a whole we should expect an argument that goes in the opposite direction.

Such an argument Wolff attempts to provide, by finding four parts of the Subjective Deduction which are related as developing stages of one argument [A104-110; 95-97; 97-104; 110-114]. This is an argument which, in the first two stages, operates from the two premises:

(1) 'All the contents of my consciousness are bound up in a unity', which is to be explained through the fact that 'representations (for instance the single words of a verse) distributed among different beings, never make up a whole thought (a verse)' [A352].

(2) 'The contents of my consciousness have the double nature of representations', which is to say that we must distinguish 'perception as an object of consciousness' and 'perception as consciousness of an object'.

With these two premisses the argument of the first stages moves to the conclusion that we have valid synthetic a priori judgments through the important step:

(3) 'The only way to unify a diversity of mental contents is by referring them, qua representations, to an object as ground of their unity'.

It is with the step from the second to the third stage that the most novel part of Wolff's account is introduced: an analysis of rule-directed activities to show that they may be spoken of as nonarbitrary, unified, and as correct or incorrect, and the consequent description of 'synthesis' as 'rule directed reproduction in imagination'. In this way steps (2) and (3) are collapsed into:

(2^1) 'The only way to introduce synthetic unity into a manifold of contents of consciousness is by reproducing it in imagination according to a rule'.

This move is the heart of the Deduction, for, by losing the second premiss, we move from 'correspondence' to 'coherence'; and

> to say that mental content R represents object O is to say that R is one of a variety (=manifold) of mental contents which has been, or can be, reproduced in imagination according to the rule which is the concept of O [133-144].

The fourth stage is a preliminary refutation of Hume, where the categories, as a priori rules of synthesis, are held to be necessarily applicable to the contents of consciousness. The fifth stage, contributed by the Second Analogy, completes the refutation with the aid of a subsidiary premiss to the effect that the form of inner sense is time, by showing how the distinction between subjective association and objective connection is made possible through the concept of causality.

The strength of Wolff's book lies in his grasp of the outline of Kant's argument, and in his bringing together with this the insights that we have gained through the long discussions of the private language argument. Wolff could have made this very much clearer if he had continually observed the distinction between general and particular statements—a distinction which has to be considered even in our account of synthesis. When Kant, for example, speaks of synthesis as "putting different representations together" [A77= B103; cf. Wolff 68-70], we can take him to mean either (and perhaps both) of 'putting numerically and qualitatively different representations together' and 'putting numerically but not qualitatively different representations together'. In the first case we shall speak of the apprehension of a particular, and in the second of the apprehension of an objective similarity or universal. Wolff does not make these alternatives clear, and consequently there are suspicious looking movements like the one in the following passage:

> To say that A really preceded B is to deny that their order can be changed, now that it has occurred. The real is precisely what we cannot tear up or rewrite. If the order cannot be altered, then it must be represented in that way and no other. In other words, we must always so represent it. Thus the objective reality of a

temporal succession of A and B is expressed by a necessary and universal rule for their representation [266-7].

There is here a half-concealed shift, which, if it can be made at all, ought surely to be made proudly and openly, from 'If A occurred before B, then A always and eternally will have occurred before B' to 'If A occurred before B, then A's always and eternally will occur before B's'. Wolff certainly thinks that Kant got from the first to the second, for he says that one of Hume's challenges is "to prove that the observable associations of events are invariable and universal, and hence constitute a sound basis for inferring the future from the past," and also that it is fair to say that Kant met this challenge [163]. I would agree with Wolff that Kant came very close to proving that the first of these statements would not be true unless the second were also true, although not so close as to remove all problems over induction. This may be seen minimally in that if the argument from Bennett that we have considered is correct, then such a complete proof would be a proof that it is necessary that these should be necessary, i.e. strictly universal, causal laws.

If we eliminate this confusion then we get a reply to Hume whose outline has been definitively sketched by Beck, and whose detail has been independently filled in by Dryer. Beck [4] replies to a charge of Wolff that he had been confused in a succinct account of Kant's argument that he had given, and incidentally criticises the papers by Schipper and Williams on the subject. His argument turns around the following statements:

K: Everything that happens, that is, begins to be, presupposes something upon which it follows by rule.

P: Events can be distinguished from objective enduring states of affairs, even though our apprehension of each is serial.

H: Among events, we find empirically some pairs of similar ones that tend to be repeated, and we then make the inductive judgment: events like the first members of the pairs are causes of events like the second.

Here H, the inductive task, presupposes P, for unless we can distinguish events we cannot establish correlations between them. But P implies K, by the argument of the Second Analogy, and therefore H implies K.

This does seem to me to be Kant's reply to Hume. The implications of the argument are still an open question—does it, for example, imply that we must know a causal rule in order to distinguish an event, and thus know a causal rule prior to discovering it?—and although an article by Buchdahl [1] to some extent deals with this, I shall leave it on one side in order to consider the validity of the argument. Does P imply K? I think the peculiarity of Kant's 'irreversibility' argument is now sufficiently marked in English literature, though often slipped over on the Continent (cf. Gueroult [3]). By this I mean the fact that if we take a series of noetic acts, or of particulars whose individuation is tied to that of their corresponding noetic acts, then *neither* a set of perceptions of an objective succession *nor* a set of perceptions of an objective co-existence is reversible. If, on the other hand, we refer to a series of perceptions exactly like a previous set except in the reverse order, then *both* a set of perceptions of an objective succession *and* a set of perceptions of an objective coexistence are reversible. In the light of this, can anything be made of Kant's argument? I think that it can, and that Dryer has in fact shown that it can [3:380-446]. The merits of Dryer's long and patient examination of the argument may well reconcile the reader to what often appears to be the quite excessive length of his book.

Dryer's discussion of the metaphysical deduction is also stimulating, being more sympathetic than most, while in the end rejecting the view that Kant has a list of all and only the basic categories. Such an examination was perhaps necessary in that so distinguished a scholar as Ebbinghaus was inclined to accept Reich's conclusions on the completeness of the table of judgments [4:20]. Bennett adds his own distinctive criticism of the metaphysical deduction, and while arguing for the categorical status of some of Kant's list, he at the same time produces novel views on the relative functions of the metaphysical deduction and the Principles. The details of this debate I cannot go into here; neither into the historical research on the metaphysical deduction by Heimsoeth [1-1; 4-1; 5] and Tonelli [4; 6], nor into the debate on the relation of transcendental and general logic discussed by Smart, Paton [5], Grayeff, Vuillemin [2], and in a slightly wider context by Rotenstreich [4:1-25]. Instead of entering into these discussions I want briefly to indicate some different approaches that have been made to the notion of self-consciousness as found in the Transcendental Deduction: approaches between which I do not wish to arbitrate, for I feel that each is useful. In the first place, there are those of phenomenological persuasion who take seriously Kant's talk of the unity of apperception being related to and exhausted in the consciousness of the identity of the act through which the manifold is unified. Gurwitsch's essay on this theme, especially when viewed in the light of his other writings, deserves to be taken seriously. A second approach is represented by Dryer, whose account of self-consciousness is akin to that of Gurwitsch, in that it relates it to the unification of representations found in a judgment, but which is idiosyncratic in that reference to the 'I think' is judged to be unhelpful [3: 125-6]. Finally there are Strawson and Bennett. They differ, firstly, in that Strawson does find in the Transcendental Deduction considerations to support the view that unity of consciousness entails the unity of that of which we are conscious, and thus objectivity, while Bennett discovers only a set of mistakes that Kant made in trying to get from the first to the second. This difference is the result, in part, of their different accounts of self-consciousness. For Bennett, relying on his argument in *Rationality*, self-consciousness "involves whatever intellectual capacities may be required for the establishment . . . of the truth of statements about one's own past mental states" [3:119], and, because of the failure of the Metaphysical Deduction, this is as far as Kant can go in the Transcendental Deduction. The argument is completed in the Analogies, where outer experience is shown, in an interesting modification of Wittgenstein's private language argument, to be a presupposition of talk about the past. For Strawson, relying on *Individuals,* the Kantian argument provides a necessary but not sufficient condition for a possible experience, where an experience is to involve awareness of having that experience. Kant provides a necessary condition, in that it is necessary for such awareness that we should be able to distinguish a 'unified objective world' from a 'subjective route' through that world; this is not, however, sufficient, in that we would further require that the subject of experience also be an intuitable object of experience. Strawson's argument presents an interesting development of his earlier position, and through its differences from the other positions I have sketched we may expect discussion to be provoked that will illuminate not only the problem of self-consciousness, but also its Kantian role.

7. Synthetic And a Priori

The *Critique* was written to explain the possibility of synthetic and a priori judgments. For many people today this provides an insuperable barrier to their introduction to the *Critique* because, in their view, there are no synthetic and a priori judgments. The subject has now become so complex, and spread so far beyond the Kantian horizons, that I cannot here do more than indicate the outlines of the controversy, and try to point out the route that will take us back to the Kantian concept. Although it is with some hesitation that I speak of 'the' Kantian concept: nominally it is perhaps univocal, but we must beware of the fact that different kinds of statements for different kinds of reasons are held to possess this status.

Bennett implicitly challenges the Kantian concept when pointing out that a synthetic a priori proposition must be necessary, where 'necessary' must be taken as weaker than logical necessity, but stronger than empirical necessity. Can such a sense be suggested? The challenge recalls the controversy provoked by Robinson, who held that Kant's concept of a necessary proposition was nothing but a confusion of four different senses of the word 'necessary': (1) the "Aristotelian sense" in which a necessary proposition is one containing the word 'must' or some cognate expression, (2) the "compulsory belief sense" in which a necessary proposition is one which, for one reason or another, it is "necessary for us men to believe," (3) the "Leibnizian sense" involving logical consistency, and (4) the "universal sense" according to which a necessary proposition is one "which asserts a universal connection with unrestricted universality" [291]. Further, Robinson argues that because Kant departs from the Leibnizian sense he has a problem about the connection of the concepts of necessity and truth, but this need not concern us greatly, as Kant was himself aware of the problem, and showed this in asking about the possibility of synthetic and a priori judgments.

About the first two senses little need be said. Although Robinson argues for the Aristotelian sense as a distinct type of necessary proposition, Bird argues cogently that it is not [1:389-90]. He also treats nicely of the compulsory belief sense, admitting that Kant does have a compulsory belief sense of the word, but denying that Kant was confused about this [cf. A824-9=B852-7]. There is, for all that, an element of compulsory belief present more generally in necessity. It is not that a compulsive belief provides a basis for calling a proposition necessary, as Parkinson would appear to suggest [394], but rather that the negation of a necessary proposition is either inconsistent or involves some form of absurdity that would preclude its being the object of a rational belief.

The Leibnizian sense need not concern us for the moment. It is certainly true that Kant did not think of 'necessary proposition' and 'proposition whose negation is logically inconsistent' as being identical in meaning, even though he thought that any proposition whose negation was logically inconsistent would be a necessary proposition.

The universal sense is introduced on the basis of Kant's claim that we have a priori knowledge either (1) if we have a proposition which in being thought is thought as necessary, or (2) if we have a proposition which is thought in "strict universality," i.e., in such a way that "no exception is allowed as possible" [33-4]. Kant is quite clear that a proposition is thought as necessary if and only if it is thought with strict universality, and his reason for this would appear to be the same as that for which we would today say that someone who refuses to admit the possibility of recalcitrance to one of his general propositions is making it analytic. Kant did not say that all unrestrictedly universal propositions were necessary, nor did he say that all true unrestrictedly universal propositions were necessary, but that those unrestrictedly universal propositions were necessary which we would not permit to suffer recalcitrance. Vaihinger speaks of the two criteria as being based upon our concepts of a qualitative and a quantitative *Anders-sein-können,* and we might, alternatively, speak of them as the intensional and the extensional aspects of necessity. We certainly cannot speak of them as two independent and fortuitously coincident specifications of the a priori.

Kant did not therefore think of strictly universal propositions as a variety of necessary proposition, but he thought of strict universality as a feature of necessary propositions. We can avoid difficulties of intensions by putting the main weight upon the second of Kant's two criteria for apriority, treating strict universality as a means for determining when an intensional connection has been made.

The problem is now posed that the extensional consequence of necessity that we are now using as a test of necessity is today part of a behavioral test that we often apply in finding out whether someone is maintaining a statement as analytic. If this is the case, then the class of synthetic and necessary propositions is of necessity an empty one. The belief that the class is an empty one had been traced by Beck to a change of meaning that has occurred in the word 'analytic' since Kant's day. His nicely modelled argument claims that as the class of synthetic and a priori truths came to be regarded during this century as an empty one, the word 'necessary' suffered a change of meaning so that it is now equivalent to 'analytic' rather than, as formerly, to 'a priori'. If this is the case, then we should expect that if the older sense of 'analytic' (analytic$_1$) and 'a priori' did not have distinct roles, there will be some equivocation in the contemporary use of 'analytic' (analytic$_2$). Do we in fact find this?

> Let us take a theory of the analytic which holds that a statement is analytic to the extent or degree to which it will be held impregnable against revision by experience. . . . Then there are two ways in which a proposition may be found to be analytic (i.e., analytic$_2$) : (1) by inspection of the sentence itself, if it is logically or linguistically true; and (2) by investigation of its role in an organised body of experience we call knowledge [2:96].

This 'theory of the analytic' is, I would argue, the same as the extensional aspect of the Kantian theory of the a priori, and the two tests, which Beck calls the microscopic and the macroscopic tests, are, as he argues, exactly correspondent to the two bases for the attribution of necessity that distinguished analytic$_2$ from the synthetic a priori. It seems clear in outline, however unclear it may be in detail, that some such distinction is operative between the sorts of justification that someone might present for not permitting the possibility of a falsifying instance. But if someone is going to maintain a statement as necessarily true and is not going to maintain this on purely definitional grounds, then he will in effect have to answer the Kantian question about the possibility of synthetic a priori judgments.

This sort of defence of the Kantian category of the synthetic a priori is one that is today being increasingly pressed. Hanson insists that there is a distinction between 'characterizing the structure of propositions' and 'characterizing the mode of justification of propositions'. He does so in the context of the embarrassing argument by challenge: 'There are no synthetic a priori statements' is not evidently true like 'There are no married bachelors in New York', so is it therefore true in the same way as 'There are no puppet theatres in New York to rival that in Salzburg' is true? I would certainly not like to think that it is merely empirically false that there are no synthetic and a priori geometrical statements, but believe that his argument can be met, after we have stripped 'a priori' of its confusions as regards the entailments 'not answerable to' and 'not derived from', on the grounds that 'there are no synthetic a priori geometrical statements' involves a type of incoherence which distinguishes it both from the logical and the empirical existential statement.

I have used the example of geometrical statements because here I think the existential denial is true. But I think that something can be done for those statements Kant defends in the *Analytic,* and perhaps in the second *Critique.* The argument so far has been that there is a difference between (1) being analytic as being held to be unfalsifiable, which is the Kantian a priori, and (2) being analytic as being reducible to a truth of logic by means of definitions, which is fairly close to the Kantian analytic. While there has been at times a tendency to confuse the two, some have noticed the gap and closed it with a concept of being complicatedly analytic, i.e., while seeing that there are many statements which are apparently unfalsifiable, and also seeing that it would be implausible to suggest some definitional equation as the basis of this unfalsifiability, vague appeal is made to some more recondite form of definition that will take us from one to the other. In this way an amorphous concept of definition is allowed to occupy all the territory that was to be held by Beck's macroscopic test for being analytic.

Concentrating on the concept of definition can help us to concentrate the dispute, because most of the articles dealing with the distinction between analytic and synthetic propositions can be interpreted in terms of it. The important contribution of Waismann's classic articles has come to be seen in their demonstration that the meaning of a word cannot always be given (and cannot perhaps ever be given) through a definitional equation. Yet it is such an equation that is required as a substitution license in the reduction of nonlogical to logical truths. Weitz, developing the view, claims that there are all sorts of statements "whose analytic character has nothing to do with their reducibility to logical truths" [490], and this resistance to the definitional account is produced by his recognizing that analytic character depends on meanings, and meanings cannot be measured by definitions as these are ordinarily understood. If, however, we extend the concept of definition, we can reallocate the analytic character of these statements in their definitional role. Thus H. G. Alexander says that "one might attempt to distinguish different types of necessary statement . . . by considering the different methods of defining the constituent words," [517], and then, distinguishing three main means of definitions, he points out that the notion of substituting definiens for definiendum makes sense only in the case of verbal definition, and not in the cases of ostensive definition or definition in use.

Faced with this difficulty we must either choose to say that there are some necessary truths which are not analytic by definition, or to say that 'analytic' and 'necessary' are coextensional terms, but not all analytic truths are reducible to truths of logic by means of definitions. A strong case can be made for adopting the first of these alternatives, although to adopt it is not to accept a sharp line between analytic and necessary propositions. This, of course, must go.

If our previous argument can be sustained, then we have indicated a class of propositions which are necessary but which are not analytic, and this class will probably contain such a favoured example as 'Nothing can be red and green all over at the one time' as well as 'Every happening has a cause'. The question arises of how we are to delimit within this class those propositions that were of particular concern to Kant.

The question may be taken together with another attack that has been launched upon the notion of an analytic proposition, and which has been taken to introduce a blurring of the line between analytic and synthetic propositions rather than the line between analytic and necessary propositions. This is the attack made by Quine, and which may be broken into two parts. The first part may be represented as accepting the account of analytic propositions as those reducible to truths of logic by means of definitions, and then stipulating that the definitions involved will either be stipulative or lexical, and so concluding that analytic propositions will either be trivial or their analytic nature will founder on one idiosyncratic idiolect. Quine does not find problematic those analytic propositions which are based upon explicit stipulative definitions ('nominal synthetic definitions' in the Kantian scheme), and we may accept these as the paradigm of analytic propositions. We may extend the notion to include analytic propositions which are so because of implicit stipulative definitions by saying that those propositions which a given person holds as necessary, and for which he will accept a suggested stipulation as the basis of their necessary truth, are to be taken as analytic. Such an extension is not an easy one to make, but I think that it can be made, and, if so, we shall still have a class of propositions which are not analytic but which are necessary.

In the second part of his attack Quine takes 'analytic' to be equivalent to the sense of 'necessary' that we have taken to be the Kantian usage. He here argues against the idea that we can speak of analytic or synthetic statements on the grounds that the former are 'verbally' rather than 'factually' true. If we should meet recalcitrance, then some change must be made in our conceptual scheme, but this change can be made at more than one point; and, in theory, there is no statement which is immune from revision. We may, he allows, draw distinctions between statements on the grounds of their relative immunity from revision, but this will be to make the distinction between analytic and synthetic statements one of degree and not of kind.

This view has been variously and continuously attacked—particularly good treatments being those by Grice and Strawson and by Bennett [1]—but from a Kantian point of view it is wholly acceptable once we have remarked that Quine is not talking about the class of analytic, but about the class of necessary propositions. Of course, Kant was inclined, in his talk of the separate contributions of sensibility and understanding, to think of a verbal and a factual component entering into the meaning of any given proposition, but this, with all its corollaries, has long been an object of distaste to the commentators. A particularly original treatment has been given by Schrader, who points out that common to both pure and empirical concepts are the features (1) that they are rules of combination, and (2) that they originate in the understanding (obtain there the "form of generality"). Kant's attempt to link empirical concepts with abstraction from experience must be rejected as un-Critical, for

> the essential difference between empirical and a priori concepts in the *Critique* is not that the former are abstracted from intuition whereas the latter are contributed by the understanding, but rather that the former are contingent while the latter are necessary [4:270-1].

Will this do as a distinction? Schrader argues that the a priori concepts are "contingently necessary" as they are "necessary as conditions for the possibility of experience and contingent in that they are valid only for possible experience." Yet the same thing may also be said of the empirical concepts. The difference is not a difference in kind, but involves a continuum of changing degrees of universality. We are simply generalizing in this spirit when we come to see that there is no sharply delimited class of synthetic a priori propositions. If Quine is right there will be no statements that are totally immune from revision in the face of recalcitrant experience. We may retain, however, an essential Kantian insight that there are propositions which are held to be necessary, i.e. strictly universal, because they are necessary for some, or all, conceptual activity. A non-Kantian example of such a proposition would be 'There are analytic propositions'. We could never be in a position to truly assert the negation of this, for to do so would be to use words with a meaning that would *ipso facto* generate analytic propositions. Yet the proposition could become false, namely if there ceased to exist language users. The example is interesting, for it brings out the existential interest of Kant's synthetic and a priori propositions: something that we could as well have done had we followed the route to Kant's concept not from our concepts of definitions, but from his own. These are admirably explained and employed in two articles by Beck [cf. 2].

8. *The Categorical Imperative*

Beck's *Commentary on Kant's Critique of Practical Reason,* where scholarship in the service of philosophical intelligence has created a book that will remain as indispensable to students of Kant's ethics as are the works of Vaihinger, Kemp Smith, and Paton to students of the first *Critique,* reflects, together with Gregor's study of the *Metaphysics of Morals,* the increased tendency to study Kant's ethics as much through his later writings as through the *Foundations.* Paulsen's conclusion that the *Metaphysic of Morals* was *freilich geringwertig* is now a contestable one: although it is contested on various grounds. Brown, for example, takes it to show that when Kant comes to deal with casuistical questions he is found to have "no principles other than formal consistency on the one hand and *ad hoc* convictions on the other" [44], and accordingly he gives credence to Duncan's interpretation of the *Foundations.* Here 'ethical', 'metaphysical', and 'critical' interpretations are opposed to one another, and it is argued that the categorical imperative is not a moral criterion, but merely a description of an agent's motive when he is acting in a morally good manner. In brief: the status of the categorical imperative is still a disputed one.

There is no difficulty in allowing Duncan's contention that the *Foundations* is intended to further Kant's Critical scheme, but, as Paton [3] has argued, the idea is scarcely tenable that Kant did not intend the categorical imperative as a formula, that is, as a recipe for constructing particular categorical imperatives. That it may be an inadequate formula without extra assumptions is not ground for denying Kant's intention to use it as such.

In two important articles Haezrahi has argued that there must be such assumptions. She claims that the categorical imperative allows as permissible the maxim 'Establish a world dictatorship for the sake of ideal power', in that somebody acting on this maxim has a will which is consistent, free, autonomous, of universal validity, and capable of imposing a definite, rationally consistent order on the world. What provides the categorical imperative with content is given by the proposition: 'in the moral domain all members of the human race enjoy equality of status and hence possess a certain instrinsic worth *qua* human beings' [1:167]. In a second article Kant's reasons for accepting the notion of man as a creature possessed of dignity are examined and compared with those of other writers. Haezrahi insists on the importance of the concept as the real as well as formal cause of moral experience, but is equally sure that "an act of faith, and a gratuitous act of faith at that, is needed for its acceptance" [2:223].

These articles are stimulating and, in the main, correct. My one difficulty with them is almost a technicality, and concerns what we are to use as the *typic* of the abstract principle 'Act only according to that maxim by which you can at the same time will that it should become a universal law'. That it needs a typic to gain application is insisted on by Beck, as well as Hall and Dietrichson [2]. As a typic Haezrahi goes to the formula of man as an end in himself. Gregor goes farther, saying that we must "analyse the nature of man as a composite, animal, rational, and moral being, and compare the maxim in question with the order which reason finds among these elements in his being" [205]. This sounds to me more like Wolff or Crusius than Kant, but it has as a consequence, Gregor believes, that we discover the connection between being free and being rational, and being rational becomes acting in accordance with the formula 'Act only on that maxim which, if it became universal law, would advance systematic harmony amongst human beings'. Any maxim which fails to fit this formula is one that we "cannot consistently will."

Gregor thus goes to the formula of the Kingdom of Ends, but, for Kant, both this and the formula deployed by Haezrahi are derivable from the formula of the law of nature. Whether this is the case, and whether the three formulae as found on Ak.IV.436 are in fact equivalent, is not something discussed in recent literature. But there has been a great deal of work on what is perhaps a precondition of this, namely the question of whether the formula 'Act as though the maxim of your action were by your will to become a universal law of nature' can be made workable as a moral criterion.

A number of examples have been debated in an attempt to show that it can. Not the least important is Kant's case of lying to a murderer, for this introduces all the difficulties of alternative descriptions of an action. Useful discussions can be found in Beck [1] and Moritz [2], while Singer argues persuasively that Kant misapplies his own criterion by slipping from a sense of 'unconditional' meaning 'not conditional upon the desires of the agent' to one meaning 'not conditional upon anything'. A consequence of this must be that we take account of features of the situation in which an agent is placed when we declare his maxim and assess his action, but whether these situational features must be known to the agent, as whether he can make an action permissible or impermissible at will by expanding or contracting his description of his action to make it fall within a narrower or a broader class, are matters that urgently call for discussion.

Attention otherwise has tended to remain with Kant's own four examples in the *Foundations*, which, because they are good examples, does not limit the importance of their discussion. Suicide and neglected talents, the avoidance of which are duties we owe ourselves, are the more difficult cases, and Harrison, in an exchange with Kemp, seems to me to get the better end of the debate in maintaining that these do not fit evenly into the Kantian theory. Certainly, the perfect and imperfect duties to others of avoiding breaking promises and nonbenevolence seems more favourable for obtaining light enough to extend to other examples. The distinction between them has been discussed by Gregor, who shows that it was at first that of legal as opposed to ethical obligation, but that Kant in the *Foundations*, recognizing perfect duties to ourself, came to construe it in terms of duties which did or did not allow exceptions in the interest of inclination. This seems reliable, although I do not clearly perceive how it relates further to the "two criteria" that Kant gives, whereby correlated with perfect and imperfect duties we have (1) maxims which cannot be *thought*, and (2) maxims which cannot be *willed*, without involving inconsistency.

Of these two criteria, there is more agreement over the second, although critics do not by any means speak with one voice. Ebbinghaus is a fair representative of the majority view when he says that the "inconsistency of the will" involved in adopting the maxim of never giving aid to others is that the agent is, in the universalisation of his maxim, willing behaviour on the part of others which could cut across his own self-interest. And, as Ebbinghaus believes, "a man cannot in harmony with his own will choose to be abandoned in misfortune by those who could give him help" [2:106].

There is nobody today who would want to argue that Kant is here introducing an appeal to self-interest, for there is no question, as there is for the naive utilitarian, of the person having to consider the possible consequences of his action in terms of other people actually following his example. Yet despite this, I am not sure that there is not a complexedly prudential type of reasoning going on here—something that is half-moral, and yet not quite moral. This becomes more apparent in Harrison, who takes Kant to mean by 'inconsistency in this will' in this context that "though there is a motive for willing the universal adoption of the maxim [not to help others], for if my maxim were universally adopted, I should not have the disagreeable task of helping others in distress, there is also a motive against, for I would in this case not have the agreeable experience of being helped by others" [1:56]. Surely it is clear that someone who willed the universal adoption of the con- trary maxim, namely *always* to help others, would also, on this criterion, have an inconsistency in his will? It is just that what was previously 'for' is now 'against'. The same objection may be lodged against Dietrichson, who argues that a person has an incon- sistency of the will if, were his maxim to become a law of nature, there would ever, even once, be an occasion on which he would wish or want it not to be so [2:161]. Surely a suitable form of 'Always help others' will be ruled out by this, for there will be occasions on which I would wish it were not a law of nature?

In the face of this apparent inconsistency in either direction, a man might well choose to be abandoned in misfortune if he were sufficiently well endowed with the gifts of nature and of human art to be sure that his self-interest would best be advanced by a policy of never helping others and never being helped by them. Nor would he be willing the abolition of mutual aid, for those who would honestly be prepared, the world being as it is, to waive their right of protest, is only a small one.

In fact, I believe the inconsistency is not that of being unable to give an affirmative answer to 'Are you honestly prepared to face the concrete consequences of people not helping you because of your acting on this maxim?' or 'Are you honestly prepared, in the world as currently arranged, to waive your right of protest?' The first would make it a simple prudential inconsistency, and the second what I have called a complexedly prudential inconsistency. Many people would be able to get through these questions who would not be able to give a positive answer to 'Are you honestly prepared, in the world as it conceivably might be or might have been, to waive your right of protest?' There is this second counter-factual condition involved, such that, in answering the question, we really have to adopt that "common standpoint." As a consequence, there is no longer possible any simple dependence of the test for consistent willing on the desires of the agent, as is suggested in the current literature. There is, as Kant insisted, a sharp break between the consistent deploying of my own desires, and the consistent interaction of the desires of a group of people. A further consequence is that the categorical imperative reduces to the Golden Rule, and as the Golden Rule reduces to the Generalisation Principle, so does the categorical imperative. But there are too many voices against me on this point for me to be able to argue it here.[9]

The status of Kant's 'strong' criterion remains insecure. There is certainly a difference between falsely promising and failing to be benevolent. In the former case my present purpose, which involves making a false promise, would not be possible if it had *always* been the case that all promises (or all promises in that area) were broken. Here the present action is legislated *out* of existence by the universalised maxim, whereas in the latter case my nonbenevolent action is legislated *into* existence, although other actions which I should like to have seen are unfortunately therewith legislated out of existence. A lot of the controversy has centred on the question of whether Kant is making a purely logical point (Kemp), or whether it involves causal argument (Harrison). This seems to me to be resolvable in either direction depending on whether the initial conditions onto which the willed law of nature is grafted are provided by the present day or of the dawn of the world: in the first case causal argument is needed to show that there would soon be no promises, while in the second logical argument suffices to show that there would never have been any promises. The point is confused by questions of the description of the proposed broken promise, for if the maxim is 'Always to break promises to repay

---

[9] I have gone into this a short distance in the original version of this paper (pp. 198-200) but am no longer satisfied with certain points in the position there taken.

money' rather than 'Always to break promises', then the logical argument would fail to function, and the causal argument would have more work to do. But there are still distinctions to be made in this area, and perhaps a total pattern to be found, and what is certain is that both will continue to be sought after.

9. *Freedom and the Highest Good*

I want to finish by remarking some articles that seem to me to be particularly noteworthy and which deal with a number of topics in Kant's treatment of ethics. Schrader, whose work intelligently confronts Kant with developments in modern Continental philosophy, focuses upon the early and unsatisfactory account of freedom when he asks the question: Why does the Aesthetic play such a minor role in the ethical work? He suggests that in the second *Critique* Kant (i) thought of practical reason as determining the will directly, and not needing the senses to mediate a connection with the external world, (ii) believed practical reason to produce its object, and (iii) was more concerned to establish the purity of pure reason than to limit its claims to autonomy. He was therefore not concerned to show that "practical reason is essential for and constitutive of empirical desire as such," so that there is a certain lack of balance in the second *Critique* which Schrader believes needs the correction of some doctrine analogous to the unity of apperception, for "if the 'I think' must accompany every sensation, the 'I will' or its equivalent must surely accompany every empirical desire. For a desire to be in any meaningful sense my desire, it must be integrally related to my consciousness." [7:110]. We must therefore not treat reason as a faculty in itself standing rather loftily above the tugs of particular passions, but ought to immerse it in the flood of experience by providing a new ethical Aesthetic—that of the first *Critique* will not do the job because "when the shift is made from the objective-cognitive perspective on the world to that of practical reason, there is a change of signature for all data to be considered." [7:109]. Put in other terms, the rough material equivalence of being responsible and being free, and the connection between the concept of action and the concept of answerability, imply that an at least possible 'I will' must accompany every action.

This lack of an Aesthetic—a lack denied to exist by Beck in his *Commentary* (chapter 12) —is something which is, to some extent, made up in the later writings, where the will is more fully incorporated into the phenomenal world. Silber argues bluntly that Kant's early attempt to resolve the problems of the Third Antinomy through the distinction between phenomena and noumena is plainly inadequate, in that this would demand what Kant cannot admit, namely, a pre-established harmony between the two worlds [5:xcviii]. An alternative solution is plainly necessary because moral experience involves an awareness of what ought to be done and, at least in some cases, an action on that awareness where both of these are dateable events. This is not to say that the earlier writing is without philosophical value, in that we may gain some observations from it upon the difference between an agent's and a spectator's attitudes to the world, but the full theory will not do as it stands. And it is arguable that Kant did himself point the way to another theory in his later distinction between the concepts of *Wille* and *Willkür*.

A good introduction to the reasons for which Kant introduced this distinction is provided by Fackenheim's treatment of the *Religion*, which begins by pointing out how Kant, who had appealed to many of his contemporaries by showing how man could rise above nature, suddenly shocked them with his doctrine of the radical evil in human nature. Fackenheim traces the doctrine out of a deficiency in the views of the earlier ethical writings where Kant maintains that only a free will can be a good will. At this point Kant was well entrenched in the Platonic tradition, a tradition perfectly expressed by Whichcote's remark that "he is least of all free; nay, he is the veriest slave in the world; who hath either will or power to vary from the law of right."[10] But granted that in ascribing evil to a person we are ascribing responsibility, and in ascribing responsibility we are presupposing freedom, this view "is compelled to deny that there can be such a thing as an evil will. Along with the evil will it must deny evil itself. And in denying both, it cannot justify moral responsibility for moral evil." [345]. After the *Grundlegung*, however, Kant struggles towards the idea of heteronomy as a true mode of willing, so that the will can be defined in terms of

---

[10] *Aphorisms* (1753), A725; cf. *Sermons* (1698), p. 307.

both practical reason and desire instead of merely in terms of practical reason, although this idea has an undesirable consequence, namely

> that a person is still a person in possession of his freedom even if he rejects the law. Thus the law no longer appears to be related to the will as a condition of its being. The categorical imperative seems to resolve itself into a hypothetical one: if one wishes to be moral, he must obey the moral law. . . . [Silber 5:lxxxv].

Kant's reluctance to accept this conclusion leads to the equivocation of the second *Critique,* and is only settled with the introduction of the distinction between *Wille* and *Willkür,* and the concept of *Gesinnung.*

The detailed articulation of these concepts is still a matter of debate. Fackenheim does little to clarify them, in that it is not clear in his account how Kant gets his disjunction that man must be either radically evil or radically good out of his statements about the relation of motives and dispositions, nor is it clear how Fackenheim thinks Kant reconciles the statements that radical evil is both innate and is also brought upon man by himself. There is for all that a clear distinction drawn between Kant's doctrine of radical evil and the Christian doctrine of original sin: for Kant there is the possibility of recreation in every act of decision. This possibility carries as a consequence that man is no longer free only in so far as he is good: he is also free to choose evil.

Nevertheless, the older concept of freedom still finds its place in the later theories. It could be said that man is free to choose to be free. In its first occurrence, 'free' refers to the activity of *Willkür,* which is able to choose to follow the dictates of inclination or of reason. Its second occurrence refers to the consideration that man is only really free when *Willkür* is determined by *Wille.* Strictly, as Silber argues, we should not speak in this way, in that *Wille* does not really act at all, but simply provides an incentive which, if strong enough, is adopted by *Willkür.* Both these faculties are spontaneous in their activity, but it is only in *Willkür's* submission to or free election of the dictate of *Wille* that man may be spoken of as behaving autonomously. There remains, in all this, the question to my mind of whether this terminology is really anything more than terminology, and whether we may not be just as well off if we remain with Hume's talk about reason and the passions. This shifting terminology may perhaps best be viewed in the light of an attempt to reconcile various pressures, without providing a particularly apt way of handling them. Certainly, in the extreme complexity of the relation of disposition to individual performance it becomes somewhat naive to speak of *Willkür* electing not only individual acts but also dispositions, and it illustrates nothing except Kant's demand for unity that he should speak of there being a single disposition of which the sum of any person's acts are, in some way, an expression. Nevertheless the *Religion* is an important document, in that it is virtually the only place where Kant deals with the continuous aspects of personality and will, and we must be grateful to Silber for his courageous plunge into these muddy waters, and for coming out with an answer as to how the categorical imperative is possible in terms of the concept of personality [5:cxxiv].

Silber has also been publishing several studies of the concept of the highest good in Kant's ethics that are intrinsically connected to his interest in the *Religion* and which are enough to raise keen hopes of his book on the ethics. In one argument he points out that Kant was inconsistent in holding the three following statements:

(1) Man is morally obligated to attain in full the highest good.
(2) That to which man is obliged must be possible.
(3) The full attainment of the highest good by man is, in fact, not possible.

Silber argues that it is the inconsistency of these three that led Kant to postulate God and immortality as necessary conditions of the moral law, but he also argues that even with these postulates they are not rendered consistent. If we concede this, we must also concede that one of (1)-(3) is false. That (3) might be false is rejected out of hand, and that (2) is false is argued against on the grounds that 'ought' implies 'can' only because 'can' is a presupposition of 'ought'. Silber's choice therefore falls on (1), which must be changed to say only that man is obligated "to approximate the highest good to the fullest possible degree" [2:478]. In this way the importance becomes apparent of Kant's statement that "nothing is more reprehensible than to derive the laws prescribing what ought to be done from what is done, or to impose upon them the limits by which the latter is circumscribed" [A319=B375]: the highest good becomes a regulative idea against which we can estimate our freedom. The argument is pushed further by Dietrichson [1], who argues from Kant's view that we can never know that our actions are determined by a pure moral motive to an infinitely extensible duty against which our freedom may be gauged. Our duty is not to achieve purity of heart, but only to strive for it. "You never know what you can do until you try" becomes an essential statement in Kant's ethics.

Essentially the same ground is covered in a second question that Schrader puts in his review of Beck's *Commentary*, for, agreeing with Beck that there is no proper Dialectic of pure practical reason, he asks: Is there a moral dialectic as such? If we were to argue by analogy from the first *Critique*, which is concerned with the finitude of the human understanding, we should expect some similar tensions involving the finitude of the human will. Schrader argues in the direction of Kierkegaard that the categorical imperative is not "the injunction to will the law but rather to will in conformity with the demands of the law and hence to will an objective state of affairs" [7:115]. But the highest good, as the final object of man's moral will, is impossible of attainment, and man's will tends to fall to moral futility in the face of this impossibility.

> At times [Kant] was inclined to accept a stoical resolution of the problem which would put the stress upon moral volition as a second-intentional act directed toward the will which is engaged in world process. But at other times he struggled with the problem of the realisability of the moral good as an objective state of affairs beyond the power of human freedom to achieve [7:116].

God, he argues, is needed within the Kantian system for this second problem, to provide assurance that a moral order could be achieved through the exercise of human freedom. It is a persuasive argument even though, when carried through, would seem to require either an identification of the interests of a man with the interests of mankind in an Hegelian manner, or a blind faith that everything turns out for the best in the manner of Kierkegaard.

Attention has always tended to focus more on the 'second intentional act', and a valuable corrective to this can be found in the work of Silber. In a first article we find an argument that is as philosophically cogent as it is historically accurate to the effect that the good must be defined consequently to the law.

> The attempt to ground the principle of morality on a previously defined material concept of good founders on this dilemma: either the good stands in no relation or in a contingent relation to the will, or the good itself has the power to determine the will to action and thereby destroys itself. In neither case can the moral law be derived from the good and, therefore, no relation of obligation can be effected between the good and the will [3:86-7].

Again, if good is defined prior to the law,

> it becomes a homogeneous concept and is related to the will as the object of its desire. But if the good is the object of desire the good is always sought, and virtue and happiness become identified since to the extent that one attains the good he is both virtuous and happy [3:98].

Emphasis must therefore be placed upon the heterogeneity of the good: upon its unification of the formal and the material which, elsewhere, Silber argues as essential to the Kantian theory [Cf. 4]. In a third article Silber specified these formal and material elements more precisely. As one element of the highest good we have the good will, which "is itself the object of the will, and in its act of volition it wills nothing more or less than its own perfection (free willing) as an end which is also a duty" [7:186]. Contingent upon this there is the material demand, which is the foundation for duties to oneself, for the "functional completeness of all our powers" which are necessary for, in so far as they are necessary for, the exercise of moral volition. Yet further content needs to be given if we are to determine the concept of the highest good, and Kant therefore insists that "one is likewise obligated to seek the happiness of others as a second end which is also a duty" [7:191]. The highest good is produced through the combination of these two ends: it is the

> synthesis of the moral good and the natural good. And since the moral good is the supreme condition of this unity, we find that in the fulfilment of the highest good happiness must be present in exact proportion to morality [7:195].

It is the balance of happiness and worthiness to be happy that distinguishes Kant's good from many utilitarian ideals, and it is something which we can go some way toward achieving, although Kant argues that God, and an after life, are necessary for the final balancing of the books. It is interesting to notice that the appeal to God is made not only because we are unable to balance the books, but also that a part reason for this is that we have no sure method of checking the balance sheets. We have the two propositions (1) that happiness ought to be distributed according to virtue, and (2) that virtue is not to be assessed in terms of its effects. The problem has its modern legacy in a distinction which we may make between moral optimists and moral pessimists. The first are those who believe that actions are the best index of virtue that we possess, and therefore advocate distributing the material component of happiness accordingly. The moral pessimists, on the other hand, are those who argue for equal distribution on the grounds either (1) that our safest course is to assume virtue to be distributed equally, or (2) that although virtue is not equally distributed it is, in any case, its own reward, or, less consequentially although primarily, (3) that there is no such thing as freedom or virtue. Although I have drawn them crudely, these are opposed positions which are the modern inheritance of the problem that Kant attempted to solve with his moral argument for the existence of God.

M. J. Scott-Taggart

University of East Anglia,
Norwich

SELECTED BIBLIOGRAPHY

I have made use of the following abbreviations:

AGP   *Archiv für Geschichte der Philosophie*
ANT   *Algemeen Nederlands Tijdschrift voor Wijsbegeerte en Psychologie*
AP   *Archiv für Philosophie*
BJA   *British Journal of Aesthetics*
BJPS   *British Journal for the Philosophy of Science*
F   *Filosofia*
JHI   *Journal of the History of Ideas*
JP   *Journal of Philosophy*
KM   *Kritik und Metaphysik. Studien* [Heimsoeth *Festschrift*]
       (Berlin, de Gruyter, 1966).
KS   *Kant-Studien*
KSE   *Kant-Studien Ergänzungsheft*
PAS   *Proceedings of the Aristotelian Society*
PPR   *Philosophy and Phenomenological Research*
PQ   *Philosophical Quarterly*
PR   *Philosophical Review*
RIP   *Revue internationale de Philosophie*
RM   *Review of Metaphysics*
TSP   *Tulane Studies in Philosophy*
ZPF   *Zeitschrift für philosophische Forschung*

ADDIS, L. C. "Kant's First Analogy," KS vol. 54 (1963) pp. 237-242.

ALBRECHT, W. "Die sogenannte neue Deduktion in Kants Opus Postumum," AP vol. 8 (1954) pp. 57-65.

ALEXANDER, H. G. "Necessary truth," *Mind* vol. 66 (1957) pp. 507-521.

ALEXANDRE, Michel *Lecture de Kant* (Paris, 1961).

ANCESCHI, Luciano D. *Hume e i presupposti empiristici della estetica Kantiana* (Milano, 1956).

ANTONOPOULOS, Georg *Der Mensch als Bürger zweir Welten. Ein Beitrag zur Entwicklungsgeschichte von Kants Philosophie* (Bonn, 1958).

AXINN, Sidney "Kant, Logic, and the Concept of Mankind," *Ethics* vol. 48 (1958) pp. 286-291.

............"And Yet: A Kantian Analysis of Aesthetic Interest," PPR vol. 25 (1964) pp. 108-116.

BALLARD, Edward G. "The Kantian Solution to the Problem of Man within Nature," TSP vol. 3 (1954), pp. 7-40.

BALLAUF, Theodor *Vernünftiger Wille und gläubige Liebe* (Meisenheim, Hain, 1957).

BARBER, Richard L. "Two logics of modality," TSP vol. 3 (1954), pp. 41-54.

BARONE, Francesco "Kant e la logica formale," F vol. 8 (1957) pp. 697-758.

.... "I problemi e il problema della logica transcendentale kantiana," F vol. 8 (1957) pp. 19-68.

BAUMER, William H. "Kant and 'God is': A Reply to Mr. Engel," KS vol. 51 (1959) pp. 27-33.

BECK, L. W. *Commentary on Kant's Critique of Practical Reason* (Chicago, 1960).

.... *Studies in the philosophy of Kant* (New York, Bobbs-Merrill, 1965).

Contains, with other studies:
(1) "Can Kant's Synthetic Judgements be made Analytic," (1955).
(2) "Sir David Ross on Duty and Purpose in Kant," (1955).
(3) "Kant's Theory of Definition," (1956).
(4) "Apodictic Imperatives," (1957).
(5) "The Meta-semantics of the Problem of the Synthetic A Priori," (1957).
(6) "The Fact of Reason," (1960).
(7) "Kant's Two Conceptions of the Will in their Political Context," (1962).

.... "The Second Analogy and the Principle of Indeterminacy," KS vol. 57 (1966) pp. 199-205.

.... "Once more unto the breach," *Ratio* vol. 9 (1967) pp. 33-37.

.... "Kant's Strategy," JHI vol. 28 (1967) pp. 224-236.

BELEVAL, Yvon "Sur un point de comparison entre Kant et Leibniz," KM pp. 1-9.

BENNETT, Jonathan "Analytic and Synthetic," PAS vol. 59 (1958-9) pp. 163-188.

.... "The Status of Determinism," BJPS vol. 14 (1963) pp. 106-119.

.... *Kant's Analytic* (Cambridge, 1966).

BERNAYS, Paul "Zur Frage der Anknüpfung an die Kantische Erkenntnistheorie," *Dialectica* vol. 9 (1955) pp. 23-65; 195-221.

BETH, E. W. "Kants Einteilung der Urteile in analytische und synthetische," ANT vol. 46 (1954) pp. 253-264.

BIEMEL, W. *Die Bedeutung von Kants Begründung der Ästhetik für die Philosophie der Kunst* (KSE, Nr. 77, 1959).

BIRD, Graham "The Necessity of Kant," *Mind* vol. 68 (1959) pp. 389-392.

.... "Analytic and Synthetic," PQ vol. 11 (1961) pp. 227-237.

.... *Kant's Theory of Knowledge* (London, Routledge, 1962).

.... "Logik und Psychologie in der transzendentalen Deduktion," KS vol. 56 (1965) pp. 373-384.

BLACKER, Harry "Kant's Theory of the relation of Imagination and Understanding in Aesthetic Judgements of Taste," BJA vol. 5 (1965) pp. 37-45.

BLAU, J. L. "Kant in America," JP vol. 51 (1954) pp. 874-880.

BROWN, Stuart M. "Has Kant a Philosophy of Law?" PR vol. 71 (1962) pp. 33-48.

BRUGGER, Walter S. J. "Kant und das höchste Gut," ZPF vol. 18 (1964) pp. 50-61.

BUCHDAHL, G. "Causality, Causal Laws and Scientific Theory in the Philosophy of Kant," BJPS vol. 16 (1965) pp. 187-208.

.... "The Relation between 'Understanding' and 'Reason' in the Architectonic of Kant's Philosophy," PAS vol. 67 (1967) pp. 209-226.

BUTTS, Robert E. "Hypothesis and Explanation in Kant's Philosophy of Science," AGP vol. 43 (1961) pp. 153-170.

.... "Kant on Hypotheses in the 'Doctrine of Method' and the Logik," AGP vol. 44 (1962) pp. 185-203.

CAMPO, Mariano "Il problema della totalitá e Kant," Rivista di filosofia neoscolastica vol. 49 (1957) pp. 10-24.

.... Schizzo storica della esegesi e critica kantiana dal 'ritorno a Kant' allo fino dell'ottocento (Varese, Editrice Magenta 1959).

CASTAÑEDA, H. " '7 + 5 = 12' as a Synthetic Proposition," PPR vol. 21 (1960) pp. 141-158.

CASULA, M. Marechal e Kant (Roma, 1955).

.... Studi kantiani sul transcendente (Milano, 1963).

CHIODI, Pietro "La dialletica in Kant," Rivista di filosofia vol. 49 (1958) pp. 254-283.

.... La Deduzione nell' opera di Kant (Torino, 1961).

COBURN, Robert C. "Animadversions on Plantinga's Kant," JP vol. 63 (1966) pp. 546-548.

COLOMBRES, C. A. I. "Diversion significados de libertad en Kant," Sapientia vol. 15 (1960) pp. 54-68.

COMBES, J. "Reflexions sur la logique de la liberté kantienne," Études philosophiques vol. 16 (1961) pp. 261-264.

CONINCK, A. de L'analytique transcendentale de Kant vol. 1 (Louvain, Nauwelaerts, 1955).

.... "L'analytique transcendentale de Kant est-elle coherente?" Revue philosophique de Louvain vol. 54 (1956) pp. 347-361.

COUSIN, D. R. "Kant on the Self," KS vol. 49 (1957) pp. 25-35.

CRAMER, W. Die Monade. Das philosophische Problem vom Ursprung (Stuttgart, 1954).

CRAWFORD, Patricia A. "Kant's Theory of Philosophical Proof," KS vol. 53 (1961) pp. 257-268.

DELEKAT, Friedrich "Das Verhältnis von Sitte und Recht in Kants grossen 'Metaphysik der Sitten' (1797)," ZPF vol. 12 (1958) pp. 59-86.

............*Immanuel Kant* (Heidelberg, Quelle & Meyer, 1963).

DELIUS, Harald *Untersuchungen zur Problematik der sogenannten synthetischen Sätze a priori* (Göttingen, Vandenhoeck & Rupprecht, 1963).

.... "Kategorischer Imperativ und individuelles Gesetz," *Argumentationen Festschrift für Josef König* (Göttingen, Vandenhoeck & Rupprecht, 1964).

DERGGIBUS, A. *Il problema morale in J. J. Rousseau e la validitá dell' interpretatione kantiana* (Torino, 1957).

DIEMERS, A. "Zum Problem des Materialen in der Ethik Kants," KS vol. 45 (1953) pp. 21-32.

DIETRICHSON, Paul "What does Kant Mean by 'Acting from Duty'?" KS vol. 53 (1961) pp. 277-288.

.... "When is a Maxim Fully Universalisable?" KS vol. 55 (1963) pp. 143-170.

DRYER, Douglas P. "Kant on the Verifiability of Metaphysics," JP vol. 54 (1957) pp. 143-4.

.... "The Concept of Existence in Kant," *Monist* vol. 50 (1966) pp. 17-33.

.... *Kant's Solution for Verification in Metaphysics* (London, Allen & Unwin, 1966).

DUNCAN, A. R. C. *Practical Reason and Morality* (London, Nelson, 1957).

DUSSORT, Henri, *L'école de Marburg* (Paris, Presses universitaires 1963).

EBBINGHAUS, J. "Kants Ableitung des Verbotes der Lüge aus dem
.... Rechte der Menschheit," RIP vol. 8 (1954) pp. 409-422.

.... "Kant und das 20. Jahrhundert," *Studium Generale* vol. 7 (1954) pp. 513-524.

.... "Interpretation and Misinterpretation of the Categorical Imperative," (trans. H. J. Paton), PQ vol. 4 (1954) pp. 97-108.

.... "Four Lectures on Kant," *Journal of the Karnatak University* vol. 2 (1958) pp. 1-30.

.... "Kants Rechtslehre und die Rechtsphilosophie des Neukantianismus," *Erkenntnis und Verantwortung. Festschrift für Theodor Litt* (Düsseldorf, Schwann, 1960).

.... "Das kantische System der Rechte des Menschen und Bürgers in seiner geschichtlichen und aktuellen Bedeutung," *Archiv für Rechts- und Sozialphilosophie* vol. 50 (1964) pp. 23-35.

EISENBERG, Paul D. "Basic Ethical Categories in Kant's *Tugendlehre*," *American Philosophical Quarterly* vol. 3 (1966) pp. 255-269.

ENGEL, S. Morris "Kant's Copernican Analogy: A Re-examination," KS vol. 54 (1962) pp. 243-251.

.... "Kant's Refutation of the Ontological Argument," PPR vol. 24 (1963) pp. 20-35.

58 KANT STUDIES TODAY

.... "On the 'Composition' of the *Critique:* A Brief Comment,"
Ratio vol. 6 (1964) pp. 81-91.
EWING, A. C. "Kant's Attack on Metaphysics," RIP vol. 8 (1954) pp. 371-391.
.... "Kant's Views of Immortality," *Scottish Journal of Theology*
vol. 17 (1964) pp. 385-395.
FACKENHEIM, Emil "Kant and Radical Evil," *University of Toronto Quarterly* vol. 23 (1954) pp. 339-353.
.... "Kant's Concept of History," KS vol. 48 (1956) pp. 381-398.
FEIBLEMAN, James K. "Kant and Metaphysics," TSP vol. 3 (1954), pp. 55-88.
FERRARI, Jean "Kant et la récension Garve-Feder de la 'Critique de la raison pure'," *Études Philosophiques* vol. 19 (1964) pp. 12-32.
FLEISCHER, Margot "Die Formeln des kategorischen Imperatives in Kants Grundlegung zur Metaphysik der Sitten," AGP vol. 46 (1964) pp. 201-226.
FLEISCHMANN, Eugene J. "Hegels Umgestaltung der Kantischen Logik," *Hegel-Studien* vol. 3 (1965) pp. 181-207.
FRIEDMANN, Lawrence "Kant's Theory of Time," RM vol. 7 (1954) pp. 379-388.
GAHRINGER, E. "The Metaphysical Aspects of Kant's Moral Philosophy," *Ethics* vol. 44 (1954) pp. 277-291.
GALLINGER, August "Kants Geschichts—und Staatsphilosophie," ZPF vol. 19 (1955).
GOTSHALK, D. W. "Form and Expression in Kant's Aesthetics," BJA vol. 7 (1967) pp. 250-60.
GRABAU, M. J. "Kant's Conception of a 'Metaphysic of Morals'," RM vol. 15 (1962) pp. 770-779.
GRAM, Moltke S. [Ed] *Kant: Disputed Questions* (Chicago, Quadrangle, 1967).
GRAYEFF, F. "The Relation of Transcendental and Formal Logic," KS vol. 51 (1959) pp. 349-352.
GREGOR, Mary J. *Laws of Freedom* (Oxford, Blackwell, 1963).
GRICE, H. P. & STRAWSON, P. F. "In Defence of a Dogma," PR vol. 65 (1956) pp. 141-158.
GOODMAN, Nelson "On Likeness of Meaning," *Analysis* vol. 10 (1949) pp. 1-7.
GUEROULT, Martial "Canon de la raison pure et Critique de la raison pratique," RIP vol. 8 (1954) pp. 331-357.
.... "Vom Kanon der Kritik der reinen Vernunft zur Kritik der praktischen Vernunft," KS vol. 54 (1963) pp. 432-444.
.... "Die Struktur der zweiten Analogie der Erfahrung," KM pp. 10-20.
GUPTA, R. K. "Eine Schwierigkeit in Kants 'Kritik der reinen Vernunft' und Heideggers Kant-Interpretation," ZFP vol. 16 (1962) pp. 429-450.

GURWITSCH, Aron "Der Begriff des Bewusstseins bei Kant und Husserl," KS vol. 55 (1964) pp. 410-427.

HAEZRAHI, Pepita "The Avowed and Unavowed Sources of Kant's Theory of Ethics," *Ethics* vol. 61 (1952) pp. 157-168.

.... "The Concept of Man as an End in Himself," KS vol. 53 (1961) pp. 209-224.

HALL, Robert C. "Kant and Ethical Formalism," KS vol. 52 (1960) pp. 433-439.

HAMBURG, Carl H. "Kant, Cassirer, and the Concept of Space," TSP vol. 3 (1954), pp. 89-112.

HAMLYN, D. W. "Analytic Truths," *Mind* vol. 65 (1956) pp. 359-376.

.... "On Necessary Truth," *Mind* vol. 70 (1961) pp. 514-525.

HANCOCK, R. N. "Ethics and History in Kant and Mill, *Ethics* vol. 68 (1957) pp. 56-60.

.... "A Note on Kant's Third *Critique*," PQ vol. 8 (1958) pp. 261-265.

.... "Kant and the Natural Right Theory," KS vol. 52 (1960) pp. 440-447.

HANSON, N. R. "Copernicus' Role in Kant's Revolution," JHI vol. 20 (1959) pp. 274-281.

.... "The Very Idea of a Synthetic A Priori," *Mind* vol. 71 (1962) pp. 521-524.

HARRISON, Jonathan "Kant's Examples of the First Formulation of the Categorical Imperative," PQ vol. 7 (1957) pp. 50-62.

.... "The Categorical Imperative," PQ vol. 8 (1958) pp. 360-364.

HARTNACK, Justus *Kant's Theory of Knowledge.* (New York, Harcourt, Brace & World, 1967).

HEIDEGGER, Martin *Kant and the Problem of Metaphysics* (1929) Translated with an introduction by J. S. Churchill (Bloomington, Indiana University Press, 1962).

HEIDEMANN, Ingeborg "Der Begriff der Spontaneität in der Kritik der reinen Vernunft," KS vol. 47 (1955) pp. 3-30.

.... "Person und Welt. Zur Kantinterpretation von Heinz Heimsoeth," KS vol. 48 (1956) pp. 344-360.

.... "Zur Kantforschung von H. J. Paton," KS vol. 49 (1957) pp. 107-142.

.... *Spontaneität und Zeitlichkeit* (KSE, Nr. 75, 1958).

.... "Prinzip und Wirklichkeit in der kantischen Ethik," KS vol. 57 (1966) pp. 230-250.

.... "Die Funktion des Beispieles in der kritischen Philosophie," KM pp. 21-39.

HEIMSOETH, Heinz *Studien zur Philosophie Immanuel Kants* (KSE, Nr. 71, 1956). Contains:

  (1) "Chr. Wolffs Ontologie und die Prinzipienforschung I. Kants," (1956).

  (2) "Der Kampf um den Raum in der Metaphysik der Neuzeit," (1925).

(3) "Metaphysik und Kritik bei Chr. A. Crusius," (1926).
(4) "Metaphysische Motive in der Ausbildung des kritischen Idealismus," (1925). This translated in *Gram* above.
(5) "Persönlichkeitsbewusstsein und Ding an sich in der kantischen Philosophie," (1924).
.... "Vernunftantinome und transzendentale Dialektik in der geschichtlichen Situation des kantischen Lebenswerkes," KS vol. 51 (1959) pp. 131-141.
.... *Atom, Seele, Monade* (Mainz Akademie der Wissenschaften und der Literatur; Abhandlungen der Geistes- und Sozialwissenschaften Klasse, Nr. 3, 1960).
.... "Problemverflechtungen in der zweiten Antinome und die Bedeutung der Thematik für Kants Werdegang," ZPF vol. 14 (1960) pp. 3-15.
.... *Studien zur Philosophiegeschichte* (KSA, Nr. 82, 1961). Contains amongst much else:
(1) "Zur Geschichte der Kategorienlehre," (1952).
(2) "Zeitliche Weltunendlichkeit und das Problem des Anfangs," (1960).
(3) "A. Colliers 'Universaler Schlüssel' und der Durchburch des neuzeitlichen Bewusstseinsidealismus," (1960).
.... "Zur Herkunft und Entwicklung von Kants Kategorientafel," KS vol. 54 (1962) pp. 376-403.
.... *Astronomisches und Theologisches in Kants Weltverständnis* (Mainz Akademie der Wissenschaften und der Literatur; Abhandlungen der Geistes- und Sozialwissenschaften Klasse, Nr. 9, 1963).
.... "Zum kosmologischen Ursprung der Kantischen Freiheitsantinomie," KS vol. 57 (1966) pp. 206-229.
.... *Transzendentale Dialektik. Ein Kommentar zu Kants Kritik der reinen Vernunft.* Part I. *Ideenlehre und Paralogismen* (de Gruyter, Berlin, 1966). Part II. *Vierfache Vernunftantinomie* (de Gruyter, Berlin, 1967).
HENDEL, C. W. [Ed.] *The Philosophy of Kant and Our Modern World* (New York, Liberal Arts, 1957).
HENRICH, Dieter "Hutcheson und Kant," KS vol. 49 (1957) pp. 49-69.
.... "Der Begriff der sittlichen Einsicht und Kants Lehre vom Faktum der Vernunft," *Die Gegenwart der Griechen in neuren Denken. Festschrift für Hans Georg Gadamer* (Tübingen, Mohr, 1960).
.... "Über Kants früheste Ethik," KS vol. 54 (1963) pp. 403-431.
.... *Der ontologische Gottesbeweis* (Tübingen, Mohr, 1960).
.... "Zu Kants Begriff der Philosophie," KM pp. 40-59.
HERRING, Herbert *Das Problem der Affektion bei Kant* (KSE, Nr. 67, 1953).
.... "Leibniz' *principium identitatis indiscernibilium* und die Leibniz-Kritik Kants," KS vol. 49 (1957) pp. 389-400.

HILDEBRANDT, Kurt "Kants Verhältnis zu Leibniz in der vorkritischen Periode," ZPF vol. 8 (1954) pp. 3-29.

HINSKE, Norbert "Kants Idee der Anthropologie," *Festschrift für Max Müller* (Freiburg & München, Alber, 1966).

.... "Kants Begriff der Antinomie und die Etappen seiner Ausarbeitung. KS vol. 56 (1966) pp. 485-496.

HOLLIS, Martin "Box and Cox," *Philosophy* vol. 62 (1967) pp. 75-8.

HOLMES, Eugene C. "The Kantian views on Space and Time re-evaluated," PPR vol. 16 (1965) pp. 240-244.

HÜBNER, K. "Leib und Erfahrung in Kants Opus Postumum," ZPF vol. 7 (1953) pp. 204-219.

JANOSKA, George "Der transzendentale Gegenstand," KS vol. 46 (1954) pp. 193-221.

.... "Abgrenzung und Grundlegung der *metaphysica specialis* bei Immanuel Kant," KS vol. 56 (1965) pp. 277-288.

JASPERS, Karl *Kant* (translated from *Die grossen Philosophen*, vol. 1, by Karl Manheim). New York, Harcourt, Brace & World, 1962.

KAESTNER, Heinrich "Das Erkenntnisvermögen als Objekt seiner selbst," *Ratio* vol. 4 (1962) pp. 100-125.

.... "Kant und die moderne Naturwissenschaft," ZPF vol. 18 (1964) pp. 119-125.

KAHL-FURTHMANN, G. "Subjekt und Objekt; Ein Beitrag zur Vorgeschichte der Kant'schen Kopernikanischen Wendung," ZPF vol. 7 (1953) pp. 326-339.

KAMINSKY, J. "Kant's Analysis of Aesthetics," KS vol. 50 (1958) pp. 77-88.

KANTZENBACH, F. W. "Kants Philosophie und ihre vierfache Wirkung auf Christen seiner Zeit," *Zeitschrift für Religions und Geistesgeschichte,* vol. 11 (1959) pp. 327-342.

KAULBACH, Friedrich "Kants Beweis des 'Daseins der Gegenstände im Raum ausser mir," KS vol. 50 (1958) pp. 323-347.

.... "Geist und Raum," *Wissenschaft und Weltbild,* vol. 12 (1959) pp. 523-533.

.... *Die Metaphysik des Raumes bei Leibniz und Kant* (KSE, Nr. 79, 1960).

.... "Das Prinzip der Bewegung in der Philosophie Kants," KS vol. 54 (1963) pp. 3-16.

.... "Leibbewusstsein und Welterfahrung beim frühen und späten Kant," KS vol. 54 (1963) pp. 464-490.

.... "Der Begriff des Standpunktes im Zusammenhang des Kantischen Denkens," AP vol. 12 (1963) pp. 14-45.

.... "Atom und Individuum. Studien zu Heimsoeths Abhandlung 'Atom, Seele, Monade'," ZPF vol. 17 (1963) pp. 3-41.

.... *Der philosophische Begriff der Bewegung* (Köln, Böhlau, 1965).

.... "Weltorientierung, Weltkenntnis und pragmatische Vernunft bei Kant," KM pp. 60-75.

KEMP, J. "Kant's Examples of the Categorical Imperative," PQ vol. 8 (1958) pp. 63-71.
.... *Reason, Action, and Morality* (London, Routledge, 1964).

KERN, Iso *Husserl und Kant* (Hague, Nijhoff, 1964).
KIBED, A. V. von "Der Widerstand gegen den Verstand bei Kant," *Philosophisches Jahrbuch der Görresgesellschaft* vol. 68 (1960) pp. 394-405.
.... "Vom Nutzen und Nachteil einer philosophischen Ethik," *Philosophie und Christentum* (Kampen, 1965) pp. 124-140.
.... *Macht und Ohnmacht der Vernunft* (München, Hueber, 1967).
KLAUSEN, Sverre *Kants Ethik und ihre Kritiker* (Oslo, Jacob Dybwad 1954).
.... *Grundgedanken der materialen Wertethik bei Hartmann und Scheler in ihrem Verhältnis zur Kantischen* (Oslo, 1958).
.... *Das Problem der Erkennbarkeit der Existenz Gottes bei Kant* (Oslo, 1959).
KNITTERMEYER, H. "Zu Heinz Heimsoeths Kantdeutung," KS vol. 49 (1957) pp. 293-311.
KNOX, T. M. "Hegel's Attitude to Kant's Ethics," KS vol. 49 (1957) pp. 70-81.
KOLENDA, Konstantin "Professor Ebbinghaus' Interpretation of the Categorical Imperative," PQ vol. 5 (1955) pp. 74-77.
KONRAD, Johanna "Inwieweit hat Kants Personenbegriff Bedeutung und Gültigkeit für unsere Zeit?" *Jahrbuch der Albertus-Universität Königsberg/Pr* vol. 5 (1954) pp. 97-112.
KOPPER, Joachim "Kants Gotteslehre," KS vol. 47 (1955) pp. 31-61.
.... "Antwort an W. A. Schulze," KS vol. 48 (1956) pp. 84-5.
KÖRNER, S. *Kant* (Penguin Books, 1955).
KRIEGER, Leonard "Kant and the Crisis in Natural Law," JHI vol. 26 (1965) pp. 191-210.
KROEBEL, Werner "Kant und die moderne Physik," *Studium Generale* vol. 7 (1954) pp. 524-533.
LACHIÈZE REY. P. "Réflexions historiques et critiques sur la possibilité des jugements synthétiques à priori," RIP vol. 8 (1954) pp. 358-370.
LAKEBRINK, Bernard "Der kantische Begriff einer transzendentalen Analogie," *Philosophisches Jahrbuch der Görresgesellschaft* vol. 68 (1960) pp. 244-257.
LANDGREBE, Ludwig "Die Geschichte im Denken Kants," *Studium Generale* vol. 7 (1954) pp. 533-544.
LANGE, H. "Über den Unterschied der Gegenden in Raume," KS vol. 50 (1958) pp. 479-499.
LAWRENCE, N. "Kant and Modern Philosophy," RM vol. 10 (1957) pp. 441-456.

LEE, Harold N. "The Rigidity of Kant's Categories," TSP vol. 3 (1954), pp. 113-22.

LEHMANN, Gerhard "Erscheinungsstufung und Realitätsproblem in Kants Opus Postumum," KS vol. 45 (1953) pp. 140-154.

. . . . "Kritizismus und kritische Motive in der Entwicklung der kantischen Philosophie," KS vol. 48 (1956) pp. 25-54.

. . . . "Voraussetzungen und Grenzen systematischer Kantinterpretation," KS vol. 49 (1957) pp. 364-388.

. . . . "System und Geschichte in Kants Philosophie," Il Pensiero vol. 3 (1958).

. . . . Kants Widerlegung des Idealismus," KS vol. 50 (1958) pp. 348-362.

. . . . "Zur Problemanalyse von Kants Nachlasswerk," Il Pensiero vol. 6 (1961).

. . . . "Zur Frage der Spätentwicklung Kants," KS vol. 54 (1963) pp. 491-507.

. . . . "Kant im Spätidealismus und die Anfänge der neukantischen Bewegung," ZPF vol. 17 (1963) pp. 438-456.

LOTZ, J. B., S. J. "Die Raum-Zeit Problematik in Auseinandersetzung mit Kants transzendentaler Ästhetik," ZPF vol. 8 (1954) pp. 30-43.

. . . . [Ed.] Kant und die Scholastik Heute (Pullach, Berchmanskolleg, 1955).

LUPORINI, Cesare Spazio e materia in Kant (Firenze, 1961).

MALGAUD, W. "Kants Begriff der empirischen Realität," KS vol. 54 (1963) pp. 288-303.

MARC-WOGAU, Konrad "Kants Lehre vom analytischen Urteil," Theoria vol. 42 (1951) pp. 140-154.

. . . . "Bemerkungen zu Kants Kritik des ontologischen Gottesbeweises," Danish Yearbook of Philosophy vol. 1 (1964) pp. 85-95.

MARGOLIS, J. "Kafka vs. Eudaimonia and Duty," PPR vol. 19 (1958) pp. 27-42.

MARQUARD, O. "Kant und die Wende zur Ästhetik," ZPF vol. 16 (1962) pp. 231-243; 363-374.

MARQUARDT, C. Skeptische Methode in Blick auf Kant (Freiburg, 1958).

MARTIN, Gottfried Kant's Metaphysics and Theory of Science (trans. Lucas P.G. Manchester, 1955).

. . . . Gesammelte Abhandlungen und Vorträge I (KSE, Nr. 81, 1961).

. . . . "Probleme der Prinzipienlehre in der Philosophie Kants," KS vol. 52 (1960) pp. 173-184.

. . . . "L'élaboration par méthodes électroniques d'un index complet de Kant," Archives de Philosophie vol. 28 (1965) pp. 23-36.

. . . . "Kants Auseinandersetzung mit der Bestimmung des Phänomens durch Leibniz und Wolff als verworrene Vorstellungen," KM pp. 99-105.

MATHIEU, Vittorio "La deduzione transcendentale di Kant," F vol. 7 (1956) pp. 405-440.
.... La filosofia transcendentale e l'Opus Postumum di Kant (Torino, 1958).
MATHUR, G. B. "Hume and Kant in their Relation to the Pragmatic Movement," JHI vol. 16 (1955) pp. 198-208.
MATSON, W. L. "Kant as Casuist," JP vol. 51 (1954) pp. 855-890.
MAVRODES, George I. "Properties, Predicates, and the Ontological Argument," JP vol. 63 (1966) pp. 549-550.
MAYO, Bernard "Incongruity of Counterparts," Philosophy of Science vol. 25 (1958) pp. 109-115.
McRAE, Robert "Kant's Conception of the Unity of the Sciences," PPR vol. 18 (1957) pp. 1-17.
MEIKLEJOHN, Donald "Kantian Formalism and Civil Liberty," JP vol. 51 (1954) pp. 842-848.
MENGÜŞOĞLU, Takiyetten "Der Begriff des Menschen bei Kant," KM pp. 106-119.
MILMED, Bella K. Kant and Current Philosophical Issues (New York University Press 1961).
MIYATA, M. "A reflection on the political philosophy of Kant," Kokka gakkai zasshi vol. 70 (1956) pp. 123-187.
MONRO, D. W. "Impartiality and Consistency," Philosophy vol. 36 (1961) pp. 161-176.
MORITZ, Manfred Kants Einteilung der Imperative (Copenhagen, Munksgaard, 1960).
.... "Pflicht und Moralität. Eine Antinomie in Kants Ethik," KS vol. 56 (1965) pp. 412-429.
MÜLLER-LAUTER, Wolfgang "Kants Widerlegung des materialen Idealismus," AGP vol. 46 (1964) pp. 60-82.
MUNITZ, Milton K. "Kantian Dialectic and Modern Scientific Cosmology," JP vol. 48 (1951) pp. 325-338.
MURALT, A. de La conscience transcendentale dans le criticisme kantien (Paris, 1958).
MURPHY, Jeffrie G. "The highest good as content for Kant's ethical formalism (Beck versus Silber)," KS vol. 56 (1965) pp. 102-116.
NAHM, Milton C. "'Sublimity' and the 'Moral Law' in Kant's Philosophy," KS vol. 48 (1957) pp. 502-524.
NAWRATIL, K. "Wie ist Metaphysik nach Kant möglich?" KS vol. 50 (1958) pp. 163-177.
NEGRI, Antonio La communita estetica in Kant (Galatine, 1957).
.... Alle origine del formalismo giuridico. Studio sul problema della forma in Kant e nei giuristi kantiani tra il 1789 e il 1802 (Padova, 1962).
NICOLIN, F. "Die Schriften Heinz Heimsoeths," ZPF vol. 15 (1961) pp. 579-591.
NIKAM, N. A. Sense, Understanding, and Reason (New York, Asia Publishing House, 1966).

OLIVER, J. W. "Kant's Copernican Analogy: an examination of a re-examination," KS vol. 55 (1964) pp. 505-511.

PANETH, F. A. "Die Erkenntnis des Weltbaus durch Thomas Wright und Immanuel Kant," KS vol. 47 (1955) pp. 337-349.

PANNENBERG, G. "Theologische Motive im Denken Immanuel Kants," Theologische Literaturzeitung vol. 89 (1964) pp. 897-906.

PARKINSON, G. H. R. "Necessary Propositions and A Priori Knowledge in Kant," Mind vol. 69 (1960) pp. 391-397.

PARSONS, Charles "Infinity and Kant's Conception of a Possible Experience," PR vol. 73 (1964) pp. 182-197.

PASINI, D. Diritto, societa e stato in Kant (Milano 1957).

PATON, H. J. "An alleged right to lie: A problem in Kantian ethics," KS vol. 45 (1953) pp. 190-203.

.... "Kant on Friendship," Proceedings of the British Academy vol. 42 (1956) pp. 45-66.

.... "The Aim and Structure of Kant's Grundlegung," PQ vol. 8 (1958) pp. 112-130.

.... "Formal and Transcendental Logic" KS vol. 49 (1957) pp. 245-263.

PATZIG, G. "Die logischen Formen praktischer Sätze in Kants Ethik," KS vol. 56 (1965) pp. 237-252.

PEACH, B. "Common Sense and Practical Reason in Reid and Kant," Sophia vol. 24 (1956) pp. 66-71.

PEARS, D. "The Incongruity of Counterparts," Mind vol. 61 (1952) pp. 78-81.

PELLEGRINO, U. L'Ultimo Kant. Saggio critica sull' Opus Postumum (Milano, 1957).

.... "La filosofia transcendentale e l'Opus Postumum di Kant," Rivista di filosofia neoscolastica vol. 50 (1958) pp. 356-367.

PICHLER, Hans Über den Sinn des kategorischen Imperativs," ZPF vol. 14 (1960) pp. 626-629.

PLAASS, Peter Kants Theory der Naturwissenschaft (Göttingen, Vandenhoeck & Rupprecht, 1965).

PLANTINGA, Alvin "Kant's Objection to the Ontological Argument," JP vol. 63 (1966) pp. 537-546.

PLAT, J. "Ethiek van Kant in de kritische werken," Tijdschrift voor Philosophie vol. 22 (1960) pp. 205-268.

PONCELET, A. "God in het Opus postumum van Immanuel Kant," Bijdragen. Tijdschrift voor philosophie en theologie vol. 22 (1961) pp. 55-69.

QUINE, W. V. O. "Two Dogmas of Empiricism," PR vol. 60 (1951) pp. 20-43.

QUINTON, Anthony "Spaces and Times," Philosophy vol. 37 (1962) pp. 130-174.

REDMAN, Horst G. Gott und Welt. Die Schöpfungstheologie der vorkritischen Periode Kants (Göttingen, 1962).

REES, D. A. "Kant's 'Physiology of the Human Understanding'," JHI vol. 15 (1952) pp. 112-130.

.... "Kant, Bayle, and Indifferentism," PR vol. 63 (1954) pp. 592-595.

REICH, Klaus "Die Tugend in der Idee. Zur Genese von Kants Ideenlehre," *Argumentationen. Festschrift für Josef König* (Göttingen, Vanderhoeck & Rupprecht, 1964).

REINER, Hans *Pflicht und Neigung* (Meisenheim, Hain, 1951).

.... "Die goldene Regel," ZPF vol. 3 (1948) pp. 74-105.

.... "Kants Beweis zur Widerlegung des Eudämonismus und das A Priori der Sittlichkeit," KS vol. 54 (1962) pp. 129-165.

REISS, H. S. "Kant and the Right of Rebellion," JHI vol. 17 (1956) pp. 179-192.

REMNANT, Peter "Kant and the cosmological argument," *Australasian Journal of Philosophy* vol. 37 (1959) pp. 152-155.

.... "Incongruent Counterparts and Absolute Space," Mind vol. 73 (1963) pp. 393-399.

RESCHER, N. "Presuppositions of Knowledge," RIP vol. 13 (1959) pp. 418-429.

RICHMAN, R. J. "Why are Kant's Synthetic A Priori Judgements Necessary?" *Theoria* vol. 30 (1964) pp. 5-20.

ROBINSON, Richard "Necessary Propositions," *Mind* vol. 67 (1958) pp. 289-304.

ROGERS, W. K. "On a Comprehensive Principle in the Kantian Critiques," KS vol. 52 (1960) pp. 448-451.

ROMBACH, H. "Die Frage nach dem Menschen," *Festschrift für Max Müller* (Freiburg & München, 1966).

ROTENSTREICH, Nathan *Experience and its Systematization* (Hague, Nijoff, 1965).

RUST, Hans "Kritisches zu Kants Religionskritik," *Jahrbuch der Albertus-Universität zu Königsberg/Pr* vol. 6 (1955) pp. 73-106.

SAARNIO, U. "Die logischen Grundlage der formalen Ethik Immanuel Kants," KS vol. 57 (1966) pp. 484-499.

SCHÄFER, Lother *Kants Metaphysik der Natur* (Berlin, de Gruyter, 1966).

SCHAPER, Eva "Kant's Schematism Reconsidered" RM vol. 18 (1964) pp. 267-292.

.... "The Kantian 'As-if' and its Relevance for Aesthetic" PAS vol. 65 (1965) pp. 219-234.

.... "The Kantian Thing-in-Itself as a Philosophical Fiction," PQ vol. 16 (1966) pp. 233-243.

SCHIPPER, E. W. "Kant's Answer to Hume's Problem," KS vol. 53 (1961) pp. 68-74.

SCHMUCKER, Josef "Der Einfluss des Newtonschen Weltbildes auf die Philosophie Kants," *Philosophische Jahrbuch* vol. 65 (1951) pp. 52-59.

.... "Der Formalismus und die materialen Zweckprinzipien in der Ethik Kants," *Kant und die Scholastic Heute* (Ed. Lotz q.v.) pp. 155-205.

.... *Die Ursprünge der Ethik Kants* (Meisenheim, Hain, 1961).

.... "Die Gottesbeweise beim vorkritischen Kant," KS vol. 54 (1963) pp. 445-463.

.... "Die Originalität der ontotheologischen Argumentes Kants," KM pp. 120-133.

SCHNEEBERGER, Guido *Kants Konzeption der Modalbegriffe* (Basel, 1952).

SCHNEIDER, F. "Kants *Allgemeine Naturgeschichte* und ihre philosophische Bedeutung," KS vol. 57 (1966) pp. 167-177.

SCHOELER, W. F. *Die transzendentale Einheit der Apperzeption von Immanuel Kant* (Bern, 1959).

SCHOLZ, Heinrich "Eine Topologie der Zeit im Kantischen Sinne," *Dialectica* vol. 9 (1955) pp. 66-113.

SCHRADER, George "Kant's Presumed Repudiation of the 'Moral Argument' in the *Opus Postumum:* An Examination of Adickes' Interpretation," *Philosophy* vol. 26 (1951) pp. 228-241.

.... "The Transcendental Ideality and Empirical Reality of Kant's Space and Time," RM vol. 4 (1951) pp. 507-536.

.... "The Status of Teleological Judgement in the Critical Philosophy," KS vol. 45 (1953) pp. 204-235.

.... "Kant's Theory of Concepts," KS vol. 49 (1957) pp. 264-278.

.... "Ontology and the Categories of Existence," KS vol. 54 (1963) pp. 47-62.

.... "Autonomy, Heteronomy, and the Moral Imperatives," JP vol. 60 (1963) pp. 65-77.

.... "Basic Problems of Philosophical Ethics," AGP vol. 46 (1964) pp. 102-117.

SCHULLER, Herbert M. "Immanuel Kant and the Aesthetics of Music," *Journal of Aesthetics and Art Criticism* vol. 14 (1955-56) pp. 218-247.

SCHULZE, W. A. "Zu Kants Gotteslehre," KS vol. 48 (1956) pp. 80-84.

SCHWARZ, W. "Kant's Philosophy of Law and International Peace," PPR vol. 23 (1962) pp. 71-80.

SILBER, J. R. "The Metaphysical Importance of the Highest Good as the Canon of Pure Reason in Kant's Philosophy," *Texas Studies in Literature and Language* vol. 1 (1959) pp. 233-244.

.... "Kant's Conception of the Highest Good as Immanent and Transcendent," PR vol. 68 (1959) pp. 469-492.

.... "The Copernican Revolution in Ethics: the Good Re-examined," KS vol. 51 (1959) pp. 85-101.

.... "The Context of Kant's Ethical Thought," PQ vol. 9 (1959) pp. 193-207; 309-318.

.... "The Ethical Significance of Kant's *Religion*," *Religion Within the Limits of Reason Alone* (trans. Greene and Hudson, New York, Harper, 1960) pp. lxxix-cxxxiv.

.... "Die Analyse des Pflicht- und Schuld- Erlebnisses bei Kant und Freud," KS vol. 52 (1960) pp. 259-309.

.... "The Importance of the Highest Good in Kant's Ethics," *Ethics* vol. 73 (1962) pp. 179-197.

.... "Der Schematismus der praktischen Vernunft," KS vol. 56 (1965) pp. 253-273.

SINGER, Marcus G. "The Categorical Imperative," PR vol. 63 (1954) pp. 577-591.

.... *Generalisation in Ethics* (New York, Knopf, 1961).

.... "The Golden Rule," *Philosophy* vol. 38 (1963) pp. 293-314.

SKILLEN, A. "The Myth of Temporal Division," *Analysis* vol. 26 (1965) pp. 44-47.

SMART, Harold R. "Two Views on Kant and Formal Logic," PPR vol. 16 (1955) pp. 155-191.

STADLER, Ingrid "Perception and Perfection in Kant's Aesthetics," *Kant* (Ed. Wolff, Doubleday, New York, 1967) pp. 339-384.

STEGMÜLLER, Wolfgang "Der Begriff des synthetischen Urteils A priori und die moderne Logik," ZPF vol. 8 (1954) pp. 535-563.

STENIUS, Erik "On Kant's Distinction between Phenomena and Noumena," *Philosophical Essays Dedicated to Gunnar Aspelin* (Lund, 1963) pp. 230-246.

.... "Are True Numerical Statements Analytic or Synthetic?" PR vol. 74 (1965) pp. 357-372.

STERN, A. "Kant and our Time," PPR vol. 16 (1955) pp. 531-539.

STRAWSON, P. F. *Individuals* (London, Methuen, 1959).

.... & GRICE, H. P. "In Defense of a Dogma," PR vol. 65 (1956) pp. 141-158.

.... *The Bounds of Sense* (London, Methuen, 1966).

SWINBURNE, R. G. "Times," *Analysis* vol. 25 (1964) pp. 185-191.

.... "Conditions for Bitemporality," *Analysis* vol. 26 (1965) pp. 47-50.

TODES, Samuel J. "Knowledge of the Ego," *Kant* (Ed. Wolff, New York, Doubleday, 1967) pp. 166-171.

TONELLI, Giorgio "La formazione del testo della Kritik der Urteilskraft," RID vol. 8 (1954) pp. 423-448.

.... "Der Streit über die mathematische Methode in der Philosophie der ersten Hälfte des XVIII Jahrhunderts und die Entstehung von Kants Schrift über die 'Deutlichkeit'," AP vol. 9 (1955) pp. 37-66.

.... *Dall'estetica metafisica all' estetica psicoempirica. Studi sulle genesi del Criticismo (1754-1771) e sulle sue fonti* (Memorie dell Academia delle Scienze di Torino, Ser. 3, Tom. 3, Pt II, 1955).

.... "L'origine della tavola dei giudize e del problema della deduzione delle categorie in Kant," F vol. 7 (1956) pp. 129-138.

.... "Von den verschiedenen Bedeutungen des Wortes 'Zweckmässigkeit' in der Kritik der Urteilskraft," KS vol. 49 (1957) pp. 154-166.

.... "La tradizione delle categorie aristotelische nelle filosofia moderna sine a Kant," *Studi Urbinati,* Ser. B vol. 32 (1958) pp. 121-143.

.... *Elementi metafisici e metodologici in Kant* (1754-1768) Vol. I (Torino, Edizioni di 'Filosofia', 1959).

.... "La question des bornes de l'entendement humain au XVIIᵉ siècle et la genèse du criticisme kantien," *Revue de metaphysique et de Morale* vol. 62 (1959) pp. 396-427.

.... "La nécessité de lois de la nature en XVIIIᵉ siècle et chez Kant en 1762," *Revue d'histoire des sciences et de leurs applications* vol. 12 (1959) pp. 225-241.

.... "Critiques of the Notion of Substance Prior to Kant," *Tijdschrift voor Philosophie* vol. 23 (1961) pp. 285-301.

.... "Der historische Ursprung der kantischen Termini 'Analytik' und 'Dialektik'," *Archiv für Begriffsgeschichte* vol. 8 (1963) pp. 120-139.

.... "Das Wiederaufleben der deutsch-aristotelischen Terminologie in der Entstehung der Kritik der reinen Vernunft," *Archiv für Begriffsgeschichte* vol. 8 (1963) pp. 233-242.

.... "Die Umwälzung von 1769 bei Kant," KS vol. 54 (1962) pp. 369-375.

.... "Deux sources britanniques ou oubliées de la morale kantienne," *Mélanges Alexandre Koyré* (Paris, Hermann, 1964) pp. 496-505.

.... "Kant's Early Theory of Genius" *Journal of the History of Philosophy,* vol. 4 (1966) pp. 109-131; 209-224.

.... "Die Anfänge von Kants Kritik der Kausalbeziehungen und ihre Voraussetzungen im 18. Jahrhundert," KS vol. 57 (1966) pp. 417-456.

.... "Die Voraussetzungen in der Logik des 18. Jahrhunderts," KM pp. 134-158.

TURBAYNE, Colin M. "Kant's Refutation of Dogmatic Idealism," PQ vol. 5 (1955) pp. 225-244.

VALLENILLA, E. M. *El problema de la nada en Kant* (Madrid, 1965).

VANCOURT, R. "Kant et la solution rationaliste du problème des religions," *Mélanges de science religieuse* vol. 22 (1965) pp. 153-192.

VLACHOS, Georges K. *La Pensée politique de Kant* (Paris, 1962).

VLEESCHAUWER, H. J. de *The Development of Kantian Thought* (trans. Duncan A. R. C., London, Nelson, 1962).

.... "A Survey of Kantian Philosophy," RM vol. 11 (1957) pp. 122-142.

.... "Études kantiennes contemporaines," KS vol. 54 (1962) pp. 63-119.

.... "Wie ich jetzt die Kritik der reinen Vernunft entwicklungsgeschichtlich lese," KS vol. 54 (1962) pp. 351-368.

.... *La 'Nachricht von der Einrichtung seiner Vorlesungen in dem Winterhalben Jahre von 1765-6' d'Immanuel Kant* (Pretoria, University of South Africa, 1965) .

.... "La Doctrine der Suicide dans l'éthique de Kant," KS vol. 57 (1966) pp. 251-265.

.... "Logica genuina ou le purisme logique. Kant et Geulincx," KM pp. 159-173.

VUILLEMIN, Jules *Physique et métaphysique kantiennes* (Paris, 1955) .

.... "Reflexionen über Kants Logik," KS vol. 52 (1960) pp. 310-335.

WAGNER, Hans "Zur Kantinterpretation der Gegenwart. Rudolf Zocher und Heinz Heimsoeth," KS vol. 53 (1961) pp. 235-254.

WAISMANN, F. "Analytic-Synthetic," *Analysis* vol. 10 (1950) pp. 25-40.

WALSH, W. H. "Schematism" KS vol. 49 (1957) pp. 95-106.

.... "Kant's Moral Theology," *Proceedings of the British Academy* vol. 49 (1963) pp. 263-289.

.... "Philosophy and Psychology in Kant's *Critique*," KS vol. 57 (1966) pp. 186-198.

.... "Kant," *The Encyclopedia of Philosophy* (New York, Glencoe, 1967) vol. 4 pp. 305-324.

WARD, K. "The Unity of Space and Time," *Philosophy* vol. 62 (1967) pp. 68-74.

WARNOCK, G. J. "Kant," *A Critical History of Western Philosophy* (edited by D. J. O'Connor, New York, Free Press, 1964) pp. 296-318.

WASSMER, Thomas A. "Responsibility and Pleasure in Kantian Morality," KS vol. 52 (1960) pp. 452-466.

WEILER, Gershon "Kant's 'Indeterminate Concept' and the Concept of Man," RIP vol. 59 (1962) pp. 432-446.

WEITZ, Morris "Analytic Statements," *Mind* vol. 63 (1954) pp. 487-494.

WEIZSÄCKER, C. F. von "Kants 'Erste Analogie der Erfahrung' und die Erhaltungssätze der Physik," *Argumentationen. Festschrift für Josef König* (Göttingen, Vandenhoeck & Rupprecht, 1964) .

WELDON, T. D. *Kant's Critique of Pure Reason*. Second ed., Oxford, Clarendon Press, 1958.

WENZL, Alois *Immanuel Kants bleibende Bedeutung* (München, 1954) .

WEYAND, Klaus *Kants Geschichtsphilosophie* (KSE, Nr. 85, 1963) .

WHITE, Morton G. "The Analytic and the Synthetic: An Untenable Dualism," *John Dewey: Philosopher of Science and Freedom* (New York, Dial, 1950) .

WHITELY, C. H. "Universalisability," *Analysis* vol. 27 (1966) pp. 45-49.

WHITTEMORE, R. "The metaphysics of the seven formulations of the Moral Argument," TSP vol. 3 (1954) , pp. 133-161.

WILKINS, B. T. "Teleology in Kant's Philosophy of History," *History and Theory* vol. 5 (1966) pp. 172-185.

WILLIAMS, M. E. "Kant's Reply to Hume," KS vol. 66 (1965) pp. 41-48.

WITTHANSEN, Johannes *En Kritisk analyse af materiebegreket hos Newton, Kant, og Einstein* [with English summary] (Copenhagen, 1958).

WOLFF, R. P. "Kant's Debt to Hume via Beattie," JHI vol. 21 (1960) pp. 117-123.

.... *Kant's Theory of Mental Activity* (Harvard, 1963).

.... [Ed.] *Kant* (New York, Doubleday, 1967).

ZOCHER, Rudolf "Kants transzendentale Deduktion der Kategorien," ZPF vol. 8 (1954) pp. 161-194.

.... "Zu Kants transzendentaler Deduktion der Ideen der reinen Vernunft," ZPF vol. 12 (1958) pp. 43-74.

.... *Kants Grundlehre* (Erlangen, Erlangener Forschungen, 1959).

.... "Der Doppelsinn des kantischen A priori," ZPF vol. 17 (1963) pp. 66-74.

ZWEIG, Arnulf *Kant's Philosophical Correspondence* (Chicago, 1967).

KANT ON THE ERRORS OF LEIBNIZ

1. *Amphiboly of the Concepts of Reflexion*

In Kant's *Critique of Pure Reason* 'the categories of the understanding' are the fundamental concepts under which every object must be thought if it is to be an object of experience. He believes himself to have established a complete list of such categories; and he hardly bothers to discuss, except perfunctorily, any other concepts which might also be supposed to be categories. He does, however, discuss certain other fundamental concepts, which he calls 'concepts of reflexion' or 'concepts of comparison'. These are sometimes supposed—entirely by themselves and without any aid from the senses—to give us knowledge of reality. A reality known solely by such concepts would have to be regarded as an intelligible reality (a *noumenon*); and such an intelligible reality has even been assumed to be reality as it is in itself.

Kant discusses these concepts in an Appendix to the *Analytic* (A260 ff.=B316 ff.). This appendix has been curiously neglected by his critics and commentators—perhaps partly because it is an appendix and perhaps also because of its repellent title: *The Amphiboly of the Concepts of Reflexion*'. But the word 'amphiboly' is only the Greek for 'ambiguity'; and Kant often consigns his most fundamental thoughts to appendices and even to footnotes. This particular appendix throws light on his own central doctrines; but its special value is that it contains what the Germans call his *Auseinandersetzung*—his coming to terms—with the philosophy of Leibniz.

He argues that the whole Leibnizian doctrine rests on a failure to grasp the ambiguity of these so-called 'concepts of reflexion'; and he professes to show how all the main errors of Leibniz follow systematically and necessarily from this fundamental failure. Seldom can so damaging a criticism have been made in so short a space. Whether we are able to accept it or not, it at least demands an answer. Kant, it must be remembered, might claim to have an inside knowledge of Leibnizian philosophy, at least in the form given it by Christian Wolff; for this was the philosophy in which he himself was brought up. Hence we have here the spectacle of one powerful mind struggling to re-think the philosophy of another from its foundations and, so to speak, to disrupt it from within.

All that can be attempted here is to pull together an argument which is oddly repetitive and to simplify (perhaps to over-simplify) its troublesome complexity. Modern science and modern logic have moved so far since Kant's time that it would require a treatise—not a short article—to translate him into modern terms. In any case we have first to understand Kant as a thinker of the Eighteenth Century before we can begin to improve on his doctrines in the light of the new knowledge. If I can help to stimulate attempts at such understanding, this is as much as I can hope to do. I fear also that I have to take over many of Kant's technical terms without adequate explanation. Some efforts to explain them may be found in my book, *Kant's Metaphysic of Experience* (which I refer to as KME).

2. *The Concepts of Reflexion*

Presumably any concepts whatever can be compared or reflected upon; but this of itself does not make them concepts of comparison or reflexion. Kant is concerned with concepts of a higher order, concepts functioning in all our comparisons and reflexions. For our present purposes we need not attempt to distinguish between comparing concepts with one another and reflecting upon them.

Let us assume that it is possible to think unreflectively about the world, as we do in ordinary experience and even to some extent in science. When we, so to speak, turn our mind back on our unreflective thinking, we are already beginning to reflect; but we are faced with the difficulty that there are at least two different ways of reflecting—there may be more.

First of all we may compare our concepts in abstraction, and this may be described as a process of purely *logical* reflexion. Here we do not take into account the nature of their supposed objects: we do not ask whether these are merely objects of thought or are possible objects of experience; nor do we ask—for Kant this is another aspect of the same question—whether our concepts have their origin in understanding or in sense. When we begin to ask these questions we have passed from purely logical reflexion to what he calls *transcendental* reflexion.

The central point is this. In what ought to be purely logical reflexion we may take it for granted that what we say about our concepts must be true also of their assumed objects. This is a fruitful source of philosophical fallacies. The only cure is to be found in transcendental reflexion.

The whole *Critique of Pure Reason* may be regarded as a work of transcendental reflexion. It seeks to trace the origin of our concepts to the different capacities and powers of the human mind: and in this way it seeks to determine the character of their supposed objects. In particular it stresses the difference between sense and understanding as sources of our ideas; and its central principle is that without sensuous intuition as well as concepts or categories of the understanding there can be no knowledge of real objects.

The same principle must be applied to the concepts of reflexion. Otherwise we may be misled by their ambiguity into thinking that by themselves they can give us knowledge of reality.

What then are these mysterious concepts of comparison or reflexion?

According to Kant there are four main headings under which concepts have to be compared: (1) identity and difference; (2) agreement and opposition; (3) inner and outer; and (4) form and matter (or the determinant and the determinable). Our concepts of these headings are the concepts of comparison or reflexion which we seek.

This list of the concepts of comparison follows the same order (Quantity, Quality, Relation, and Modality) as is found in the list of the forms of judgement and of the categories: it too is supposed to be exhaustive, presumably because to compare is essentially to judge.

All of this produces a nest of puzzles which cannot here be discussed.

3. *The Central Error of Leibniz*

Our primary concern is with the details of Kant's argument, but before going on to these it may be well to look briefly at what he regards as the central error of Leibniz. Bertrand Russell maintains that Leibniz went wrong because he rested his metaphysics on a subject-predicate logic. It may be argued that Kant also rests upon a subject-predicate logic, but this need not necessarily vitiate his criticism of Leibniz—at least as an *argumentum ad hominem*. What Kant holds is that Leibniz went wrong because he had a false view of the subject-predicate relation: he supposed that in a true proposition the predicate was in the subject; and he took this vague phrase to mean that the predicate was in the *notion* or *concept* of the subject. That is to say, he failed to distinguish between the subject and the concept of the subject (or the subject-concept) —thus blurring the difference between analytic and synthetic propositions; and from this confusion all the doctrines of the *Monadology* follow.

The same criticism may be put—perhaps too simply—in another way. Leibniz assumed that there is no more in an object than is contained in the concept of the object. Hence he compared things merely by comparing their concepts, and naturally he found in things only the differences to be found in their concepts—particularly in the pure concepts of comparison or reflexion. This led him to confuse the object of pure conception (the noumenon, which for Kant is no real object at all) with sensible or phenomenal objects (which are the only real objects of knowledge). In Kant's own words (A270 = B326) : he compared all things with one another merely by concepts and found, as is natural, no other differences than those by which understanding distinguishes its pure concepts from one another.

That is to say, Leibniz *intellectualised* phenomena, whereas Locke had chosen the reverse way and *sensified* the concepts of pure understanding by deriving them from sensuous impressions. As against these errors Kant insists that understanding and sensibility are two entirely different sources of ideas and only in combination can they give us knowledge of objects. For him the fundamental mistake of Leibniz lay in supposing that pure concepts by themselves can give us knowledge both of intelligible things in themselves and also of sensible or phenomenal objects. He failed to ask how the objects of such concepts can be given and supposed that our senses merely confuse and distort the concepts of understanding.

4. *The Identity of Indiscernibles*

The meaning of Kant's criticism becomes more clear under the heading of identity and difference. Leibniz maintained that if two objects—say, two drops of water—had exactly the same quality and quantity, then they were the same object: they were numerically identical and so must be one object and not two.

This conclusion is inevitable on his intellectualistic presuppositions; and it has been glorified by being called the 'principle of the identity of indiscernibles'. If individual objects can be known by means of concepts alone, then where, as in the present illustration, the concept is the same, the alleged objects must be regarded as one and the same object; and—as Kant says in A280 = B336—all that can be done is to set one and the same thing in different relationships (which for the two drops, or rather one drop, of water in question are different spatial relationships).

Once we recognise that if an object is to be known, it must be given to sense and not merely conceived, this artificial difficulty disappears. Drops of water, if they are to be known, must be given to sense under the form of space; and even if they are exactly alike, the mere fact that they are in different parts of space means that they must be numerically different: there must be two drops and not one. So too if we consider different parts of space—for example, two cubic feet; so far as the concept of them is concerned, they are identical; but they are still numerically different because of their different location.

All of this bears out Kant's central contention. If we first of all make comparisons merely between concepts and then transfer these comparisons to the objects of these concepts without reflecting on the way in which the objects can be known, we are in danger of falling into absurdities.

5. *Agreement and Opposition*

Similar absurdities arise if we pass unreflectively from the merely logical agreement and opposition of concepts to the real agreement and opposition of things. Even if we can say that there is no logical opposition between affirmations, we are not entitled to infer from this that there is no opposition either between things in themselves (of which we have no knowledge at all) or between objects in nature, which we know by means of sense. Yet this was precisely the inference made by Leibniz and still more by his followers, although it was not proclaimed with all the pomp of a new principle as in the previous case.

Here again if we confine ourselves to the purely logical comparison of concepts, we can say that no opposition between realities is conceivable. According to Kant (A283n=B339n) this means merely that a concept which contains only affirmations contains no negations—a proposition which he admits he has never doubted. But it was on this fragile basis that the Leibnizians inferred that all evil was merely negative—it was simply a consequence of the limitations of created beings. Similarly they inferred that all reality could be combined without conflict in one being. This refers, I think, to the way in which some philosophers arrived, by purely logical considerations, at the concept of God as the original being, the highest being, the most real being, the being of beings, and so on. See A571 ff. = B599 ff.

This way of thinking is inevitable if we suppose that things can be known merely by means of concepts and so are to be considered as noumena. When we remember that objects of knowledge are only phenomena or appearances, the absurdity of the argument again becomes obvious. Pain, for example, may outweigh and cancel pleasure. One phenomenal reality can cancel another in whole or part, as when two moving forces in the same straight line pull or push a point in opposite directions. Thus there may be real opposition between realities even when there is no logical opposition between their concepts.

6. *Monads*

The remaining fallacies have a greater interest, not only because they concern the central core of the Leibnizian philosophy, but also because they enable Kant to clarify his own relational doctrines of substance and space.

If under the head of 'relation' we compare concepts from a purely logical point of view, we are faced with an absolute distinction between the inner and outer—the internal and external; for one concept either contains or does not contain what is contained in the other. Here again we fall into an amphiboly if we transfer these distinctions unreflectively from concepts to objects or things. From a purely intellectual point of view all relations, according to Kant, must be external: they presuppose something to be related which is itself absolutely independent of external relations. Such a 'something' must be conceived as a substance which is, so to speak, entirely internal. In being free from all external relations, there can be in it no composition, no parts outside other parts. That is to say, only a simple substance can stand in relations; and so we arrive inevitably at the view of Leibniz that the stuff of reality is made up entirely of simple substances, that is, of monads.

But how are we to conceive of such monads? If we look for simple substances in space, we cannot find them. The inner determinations of substances in space, that is, of phenomenal substances, consist entirely in relations—relations of space, of shape, of motion, and of causality. We know substances only by their powers of attraction, repulsion, and impenetrability—that is, by their relations to other things in space. These qualities are only relatively, not absolutely, internal; and in space we know no other qualities which can constitute a substance. Since from an intellectualistic point of view like that of Leibniz we must regard our simple substances as possessing wholly internal powers and characteristics, it is inevitable that we should regard our monads as minds or as analogous to minds; and we must take their internal states or characteristics to be thoughts or analogous to thoughts, for these as known by inner sense are the only absolutely inner characteristics with which we are acquainted. The internal power of a monad can consist only in having ideas, and such monads must constitute the fundamental stuff of which the entire universe is made. A monad may be defined as a simple being possessed of ideas.

Once this is assumed, it becomes obvious that there can be no real reciprocal connexion—no real community or communion—between monads. Whatever communion there may be cannot be one of physical influence or interaction, but must spring from a pre-established harmony. Since the ideas of the monads are wholly internal, there can be no real connexion between the ideas of two different monads, and so there must be some third cause which influences them and makes their states of mind correspond. This result, on the view of Leibniz, is not produced separately on each occasion: he rejects the doctrine of occasionalism or of supernatural assistance. The pre-established harmony must follow from the unity of the idea of one valid cause for all states of the monads. From this cause all monads must receive, in accordance with universal laws, both their existence and their permanence, and consequently also their mutual correspondence.

According to Kant this doctrine rests upon the same false abstraction as the others: it follows inevitably from supposing that objects or things can be known by pure conception, and from forgetting that they must also be given to sense under the forms of time and space. While it is true that solely by means of concepts we cannot think of anything external except by reference to something internal, this does not apply to our intuitions of objects in space. Our intuition of an object always contains something more than is present in the mere concept of an intelligible object as such; for it is by intuition that we are aware of space and of permanent appearances in space. Space, with all it contains, consists only of formal relations between spaces or of real relations between bodies; and a permanent appearance in space—that is, impenetrable extension—contains mere relations and nothing whatever that is absolutely internal; yet in spite of this it can be the ultimate substratum of all our outer perceptions. In actual objects as phenomena it is simply not true that what is external or relational must be based on something absolutely internal; and so the whole elaborate structure of Leibniz must fall to the ground.

It is sometimes assumed to-day, perhaps by a lack of transcendental reflexion, that if we accept a relational theory of space we must reject Kant and follow Leibniz; but it should already be clear that Kant's theory of space is at least as relational as that of Leibniz. This will become more obvious under the next heading.

7. Form and Matter

Kant regards the concepts of form and matter as the basis of all our reflexions, and indeed as bound up inseparably with every use of the understanding. In his most general or abstract account of them he is, I think, trying to state clearly a traditional distinction, not to put forward a special theory of his own; but it is not always easy to be certain where the traditional account ends and his own modifications of it begin.

Broadly speaking, matter is for him the 'determinable' *(Bestimmbar)* and form the 'determinant' *(Bestimmung)*. It may seem only an extension of this usage to say that the matter is what is given (whether to thought or sense) and the form is the way in which the given is thought (A279 = B335). Here thought is supposed to determine or even to combine what is given. This seems to be good Kantian doctrine, even if it requires some further extension or qualification.

The concepts of form and matter may be applied relatively to one another. Thus in a statue the form may be regarded as the shape, and the matter as the stuff or material to which the sculptor has given a shape. But the material he uses has already a shape, so that what is regarded as form in one relation may be regarded as matter in another relation. Kant is not here concerned with such empirical form and matter in particular objects. He is using the words in their transcendental sense (A266 = B322). By this intimidating expression he appears to mean that he is not concerned with particular differences in objects, but only with the distinction between form and matter so far as this must apply to every concept and so to every object as such.

So far we are concerned only with the general difference between form and matter; and Kant, as usual, recognises that we can compare concepts as regards their form and matter from a purely logical point of view. If we go on to suppose that what we say in comparing concepts can be transferred without further reflexion to objects or things, we must fall into further fallacies, of which Leibniz again was guilty.

From the point of view of pure logic—the only one adopted by an intellectualistic philosopher—the matter is prior to the form; something must be given (at least in a concept) if we are to determine it in a definite way; and this must apply to all pure concepts of the understanding so far as they are supposed—entirely by themselves—to give us knowledge of objects.

Kant illustrates this contention in various ways. Logicians, he tells us, have taken the universal to be the matter and the specific difference to be the form—he is presumably thinking of definition by means of genus and differentia. So too in judgement the given concepts are supposed to be the logical matter or material for the judgement, while the relation between them (by means of the copula) is considered to be the form. These doctrines are presumably accepted by Kant himself, but the following examples may be illustrations of the intellectualistic fallacy. In every being the constituent parts (known as the *essentialia*) are supposed to be the matter; the way in which they are combined into one thing is supposed to be the form. This principle is extended to cover things in general or things as such (including presumably things in themselves as alleged to be known or knowable by the pure concepts of the understanding). Here—although Kant may be translating the doctrine into his own terminology—unlimited reality is said to be the matter (the matter of all possibility), while limitation (or negation) is said to be the form by which one thing is distinguished from another in accordance with transcendental concepts. If we want an illustration of this (which may, however, be misleading), particular spaces may be regarded as limitations of one total possible space, and they are to be distinguished from one another by their different limitations, by the different ways in which the one possible space is limited or negated. But this should perhaps be taken as an analogy rather than as an illustration, since it seems to assume a Kantian rather than a Leibnizian view of space.

8. *Space and Time*

Because Leibniz took it for granted that matter must precede form, he had to assume first of all that there were monads possessed of a purely internal power of entertaining ideas, and then to base on this—by the aid of a pre-established harmony—their external relations and the mutual correspondence of their states (namely, their ideas). So much we have already seen under the heading of the internal and the external. But the same intellectualistic view was also at the root of his theories of time and space. Space for him was possible only because of the relations of substances, and time was possible only through combining the states of substances as grounds and consequents. This view, according to Kant, is inevitable if space and time are intellectualized instead of being regarded as the forms of our sensibility. If you try to understand the external relations of things by concepts independently of sensuous intuition, the only concept you can use is that of reciprocal action; and if you try to understand the combination of different states in one thing, the only concept you can use is that of ground and consequent. Hence Leibniz was compelled to think of space as a certain order in the community of substances, and of time as the dynamic succession of their states (A275 = B331).

I must confess that I find these sayings very dark. We should expect the concepts used to be logical concepts or pure (as opposed to schematized) categories. Perhaps as regards time they are, since ground and consequent is a logical concept even if it is sometimes confused with cause and effect. There are greater difficulties about space. The concept we should expect to be used is the pure category of community or communion—that is, the concept of the synthesis of ultimate subjects such that the predicates of the one subject have their *ground* in the other and vice versa (see KME, II 55). Perhaps this is the concept Kant has in mind—with possibly the further qualification that it may be confused by Leibniz with the real or schematized category of interaction by which substances are thought to be causes of determinations in each other; Kant even says—strangely enough—that this is our pure concept of relations (A285 = B342). But then we have to face the further difficulty that there can be for Leibniz no real interaction between the monads, and any correspondence between them must spring from a harmony pre-established by God. I cannot see the consistency of all this.

Even Leibniz had to recognise that there was something peculiar about time and space—something which made them look as if they were independent of things. This, however, he attributed to the fact that the concepts of space and time were confused or rendered indistinct by the senses—on his view the only function of sense was to confuse the clear concepts of the understanding. Because of this confusion some thinkers, according to Leibniz, were led to conceive time and space, not as a mere form of dynamic relations, but as a self-subsistent intuition prior to things—the reference here is, I think, not to the views of Kant (which Leibniz had no means of knowing) but to the absolute time and space of Newton. (This Newtonian doctrine Kant regarded as so absurd that it would be accepted only by Englishmen.)

The double doctrine of Leibniz is so extraordinary that it may remind the flippant of the Mohammedan holy man who was asked by his disciples why he persisted in drinking wine contrary to the commands of the Prophet. He explained that he did so because when the wine touched his lips, it was turned by a miracle into water. 'How then', asked his disciples, 'does it have the effect of making you drunk?' 'Ah', replied the holy man, 'that is a second miracle'.

Kant's criticisms are the same as under the previous headings. If we suppose that we can know objects directly by pure concepts and in this way can know things as they are in themselves; if further we suppose that space and time are determinations of things as they are in themselves; then the doctrines of Leibniz are inevitable; for there can be nothing in the objects which is not already contained in our pure concepts. But for Kant all these suppositions are false abstractions. We cannot know objects solely by means of pure concepts: we can know them only if they are also given to sense under the forms of time and space. This means in turn that there is always more in the known object than is contained in our pure concepts. Space and time are not universal characteristics of things in themselves nor are they known by means of pure concepts which originate in thought and are then obscured by means of sense in such a curious way that they begin to look like individual things. On the contrary they look like individual things because, unlike the pure categories, they are not derived from thought at all. They are, so to speak, analysed out of objects given to sense; they are the forms of intuition which are left when we think away the matter of sensation that is given under these forms. Once it is recognized that they have their origin, not in thinking, but in sensibility, it is easy to see that as forms of intuition they are prior to all the matter given to sense, and so prior to all phenomena and all the data of experience. If we accept the distinction between thought and sense and do not muddle these up, then so far as sense is concerned, it is the form which makes the matter possible—not the matter which makes the form possible. The view that only the matter can make the form possible springs solely from an intellectualistic prejudice.

These are difficult questions on which it is unwise to be dogmatic; but it seems clear that Kant has a case, and indeed that he appears to be more empirical than Leibniz and closer to the facts of experience—he ought not to be dismissed off hand without any attempt to understand his position. I do not know how far modern physics can be used to support Leibniz and dispose of Kant; but perhaps we should at least ask ourselves whether some common assumptions of today spring from a deeper insight into physics or from a lack of transcendental reflexion.

9. *Matter and Substance*

If we set aside the problem of minds (the matter of which is to be found in feeling or sensation) and consider only external objects, we must say that for Kant matter is the permanent reality which fills space with different degrees of intensity. In other words, matter is substance and substance is matter; but the substance in question is substance as a phenomenon *(substantia phaenomenon)* —not *substantia noumenon* as supposed to be conceived, and indeed known, solely by the pure thought of an ultimate subject which can never be a predicate. As filling space, matter is real; as permanent, it is substance; and as having a determinate position in time and space, it and its qualities are said to exist.

Although for Kant the concept of substance is a pure concept, not derived from sense but from thought (at least in so far as substance is taken to be the subject of which we predicate the qualities given to sense), our knowledge of substances is as empirical as our knowledge of causes and effects. In our ordinary everyday experience we take bodies to be permanent and attribute to them the qualities we perceive by sense, and unless we did so experience would be impossible; but for exact knowledge of substances we must look to science and particularly to physics. The view that there is, or must be, something absolutely internal in physical substances Kant regards as a pure illusion. As we have seen, all we can know of physical substances consists of relations— relations of space, shape, motion, and causality—and these are only relatively internal (compare also B67). Kant naturally enough accepts the Newtonian science of his time, and indeed seeks to find for it a philosophical basis. Hence he takes substances to be characterized by attraction and repulsion and impenetrability. But he is in no way committed to any doctrine of atoms as solid particles. On the contrary, he rejects as purely metaphysical the doctrine of atoms and the void, although he never claims to disprove it a priori. He accepts a dynamical theory of matter, not a mechanical one, but mainly, if not entirely, on empirical grounds—although he insists that an empty time and an empty space (such as was assumed by the atomists) can never be proved by experience (A172 = B214). He is far from holding that the science of his time has said the last word on these topics. On the contrary, he not only believes that the function of science is to describe by the observation and analysis of phenomena the internal character of nature (so far as nature can be said to have an internal character); he also asserts that we can never know how far this process may go in the course of time (A278 = B334), although it can never give us knowledge of reality as it is in itself. Only a physicist who also understands Kant—and to expect this is to expect a great deal—can say whether it is possible to adjust Kant's theories to modern physics; but of one thing we can be sure—if Kant were alive today, this is what he would be trying to do.

10. *Phenomena and Noumena*

For Kant all claims to know the inner nature of reality, and all complaints that we are unable to do so, are equally out of place. They are alike in supposing that by pure conception we are able—or at least should be able—to know reality as it is in itself. But the only objects we can know are phenomenal objects given to sense, and these, so to speak, have no absolutely inner nature: they do not contain reality as it is in itself, but only reality as it is relatively to our finite cognitive powers of understanding and sense.

If we claim to know reality by means of pure conception, we are supposing that reality is composed of purely intelligible objects (*noumena* or *intelligibilia*), which are what they are independently of our thinking, and yet can be known by us. This view is particularly difficult for Leibniz, since—in his criticisms of Locke in the *New Essays*—he insists that although we have no innate ideas as Locke understood them, we have an innate disposition to think in certain ways, and our a priori concepts spring from our reflective understanding of these ways of thinking. All of this may be regarded as the germ of Kant's own doctrine of the categories, but Leibniz failed to draw the necessary conclusions. If a priori concepts originate in this way, they cannot—unless by a pre-established harmony—give us knowledge of things in themselves. They are only forms of synthesis awaiting a matter to be combined; and they can give us knowledge of objects only so far as we are able to combine in one time and space the matter given to sense and to combine it in such a way that this matter accords with these forms of synthesis. But such objects are phenomenal objects or appearances, and not purely intelligible objects or things as they are in themselves.

These conclusions seem to be inevitable on the presuppositions of Leibniz himself, but because of his uncritical assumption that his pure concepts unaided by sense can give us knowledge of an intelligible world, he is able to construct a theory—a very queer theory—of reality as it is in itself. Our pure thinking, which by itself is capable of giving us knowledge of reality, is unfortunately confused by sense, which makes us seem to be aware of a world of sensible bodies in a time and space which look as if they were individual things, although they are nothing of the kind. The real world is composed of simple nonspatial monads which think with different degrees of confusion and have no direct connexion either with each other or with reality as a whole. In spite of these different degrees of confusion God has pre-established a harmony in the monads such that there is some sort of correspondence between their different ideas. This is presumably a philosophical account of reality as it is in itself; but the man who knows it seems to be both a monad cut off from all other monads, and yet a man who can know the nature of other monads and of the whole. I cannot see how this knowledge is possible: it looks like a kind of faith. But I do not speak as an expert on Leibniz, and it may be that this summary does him injustice.

Kant, on the other hand, never denies (although on this point he is often misunderstood) that our pure concepts have a prima facie claim to go beyond sense and the objects of experience. They enable us to realize that what is given to sense need not be, and perhaps cannot be, all the reality there is. We are entitled to use the concept of an intelligible reality or a noumenon as an object which is not given to our senses. But we can turn this into a positive concept only by supposing that such an object could be known by a kind of understanding or a kind of intuition different from our own—by an understanding which was also intuitive in itself or an intuition which was also intellectual in itself. Such an understanding would be infinite and creative: it would make its own objects in thinking; and indeed it would be its own object in thinking. But since we do not possess such an understanding, the concept of it is problematic: we cannot say that the object thought in it is either possible or impossible, and still less can we say that it exists or does not exist. Least of all can we say, as in the ontological argument, that it must exist.

H. J. PATON

OXFORD UNIVERSITY

KANT'S RELATION TO BERKELEY*

I

It is commonly held that because of his obvious misinterpretations of Berkeley's philosophy, which he called dogmatic or visionary and mystical idealism, Kant thereby betrayed a gross misunderstanding of that philosopher. The theory advanced to explain this is that Kant was not acquainted with any of Berkeley's writings, but obtained his knowledge from inadequate second-hand sources.[1] This theory is supported by the fact that Kant's knowledge of the English language was most imperfect. He never read a single English book. Coupled with this is the apparently acceptable fact that there were no German translations of Berkeley's works in existence before 1781, the year of publication of the first edition of the *Critique of Pure Reason*.[2] In that year, there appeared a German translation of Berkeley's *Three Dialogues between Hylas and Philonous*.[3] This work was therefore available to Kant before he published his *Prolegomena to any Future Metaphysics* (1783)[4] and the second edition of the *Critique* (1787). But such is the nature of Kant's account of Berkeley's doctrine in these works that, on the common view, Kant neglected to avail himself of the opportunity to read it. Thus, previous assessments of the evidence,

---

* Reprinted by permission of the author and the *Philosophical Quarterly*, 5, July 1955.

1 See N. Kemp Smith, *A Commentary on Kant's Critique of Pure reason*, pp. 156-7. Cf. also A. C. Ewing, *A Short Commentary on Kant's Critique of Pure Reason*, p. 182; H. J. Paton, *Kant's Metaphysic of Experience*, II, p. 376; T. D. Weldon, *Introduction to Kant's Critique of Pure Reason*, pp. 9-10; A. D. Lindsay, *Kant*, p. 15; *et al.*

2 References to the first and second editions will be by page numbers and the letters A and B respectively.

3 Hereafter referred to in notes by dialogue number as *Hylas*. Berkeley's *Principles of Human Knowledge* will be referred to in notes by paragraph numbers as *Prin*.

4 Hereafter referred to in notes by section numbers as *Proleg*.

internal and external, have produced the view that Kant knew nothing of Berkeley's writings at first hand and, accordingly, misunderstood and misinterpreted his teaching. From this, it follows, although the commentators have omitted to stress this conclusion, that Kant's many atempted refutations of dogmatic idealism fail before they begin. The above is not only the accepted view, backed by seemingly strong evidence; it is the most plausible. Nevertheless, it is almost wholly mistaken, as I shall show.

II

First, let us banish the idea that Kant could not have read any of Berkeley's writings before he published the first edition of the *Critique*. On the contrary, he could have read at least two. These are Berkeley's *Three Dialogues between Hylas and Philonous* and his *De Motu*. Professor Kemp Smith indicates that a German translation of the *Three Dialogues* was published at Leipzig in 1781, and asserts that this was the first of Berkeley's writings to appear in German.[5] Authorities on Kant have ignored a much earlier translation of the same work which was published at Rostock in 1756. Their oversight is understandable because the translation lies hidden in a larger work entitled *Die Würklichkeit der Körper*[6] which contains also Arthur Collier's *Clavis Universalis*.

---

[5] *Op. cit.*, p. 156.

[6] I have examined a copy of this work from the library of the University of Southern California. Its full title is: *Samlung der vornehmsten Schriftsteller die die Würklichkeit ihres eignen Körpers und der ganzen Körperwelt läugnen. Enthaltend des Berkeleys Gespräche zwischen Hylas und Philonous und des Colliers Allgemeinen Schlüssel. Uebersetzt und mit wiederlegenden Anmerkungen versehen nebst einem Anhang worin die Würklichkeit der Körper erwiesen wird von Joh. Christ. Eschenbach, Prof. Philos. zu Rostock.* (Rostock bey Unton Ferdinand Röse. 1756.) Eschenbach states in the Preface that since it was impossible to come upon the English original his translation of the *Dialogues* is based on the French translation of Amsterdam, 1750. T. E. Jessop, *Bibliography of George Berkeley*, no. 73, gives the same title. However, in Kayser, *Bücher-Lexicon* (now *Bücherverzeichnis*), V (S-T), Leipzig, 1835, pp. 34b-35a, an abbreviated title of undoubtedly the same book is given. It omits reference to Berkeley's and Collier's works, also the phrase *und der ganzen Körperwelt*, and names the publisher as Cnobloch of Leipzig. The translation of 1781, Leipzig, is styled *Philosophische Werke*. According to Jessop, *op. cit.*, no. 74, it contains only the *Three Dialogues*.

Hence, the *Three Dialogues,* which contains the whole of Berkeley's main doctrine, was available to Kant long before he began to compose his *Critique.* Moreover, the fact that the editor and translator of the *Dialogues,* Johann Christian Eschenbach I, was also a professor of philosophy at Rostock, who sought to refute Berkeley's doctrine and who subsequently published works of his own on logic and metaphysics,[7] increases the chances that the book attracted Kant's attention. Laying aside, for the time being, all the claims adduced from the internal evidence to the effect that Kant was wholly unacquainted with Berkeley's writings, it seems to me highly unlikely that Kant, who lived with the book-dealer Kanter for a considerable time prior to the eighties,[8] and who was sufficiently curious to buy and study Swedenborg's *Arcana Coelestia,*[9] should not have availed himself of the opportunity to examine a book containing the official doctrines of two other exponents of 'mystical and visionary idealism',[10] and indeed, as the title indicates, the most eminent repudiators of the reality of the entire corporeal world.

Another important work of Berkeley's which Kant might also have read, is the former's *De Motu,* published in London in 1721 and again in 1752. This Latin treatise did not have a wide circulation on the continent. However, it opposes the doctrines of Newton and Leibniz on the subject of motion in space, a subject which was Kant's special concern in his pre-Critical period. To a diligent enquirer, Berkeley's *De Motu,* which, as far as Kant was

---

[7] *Metaphysik, oder Hauptwissenschaft* (1757) ; *Elementa Logices* (1766) ; both written at Rostock and published at Leipzig by Cnobloch.

[8] See F. Paulsen, *Immanuel Kant,* Scribners (1902) , p. 45.

[9] Kant's work on Swedenborg, *The Dreams of a Visionseer,* appeared in 1766. Kant was, of course, extremely sceptical of Swedenborg's theories. However, the Russian philosopher, Vladimir Sergeivitch Soloviev, in his article on Kant (Brockhaus and Ephron's encyclopaedic dictionary) attributes Kant's renunciation of Newton's absolute space and his corresponding adoption of the ideality of space in his *Dissertation* (1770) to the influence of Swedenborg. See A. V. Vasiliev, *Space, Time, Motion* (1924) , pp. 74-5.

[10] Kant uses this phrase to describe Berkeley's position in *Proleg.* 13. Kemp Smith notes that such a description is doubtless partly due to the old-time association of idealism in Kant's mind with Swedenborg's teaching. *Op. cit.,* p. 158, note 4.

concerned, required no translation, would most assuredly have been accessible.

Having removed the supposed impossibility of Kant's direct acquaintance with Berkeley's works prior to the publication of the first edition of the *Critique,* by showing that at least two of them were available to Kant, and one of these readily so, let us now proceed to examine Kant's attempted refutations of idealism.

III

There are eight separate passages in the first and second editions of the *Critique* and in the *Prolegomena* which are specific attempts by Kant to refute idealism. These passages, approximately in the order in which they were written, and accompanied by brief comments upon the kinds of idealism Kant opposes, are as follows:

FIRST EDITION OF *CRITIQUE*

I *Section 7 of the Transcendental Aesthetic* (A36-41) .
Explicit against 'idealism'.

II *The Fourth Paralogism: Of Ideality* (A366-80) .
Explicit against all 'empirical' idealism, and, in particular, against the 'sceptical' idealism of Descartes. 'Dogmatic' idealism is merely mentioned.

III *Section 6 of the Antinomy of Pure Reason* (A491-97) .
Explicit against 'empirical' idealism.

THE *PROLEGOMENA*

IV *Section 13, Remarks II and III.*
Explicit against the 'mystical and visionary' idealism of Berkeley. The 'empirical' or 'dreaming' idealism of Descartes is mentioned.

V *Section 49.*
Explicit against 'material, or Cartesian' idealism.

VI *Appendix, Second Part.*
Explicit against all 'genuine' idealism from the Eleatics, through Plato, to Berkeley, and particularly against the

'dogmatic' idealism of Berkeley. The 'sceptical' idealism of Descartes is mentioned.

SECOND EDITION OF *CRITIQUE*

VII *Section 8, Parts III and IV of the Transcendental Aesthetic* (B69-72).
Explicit against Berkeley.

VIII *Refutation of Idealism* (B274-9) supplemented by *note to Preface* (Bxxxix-xli).
Explicit against the 'problematic' idealism of Descartes. The 'dogmatic' idealism of Berkeley is described. Both are called instances of 'material' idealism.

The idealism which Kant seeks to refute is material or empirical idealism, that is, any doctrine which doubts or denies the existence of objects in space outside us. The former is called 'sceptical' or, though not until the last passage, 'problematic' idealism. Descartes' name is the only one explicitly associated with it. The latter is the dogmatic idealism of Berkeley. It is only once described as 'mystical and visionary'. From the above, Kant distinguishes his own critical or transcendental idealism, a doctrine which denies the *absolute* reality of space and time, and the external bodies in them. It involves empirical realism or dualism, according to which, bodies in space outside us, as well as ourselves who perceive them, are considered to be empirically real. In the first edition of the *Critique*, the most important passage is the fourth *Paralogism* which, by adopting a position resembling Berkeley's, tries to refute Descartes. Although Kant promises to deal with dogmatic idealism, Berkeley is neither named nor opposed in this edition. The first edition of the *Critique* appeared in the early summer of 1781. Kant waited many anxious months for the response of the learned world. He was most disappointed by the contents of the first, the Garve-Feder or Göttingen review, which appeared in January, 1782. Garve described the *Critique* as 'a system of higher idealism', and classified Kant with Berkeley. This was anathema to Kant. Accordingly, in the *Prolegomena* (published Easter, 1783), Kant, for the first time, is at pains to show that his position is the 'very contrary' of Berkeley's. Two of the three 'refutations' in the *Prolegomena* are directed against Berkeley. Kant asserts that Berkeley's doctrine is 'an objectionable idealism', against which and other such 'chimeras of the brain', his *Critique* contains the 'proper antidote'. In the second edition of the *Critique* (1787), Kant suppresses what Schopenhauer called 'the principal idealistic passage', i.e., the fourth *Paralogism,* and replaces it by the *Refutation of Idealism* which answers Descartes' view without appearing to fall into subjectivism. The other passage, added to the *Aesthetic,* is, as we have seen, directed against Berkeley. In these passages, occur those well-known obvious misinterpretations of Berkeley. To 'the good Berkeley' is ascribed the view that the things in space are 'merely imaginary entities' or that he degrades bodies in space to 'mere illusion'.

It appears from the above summary that the eight 'refutations' of idealism are directed against either Descartes or Berkeley. This, however, is mere appearance. If one ponders on these passages in the order in which they were written, one may discern an underlying central argument to which the attacks on Descartes and Berkeley are merely incidental. This central argument begins by outlining a position common to most previous metaphysicians and natural philosophers. It is, in fact, the prime feature of the Newtonian World-View. Kant calls it 'transcendental realism'. Omitting details, the argument continues by showing that such a view leads inevitably to idealism, and culminates by turning the argument of idealism against itself to provide a positive proof of the external world. This is the real argument of the 'refutations'. Depending on the point of emphasis, it has been regarded either as a refutation of realism or (as Kant treats it) as a refutation of idealism with its corresponding proof of the external world which exhibits his empirical realism. Although the argument is discernible in all the 'refutations' except the last, it is most clearly seen in the fourth *Paralogism.* In the last 'refutation', Kant uses a method of proof of the external world different from that of the preceding seven. Because only one of these passages was subsequently suppressed by Kant, the central argument must be considered official Kantian doctrine. In this paper I shall, accordingly, ignore the *Refutation of Idealism* except in so far as it presents Kant's views on Berkeley.

It is my view that the central argument of the 'refutations' has a systematic similarity, in its principal features, with the main argument of Berkeley's *Principles* and *Dialogues.* Berkeley is concerned to expose the fallacies inherent in a certain way of thinking to

which the metaphysicians and physicists of his age were prone. He
calls this doctrine 'materialism' and those who teach it, 'materi-
alists', or, more often, 'the philosophers'. He shows that it leads
inevitably to scepticism, and, in fact, joins the sceptics for much of
the way. Then he turns the argument of scepticism against itself to
provide (up to his time) a unique proof of the external world.
Since Berkeley's death, commentators have tended to emphasize the
first half of his argument, which they have seen as an attempt to
refute materialism or realism, and have been notorious in their
neglect of the last. Consequently, Berkeley has been presented to
the world as an idealist. Few have dwelt upon his refutation of
scepticism and his corresponding proof of the external world which
exhibits his empirical realism. The whole argument appears most
clearly in that paradigm of dramatic unity, the *Three Dialogues*. It
is seen, of course, in the *Principles,* but here the dissentient side of
immaterialism is so protested at the expense of Berkeley's empirical
realism that one can readily understand the mistaken judgement of
history.

IV

In order to prove my point, I shall now present, in more detail,
the main steps of this argument. I shall juxtapose the key assertions
of Kant and Berkeley. For reasons only of conciseness, quotations
from the *Principles* will preponderate over those from the *Dialogues:*

First Step

The philosophers assert the absolute reality of space and time, and
hold that external objects exist by themselves independently of our
senses.

> Kant: [The transcendental realists] . . . maintain the absolute reality
> of space and time, whether as subsistent or only as inherent
> (A39) . . . wrongly supposing that objects of the senses, if they
> are to be external, must have an existence by themselves, and
> independently of the senses (A369) .

> Berkeley: [The philosophers assert] the being of an absolute space,
> distinct from that which is perceived by sense (*Prin.* 116) .

> [They hold] that there are certain objects really existing
> without the mind, or having a subsistence distinct from
> being perceived (*Prin.* 56).

Kant specifically refers to certain 'mathematical' and 'metaphysical'
students of nature; probably Newton and Leibniz. Berkeley elsewhere refers to 'absolute space, that phantom of the mechanic and
geometrical philosophers' (*Siris* 271). However, in the above passages, he has in mind, not only Newton, but Locke, Descartes,
Malebranche, More and Raphson. The views of these thinkers and
many others (whom I shall continue to refer to as 'the philosophers') make them advocates of the prevailing doctrine, called by
Kant 'realism' and by Berkeley, 'materialism'. Berkeley only barely
considers the subject of time, but doubtless intends to ascribe to his
opponents the belief in absolute time, which notion he calls 'duration in abstract' (*Prin.* 97).

Kant and Berkeley observe that the transcendental realist or
materialist distinguishes between the primary and the secondary
qualities of bodies. The former, such as extension and shape, really
inhere in external bodies. The latter, such as heat, colour and taste,
belong only to appearances and are held to have no proper exis
tence 'outside us' (in the transcendental sense) but to be entirely
relative to our sensibility (*Proleg.* 13, A373; *Prin.* 9).[11]

Second Step

This doctrine of the philosophers makes them victims of the common delusion that the human mind can venture beyond all possible experience.

> Kant: [Transcendental realism involves] the transcendental illusion,
> by which metaphysics has hitherto been deceived and led to the
> childish endeavour of catching at bubbles, because appearances,
> which are mere ideas,[12] were taken for things in themselves.
> (*Proleg.* 13. Cf. A369, 491).

---

[11] This observation by Kant and Berkeley oversimplifies Locke's official
position. For him, the secondary qualities are not in us, but are powers of the
primary qualities which produce *ideas of* secondary qualities in our minds.

[12] Throughout this paper, following Caird, *The Critical Philosophy of
Kant,* I translate the term *Vorstellung* by 'idea'. This is more appropriate than
the 'representation' of most translations because Kant is referring to the same
entities as Locke, Berkeley and the Cartesians, who use the term 'idea' or *'idée'.*

Berkeley: When we do our utmost to conceive the existence of external bodies, we are all the while only contemplating our own ideas. But the mind taking no notice of it self, is deluded to think it can and doth conceive bodies existing unthought of or without the mind; though at the same time they are apprehended by or exist in it self (*Prin.* 23).

Kant and Berkeley provide similar analyses of the error committed by the philosophers; it is manifested in the deluded attempt to venture beyond the limits of possible experience. Dealing directly with this symptom, Kant observes that 'our knowledge of the existence of things reaches only so far as perception' (A226), and that, 'in the absence of perception even imagining and dreaming are not possible' (A377). Berkeley notices the same truth, 'My conceiving or imagining power does not extend beyond the possibility of real existence or perception' (*Prin.* 5), and again, 'Many things, for aught I know, may exist . . . but then those things must be possible' (*Hylas* III). Kant names the error, 'the transcendental illusion', here defined as treating ideas as things in themselves. This instance of the illusion he calls, on one occasion, 'dreaming idealism' (*Proleg.* 13). On Berkeley's analysis also, our supposed conception of external bodies (material substance) in absolute space outside us[13] is shown to be nothing but a contemplation of our own ideas. The error of the philosophers is therefore revealed as interpreting these ideas as external bodies. Yet for him, the analysis goes further. In the quoted passage, he describes the source of the error as 'the mind taking no notice of itself'. We forget that we are chained to a human sensibility. We forget ourselves as observers.[14]

Third Step

The philosophers' distinction of things from ideas leads inevitably to scepticism.

---

13 'Your belief in matter', Philonous remarks to Hylas, 'makes you *dream* of those unknown natures in everything' (*Hylas* III).

14 Berkeley discovered this Idol of the Tribe whilst working on a particular problem in the psychology of vision, viz., the problem of the inverted retinal image, in which he exposes the same delusion in the writers of optics, including Newton and Molyneux. (See his *New Theory of Vision*, pp. 116-118.)

Kant: Transcendental realism inevitably falls into difficulties, and finds itself obliged to give way to empirical idealism, in that it regards the objects of outer sense as something distinct from the senses themselves (A 371). [On this view] it is quite impossible to understand how we could arrive at a knowledge of their reality outside us, since we have to rely merely on the idea which is in us (A 378. Cf. *Proleg.* 49).

Berkeley: All this scepticism follows from our supposing a difference between *things* and *ideas*. . . . So long as we attribute a real existence to unthinking things, distinct from their being perceived, it is not only impossible for us to know with evidence the nature of any real unthinking being, but even that it exists. . . . We see only the appearances, and not the real qualities of things (*Prin.* 87-8).

As we have seen, Kant is opposed to empirical or material idealism. Its two sub-divisions are sceptical idealism (that which doubts) and dogmatic idealism (that which denies) the existence of bodies in space outside us. The meaning Kant intends to give to 'idealism' is partially obscured by his various definitions and by the ambiguity of the phrase 'bodies in space outside us'. Is Kant referring to material substance or to sensible things in empirical space? A careful reading of all the 'refutations' indicates that Kant intends the latter. We shall see that Kant's own official doctrine, transcendental idealism, denies the absolute reality of bodies in absolute space. Moreover, Kant's use of the title 'empirical' reveals the nature of the idealism he opposes. Finally, although on one occasion Kant defines 'dogmatic idealist' as 'one who denies the existance of matter', and 'sceptical idealist' as 'one who doubts its existence' (A377), in the same passage he defines 'matter' as 'only a species of ideas' (A370). From all this it is evident that the idealism Kant opposes is the doctrine which doubts or denies the reality of the sensible world. Since once transcendental realism is upheld, sceptical idealism is 'inevitable' (A371) and dogmatic idealism 'unavoidable' (B274), it follows that Kant regards these doctrines as two different stages in the logical decline of transcendental realism.

On my view, in spite of a different terminology, the same two stages can be distinguished in Berkeley's analysis of the logical decline of materialism. This is true of the *Dialogues,* not of the

Principles in which only one stage is discernible. Hylas vacillates between doubt and denial of the reality of the external world. The former position, Berkeley calls 'scepticism'. However, when Hylas is 'plunged yet deeper in uncertainty' and is forced, 'positively to deny the real existence of any part of the universe', Berkeley names this further stage, 'the deepest and most deplorable scepticism' (*Hylas* III). Thus, that position which Kant calls 'sceptical idealism', Berkeley calls 'scepticism', and what Kant calls 'dogmatic idealism', Berkeley calls 'the deepest scepticism'. It is the latter position of extreme scepticism that both men are most anxious to ridicule and escape from. The one thinks of it as a chimera of the brain, the other, as an extravagancy.

In similar fashion, Kant and Berkeley expose the consequences of the philosophers' corresponding distinctions between two spaces and two times—absolute and relative. Kant observes that absolute space and time, 'two eternal and infinite self-subsistent non-entities *(Undinge)* . . . must be the necessary condition of the existence of all things, and moreover must continue to exist, even although all existing things be removed. . . . As conditions of all existence in general, they must also be the conditions of the existence of God' (A39, B71). Since the existence of all things thus depends on nothing, the whole universe is thereby 'transformed into mere *illusion*' (B70). This consequence would belong to a doctrine lying beyond even extreme scepticism or dogmatic idealism since our own selves would also vanish from existence. All such notions, Kant calls 'absurdities' (B70). Berkeley's account is similar. As we have seen, he barely considers time. He ascribes to the philosophers the view that 'absolute space continues to exist after the annihilation of all bodies'. He remarks that it 'necessarily exists of its own nature' (*De Motu* 54), and that we are, accordingly, reduced to thinking that 'there is something beside God which is eternal, uncreated, infinite, indivisible, immutable' (*Prin.* 117). Since all its attributes are negative, he concludes, 'it seems therefore to be nothing' (*De Motu* 53). All such views, Berkeley calls 'absurd notions' (*Prin.* 117).

We have arrived at that stage of the argument in which the diagnosis of the malady afflicting modern philosophy is complete. Dogmatic idealism (extreme scepticism) is seen as the inevitable consequence of a certain way of thinking (transcendental realism or materialism) which must be deluded because its consequences are either absurd or impossible. The last half of the argument contains the remedy. So deceptive in nature are the early stages of this remedy that it appears as though Kant and Berkeley are victims of a self-inflicted malady—the very same malady they seek to cure. The argument proceeds by accepting, what are, in fact, idealist or sceptical premisses.

Fourth Step

The remedy consists first, in pointing out to the philosophers a truth they already know, namely that the *esse* of ideas or appearances is *percipi*.

> Kant: Sceptical idealism thus constrains us to have recourse to the only refuge still open, namely, the ideality of all appearances . . . for we cannot be sentient of what is outside ourselves, but only of what is in us (A378). All appearances are not in themselves *things;* they are nothing but ideas, and cannot exist outside our mind (A492).

> Berkeley: The philosophers . . . being of the opinion that . . . the things immediately perceived are ideas which exist only in the mind (*Hylas* III).

The philosophers must admit the truth of this premiss because it is their own. They had used it whilst correcting the views of the common man, who holds that the things immediately perceived are external bodies which exist independently of being perceived. The philosophers corrected this 'mistake of the vulgar'.[15] In the above passages, Kant and Berkeley use the terms '*Vorstellung*' and 'idea' to refer to the immediate data of sense. Things immediately perceived, i.e., appearances, are identified with these ideas. No claim is made at this stage that these ideas are real or permanent. No criterion is provided to distinguish reality from the idle visions of fancy or from dreams. As a result of the next step, the denotation of 'idea' increases enormously.

---

15 E.g., Malebranche, *Recherche* . . . , VI⁰ *Éclaircissement,* 'Les hommes ont toujours consulté leurs yeux pour s'assurer de l'existence de la matière. . . . Ils pensent qu'il ne faut qu'ouvrir les yeux pour s'assurer qu'il y a des corps. . . . Cependant il est certain (que toutes les qualités sensibles dans les corps qui semblent les exhaler ou les répandre) ne sont point hors de l'âme qui les sent'.

Fifth Step

The remedy continues by assimilating the so-called external bodies of the philosophers into the realm of ideas or appearances.

> Kant: External bodies are mere appearances, and are therefore nothing but a species of my ideas, the objects of which are something only through these ideas. Apart from them they are nothing (A370. Cf. A491, *Proleg.* 13).

> Berkeley: As to what is said of the absolute existence of unthinking things without any relation to their being perceived, that seems perfectly unintelligible. Their *esse* is *percipi,* nor is it possible they should have any existence, out of the minds or thinking things which perceive them (*Prin.* 3).

This is the point of departure from the doctrine of the philosophers, and it would seem to plunge Kant and Berkeley even deeper into scepticism. Berkeley may be conscious of this association but does not admit it. Kant, however, concedes, 'Up to this point I am one in confession with the above idealists' (*Proleg.* Appx.). In fact, the above passage is Kant's explicit formulation of what he calls his 'transcendental idealism' (A491). In this step, the realm of ideas has been extended radically to accommodate the contents of all possible outer experience. Its significance is most clearly grasped in its application to the distinction of the philosophers between the primary and secondary qualities. Kant observes that since Locke's time it has been generally assumed that the secondary qualities of bodies, such as heat, colour and taste, belong only to their appearances and do not exist outside our ideas. He adds, 'I go farther and, for weighty reasons, rank as mere appearances the remaining qualities of bodies also, which are called primary—such as extension, place, and, in general, space, with all that which belongs to it' (*Proleg.* 13). Berkeley has at least three different arguments against this distinction, but the one which is uniquely his, and on which he rests his whole case, is the argument: 'It is evident . . . that extension, figure and motion are only ideas existing in the mind, and that an idea can be like nothing but another idea, and that consequently neither they nor their archetypes can exist in an unperceiving substance' (*Prin.* 9). This is an application of Berkeley's main argument against the doctrine of material substance.

The latter is used repeatedly in the *Principles* and the *Dialogues*. It is a sceptical or idealist argument, but has more power than any of the relevant arguments of the great sceptical precursors of Berkeley, such as Bayle. Their arguments from relativity cannot affect Locke's official position (see above, note 11), whereas I think Berkeley's argument demolishes it.

From all this, it is readily seen that the fourth and fifth steps of this central argument represent the idealism of Kant and Berkeley. The fourth step showed that the *esse* of ideas or appearances is *percipi*. The fifth shows that the *esse* of the external bodies of the philosophers is also *percipi*. The term 'idea' or '*Vorstellung*' has snowballed in meaning. As before, no claim is yet made that these ideas are real or permanent. They are phantasms, of the same stuff as dreams, having the same ontological status as the ideas of Locke and the Cartesians. All that has occurred is a notable increase in the denotation of the term. The early critics of Kant and Berkeley evidently interpreted this temporary stage as their final position. We have noticed this response in Kant's case (see above p. 92). It was voiced more confidently and widely in the case of Berkeley. James Beattie wrote of 'this absurd doctrine'.[16] David Hume considered Berkeley the best of all teachers of scepticism: 'All his arguments, though otherwise intended, are, in reality, merely sceptical'.[17] Either Hume neglected the important final step in the whole argument, or he thought it failed.

Sixth Step

And all these appearances are real.

> Kant: I leave things as we obtain them by the senses their reality (*Proleg.* 13). In order to arrive at the reality of outer objects, I have just as little need to resort to inference as I have in

---

[16] In his *Essays* (Edinburgh 1776), p. 183, he continued, 'If all men were in one instant deprived of their understanding by almighty power, and made to believe that matter has no existence but as an idea in the mind, all other earthly things remaining as they are . . . I am certain that, in less than a month after, there could not without another miracle, be one human creature alive on the face of the earth', and added in a footnote that whilst a blind or deaf man can survive, it would be impossible for all mankind if they lost their percipient faculties.

[17] *Inquiry*, XII, i, note.

regard to the reality of the object of my inner sense. . . . For in both cases alike the objects are nothing but ideas, the immediate perception of which is at the same time a sufficient proof of their reality (A371).

An empirical realist allows to matter, as appearance, a reality which does not permit of being inferred, but is immediately perceived (A371).

Berkeley: I am of a vulgar cast, simple enough to believe my senses, and leave things as I find them (*Hylas* III).

I might as well doubt of my own being, as of the being of those things I actually see and feel. . . . Those immediate objects of perception, which, according to you, are only appearances of things, I take to be the real things themselves (*Hylas* III).

If by *material substance* is meant only sensible body, that which is seen and felt . . . then I am more certain of matter's existence than you, or any other philosopher, pretend to be (*Hylas* III).

This step concludes the argument. Having consorted with idealism in order to refute transcendental realism, a procedure which was, for Kant, the 'only alternative' (B72), a 'recourse to the only refuge' (A378), and for Berkeley, an appeal to a truth, 'so near and obvious to the mind' (*Prin.* 6) ; and, on the face of it, having left no avenue of escape from the negative conclusions of the sceptics, the two men now divorce themselves from it. Accordingly, this final step in the central argument constitutes Kant's and Berkeley's refutation of idealism or scepticism and, by the same token, their proof of the external world. From it, emerges their empirical realism. The argument achieves this in a most ingenious yet simple way, by accepting the sceptical conclusion of one such as Hylas, that all we can ever know of the external world are certain ideas or appearances, and then admitting, as any consistent empiricist must, that these appearances are real. After all, it is a jest to hold, as do the philosophers, that the things we see and touch are mere illusions.[18]

---

[18] This final step illuminates the irony inherent in Dr. Johnson's notorious ostensive refutation of Berkeley's 'ingenious sophistry', by exclaiming, while 'striking his foot with mighty force against a large stone, till he rebounded from it "I refute it thus"'. Such an argument, and also G. E. Moore's

There are, of course, difficulties in such a proof of the external world as this, the main one being the problem of error or illusion. If external bodies are reduced to mere ideas, it might seem that the external world is thereby reduced to the level of dreams. Locke had said, 'To make our knowledge real, it is requisite that the ideas answer their archetypes'.[19] It might seem that neither Kant nor Berkeley, in spite of the ingenuity of their final step, has escaped from that extreme form of scepticism which each was most anxious to avoid, to wit, dogmatic idealism. Both men posed and answered this objection (in the first edition of the *Critique* and in the *Principles,* respectively) long before it was made in fact by their detractors. Berkeley had the prescience, remarkable but unavailing, to give it pride of place as the First Objection in the *Principles* (34-40). The critics, however, in both cases, proved to be either negligent or unconvinced. As Kant said about Hume, both men 'suffered the usual misfortune of metaphysicians, of not being understood'. In answering the critics, Kant asserts that the above objection rises from an 'almost intentional misconception, as if my doctrine turned all things of the world of sense into mere illusion' (*Proleg.* 13). The same objection prompts Berkeley's: 'It is a misapprehension that I deny the reality of sensible things' (*Hylas* III). Both men then proceed to reaffirm their previous answer.

The distinction between reality and illusion retains its full force. Its criterion is not the futile correspondence of our ideas with external archetypes, but merely their coherence within our experience. In effect, there are no illusions of sense, only delusions of the understanding, because the senses tell no lies. Kant declares, 'It is not the senses, however, which must be charged with the illusion, but the understanding' (*Proleg.* 13). Error occurs on the level of judgment. Thus, when we connect our ideas 'according to the rules of the coherence of all knowledge in experience, illusion or truth

---

celebrated proof of an external world, 'By holding up my two hands, and saying, as I make a certain gesture with the right hand, "Here is one hand", and adding, as I make a certain gesture with the left, "and here is another"', amount to nothing but vindications of the empirical realism of Kant and Berkeley. See *Life of Johnson,* Globe Edition, Macmillan, London, 1929, p. 162; and G. E. Moore, 'Proof of an External World', *Proceedings of the British Academy,* Vol. 25, 1939, p. 295.

19 *Essay,* IV, iv, 8.

will arise according as we are negligent or careful'.[20] He illustrates an 'illusion of sense' by the apparent progressive and retrogressive motion of the planets [*ibid.*]. Berkeley tells us that the objection vanishes once we but place 'the reality of things in ideas, fleeting indeed, and changeable; however not changed at random, but according to the fixed order of Nature' (*Hylas* III). Real things are 'more strong, orderly and coherent' than the irregular visions of fancy (*Prin.* 33). A man's 'mistake lies not in what he perceives immediately', for error here is impossible, 'but in the wrong judgment he makes'. He illustrates an 'illusion of sense' by the apparent lack of motion of the earth (*Hylas* III).

V

The central argument, which I have drawn attention to, constitutes the common ground of Kant and Berkeley. They did, of course, proceed to supplement it along different lines peculiar to their separate systems. Before we consider what conclusions may be drawn from the fact that the two men share the central argument, let us notice the important ways in which Kant differs from Berkeley as exhibited in the passages of the 'refutations'. These ways are concerned with Kant's treatment of: the self, the reality of common things and the nature of space.

First, although Kant and Berkeley agree that we know the external world as immediately as we know ourselves, the self which Kant refers to here is merely the empirical self. From it he distinguishes the self proper, the transcendental subject, which is an unthinking, and, to us, an entirely unknown, being (A380, 492). Berkeley makes no such distinction, holding that we know our real selves, not in the same way as we know ideas, but, still immediately, by reflex act and notionally (*Hylas* III). This important difference does not affect the central argument because, in it, the nature of that self which is known immediately is not in question. All that is sought is the equality in immediacy of knowledge of the outside world with it.

Secondly, at the close of the argument, we saw that the reality of common things was secured by appealing to the criteria of their

---

20 *Cf.* B69, 'It would be my own fault, if out of that which I ought to reckon as appearance, I made mere illusion', also A376-7, A492, *Proleg.* 49.

immediate perception and their coherence within experience. The questions of their cause and of the ground of the coherence of our ideas were not treated, because in these matters, Kant and Berkeley differ. In Berkeley's case, the cause of the sensible world is God. He is the ground of its 'steadiness, order, and coherence'. Our ideas change, not at random, but according to the fixed order of Nature, the rules or laws of which, open to discovery by us, constitute God's will. For Kant, the non-sensible, but purely intelligible, 'cause of appearances in general' is the transcendental object. This is not material substance, but is the 'ground (to us unknown) of the appearances'. To it 'we can ascribe the whole extent and connection of our possible perceptions' (A380, 494). It is, therefore, the cause, not only of real things (those connected in accordance with the laws of empirical advance) but of the fixed order of Nature. The transcendental object, therefore, replaces Berkeley's God.[21]

Kant, however, provides additional criteria of the reality of outer objects. I have so far considered only those which he shares with Berkeley. The first of these was immediate perception. Kant often speaks as if nothing else is needed. He asserts that it is 'a sufficient proof' of the reality of outer objects. He accepts the existence of matter on the 'unaided testimony of our mere self-consciousness'. The other criterion shared with Berkeley was coherence within experience. This involves, not only actual perception,

---

[21] Whether Kant intends to identify the transcendental object with the thing-in-itself is doubtful. Authorities differ. Kemp Smith, *op. cit.*, p. 204, regards the doctrine of the transcendental object as a pre-Critical, or semi-Critical, survival. Paton, *op. cit.*, p. 423, disagrees, and identifies it with the thing-in-itself. Whether Kant intends to identify it with God is equally doubtful. However, Kant's God, whose existence 'we not only may, but *must*, assume', has the same role as that of the transcendental object as described in the text to this note. Not in any of the passages of the 'refutations' but in the appendix to the *Transcendental Dialectic*, Kant argues that 'the world is a sum of appearances; and there must therefore be some transcendental ground of the appearances', responsible for 'the order of the world and of its connection in accordance with universal laws'. But, by assuming this 'all-sufficient cause', Kant asks, 'Do we then extend our knowledge beyond the field of possible experience?' and answers, '*By no means.* All that we have done is merely to presuppose a something, a merely transcendental object, of which, as it is in itself, we have no concept whatsoever' (A696-8). It is needless to indicate, however, that for Kant, such an object is only an 'object in *idea* and not in reality', which must be used regulatively and not constitutively.

but judgment by the understanding. Thus, for example, the dagger before Macbeth's eyes is certainly perceived. However, unlike the dagger which he draws, it lacks objective reality, and Macbeth is able to correct his earlier judgment, and to regard the former dagger as a mere 'dagger of the mind'. Whilst this example illustrates the criterion of coherence within experience for both men, the coherence is differently explained. Berkeley rests it upon the comparison of ideas. Kant accepts such comparison, but states that *a priori* concepts of the understanding must be 'superadded' (*Proleg.* 20). In the passages of the 'refutations', however, the formal conditions underlying the criterion are implied, rather than stated, giving the impression that they are, indeed, superadded.[22] A typical statement of the criterion is: 'Whatever is connected with a perception according to empirical laws, is actual' (A376).[23] This accords with the second *Postulate of Empirical Thought*,[24] in which it is shown that, under the guidance of the *Analogies of Experience,* we can know that an object is real. In the *Analogies,* it is shown that knowledge must conform to *a priori* concepts.[25] According to Kant, we are thus able to make the transition from awareness of our own ideas to cognition of outer objects, or, in other words, from our perceptions to objectively valid judgments. Apart from this condition, there can be no knowledge, but merely 'a rhapsody of perceptions'.[26] The above criterion is stressed in the

---

22 For example, *Proleg.* 49, 'This doubt [regarding reality] may easily be disposed of, and we always do so in common life by investigating the connection of appearances in both space and time according to universal laws of experience'.

23 *Cf.* A493; *Proleg.* 13, 49.

24 'That which is bound up with the material conditions of experience, that is, with sensation, is actual' (A218).

25 Specifically, to the '*a priori* transcendental unity of apperception' (A177).

26 In spite of such seemingly sure guidance, Kant encounters difficulties in distinguishing, in fact, an objectively valid judgment from a subjective perception. In the *Prolegomena,* he distinguishes between judgments of perception and judgments of experience. The former, e.g., 'Sugar is sweet', involves merely the comparison of ideas and contains no necessity or universality. The latter, e.g., 'The sun warms the stone', has undergone the addition of a concept of the understanding, and is inter-subjectively valid (*Proleg.* 19, 20). This tenuous distinction is relinquished in the second edition

early 'refutations'.[27] It is used directly against the sceptical idealism of Descartes on three occasions. Since the formal conditions of this criterion are, as Kant states, 'superadded', the central argument is not affected thereby. They do mark an important divergence from Berkeley's 'pre-Critical' doctrine, but Kant never directly developed it against Berkeley. An additional criterion is the assumption of the thing-in-itself. In the passages of the 'refutations' this is stressed on only one occasion (*Proleg.* 13). It is the existence of the things behind the appearances, causing these appearances in us, which makes Kant's doctrine 'the very contrary' of idealism. Berkeley's idealism fails because it denies, not the existence of bodies in space, but things-in-themselves. This recourse is completely out of line with the other 'refutations', and indeed, with the Critical philosophy. The illegitimate appeal to this criterion, coming as it does, just after Kant had read the Garve-Feder review, gives the impression of desperation. Kant has not yet found his 'certain criterion' which distinguishes his doctrine from that of Berkeley.

Thirdly, although in the penultimate step of the central argument we saw that Kant and Berkeley are as one on the question of the *ideality* of space and its appearances (that is, all things perceived or perceivable have no existence outside our minds), Kant proceeds to superimpose his characteristic doctrine that space (but not the things in it) is not only ideal, but inheres in us as a pure form of sensibility prior to all experience. Kant uses the *a priori* character of space as an additional criterion of reality, but not until late in the 'refutations'. It turns out to be the essence of Kant's answer to Berkeley. Unlike the other divergences, which occur after the conclusion of the central argument, this one may affect the final step. It is, therefore, significant to my thesis, and will be considered in the next section.

In spite of these differences, the central argument is unified and complete. Before we proceed to consider Kant's direct treatment of Berkeley's doctrine, let us see what conclusions may be drawn from the fact that the above argument, as it now stands, is shared by both men. In the history of philosophy, this argument is the

---

of the *Critique,* for it is clear that if one kind of judgment must conform to the formal condition, so must the other.

27 See note 22 and accompanying text.

unique property of Kant and Berkeley. Whilst no other philosopher, to my knowledge, has produced it, many have asserted some
of the individual steps, some, like the sceptics or idealists, more
than others; but none has either presented these steps in such a
characteristic fashion or conjoined them. First, there is the incisive
analysis of the existing situation, which, by its complete antagonism
to the tone of the age, separates Kant and Berkeley from the vast
majority of other thinkers. Allied to this, is their exclusive disclo-
sure of the source of the delusion inherent in modern philosophy,
and their singular deduction of its inevitable consequences, temporarily in sceptical, and ultimately in dogmatic, idealism. Next,
there is the deliberate acceptance (one may almost add, exploitation) of sceptical arguments. Kant and Berkeley develop this stage
in different directions,[28] but what they share, viz., 'the ideality of
all appearances', and the consequent assimilation of the external
bodies of the philosophers into the realm of mere appearance, they
share only with the sceptics. Finally, in their refutation of dogmatic
idealism (the deepest scepticism) with its attendant proof of an
external world, they leave the whole field far behind. Berkeley's
refutation of scepticism, with his parallel vindication of commonsense, was one of his main aims. His argument to implement it,
developed in the *Dialogues* rather than in the *Principles,* is perhaps
the most singular feature in his whole philosophy. This simple, but
devastating, turning of the game played by scepticism against
itself[29] was original with Berkeley. When this is conjoined with the
other steps to make his main argument, Berkeley's contribution
must be considered as unique up to his time.

Seventy years later, Kant developed an argument in which the
parallel with Berkeley's is exact in some features and close in
others. This becomes more evident once we realize the fact
(strangely neglected by commentators) that Kant most often uses
the term 'idealism' (a word which Berkeley never used) to mean
what Berkeley means by the term 'scepticism'. Kant shares with
Berkeley what is perhaps the latter's most singular feature and uses

---

[28] As we have seen, and as Hume implies, Berkeley provides stronger
arguments than any of his sceptical precursors. (See above, p. 101.)

[29] See Richard H. Popkin, 'Berkeley and Pyrrhonism', *Review of Metaphysics,* 2, (Dec., 1951) , who brings out this point with great clarity.

it to turn the tables on idealism. He conjoins with it the other steps of the argument in a fashion characteristic of none of his precursors (including Hume) except Berkeley.

From the considerations summarized above, and, for the time being, from these alone, I may say at once that Berkeley anticipated Kant in the latter's central argument of the 'refutations'. I go further and, for weighty reasons, conclude that it is inherently likely that Kant was thoroughly familiar with Berkeley's doctrine and learned from it.

VI

There are four difficult sets of facts which my theory must explain. These are: (1) Kant's many obvious misinterpretations of Berkeley's doctrine; (2) Kant's vehement denial that his own doctrine resembles Berkeley's; (3) Kant's extreme animus, reserved, amongst philosophers, for Berkeley alone; (4) Kant's omission of any direct treatment of Berkeley's doctrine in the first edition of the *Critique;* his promise to deal with it, and his failure to do so; his belated indication, in the appendix of the *Prolegomena* and in the second edition of the *Critique,* that Berkeley's doctrine had already been undermined in the *Aesthetic.* Of these, the first three are readily accounted for on the accepted theory, according to which, Kant was largely ignorant of Berkeley's philosophy. This theory can, not quite so readily, explain the fourth. On the face of it, none of them supports my theory. The most important is the first, which seems to demolish my theory. Clearly, Berkeley did not deny the reality of the sensible word; Kant says that he did. Such gross misinterpretation surely indicates profound misunderstanding. However, this first set of facts, when properly assessed and interpreted, yields a contrary view. The remaining facts are so illuminated thereby, that the accepted theory is rendered improbable, whilst my view, that Kant was thoroughly familiar with Berkeley's doctrine and understood it well, becomes the only adequate explanation.

Kant's official view of Berkeley's doctrine is found in five short passages, one in the first edition of the *Critique,* and two each in the *Prolegomena* and the second edition of the *Critique.*[30] The

---

[30] Numbered by me, II, IV, VI, VII, VIII. See above, p. 91.

objection to Berkeley's doctrine, common to all the passages, is that it is a philosophy of illusionism: Berkeley denies the reality of bodies. In only one passage *(Proleg. 13)*,[31] are these bodies held to be external, in the sense of being transcendentally outside us. Therefore, the burden of Kant's official view is that Berkeley denies the reality of bodies *in space,* or, in Kant's words, he 'regards the things in space as merely imaginary entities *(Einbildungen)'* (B274). Kant's official view does seem to arise from a misconception of Berkeley's doctrine, and therefore to stem from ignorance. This accords with the accepted theory. However, such a theory loses weight immediately, when it is pointed out that Kant rarely agrees with anyone,[32] and that his customary procedure in discussing the views of other philosophers, is to present, not their real views, but rather the consequences he considers to be entailed by them. These Kantian consequences are then ascribed to the philosophers as their own views. For example, although Kant studied Leibniz's works carefully, he ascribes to him views which Leibniz never held.[33] Therefore, even if Kant had studied Berkeley's writings as carefully as he studied those of Leibniz, it is likely that his account of Berkeley's doctrine would be distorted. From this consideration, it may be safely observed that Kant's misinterpretations of Berkeley's doctrine are, at least, compatible with the theory that he was thoroughly familiar with it.

Of the five passages, the last three are most relevant, because, not until he began them, had Kant finally settled on a way to treat Berkeley. Although they seem to indicate misconception, nevertheless they secrete Kant's real view of Berkeley. Kant's final account of Berkeley's doctrine is as follows:

> He maintains that space, with all the things of which it is the inseparable condition, is something which is in itself impossible; *and he therefore regards the things in space as merely imaginary*

---

[31] See above, p. 107.

[32] Hume is about the only philosopher to whom he acknowledges a debt. See *Proleg.,* Introduction.

[33] Cf. A39-40. On this matter, Kemp Smith, *op. cit.,* p. 140, note 6, observes: 'Kant, following his usual method in the discussion of opposing systems, is stating what he regards as being the logical consequences of certain of Leibniz's tenets, rather than his avowed position'. Similar considerations apply to Kant's account of Newton (A39-40).

entities. Dogmatic idealism is unavoidable, if space be interpreted as a property that must belong to things in themselves. For in that case space, and everything to which it serves as condition, is a nonentity. The ground on which this idealism rests has already been undermined by us in the Transcendental Aesthetic [B274, my italics].

It will be noticed that this passage contains an essential part of Kant's own doctrine. It is, in fact, a summary of the logical decline of transcendental realism, presented in the first three steps of the central argument of the 'refutations', doctrine which, as we have seen, is just as much Berkeley's as it is Kant's. The important question is: Does Kant know that Berkeley shares it? I think he does. It is certain that Kant ascribes to Berkeley his own denial of the absolute reality of space and the external bodies in it, i.e., his denial of transcendental realism. This is evident from the first sentence. But Kant holds also that Berkeley had drawn the ultimate logical consequence from the realist position, viz., dogmatic idealism, with its denial, not only of the reality of absolute space, but of the reality of the whole sensible world. In other words, Kant ascribes to Berkeley his own doctrine, that once transcendental realism is upheld, dogmatic idealism (complete illusion), is unavoidable. The only other passage which treats of Berkeley directly in the second edition of the *Critique* bears this out. The passage was added at the end of the *Aesthetic.* Here, Kant asserts that his principle of the ideality of appearances does not entail illusion. The contrary is the case: 'It is only if we ascribe objective reality' to space and time, 'that it becomes impossible for us to prevent everything being transformed thereby into mere illusion' (B70). Then, after indicating the absurdities involved in the notion of such entities, he concludes that, accordingly,

We cannot blame the good Berkeley for *degrading bodies to mere illusion* [B71, my italics].

Since Kant asserts by implication that dogmatic idealism or illusionism is avoidable if one does not uphold the absolute reality of space, it follows that a way of escape is left open for himself and Berkeley; not so for the transcendental realists. Kant would have to admit that we must 'blame' Newton, Leibniz, More, Clarke and Locke for inconsistency, and Descartes and Malebranche for refraining from taking the last logical step; he would have to admit that we must 'blame' all transcendental realists for not seeing what he and Berkeley saw. From all this, it is evident that Kant is consciously ascribing to Berkeley his own insights which are presented in the first three steps of the central argument of the 'refutations'.[34]

We have seen that another essential part of Kant's doctrine is his principle, called by him, 'the ideality of all appearances', a principle also shared with Berkeley. But of even more significance than the fact that they share it, is the additional fact that Kant is aware of it. This is evident from the remaining relevant passage on Berkeley in the appendix to the *Prolegomena*. Here, Kant makes a striking admission—one he makes nowhere else. He attributes to Berkeley the view that space and its contents have no absolute reality, but instead, are nothing but appearances; then he admits that he is 'one in confession' with Berkeley on this doctrine. In other words, Kant is here consciously ascribing to Berkeley what amounts to his own insights embodied in the fourth and fifth steps of the central argument.[35] In the same passage Kant reveals additional knowledge:

> Berkeley regarded space as a mere empirical idea that, like the appearances it contains, is, together with its determinations, known to us only by means of experience or perception.

A line later, he adds that 'Berkeley did not consider' the subject of time. Kant's account of Berkeley on space is accurate, and his remark on time would be accurate, had he read only the *Dialogues*[36] and *De Motu*. We now know, therefore, not only that Kant and Berkeley hold in common the central argument, but that Kant is aware he shares almost all of it with Berkeley; and we also know that Kant has reliable additional knowledge. My assessment

---

[34] See above, pp. 94-99.

[35] See above, pp. 99-101.

[36] In these, however, occurs the one significant observation: 'Do I not acknowledge a two-fold state of things, the one ectypal or natural, the other archetypal and eternal? The former was created in time; the latter existed from everlasting in the mind of God' (*Hylas* III). The subject is accorded only two paragraphs (97-98) in the *Principles*.

of the evidence reveals on Kant's part, not ignorance of Berkeley's philosophy, but sure comprehension.

Although Kant must admit that illusionism is avoidable by himself and Berkeley, he means that, while he succeeds, Berkeley fails. The italicized portions of the above passages reveal this. Since Berkeley does not intend to degrade bodies to mere illusion, Kant's assertion that he does is a misinterpretation. Kant, almost throughout, speaks as though he really believes that Berkeley intends to be a whole-hearted dogmatic idealist; but there is one exception. In the last passage we have been considering, Kant gives more detailed treatment of the difference between him and Berkeley than anywhere else. Here we see that Kant departs from Berkeley's view, not on the question of the ideality of space and its appearances, but on its *a priori* nature. The distinction between *ideality* and the *a priori* (often neglected by authorities) is clarified in this passage. Kant agrees with Berkeley that space is ideal, but whereas the latter holds that it is learned from experience, Kant holds he has proved that 'it inheres in us as a pure form of our sensibility before all perception or experience'. Because of this, it can 'afford the certain criterion for distinguishing truth from illusion therein'. He adds:

> *It follows* from this that . . . experience, according to Berkeley, can have no criteria of truth because its phenomena (according to him) have nothing *a priori* at their foundation, whence *it follows* that experience is nothing but sheer illusion [my italics].

Kant thus holds that illusion is a necessary consequence of Berkeley's view, not that it is Berkeley's view. This highly significant admission makes it more than likely that Kant's repeated assertions elsewhere to the effect that Berkeley actually believes in dogmatic idealism are instances of Kant's habit of ascribing to other philosophers what are, in fact, consequences drawn by Kant himself.[37] It follows that Kant's knowledge of Berkeley's philosophy is still more accurate than was previously thought. Since the misinterpretations stem from accurate knowledge, they are deliberate, and are, therefore, more properly called 'perversions'. The same analysis comprehends Kant's denial that his doctrine at all resembles Berkeley's.

---

[37] See above, note 33 and text. In the case of Newton and Leibniz, however, Kant is usually more careful. For them, he uses phrases such as: 'They have to admit', and 'They are obliged to deny'. Cf. A39-40.

For this just is not so. We have Kant's own admission that it is not. One would also expect misinterpretation and denial of resemblance, both of which stem from full knowledge, to be symptoms of animus. This is most likely the case. We have already noticed remarks which indicate that Kant desires his readers to know that he finds Berkeley's teaching abhorrent.[38]

This brings us to the question of Kant's promise, in the first edition of the *Critique,* to deal with Berkeley's doctrine, and his failure to do so. In the fourth *Paralogism,* Kant's position is made to resemble Berkeley's more closely than anywhere else. We now know that there is, not only resemblance, but Kant's awareness of it. If he had sought to refute Berkeley in the next section, he must have ended in hopeless confusion, for he would have been refuting himself. He therefore did not even try. A niggardly description of Berkeley's doctrine was his only recourse. However, the Göttingen review and similar criticisms made it imperative for Kant to define his difference from Berkeley. He appealed first, to his assumption of the thing-in-itself, and then to the *a priori* character of space. Although the latter is a legitimate difference, Kant's appeal to it in this connection (as a guard against illusion, which Berkeley lacked), creates difficulties. We have seen that, throughout the 'refutations', transcendental realism entails illusion, not because it lacks the assumption of space as a prior condition of all experience (because he already makes this assumption), but because it distinguishes outer appearances from the senses. The Kantian antidote to this is not the *a priori* nature of space, but its ideality or subjectivity, which assimilates space and its contents into the realm of ideas, and thus *prevents* illusion.[39]

---

38 See above, p. 92. In addition, the epithet, 'the good Berkeley', should be contrasted with 'the illustrious' or 'the celebrated', which are reserved for other philosophers. He calls the sceptical idealist 'a benefactor of human reason'.

39 This is made clear at A378, *Proleg.* 13, B69-70. It is, moreover, the principle of ideality which saves *all* outer appearances, i.e. all possible experience, for the application of mathematical knowledge. Kant's additional doctrine of the *a priori* character of space is designed to give this mathematical knowledge its apodeictic certainty. However, in certain passages of the second edition (particularly B44), Kant seeks to confuse the *a priori* and the *subjective* elements, using the word 'ideality' to embrace both.

Finally, my suggestion that Kant's deliberate misinterpretations of Berkeley's doctrine were prompted by animus calls for further explanation. The vulgar view of Berkeley, then as now, was of a befooled enthusiast who sought notoriety by his paradoxes.[40] Moreover, Kant abhorred all things mystical[41] and visionary, and classified Berkeley's idealism as such. To acknowledge debt to such a man, or even to admit affinity, was quite out of the question for Kant. However, in the history of philosophy, instances of Catullus' *odi et amo* are by no means rare; the prime example being the relation between Aristotle and Plato. As a result of my reassessment of the evidence, I hold that Kant carefully studied and fully comprehended the writings of the eccentric Irishman. I also suggest that, whilst he may very well have deplored some of Berkeley's conclusions, nevertheless he noted those insights which contributed to the solution of the problem of modern philosophy, and made

---

[40] The remark of Leibniz is representative: 'I suspect that he is one of those people who seek to become famous by their paradoxes' (Letter to des Bosses, 15 Mar. 1715).

[41] Kant's reactions to the impressions of his friend, Georg Hamann, after reading the first edition of the *Critique,* are recorded: 'Owing to its high ideals, he thought the book might be called "Mysticism" as well as the *Critique of Pure Reason.* He told Kant that he liked his work, "all except the mysticism". Kant, who had a dread of everything of the kind, was astonished' (J. H. W. Stuckenberg, *Life of Immanuel Kant,* Macmillan, London, 1862, p. 269).
I am indebted to Lewis White Beck for the following note from Hamann's *Metakritik über den Purismus der Vernunft* (written in 1784 but not published until 1800), and for the concluding observation:
"A great philosopher has asserted that 'general and abstract ideas are nothing but particular ideas, but bound to a certain word, which gives a greater scope or extension to their meaning, and at the same time reminds us of that meaning in individual things'. This assertion of the Eleatic, mystic, enthusiastic Bishop of Cloyne, George Berkeley, is described by Hume as one of the greatest and most valuable discoveries made in our time in the republic of letters. First and foremost, it seems to me that the new skepticism owes more to the older idealism than this casual, single occasion would incidentally give us to understand, and that without Berkeley Hume would scarcely have become the great philosopher which criticism, in unanimous gratitude, makes him out to be. . . ."
Hamann had been in England, and maybe it was he who gave Kant the notion that Berkeley was an "Eleatic."

them his own. My thesis is summarized by Ernst Mach: 'Berkeley's point of view [was] secretly preserved by Kant'.[42]

COLIN MURRAY TURBAYNE

UNIVERSITY OF ROCHESTER

---

[42] Quoted by A. V. Vasiliev, *op. cit.*, p. 85. See Ernst Mach, *Die Analyse der Empfindungen* (9th edition, Jena, 1922) , p. 299.

KANT ON THE MATHEMATICAL METHOD

According to Kant, "mathematical knowledge is the knowledge gained by reason from the construction of concepts." In this paper, I shall make a few suggestions as to how this characterization of the mathematical method is to be understood.

The characterization is given at the end of the *Critique of Pure Reason* in the first chapter of the *Transcendental Doctrine of Method* (A 713 = B 741).[1] In this chapter Kant proffers a number of further observations on the subject of the mathematical method. These remarks have not been examined very intensively by most students of Kant's writings. Usually they have been dealt with as a sort of appendix to Kant's better known views on space and time, presented in the *Transcendental Aesthetic*. In this paper, I also want to call attention to the fact that the relation of the two parts of the first *Critique* is to a considerable extent quite different from the usual conception of it.

To come back to Kant's characterization: the first important term it contains is the word 'construction'. This term is explained by Kant by saying that to *construct* a concept is the same as to exhibit, a priori, an *intuition* which corresponds to the concept.[2] Construction, in other words, is tantamount to the transition from a general concept to an intuition which represents the concept, provided that this is done without recourse to experience.

How is this term 'construction' to be understood? It is not surprising to meet it in a theory of mathematics, for it had in Kant's time an established use in at least one part of mathematics,

---

[1] In referring to the *Critique of Pure Reason*, I shall use the standard conventions A = first edition (1781), B = second edition (1787). All decent editions and translations give the pagination of one or both of these editions. In rendering passages of the first *Critique* in English, I shall normally follow Norman Kemp Smith's translation (London and New York: Macmillan Co., 1929).

[2] *Loc. cit.*

viz. in geometry. It is therefore natural to assume that what Kant primarily has in mind in the passage just quoted are the constructions of geometers. And it may also seem plausible to say that the reference to intuition in the definition of construction is calculated to prepare the ground for the justification of the use of such constructions which Kant gives in the *Transcendental Aesthetic*. What guarantee, if any, is there to make sure that the geometrical constructions are always possible? Newton had seen the only foundation of geometrical constructions in what he called 'mechanical practice' (see the preface to *Principia*). But if this is so, then the certainty of geometry is no greater than the certainty of more or less crude 'mechanical practice'. It may seem natural that Kant's appeal to intuition is designed to furnish a better foundation to the geometrical constructions. There is no need to construct a figure on a piece of paper or on the blackboard, Kant may seem to be saying. All we have to do is to represent the required figure by means of imagination. This procedure would be justified by the outcome of the *Transcendental Aesthetic,* if this can be accepted. For what is allegedly shown there is that all the geometrical relations are due to the structure of our sensibility (our perceptual apparatus, if you prefer the term) ; for this reason they can be represented completely in imagination without any help of sense-impressions.

This interpretation is the basis of a frequent criticism of Kant's theory of mathematics. It is said, or taken for granted, that constructions in the geometrical sense of the word can be dispensed with in mathematics. All we have to do there is to carry out certain logical arguments which may be completely formalized in terms of modern logic. The only reason why Kant thought that mathematics is based on the use of constructions was that constructions were necessary in the elementary geometry of his day, derived in most cases almost directly from Euclid's *Elementa*. But this was only an accidental peculiarity of that system of geometry. It was due to the fact that Euclid's set of axioms and postulates was incomplete. In order to prove all the theorems he wanted to prove, it was therefore not sufficient for Euclid to carry out a logical argument. He had to set out a diagram or figure so that he could tacitly appeal to our geometrical intuition which in this way could supply the missing assumptions which he had omitted. Kant's theory of mathematics, it is thus alleged, arose by taking as an essential feature of all mathematics something which only was a consequence of a defect in Euclid's particular axiomatization of geometry.[3]

This interpretation, and the criticism based on it, is not without relevance as an objection to Kant's full-fledged theory of space, time, and mathematics as it appears in the *Transcendental Aesthetic*. It seems to me, however, that it does less than justice to the way in which Kant actually arrived at this theory. It does not take a sufficient account of Kant's precritical views on mathematics, and it even seems to fail to make sense of the arguments by means of which Kant tried to prove his theory. Therefore it does not give us a chance of expounding fully Kant's real arguments for his views on space, time and mathematics, or of criticizing them fairly. It is not so much false, however, as too narrow.

We begin to become aware of the insufficiency of the above interpretation when we examine the notion of construction somewhat more closely. The definition of this term makes use of the notion of *intuition*. We have to ask, therefore: What did Kant mean by the term 'intuition'? How did he define the term? What is the relation of his notion of intuition to what we are accustomed to associate with the term?

The interpretation which I briefly sketched above assimilates Kant's notion of an a priori intuition to what we may call mental pictures. Intuition is something you can put before your mind's eye, something you can visualize, something you can represent to your imagination. This is not at all the basic meaning Kant himself wanted to give to the word, however. According to his definition, presented in the first paragraph of his lectures on logic, every particular idea as distinguished from general concepts is an intuition. Everything, in other words, which in the human mind

---

[3] A paradigmatic statement of this view occurs in Bertrand Russell's *Introduction to Mathematical Philosophy* (London: George Allen and Unwin, 1919), p. 145: "Kant, having observed that the geometers of his day could not prove their theorems by unaided arguments, but required an appeal to the figure, invented a theory of mathematical reasoning according to which the inference is never strictly logical, but always requires the support of what is called 'intuition'." Needless to say, there does not seem to be a scrap of evidence for attributing to Kant the 'observation' Russell mentions.

represents an individual is an intuition. There is, we may say, nothing 'intuitive' about intuitions so defined. Intuitivity means simply individuality.[4]

Of course, it remains true that later in his system Kant came to make intuitions intuitive again, viz. by arguing that all our human intuitions are bound up with our sensibility, i.e., with our faculty of sensuous perception. But we have to keep in mind that this connection between intuitions and sensibility was never taken by Kant as a mere logical consequence of the definition of intuition. On the contrary, Kant insists all through the *Critique of Pure Reason* that it is not incomprehensible that other beings might have intuitions by means other than senses.[5] The connection between sensibility and intuition was for Kant something to be proved, not something to be assumed.[6] The proofs he gave for assuming the connection (in the case of human beings) are presented in the *Transcendental Aesthetic*. Therefore, we are entitled to assume the connection between sensibility and intuitions only in those parts of Kant's system which are logically posterior to the *Transcendental Aesthetic*.

My main suggestion towards an interpretation of Kant's theory of the mathematical method, as presented at the end of the first *Critique,* is that this theory is not posterior but rather systematically prior to the *Transcendental Aesthetic*. If so, it follows that, within this theory, the term 'intuition' should be taken in the 'unintuitive' sense which Kant gave to it in his definition of the

---

4 See e.g. Kant's *Dissertation* of 1770, section 2, § 10; *Critique of Pure Reason* A 320 = B 376-377; *Prolegomena* § 8. Further references are given by H. Vaihinger in his *Commentar zu Kants Kritik der reinen Vernunft* (Stuttgart: W. Spemann, 1881-1892), Vol. 2, pp. 3, 24. Cf. also C.Ch. E. Schmid, *Wörterbuch zum leichteren Gebrauch der Kantischen Schriften* (4th ed., Jena: Cröker, 1798) on *Anschauung*.

5 "We cannot assert of sensibility that it is the sole possible kind of intuition" (A 254 = B 310). Cf. e.g. A 27 = B 43, A 34-35 = B 51, A 42 = B 59, A 51 = B 75 and the characteristic phrase "uns Menschen wenigstens" at B 33.

6 The opening remarks of the *Transcendental Aesthetic* seem to envisage a hard-and-fast connection between all intuitions and sensibility. As Paton points out, however, they have to be taken partly as a statement of what Kant wants to prove. See H. J. Paton, *Kant's Metaphysic of Experience* (London: George Allen and Unwin, 1936), Vol. I, pp. 93-94.

notion. In particular, Kant's characterization of mathematics as based on the use of constructions has to be taken to mean merely that, in mathematics, one is all the time introducing particular representatives of general concepts and carrying out arguments in terms of such particular representatives, arguments which cannot be carried out by the sole means of general concepts. For if Kant's methodology of mathematics is independent of his proofs for connecting intuitions and sensibility in the *Aesthetic* and even prior to it, then we have, within Kant's theory of the method of mathematics, no justification whatsoever for assuming such a connection, i.e., no justification for giving the notion of intuition any meaning other than the one given to it by Kant's own definitions.

There are, in fact, very good reasons for concluding that the discussion of the mathematical method in the *Doctrine of Method* is prior to, and presupposed by, Kant's typically critical discussion of space and time in the *Transcendental Aesthetic*. One of them should be enough: in the *Prolegomena,* in the work in which Kant wanted to make clear the structure of his argument, he explicitly appeals to his discussions of the methodology of mathematics at the end of the *Critique of Pure Reason* in the beginning and during the argument which corresponds to the *Transcendental Aesthetic,* thus making the dependence of the latter on the former explicit. This happens both when Kant discusses the syntheticity of mathematics (Academy edition of Kant's works, Vol. 4, p. 272) and when he discusses its intuitivity (*ibid.* p. 281; cf. p. 266).

Another persuasive reason is that at critical junctures Kant in the *Transcendental Aesthetic* means by intuitions precisely what his own definitions tell us. For instance, he argues about space as follows: "Space is not a . . . general concept of relations of things in general, but a pure intuition. For . . . we can represent to ourselves only one space. . . . Space is essentially one; the manifold in it, and therefore the general concept of spaces, depends solely on the introduction of limitations. Hence it follows that an . . . intuition underlies all concepts of space" (A 24-25 = B 39). Here intuitivity is inferred directly from individuality, and clearly means nothing more than the latter.

But I am afraid that, however excellent reasons there may be for reversing the order of Kant's exposition in the first *Critique* and for putting the discussion of mathematics in the *Methodenlehre* before the *Transcendental Aesthetic,* my readers are still likely to be incredulous. Could Kant really have meant nothing more than this by his characterization of the mathematical method? Could he have thought that it is an important peculiarity of the method of mathematicians as distinguished from the method of philosophers that the mathematicians make use of special cases of general concepts while philosophers do not? Isn't suggesting this to press Kant's definition of intuition too far?

The answer to this is, I think, that there was a time when Kant did believe that one of the main peculiarities of the mathematical method is to consider particular representatives of general concepts.[7] This view was presented in the precritical prize essay of the year 1764. Its interpretation is quite independent of the interpretation of Kant's critical writings. In particular, the formulation of this precritical theory of Kant's does not turn on the notion of intuition at all. It follows, therefore, that the idea of the mathematical method as being based on the use of general concept *in concreto,* i.e., in the form of individual instances, was the starting-point of Kant's more elaborate views on mathematics. Whether or not my suggested reading of Kant's characterization of mathematics is exhaustive or not, that is, whether or not intuition there means something more than a particular idea, in any case this reading is the one which we have to start from in trying to understand Kant's views on mathematics.

It is useful to observe at this point that the reading of Kant which I am suggesting is not entirely incompatible with the other, more traditional, interpretation. On one hand, a fully concrete mental picture represents a particular, and therefore an intuition in the sense of the wider definition. On the other hand, particular instances of general concepts are usually much easier to deal with than general concepts themselves; they are much more intuitive in the ordinary sense of the word than general concepts. The

---

[7] This has been brought out clearly and forcefully by E. W. Beth, to whose writings on Kant I am greatly indebted, although I do not fully share Beth's philosophical evaluation of Kant's theories. See "Kants Einteilung der Urteile in analytische und synthetische," *Algemeen Nederlands Tijdschrift voor Wijsbegeerte en Psychologie,* **46** (1953-54), 253-264; *La crise de la raison et la logique* (Paris: Gauthier-Villars, 1957); *The Foundations of Mathematics* (Amsterdam: North-Holland Publishing Company, 1959), pp. 41-47.

two interpretations therefore don't disagree as widely as may first seem. What really makes the difference between the two is whether Kant sometimes had in mind, in addition to 'usual' intuitions in the sense of mental pictures or images, some other individuals that are actually used in mathematical arguments. This, I think, is something we must make an allowance for.

In fact, if we have a closer look at Kant's actual theory of mathematics as presented at the end of the *Critique of Pure Reason,* we shall see that many things become natural if we keep in mind the notion of intuition as a particular idea in contradistinction to general concepts. Usually, people read Kant's theory of the mathematical method in the light of what he says in the *Transcendental Aesthetic.* In other words, they read 'intuition' as if it meant 'mental picture' or 'an image before our mind's eye' or something of that sort. But then it becomes very difficult to understand why Kant refers to algebra and to arithmetic as being based on the use of intuitions. The point of using algebraic symbols is certainly not to furnish ourselves with intuitions in the ordinary sense of the word, that is, its purpose is not to furnish ourselves with more vivid images or mental pictures. Scholars have tried to reconcile Kant's remarks on algebra and arithmetic with his critical doctrines as they are presented in the *Transcendental Aesthetic.* The outcome of these attempts is aptly summed up, I think, by Professor C. D. Broad in a well-known essay on "Kant's Theory of Mathematical and Philosophical Reasoning," where he says that "Kant has provided no theory whatsoever of algebraic reasoning."[8] This is in my opinion quite correct if we read Kant's description of the mathematical method in the light of what he says in the *Transcendental Aesthetic.* But then Broad's view becomes, it seems to me, almost a *reductio ad absurdum* of the assumption that the *Transcendental Aesthetic* is, in Kant's mind, logically prior to the discussion of mathematics at the end of the first *Critique.* For on this assumption the statements Kant makes on arithmetic and algebra are not only deprived of their truth but also of their meaning. If the *Transcendental Aesthetic* were logically prior to Kant's methodology of mathematics, it would become entirely incomprehensible what on earth Kant could have

---

[8] *Proceedings of the Aristotelian Society,* 42 (1941-42), 1-24.

meant by his remarks on arithmetic and algebra which so obviously are at variance with his professed theories.

On the other hand, if we assume that by 'intuition' Kant only meant any representative of an individual when he commented on arithmetic and algebra, a number of things, although not necessarily everything, becomes natural. If we can assume that the symbols we use in algebra stand for individual numbers, then it becomes trivially true to say that algebra is based on the use of intuitions, i.e., on the use of representatives of individuals as distinguished from general concepts. After all, the variables of elementary algebra range over numbers and don't take predicates of numbers as their substitution values as the variables of a formalized syllogistic may do. Then we can also understand what Kant had in mind when he called algebraic operations, such as addition, multiplication and division, constructions. For what happens when we combine in algebra two letters, say a and b, with a functional sign, be this f or g or $+$ or $\cdot$ or:, obtaining an expression like $f(a,b)$ or $g(a,b)$ or $a + b$ or $a \cdot b$ or $a : b$? These expressions, obviously, stand for individual numbers or, more generally, for individual magnitudes, usually for individuals different from those for which a and b stood for. What has happened, therefore, is that we have introduced a representative for a new individual. And such an introduction of representatives for new individuals, i.e. new intuitions, was just what according to Kant's definition happens when we construct something. The new individuals may be said to represent the concepts 'the sum of a and b', 'the product of a and b', etc.

Kant's remarks on algebra therefore receive a natural meaning under my interpretation, quite apart from the question whether this meaning is ultimately reconcilable with what Kant says in the *Transcendental Aesthetic*. We might say that the purpose of Kant's use of the term 'intuition' here is to say that algebra is *nominalistic* in Quine's sense: the only acceptable values of variables are *individuals*.

Kant's remarks on arithmetic present a somewhat more complicated problem. I shall not deal with them fully here, although they can be shown to square with the view I am suggesting. There is only one point that I want to make here.

In the case of the arithmetic of small numbers, such as 7, 5, and 12, the ordinary reading of Kant's remarks is not without plausibility. What Kant seems to be saying is that in order to establish that $7 + 5 = 12$ we have to visualize the numbers 7, 5, and 12 by means of points, fingers, or some other suitable illustrations so that we can immediately perceive the desired equation. He goes as far as to say that equations like $7 + 5 = 12$ are immediate and indemonstrable (A 164 = B 204). This is not easy to reconcile with the fact that Kant nevertheless described a procedure which serves, whether we call it a proof or not, to establish the truth of the equation in question and that he said that his view is more natural as applied to large numbers (B 16). I hope to be able to show later what Kant meant by saying that equations like $7 + 5 = 12$ are 'immediate' and 'indemonstrable'. He did not mean that the equation can be established without an argument which we are likely to call a proof. 'Immediate' and 'indemonstrable' did not serve to distinguish immediate perception from an articulated argument, but to distinguish a certain subclass of particularly straightforward arguments from other kinds of proofs. The ordinary interpretation of Kant's theory therefore fails here too. Of the correct view I shall try to give a glimpse later.

One good way of coming to understand Kant's theory of mathematics is to ask: What were the paradigms on which this theory was modelled? The most obvious paradigm, and in fact a paradigm recognized by Kant himself, was Euclid's system of elementary geometry.[9] In the beginning of this paper, we saw that a usual criticism of Kant's theory of mathematics is based on a comparison between Kant's theory and Euclid's system. It seems to me, however, that it is not enough to make a vague general comparison. It is much more useful to ask exactly what features of Euclid's presentation Kant was thinking of in his theory. In view of the interpretation of Kant's notion of intuition that I have suggested, the question becomes: Is there anything particular in Euclid's procedure which encourages the idea that mathematics is based on the use of particular instances of general concepts?

---

[9] See the Academy Edition of Kant's works, Vol. 2, p. 307. Concerning the *Elementa*, see Sir Thomas Heath's translation and commentary *The Thirteen Books of Euclid's Elements* (Cambridge: Cambridge University Press, 1926).

It is easy to see that there is. For what is the structure of a proposition in Euclid? Usually, a proposition consists of five (or sometimes six) parts.[10] First, there is an *enunciation* of a general proposition. For instance, in proposition 20 of the *Elementa* he says: "In any triangle two sides taken together in any manner are greater than the remaining one." This part of the proposition was called the πρότασις.

But Euclid never does anything on the basis of the enunciation alone. In every proposition, he first applies the content of the enunciation to a particular figure which he assumes to be drawn. For instance, after having enunciated proposition 20, Euclid goes on to say: "For let ABC be a triangle. I say that in the triangle ABC two sides taken together in any manner are greater than the remaining one, namely, BA, AC greater than BC; AB, BC greater than CA; BC, CA greater than AB." This part of a Euclidean proposition was called the *setting-out* or *ecthesis* (ἔκθεσις, in Latin *expositio*). It is perhaps no accident that Kant used the German equivalent for setting-out (*darstellen*) in explaining his notion of construction, and that he used the term exposition for a process analogous to that of mathematical construction.

The setting-out or *ecthesis* is closely related to the following or third part of a Euclidean proposition. This part was called the *preparation* or *machinery* (κατασκευή). It consisted in stating that the figure constructed in the setting-out was to be completed by drawing certain additional lines, points, and circles. In our example, the preparation reads as follows: "For let BA be drawn through the point D, let DA be made equal to CA, and let DC be joined."

The construction was followed by the *apodeixis* or *proof proper* (ἀπόδειξις). In the proof, no further constructions were carried out. What happened was that a series of inferences were drawn concerning the figure introduced in the setting-out and completed in the 'preparation'. These inferences made use (1) of the axioms, (2) of the earlier propositions, and (3) of the properties of the figure which follow from the way in which it was constructed.

After having reached the desired conclusion about the par-

---

10 Heath, *op. cit.*, Vol. 1, pp. 129-131.

ticular figure, Euclid returned to the general enunciation again, saying, e.g. "Therefore, in *any* triangle, etc."

When this structure of a Euclidean proposition is compared with Kant's account of the mathematical method, the agreement is obvious. Kant's idea of geometry was, it may be said, Euclidean in more than one sense of the word. When Kant says that it is the method of mathematicians always to consider general concepts *in concreto,* in a particular application, he has in mind the setting-out or *ecthesis* of a Euclidean proposition where a general geometrical proposition is 'exhibited' or 'set out' by means of a particular figure. This is borne out by the examples by means of which Kant explains his theory of the mathematical method. He says that the superiority of the mathematical method over the philosophical one in geometry lies in the fact that the mathematician can draw actual figures and carry out proofs in terms of such figures. For instance, if a philosopher (*qua* philosopher) tries to prove that the sum of the internal angles of every triangle is equal to two right angles, he is reduced, Kant says, to analysing the concepts 'straight line', 'angle', and 'three', and is unable to get anywhere. A mathematician, in contrast, can draw a figure of a triangle, complete it by means of suitable additional constructions (i.e., introduce suitable new lines, circles, etc. into the argument) and thereby make the proposition to be proved obvious. (See A 716-717 = B 744-745.) [11]

This example shows that, in addition to the setting-out or *ecthesis* of a Euclidean proposition, Kant also had in mind the part of the proposition which follows the *ecthesis,* viz. the preparation or 'machinery'. Setting-out and preparation were the two parts of a Euclidean proposition where constructions in the usual sense of the word were made; and we have seen that these two parts were also the ones in which constructions in Kant's abstract sense of the word were needed, i.e. where new individual points, lines, etc. were introduced. This, then, means that within geometry Kant's notion of construction coincides with the ordinary usage of the term 'construction'.

---

[11] We can see here that according to Kant the peculiarity of mathematics does not lie in the *axioms* and *postulates* of the different branches of mathematics, but in the mathematical mode of argumentation and demonstration.

This outcome of our comparison between Kant and Euclid supports what was said earlier. It shows that Kant's notion of a construction accommodates as a special case the usual geometrical notion of construction. Now the constructions of the geometrical kind need not take place in the human mind. More often than not, they are carried out on a piece of paper or on the blackboard. What is common to all such constructions is that some new lines, points, or circles are introduced. If these geometrical entities are conceived of as individuals, they fit into Kant's general definition of an intuition. There is no need, therefore, to assume that the constructions of geometry mean for Kant something else than what we are prepared to call constructions.

But this is not all we can get out of the comparison. If we have a somewhat closer look at the relation between Kant's theory of the mathematical method and Euclid's practice, the relation serves to suggest several insights into Kant's theory. Here I shall only mention a few of them.

(1) There is in geometry an ancient distinction between two kinds of methods. There is, on one hand, the method of assuming a desired result to be achieved, for instance, of assuming that we have succeeded in making a desired construction, in the ordinary sense of 'construction'. From these assumptions one then argues 'backwards', so to speak, to the conditions on which this construction is possible and to the ways in which it can be effected. This is called the analytic method. It was sometimes ascribed to Plato, but it was not to be employed explicitly and systematically in a large scale until the analytic geometry of Descartes, the very name of which is derived from the 'analytic' method in question. The other method was the synthetic one. In applying it one tries to effect the desired result, for instance, to make a desired construction, by actually carrying out constructions. What distinguishes the two methods, therefore, is broadly speaking the fact that in the analytic method no constructions are made while the synthetic method is based on the use of actual constructions.[12]

---

12 We have to realize, however, that the mere difference of the directions in which one is proceeding in an analysis and in a synthesis, respectively, was sometimes emphasized at the expense of the questions whether constructions are used or not. One could thus distinguish between a 'directional' and a

Kant indicates that what makes mathematics in general and geometry in particular *synthetic* is the use of intuitions, i.e., the use of constructions. We have seen that his notion of construction coincides, in geometry, with the ordinary mathematical usage of the term 'construction'. What this means, then, is that Kant's distinction between analytic and synthetic is modelled, within mathematics at least, on a usage of mathematicians which was current at his time. (Mathematicians to-day still speak of synthetic geometry, meaning geometry which turns on the use and study of geometrical constructions.) This suggestion is supported by Kant's own comments on the subject, which serve to narrow down his sense of synthetic so as to connect it explicitly with constructions in an almost geometrical sense. The distinction between analytic and synthetic in geometry was earlier often used to separate two methods of *finding a desired proof or construction,* or, in some cases, to separate two methods of exposition. What Kant needed was a distinction between two different means of *carrying out a proof.* For him, the paradigm of synthesis was precisely synthesis in the geometrical sense of the word, i.e. the completion of a figure by means of the introduction of new geometrical entities. This he distinguished from the other usage which was based on the paradigm of proceeding 'inversely' from a ground to a consequence. This difference is stated by Kant, if not in so many words, in a footnote to the first paragraph of his *Dissertation* of the year 1770.[13]

(2) There is another way in which an awareness of the respective geometries of Euclid and Descartes helps us to understand Kant. We can make a particularly interesting observation if we compare Euclid's geometry with Descartes'. According to Descartes, the main idea of the analytic geometry was a correlation or analogy between algebraic and geometrical operations. Just as all we need in arithmetic are the four or five basic operations of addition, sub-

---

'constructional' (or 'problematic') sense of analysis and synthesis. Cf. my paper, "Kant and the Tradition of Analysis," in *Deskription, Existenz und Analytizität,* ed. P. Weingartner (Munich: Pustet, 1966).

[13] Cf. also, *Prolegomena,* § 5 (*Academy Edition,* Vol. 4, p. 276, footnote). We can also say that Kant's remarks in effect serve to distinguish between the directional and the constructional (problematic) sense of analysis and synthesis, and to indicate that Kant opts for the latter. (See the preceding footnote and the article mentioned there.)

traction, multiplication, division, and the extraction of roots, exactly in the same way we need in geometry only a few basic constructions, Descartes says.[14] What we are interested in here is the analogy between algebraic and geometrical operations, in particular the fact that algebraic operations correspond to certain geometrical constructions. This gives, I think, the key to what Kant means by saying that simple arithmetical equations, such as $7 + 5 = 12$ are 'immediate' and 'indemonstrable'. We see this if we try to cast the argument by means of which $7 + 5 = 12$ is verified into the form of a Euclidean proposition. Because of the analogy between algebraic operations and geometrical constructions, the actual addition of 7 and 5 corresponds to the third stage, i.e., the preparation or 'machinery', of a Euclidean proposition. Kant's explanations also show that, according to him, the numbers 7 and 5 must somehow be 'set out' or 'exhibited' before the actual operation of addition, in analogy to the 'ecthesis' of a Euclidean proposition. (This is what his remarks on "points or fingers" illustrate.) But what, then, corresponds to the proof proper, to the *apodeixis*? Obviously, all that we have to do in order to show that $7 + 5 = 12$ is to carry out the operation of addition; the proof proper is reduced to a mere minimum, to the mere observation that the result of the addition equals the desired result 12. In a perfectly good sense, therefore, one can say that no proof (proper), no *apodeixis* is needed to establish that $7 + 5 = 12$. This equation is 'immediate' and 'indemonstrable' in the precise sense that it can be established by the mere preparation or 'machinery' of a Euclidean proof. This is all that Kant's statement amounts to. And the fact that this really was Kant's idea is shown by a letter of his to Schultz, dated November 25, 1788. The main difference is that, instead of using the terminology which pertains to the *theorems* of the Euclidean geometry, Kant in this letter makes use of the parallel terminology pertaining to geometrical *problems*.

This is important, I think, over and above the interpretation of particular passages, for it shows how Kant intended the intuitivity of arithmetic to be understood. The immediacy of arithmetical truths is not due to the fact that simple equations like $7 + 5 = 12$ are perceived to be true and not argued for, but to the fact

---

14 See *La Géométrie*, the first few statements (pp. 297-298 of the first edition).

that the only thing we have to do in order to establish such equations is to carry out the computation. This serves to explain why Kant said his account of the equations is more readily understood in the connection of large numbers (B 16; cf. A 78 = B 104) .

(3) I suspect that a particularly perplexing passage in the first *Critique* receives a natural explanation pretty much in the same way as the remarks on arithmetic. I mean the statement Kant makes in B 14 to the effect that all the inferences (*Schlüsse*) of the mathematicians are based on the principle of contradiction "which the nature of all apodeictic certainty requires." This passage becomes very natural if we take Kant for his word and understand him as referring solely to the apodeictic or 'proof proper' part of a Euclidean proposition. Taken literally, the proof proper or apodeixis is after all the only part of a Euclidean proposition where inferences are drawn. Taken in this way Kant's statement expresses precisely what he would be expected to hold on my interpretation, viz. that the distinction between on one hand *apodeixis* and on the other hand *ecthesis* and the auxiliary construction separates the analytic and the synthetic parts of a mathematical argument.

What have we accomplished so far? We have seen that in Kant's theory of the mathematical method, presented towards the end of the first *Critique*, one has to keep in mind the possibility that by intuitions Kant means particular representatives of general concepts. We have seen that a number of things about Kant's theory of algebra, arithmetic, and geometry become natural from this point of view. But, it may be said, the possibility of intuitions which are not sensible is ruled out in the *Transcendental Aesthetic*. Kant argues there that all the use of intuitions in mathematics is based on the intuitions of space and time, and that these intuitions are due to the structure of our sensibility. There is, therefore, no room left in mathematics for intuitions that are not connected with sensibility.

I have no desire to deny that this is what Kant says. But I want to point out that the disagreement between the above interpretation of Kant's methodology of mathematics and his theory of space and time in the *Transcendental Aesthetic* does not disprove my interpretation. The discrepancy between the two parts of Kant's system belies my reading of Kant only if the account of mathematics given in the *Transcendental Aesthetic* is correct. Kant claims there that the use of intuitions in mathematics can only be understood if we assume that all these intuitions are due to our sensibility. If there now are intuitions, say the individual variables or 'intuitions' of algebra, which have no relation to our sensibility, then the only possible conclusion is not that these alleged intuitions are not intuitions at all in Kant's sense. The other possibility is to say that they are genuine intuitions but that Kant just was wrong in saying that all the intuitions used in mathematics are *sinnlich,* i.e. due to our sensibility.

But then it remains to be explained how Kant came to entertain the mistaken doctrine. I have implied that the notion of the mathematical method as being based on the use of individual instances was the starting-point of Kant's better-known theory that all the intuitions we use in mathematics are due to our sensibility. What is there in the notion of an intuition as an individual instance which made Kant think that this conclusion is inevitable? We have discussed the rôle of intuitions, in the sense of representatives for individuals, in algebra, in arithmetic, and in geometry. What is the common feature of these uses which can only be explained, according to Kant, by assuming that the mathematical intuitions are sensuous? What is the common denominator of all the mathematical 'constructions' we have discussed?

(4) It seems to me that a natural generalization is virtually contained in the above analysis of Euclid's propositions. The most important part of a Euclidean proposition which is intuitive in Kant's sense is the setting-out, the *ecthesis.* Now this notion of *ecthesis* occurs not only in Greek geometry. It also occurs in the Aristotelian logic. Aristotle never explains explicitly what the procedure called *ecthesis* is, but we can perhaps say that it was a step in which Aristotle moved from considerations pertaining to a general term over to considerations pertaining to a particular representative of this general term. For instance, in *An. Pr.* I, 2, 25a15 Aristotle seems to argue as follows: If no *A* is a *B*, then no *B* is an *A*. For if not, then some *B*'s are *A*'s. Take a particular *b* of this kind. This particular *b* has both the property *B* and the property *A* and shows, therefore, that it is impossible that none of the *A*'s is a *B* as we assumed. This contradiction proves the conclusion. A later passage (*An. Pr.* I, 41, 49b33ff.) seems to indicate that Aristotle

took the logical *ecthesis* to be essentially the same as the geometrical one.[15]

I suggest that this notion of *ecthesis* offers a very good reconstruction of Kant's notion of construction, i.e., of the notion of the exhibition of a general concept by means of particular representatives. It agrees, as we see, very well with the way in which Kant defines the notion of construction. Its use in the Aristotelian logic may perhaps explain why Kant criticized (in the essay on the "False Subtlety of the Four Syllogistic Figures") certain parts of this logic. He went as far as to reject, in effect, all the syllogistic modes except the first two modes of the first figure. The explanation may perhaps lie in the fact that the particular application of *ecthesis* I just outlined was calculated to prove one of the rules of conversion which Aristotle needed in order to reduce all the syllogistic modes to the first two modes. Since the use of *ecthesis* was for Kant a typically mathematical method of reasoning, he could not use it in logic in the way Aristotle did. For this reason, Kant could not reduce all the syllogistic modes to the two modes of *Barbara* and *Celarent* which he recognized as the basic ones, and was bound to reject all the others as being 'impure' and 'confusing'.

The notion of *ecthesis* can be made precise in terms of modern logic.[16] It becomes, in effect, identical with one of the most

---

[15] Concerning the notion of *ecthesis* in Aristotle, see W. D. Ross, *Aristotle's Prior and Posterior Analytics: A Revised Text with Introduction and Commentary* (Oxford: The Clarendon Press, 1949) pp. 32-33, 412-414; Jan Łukasiewicz, *Aristotle's Syllogistic from the Standpoint of Modern Formal Logic* (Oxford: The Clarendon Press, 1951), pp. 59-67; Günther Patzig, *Die Aristotelische Syllogistik* (Göttingen: Vandenhoeck & Ruprecht, 1959), pp. 166-178; B. Einarson, "On Certain Mathematical Terms in Aristotle's Logic," *American Journal of Philology* 57 (1936), 34-54, 151-172, esp. p. 161. As will be seen from these discussions, the precise interpretation of the Aristotelian notion of *ecthesis* (as used in his logic) is a controversial problem to which an unambiguous solution may be unavailable. The interpretation which I prefer (and which I shall rely on here) assimilates logical *ecthesis* to the "existential instantiation" of modern logic. I cannot argue for this interpretation as fully here as it deserves. For Aristotle's use of the term *ecthesis* in geometry, which seems to me to be closely related to the logical *ecthesis*, cf. e.g. *An.Pr.* I, 41 49b30-50a4; *An. Post.* I, 10, 76b39-77a2.

[16] I am here presupposing the interpretation mentioned in the preceding footnote. For further remarks on this interpretation, cf. my paper, "Are Logical Truths Analytic?," *Philosophical Review* 74 (1965), 178-203, and E. W. Beth's

important rules of inference of quantification theory (existential instantiation). And, in terms of the notion of *ecthesis* so reconstrued, we can see in what sense the equation $7 + 5 = 12$ can be said to be based on the use of particular representatives of general concepts, i.e., on the use of *ecthesis*. It would take us too far, however, to go into this question here.[17]

I shall conclude this paper by sketching very briefly and in un-Kantian terms how the reconstruction of Kant's notion of construction in terms of *ecthesis* or in some similar way makes sense of his attempt to connect the mathematical method with sensibility. It was already suggested that the notion of construction may perhaps be identified with certain methods of proof in modern logic. If this is so, then Kant's problem of the justification of constructions in mathematics is *not* made obsolete by the formalization of geometry and other branches of mathematics. The distinction between intuitive and nonintuitive methods of argument then reappears in the formalization of mathematical reasoning as a distinction between two different means of logical proof. But does there remain any sense in which the use of such 'intuitive' methods is problematic? Would Kant have accepted such a reconstruction of the notion of intuition as a premise of his argument that all intuitions are due to our sensibility?

The answer to the questions is, I think, yes. We can see why it was natural for Kant to make the transition from the use of individual instances of any kind to their connection with sensibility. I shall briefly outline two explanations.

Historically, it may be said, nothing was more natural for Kant than to connect individuals with the use of our senses. Aristotle already held that "it is sense-perception alone which is adequate for grasping the particulars" (*An. Post.* I, 18, 81b7). All knowledge, therefore, which is obtained by means of particulars, must be perceptual. How natural the application of this general Aristotelian

---

discussion of the relation of *ecthesis* and modern logic in "Semantic Entailment and Formal Derivability," *Mededelingen van de Koninklijke Nederlandse Akademie van Wetenschappen, Afd. Letterkunde*, N.R., 18, no. 13 (Amsterdam, 1955), pp. 309-342.

17 Some remarks on these points are contained in my paper, "Kant Vindicated," in *Deskription, Existenz und Analytizität*, ed. P. Weingartner (Munich: Pustet, 1966).

idea to the case of constructions in Kant's sense was, is perhaps shown by the fact that Alexander the Commentator already applied Aristotle's idea to the process of *ecthesis*. Alexander held that the singular term introduced in the *ecthesis* is given by perception, and that the proof by *ecthesis* therefore consists in a sort of perceptual evidence.[18] And the general Aristotelian assumption about individuals and senses was echoed by Kant's German predecessors.

Another, and perhaps a more important way of making Kant's ideas plausible may be derived from the division of the Euclidean propositions into parts. We have seen that for him, the use of constructions took place in the second and the third part of a Euclidean proposition, while in the fourth part the argumentation was purely nonconstructive or, which amounts to the same, purely analytic. Now the distinction between these parts of a Euclidean proposition corresponds, according to a widespread view of which Kant seems to have accepted, to a distinction between two kinds of principles of Euclid's system. The principles of construction are the so-called postulates, while the principles of proof proper are called axioms (common notions). It is significant that the examples Kant gives of analytic principles used in geometry (B 17) obviously fall into the second category. (This shows, incidentally, that Kant's notion of construction in geometry was not, as sometimes has been suggested, something alien to the axiomatic treatment of geometry. The very examples Kant gives of geometrical constructions are based either directly on Euclid's postulates, or else on explicit propositions Euclid has proved earlier; a fact of which Kant scarcely could have been unaware. In point of fact, the main

---

18 Alexander of Aphrodisias, *In Aristotelis Analyticorum Priorum Librum I Commentarium*, ed. M. Wallies, in *Commentaria in Aristotelem Graeca*, Vol. 2 (a) (Berlin 1883), p. 32, cf. pp. 32-33, 99-100, 104; Łukasiewicz, *op. cit.* pp. 60-67. An attempt to explain and to justify the mathematical *ecthesis* from an Aristotelian point of view also easily gives rise to striking anticipations of Kantian doctrines. Thus we find, for instance, that according to Theophrastus mathematical objects "seem to have been, as it were, devised by us in the act of investing things with figures and shapes and ratios, and to have no nature in and of themselves . . ." (Theophrastus, *Metaphysica* 4a18 ff., pp. 308-309 Brandisii). Cf. also Anders Wedberg, *Plato's Philosophy of Mathematics* (Stockholm: Almqvist & Wiksell, 1955), p. 89, who emphasizes that Aristotle likewise seems to anticipate some of the most salient features of Kant's theory of mathematics.

construction needed in Kant's favourite example, the theorem about the internal angles of a triangle, is based on the postulate of parallels which Kant himself had tried to prove.)

Hence, the distinction between intuitive and logical ways of reasoning was for Kant, within geometry at least, equivalent with the distinction between the use of postulates, i.e., principles of construction, and the use of axioms, i.e., principles of proof. What, then, constitutes the latter distinction? According to a wide-spread view which may be traced back to Aristotle and certainly back to the Greeks, postulates are assumptions of *existence*. Kant's problem of the justification of constructions, therefore, amounts to the problem of justifying the use of existential assumptions in mathematics.

Stated in this form the whole problem may seem spurious. There is certainly nothing that could prevent a mathematician from studying axiom systems which incorporate general existential assumptions.

The problem only makes sense if we are concerned with the applicability of mathematical reasoning to reality. But this certainly is something Kant was concerned with in the *Transcendental Exposition,* in spite of the fact that he insists that he is speaking of pure mathematics only. (This appears particularly clearly from paragraphs 8-9 of the *Prolegomena*; cf. Vaihinger's discussion of these paragraphs.) We may ask: what happens when we apply to reality a particular mathematical argument in the course of which a postulate, i.e., a general existential assumption, has been used? In applying it, we have to introduce a representative for a new individual, as Kant puts it "without any object being present, either previously or now, to which it could refer." The introduction of the new representative for an individual is carried out a priori. The existence of the individual object in question, in other words, is not given by experience. Kant describes the situation by saying that the intuition or, in our terms, the representative for an individual object precedes its object. The only thing to make sure that there is any object at all corresponding to the representative is the general existential assumption. But it may seem as if there is no general justification for the application of existential assumptions at all unless we are in fact acquainted with the objects that are assumed to exist, which simply is not the case with applications of our a priori knowledge. It seems, as Kant puts it, impossible to intuit anything a priori. For in the absence of actual acquaintance there is in reality nothing to make sure that we can always find objects which the representatives we have introduced really stand for or that they have the properties we expect them to have.[19]

Kant's solution of this (real or apparent) problem consists in saying that there is one and only one case in which we can be sure that the individuals we have assumed to exist really do so and have the desired properties. This is the case in which we have ourselves created the objects in question or ourselves put the desired properties and relations into them.[20] And he seems to think that there is only one stage of our coming to be aware of objects in which this kind of 'putting properties into objects' can take place. Or, rather, there is only one stage in which we can 'put properties' into *all* (individual) objects. This stage is sense-perception. For sensible perception is the only way in which an individual object can 'make its way' into our consciousness. Outer sense is the only way in which we can become aware of external objects. For this reason, it is the only stage of our coming to know objects at which we can ourselves give spatial relations to *all* external objects. Therefore, the spatial relations postulated in geometry must be due to the structure of our outer sense.

---

[19] This difficulty was emphasized by Kant's early critics. For instance, J. G. E. Maas writes in his long paper, "Ueber die transscendentale Aesthetik," *Philosophisches Magazin* 1 (1788), 117-149, as follows, *apropos* Kant's notion of an a priori intuition: "Hierbey kann ich (I) die Bemerkung nicht vorbeglassen, dass eine Anschauung *a priori* . . . nach Kants eigenen Erklärungen nicht denkbar sey. Eine Anschauung ist eine Vorstellung. Sollte sie *a priori* seyn, so müsste sie schlechtendings nicht von Objecte hergenommen werden, und eine Anschauung ist doch nur möglich, sofern uns der Gegenstand gegeben wird, dieses aber ist wiederum nur dadurch möglich, dass er das Gemüth auf gewisse Weise afficiere. Eine Anschauung *a priori* ist demnach unmöglich, und kann mithin auch in Ansehung des Raumes nicht zum Grunde liegen" (pp. 134-135). Maas does not realize, however, that the possibility of a successful use of a priori intuitions is precisely the problem Kant was trying to solve in the *Transcendental Aesthetic*.

[20] In B xviii Kant says that he is "adopting as our new method of thought . . . the principle that we can know a priori of things only what we ourselves put into them." Cf. also B xiii-xiv. I have commented briefly on the historical background of this Kantian assumption in "Kant's 'New Method of Thought' and his Theory of Mathematics," *Ajatus*, 27 (1965), 37-47, and in *"Tieto on valtaa," Valvoja*, 84 (1964), 185-196.

I am putting forth this partial reconstruction only as a first approximation to what Kant had in mind in the *Transcendental Exposition*. This reconstruction is related fairly closely to Kant's 'transcendental argument' for his theory of space and time especially as it is presented in the *Prolegomena*. I have merely tried to fill in those steps which Kant does not himself emphasize in the light of his general assumptions. The relation of my partial reconstruction to Kant's other arguments for his views is more complicated, and requires a longer discussion than I can undertake here.

I want to emphasize that I am not at all claiming that Kant's argument is correct. The main purpose which the reconstruction serves here is to suggest that Kant's problem of the possibility of constructions in mathematics, and his attempted solution to the problem, makes perfectly good sense even when by 'construction' one only means 'the introduction of a new individual representative for a general concept'.

The structure of Kant's argument in the form presented here is nevertheless worth a closer look. Its several stages may be represented in the light of what has been said somewhat as follows:

(1) Mathematical reasoning is principally concerned with the existence of individuals.

(2) The results of mathematical reasoning are applicable to all experience a priori.

In virtue of Kant's general 'Copernican' assumptions ("we can know *a priori* of things only what we ourselves put into them") (1) and (2) force us to conclude:

(3) The existence of the individuals with which mathematical reasoning is concerned is due to the process by means of which we come to know the existence of individuals in general.

Of course, what really matters is not the existence of the individuals as such (there are plenty of individuals existing in the world) but the existence of individuals having the appropriate relations to each other. Hence we may perhaps paraphrase (3) as follows:

(4) The mutual relations of the individuals with which mathematical reasoning is concerned is due to the process by means of which we come to know the existence of individuals.

These systems of mutual relations may be expected to be reflected by the structure of mathematical reasoning.

Now Kant has been seen to assume that

(5) the process by means of which we come to know the existence of individuals in general is sense-perception.

From (4) and (5) it follows that

(6) the structure of mathematical reasoning is due to the structure of our apparatus of perception.

Now (6) is in effect a basic feature of Kant's full and final doctrine of the mathematical method, as complemented by the results he thought he had achieved in the *Transcendental Aesthetic*.

This line of thought (1) — (6) is not without interest and even without certain plausibility. Since we have seen that Kant's point can be translated so as to apply to modern logic, we are therefore led to ask what the corresponding argument will look like as applied to symbolic logic. Steps (1) — (2) and (4) do not seem to me completely implausible as applied to logic instead of mathematics. It is in (5) that Kant really goes wrong. It is simply not true that we usually or always come to know the existence of individuals in the world by means of perception in the sense that perception is the whole of the process involved. It may even be asked whether any perception at all need be involved. When we come to establish the existence of a number of a certain kind, it is mistaken to assume that perception is always involved. (But is a number really an individual? Maybe not; but certainly a number was an individual for Kant when he called the symbols of algebra intuitions, i.e., representatives of individuals. Kant's account of algebra stands or falls with the assumption that 'individuals' of the sort represented by the variables of algebra are also known by the sole means of perception.) The concept of an inner sense to which Kant resorts here is one of the weakest points of his system. To think of all knowledge of individual objects as being due to perception is to succumb to a temptation which for Kant may have been very real but which it is important to get rid of. This is the temptation to think that the basic materials of human knowledge are *given to* us passive receivers who do not have to actively search for these materials. On this fallacious idea the human mind, often conceived of as a disembodied spirit inhabiting an alien machine, has to wait until the signals from the outside strike its receptors. (It is interesting in this connection to observe the way in which Kant stressed the passive nature of perception, speaking, e.g., of how objects are *given to us* in perception.) The fact that the mind can indirectly spur the machine into a movement is not thought to alter the situation materially. Nor is the situation essentially changed by the fact that according to Kant the human mind can in many ways actively organize the raw-materials thus obtained, add to them and perhaps even modify them.

I hope that I do not have to argue here that this picture is *grundfalsch*, thoroughly false. It is more interesting to ask for a better account. If perception is not the general concept which covers all that we want, what is? It seems to me that insofar as we can give a general name to all the processes by means of which we come to know the existence of individuals, they may rather be called processes of searching for and finding than acts of perception, albeit we have to accommodate the accidental perception of an object as well as the deliberate construction of an object as special cases of 'searching' and 'finding' in this broad (broadest possible) sense. Hence we have instead of (5) :

(5) The process by means of which we come to know the existence of individuals is that of searching for them.

Instead of (6) we thus have to conclude:

(6) The structure of a logical argument is due to the structure of the processes of searching for and finding.

My attempted partial reconstruction of the main point of Kant's philosophy of mathematics as applied to modern symbolic logic instead of mathematics thus gives rise to an interesting suggestion for our present-day philosophy of logic. The suggestion is to consider the logic of quantification as being essentially the logic of the notions of searching for and finding (suitably generalized). It seems to me that this suggestion is likely to give rise to interesting and important considerations, if carried out systematically.

JAAKKO HINTIKKA

STANFORD UNIVERSITY AND
THE UNIVERSITY OF HELSINKI

THE KANTIAN THEORY OF SPACE IN THE LIGHT OF GROUPS OF TRANSFORMATIONS*

1. *On Kantian Space as a Group of Motions: Continuity and Constancy Curvature*

Two difficulties arise in the study of the Kantian theory of space. The first turns on the intrinsic significance of this theory, and the second on the possibility of assessing it in terms of the theory of groups of motions.

To be sure, Kant excludes the concept of the motion from geometry and assigns it to kinematics[1]; all objective movement is in fact empirical, but we must make two modifications to this statement. First, movement as a description of a space is a pure act of successive synthesis of diversities, and this act of the subject is absolutely necessary in order to conceive both geometrical figures and time itself. Moreover, this description is not merely an accessory of geometric thought, for it defines the nature of extensive magnitudes, the representation of whose parts makes possible that of the whole. It is upon the successive synthesis of the productive imagination, when it engenders figures, that geometry with all its axioms is founded.[2]

But we must go further. In order to measure space, the progression of intuition must be regarded as limitless.[3] What, then does this progression signify if not that I must be able to move the unit that I have arbitrarily chosen, be it an ell or a foot, along the length of a segment. The unit of measurement is, consequently, mobile.

In the end, the Transcendental Methodology requires that, no matter what the nature of the geometric axioms, the demonstra-

---

* Translated by Natalie F. Tarbet.

[1] A 41 = B 58; on this point, see Vuillemin, *Physique et métaphysique kantienne* (Presses universitaires de France, 1955), § 2, pp. 25-42.

[2] A 163 = B 204.

[3] A 25 (5).

tions of theorems, far from being able to proceed in a purely logical fashion, must proceed according to the construction of concepts.[4] These constructions are movements. It is therefore not illegitimate to ask if the Kantian doctrine implies *in nuce* a theory of groups of transformations.

Two questions must, however, be dealt with before we proceed with our examination.

(a) The theory of groups of motions implies continuity. But the word is not even pronounced in the Transcendental Aesthetic.

This objection is all the more serious because, if we wish to establish the apodictic character of the construction, we have to invoke the principle of continuity. Now in Kant's thought, the latter is either totally deprived of any constitutive role or it is confused with the principle of the Anticipations of Perception; and then it no longer corresponds to an intuition of the sensibility,[5] but to a category of the understanding.[6] But the principle of the Anticipations has itself remained extremely obscure in critical philosophy.

There is lacking in Kant's Transcendental Aesthetic, then, a postulate concerning the continuity of space. However, as Kant recognizes when trying to find a place for it in the Analytic of Principles of the understanding, this postulate is not intuitive by nature. By itself, intuition is incapable of proving that space is three-dimensional,[7] because the notion of dimension implies that of continuity. It is this principle which Lie is expressing when he says that space is a *Zahlenmannigfaltigkeit*. The intuitive axiom with which Kant replaces it must then be held to be necessary but not sufficient, contrary to what the transcendental method requires.[8]

(b) The second question refers to spaces with no constant curvature. It requires that we effect a dissociation of Kantian axioms.

The second edition of the *Critique of Pure Reason* includes two deductions of the concept of space. The first is metaphysical and

---

4 A 719-722 = B 747-750.

5 A 666 = B 696.

6 A 169-70 = B 211-212.

7 A 24 (3) = B 41.

8 B 40, § 3.

consists of demonstrating what is given *a priori* in this concept[9]; it avoids any reference to geometry.[10] We will call the axioms of this exposition M′.[11] The second deduction is transcendental and turns on the concept of space considered as a principle permitting us to comprehend the possibility of other synthetic *a priori* knowledge[12]; in other words, with the concept of space made a principle, we must be able to deduce from its properties, as necessary and sufficient conditions, the possibility of geometry and *its applicability to physics.*

This encroachment of one science on another warrants reflection. In effect, Kant is talking about two different levels, or, rather, two different requisites within the transcendental deduction.[13] The transcendental deduction may not be absolutely necessary when we are dealing with simple intuitions, which turn on the essence and not on the existence of objects, properly speaking. A metaphysical deduction may therefore suffice, for the geometer runs no risk of error as long as he limits himself to his pure science. Intuition here has indeed the character of immediate evidence. But when we are dealing with concepts of pure understanding and therefore with indirect and mediate synthetic *a priori* judgments concerning existing objects, this evident character terminates and a transcendental deduction becomes absolutely necessary. But, for the same reason a transcendental deduction of the concept of space is seen to have been necessary, and thus the additions made in the second edition are seen to be legitimate. As a matter of fact, the geometer, insofar as he applies the concept of space, is subject to the same errors as the physicist, and he needs the philosopher's critique if he too is not to fall into the antinomies of pure reason.

---

[9] B 38.

[10] As the suppression of A 24 (3) in the second edition proves, but the argument is incorporated in B 41.

[11] We shall call the axioms of the Metaphysical Exposition of the first edition M, and those of the Metaphysical Exposition of the second edition M′, followed by a number referring to the numbered paragraphs of the respective editions. We shall call the axioms of the Transcendental Exposition (second edition only) T.

[12] B 40.

[13] A 87-89 = B 119-121. On this fundamental point, see Vuillemin, *op. cit.,* § 1, pp. 11-25.

Now, we find again in the transcendental exposition of space in the Aesthetic the two different requisites of deduction in general. The transcendental exposition has four axioms:

T_1. The representation of space is intuitive.

T_2. The representation of space is *a priori*.

T_3. The representation of space permits us to determine *a priori* the concept of objects.

T_4. The representation of space is a formal property of the subject.

Now T_1 and T_2 bear on the possibility of geometry, T_3 on the relationship between geometry and physics and T_4 on the limits of the application of geometry. The latter two axioms are reciprocal, so to speak. T_3 signifies there is no physical object without the application of geometric forms; T_4 that there is no application of geometric forms outside of the physical object, that is to say, outside of the phenomenon. These are, however,[14] principles rather than axioms, and they are deprived of that character of immediate evidence which, according to Kant, is a characteristic of T_1 and T_2. It is, therefore, logical to analyse them separately at the same time as the "principle" of continuity.

2. *On Space as the Subjective Form of Exteriority*

The metaphysical exposition itself contains an axiom ($M_2 = M'_2$) equivalent to T_3. Or rather, M'_2 has two parts:

M'_{21}. It is impossible for me to abstract from space in order to obtain objects, as residue. This axiom is a kind of reciprocal of M'_1 ($=M_1$).

M'_{22}. Space is the necessary form of exteriority. This axiom is identical to T_3, and it is therefore permissible to criticize M'_{22} and T_3 at the same time.

Now these two axioms affirm that space is the form of exteriority and that one has the right, therefore, to distinguish the form of the intuition from its matter and to distinguish mathematics from physics. Thus Kant predetermines the character of the metric: he makes it a form characteristic of space. The theory of relativity requires us, in every case, to see an essential difference between an

---

[14] A 733 = B 761; Vuillemon, *op. cit.*, p. 38.

axiom like the one about dimensions and an axiom like the one about distance and free motion. That space is a manifold of numbers [*Zahlenmannigfaltigkeit*] is a truth belonging *a priori* to its nature. That it has a metric is a truth which physics communicates to it, and it consequently pertains to problems of existence and concepts.

At this point we must analyse the rule of T_4. When we compare T_4 to M'_4 which defines space as an infinite given magnitude,[15] we see that T_4 intervenes to prevent M'_4 from producing antinomies. By itself, the metaphysical exposition is compatible with the Newtonian concept of an absolute space regarded as the *sensorium Dei*. This conception has the advantage of preserving the apodictic character of geometry, while the contrary idea of Leibniz, for whom space is a relationship between objects, renders the idea of pure geometry impossible. But the former, according to Kant, leads to antinomies of reason. M'_4 certainly does not imply any such antinomies, but neither is it sufficient to exclude them. T_4 is therefore required for this purpose.

Newton's doctrine of absolute space consists of putting space beyond phenomena.[16] It leads us to declare the world infinite in extension,[17] and to give an apparent basis of meaningless determinations of external intuition, not being determinations of possible perceptions, such as, for instance, the motion or rest of the world in infinite empty space.[18] Finally, it induces us to regard matter as indefinitely divisible.[19]

Now these two affirmations, contrary to what Kant says, cannot be reduced to absurdity by counter-arguments. As far as the infinity of absolute space is concerned, the theory of groups refutes this preconception. As for the infinite divisibility of space, it is itself a dogma[20] only if we add that one can also say that space is made up of simple and indivisible entities, or points. These two considerations are compatible from the moment we state precisely the notion of the powers of infinite sets.

---

15 B 40.

16 A 431 = B 457.

17 A 427-9 = B 455-57.

18 A 429 = B 457.

19 A 435-437 = B 463-465.

20 A 524-525 = B 552-553.

Consequently, there is no decisive reason obliging us to use T_4 to avoid antinomies which might derive from M'_4, since these antinomies do not really arise. The transcendental doctrine of space is compatible with the Newtonian hypothesis of absolute space.

3. On the Synthetic Character of Geometry

At this point we may examine the axioms which, according to Kant, establish the possibility of geometry. These axioms include besides M_3, T_1, and T_2, the last two axioms of the metaphysical exposition in the first edition, viz., M_4 and M_5. On the other hand, as $M_3 = T_2$, $M_4 = M'_3$ and $T_1+T_2 = M'_3$, (details apart) it be logical to examine successively, T_1, T_2, M_5 and M'_4.

Then let this be the system:

T_1. Geometry proceeds synthetically, that is, by sensible intuition.

T_2. Geometry proceeds apodictically, that is, a priori.

M_5. Space is represented as given as an infinite magnitude [eine unendliche Grösse gegeben].

M'_4. Space is represented as an infinite given magnitude [eine unendliche gegebene Grösse].

The first of these postulates is based on the distinction between analytic judgments, which simply clarify a given concept, and synthetic judgments, which add to a concept a determination it formerly did not contain. This addition implies a source other than knowledge by concepts. Kant calls it intuition whether it be empirical or pure. Because of its relation with geometry, such a doctrine merits a three-fold examination of how we analyse the proofs of this science, of its axioms or postulates, and finally, of the sensible representations it uses.

The examples of the proofs Kant uses to legitimize T_1 are of two kinds. Some use the fifth Euclidian postulate,[21] but they are only to be found in the Transcendental Methodology, which is considered to be the oldest section of the Critique, thereby letting us think that through inadvertence alone did Kant abandon this example, which would imply that geometric intuition is, for him, Euclidian. The other examples carefully avoid appeal to the fifth

---

21 A 716-717 = B 744-745; Euclid, Elements, I, Prop. 32.

postulate. They are: "In a triangle, two sides together are greater than the third"[22]; "Two straight lines could not enclose a space"; and "Three straight lines make possible a figure."

These examples, therefore, leave open the question of knowing which geometry is implied by the Kantian exposition. But do they show the intuitive nature of geometry? Is not demonstration reduced to a simple logical sequence by reduction to axioms?

Intuition then reverts to the axioms themselves. Does Kant mean that the postulates, in the Euclidian sense, are logically unprovable, while "common notions" are "logically provable" signifying "reducible to principles of identity and non-contradiction"? Thus,[23] among the principles of pure geometry, he opposes those belonging to the second class, such as "$a=a$," "$a+b>a$," "The whole is greater than its parts," to those which logical analysis is insufficient to establish and which require an intuition, such as: "A straight line is the shortest distance between two points."

But insofar as common notions are concerned, we note that geometric equality, for example, is not reducible to logical identity since it only takes place relative to a definite group of displacements, since the relation "$>$" cannot be derived from the relation "$=$", and since, in the last analysis, the proposition "The whole is greater than its parts" is true by identity only in the particular case of finite sets. As for the definition of the straight line, it implies that the axiom[24] "From one point to another, only one straight line may be drawn"[25] is added and that we prove the theorem: "Two straight lines with two points in common coincide for their full length and in fact make one and the same straight line." Now, of which, the definition, the axiom, or the theorem, are the elements most intuitive? There is necessarily something arbitrary

---

[22] A 25 $=$ B 39; 44 Euclid, *The Thirteen Books of Euclid's Elements*, trans. from the text of Heiberg by T. L. Heath, 2d ed., revised (three volumes, New York: Dover, 1956), I, prop. 20.

[23] B 16-17.

[24] Let us postulate that in a triangle, two sides taken together are greater than the third, and prove that two straight lines having two common points coincide for their full length. Euclid, I, p. 169.

[25] This proposition figures in M_3 but is abandoned in T_2 in which only the axiom of dimensions is kept.

about dividing intuition and logic. Besides, Hilbert has analysed the notion of the straight line as the shortest distance between two points.[26] It implies: 1) axioms concerning the connections of the elements (points, straight lines, planes), 2) axioms introducing the concept of segment (*Strecke*) and the series of points of a straight line, 3) the continuity axiom, and 4) the elementary properties of the concept of magnitude. Thus, the "global" and immediate element in Kant's concept of intuition is reduced to several distinctly different notions. Furthermore, because these elements are only implicitly defined by the axioms, it is impossible to bring intuition to bear on them. We can certainly see that the union of different groups of axioms revealed by analysis to be necessary for establishing Lie's geometries—or Euclid's in a more restricted way—conforms to the "global" intuition we have of space. We can then reject the other logical possibilities which result from choosing a different group of axioms, by pretending that they would change the intuition. But such a decision is entirely foreign to mathematics.

It remains, therefore, to see to what extent our faculty of sensible representation is capable of choosing from among logically possible axioms those giving rise either to Lie's three geometries or to Euclid's single one. Did Beltrami resolve this problem, as Helmholtz claimed? We could object that the correspondence established between non-Euclidian spaces and ordinary space only proves that the geometries of these spaces are not contradictory or, at least, that they all have the same degree of consistency that Euclid's geometry has; but we could also object that these logical proofs remain insufficient, according to Kant, and that the synthetic intuition of space in reality pertains, in all these correspondences, to Euclidian space alone. Strictly speaking, the models of Beltrami and other geometers would then ruin Kant's transcendental proofs; but they would leave the metaphysical proofs intact.[27] Nonetheless, it would seem that these models prove more than we would like to admit. If we infer from the known laws of our sense perceptions that series of sense impressions which without change of our sense organs a spherical or pseudo-spherical world would give us, not

---

26 Letter to Felix Klein, *Math. Ann.* Bd. 46.

27 Bertrand Russell, *An Essay on the Foundations of Geometry* (1st ed., 1897; New York: Dover, 1956), p. 56.

only do we not discover any inner contradictions in the calculation of metric propositions, but we can very well imagine the appearance of such worlds in all directions just as we can conceive them through our understanding.[28]

In the end, we note that these correspondences must be *complete*, but that this final consideration forces us to intervene with abstract *"Mannigfaltigkeiten."*[29] The intuitive aspect we lend to the non-Euclidian geometries would not apply except in normal regions, and Euclidian space would be mathematically "distinguished" as soon as we envisaged the complete space. Lie has shown what difficulties such a distinction causes in Helmholtz's system of axioms. Now, when Kant invokes Archimedes' definition of the straight line without specifying whether this definition is viable in a complete space (as it seems to be) or only in a limited region, the resulting incertitude throws us upon the following alternative: if it is valid for the complete space, we exclude *a priori* the possibility of Riemann's geometry; or if it is valid for a limited region, we retain the possibility of Riemann's geometry.

Consequently, if T_1 implies recourse to intuition in geometric reasoning, it must be rejected. If this same recourse takes place in the axioms, T_1 no longer appertains to the intrinsic conditions of the possibility of geometry. If, last of all, T_1 simply signifies the possibility of intuitive representation of geometric propositions, insofar as this representability adds something sensible to them, it can distinguish the Euclidian group among Lie's three groups only if we impose on intuition the requirement that it be complete.

4. *On the A Priori Character of Space*

T_2 affirms the *a priori* and therefore universal and necessary character of the representation of space.

The only example kept in the second edition is the one about the three-dimensional character of space. We will consider this example as a special axiom, D.

---

[28] H. Helmholtz, "Ueber die tatsächlichen Grundlagen der Geometrie," *Wissenschaftliche Abhandlungen* (Leipzig, 1883), vol. 2, pp. 610-617, 614.

[29] R. Bonola, *Non-Euclidean Geometry* (with translations of Bolyai and Lobatchewsky), ed. R. Carslaw (LaSalle, Ill.: Open Court, 1906). Reprinted (New York: Dover, 1955).

Now, Kant claims that the tri-dimensionality of space is a "necessary truth." He abandons in the *Critique of Pure Reason* the argument concerning the incongruity of symmetrical figures. In his pre-critical writings he had linked this argument with the one on the specificity of dimensions. But, he abandoned the accessory in order to save the essential in this example. And in the *Dissertation* (1770) he attempted to give a demonstration of the tri-dimensionality of space.

This demonstration depends on two essential ideas: 1) the three-dimensional Euclidian system is complete. This shows the difference between the notion of symmetry in the plane and in space. Men have wanted to "prove" that space has to have three dimensions by basing their arguments on Helmholtz's free-motion postulate. If we consider group Δ_0 of Euclidian rotations, including all the linear transformations which leave the squares of distances invariable, this group can be represented by the mobility of a rigid body. But when this representation is no longer valid, the characterization ceases to be convincing. It would therefore be better to regard Δ_0 as an abstract group whose various representations by linear transformations are characteristic of different physical quantities: For example, the representation made by orthogonal transformations would be characteristic for the vectors, a tensor representation would be characteristic for the electromagnetic field strength, and the "spinor" representation for the electronic-wave field. But such an abstract analysis of group Δ_0 would have nothing more in common with concrete intuitive analysis that the Transcendental Aesthetic suggests.

2) Kant perceived the topological nature of the problem and, foreseeing the bond uniting the notions of continuity and dimension, began to supply the elements needed for analysing the second by means of the first. Poincaré formulates the problem in terms in which the spirit of Kant's *Dissertatio* revives in rather curious fashion. It is impossible to break space down into several parts "either by forbidding passage beyond certain points or by forbidding the crossing of certain lines; these obstacles could be overturned. It is necessary to prevent going through certain surfaces,

that is, two-dimensional sections; it is on this account that we say space has three dimensions. . . ."[30]

Now such a conception is dealing with a much more general and primitive space than metrical space, and we can thereby rigorously hold it as being given *a priori* in relation to the latter. If one then keeps the example provided by M_3 describing the straight line as the shortest distance between two points, and thereby defining the geodesics, this special new axiom, G—though it be compatible with the three Lie groups when applied in normal regions or with the group of Euclid and Lobatschewsky-Bolyai when considering complete space—is no longer on the same level as the axiom of dimensions. Since Kant has isolated the latter in the second edition, it must be noted that he had a sense of the Riemannian distinction between the relations of extension or of region, and the metrical relations, and, furthermore, that he probably envisaged the possibility of geometries other than Euclid's, even if only to eliminate them in the end, as Lambert had done. The comparison of the two editions of the *Critique* on these points produces the following results:

D is *a priori*.

In the first edition G is *a priori*. The second leaves the question open.

5. *Space Represented as Given as an Infinite Magnitude*

In M_5, Kant refrains from speaking of space as an infinite given magnitude. He only invokes the necessity of being able to pursue indefinitely a spatial construction. Therefore this axiom can be broken down into two parts, M_{51} and M_{52}.

M_{51}. The axiom of free motion, permitting movement of the metric standard.

Axioms G, M_{51} and D, taken together, complete the definition of Lie's three groups. Moreover, we quickly note that M_{51} is more general than G. Though it has disappeared like G from the second edition, the reason cannot, as we shall see, be imputed to M_{51} itself. Without it, it would be impossible for the productive imagination to function. We then have the feeling that the very order

[30] Henri Poincaré, *Science et hypothèse* (Paris: Flammarion, 1902) , p. 45.

of Lie's axioms is foreseen by Kant, D preceding M_{51} which in turn precedes G. But, if this analysis is correct, apriority ceases to pertain absolutely and in its own right to knowledge; *it can only be recognized relatively.*

M_{52}. The boundlessness[31] of intuition is necessary to determine the nature of space. "A general concept of space which is common to the foot as well as to the ell can determine nothing with regard to magnitude."[32]

This axiom can be interpreted in two ways. (a) It signifies that intuition alone gives absolute meaning to measurement, scientific concepts being able to grasp only the relationships between things.

But is it not Kant himself who, in order to show the subjectivity of space and time, recalls that "everything in our knowledge which belongs to intuition . . . contains nothing but mere relations; namely, of locations in an intuition (extension), of change of location (motion), and of laws according to which this change is determined (moving forces) "?[33] To pretend the contrary would be to sacrifice the spirit of geometry and to deny the principle of the relativity of measurement.

(b) It would appear, then, that Kant simply wishes to join the notions of intuition and measurement by a necessary link. Let there be a segment of a straight line AB which I divide in ten parts, one tenth of which I designate as a unit. How does AB contain these parts?, queries the second edition (M'_4). The answer to this question can be found, though more generally, in M_3: any determination of space is a limitation of it.[34] In space, the relation of parts—and *a fortiori* of limits—to the whole is entirely different from the relation between individual things and the concept under which they are subsumed.

Nevertheless, the *Dissertatio* defines space as an infinite given magnitude[35] and denies that every actual aggregate can be given a number (i.e., that every *quantum* is finite).[36] On the other hand,

---

31 *Grenzenlosigkeit,* which corresponds to *Uneingeschränktheit* for time (A 32 = B48).

32 A 25.

33 B 66-67.

34 A 25 = B 39.

35 *Inaugural Dissertation,* § 15, Corollary.

36 *Ibid.,* § 28.

in the first edition of the *Critique*, Kant contents himself with the necessity for the infinite progression of intuition. M_{52} asserts, with $M_3 = M'_2$, not only that intuition differs from concept in that a concept does not contain *in itself* the specific differences of the things it subsumes, while the intuition does; it asserts also that the enumeration of the parts is, for intuition, unlimited whether it be in the order of the infinitely large or of the infinitely small. Consequently, unlike some other *quanta,* space represented as infinite is not determinable by composition[37]; the whole here precedes its parts. To illustrate this peculiarity of space, Kant adduces a concept of relations which in themselves imply a principle of infinity,[38] that is, the concept of irrational magnitudes.[39] The anteriority of an indefinite whole with regard to the parts it contains without designating them, which makes the representation of space an intuition. This conclusion, however, is illusory, since the thought of an infinite set is legitimate and requires of its principle only the purely intellectual notion of a one to one correspondence; hence it is useless to appeal to an intuition in order to compose space from its point-elements.

6. *On Space Represented as an Infinite Given Magnitude*

With M'_4, the second edition eliminates all allusion to the unlimited character of intuition and specifies that we represent space as an infinite given magnitude. As the addition to M_1 of the words "along side of" well indicates, Kant wishes to distinguish the successive exteriority of instants in time and the simultaneity of parts of space. In the Transcendental Deduction of Pure Concepts of the Understanding (second edition), he shows that (1) we cannot *think* any fundamental element of space without drawing it in thought, the action of the subject necessarily implying the concept of succession which determines the inner sense with regard

---

[37] A 165 = B 204; Letter to Johann Schultz, February 17, 1784 (translated in Arnulf Zweig, *Kant's Philosophical Correspondence* [Chicago, 1967] pp. 111-112).

[38] A 25.

[39] Letter to August Wilhelm Rehberg, September 25, 1790 (Zweig, *op. cit.*, p. 166) in which Kant wishes to show that the determination of $\sqrt{2}$ requires intuition and cannot take place through pure concepts of the understanding.

to its form; (2) the determination of the elements requires—just as much for elements of space as for instants of time—that we describe them in space, which is the form of exteriority insofar as it is simultaneous.[40] This precision aims at subordinating the psychological cognition of "I" to the given of an external affection, at rendering *a priori* impossible all rational psychology as a consequence, and thus at refuting idealism.[41] By insisting on the actually given character of the infinity of space, Kant separates it from the purely temporal act of construction. He therefore prefers the form of the intuition to formal intuition and abolishes the Cartesian illusion that knowledge of the soul is more readily attainable than that of the body.

Now this theme belongs to the architectonic of the Kantian system and not to the metaphysical exposition of the concept of space. If M_5 is compatible with Riemann's geometry, while M'_4 excludes it, nothing permits us to say that Riemannian space would be more "formal" and less "intuitive" than Euclidean space. Moreover, in going from the first to the second edition, Kant did not have in mind restricting the hypotheses which are the foundations of geometry. As a matter of fact he declares: "Of a straight line we may rightly say that it can be produced to infinity. In this case the distinction between an infinite and an indeterminately great advance (*progressus in indefinitum*) would be mere subtlety."[42] Herein is the prejudice he shares with Saccheri and Lambert. According to Kant, the distinction between infinite and unlimited applies only to the regress, not the advance, by which one goes from the given to its conditions.[43] Now, this application is itself foreign to geometry. Consequently, if we wish to confine ourselves to the intrinsic analysis of Kant's notion of space, nothing permits us to prefer the second edition text to the first, although in reality the latter is compatible with Lie's three groups while the former excludes spaces with negative curvature. Within the Kantian analysis, there are no geometric reasons but only reasons derived from

---

40 B 154-157.

41 Buillemin, *op. cit.*, p. 15, § 1.

42 A 511 = B 539.

43 A 512 = B 540; Vuillemin, "Reflexionen über Kants Logik," *Kant-Studien* 52 (1960-61), pp. 310-335.

the antinomies and from the possibility of the physical object which make the infinite preferable to the unlimited.

Dehn has shown that the hypothesis of the obtuse angle is compatible with the infinity of the straight line in a non-Archimedean system. Here too we perceive the confusion of Archimedes' postulate (Anticipation of the understanding, according to Kant) with the postulate of extension (intuitive, according to Kant). Now properly speaking, intuition by itself is incapable of producing a clarification, which we could expect from logical analysis alone. And this analysis, by dissociating the connections Kant took to be evident, destroys the necessity and absoluteness not only of transcendental proofs but of metaphysical proofs as well.

Does Kant, then, accept the geometry of Lobatschewsky-Bolyai since it is compatible with D, G and M_{51}? Nothing in the Transcendental Aesthetic allows us to put it aside. However, the theory of schematism appears to prove that Kantian geometry is only Euclidian. We have to impose the schema of geometric figures, the "triangle in general," on particular images which cannot themselves be made adequate to the schema.[44] What, then, does it mean for the image to be geometrically inadequate to the schema? For it to be possible the equivalence of figures must not result from their identity, as happens in arithmetic formulae, but from the invariability of certain properties in relation to a definite group of transformations. When it is the group of Helmholtz's rigid displacements, it is compatible with the geometry of Lobatschewsky-Bolyai. When it is the group of affinities, it excludes it, since only Euclidian geometry allows a figure to keep its form when the lengths of its sides change proportionately. This, now, is what Kant requires not only in the Transcendental Methodology, or when he evokes Thales' theorem,[45] but when he affirms that the unity of the transcendental apperception makes possible the distinction between the form (Gestalt) of a triangle and its image.[46] There is here a reminiscence of the word "idea," which signified first the independence of form in relation to magnitude—the postulate distinguishing the geometry of Euclid.

---

[44] A 140-143 = B 179-182 and A 164-5 = B 204-206.

[45] B xi-xii.

[46] A 124; Vuillemin, op. cit., p. 32.

7. *The Ambiguities in the Exclusion of Empiricism*

These axioms remain:

M'_1. Space is not an empirical concept.

M'_{21}. One cannot make a representation of the absence of space [*eine Vorstellung davon machen, dass kein Raum sei*].

These two axioms make a whole. The first affirms that no element taken from experience enters into the necessary and sufficient conditions of the form of exteriority. The second adds that, our power of abstraction, being without effect upon this form itself, the form is a necessary representation and, for this reason, *a priori*. Although T_2 expresses the transcendental analogue of these two metaphysical axioms, they are conspicuous for leaving entirely undecided the question of knowing whether this *a priori* representation is by nature conceptual or intuitive.

The argument which these axioms have given rise to permits us to divide the possible choices regarding them in the following way. Some, like Helmholtz and Riemann, uphold the *a posteriori* character of the representation of space against Kant. Others, with Russell,[47] keep only the following general affirmation in Kant's system: the universal form of all exteriority is *a priori*. They refuse to hold as true T_2 which reduces geometric axioms to *a priori* synthetic judgments. Still others, like Poincaré, ally with the second group to recognize a pure representation in the general matrix of the diverse forms of exteriority[48]; but when it comes to proceeding from the general matrix to the particular groups enumerated by Lie, they do not invoke experience, as the second group does, but convenience alone, that is, an intrinsic mathematical criterion.

The discussion is often confused because the empirical thesis concerning space is itself ambiguous. It can signify either that the form of exteriority cannot be conceived independently of matter, as Riemann suggests at the end of his *Dissertation* or else that from among the three groups corresponding to spaces with constant curvature, experience permits us to choose the one that is "true," that is, realized in nature, as Helmholtz and (most of the time) Riemann himself understand it. But these two interpretations are

---

47 Russell, *op. cit.*

48 H. Poincaré, "Sur les hypothèses fondamentales de la Géometrie," *Bull. de la Société math. de France*, t. XV, pp. 203-216 at p. 215.

extremely different. The first takes exception to $T_3 = M'_2$, the second denies $M_1 + M'_{21}$.

The Kantian theory of space, reduced to $M_1 = M'_{21}$, is apparently compatible with both Russell's and Poincaré's doctrines, since it excludes only empiricism. However, when we add T_2 or M'_3 we see that the Kantian theory is identifiable with neither one and that, by making geometric judgments *a priori* syntheses, it prohibits Russell's analytical point of view and simultaneously Poincaré's conventionalism.

It seems that a triple opposition will allow us to define the criteria that mathematical judgments satisfy. The first is that of intuition and understanding, which figures in T_2 or M'_3. The second Kant does not make explicit; it splits Poincaré and Russell when they interpret in two different ways the apriority which they both recognize in these judgments. In reality, it is concerned with the opposition between a science of truth which considers an argument as true only when it can correspond to reality taken either from real experience of intuition, or at least from an idea of the understanding; and a formal science, such as formal axiomatic conceives it, which limits its desires to requiring of a system that it not be contradictory, redundant, or possibly categorical. Finally, we can imagine that arithmetic and geometry possess a similar status and method as to the form of their judgments, however different their objects may be, or else we can regard them on the contrary as two entirely distinct sciences.

Criterion / Author	Identification (+) or distinction (−) of arithmetic and geometry	Science of truth (+) or formal science (−)	Intuition (+) or understanding (−)
Kant	+	+	+
Russell	+	+	−
Hilbert	+	−	±[49]
Poincaré	−	Arithmetic +	+
		Geometry −	−

[49] "+" in the *Beweistheorie*.

(In this table the sign "+" means that the author's doctrine satisfies the first of the two criteria; the sign "−" that it satisfies the second. For example, line four of the second column reads "according to Poincaré, arithmetic is a science of truth and geometry a formal science.")

The specificity of the Kantian doctrine immediately stands out from this table. It holds to the connection among the three positive criteria. Poincaré's is Kantian in arithmetic, but for the same reason he is not Kantian in geometry. In other words, Kantian intuitionism remains extrinsic. The intuitive experience claimed by the principle of complete induction is put on the same level as "pure" sensible perception of the square or cube. Thus, it is necessary, in order to specify $M_1 + M_{21}$, to add the following axioms:

K_1. Geometry and arithmetic use judgments of the same form.

K_2. Mathematical judgments turn on essences (*Wesen*); they go beyond simple formal logic. This axiom is a consequence of T_1, but is less "strong."

The question is, then, to know if $(K_1 + K_2)$ is compatible with M'_3 or T_2. Now, the *Dissertatio* of 1770 identifies mechanics with the science of time, geometry with that of space, and arithmetic with a science purely intellectual in itself but whose concrete realization would utilize representations of time and space conjointly. The *Critique* changes this conception. If space remains the object of geometry, time becomes the object of arithmetic, which justifies K_1. But we immediately raise this objection: how, even if we admit that from a psychological standpoint it results from the successive addition of units, does number preserve the memory of its intuitive origins, since, in order to use it, none of precisely that thought-process which formed it must remain? How, consequently, does the intellectual become sensible? Inversely, how does the spatial figure, which is particular, become intellectualized? We would understand this transformation if, as the axiomatic method requires, geometric laws pertained only to the world of the understanding and to formal logic. But, as K_2 is applicable to geometry thanks to K_1, such a solution is impossible and the inadequacy noticeable between schema and image raises the question of knowing how particular constructions establish general laws or how such laws preserve the necessary connection with figures.

8. *Conclusion*

These, then, are the clarifications which the philosophic doctrine of space can gain from the mathematical theory of groups, when it is especially applied to the Helmholtz-Lie problem.

The Kantian theory anticipates with D, M_{51} and G, Helmholtz's three principal axioms: those of dimensions, free motion, and the invariability of distance by the group of displacements. It also allows us to understand that much more profoundly the organization of these three axioms, though such a conception requires the reworking of the notion of the a priori. Kant foresees the bond between continuity and dimension and their topological significance, but his theory of continuously varying magnitudes compromises the value of his foresight.

The Transcendental Aesthetic produces the same difficulties as Helmholtz: can we effectively conceive space independent of matter, as $M'_{22} = T_3$ does? Moreover, the confusion between infinite and unlimited implicitly excludes Riemann's interpretation $(M_5 = M'_4)$. The theory of schematism excludes, probably deliberately, that of Lobatschewsky-Bolyai.

The principal difficulty with the Kantian doctrine lies in its notion of intuition. Contrary to what T_1 affirms, it does not necessarily come into geometric demonstrations, it does not belong to the intrinsic significance of axioms, and, if it serves to facilitate the representation of propositions, it still does not permit us to prefer Euclid except on the condition that it is not only normal but complete. Contrary to what K_1 supposes, there is nothing common to arithmetical intuition and geometrical intuition; the theory of the apriority of space is burdened with this confusion. Finally, contrary to what T_4 implies, it is possible to avoid the difficulties of "absolute space" as soon as we admit the existence of infinite sets.

J. VUILLEMIN

COLLÈGE DE FRANCE

KANT ON THE PERCEPTION OF TIME

This essay amounts to a commentary on some of the leading doctrines of the Analogies of Experience, whose main contention I take to be that we should not be in possession of a unitary time-system unless certain things were true, and indeed necessarily true, of the world of experienced fact. A unitary time-system is one in which all temporal ascriptions—all dates and durations—are directly relateable; it makes sense inside such a system to ask of every supposed happening whether it preceded, followed or was simultaneous with anything else which is taken to happen. Kant assumes, obviously correctly as it seems to me, that the temporal system we have at least purports to be unitary in this way. He also assumes, again as I see it uncontrovertibly, that statements assigning dates to events or durations to processes are intended to say something about the objective world, instead of to record what particular persons happen to feel. We do contrast real with apparent duration ("the struggle lasted for ten minutes, though it felt like an age"), but it is the former which necessarily occupies our primary attention, for only if we first fix the real position of some things in the temporal process can we speak effectively of the apparent position of other things. The real, here as elsewhere, is the normal, the apparent the deviant, and you cannot understand the deviant until you grasp that from which it deviates. Our chief aim in operating a system of temporal concepts must accordingly be to say what objectively is the case.

It turns out, however, that the achievement of this aim is less easy here than in some other instances. Direct perception, at least if we correlate the data of different senses, or even of one sense at different times, enables us to say that physical objects possess certain properties. But time, as Kant himself is constantly saying, "cannot be perceived": events do not come to us with their dates stamped on them, and the fact that a precedes b in my experience does nothing to show that a precedes b in reality. The special difficulties of the establishment of objective time-determinations are such, Kant believes, that we can make genuine temporal judgments only if the experienced world has a certain necessary form. It must be a world in which nothing is absolutely created or absolutely annihilated, one where all change is transformation. It must be a world in which events are not loose and separate in the way Hume took them to be, but rather where the very fact that something occurs means that something else *must* have occurred or be about to occur, i.e. one where there are necessary connections between events. Finally, it must be a world in which different physical things do not operate in causal independence of one another, but form part of a system all of whose members are in thoroughgoing causal reciprocity. That these things are the case in the world we have to deal with Kant says is not just a fact but a necessary fact: it is bound up with our having a certain consciousness of time whose characteristics we all recognise.[1]

In what follows I shall be trying to sketch and evaluate Kant's arguments for these striking conclusions. As he says himself, many persons before him had accepted them as true, but few, if any, had subjected them to serious examination and none had offered a

---

[1] The general principle of the Analogies is best stated in the formula Kant uses in the first edition (A 176-7): "All appearances are, as regards their existence, subject *a priori* to rules determining their relation to one another in one time." I take it that the last three words here are the crucial ones. The formula in the second edition ("Experience is possible only through the representation of a necessary connection of perceptions"—B 218) would apply to the Transcendental Deduction as well as to the Analogies, and does not bring out the special concern of the latter with dates and duration. Kant's reference in the first edition passage to "existence" is in contrast to what he had tried to establish in the Axioms of Intuition and Anticipations of Sense-Perception, where it was the internal structure of appearances which occupied his attention. In the Analogies he seeks to show that, quite apart from their internal structure, the very fact that certain items occur in our experience commits us to the belief that other items will occur or have occurred, and so permits us to move necessarily from the existence of one thing to that of another. Naturally, he finds something paradoxical in our ability to make demands on fact in this way; his solution to the paradox is to argue that we are dealing not with an independently existing world, but with one which is merely phenomenal. I shall not be concerned with this issue in the present discussion, but I try to bring out Kant's caveat that he is dealing only with "phenomena" or "appearances" by speaking of "the experienced world" or "the world of experienced fact."

satisfactory proof of their validity. The 'philosopher' who, asked how much smoke weighs, replied that you could get the answer by subtracting the weight of the ashes left from the weight of the wood burnt (B 228/A 185) was in fact assuming the principle of the first Analogy; so were the ancients when they produced their formula *Gigni de nihilo nihil, in nihilum nil posse reverti.* Similarly the principle that nothing happens without a cause is accepted as axiomatic by philosophers and nonphilosophers alike in daily life. One can call attention to the special necessity we attach to such principles by pointing out that, if someone says that something happened for no reason at all (without any connection with anything that preceded) or that something may have gone clean out of existence, this is taken as a joke: the implication is that we are not prepared to subject principles of this kind to serious doubt. But it is one thing to establish this as a matter of fact, and quite another to find a justification for treating them in this way. What makes Kant's position intriguing is just that he thinks he can provide such a justification. Still more impressively, the justification he offers of one principle is, as we shall see, closely bound up with those he gives of the others: the three Analogies, although formally separate, belong intimately together, with the result that the argument in any one case derives support from the argument in the others. This is not to say that it has to be accepted, either as a whole or in part; it is merely to call attention to an immediate point of strength in Kant's case and to suggest that its rejection may involve more far-reaching consequences than may at first appear.

Kant makes remarks both at the beginning and at the end of the Analogies about the form of the proofs he offers. He maintains that neither a conceptual nor an empirical proof is in point here, what is wanted being rather a "transcendental" proof, "from the possibility of experience." We need to start from the fact that we are able to apply a certain system of concepts, and then ask what must be true if this situation is to obtain. I have drawn attention elsewhere[2] to some of the difficulties in this notion, and shall merely say now that, for all Kant's disclaimers, the suspicion must remain

---

2 See my article "Philosophy and Psychology in Kant's *Critique*," *Kant-Studien,* 57 (1966) , 186-198.

that he offers a series of analytic arguments after all, built largely round his idea of what is involved in being an *event*. I do not mean this to imply that his contentions are, in my opinion, essentially arbitrary: he could and would assert that his concept of an event was framed to fit the facts of our actual temporal experience. But even if this is true, as no doubt it is, the form of the argument would not be unique in the way Kant says it is.

With this by way of preliminary let us now proceed to the details of Kant's case. The reason why the Analogies, unlike the Axioms and Anticipations, involve three special principles in addition to the general principle already referred to is that time has three *modes*, duration, succession and coexistence (B 219/A 177). The obvious inference from this would be that the first Analogy is concerned with the perception of duration. In fact, its purpose is wider than this: it seeks to lay down a general condition which must be satisfied if we are to have a single, continuing time-system, as opposed to a set of particular temporal judgments which can be brought into no relationship with one another. If all times are to belong to a single series (and we all behave as if they must) we must believe, Kant maintains, that there is something in the experienced world which endures through all time, something which persists as the underlying substance of things, though its manifestations or modifications constantly change. At bottom, in this scheme of things, nothing is created or annihilated; what is fundamentally there continues to exist, unchanged in quantity. The idea is perhaps most easily made intelligible if we take it, as Kant himself was inclined to do, in terms of the classical doctrine of matter, the configurations of which were supposedly constantly changing though it was itself indestructible and though its quantum in nature was neither increased nor diminished whatever changes occurred. But it is important to notice that all Kant needs to make good his point is that there is *something* in the world of experience which endures through all time; he has no call, nor indeed any authority, to say what that something is. To put it in his own terms: *that* the concept of substance has application in the experienced world is a truth we can know a priori; *what* its application is we can find out only by empirical means. Kant's position about substance is in fact exactly parallel to his position in the rest of the Analytic of Principles. In the Anticipations of Sense-Perception, for example, he tries to show that every sensation must have a determinate degree; only on this presupposition, he argues, are we justified in asking quantitative questions about, e.g. the intensity of an illumination or the depth of a colour. But he never pretends that we can anticipate experience here in more than formal terms: to find out in what degree a sensation is present we need to have recourse to experience. Similarly in this passage: to discover what form the permanent takes we must go to the scientist, not the critical philosopher.[3]

In the summary proof he added in the second edition at the beginning of the first Analogy (B224-5) Kant first remarked that time itself "remains and does not change," since it is in time that all changes must be thought to take place. But time itself cannot be perceived, and hence it follows that "there must be found in the objects of perception . . . the substratum which represents time in general." To say the least, this is not very lucid. The case is put rather more convincingly in the opening paragraph of the first edition version, where we read that, in order to determine whether "the manifold of appearance" is, as "object of experience," coexistent or successive, "we require an underlying ground which exists *at all times,* that is, something *abiding* and *permanent,* of which change and coexistence are only so many ways (modes of time) in which the permanent exists" (A 182/B 225-6). But for anything like an effective argument in support of Kant's conclusion we have to turn to the last pages of the first Analogy. If we were willing to allow that "new things, that is, new *substances,* could come into existence," we read in one passage (B 229/A 186), we should "lose that which alone can represent the unity of time, namely the identity of the substratum." The reason for this, as given in a later paragraph (B 231/A 188), is that "this permanent is what alone makes possible the representation of the transition

---

[3] It was in his *Metaphysical First Principles of Natural Science* (1786) that Kant laid down as the "first law of mechanics" that "in all changes of corporeal nature the quantity of matter on the whole remains unchanged, neither increased nor diminished" (Berlin edition, IV 541). In this work Kant professes to apply the results of the critical philosophy, but not without introducing empirical concepts, in particular that of motion. The concept of matter involves the concept of motion in its definition, according to *Metaphysical First Principles,* IV, 480.

from one state to another." "A coming to be or ceasing to be that is not simply a determination of the permanent but is absolute, can never be a possible perception" (*ibid.*). "If we assume that something absolutely begins to be, we must have a point of time in which it was not. But to what are we to attach this point, if not to what already exists? For a preceding empty time is not an object of perception" (same paragraph). If substances could come into being or cease to exist, "appearances would relate to two different times, and existence would flow in two parallel streams—which is absurd" (B 231-2/A 188).

I shall now attempt a free reconstruction of this somewhat elusive line of thought, designed to bring out what I take to be its main points. Let me remark first that inspection of the whole passage reveals that Kant is concerned not just with the unity but also with the continuity of time, which he says can be assured only if we suppose that the underlying substance or stuff of the experienced world—whatever it is that undergoes change—persists unaltered in quantity. Without continuity of substance in this sense we could not have continuity of time. Why not? First, for the general reason that "only the permanent can change": we can take cognizance of alterations only if we see them against a background that persists. If there were nothing stable in our experience—if we lived in a world more Heracleitean than that of Heracleitus, with everything 'flowing' at the same rate—we could not even appreciate its instability. Kant makes use of this argument in the second edition Refutation of Idealism when he claims that knowledge of our inner states is possible only if we also have outer experience. The mental world, as Hume put it (*Treatise,* p. 252, ed. Selby-Bigge), is one where perceptions "succeed each other with an inconceivable rapidity, and are in a perpetual flux and movement." In these circumstances, to say no more than that different perceptions are related as earlier and later we require to be conscious of something permanent, and this must be something outside the series of perceptions (B 275-6). However, this argument alone will certainly not give Kant all he wants in the first Analogy, for the persisting things it demands need only be relatively persistent. We all know that as a matter of fact a dating system is possible only because the physical world contains relatively stable and long-lasting objects like the earth and the sun; that there are such objects is, one supposes, an empirical matter. But the first Analogy puts forward what is claimed to be an a priori as opposed to an empirical requirement; the permanence or persistence it speaks of is absolute, persistence *through all time* rather than *for a long time*. Kant must therefore have, or suppose himself to have, further arguments in support of his case.

In fact, these arguments are all indirect: they take the form of asking what the situation would be if the principle of the first Analogy did not hold. Suppose in the first place that the principle were to be breached by the creation of a new substance, which would then presumably manifest itself in what, in our present language, we should describe as a series of happenings. How should we integrate these happenings with the rest of our experience? How indeed should we be justified in speaking of them as happenings at all? Since by definition they would be accidents of a substance which was totally unrelated to anything else in existence, their history would be separate from that of the rest of the experienced world. We could not accordingly say whether what happened to this new substance was happening before, after or simultaneously with any other events; we should find ourselves in the paradoxical position of having two wholly unrelatable time-series, one which we had already, the other which we had newly acquired. But would even this language be legitimate in the circumstances sketched? It is surely plain that it would not. We could not date the emergence of the new substance, and in consequence would not be justified in saying that the "new" time-series had "just been acquired." We can say things like "At such-and-such a time Vesuvius first erupted" because we can see this occurrence as part of the history of the earth, which in turn is part of the history of the supposedly persistent physical universe. But we could not say "At such-and-such a time a new substance began to manifest itself," since *ex hypothesi* other happenings would have no connection with this supposed event. The first appearance of a new substance would accordingly be preceded by nothing but empty time which, as Kant says, is not a possible object of perception.

Consider now the opposite contingency in which substance is thought of not as being created but as annihilated. It might be supposed that the annihilation of substance—its going clean out of existence—could be a dateable occurrence, since it would follow on a regular series of happenings in which something taken to be permanent changed in an orderly way. Provided that events of this sort were relatively rare—if transformation were the general rule and annihilation only exceptional—we could at least recognise them as events. But there are difficulties about this too. Unlike all other events, an occurrence of this sort would have predecessors but no successors; as the absolute termination of a series it could not be said to belong to the history of anything. More seriously, it is hard to see how what *we* should describe as subsequent to it could be said to be really subsequent to it; as an event with no outcome it could not be seen as a regular part of the time-series. Once more, it would be followed by nothing but empty time, and as such could not be perceived.

Substance then must be taken as permanent because neither the creation nor the annihilation of substance can be experienced. It follows that we must suppose that everything that happens must belong to a single history, the history of eternal (phenomenal) substance. Were this not so we should be without a framework inside which to elaborate a unitary system of temporal relations. The position would be that we should be presented with a series of distinct histories which could be brought into no relationship to one another; the temporal questions we now think it appropriate to raise on all occasions simply could not be posed. It is important to observe that the same predicament would threaten us if we followed the lead of some commentators and argued that relatively persistent objects of the kind previously referred to would be enough to meet Kant's requirements. That they would not we can see by reflecting that there might be, and doubtless are, relatively persistent physical objects in different galaxies. It would be possible in these conditions for different groups of intelligent beings to make temporal judgments which were wholly unrelatable; with nothing more to go on than is here presumed we could not ask whether events in the one galaxy were or were not simultaneous with those in another. Kant is right in holding this to be a paradox, and in arguing that we in fact make more extensive demands about the unity and continuity of time than would be possible in the conditions sketched. We need to provide for overall continuity, and that is why we need not relative but absolute permanence in the substance of things.

It scarcely needs to be emphasised that the substance for which Kant argues in the first Analogy is not metaphysical substance. He is not talking about things in general, but about the world of experience; the characteristics of *substantia phaenomenon,* as he calls it (B 186/A 146), can accordingly be quite different from those of substance in the metaphysical sense. *Substantia phaenomenon,* to mention one point only, is something which *essentially* manifests itself in time, which would certainly not be true of, for example, Leibniz's monads. Substance in the first Analogy resembles the substance of metaphysicians in that it cannot be directly experienced; you can get at phenomenal substance only through its accidents. But there the resemblance ends, for whereas metaphysical substance is empirically inaccessible because it transcends experience altogether, substance of the kind Kant here postulates is inaccessible because it is not the sort of thing which *could* be got at in itself. Just as one could not confront the social structure of a community, but only discern it in the attitudes and actions of its members, so one cannot experience phenomenal substance, but only grasp it through its manifestations. In other words, substance is an organising concept, concerned to relate different items in experience. But it is not any less respectable because of that fact.

I am inclined to think that this part of Kant's case is not only plausible, but plainly correct. But I confess to two serious misgivings about it. First, any attentive reader of the Analogies notices the way in which Kant alternates between talk of substance in the singular and talk of substances in the plural. The third Analogy in particular will make sense only if we are permitted to speak of phenomenal substanc*es*. But what could these substances be? In the third Analogy they seem to be large astronomical objects like the sun. But the sun is certainly not an eternal object with a never-ending history: it came into existence at a particular time or during a particular period, and will cease to exist at some time in the future. At this date the material of which the sun is composed will be transformed into something else. Similarly with other suggested substances, where these are identified with familiar objects whether large or small. But to attempt the identification is in any case mistaken, for the reason explained in the last paragraph: to speak of substance in the sense of the first Analogy is not to speak of an item in the world. The transition from substance to substances accordingly seems quite unjustified.

My second misgiving arises out of the awkward fact that there is a well-known theory in cosmology which involves a doctrine of the continuous creation of matter, and so seems to go directly counter to Kant's conclusions. True, this theory is not universally accepted, but it is for all that seriously discussed, which would hardly be likely if there were some a priori objection to it. Defenders of Kant seem to me to have two options as regards this theory. They might in the first place claim that the continuous creation of matter is not the continuous creation of substance in the sense Kant intends; on this I can say only that it looks uncommonly like it. Alternatively, they can argue that there is after all an a priori objection to the theory of continuous creation, though its propounders, not having considered the questions Kant raises, are not aware of this. My own inclination would be to fall back on this second defence, and at least to require the theory's supporters to explain how on their view the unity and continuity of time are to be safeguarded. But I admit that I feel an awkwardness in supposing that men as intelligent as these can make the mistake which on this interpretation they would be making.

I must now pass to the second Analogy, which I shall again discuss only from a limited point of view, omitting any proper enquiry into Kant's concept of causality and concentrating on the relevance of his arguments to the perception of time. The first Analogy, as expounded above, sought to establish a general condition for the making of temporal judgments: the continuity and unity of time had to have their counterpart in the world of experience. As we saw, Kant himself connected this requirement with the perception of duration. In the second Analogy he considers another mode or aspect of time, succession, and argues that we can say that one event really precedes another only if there are necessary connections in the experienced world. The connections in question are not the intelligible connections for which rationalist philosophers like Descartes sought; all that Kant is claiming is that, when an event occurs, there must be *some* preceding event upon which it follows according to a rule. There is no question here of our being able to attain insight into the workings of nature; in one way these remain as 'secret' on Kant's view as they do on that of

Hume. But in another way the experienced world as Kant sees it is altogether different from the world of Hume, for whilst in the latter all events are loose and separate and anything can, in principle, precede or follow anything else, in Kant's understanding of the scheme of things events are tightly linked together, and the temporal order, so far from being full of contingencies, is determinate down to the last detail. Unless this were true, Kant argues, we could never say that this objectively followed that.

To get a grip on this at first sight extravagant argument we need to observe at the outset that Kant is here making a specific application of something for which he had put up a case in the first edition version of the Transcendental Deduction, that association presupposes affinity.[4] In claiming that the categories are necessary for experience he naturally had to refute the suggestion that they are nothing but highly general concepts empirically arrived at. Hume had invoked the psychological machinery of association with a view of showing that this was true of the key concept of cause. According to this way of thinking, some of our 'perceptions' introduce others in a regular manner—there are constant conjunctions in our experience—and this leads us, when a perception of the first sort appears, to feel very strongly that one of the second sort will follow. We imagine in these circumstances that there is a necessary link between the one event and the other, but the necessity is in fact purely subjective. Kant's objection to this theory is fundamental: he denies that the process could even start unless necessary connections were presupposed. If the situation were as Hume describes it—if we had to deal with nothing but perceptions occurring in individual minds—it would be impossible to speak of one regularly following another. That our experiences are orderly depends on the fact that the world of events is orderly, and the world of events must be separated sharply from the sphere of private perceptions. Experiences do follow one another in regular sequence, but that is because necessary connections are already built in at this level: events of their nature have necessary ties with what precedes and follows. Hume succeeds in extracting causality from experience only because it is there already, and there not as a matter of fact but as a matter of necessity.

---

4 See A 112 ff., 121 ff.

Before trying to elaborate this further I should like to emphasise another relevant respect in which Kant and Hume differ fundamentally. Hume builds his whole theory of mind around the occurrence of perceptions, which he divides into the two species impressions and ideas. Asked to account for the peculiar nature of belief—to explain what it is to assent to or dissent from an idea, as opposed to merely entertaining it—Hume replies that it is to contemplate the idea in question with a special sort of feeling. So far as I know, Kant nowhere discusses this theory of belief directly, but everything he has to say on the closely connected subject of judgment goes to show that he must have rejected it in entirety. In his account of the subject the central aim in judgment is to say what is really the case, as opposed to how things seem to the individual experient. Judgment aspires to express truth, and what is true holds without distinction of persons. To see the distinctive feature of judgment as residing in a privately experienced feeling is from this point of view to pick on something utterly irrelevant. For even if it were in fact the case (as it is not) that whenever we form beliefs we experience such feelings, they clearly have nothing to do with belief as involving truth-claims. To maintain that a certain belief is true is to claim the ability to go beyond the impressions or feelings of individual believers and state what must be accepted by anyone who considers the facts. Hume displays enormous ingenuity in trying to show how on his account of the matter we could still speak of a 'system of realities'; the fact remains, even so, that his theory is broken-backed from the start. By contrast, Kant brings the notions of judgment and truth into prominence from the beginning of the *Critique,* and in so doing avoids the fantasy, if also some of the charm, of his great contemporary.

Whatever the merits of these general remarks, it is certainly true that Kant's notion of judgment has to be kept constantly in mind in reading the second Analogy. As everyone who has looked at that section knows, Kant puts his problem as that of how we are to pass from subjective to objective successions: he wants to know on what conditions we can say that one thing follows another "in the object," as opposed to in my mind or yours. Kant says notoriously that "the apprehension of the manifold of appearance is always successive" (B 234/A 189), but there was no necessity from his point of view to insist on the "always." To get the argument started it is enough to make the modest claim that the order of our apprehension does not necessarily coincide with the order of actual events; to point to the obvious fact that we sometimes apprehend successively states of affairs which we take to be really simultaneous, and at other times believe that the order of our apprehension is the same as, or corresponds to, the objective order of events. We are set a problem by the circumstances in which our experiencing takes place: we have to sort out what the world is really like from how it merely appears to us, and this problem is as urgent for time-relations as anywhere. Hume tried to hold on to appearances, here as elsewhere, as the only palpable realities; the so-called real world could in his view be no more than a necessary fiction. Not the least of Kant's merits was that he saw that this involved a reversal of the true order of things: the subjective could become intelligible in the light of the objective, and not vice versa. The conception of appearance makes no sense unless we have first given sense to the conception of reality.

The solution Kant offers to his problem is a variant of the general doctrine advanced elsewhere in the *Critique* which connects the notions of objectivity and necessity. A subjective sequence is one which is essentially arbitrary; it is like the connecting of two ideas by association. An objective sequence, by contrast, is not arbitrary but necessary; it is like the connecting of two ideas by judgment. There is a sense in which what is true may be said to be compulsive for all thinkers, whatever the nature of the content involved; everyone who thinks rationally is under obligation to accept it. Kant may well have been thinking of this sort of compulsiveness in the present discussion, but it is certainly not all he had in mind. For he wants to explicate the notion of an objective sequence as being necessary in a further, internal sense, namely that it is one which takes place in accordance with a rule. To understand this we must begin at the point he begins himself, with the conception of an event as occurring at a determinate place in time. Events are, of their nature, not self-contained, but point both backwards and forwards in the time-series. Nor is this the mere tautology that everything present has a past and a future. Something happens now *because of* something which happened in the past; its place in the time-series is not accidental, but is due to the occurrence of some preceding event. Because a thing of a certain sort happened at time t^1, a thing of another sort happens at time t^2; there is a rule connecting the two occurrences. It is not Kant's doctrine that rules of this sort can be discovered a priori. All that we can know in advance of experience is that any event will point backward to *some* event in the past and forward to *some* event in the future. But that this much can be said is entirely certain, for only on these terms can we understand what it means for one thing to succeed another as a matter of objective fact, as opposed to in our private experience.

It should be observed that Kant is not committed to the impossible proposition that every objective sequence is a causal sequence; his own instance (B 237/A 192) of the boat seen sailing downstream clearly precludes this. There is no rule to the effect that when boats are seen upstream they must subsequently be seen downstream. For the sequence to be objective what is required is that it be causally determined in a more general sense: *elements* in the later situation must be what they are because of the occurrence of the earlier one. Here as elsewhere Kant's claims are more modest than they have sometimes been taken to be. But the fact that they are modest when considered in detail should not disguise their radical character when considered more broadly. That we can know a priori that there are necessary connections between events is a sufficiently startling proposition even when all the proper qualifications have been put in. And it must be emphasised that Kant is in no doubt either about its truth or about the ubiquity of its application: he believes that it would not be possible to claim that *anything* really preceded or followed anything else unless *every* event in the experienced world pointed forwards and backwards in the way we have described. The time-series as a whole must be fixed in advance, with the position of the earlier members determining that of the later, if we are to be able to make true judgments about succession. We all know the discomfort this result caused Kant when he came to write his moral philosophy, but we are not concerned here with this aspect of the matter.

In the Discipline of Pure Reason (B 815/A 787) Kant says that it is a "peculiarity" of transcendental proofs that "only *one* proof can be found for each transcendental proposition." It is somewhat curious in view of this that he offers what seem to be six or seven separate arguments in support of the principle of the second

Analogy. But the diversity here is perhaps misleading: at bottom Kant relies throughout on a single main line of thought. He moves from a formal feature of time—the fact that past must precede present and present future is what is taken (this is the all-important point) as a single continuous series—to its counterpart in the real world, arguing that we could not "empirically apprehend this continuity in the connection of times" (B 244/A 199) unless "the appearances of past time determine all existences in the succeeding time." It seems clear that this argument has a close relationship to the main proof of the first Analogy, and indeed the difficulty is to make any sharp separation between the two. In the first Analogy Kant sought to demonstrate that whatever happens must form part of the history of something which persists through all time without increase or diminution; his emphasis there is on the unchanging subject of which all events are the history. In the second Analogy he shifts attention from the subject to its manifestations; the point which now preoccupies him is the specific place of events in time. But there is the same stress in the two passages on connectibility, and in both the conclusion is drawn that to allow exceptions to the principle argued for would jeopardise the continuity of time. Just how close the two come can be seen if we reflect that, instead of ruling out absolute creation as he does in the first Analogy by arguing that it would involve unrelateable time-series, Kant could have considered the subject in the second Analogy and declared absolute creation impossible on the ground that the first manifestation of a new substance would not follow on any preceding event according to a rule and could not therefore be said to have a determinate place in time. Absolute annihilation could similarly have been proscribed on causal grounds: if something went clean out of existence we should have an event which had no effects, a possibility which Kant believed would have fatal results for our perception of objective succession. From the point of view of the second Analogy the creation of a new substance would involve what was in effect a random occurrence, whilst the annihilation of some existing substance would issue in what might perhaps be called a random nonoccurrence. Both would involve inexplicable breaches of regular temporal sequences, and as such would constitute a threat to the very possibility of making true judgments about the objective order of events.[5]

Few philosophers today are prepared to take the threat just spoken of with entire seriousness; indeed, the prevailing view is that conclusions such as Kant tries to establish in the Analogies must be viewed with profound suspicion. It is not denied that experience is as a matter of fact full of regularities, as even Hume was prepared to admit; what is questioned is the contention that we need to provide for total regularity, on pain of losing all ability to discriminate the real from the imaginary. Two quite distinct factors combine to build up and sustain this attitude. First, the widely-shared empiricist prejudice against principles which claim to be synthetic a priori: it is felt that only someone deplorably ignorant of or insensitive to the most elementary distinctions in philosophy could commit himself to these. Reflection on the special character of the principles Kant advocates in the Analogies will perhaps go some way to dispel this prejudice, for whatever account we finally give of them they can scarcely count as ordinary truths of fact, miraculously known apart from experience. But even if this defence succeeds, the general attitude to this part of Kant's work is not likely to change. For there is a second factor in operation here, namely a persistent belief that Kant is making a lot of fuss about nothing. He confronts us, on this account, with possibilities which he himself describes as alarming, but which can be seen, if contemplated coolly, to be nothing of the sort. Why should there *not* be an occasional random occurrence, or an occasional

---

[5] It is interesting to observe that there is very little in the second Analogy to correspond to the indirect arguments of the first (see above, p. 382). In B 239-40/A 194-5 Kant has a paragraph which begins with the words "Let us suppose that there is nothing antecedent to an event, upon which it must follow according to rule," in the course of which he maintains that "we should then have only a play of representations, relating to no object; that is to say, it would not be possible through our perception to distinguish one appearance from another as regards relations of time." But there is no attempt here to discuss the case in detail. A later passage (B 247/A 201) speaks briefly of what would happen "were I to posit the antecedent and the event were not to follow necessarily thereupon": I should, Kant claims, "have to regard the succession as a merely subjective play of my fancy; and if I still represented it to myself as something objective, I should have to call it a mere dream." But there is no detailed discussion in this case either.

random nonoccurrence for that matter? Experience shows that we can take a certain amount of disorder in our stride: the aberrant can upset us, but need not cause the catastrophic consequences which Kant says must result if we take it seriously. The late Dr. Waismann is said to have believed that a hammer he once possessed went clean out of existence: what harm is there in admitting that he may have been right? Provided that most substances persist, the annihilation of one here and there will make no practical difference. And if most sequences are regular, an occasional breach of causal law can be tolerated without difficulty.

The suggestion here is that there is enough persistence and regularity in the experienced world to enable us to accommodate the exceptions which Kant wants to rule out dogmatically. But is there? The difficulty, as I see it, is to set any limit to the number of exceptions, once their possibility has been admitted. To argue that *as a matter of fact* the creation and annihilation of substance are rare, and the reign of causal law nearly if not quite universal, will not provide the necessary security. For even if it is true (and how we could know it is not obvious) that exceptions to Kant's principles have up to now been few, that will not prevent their occurring with far greater frequency in the future. How far must this process go before we have to confess ourselves totally baffled? If the reply is made that we are concerned with real and not merely logical possibilities, and so can safely discount any such contingency, the question can be asked whether without it the situation as described is free of difficulty. On the hypothesis under consideration things are occurring—few in number, admittedly, but occurring nevertheless—which we cannot integrate with the rest of our experience: events which have no antecedents, events which have no consequences, happenings that come about for no reason at all. What is there in these circumstances to distinguish these peculiar phenomena from total illusion? If some hard-headed person of a scientific cast of mind were to pronounce them entirely unreal, would there be any means of answering him? To take this line is, of course, to subscribe to Kant's principle that only what is connectible according to law is empirically real. Alternatively, an attempt might be made to hold on to the reality of the phenomena whatever the consequences: the effect of this, if it were seriously persevered with, would be to cast doubt on what had hitherto been taken as the system of realities. We cannot, in fact, do justice at the same time to those happenings which conform to rule and those happenings which do not; it is a case of choosing the one or the other. In this respect our position is like that Kant described when he spoke of the creation of substance involving time flowing in two different streams. And just as in that case, we should have no reason for preferring either to the other.

I do not myself believe that those who think we could (or can) get on with a moderately disorderly world have thought through the consequences of their hypothesis. One merit of Kant's discussion in the Analogies is that it makes these consequences clear.

It remains to say something about the third Analogy, the part of Kant's case which has received least attention from commentators. Here Kant tries to do for coexistence what he had, to his own satisfaction at least, already done for succession in the second Analogy. It would be impossible, according to the argument of the latter, for us to say that one event is really prior or posterior to another unless, in general, events had necessary connections, the occurrence of one at a determinate point of time necessitating the occurrence of another at some subsequent point. Irreversibility of perception is on this view a sign of objective succession, but itself needs to be explained by something more fundamental, which turns out to be the ubiquity of causal connections between earlier and later members of the temporal series. Similarly in the third Analogy Kant starts from the reversibility of perceptions as empirical evidence of coexistence, but argues that two things can be judged to coexist only if a further and deeper condition is fulfilled, namely that they should stand in mutual causal interaction. The perception of coexistence is thus possible only if we can know a priori an important and surprising truth about the world of experienced fact.

The first difficulty in assessing this argument is to know what Kant is talking about. In the second Analogy he was concerned with the succession of *events*; here he speaks not about events being simultaneous but of *substances* coexisting. We have already seen that serious problems are involved when Kant passes from the singular to the plural in his discussion of substance: the first Analogy seems to argue for the existence of a *single* continuing substance, and makes no provision for this to exist in separate bits.[6] Moreover, the substances of the third Analogy are perceived to coexist *in space*; they are, in fact, familiar objects like the moon and the earth. Things of this sort are, of course, only relatively persistent; they cannot, as we have seen, fulfill the function in our knowledge of temporal relations which Kant assigns to substance in the first Analogy. Nevertheless, it seems clear enough that it is of them that Kant is thinking in this part of his work: he wants to show that physical things are in dynamical interaction, and to maintain that this is a necessary condition of our being able to make any judgments about real coexistence.

How do we in fact know that the earth and the moon coexist? We can look first at the earth and then at the moon, or we can look first at the moon and then at the earth, and the order of our perceptions will be without effect on their content. But this, according to Kant, would not suffice to show that the two are really coexistent. For something of the kind might be true if we each lived in a world of his own private experience, in which everything would be what it seemed to be and nothing could be said about objective dates. Just as the perception of succession demands the universal operation of the category of causality as regards successive members of any temporal series, so the perception of coexistence demands that there shall be no temporal series which are wholly self-contained. It cannot, for instance, be the case that what we may perhaps call the life-histories of the earth and the moon are each determined throughout by causal law, but nevertheless remain entirely without influence on one another. For if this situation obtained we should once more be in the position of having separate temporal orders with no means of bringing them into relationship with one another; in these circumstances we should not be able to operate a unitary temporal system. The fact is, however, that we do take our temporal system to be unitary, and must therefore accept as true whatever is necessary for it to be so. In Kant's eyes this means that we are committed to the category of reciprocity as well as to the categories of substance and causality.

---

6 What makes this still more curious is that Kant was strongly opposed to atomism in physical theory. He thought it a mere prejudice to assume that matter must exist in packets which differed only in size. See e.g. B 215/A 173 ff.

It might be thought that this argument evidently claims too much. Many very different kinds of event are thought of as happening at the same time; many different kinds of substance, in the loose sense of 'substance' used in the third Analogy, are taken to be coexistent. If, to take an instance, Mr. Harold Wilson coexists with the Taj Mahal, must we suppose them to be in thoroughgoing causal interaction? It should be noticed, however, that Kant says only that "each substance . . . must contain in itself the causality of *certain* determinations in the other substance" (B 259/A 212; my italics). I take this to mean that the Taj Mahal need not affect the whole of Mr. Wilson's life-history, nor vice versa; the influence of the one on the other need not be significant, provided it is real. That it is real, though slight, insofar as Mr. Wilson and the Indian monument are both physical bodies, would be generally admitted. The point Kant wants to add is that it *must* be real.

The argument here becomes altogether more plausible if we observe the emphasis placed in the third Analogy on substances coexisting *in space*; the causal interaction Kant postulates is clearly between objects in a physical universe, united by, for example, gravitational force. But though this illustrates what Kant was after, I do not think it necessarily exhausts it. Just as in the first Analogy the notion of continuing substance can, but need not, be illuminated by referring to indestructible matter, so here reference to the dynamical community of objects in a gravitational system is helpful but not compulsive. If scientists have abandoned the conception of matter as Kant himself understood it, the argument of the first Analogy is not invalidated, for it requires only that there be *something* in the experienced world which persists through all change; as was emphasised earlier, it is for scientists to say what form it will take. Similarly in the third Analogy. It could be that physical objects have to be thought of in ways which were not suspected in Kant's day, and that the principles which unite them in a single physical system are very different from what men thought them then. But even if this is true it does not alter the situation in essentials, for there will still be an a priori reason, connected with our perception of time, for supposing that nothing in the universe can be totally independent of anything else. How the concept of reciprocity applies must be found out empirically; that it applies can be shown from the principles of the critical philosophy.

Is this the beginning of *Naturphilosophie?* Historically no doubt it is. We all know that the *Critique* led on to the *Metaphysical First Principles of Natural Science,* and that the latter was the starting-point for the wild speculations of the *Opus Postumum.* That Kant, for all his suspicion of metaphysics, had a taste for the constructivism fashionable in his later years could scarcely be denied. Nor is it easy to refute the suggestion that he might never have started on this slippery slope if he had not believed himself to have a good case in the Analogies. But however regrettable the later steps in this progress, the fact that they occurred cannot in itself discredit its beginning. I suggest that the argument of the Analogies deserves attention for its own sake, and that its conclusions, which are both clearly stated and closely reasoned, cannot be set aside for any general reason, as that they involve a claim to intellectual intuition (which they do not) or conflict with the plain truth of empiricism. If they are to be refuted at all, they must be refuted on their own ground and in their own terms. And the critics must tell us how the problems about continuity, succession and coexistence which Kant raises are to be solved, if they are not to be solved along Kantian lines.

W. H. WALSH

UNIVERSITY OF EDINBURGH

KANT'S VIEWS ON
SENSIBILITY AND UNDERSTANDING*

I

3. One of the most striking features of Kant's epistemology is his insistence on the need for a sharp distinction between sensibility and understanding. "Our knowledge," he tells us (A50; B74), "springs from two fundamental sources of mind; the first is the capacity of receiving representations (receptivity for impressions), the second is the power of knowing an object through these representations (spontaneity [in the production of] concepts). Intuitions and concepts constitute, therefore, the elements of all our knowledge. . . ." In spite of this radical difference in role, both sensibility and understanding are construed as, in a broad and ill-defined sense, faculties of representation. It is this, perhaps, which leads him to suggest (A15; B29) that they may "spring from a common, but to us unknown, root."

4. It is tempting to think that Kant's distinction between the representations of the understanding and the representations of sensibility is essentially the same as that which many philosophers have drawn between conceptual and nonconceptual representations; and therefore to construe his distinction as a clear-cut advance on the notorious tendency of his predecessors on both sides of the Channel, is to run these together.

5. Yet an examination of the use to which Kant puts his distinction soon makes it evident that while there is *something* to this interpretation, there is little which is 'clear-cut' about the way in which the distinction is drawn. One is tempted to say that here, as

* The first of six (6) John Locke lectures given at Oxford in the Spring of 1966. It is Chapter I of *Science and Metaphysics: Variations On Kantian Themes* (London: Routledge and Kegan Paul, 1968), and is printed here by kind permission of the publishers. [This book will be referred to hereinafter as SM. The first two sections of the original lectures have been omitted but the numbering of the sections has been retained.—Editor's note.]

in so many aspects of his argument, Kant is fighting his way towards a clarity of structure which he never achieves, and which is in his thinking only as the oak is in the acorn. A strong indication of this is found in the close relationship which exists in Kant's mind between the two dichotomies: sensibility, understanding; intuition, concept. The first item on each pair is introduced under the heading of 'receptivity', the second under that of 'spontaneity'. Alas! this neatness soon falls victim to the exigencies of argument. 'Intuition' turns out to be Janus-faced, and the understanding to have its own mode of receptivity.

6. Indeed the moment we note that Kant's *primary* use of the term 'concept' is to refer to general concepts, whether sortal or attributive, a priori or empirical, it is bound to occur to us that what he speaks of as 'intuitions', at least in certain contexts, might well be, in a broader but legitimate sense, *conceptual*. And since it is clear that Kant thinks of intuitions as representations of individuals, this would mean that they are conceptual representations of individuals rather than conceptual representations of attributes or kinds. Indeed Kant refers in the *Aesthetic* to the individuals Space and Time as concepts (A24; B38; A32; B48).

7. On the other hand, since it is clear that not all conceptual representations of individuals can plausibly be construed as Kantian intuitions, additional restrictions must be placed on this interpretation before it can be seriously entertained. A plausible suggestion is that 'intuitions' differ from other conceptual representations of individuals by not being mediated by general concepts in the way in which, for example,

the individual which is perfectly round

is mediated by the general concept of being perfectly round. A more positive clue is provided by Kant's reference to intuitions as "in immediate relation to an object" (A58; B93). Unfortunately, this clue, though it reinforces the above suggestion, is not without ambiguity. It might be interpreted along causal lines, telling us that intuitions are generated by the immediate impact of things in themselves in our receptivity. An intuition is *caused* by its 'object'. I think that there is *something* to this suggestion, and I shall return to it later. On the other hand, "immediate relation" can be construed on the model of the demonstrative 'this'. On this model, intuitions would be representations of *thises* and would be conceptual in that peculiar way in which to represent something as a *this* is conceptual. This, I believe, is the correct interpretation.

8. Another consideration which should make us wary about the supposed clarity with which Kant is distinguishing conceptual from nonconceptual representations is the fact that he allows for 'intuitions' which belong to the 'intellect' (and hence spontaneity), rather than to sensibility (and hence receptivity), though he emphasizes that 'intellectual intuitions' are not enjoyed by human minds nor, presumably, finite minds generally.

9. Our intuitions, unlike God's, essentially involve receptivity. I say 'involve' because, as begins to emerge, the connection of *intuition* with *receptivity* is not as simple as Kant's initial formulations imply. It would, for example, be puzzling in the extreme to assert that the representation of Space is in *no* sense intellectual. Furthermore, Kant clearly commits himself to the view that some representations of individuals are intuitions and *yet* involve a 'synthesis' which, if not a function of the understanding in its role of subsuming representations under general concepts, is certainly no matter of sheer receptivity, but rather of that interesting meeting ground of receptivity with spontaneity which is the 'productive imagination'.

10. We seem, therefore, to be led to a distinction between intuitions which do and intuitions which do not involve something over and above sheer receptivity. It is the former, Kant tells us in the metaphysical deduction (A78; B104), which the understanding subsumes under general concepts. And since he tells us shortly afterward that it is "the same function which gives unity to the various representations *in a judgment*" which "also gives unity to the mere synthesis of various representation *in one intuition*" (A79; B104-5), we are not surprised when, after vaguely characterizing 'synthesis' as "the mere result of the power of imagination, a blind but indispensible function of the soul" (A78; B103), it turns out, most clearly in the second edition (B151-3), that this imagination, under the name 'productive imagination' is the understanding functioning in a special way. Since what we typically speak of as 'imagined' are individual states of affairs, the use of this phrase to refer to the understanding *qua* engaged in that representing of individuals which involves receptivity, and is basic to experience, is not inappropriate. The idea that the understanding *qua* produc-

tive imagination works 'unconsciously' should undoubtedly be interpreted by contrast with the understanding *qua* engaged in the question-answering activities of classifying and relating intuitively represented objects of experience, which Kant refers to in this passage as 'analysis'.

11. We are now in a position to elaborate the earlier suggestion that to 'intuit' is to represent a *this*. For of intuitions those, at least, which are synthesized by the productive imagination would seem to have a form illustrated by

>this-cube

which, though not a judgment, is obviously closely connected with the judgment

>This is a cube.

If this suggestion is correct, we are at once struck by the kinship of Kant's view that the basic *general* concepts which we apply to the objects of experience are derived (by the analytic activity of the understanding) from the intuitions synthesized by the productive imagination, with classical Aristotelian abstractionism. The two positions have in common the idea that we move from representations of the form

>this-cube

which is a representation of a *this-such* nexus, specifically of *this as a cube*, though it is not a judgment and does not involve 'cube' in a predicative position, to representations in which the same nexus and the same content occur in explicitly propositional form

>This is a cube.[1]

12. A key difference would be that for Kant (unlike the Aristotelian) the nexus is 'in' the intuitive representation because it has, so to speak, been put there, not being present in the representations of *sheer* receptivity on which, in some sense, the synthesized intuition is founded.

---

[1] I have explored this feature of Aristotelian theories of concept formation in "Aristotle's Metaphysics: An Interpretation," which is Chapter IV of *Philosophical Perspectives* (Springfield, Illinois: Charles C Thomas, 1967).

13. The view that before we can have representations of the form

    x is a cube

we must have representations of the form

    this-cube

is a puzzling one. The different ways in which the representations *cube* and *white* occur in

    This cube is a die. This white thing is a man,

on the one hand, and

    This is a cube. This is white

on the other, once as part of the subject, once as predicate should, indeed, be taken seriously. But they should not be interpreted in terms of genetic priority. For, surely, the representations

    this cube
    this white thing

are essentially *incomplete* in that while they can occur in a mental listing, they would be unable to play even this role unless one knew how to complete them to form such representations as

    This cube is a die
    This white thing is a man

14. The point stands out even more clearly with respect to our representations of Space and Time. These representations are representations of 'individuals' in that sense of this term according to which anything referred to by a singular term of whatever logical level is an individual. I shall shortly be calling attention to key ambiguities in Kant's treatment of Space and Time. What concerns me now is the implausibility of the idea that general concepts pertaining to Space, e.g. the concepts of line, intersection, surface, etc., are genetically posterior to such representations as

    this-line
    this-intersection
    this-surface
    etc.

15. Notice that what I am attacking is not the idea that the occurrence of *universal* representations within the subject terms of

actual or possible judgments is genetically prior to their occurrence in a predicative position, though this idea certainly merits attack. The *this-ness* is essential. For the traditional claim was that in the representation

    this-cube

cube is not occurring as a *general* at all. The hyphenated phrase 'this-cube' expresses a representing of something *as a cube* in a way which is conceptually prior to *cube* as a general or universal representation; that is, in a way which is conceptually prior to predication or judgment. The strength of the position lies in the fact that the individual represented in perception is never represented as a mere *this,* but always, to use the classical schema, a *this-such.*

16. On the other hand, it is clear that in mature experience, the *'this-suches'* which typically get expressed in language are conceptually rich, even 'theory laden', and presuppose the predicative use of general representations. Kant's thesis, like the Aristotelian, clearly requires the existence of perceptual *this-suches* which are limited in their content to what is 'perceptible' in a very tough sense of this term (the 'proper sensibles'). It requires the existence of completely determinate 'basic' perceptual this-suches.

17. All this suggests that Kant's use of the term 'intuition', in connection with human knowledge, blurs the distinction between a special sub-class of *conceptual* representations of individuals which, though in some sense a function of receptivity, belong to a framework which is in no sense prior to but essentially includes general concepts, and a radically different kind of representation of an individual which belongs to sheer receptivity and is in no sense conceptual.

18. In any event, it is clear that Kant applies the term 'intuition' to both the representations which are formed by the synthesizing activity of the productive imagination and the purely passive representations of receptivity which are the "matter" (A86; B108) which the productive imagination takes into account. Yet if he is not unaware that he is using the term 'intuition' somewhat ambiguously, he does not seem to be aware of the radical nature of the ambiguity.

19. It is implicit in the preceding remark, but needs to be emphasized, that Kant attributes to the representations of sensibility as

such, which, following the tradition, he calls impressions (A86), the character of not being 'of' anything complex. Thus (A99ff.) we find a principle to the effect that receptivity provides us with a *manifold of representations,* but not with a *representation of a manifold,* which latter he proceeds to equate with *representation of a manifold as a manifold.* Other passages in both editions make essentially the same point. It is, indeed, the opening theme of the second edition *Deduction.* It might be thought that Kant is simply denying that the representations of sheer receptivity represent anything as having what might be called a *categorial* structure or complexity. Certainly the distinction between categorial structure and, say, spatio-temporal structure is essential to his argument, but it does not operate in this way. It might be thought, in view of his thesis that Space is the form of outer sense, that he would admit that sheer receptivity can provide us with a representation of a spatial structure. I am convinced, however, and shall argue that this is not the case. He is committed to the stronger claim that what the representations of sheer receptivity are *of* is in no sense complex, and hence that the representations of outer sense as such are not representations of spatial complexes. If I am right, the idea that Space is the form of outer sense is incoherent. Space can scarcely be the form of the represent*ings* of outer sense; and if it is not the form of its represent*eds,* i.e. if nothing represented by outer sense as such is a spatial complex, the idea that Space is the form of outer sense threatens to disappear. The explanation of this incoherence as we shall see, is the fact that his treatment of the 'form' of outer sense shares the ambiguity of his treatment of 'outer intuition'.

20. Thus, the above considerations would not count against the idea that Space is the form of outer *intuition,* i.e. of outer intuit*eds,* if we attribute *all* "outer intuition" to the "figurative synthesis" (B151) of the productive imagination. But, then, Space would seem to disappear altogether from receptivity as such. To reconcile the insights contained in Kant's treatment of 'sensibility' and 'intuition', the distinction we have been drawing between the impressions of sheer receptivity and the intuitions of the productive imagination must be paralleled by a corresponding distinction between two radically different senses of spatial terms, in one of which we can speak of *impressions* as having a spatial form, while in the

other we can speak of *the objects of intuition* as having a spatial form.

II

21. I have been arguing that of the items Kant calls 'intuitions', those which are representations of a manifold *as a manifold* constitute a special class of representations of the understanding. They belong, as such, to spontaneity. Their 'receptivity' is a matter of the understanding having to cope with a manifold of representations characterized by 'receptivity' in a more radical sense, as providing the 'brute fact' or constraining element of perceptual experience.

22. The latter manifold has the interesting feature that its existence is postulated on general epistemological or, as Kant would say, transcendental grounds, after reflection on the concept of human knowledge as based on, though not constituted by, the impact of independent reality. It is postulated rather than 'found' by careful and discriminating attention. The concept of such a manifold is, in contemporary terms, a theoretical construct. Let us, following Kant (and a long tradition which goes back at least to Aristotle), call the items which make up such a manifold 'sense impressions', and let us explore independently the idea that it is reasonable to postulate the existence of sense impressions. As usual the case will be argued in terms of visual perception, but the conclusions reached can readily be extended to all modes of perception.

23. Among the themes which can be distinguished in the classical treatment of sense impressions, the following three can be shown, I believe, to be fundamental, however entangled they became with other lines of thought. I shall assume, as a working hypothesis, that the standard form of expressions referring to sense impressions is that illustrated by

an impression of a red rectangle.

In terms of this example, the three themes can be formulated as follows:

(a) Impressions of a red rectangle are states of consciousness.

(b) Impressions of a red rectangle are brought about in

> normal circumstances by physical objects which are red
> and rectangular on the facing side.[2]

(c) Impressions of a red rectangle *represent*, in a sense to
be analyzed, red and rectangular physical objects.

24. The phrase 'state of consciousness' is both ambiguous and obscure. The obscurity, I believe, is an honest one, the result of the coming together of many ideas at different levels of description and explanation. The conception of visual impressions as states of consciousness can be clarified to some extent by pointing out that they were assimilated to bodily sensations and feelings. The ambiguity I have in mind is manifold. There is, in the first place, the distinction between conceptual and nonconceptual states of consciousness, which it is the purpose of this chapter to explore. Sense impressions are nonconceptual states of consciousness. Then there is the distinction between 'states' and 'objects' of consciousness. The phrase 'object of consciousness' is itself highly ambiguous but for the moment, at least, I shall use it as roughly equivalent to 'noticed'. Like bodily sensations, visual impressions were construed as not only *states* but as, at least on occasion, *objects* of consciousness. Whatever Descartes himself may have thought, there is nothing absurd in the idea that states of consciousness occur which are not apperceived, a fact which was appreciated by Leibnitz.[3] More startling, and to many absurd, is the idea that there are broad classes of states of consciousness *none* of the members of which are apperceived. Startling or absurd, the idea is at least not obviously self-contradictory. (This *may* be due to its obscurity.) In any case, I shall push it to the hilt.

25. I must hasten to add that, according to the position I shall defend, even if visual sense impressions are never apperceived, they

---

[2] In the following I shall abbreviate 'physical object which is red and rectangular on the facing side' by 'red and rectangular physical object'.

[3] Though Leibnitz appreciated the fact of unapperceived representings, his account of the distinction between apperceived and unapperceived representings is by no means unambiguous. He fails to nail down the point that the apperception of a representing involves a numerically distinct representing, i.e. a distinction between an apperceptive representing and the representing it apperceives. At times the distinction between apperceived and unapperceived representings seems to coincide with a 'qualitative' distinction between *grandes* and *petites* representings. He may, however, have intended it to be a synthetic *proposition* that *petites* representings are (usually?) unapperceived.

are so intimately related to certain *other* inner episodes which *are* apperceived, that the temptation, for one who grants their existence, to say that they are themselves apperceived is difficult indeed to resist, particularly when all of the relevant distinctions have not been drawn.

26. To avoid saying that there are visual sense impressions but that they are never apperceived, one might be tempted to take a familiar weapon from the Cartesian arsenal and put it to a new use. Appealing to the fact that (Cartesian confusions aside) the apperception of a representing always involves a conceptual act which, however intimately related to the apperceived representing is numerically distinct from the latter, one might suggest that visual impressions *are* apperceived, but "inadequately" in that the conceptual framework of the apperceptive act does not 'adequately' represent the state of which it is the apperception.

27. Thus philosophers have been known to claim that we perceive the world inadequately *sub specie Strawsonii*, but would perceive it adequately *sub specie Smartii* as whirls of atoms in the void. It might, therefore, be claimed that there are states of consciousness which are inadequately apperceived *sub specie Warnockii* ("it seems to me as if I were seeing an orange") but which we might someday apperceive under a more adequate *ratio*. And, indeed, in spite of modern reinterpretations of the contrast between scientific reason and common sense, the Cartesian view that concepts which are subtly adapted to the demands of everyday living might yet be "inadequate" retains its vitality.

28. Since, however, the respect in which apperception *sub specie Warnockii* is 'inadequate' turns out to be exactly what the postulation of sense impressions is designed to correct, I shall drop this theme of 'inadequate conceptual frameworks' (at least for the present) and concentrate on the original task of exploring the idea that it might be reasonable to postulate the existence of states of consciousness which are not apperceived at all. I have already indicated that this was, in essence, the Kantian position, though he tends to restrict the term 'consciousness' to apperceiving and to the apperceived as such. I shall argue that Kant was right to postulate the existence of a manifold of outer sense on epistemological ('transcendental') grounds—even if the details of his argument are open to serious objection.

29. There are, of course, many who would say that it is the business of science to introduce hypothetical entities, and *therefore* not the business of philosophers to do so. The pragmatically useful division of intellectual labor, reflected in the proliferation of academic departments and disciplines has been responsible for many necessary evils, but none more pernicious than this idea. Philosophy may perhaps be the chaste muse of clarity, but it is also the mother of hypotheses. Clarity is not to be confused with insight. It is the latter which is the true final cause of philosophy, and the insight which philosophy seeks and which always eludes its grasp is total insight. If the maxim *hypotheses non fingo* had captured classical and medieval philosophy, there would have been abundance of clarity but no science, and, in particular, no theoretical science as we know it today.

30. Unless a purely instrumentalist account of the language game of hypothetical entities is to be taken for granted, philosophers must concern themselves with the ways in which these entities are related to the more familiar objects of everyday life. It is clear that if a scientific psychology untrammeled by philosophical traditions were to postulate non-Warnockian states of consciousness in their explanation of certain features of perception, philosophers would regard this step as an eminently suitable topic for philosophical reflection. That 'behavioristics' as a separate discipline was precluded from moving in this direction when behaviorism was substantive rather than methodological, is, of course, no guarantee that it will not do so, now that its conceptual straight jacket has been loosened.

31. In any event, the time for philosophers to cease looking for explanatory hypotheses will come when the puzzles which demand them are adequately taken care of under another professional tag. No doubt the *distinctive* talent of philosophers today, as in the late middle ages, is concept chopping, but there just may be the same need today as there was then for hardy souls to dig up new concepts to chop, as did the great protoscientists of medieval schools.

III

32. It is, I suppose, as noncontroversial as anything philosophical can be that visual perception involves conceptual representations.

And if one accepts the idea that candid overt speech is the expression, in a broadly causal sense, of non-Rylean conceptual episodes, it is reasonable to take the considered verbal reports of one who is scrutinizing his environment in a "what do we have here?" frame of mind, to be the expression of conceptual episodes which are a function of (a) his perceptual capacities and set; (b) the impingement of the environment on his visual apparatus.

33. We have already noted that the vocabulary of these verbal reports is far richer than classical philosophers would admit into the proper philosophical description of sense impressions. Thus, people report that they see a red book on a brown table, but while it is appropriate to say of a third party that he is under the (visual) impression that there is (in front of him) a red book on a brown table (i.e. that he visually takes this to be the case), and that he has the (visual) impression of there being (in front of him) a red book on a brown table, philosophers have been notoriously reluctant to speak of sense impressions of a book on a table. If we think of sense impressions as belonging to the category of conceptual episodes expressed by perceptual reports, this fact is rather a puzzle. According to the tradition, sense impressions are present in all perception, however sophisticated, and it is surely odd to suppose that such rich conceptual episodes as that expressed by "here is a red book on a brown table" are invariably accompanied by such thin conceptual episodes as that expressed by "here is a red rectangle standing out from a brown background."

34. In certain circumstances of perception, however, as has often been pointed out, even the verbal expression tends to become minimal, thus as the speaker becomes more cautious or puzzled. There are, however, two ways in which reports may be minimized which must be carefully distinguished, though they may both be present in any given situation. Compare the following:

Tom: See that red book over there.

Dick: [I don't see a book over there but] there is a red and rectangular physical object over there.

Harry: [I don't see a red book over there, though I grant that] it looks to me as though there were a red book over there.

Dick's report is a minimal *objective* report, minimized with respect

to the physical state of affairs it claims to obtain. Harry's report repeats the content of Tom's assertion but places it in the rubric 'it
looks (to me) . . . ' A still more cautious report might be made
by Jones, thus

> Jones: [I grant that] it looks to me as though there were a
> red and rectangular physical object over there.

Dick made an objective assertion which is extremely limited in its
content. Jones suspends even this limited claim by his use of the
'looks (to me) . . .' rubric.

35. There are interesting differences between the statements made
by Dick and Jones, and, correspondingly, between the conceptual
representation they express. For our purposes, the most interesting is that Jones' statement is on a higher level, much as belief
statements, e.g.

> Mary believes that it is raining

are on a higher level than the statements they in some sense contain,
in this case

> It is raining

Jones is saying of himself what we might say of Dick if we thought
that his statement was considered but false. And it seems clear that
if we were to say

> It looks to Dick as though there were a red and rectangular
> physical object over there.

part of what we would be expressing would be *our* conceptual
representation that *Dick* is conceptually representing that there is,
in front of him, a red and rectangular physical object. Presumably,
therefore, Jones' statement expresses a conceptual representation,
part of which consists in attributing to *himself* a conceptual representation that there is (in front of him) a red and rectangular
physical object. And if we ask what kind of representation this is,
the answer must surely be 'that kind of conceptual representation
which is being under the visual impression that (visually taking it
to be the case that) there is (or of their being) a red and rectangular physical object in front of one'.

36. But if it were not for the recurring puzzles of sense percep-

tion, there would be no reason to think that even when candid reports, and, therefore, the conceptual representations they express, are unguarded and conceptually rich, they are accompanied by unverbalized minimal conceptual representations of either the objective or 'looks (to me)' variety. Yet many philosophers have been strongly inclined to say that visual perception always involves representations which are appropriately described in objectively minimal terms, and are appropriately called impressions, as being in some sense, functions of 'receptivity'. I think that these philosophers are right, and that the point is of great importance. I also think, however, that most influential accounts mistakenly assimilate impressions, thus understood, to minimal conceptual representations, minimal both with respect to the physical content in terms of which they are described, and in being bracketed by *looks* or *seems*.

37. That the idea that visual perception always involves minimal conceptual representations is false does not, I believe, need to be argued. On the other hand, the idea that visual perception always involves sense impressions properly described by a special use of a minimal physical vocabulary does seem to me eminently capable of defense, once the confusion of sense impressions with the minimal conceptual representations which do occur in extremely guarded perception has been overcome.

38. Before taking steps in this direction, let me note that even on the hypothesis, contrary to fact, that visual perception as such involves minimal conceptual episodes, reflection on the nature of perceptual experience would lead us to the idea that the receptivity or secondness (Peirce) involved in visual perception has three distinguishable aspects:

> 1. a purely physical aspect which could, in principle, be described in terms of physical theory—though it can also be described (as by Aristotle) in common sense terms.

This physical aspect would bring about

> 2. the primary mental aspect, construed by this account as a minimal conceptual episode, which latter in turn would bring about, given the set of the perceiver, and in a way which is no matter of sheer receptivity,

3. a rich conceptual episode involving such concepts as those of cabbages and kings and pigs in barnyards.

39. My objection to this analysis is not to the idea that some such trichotomy is involved, nor to the contrast between the 'receptivity' of sense impression and the *guidedness,* to use a relevant concept from the *Investigations,* of the flow of conceptual representations proper involved in normal perceptual activity. Indeed, I think that the latter distinction is exactly what Kant needs to make his theory work. Thus, when he speaks of the productive imagination as "taking up" (A120) the manifold of outer sense into its activity (the synthesis of apprehension), the metaphor implies, of course, that the manifold is an independent factor which has a strong voice in the outcome. On the other hand, it is only if the manifold is mistakenly construed as belonging to the conceptual order that it *makes sense* to suppose that it, so to speak, bodily or literally becomes a part of the resulting intuitive representation. As nonconceptual it can only guide 'from without' the unique conceptual activity which is representing of *this-suches* as subjects of perceptual judgment.

40. Indeed, it is only if Kant distinguishes the radically nonconceptual character of sense from the conceptual character of the synthesis of apprehension in intuition [which is, of course, to be distinguished from the conceptual synthesis of recognition in a concept, in which the concept occupies a predicative position] and, accordingly, the *receptivity* of sense from the *guidedness* of intuition, that he can avoid the dialectic which leads from Hegel's *Phenomenology* to 19th Century idealism.

IV

41. But is it genuinely necessary to interpose nonconceptual representations *as states of consciousness* between the 'physical' impact of the sensory stimulus and the conceptual representations (guarded or daring) which find verbal expression, actually or potentially, in perceptual statements? Can we not interpret the receptivity involved in terms of 'purely physical' states, and attribute to these the role of guiding conceptualization? Why should we suppose that receptivity culminates in a state which is neither 'purely physical' *nor* conceptual? Yet to do just this is, I shall argue, of the greatest im-

portance for the philosophy of mind, and in particular, for an understanding of how the framework of physical science is to be integrated with the framework of common sense.

42. If what might be called the 'sense impression inference'[4] is an inference to an explanation, what specifically is it designed to explain? Clearly not, at least in the first instance, facts of the form 'it seemed to Jones that O was red, when it wasn't', for we can do this without invoking sense impressions, appealing instead to the specific abnormalities of either Jones or his circumstances. Nor, at least primarily, is it designed to explain 'discrimination behavior' of the type which can be acquired by flatworms and encouraged in white rats, a 'consecutiveness' which in Leibnitz' phrase "apes reason." Rather its primary purpose is to explain the occurrence of certain *conceptual* representations in perceptual activity. The representations I have in mind are those which are characteristic of what we have called 'minimal conceptual representations'.

43. If we construe physical objects, for the moment, in Strawsonian terms, we can say that the aim is to explain the correlation of the conceptual representations in question with those features of the objects of perception which, on occasion, both make them true and are responsible for bringing them about.

44. Thus, the sense impression inference is an attempt to account for the fact that normal perceivers have *conceptual* representations of a red and rectangular object both

(a) when they are being affected in normal circumstances by a red and rectangular object; and

(b) when they are being affected in abnormal circumstances by objects which have other, but systematically related characteristics.

It is essential to note that the *explanandum* concerns *conceptualization* rather than behaviorial discrimination as such. It is also essential to note that the correlation of the correct conceptual response with objects perceived in normal circumstances by normal perceivers is as much in need of explanation as the correlations of

---

4 Note that unlike the 'sense-datum inference' it is not a matter of explaining the fact that an object looks red (or that there looks to be a red object) in terms of the idea that there is something, a sense-datum, which actually *is* red; for a sense impression of a red rectangle is neither red nor rectangular.

conceptual responses with abnormal perceptual situations. It is not enough, for reasons which I shall give in a moment, to explain the latter by saying that the proximate physical stimulus caused, e.g. by a black object in normal circumstances is the same as that caused by a red object in abnormal circumstances. For even in normal cases there is the genuine question, 'Why does the perceiver *conceptually represent* a red (blue, etc.) rectangular (circular, etc.) object in the presence of an object having these qualities?' The answer would seem to require that all the possible ways in which *conceptual representations* of color and shape can resemble and differ correspond to ways in which their *immediate nonconceptual occasions,* which must surely be construed as states of the perceiver, can resemble and differ.

45. Thus, these nonconceptual states must have characteristics which, *without being colors,* are sufficiently analogous to color to enable these states to play this guiding role. If the notion of one family of characteristics being *analogous* to another family of characteristics is obscure and difficult, it is nevertheless as essential to the philosophy of science as it has been to theology and, it would seem, somewhat more fruitful. That it is a powerful tool for resolving perennial problems in epistemology and metaphysics is a central theme of SM.

46. If the *explanandum* formulated above is a genuine one, there are, it would seem, other possible accounts than the one I am recommending. Thus either of the following lines might be taken:

(a) The tendency to have conceptual representations of a red (blue, etc.) and rectangular (circular, etc.) physical object under certain stimulus conditions, although, as Aristotle pointed out, the eye does not assume a red and rectangular state and no red and rectangular object may be present, is innate.

(c) One is taught by one's linguistic peers who already have the relevant concepts and propensities, to play the color-shape language game and, by so doing acquire these concepts and propensities.

47. I shall ignore the former suggestion. As for the latter, I do not wish to deny the insights it contains. Nevertheless, the ability to teach a child the color-shape language game seems to imply the existence of cues which systematically correspond, in the manner

adumbrated above, to the color and shape attribute families, and are also causally connected with combinations of variously colored and shaped objects in various circumstances of perception. If so, the account in terms of the *transmission* of the color-shape language game from generation to to generation supplements, but does not replace, the original suggestion. If we adopt this suggestion, however, we are faced with the task of explicating the idea that physical objects bring about states of perceivers which have attributes systematically analogous to perceptible color and shape, without literally *having* perceptible color and shape.

48. I have, it will be remembered, taken as my paradigm of a sense impression

> an impression of a red rectangle

where this locution is carefully distinguished from one which says, for example of Jones that he has

> an impression of a man lurking in the corner.

The latter clearly attributes to Jones a conceptual state. Thus the above paradigm should not be taken as a truncated form of

> an impression of a red rectangle being (for example) over
> there.

49. Since the sense impression of which we are speaking is clearly described in terms of its standard cause, one might be inclined to think that we should refer to it as

> an impression of a physical object which is red and rectangular on the facing side.

But although this would have been in the spirit of what might be called the Aristotelian phase of the concept, reflection on the nature of the proper remote cause of impressions resulted in a tendency increasingly to *minimize* their description. It is this minimizing tendency, inspired by what I referred to (in paragraph 23 above) as the causal theme, which, combined with empiricist abstractionism, led directly to Hume. The description of impressions loses those features which made it plausible to think that a Jack Horner intellect could pluck from them the categories of physical object discourse.

50. Thus, since only the surface of an opaque object is relevant to the description of the corresponding sense impression, the latter tends to become an

> impression of a facing red and rectangular expanse.

Again, since the causal powers of an object are not themselves causes, the description of impressions tends to be purged of all expression which logically imply causal properties: an impression of a pink ice cube tends, in view of the causal properties implied by 'ice', to become an impression of a pink cube.

51. Again, where the cause of an impression is one billiard ball knocking another into a pocket, the impression description tends to be watered down into

> impression of a white sphere moving toward another white sphere followed by a motion of the latter

and this, in turn, into

> an impression of a facing white hemispherical surface moving toward another facing white hemispherical surface folowed by a motion of the latter.

V

52. If we accept this way of looking at the receptivity involved in visual perception, a number of things fall into place. To begin with, we can understand the temptation to assimilate sense impressions to minimal conceptual representations. For neither the sense impression of a red rectangle nor the conceptual representation of a red rectangle is either red or rectangular.

53. In the *second* place, the interpretation of the framework of sense impressions as a theoretical framework suggests that the analogy between the attributes of impressions and the perceptible attributes of physical objects is but another case of the role of analogy in theoretical concept formation. Analogical concepts in science are methodologically dependent on a conceptual base to which they are not reduceable.[5]

---

[5] For an account of analogical concept formation in science see my essay on "Scientific Realism or Irenic Instrumentalism" in, *Boston Studies in the Philosophy of Science*, eds. Robert S. Cohen and Marx W. Wartofsky (New York, 1965).

54. Thus, when we characterize a visual impression as

>an impression of a red rectangle

the use of the word 'red' and 'rectangle' is derivative from the use of the corresponding predicates in the context

>a physical object, the facing side of which is a red rectangle.

In this derivative use they form an adjectival expression

>of a red rectangle

which, when joined to the category word 'impression' forms the sortal expression

>(an) of-a-red-rectangle impression.

55. Here we must note that there are many who would grant

(a) that there are visual sense impressions;
(b) that they are nonconceptual representations;
(c) that they can be described only in terms of their standard physical causes;

but who take (c) to be equivalent to the idea that the sense of the phrase

>a visual impression of a red rectangle

is simply that of

>a nonconceptual state of the perceiver (mediating between the stimulus and the conceptual outcome) of *the kind which* has as its standard cause a red and rectangular physical object.

This is a radical mistake, for by construing the reference to the characters of the nonconceptual state as a definite description of unknown attributes in terms of their causal connections, *rather than as the analogical introduction of new predicates,* it takes an agnostic stance which plays into the hands of a crude physicalism. Might not *the kind of state* which, etc., be a complicated pattern of the kind of physical processes which go on in hedges and stones?

56. In the *third* place, since in the causal context

>normally caused by a red rectangular (physical) surface

which is the basis (though not the sense) of the description of the corresponding impression; the phrase

> a red rectangular (physical) surface

clearly refers to no particular physical surface, the *apparent* reference of the expression

> an impression of a red rectangle

to a particular red rectangle, which has bemused sense datum theorists, is both explained and explained away. We can understand why impressions are *in their way* 'of individuals', and why they have been construed as 'direct' or 'intuitive' representations of individuals as contrasted with representations mediated by general concepts. When, therefore, we understand the role of the phrase 'a red rectangle'; in references to sense impressions proper, we see that the question

> Impression of *which* red rectangle?

makes sense only as a request to know which red and rectangular object is *causing* the impression, rather than how the impression is to be described.

57. In the *fourth* place we understand why the fact that philosophers use 'of' constructions involving the same physical object predicates to modify both the category word 'conception' and the category word 'impression', thus

> impression of a red rectangle
> conception of a red rectangle

does not commit them to the idea that these physical object predicates are doing the same kind of job in both contexts.

58. Thus, in the *fifth* place, we understand why the temptation to conflate sense impressions proper with minimal conceptual representations is a temptation to construe an impression of a red rectangle as though it were a special kind of conceptual representation of a particular red rectangle, as though it were a *token* (in Peirce's sense) of the Mentalese phrase

> this red rectangle

or

> this red rectangular thing

that is, as though, in describing sense impressions, the words 'rea
and 'rectangle' were being used to mention conceptual items in
the vocabulary of inner speech.

59. *Finally*, we understand why, although both the contexts

impression of . . .

and

conception of . . .

are, from a logical point of view, intensional (note the 's') for
from neither

Jones has an impression of a red rectangle

nor

Jones is conceiving of a red rectangle

can we infer that there is a red rectangle in the neighborhood.
Only the latter is 'intentional' (note the 't') from the point of
view of the philosophy of mind, where the intentional is that which
belongs to the conceptual order.

VI

60. Before I return to Kant with this apparatus in mind, one
further consequence of the 'causal theme' needs to be noticed, for
it reveals additional possibilities of confusion—thoroughly exploited
by Hume and not entirely absent in Kant. We are all familiar with
Wittgenstein's thesis in the *Tractatus* that at the level of atomic
propositions the conceptual representation of a complex state of
affairs is a complex of conceptual representations. Thus, a representing that

x_1 precedes (temporally) x_2

consists of a representing of x_1 related (though not, presumably,
by the same relation) to a representing of x_2. I wish to call attention
to the fact that a comparable thesis can be (and has been) advanced
with respect to sense impressions.

61. Let me begin by postulating a Descartes (let us call him
Renatus) who (unlike the historical Descartes) draws a clear cut

distinction between conceptual and nonconceptual states. He rejects, of course, the idea that the sense impression of a red rectangle is literally red or literally rectangular. As we have done, he argues that 'of a red rectangle' combines with 'impression' to form a sortal predicate for a certain kind of mental state. Thus he speaks of

An (of a red rectangle) impression

but proposes a convention, illustrated by the equivalence in ordinary language of 'warm sensation' with 'sensation of warmth', according to which

a red rectangle impression

is to have the sense of

an (of a red rectangle) impression.

62. We now ask him to suppose that someone (Jones) is looking, in normal circumstances, at a green square one side of which coincides with a red square, and as a result has

an impression of green square adjoining a red square.

Before exploring the logic of this locution, let us note that language provides us with a way of making complex common nouns out of simple ones, thus from '(a) cat' and '(a) mat' we can form the complex common noun

cat-on-a-mat

which occurs in the sentence

This is a cat-on-a-mat.

It is essential to note that the expression

aK_1-R-a-K_2

is an instance of the same general form as that exemplified by

a cat.

It is *not* a propositional expression illustrating the form

x R y.

A confusion of references to complex objects with relational statements has had serious consequences in both metaphysics and epistemology.

63. Let us return to the above example of

an impression of a green square adjoining a red square

Otherwise put

an (of a green square adjoining a red square) impression

or, by the proposed convention

an (a-green-square-adjoining-a-red-square impression).

We now ask Renatus if having this impression entails having an impression of a green square and an impression of a red square. He answers, predictably, yes. We then ask if the original impression *consists of an* of-a-green-square impression and an of-a-red-square impression. Again the answer is yes. Finally we ask whether, for these two impressions to be parts of the embracing impression, they must be related. The answer is yes; but this time even our cooperative Renatus is recalcitrant enough to insist that the relation of the two impressions is not the

adjoining

relation—nor any kind of spatial relation. Mental states, he insists, are neither red, green, square, juxtaposed, nor spatial in any way.

64. When, however, it is pointed out that there must be *something* about the relation between the impressions which makes it that they constitute an impression of *adjoining* squares, rather than of *separated* squares, or squares which *meet at corners,* he grants that the relation of the impressions must 'correspond' to *adjoining* in a sense of 'correspond' which turns out, from our point of view, to be just the *analogy* which has already cropped up in our discussion of the *qualitative* character of impressions. If we represent the genuinely spatial relation of adjoining by 'R_1', we can represent the 'corresponding' relation between the component impressions by 'R_1''.

65. Thus we must add to our earlier point that the impression of a red rectangle, though neither red nor rectangular, has counterpart attributes, the idea that the impression of a relational complex is a complex (involving a counterpart relation) of impressions. Succinctly put, impressions have attributes and stand in relations

which are counterparts of the attributes and relations of physical objects and events.

66. These considerations give us the identity,

$$\left.\begin{array}{l}\text{An impression of a green}\\ \text{square } R_1 \text{ a red square}\end{array}\right\} = \left\{\begin{array}{l}\text{An impression of a green}\\ \text{square } R_1' \text{ an impression of a}\\ \text{red square.}\end{array}\right.$$

Or, using the above convention,

$$\left.\begin{array}{l}\text{an (a green square } R_1 \text{ a}\\ \text{red square) impression}\end{array}\right\} = \left\{\begin{array}{l}\text{An (a green square) impres-}\\ \text{sion } R_1' \text{ an (a red square)}\\ \text{impression.}\end{array}\right.$$

67. Still more schematically we have

$$\text{an (} \ldots R_1 \text{---) impression } = \left\{\begin{array}{l}\text{an (} \ldots \text{) impression } R_1'\\ \text{an (---) impression.}\end{array}\right.$$

This schema, it will be noted, provides a way of transforming contexts in which relation words appropriate to physical objects occur in phrases which characterize a single impression into contexts in which two (or more) impressions are characterized as related by a counterpart relation.

68. If, as Wittgenstein held (in the *Tractatus*) it is also true that conceptual representations of relational states of affairs are to be construed as complexes of conceptual representations of their terms, the question obviously arises 'What is the connection between the counterpart relations which bind conceptual representations of terms into conceptual representations of complex states of affairs, thus the conceptual representation that x_1 adjoins x_2, and the counterpart relation which binds nonconceptual representations into nonconceptual representations of relational wholes, thus the impression of a green square adjoining a red square'. I shall have something to say on this topic in Chapter 4 [SM].

69. The above schema can be seen to amount to the idea that an impression of a complex is a complex of impressions. If we add to this the idea that the latter is the 'true' description, we have a characteristically Humean thesis which reappears in Kant.

70. A philosopher who is prepared to insist that at least some of our concepts are derived by abstraction from the contents of sense impressions, and who takes the above thesis seriously, would obviously be hung up on concepts of relation. He might be impelled to say that concepts of relations have a different 'source' from concepts of qualities. This, however, would be because has he failed to note that

the same move which takes 'R$_1$' out of the context 'impression of' also, as we previously saw, takes 'red' and 'rectangular' out of this context and turns them into counterpart predicates.

71. Hume, in any case, strode over all these complexities with seven league boots, for, as is notorious, he confused between

    (1) an impression of a green square
    (2) a conviction that a green square exists
    (3) a green square

And, correspondingly, between

    (1) an impression of a green square adjoining a red square
    (2) a conviction that a red square adjoining a red square exists
    (3) a green square adjoining a red square.

72. These confusions also blurred the distinction between 'abstracting' the concept of ϕ from a representation of a ϕ item, and 'abstracting' it from an actually ϕ-item. In this connection it should be noted that an interesting strand in 17th and 18th Century theories of concept formation is a distorted form of the sound principle that concepts are *caused* rather than abstracted. Thus Descartes held that the cause of a concept must be something actually existent which is at least as 'perfect'—in the medieval sense—as what the concept is 'of'. This formulation is clearly designed to permit God to be the cause of mathematical and metaphysical concepts. But many philosophers who rejected innate ideas (e.g. Berkeley and Locke) clearly assumed that our ability to conceive of the various kinds of mental act is caused by the actual occurrence of these acts in our minds, though this causation was usually not distinguished from abstraction. The most interesting example is Hume, who clearly thinks that the concept of an impression is an empirical concept caused by the occurrence of impressions, and the concepts of an idea is an empirical concept *caused* by the occurrence of ideas. That he confuses between an impression of a red dot causing an idea of a red dot, and its causing an idea of an impression bears out the picture of total but useful confusion described above.[6]

---

[6] *A Treatise of Human Nature*, edited by Selby-Bigge, Part I, Book I, Section I, p. 6: "as our ideas are images of our impressions, so we can form secondary ideas, which are images of the primary; *as appears from this very reasoning concerning them.*" (italics mine).

VII

73. We are now in a position to comment on some of the more obscure themes in Kant's treatment of sensibility. I shall begin by making the contrary to fact assumption that Kant was clear about the radical difference between sense impressions proper and the intuitions synthesized by the productive imagination. Such a Kant would then have distinguished between:

(a) the nonconceptual representations of outer sense proper which, although conveniently described as impressions of spatial complexes, are strictly speaking nonspatial complexes of unextended and uncolored impressions;

(b) the intuitive (but conceptual) representations of extended structures located in space.[7]

74. This splitting up of the representations initially lumped together under the heading of 'sensible intuition' into conceptual and nonconceptual representations demands a corresponding splitting in two of the concept of a 'form of sensible intuition'. On the one hand, there would be the intuitive (but conceptual) representations of Space (and Time) which serve as frameworks for the conceptual representation (intuitive or discursive (A68: B93)) of individual objects and events. On the other hand, there would be the attributes of and relations between the impressions of pure receptivity. Though, as has been pointed out, we conceive of certain of these attributes and relations as *counterparts* of spatial attributes and relations proper, they would not literally be the spatial attributes and relations in terms of which we conceptually represent physical objects and events. (That color and color relations should have been given a similar treatment is clearly part of the burden of my argument.)

75. Kant's failure to distinguish clearly between the 'forms' of receptivity proper and the 'forms' of that which is represented by the intuitive conceptual representations which are 'guided' by receptivity—a distinction which is demanded both by the thrust of

---

[7] It will have been noted that I have had little to say about temporal attributes and relations. For my present purposes, however, it is sufficient to note that the problems posed are, as Kant saw, parallel to those of Space, and his treatment succeeds and fails in parallel ways.

his argument, and by sound philosophy—had as its consequence that no sooner had he left the scene than these particular waters were muddied by Hegel and the Mills, and philosophy had to begin the slow climb "back to Kant" which is still underway.

VIII

76. It is to be noted that although Kant denies, in the spirit of Hume's principle, that any representation of sheer receptivity is a representation of a complex, and, accordingly, construes all representations of complex items (which he equates with representations of a complex *as* complex, of a manifold *as* manifold) to be acts of spontaneity or the understanding, he nowhere denies, and is not committed to denying, that the manifold of external sense as such is a relational structure. Indeed, the more general point can be made that Kant nowhere denies or need deny that the in-itself has a relational structure. What he does deny, whether for good reasons or for bad, a topic for subsequent discussion, is that the relations we conceptually represent are the relations which the in-itself exemplifies.

77. With respect to the manifold of outer sense, Kant does not seem to have found the happy medium between the absurdity of saying that Space is a form of outer sense in that the manifold of outer sense is literally spatial, and the overly strong claim that the only way in which spatial relations enter into perceptual states is as contents of *conceptual* representations. This means that the characteristics of the representations of receptivity as such, which is what should *properly* be meant by the forms of sensibility, are never adequately discussed, and the so-called forms of sensibility become ever more clearly, as the argument of the *Critique* proceeds, forms of conceptual representations. By overlooking the importance of analogical concepts—save in theological contexts—and hence by failing to note the analogical character of our concepts of the attributes and relations which sense impressions *must* have to perform their explanatory role, Kant reduces the concepts of receptivity and sensibility to empty abstractions.

78. If, *per impossible*, Kant had developed the idea of the manifold of sense as characterized by analogical counterparts of the perceptible qualities and relations of physical things and events,

he could have given an explicit account of the ability of the impressions of receptivity to guide minds, endowed with the conceptual framework he takes us to have, to form the conceptual representations we do of individual physical objects and events in Space and Time. He could thus have argued that when on a certain occasion we come to have an intuitive conceptual representation that this green square adjoins that red square, we do so by virtue of having a complex of nonconceptual representations which, although nonspatial and without color, have characteristics which are the counterparts of *square, red, green* and *adjoining,* and which make them such as to account for the fact that we have *this* conceptual representation rather than that of there being a purple pentagon above an orange elipse. That he 'implicitly' gives some such account (or must have done so) has been argued by many, thus, by Professor Paton[8] though the full scope of the distinctions necessary to pull it off has not always been appreciated.

WILFRID SELLARS

UNIVERSITY of PITTSBURGH

---

[8] Kant's *Metaphysic of Experience,* Vol. I, Chapter 6, Section 8.

KANT'S FIRST ANTINOMY

In the First Antinomy of *The Critique of Pure Reason,* Kant drew two conclusions from the argument he gives. First, Kant took his argument to show that the referent of the concept of 'world' does not exist as a thing in itself. For at B532 he says:

> If we regard the two propositions, that the world is infinite in magnitude and that it is finite in magnitude, as contradictory opposites, we are assuming that the world, the complete series of appearances, is a thing in itself that remains even if I suspend the infinite or the finite regress in the series of its appearances. If, however, I reject this assumption, or rather this accompanying transcendental illusion, and deny that the world is a thing in itself, the contradictory opposition of the two assertions is converted into a merely dialectical opposition. Since the world does not exist in itself, independently of the regressive series of my representations, it exists *in itself* neither as an *infinite* nor as a *finite* whole.

Kant also thought that the same argument established yet another conclusion. For he held that the argument of the First Antinomy gives an independent proof of the transcendental ideality of time and space. This is set forth at B534:

> It affords indirect proof of the transcendental ideality of appearances—a proof which ought to convince any who might not be satisfied by the direct proof given in the Transcendental Aesthetic. This proof would consist in the following dilemma. If the world is a whole existing in itself, it is either finite or infinite. But both alternatives are false (as shown in the proofs of the antithesis and thesis respectively). It is therefore also false that the world (the sum of all appearances) is a whole existing in itself. From this it then follows that appearances in general are nothing outside our representations—which is just what is meant by their transcendental ideality.

The two inferences Kant makes here, then, are these:

(1) If the complete series of appearances is a thing in itself, then it must be either finitely or infinitely large. It is neither of these; therefore, the complete series of appearances does not exist as a thing in itself.

(2) If the complete series of appearances is neither finitely nor infinitely large, then all appearances are transcendentally ideal. The complete series of appearances is neither; therefore all appearances are transcendentally ideal.

Now I believe that neither (1) nor (2) is a valid inference. In what follows I shall, accordingly, undertake three things: to establish the invalidity of (1) and (2); to ask whether Kant's arguments can be reconstructed to prove what he wanted them to prove; and to assess some recent objections to Kant's argument in the First Antinomy.

1. *The Argument of the Antinomy*

As Kant sets it out, the argument of the First Antinomy runs as follows.[1] The thesis asserts that the world has a beginning in time and is limited spatially. Proponents of this view argue for it by assuming the opposite view and reducing it to absurdity. We begin, accordingly, by assuming that the world has no beginning in time. And this assumption is taken to be logically equivalent to the claim that infinitely many intervals of time have elapsed. But an infinite number of moments cannot have elapsed simply because we cannot complete an actual infinity of moments by successively synethesizing them. An actual infinity of moments cannot, therefore, have existed—from which it is inferred that the world cannot be temporally infinite.

A second claim is made by the proponents of the thesis; the claim, namely, that the world is limited spatially.[2] Here we are first asked to assume that the world is unlimited in spatial extension. It is then pointed out that we could not completely synthesize the parts of such a world. And it is inferred that the world cannot be spatially infinite. The conclusions of both of the foregoing

---

[1] Beginning at A426-B454. (All references to the first *Critique* are to the translation by Norman Kemp Smith.)

[2] Beginning at A428-B456.

arguments are then conjoined to derive the further conclusion that the world is both spatially and temporally finite.

The contention of the antithesis is twofold: that the world has no beginning in time (being therefore temporally infinite) and that the world is spatially unlimited (being therefore spatially infinite). We are asked to assume that the world did have a beginning in time. On this assumption, the time at which the world began would have been preceded by a time at which the world did not exist. But the moment prior to the moment at which the world came into existence would then be an empty time. But if time is empty, no coming into existence could take place. Why? Because no part of that empty time "possesses, as compared with any other, a distinguishing condition of existence rather than non-existence."[3] Thus the world cannot have had a beginning in time.

The second part of the antithesis—that the world is not spatially limited—is defended on the ground that the world, as a limited spatial whole, would have to be related to empty space which borders it. Empty space cannot, however, be related to the world as a whole; for a relation to empty space would be a relation to nothing and hence not a relation at all. But since the world cannot be spatially and temporally finite, then the only other conclusion open to us is that it is infinite in both respects. *Tertium non datur.*

The general conclusion which Kant draws from the arguments of thesis and antithesis here is familiar: Each is right in what it denies but wrong in what it affirms. Thus the thesis is right in denying that the world is infinite but wrong in affirming that the world must therefore be finite. The antithesis is right in denying that the world is finite but wrong in inferring that it must therefore be infinite. What Kant takes the arguments to show is rather that the world is neither finite nor infinite.[4]

2. *What the First Antinomy Does Not Prove*

For the moment I do not want to ask whether Kant has succeeded in showing that the world as a whole is neither finite nor infinite. I propose to grant him that conclusion for the sake of

---

3 B454.

4 A504-B532.

argument and ask whether he has shown either that the world does not exist as a thing in itself or that appearances are transcendentally ideal.

Consider first the alleged conclusion that the world does not exist as a thing in itself. This has not been demonstrated by the argument as it stands. To see this, we need only examine what Kant means by "thing in itself." I find two senses of the term in Kant. I shall call the first the ontological conception of the term. This is found in the Transcendental Aesthetic, embedded in Kant's discussion of time:

> Time is not something which exists in itself, or which inheres in things as an objective determination, and it does not, therefore, remain when abstraction is made of all subjective conditions of its intuition.[5]

The same point is made for space when Kant says the following:

> . . . [S]pace does not represent any determination that attaches to the objects themselves, and which remains even when abstraction has been made of all the subjective conditions of experience.[6]

The argument for this conclusion is instructive because it shows the criterion according to which Kant will count anything as a thing in itself. At A33 he argues that space and time cannot be things in themselves because, on such an assumption, we would have to say that they are actual while not being actual objects. Nor can they be relational properties of substances because, on that assumption, they could not precede objects as a condition of their being objects for us. The conclusion is drawn from this when Kant says at A43 that space and time are "conditions which are originally inherent in the subject." The pattern of this argument works itself out as follows: If something can be neither a substance nor an accident of substance when separated from space and time, then it cannot be a thing in itself. A thing in itself is, then, either a substance or a property when separated from space and time. What is important for our purposes is that Kant talks of a thing in itself as a *kind of object*. It is the kind of object that remains when we abstract from the conditions under which that object is given to us.

---

[5] A33-B49.

[6] A26-B42.

But there is quite a different conception of what a thing in itself is running parallel to the ontological conception. This, too, is present in his discussion of time. For at A31 he says that time is merely "a necessary representation that underlies all intuitions." And the same point is made for space when, at A24, he says that space is an intuition which underlies all outer intuitions. To speak of things as they are in themselves is to speak of them apart from the relation they have to our means of representing them. But here what is to count as a thing in itself has changed. For here when we talk about an object as a thing in itself, we mean only to talk about it as it is apart from possible human verification. *But we do not say that such an object is nonspatial and nontemporal.* On this second view (which I shall call the criteriological conception) all that is implied is that we do not *know* whether things as they are in themselves are nonspatial and nontemporal. On the ontological view, however, what is being claimed is that things in themselves are necessarily nonspatial and nontemporal. The ontological view is the main assumption governing the argument in which Kant moves from saying that space and time do not remain when "abstraction has been made of all the subjective conditions of experience." But this claim should nonetheless be strictly separated from the other, weaker, claim according to which space and time are necessary representations which underlie all our intuitions. For this latter claim is completely neutral about the ontological issue of whether space and time do in fact exist apart from possible human experience. And the neutrality of the claim about this issue gives a second view of what is to count as a thing in itself.[7]

---

[7] There is a counterargument according to which the criteriological conception is reducible to the ontological conception of the thing in itself. Thus it might be argued that space and time define what is to count as verifiable. To admit the possibility that things in themselves might be spatial and temporal is to deny that they are things in themselves just because space and time would make them possible objects of human experience. Hence, it might be concluded that the criteriological view is not a separate view of the thing in itself at all. But there is an effective reply to this counterargument. What makes the criteriological conception so different from the ontological conception of things in themselves is that, on the criteriological conception, what defines verifiability is that we must *see* objects in a space-time matrix; nothing is said about whether they *are* in fact in a space-time matrix apart from possible human experience. And to claim that they are is not *ipso facto* to claim that they are possible objects of human experience.

Let us now go back to the conclusion of the First Antinomy. Does that conclusion show that the world cannot exist as a thing in itself in either of the two senses I have distinguished? Take the ontological conception of the thing in itself first. Does the argument of the antinomy show that the world does not exist as a nonspatial and nontemporal whole? I think not. What Kant tries to show in the antinomy is that the world is neither finite nor infinite with respect to time and space. And this is not enough to show that the world is neither finite nor infinite apart from space and time. Both the thesis and the antithesis of the antinomy assume that the world is the totality of all *appearances.*[8] And both the thesis and the antithesis assume that only the notion of a spatial and temporal world is being considered. But to show that something is or is not true of such a world is to be perfectly silent about whether the same things might be true of a nonspatial and nontemporal world. So Kant has not shown that the world of phenomena cannot exist as a thing in itself.

But perhaps the argument of the antinomy works when we interpret the notion of the thing in itself criteriologically. Perhaps Kant has succeeded in showing that the world cannot exist as a thing in itself if we interpret him to be saying that we cannot *know* whether the world as a whole is finite or infinite. But this is not a viable exegetical alternative for two reasons. For one thing, the demonstrations of both the thesis and antithesis assume a conception of 'world' according to which we can know the properties it has; for 'world' figures in the argument as equivalent to 'complete series of appearances'; and we can, on Kant's own admission, know the properties of the world when it is taken in this sense. For another, both arguments in the antinomy purport to demonstrate that we can know that the world is not finite and not infinite. So the argument of the antinomy forbids us to assume that 'thing in itself' is being used in its criteriological sense.

I turn now to the second conclusion which Kant draws from the argument of the antinomy: that it supplies independent proof of the transcendental ideality of space and time. Now Kant means several things by 'transcendental ideality', not all of which are logically equivalent. The argument he gives in the Aesthetic pur-

---

8 Cf. the definition of 'world' at A334-B391; A605-B633; A418-B446; A419-B447.

porting to show that space and time are transcendentally ideal
has already been mentioned: Space and time cannot be substances,
for they would have to be actual without being actual objects. Nor
can they be relations obtaining among substance, for then they
would not be a condition of our being presented with objects.[9] The
conclusion which Kant draws from this is likewise familiar: Space
and time are properties of human sensibility, by which is meant
that they are transcendentally ideal.[10] The pattern of the argument, then, is this: We can know that space and time are the conditions under which any object must be presented to us; therefore,
space and time cannot be properties of the things that they present
but are rather forms of our apprehension of things and are therefore transcendentally ideal. The argument here, with whose validity
I am not at present concerned, yields three characteristics of transcendental ideality: (1) Something is transcendentally ideal if it
is a property of human sensibility; (2) Something is transcendentally ideal if it is a universal condition of our being presented
with objects; (3) Something is transcendentally ideal if it is neither
a substance nor an accident of a substance. (1) is the definition
Kant himself gives of the notion. (2) and (3) are both exclusive
descriptions of the notion which emerge from the argument Kant
gives in the Transcendental Aesthetic.[11]

How does the First Antinomy give us a demonstration that
space and time are transcendentally ideal independent of the one
offered in the Transcendental Aesthetic? Let us grant for the sake
of argument that the world is neither finite nor infinite. It does
not, however, follow that space and time are properties of human
sensibility, or that they are universal conditions of our being pre-

---

9 Cf. A33.

10 Cf. A26-B42.

11 My discussion here will concentrate on (1) — what I call the definition of
'transcendental ideality'. For if it can be shown that (1) has nothing to do with
the conclusion of the First Antinomy, (2) and (3) can be immediately dismissed.
(2) follows from (1), although they are not equivalent: If anything is a property of
human sensibility, it must be a condition of our being presented with objects. (3)
likewise follows from (1) : If space and time are nothing but forms of apprehension,
then they cannot be substances or accidents of substances. As Kant understands
'substance', the self is not a substance. (Cf. B407) And since the self is not a substance, it cannot have accidents. Hence to show that the conclusion of the antinomy
is irrelevant to (1) suffices to disqualify both (2) and (3).

sented with objects, or yet that they are neither substances nor accidents of substances. There are three arguments to support this conclusion.

The first argument is as follows. Whether space and time are properties of things or merely forms of our apprehension of things is quite independent of whether the totality of phenomena is finite or infinite. For the argument that we cannot apply either of two mutually exclusive predicates to a collection depends upon certain characteristics possessed by the collection as a whole. But that space and time are forms of our apprehension does not depend upon properties of the collection as a whole but rather on the properties the collection has when taken distributively. To show that the collection as a whole is neither finite nor infinite tells us nothing about whether the parts of the collection are in fact properties of things as they are in themselves. To say that the collection of all men is not itself a man does not permit us to infer that no number of that collection is a man. Similarly, to say that the collection of all spaces and times is neither finite nor infinite does not permit us to infer the same about specific moments of time and specific intervals of space. Hence, we cannot use this conclusion to ground the further inference that space and time are merely forms of our apprehension of things.

But why should Kant have thought that he could make the inference that I have just questioned? He apparently reasoned as follows. If it could be shown that there are some things in the world which are neither finite nor infinite, then they cannot be objects. This is the case with space and time, for they are included in the world as a whole. And from this it is inferred that space and time cannot be properties of things by means of the auxiliary premise that anything which is neither finite nor infinite must be mental. Kant does not, to be sure, explicitly defend this premise. And my reason for attributing it to him is that only by means of it can he successfully move from the conclusion that the world as a whole is neither finite nor infinite to the further conclusion that space and time are transcendentally ideal. But even if this auxiliary premise is admitted, the argument still suffers from the same defect: Kant has not shown that space and time are mental properties by showing that the totality of spaces and time is neither finite nor infinite.

There is a second argument which shows that the First An-

tinomy does not give us an independent proof of the transcendental
ideality of space and time. Kant holds that the antinomy does give
us such a proof because it could arise only on the assumption that
space and time are transcendentally real.[12] His reason for saying
this follows from his discussion of the distinction between dialectical and contradictory opposition.[13] We are tempted, he says, to
take the thesis and the antithesis of the antinomy to be mutually
exclusive and exhaustive alternatives. But this can be so only on
the assumption that space and time are something in themselves:
To say that they are things in themselves is to imply that they must
have one of two contradictory predicates. The fact that neither of
two contradictory predicates applies to them shows that the opposition between these predicates is dialectical and that there is a
third alternative; namely, that space and time are just forms of our
sensibility. On this assumption, what appeared to be a pair of
contradictory propositions now becomes a pair of contraries, both
of which are false.

But does the antinomy really assume that space and time are
transcendentally real? I think not. Kant in fact assumes the very
opposite in the argument he gives. The argument for the thesis
assumes, for example, that space and time are appearances. For it is
only on this assumption that one of the crucial moves in the argument is intelligible. The move is this. Kant rejects the possibility
that the world could be infinite because of the fact that "the infinity
of a series consists in the fact that it can never be completed through
successive synthesis."[14] Kant moves here from 'cannot be synthesized by us' to 'cannot be in itself infinite'. And this move in the
argument can be explained only on the assumption that Kant is
assuming the world to be the totality of appearances and not the
totality of things as they are in themselves.[15] For if the world is
the totality of appearances, then showing that we cannot synthesize all of these appearances is equivalent to showing that the
totality itself cannot be infinite. To say that there is an appearance

---

12 Cf. B519 to B521-A491 to A493.

13 A504-B532.

14 A426-B454.

15 There is independent evidence for this in his definition of 'world'; cf. footnote
7 above.

which we could not synthesize would be to say—what is self-contradictory—that there is an appearance that cannot appear. But the assumption that the world is the sum total of appearances runs counter to Kant's claim that the antinomy assumes space and time to be transcendentally real. And it therefore cannot be the case that the antinomy can be removed by assuming space and time to be transcendentally ideal, for that assumption is already present in the antinomy as Kant states it.

The third argument showing that the antinomy does not give an independent proof of transcendental idealism is a variant of the second argument and runs as follows. Even if we do assume that space and time are forms of our sensibility, we may not infer that they are neither finite nor infinite. We could in fact hold that space and time are merely subjective forms and still hold that they are infinite. For we could say that they are infinite just in the sense that neither the temporal nor spatial series has a last member. And this would not be precluded by the fact that they are subjective forms. The totality of these series would not be exhibited in intuition. But this is not to say that there is any member of the series which could not be so exhibited. There would be no element in the series that would not be capable of being presented in possible human experience. And this is enough to fulfill the requirement implicit in saying that space and time are forms of apprehension. To say this is in part to say that they are possible objects of human experience. And both space and time could be infinite. They could not, of course, be exhibited synoptically. But this is not to say that no part of each series cannot be presented in intuition and thus be possible objects of human experience. What I have said does not *prove* that there are infinitely many spaces and times. All it does is to show that the assertion that there are such things does not violate the condition implicit in saying that space and time are nothing beyond possible human experience.[16] My conclusion, then, is that there is no connection between saying that space and time are subjective forms of apprehension and saying that they are neither finite nor infinite.

---

[16] It is not an argument against my position to say that the last member of the series cannot be exhibited. I concede that such a member cannot be exhibited *as the last member*. But this does not mean that it cannot be exhibited at all.

3. *What the First Antinomy Does Prove*

What I have been arguing so far is that the two main conclusions which Kant draws from the First Antinomy do not in fact follow from it. But can his argument be reconstructed to yield these two conclusions? I believe that the first conclusion—that the world does not exist as a thing in itself—can be made to follow from an argument which Kant gives. But, as I hope to show, although this conclusion can be established, the argument is powerless to establish the second conclusion.

I propose the following reconstruction of Kant's argument for the conclusion that the world does not exist as a thing in itself. When Kant says that the world as the totality of appearances does not exist as a thing in itself, this can be made to follow from the more general conclusion that the definite description, 'the sum of all appearances', has no referent. But how exactly can Kant's argument be made to prove this? The totality of appearances, if it exists, must be either finite or infinite. Consider each alternative in turn. It cannot be finite; and Kant gives two arguments to prove this. He holds that the world cannot be finite because such a world would have to be preceded by an empty time which lacks "as compared with any other, a distinguishing condition of existence rather than non-existence."[17] I interpret him to be arguing that the world cannot be finite just because such a world would lack the causally sufficient conditions for coming into being.

Kant's second argument against the finitude of the world runs like this. A world that is finite must be related in some way to empty space. And this for Kant is a relation to nothing. The argument is, as it stands, confusing. For 'world' here means 'totality of appearances'; and space and time are both appearances. Thus even a world that is finite logically cannot stand in relation to empty space. But Kant's argument can perhaps be reformulated as follows. The assumption that the world is finite can be said to entail a contradiction. Saying that it is finite implies, that it be related to what it does not include; otherwise such a world would not be the totality of appearances. The contradiction, then, is that a finite world must both have and not have a spatial relation to what it does not include.

---

17 B454.

If the preceding two arguments are sound, then 'the sum of all appearances' cannot have a referent that is finite. The only other alternative is, accordingly, to supply it with a referent that is actually infinite. But this alternative is as unsuccessful as the other one: the totality of appearances cannot be actually infinite. Here two quite distinct arguments for this conclusion must be disentangled. The first consists in a definition of an infinite series which Kant introduces at B544, when he says that "the infinity of a series consists in the fact that it can never be completed through successive synthesis." As it stands, the argument is inconclusive: it might very well be true that *we* cannot complete the series although the series itself is in fact infinite. But there is another argument, occurring at B459, where Kant says that "no multiplicity is the greatest, since one or more units can always be added to it. Consequently an infinite given magnitude, and therefore an infinite world (infinite as regards the elapsed series or as regards extension) is impossible." The argument here does not depend upon any assumptions that refer only to *our* ability to synthesize the successive parts of an infinite series. The reason we cannot complete an infinite series is the result of a property of the series itself: that, for any given unit you reach in the series, it is always possible to add another unit. And if it is always possible to do this, then the notion of a last member of the series is self-contradictory. A series with a final member is either not infinite or the member chosen is not the last member. From this it follows that the totality of appearances cannot be actually infinite.

The reason Kant rejects an actually infinite magnitude is that such a notion contains, strictly speaking, a contradiction. It implies a number such that it must be the last member of the series but which cannot be the last member. My evidence for attributing this position to Kant lies in what he means when he says that an actual infinity is "a quantity which is greater than any number."[18] If we combine this definition of infinity with Kant's statement that an infinite series is such that it can never be completed by successive synthesis, we can more readily see how the contradiction in the notion of an actually infinite magnitude arises. The claim that we can synthesize such a magnitude entails a contradiction, for it en-

---

[18] A432n.

tails that we can assign a number to such a magnitude as its measure. In such a case, the magnitude alleged to the infinite would both possess a number and lack it. And this is the source of the contradiction.

This interpretation of Kant's argument has, however, been disputed, principally by Kemp Smith, who says it is "all-important to observe that Kant does not, either in the *Critique* or in any other of his writings, assert that the concept of the actual infinite is self-contradictory."[19] But this is an over-simplification of Kant's position. Kant holds that the concept of what he calls an infinite *multiplicity* does not contain a contradiction. But this is to be distinguished from the very different concept of an infinite *magnitude* which figures in the argument of the First Antinomy.[20] The former concept does not entail a contradiction because it is merely the concept of a collection which cannot be numbered. The latter concept does entail a contradiction just because it entails that the collection in question can be assigned a number. And it is this latter concept which is being discussed in the antinomy.

But if Kant does make the distinction I have just pointed out, it might be asked why he appears to reject this method of disproving the existence of an actually infinite magnitude at A430. Kant says that he might have sought to disprove the existence of the actual infinite by saying that "a magnitude is infinite if a greater than itself, as determined by the multiplicity of given units which it contains, is not possible."[21] Kant could then have pointed out that there is no greatest multiplicity "since one or more units can always be added to it."[22] For this reason an infinite given magnitude is impossible. Now Kant rejects this proof because it is based on what he considers to be a defective concept of infinity. But what exactly is defective about the concept of infinity? The definition is defective because it purports to tell us how great the infinite collection is and give us the concept of a maximum. And this is not, according to Kant, what we think in the concept of infinity.

---

19 Norman Kemp Smith, *A Commentary to Kant's "Critique of Pure Reason"* (Humanities Press: New York, 1962), p. 486. Hereinafter cited as *Commentary*.

20 Cf. A432-B460; the same point is made in *De mundi sensibilis atque intelligibilis forma et principiis*, para. 1n.

21 A431-B459.

22 A431-B459.

Can we take this as evidence for the conclusion that Kant does not hold the concept of an actual infinity to contain a contradiction? What this passage says is that we cannot define infinity as a magnitude since we then imply that we can say how great the magnitude is; i.e., are able to assign it a number. The passage does not say, however, that the concept of an actually infinite *magnitude* is free from contradiction. And the way in which Kant disproves the contention that the world is temporally infinite rests on the assumption that such a concept must be assumed by those asserting the temporal infinity of the world and that such a concept does contain a contradiction. For anyone holding that an infinite collection of temporal intervals can be synthesized must assume that it is possible to assign a number to an infinite collection, which is just to assume that an infinite magnitude has a last member. And this assumption does contain a contradiction because it rests on a misunderstanding of what an infinite collection is. Hence, the argument Kant gives against the possibility of a temporally infinite world does assume that one kind of concept of an actual infinity contains a contradiction.

The referent of 'the totality of appearances' cannot, then, be infinite. And this exhausts the alternatives. From this it follows that the referent is nonexistent. Now, if this is the real structure of Kant's argument, then he has proved that the totality of appearances does not exist as a thing in itself; for he has established that it does not exist at all, and a fortiori it does not exist as a thing in itself. But this conclusion has nothing to do with the characteristics peculiar to things in themselves. Nor does it turn on the notion of transcendental ideality. It is an immediate inference from the conclusion—which Kant's argument does establish—that the object called the totality of appearances does not exist at all. I admit, of course, that Kant wanted to move from showing that the totality of appearances does not exist as an object to the conclusion that the totality of appearances exists as a form for apprehending objects. But I have already argued that the move is not supported; and the conclusion that I have drawn from Kant's reconstructed argument is, I believe, the only conclusion which the argument will support.

Thus Kant's argument will yield the conclusion that the world does not exist as a thing in itself. Will it also support the conclusion that space and time are transcendentally ideal? Kant's argument, even as reconstructed, will not license such an inference. Nothing follows about whether space and time are merely properties of human sensibility from showing that there is no such object as the totality of phenomena.

4. Recent Criticisms of the First Antinomy

The purport and success of Kant's antinomy have been persistently assailed in the literature; but I believe that Kant has generally been unfortunate in his critics. There are several objections to his argument which I believe to be unsound. Russell has, for example, raised several objections that have since become legion. The first runs like this:

> [W]hen Kant says that an infinite series can "never" be completed by successive synthesis, all that he has even conceivably a right to say is that it cannot be completed *in a finite time*. Thus what he really proves is, at most, that if the world had no beginning, it must have already existed for an infinite time. This, however, is a very poor conclusion, by no means suitable for his purposes.[23]

This objection rests on a confusion of the two arguments Kant gives for the nonexistence of actually infinite magnitudes. It confuses the argument according to which we cannot synthesize a magnitude that is infinite with the other argument according to which there are no such magnitudes. Russell's argument here holds against the former: We cannot synthesize an infinite series unless we had an infinite amount of time. But Russell's argument does not hold against the latter: For Russell is completely silent about the possibility of an actual infinity.

Although Russell is silent in the present passage about the existence of infinite sets, we need not guess about his position on the issue. He has argued that there are infinite sets and that it is a mistake to deny their existence. And lest this be thought an objection to Kant's view about infinite magnitudes, I propose to show that Russell's point does not affect Kant's argument. Russell is con-

---

23 Bertrand Russell, *Our Knowledge of the External World* (George Allen & Unwin Ltd.: London, 1952), p. 161. Hereinafter cited as OKEW.

cerned to argue against those who think that the notion of an infinite number is self-contradictory. And he holds that there are numbers which obey different rules than finite numbers and that the notion of such a number does not entail a contradiction. He argues as follows. There are series which have the properties of reflexiveness and noninductiveness. A number is reflexive when it is not increased by adding one to it.[24] A number is noninductive when it lacks at least one inductive property, one such property being that a noninductive number has no immediate predecessor.[25] The conclusion of Russell's argument is that there are numbers that are both reflexive and noninductive, that they are infinite numbers, and that the concept of such a number contains no contradiction.

Does this invalidate Kant's argument that there is no actual infinity? I do not think it does. What Russell has established is that there can be numbers which are infinite in the sense that they have certain properties other kinds of numbers lack. But to establish that there are infinite numbers is not to establish that there are infinitely many numbers. When Kant denies that there can be a last member of an infinite series, what he is denying is presumably what Russell rejects when he denies the existence of a greatest finite number. Notice that, on Russell's account of a noninductive property, we begin the infinite numbers by postulating that the first such number has no predecessor. There is, accordingly, no way to count from finite to infinite numbers. And this is precisely what Kant is claiming when he says that you cannot start a series of finite numbers and generate an infinite series. I conclude, therefore, that Russell's demonstration of the existence of infinite numbers cannot be used as an argument against Kant's view that there is not an actually infinite magnitude.

But Russell adduces another argument which he believes to be fatal to Kant's view about the impossibility of a synthesis of infinitely many units. Russell argues the following:

> As we see from the word "synthesis," he [Kant] imagined a mind trying to grasp these successively, *in the reverse order* to that in which they had occurred, i.e. going from the present backwards. *This* series is obviously one which has no end. But the series of

24 Russell, OKEW, p. 194.
25 Russell, OKEW, p. 202.

events up to the present has an end, since it ends with the present. Owing to the inveterate subjectivism of his mental habits, he failed to notice that he had reversed the sense of the series by substituting backward synthesis for forward happening, and thus supposed that it was necessary to identify the mental series, which had an end, with the physical series, which had an end but no beginning.[26]

There are two points which vitiate this objection to Kant's argument. First, even if we do make the distinction between the two kinds of series which Russell mentions, it has not been shown that Kant has confounded them. For it has not been shown that by 'beginning' Kant meant or must have meant 'beginning for us'. Secondly, to say that one of these series—namely, the series terminating in the present—has an end is not to say that it is actually infinite. An independent proof must be given of this; and, as it stands, it is completely neutral concerning whether the series terminating in the present in fact can be actually infinite.

There remain three arguments which purport to uncover serious errors in Kant's argument. The first is to be found in Norman Kemp Smith's *Commentary* and has been recently pressed by Benardete.[27] Both claim that Kant's argument against an infinite series breaks down on a simple *non sequitur*. For, it is asked, does Kant not move from the impossibility of our *thinking* the world as infinite to the conclusion that the world *is* not infinite.[28] And if he does this, it need only be pointed out that the world's *de facto* infinity is quite compatible with our inability to conceive of it as infinite. The objection fails. And it fails because both Benardete and Kemp Smith confound the two arguments which are to be found in Kant against the possibility of an infinite series. Against the weaker argument the objection holds. But this leaves the stronger one completely intact.

The second and third objections to Kant's argument are ones which Professor Benardete has added to the budget. Benardete wants to show that Kant's arguments against the infinity of an

---

26 Russell, OKEW, p. 161.

27 Norman Kemp Smith, *Commentary*, p. 486; Jose Benardete, *Infinity* (Oxford University Press: New York, 1964, p. 128; cf. p. 129. Hereinafter cited as *Infinity*.

28 Cf. Kemp Smith, *Commentary*, p. 485.

elapsed series collapse because an actually infinite magnitude is logically possible. One such argument is the following:

1. It is necessary that either a finite or an infinite number of stars exists.
2. It is not logically necessary that the number of stars be finite.
3. Therefore, it is logically possible that the number of stars is infinite.[29]

This is offered by Benardete as a proof that actually infinite magnitudes are at least logically possible. Benardete concludes:

> To conceive of an infinite world does not require, as Kant seems to suppose, some special mental act of prodigious scope. It is not at all a matter of racking one's brains. One has only to recognize two tautologies as tautologies and then to perform a simple logical inference.[30]

The argument, then, amounts to the introduction of (1) and (2) as tautologies and the claim that (3) follows from them. There is, however, one fatal difficulty with this argument: It begs the question. Premise (2) assumes that it is not logically impossible that there be infinitely many stars—which is precisely the point at issue. Now it is, of course, true that the particular finite number assigned to the collection of stars is not logically necessary. But that the number be finite is, on Kant's position, necessary. Hence Benardete derives the conclusion he wants only at the price of circularity.

But Benardete attempts to argue to the same conclusion by a somewhat different argument. There are two parts to the argument: a reconstruction of Kant's position and a demonstration that the empirical use of the concept of finitude entails the metaphysical use of the concept of the actually infinite. Consider, first, how Benardete reconstructs Kant's position:

> (1) The world as a whole is no possible object of experience; (2) Only what is a possible object of experience may be rationally supposed to exist; ergo (3) The world as a whole may not be rationally supposed to exist.[31]

So much for the reconstruction. Now Benardete holds that Kant's

---

29 Benardete, *Infinity*, p. 129.

30 *Ibid.*

31 Benardete, *Infinity*, p. 110.

proof of premise (1) is vitiated by the ability Kant grants us meaningfully to apply the concepts of the finite to objects in our experience. Benardete argues as follows:

> We may say that the correlative terms finite and infinite are peculiar in that one of the terms denotes an empirical, whereas the other denotes a metaphysical, concept. If we contrast the hard empirical thesis that *this* wall before me is finite and the clearly metaphysical thesis that the universe is infinite, it follows that the denial or falsity of the empirical thesis logically entails the truth of the metaphysical thesis. . . . Finite and infinite being correlative concepts, the empirical is seen to be unintelligible apart from the cosmological.[32]

There is one interpretation which Benardete's words will bear that can be dismissed immediately. If it is false that this wall before me is finite, then it will be true that it is infinite. But this does not show that the empirical use of the concept of finitude entails its metaphysical meaningfulness. All that has been shown is that, if any entity is not finite, it is infinite—which is tautologically true. Thus on this interpretation Benardete has not shown the logical possibility of an actual infinity.

What Benardete is saying can also be interpreted as follows. He could be saying that, when we say that a particular object is finite, we are committed to saying that it is at least meaningful to entertain the possibility that it is infinite. But if this is so, then the proof which Kant offers to show that the world as a whole cannot be a possible object of experience is vitiated. For that proof assumes that the concept of an actual infinity is self-contradictory. And if the concept of an actual infinity can be meaningfully, though falsely, applied to particular objects in experience, then Kant cannot hold that the concept is logically impossible. In this sense, then, the empirical employment of the concept of the finite might be said to presuppose the meaningfulness of the concept of the actually infinite.

But does the empirical employment of the concept of the finite really commit Kant to hold that actually infinite collections are logically possible? I do not think it does. What the empirical employment of the concept implies is this: To say of a given object in

---

[32] Benardete, *Infinity*, pp. 108-109.

experience that it is not finite is meaningful only in the sense that it is always false to make such an assertion. Thus such an assertion is meaningful in that it is formulated in a well-formed expression and its denial generates a logically necessary truth. But this does not imply that the concept of an actual infinity is free from contradiction. What vitiates Benardete's argument is an equivocation on the notion of meaningfulness according to which he moves from 'meaningful' understood as 'either true or false' to 'meaningful' understood as 'logically possible'. That something in our experience is actually infinite can be meaningfully denied without our being forced to say that the concept whose applicability is denied is free from contradiction. A concept which entails a contradiction is at least meaningful (albeit necessarily false), for the negation of that concept is logically necessary. Thus when Kant permits the empirical employment of the concept of the finite, he is not forced to grant that the concept of an actual infinity is one whit less impossible than it is.

M. S. GRAM

NORTHWESTERN UNIVERSITY

THE IMPOSSIBILITY OF
TRANSCENDENTAL DEDUCTIONS

The purpose of this paper is first to explain a general notion of transcendental deductions, of which the Kantian are special cases; next to show, and to illustrate by examples from Kant's work, that no transcendental deduction can be successful; and thirdly to put one of Kant's achievements in its proper light by substituting for his spurious distinction between metaphysical exposition and transcendental deduction, a revised notion of metaphysical exposition and of the philosophical tasks arising out of it.

I. *The General Notion of a Transcendental Deduction*

Making statements about the external world presupposes not only a prior distinction between oneself and that world, but also a method for differentiating, within one's experience of it, external objects and attributes—properties and relations of which external objects are the bearers. I shall say that such a method of external differentiation is associated with, or belongs to, a categorial schema or, briefly, a "schema" of external differentiation if, and only if, the attributes employed comprise what may be called respectively, in accordance with philosophical tradition, "constitutive" and "individuating" attributes. An attribute is constitutive (of external objects) if, and only if, it is applicable to external objects and if, in addition, its applicability to an object logically implies, and is logically implied by, the object's being an external object. I shall say, more briefly, that a constitutive attribute is "comprehensively applicable" to external objects. An attribute is individuating (for external objects) if, and only if, it is applicable to every external object and if, in addition, its applicability to an external object logically implies, and is logically implied by, the external object's being distinct from all other external objects. I shall say, more briefly, that an individuating attribute "exhaustively individuates" external objects.

Some comments on these definitions may be helpful. Although not yet fully general, they fit, for example, Kant's view of the attribute 'x is a substance' as constitutive of, and his view of the attribute 'x wholly occupies a region of absolute space during a period of absolute time' as individuating for, external objects. The term "logically implies" is used to express the converse of the relation of logical deducibility with respect to some underlying logic, which at this stage need not be made explicit. An individuating attribute the possession of which by an external object logically implies its being distinct from all others, must not be confused with any merely identifying attribute the possession of which by an external object happens as a matter of fact to distinguish it from all others. Lastly it should be emphasised that a method of prior external differentiation does not necessarily belong to a categorial schema.

Statements about the external world are not the only ones which presuppose a prior differentiation of experience into objects and attributes, and thus, possibly, a categorial schema consisting of constitutive and individuating attributes. We also make, at least prima facie, statements of other kinds, presupposing prior differentiations of other regions of experience, e.g. sensory, moral and aesthetic experience, which may or may not belong to categorial schemata. A schema of sensory differentiation would contain constitutive attributes of, and individuating attributes for, sensory objects. The same would hold analogously for schemata of moral and aesthetic differentiation, if any. Such considerations permit us to generalize the definition of a categorial schema as follows: A method of prior differentiation of a region of experience is associated with, or belongs to, a categorial schema if, and only if, the attributes employed comprise attributes which are constitutive of the region's objects, and attributes which are individuating for them. For my purpose here it is not necessary to raise, much less to answer, the question why anybody uses the methods of prior differentiation which he does in fact use, or why for him experience should fall into more or less clearly distinguishable regions and should fall into them in one way rather than in any other.

A transcendental deduction can now be defined quite generally as a logically sound demonstration of the reasons why a particular categorial schema is not only in fact, but also necessarily employed, in differentiating a region of experience. This definition is very wide indeed and will presently be shown to cover Kant's conception of a transcendental deduction. Because of its generality it must be protected against such charges of vagueness as would rob the subsequent discussion of all cogency. Such protection can be achieved by the following characterization of the key-phrases which occur in the definition. Although a "logically sound demonstration" need not be a deductive argument, it may contain deductive arguments in which case these must not be fallacious. Again, whatever else may be meant by the statement that a schema "is *necessarily* employed in differentiating a region of experience" it logically implies that any method actually or possibly employed in differentiating the region belongs to the schema. Apart from these provisos no further restrictions are imposed on interpreting the definition.

Among the most important and interesting examples of attempted transcendental deductions are, of course, those found in Kant's philosophy, on which I shall be drawing for illustrations of the general thesis that transcendental deductions are impossible. This choice will limit me to an examination of schemata of external and practical differentiation. Kant's transcendental deductions contain only such. He held that of all the methods of prior differentiation of experience which he investigated, only those of external and practical differentiation—and not, for example, any method of aesthetic differentiation—belong to categorial schemata. It would not be difficult to find, in these or other fields, many simpler or more simple-minded philosophical arguments easily recognizable as attempts at transcendental deductions in the sense of our definition.

II. *The Impossibility of Transcendental Deductions*

I shall now examine the preconditions of the possibility of any transcendental deduction, and show that at least one of them is such that it cannot be satisfied; from which result, of course, the impossibility of transcendental deductions follows immediately. Before a transcendental deduction can be attempted for any region of experience, a method of prior differentiation of the region must first be exhibited and shown to belong to a schema. This, as was pointed out by and was perfectly clear to Kant, need not be the case. But if the method of prior differentiation does belong to a schema the task of exhibiting the schema is feasible. It consists (a) in searching for nonempty attributes, e.g. an attribute P such that 'x is an object of the region' logically implies and is implied by, 'x is a P'. Sometimes one may succeed in the more ambitious task of giving a complete, finite enumeration of the simplest constitutive attributes, i.e. such as are not logically equivalent to a conjunction of other constitutive attributes. We might, following Kant, call such simple and finitely enumerable attributes the "categories" of the region and say that they are ultimately constitutive of the region's objects. But this pleasant possibility may be ignored.

The task further consists (b) in searching for at least one nonempty attribute, say Q, such that Q is applicable to every object of the region, and is such that 'x is an object of the region and a Q' logically implies, and is logically implied by, 'x is a distinct object of the region'. If another attribute say R, should also turn out to be an individuating attribute for the objects of the region then 'x is an object of the region and an R' logically implies, and is logically implied by, 'x is an object of the region and a Q'. We may again ignore this possibility. The fulfilment of the first precondition of the possibility of a transcendental deduction, i.e. of the above tasks (a) and (b) may be called "the establishment of a schema"—on the basis of investigating a particular method of prior differentiation of a region of experience into objects and attributes.

With the establishment of a schema the preconditions for its transcendental deduction are, however, not yet satisfied. For to establish a schema is to establish that a particular method for differentiating a region of experience belongs to the schema, and not that any method which might actually or possibly be thus employed, also belongs to it. Before one can show *why* any and every possible method belongs to the schema one has to show *that* any and every possible method belongs to it. One must, as I shall say, demonstrate the schema's uniqueness.

How could this be done? Prima facie three possibilities are open. First, to demonstrate the schema's uniqueness by comparing it with experience undifferentiated by any method of prior differentiation. But this cannot be done since the statements by which the comparison would have to be made, cannot be formulated with-

out employing *some* prior differentiation of experience; and even if
there were undifferentiated experience, one could at best show
that a certain schema "reflects" it, and not that some other schema
could not also reflect it. Second, to demonstrate the schema's
uniqueness by comparing it with its possible competitors. But this
presupposes that they all can be exhibited, and is self-contradictory
in attempting a "demonstration" of the schema's uniqueness, by conceding that the schema was not unique. Thirdly, one might propose
to examine the schema and its application entirely from within the
schema itself, i.e. by means of statements belonging to it. Such an
examination, at best, could only show how the schema functions in
the differentiation of a region of experience, not that it is the only
possible schema to which every differentiation of the region must
belong.

The three methods include the possible grounds for a con-
cordance between reality and its apprehension, mentioned in the
preface to the second edition of *The Critique of Pure Reason*.
In order to avoid vague appeals to demonstrations of a categorial
schema's uniqueness by other methods, e.g. some mystical insight
or some special Logic, I am prepared to reduce my claim to the
thesis that uniqueness demonstrations of a schema by comparing it
with undifferentiated experience, by comparing it with other schemata, or by examining it from within, are impossible. It should be
noted that I am speaking not of isolated concepts, such as 'permanence' or 'change', which may or may not be indispensable to
our thinking, but which by themselves are not constitutive of, or
individuating for, the objects of a region of experience—even
though a demonstration of their uniqueness is, as I should be prepared to argue, equally impossible.

It is the impossibility of demonstrating a schema's uniqueness
that renders transcendental deductions impossible. The general
argument just sketched rests mainly on two distinctions: the distinction between a method of prior differentiation and its categorial schema, if any; and the distinction between (a) establishing that a method of prior differentiation belongs to a schema and
(b) demonstrating the uniqueness of the schema. In order to illustrate my conclusion with examples from Kant's work, I shall try
to choose such as will not only serve to draw attention to errors,
but will also suggest reasons why these errors are liable to escape

undetected. I begin with what I consider to be a mistake which all the Kantian attempts at transcendental deductions have in common.

Assume that we have investigated a method of prior differentiation of a region of experience and found that it belongs to a schema. The result, as we have seen, is formulated (a) by statements to the effect that some of the attributes employed by the method are constitutive of the objects of the region, e.g. that among the attributes is one, say P, such that P is applicable to objects of the region *and* such that 'x is an object of the region' logically implies, and is implied by, 'x is a P'. (b) by statements to the effect that one (or more) of the attributes employed are individuating for the objects of the region, e.g. that among the attributes is an attribute, say Q, such that Q applies to every object of the region *and* such that 'x is an object of the region and a Q' logically implies, and is implied by, 'x is a distinct object of the region'. Let us now, as Kant did, examine the logical status of (a) statements of comprehensive applicability and (b) statements of exhaustive individuation.

Each of them is a conjunction of two statements. The first expresses that the extension of an attribute is, as a matter of fact, not empty, that something exists, the existence of which could not be guaranteed by logic or definitions alone. It is therefore a synthetic statement. The second is clearly logically necessary. Since a conjunction of a synthetic and a logically necessary statement is synthetic, the statements of comprehensive applicability and exhaustive individuation are all synthetic.

Moreover, each of these two kinds of statements in question, namely that of comprehensive applicability and that of exhaustive individuation, is compatible with any statement about objects, i.e. with any statement expressing the applicability or inapplicability of attributes to objects—*provided* that such a statement is made by a method of prior differentiation which belongs to the schema. The reason for this is that in that case no attribute can be applied or refused to any objects except such as are constituted and individuated by the schema's constitutive and individuating attributes. Thus no incompatibility can arise between the statements of comprehensive applicability and exhaustive individuation of a categorial schema on the one hand, and any statement expressed by a method of prior differentiation belonging to the schema on the other. The statements of comprehensive applicability and exhaustive individuation are thus a priori with respect to a particular schema, namely the schema which comprises them. It does not follow that they are also a priori with respect to any schema which can be claimed to be the only one possible, i.e. that they are "uniquely a priori." Thus in establishing that a method of prior differentiation belongs to a schema one shows *eo ipso* that the statements of comprehensive applicability and of exhaustive individuation are synthetic and nonuniquely a priori. To show that they are uniquely a priori would require a demonstration of the schema's uniqueness, which I have just argued to be impossible.

Kant did not see this, and he conflates uniquely a priori with nonuniquely a priori statements. This conflation not only pervades his whole philosophy, but even determines its structure, especially the division of all his principal arguments into metaphysical expositions and transcendental deductions.[1] A metaphysical exposition which exhibits a concept as, or exhibits it insofar as it is, a priori is always the result of inquiry into one actually employed method of differentiation. It can thus at best establish the schema, if any, to which the method belongs. A transcendental deduction, aimed at showing that and how a priori concepts are applicable or possible, examines only the schema which has been established by the metaphysical exposition of this particular schema. It thus does not examine a schema the uniqueness of which has been demonstrated. Kant's failure even to *consider the need* for interpolating a uniqueness-demonstration between any metaphysical exposition and a corresponding transcendental deduction and his conflation of nonuniquely and uniquely a priori statements are so intimately related that they deserve to be regarded as two aspects of the same error.

The reasons why these points, which in our own day are not too difficult to see, have escaped Kant, are partly historical and partly logical. The historical ones, are, of course, that like most of his contemporaries, Kant considered the mathematics and physics of his day and the moral code by which he found himself bound, to be true beyond doubt; he felt in no way compelled to consider, therefore, the question of schemata other than those to which be-

---

1 See *Critique of Pure Reason*, B. 38, 80, etc.

long the methods of differentiation employed by him in his mathematical, physical and moral thinking. The logical reasons are that his various attempts at transcendental deductions contain subsidiary assumptions which tend to reinforce the common error underlying all of them.

The Transcendental Aesthetic which exhibits the individuating attributes of the Kantian schema is based on the assumption that the propositions of Euclidean geometry describe the spatial relations between external objects; also the more general assumption that if—*per impossibile*—two different geometries were conceivable, then at most one of them would describe, and at least one would misdescribe, these relations. However, neither Euclidean geometry, nor any other, describes the spatial structure of external objects or the spatial relations between them. A physical triangle, for example, is not an instance of the concept 'Euclidean triangle', or for that matter 'non-Euclidean triangle', just as neither a Euclidean triangle nor a non-Euclidean one is an instance of the concept 'physical triangle'. To "apply geometry to the external world" is not to assert geometrical attributes of external objects, but to identify external objects with instances of geometrical attributes in certain contexts and for certain purposes, i.e. to treat them *as if* they were identical. The applicability, in this sense of one geometry does not exclude the applicability of another. Kant assumes the unique applicability to external objects of Euclidean geometry, without even attempting to establish the assumption. Yet the assumption of the unique applicability of Euclidean geometry to external objects is a key premiss in the very argument by which he tries to establish that spatio-temporal location in Euclidean space and Newtonian time is the principle of individuation for all external objects—a principle which he shows to be synthetic, and non-uniquely (not, as he thinks, uniquely) a priori.

Again, the Transcendental Analytic, which exhibits the constitutive attributes of the Kantian schema, assumes as a principle that the categories must be recognized as conditions a priori of the possibility of experience[2] conceived as differentiated into distinct external objects and attributes of such. Sufficient conditions are not distinguished from sufficient and necessary conditions. The former,

---

[2] See e.g. B 126.

which Kant tries to establish, are satisfied by the establishment of a schema. The latter would be satisfied only if the schema's uniqueness were also demonstrated. Failure to distinguish between the two kinds of conditions thus supports the conflation of statements synthetic and nonuniquely a priori, with synthetic and uniquely a priori statements of comprehensive applicability.

The most convincing way to expose Kant's failure to give a transcendental deduction of the schema of external differentiation established in the *Critique of Pure Reason,* is simply to provide an example of a different schema of external differentiation. Since I have gone into this point in detail elsewhere,[3] I may put it here quite briefly. Grant that determinate spatio-temporal location, as conceived by Newton and Kant, exhaustively individuates external objects of which the Kantian categories of substance, causality and the rest, are the constitutive attributes; and grant also that the statements to this effect are synthetic a priori. The existence of relativistic quantum-mechanics compels us to grant equally that determinate spatio-temporal location in a spatio-temporal continuum of an altogether different kind exhaustively individuates external objects of which the constitutive attributes are quite other than the Kantian categories; and to grant equally that the statements to this effect are synthetic a priori. But neither schema of external differentiation is unique; and the synthetic a priori statements about the comprehensive applicability of, and the exhaustive individuation for, external objects with respect to either schema are non-uniquely a priori.

In Kant's practical philosophy he investigates a method for differentiating objects and attributes within the experience of the practicable. The objects might be called "morally relevant" objects since their attributes include moral attributes. By exhibiting the constitutive and individuating attributes employed by the method, the method is shown to belong to a schema. Again no attempt is made to demonstrate the uniqueness of the schema. Such an attempt could not, as I have argued, in any case have been successful, from which circumstance the impossibility of any transcendental deduction of the schema immediately follows.

---

3 'Zur Kantischen Begründung der Mathematik und der Naturwissenschaften' *Kant Studien,* 56, No. 3/4 (1966) .

At this point, however, Kant varies his usual procedure. Having established the schema, he does not immediately attempt its transcendental deduction. Instead he tries to derive a new principle from it, namely the categorical imperative, the applicability of which does not only characterize the merely morally relevant objects, which are constituted and individuated by the schema, but also those among the morally relevant objects which are the bearers of moral value. Only after the alleged derivation of the categorical imperative is completed, does he attempt a transcendental deduction of it and the schema.

Kant's belief that an examination of his schema of practical differentiation yields the categorical imperative, which he regarded as a necessary and sufficient criterion of the morality of any action, was one of the main reasons why, in his practical philosophy, he overlooked the circumstance that to establish a schema is not to demonstrate its uniqueness; and why consequently there too he conflated synthetic statements which are nonuniquely a priori with uniquely a priori ones. I shall not consider Kant's derivation of the categorical imperative from the allegedly unique schema of practical differentiation. Instead I shall compare that schema with a different one, thus providing the strongest possible kind of argument against the assumption of its uniqueness, and, therefore, against the soundness of the attempted transcendental deduction of it.

Since what is practicable is practicable in the external world, any method of practical differentiation will depend on, and vary with, the adopted method of external differentiation and even with substantive assumptions about the external world, formulated by means of this method. Let us ignore such variations, however important they may be. Kant's metaphysical exposition as a search for the constitutive and individuating attributes employed in his method of practical differentiation leads him to the following conclusions: (a) the attribute 'x is a morally relevant object' is not empty; and it logically implies, and is logically implied by, 'x is a type of act and x is performed in accordance with a maxim, chosen by an agent'. (b) The latter attribute is not only constitutive of morally relevant objects, but also individuates them exhaustively. The key-terms of the bilateral implication require comment.

An act is the intentional initiation (prevention or nonprevention) by a person of a change in the situation which confronts him. A maxim is a rule of the general form: 'If in a situation of type S, perform an act of type A'. S and A are not the unmanageably long, and possibly unlimited, conjunctions of attributes which are respectively characteristic of concrete situations and particular acts. They are manageable conjunctions of relevant attributes— their relevance or irrelevance being determined by the person who chooses the maxim before acting, who formulates it retrospectively or who is at least assumed to be capable of doing so. S may, and usually does, comprise some reference to the person's desires and intentions other than the intention involved in performing the act. A need not, usually does not, and—on some interpretations of Kant's theory—must not, comprise such a reference. Examples of maxims where A does not comprise it are: If in . . . help (or don't help) your neighbour, commit (or don't commit) suicide etc.

According to Kant an act by itself is not a morally relevant object. What constitutes and individuates the bearers of moral attributes, i.e. of moral value, disvalue and indifference, is the type A under which a person subsumes his act, and the maxim to which he conforms in acting. At this point a glance at the history of moral philosophy is sufficient to provide examples of schemata of practical differentiation, which are internally consistent, have been actually employed and are quite different from the Kantian. According to a whole class of such schemata a morally relevant object is a complicated relation between an act, the agent's beliefs, the truth or falsehood of his beliefs and his desires. Such a relation need not depend on the person's chosen maxims; and is quite compatible with the reasonable assumption that not every act is governed by a maxim. The Kantian schema of practical differentiation is nonunique and its transcendental deduction therefore impossible.

III. *A Revised Notion of Metaphysical Exposition*

Before arguing that the spurious distinction between metaphysical exposition and transcendental deduction should be replaced by a revised notion of metaphysical exposition and showing how much in harmony such replacement is with some of Kant's insights, another attempt must be briefly examined at reconstructing the strategy of the transcendental philosophy. It sees the fundamental error not in neglecting the problem of demonstrating the (undemonstrable) uniqueness of any schema of differentiation, but merely in a narrowness of the methods investigated by Kant of prior differentiation and a corresponding narrowness of the schemata established by him.

On this view the post-Kantian development of physics and mathematics, for example, would merely show the Kantian schema of external differentiation as having to be widened before a transcendental deduction is attempted; one need not regard a transcendental deduction as in principle impossible. Thus the individuating attribute for external objects 'x wholly occupies a region of space and an interval of time as conceived by Newton' is to be replaced by 'x wholly occupies a region of space and an interval of time as conceived by Newton or a spatio-temporal region as conceived by Einstein'. In a similar manner the Kantian constitutive attributes are to be replaced by unions of them with other corresponding constitutive attributes. But, then, how could one show that the available constitutive and individuating attributes exhaust all the conceivable ones, or that all those conceivable have been conceived? To show this, one would have to produce a demonstration of the widened schema's uniqueness and, as has been argued quite generally, such a demonstration is impossible.

In his metaphysical expositions of a particular method of prior external and a particular method of prior practical differentiation, Kant has established that they belong to schemata, i.e. that they employ constitutive and individuating attributes. The statements to the effect that the constitutive attributes are comprehensively applicable to the objects of the differentiated region of experience and that the individuating are exhaustively individuating for them, are synthetic and nonuniquely a priori—not as Kant thought uniquely a priori. These statements do not demarcate the structure of any method of external or of practical differentiation, as necessarily unchangeable; they are compatible with the assumption—and the historical truth—that schemata of external and practical differentiation can change and become obsolete.

The constitutive and individuating attributes of a schema which is no longer employed, may even turn out, or be judged, to be empty. Having e.g. abandoned the Kantian schema of external differentiation in favour of another, it becomes possible—looking as it were from the outside—to assert that the Kantian attribute of substance is empty, i.e. that the synthetic, nonuniquely a priori statement asserting its comprehensive applicability to external objects is false. A social anthropologist may in a similar manner judge that the constitutive and individuating attributes of a demonology, which he has investigated, are empty, even though a certain way of life might be inseparably bound up with it.

In order to do justice to such possibilities I now define a revised notion of metaphysical exposition, which relativizes the Kantian absolute notion in a number of ways. It is the analysis of methods for the differentiation of more-or-less-well-demarcated domains into objects and attributes which aims at the exhibition of synthetic and nonuniquely a priori statements, by exhibiting the schemata in respect of which the statements are a priori. The differentiated domain, as became clear in discussing geometrical statements, need not be a region of experience. It may be a domain of ideal objects. A method of differentiation belongs, we remember, to a schema if, and only if, it employs attributes which are constitutive of all objects of the domain and attributes which individuate all of them. The constitutive and individuating attributes are the schema. A statement is synthetic if, and only if, it is not logically valid with respect to the logic underlying the methods of differentiation being considered. Thus we must, distinguish e.g. statements synthetic with respect to classical from those synthetic with respect to intuitionist logic. A statement is a priori with respect to a schema if, and only if, it is compatible with any statement in which an attribute is applied to one or more distinct objects by means of any method which belongs to the schema.

Among the kinds of schemata which a metaphysical exposition (in the revised sense) of various methods of differentiation may establish for them are the following: Schemata (a) of external differentiation, including the schema established in the *Critique of Pure Reason* for the method of external differentiation investigated by it. But there are other methods of external differentiation belonging to the same or other schemata. Schemata (b) of practical differentiation, including the schema established in the *Critique of Practical Reason* for the method of practical differentiation investigated by it. But there are other methods of practical differentiation belonging to the same or other schemata. Schemata (c) of idealized external or, briefly, mathematical differentiation of a domain which is an idealization of some aspects of external experience. The methods of differentiating such a domain and the statements which are true about it, are sometimes expressed in axiomatic mathematical theories, even though a large class of such theories cannot, as Gödel has shown, comprise all the statements which are true about the domain. Kant, as was pointed out earlier, failed to recognize the multiplicity of possible mathematical schemata and confused mathematical with external differentiation. Schemata (d) of idealized practical differentiation, which are of interest in the study of certain normative, e.g. legal, systems. Schemata (e) of logical differentiation. Their establishment results in synthetic nonuniquely a priori statements of comprehensive applicability. Such a statement is a conjunction consisting of two statements, an analytic statement asserting that certain statement-forms are true of all objects constituted and individuated by any of the available methods of differentiation, and a synthetic statement asserting that the domain of these objects is not empty. Kant, who was not faced with the problem of alternative logics, naturally did not consider this possibility.

Every synthetic, nonuniquely a priori statement is a priori with respect to at least one schema. Thus statements of comprehensive applicability and exhaustive individuation are a priori with respect to the schema to whose constitutive and individuating attributes they refer. Next, all synthetic, ideal statements are a priori with respect to any schema of external differentiation, because no statement solely about ideal objects can be incompatible with any statements solely about external objects, however these may be constituted or individuated. Again the question how far statements which belong to a schema of practical differentiation are a priori with respect to a schema of external differentiation cannot be answered in general, since methods of external differentiation and methods of practical differentiation (and their schemata, if any) may stand in a variety of relations to each other.

The important Kantian distinction between synthetic a priori statements and regulative principles remains valid. We might define a regulative principle as being synthetic if, and only if, the statement describing the type of action prescribed by the principle is synthetic; and as a priori with respect to a schema of differentiation if, and only if, the descriptive statement is compatible with any statement in which attributes are applied to objects by a method of differentiation which belongs to the schema. Regulative principles which are in this sense synthetic and nonuniquely a priori differ, of course, from synthetic and nonuniquely a priori statements by having no truth-value. In the course of a metaphysical exposition such principles will often be uncovered, whether or not we decide to include their exhibition among its explicit aims. Epistemologically of greatest interest are those regulative principles which regulate the construction of theories and those which express preferences for some schemata over others.

Transcendental deductions of schemata and of synthetic a priori statements are, as I have argued, impossible because their uniqueness cannot be demonstrated. The Kantian question as to how synthetic and uniquely a priori judgements are possible does not arise. In its place, however, there arises another question: How are synthetic and nonuniquely a priori statements possible? To answer this question is, as we have learned from Kant, to examine the function of such statements, that is to say their relations to each other, to analytic and to empirical statements. The task is by no means simple or trivial as can be seen, for example, by considering the relation in scientific thinking between various schemata of external, ideal and logical differentiation. Moreover, since contrary to Kant's convictions, not only methods of differentiation but also the schemata to which they belong can and do change, the task cannot be completed once and for all, but must be undertaken over and over again.

S. KÖRNER

THE UNIVERSITY, BRISTOL

ANALYTICITY AND GRAMMAR

Kant's theory is not so simple
as it looks, and the nature of
analytic judgments is not altogether
clear.[1]

Kant's distinction between analytic and synthetic judgments is best known through his metaphoric definition of an analytic judgment as one in which "the predicate B belongs to the subject A, as something which is (covertly) contained in this subject A" (B 10).[2] Although this is the most famous formulation of Kant's distinction, what strikes a student most forcefully about Kant's discussion of analyticity is the variety of different ways in which he explains the idea. One can identify passages which seem to make analyticity depend upon (1) containment, (2) identity, (3) contradiction, (4) our way of knowing the judgment in question, (5) our way of thinking the judgment in question, (6) the function or role of the judgment in question. In addition to these six prima facie different conceptions of analyticity, there is also a question whether Kant intends his distinction to range over all judgments or only over subject-predicate judgments; if we apply these two alternatives to the six conceptions of analyticity, we have a total of twelve theories of analyticity contained in or suggested by Kant's discussion. This is a bewildering situation indeed, and it is no wonder that subsequent discussions of analyticity have often lacked the decisiveness that one might wish for in matters of logic.

---

[1] H. J. Paton, *Kant's Metaphysics of Experience* (London, 1936, p. 86. Hereinafter cited as KME.

[2] I. Kant, *Critique of Pure Reason*. Parenthetical references in the text are to pages in the original editions, 'A' indicating the first edition and 'B' indicating the second. The translation used is that by N. Kemp Smith (London, 1958).

I propose to give fresh consideration to what Kant said about the distinction between analytic and synthetic judgments. I shall first consider how widely we may presume Kant intended his distinction to apply, and then examine various formulations of the distinction in the *Critique*. These formulations lead to two broad lines of interpretation, in terms of logical form on the one hand and in terms of the phenomenology or function of the judgment on the other. I shall reject the first line, and offer an interpretation of Kant's notion based on the explicative function which he assigns to analytic judgments. This interpretation proves to be compatible with all that Kant has said about the analytic, and illuminating when applied to some of his puzzling remarks. It turns out that the explication achieved by an analytic judgment is very like the explication achieved by what Wittgenstein called a "grammatical" proposition, and hence that analyticity (in Kant's sense) is very like grammar (in Wittgenstein's sense). It turns out, too, that Kant's distinction is more pragmatic than is generally realized, and that it therefore remains untouched by the main thrust of recent attacks on other distinctions between the analytic and the synthetic.

1. *The Range of Kant's Distinction*

The section of the *Critique* entitled "The Distinction Between Analytic and Synthetic Judgments" begins with the words, "In all judgments in which the relation of a subject to the predicate is thought. . . ." It appears that the remainder of this section is meant to be read with the condition of this opening phrase in mind, and this immediately suggests, as Robinson and Marc-Wogau have pointed out,[3] that Kant did not conceive of his distinction as applying to any but subject-predicate propositions. It may therefore be that theorems of logic, relational propositions, and simple existential propositions are not even to be considered in the light of the distinction which Kant sets for subject-predicate propositions!

In its broadest form such a suggestion has little to recommend it and is easily rebutted. A simple existential judgment, such as 'God

---

3 R. Robinson, "Necessary Propositions," *Mind* 67 (1958), 289-304. K. Marc-Wogau: "Kants Lehre vom analytischen Urteil," *Theoria* 17 (1951), 140-154.

exists' or 'There are aardvarks', can be regarded as having a logical predicate, even though (as Kant puts it) " 'Being' is obviously not a real predicate" (B 626).[4] Kant himself, for example, explicitly discusses existential judgments in regard to analytic-synthetic distinction, and argues that they are all synthetic (B 625-626). Similarly, a relational judgment can be looked upon as having a subject and a predicate, even though such an analysis of it is not final and may not be wholly satisfactory. Theorems of logic are perhaps more difficult to fit into the subject-predicate mold, but it is in any case implausible to regard them as judgments in the Kantian sense. It would seem, therefore, as Parkinson contends,[5] that Kant may legitimately look upon his distinction as quite general and assimilate a variety of sorts of judgments to the subject-predicate pattern.

Against these considerations we must set Kant's own classification of judgments into three species, categorical, hypothetical, and disjunctive (B 95). He explains that "In the first kind of judgments we consider only two concepts, in the second two judgments, in the third several judgments in their relation to each other" (B 98). Kant's explanation of analyticity is obviously tailored to fit the first of these three species of judgments, and nowhere is it altered to fit the different dimensions of the other two. This is a matter of some significance for appreciating the distance between Kant's conception of analyticity and that of many moderns.[6] There is, for example, no obvious way for Kant to regard the judgment, 'If the Mekong is longer than the Danube and the Yangtze is longer than the Mekong, then the Yangtze is longer than the Danube' as ana-

---

[4] W. C. Salmon and G. Nakhnikian show that existence can be treated as a predicate within the framework of modern logic too, in their paper " 'Exists' as a Predicate," *Philosophical Review* **66** (1957), 535-542.

[5] G. H. R. Parkinson, "Necessary Propositions and *a priori* Knowledge in Kant," *Mind* **69** (1960), 391-397. It might also be mentioned that in the *Critique of Practical Reason* Kant extends the scope of the distinction even more by speaking of analytic and synthetic imperatives; see L. W. Beck: *A Commentary on Kant's Critique of Practical Reason* (Chicago, 1960), p. 86.

[6] The great distance between Kant's view and modern formal views is emphasized by E. W. Beth, who elaborates the point from a different perspective in his valuable article, "Kants Einteilung der Urteile in analytische und sunthetische," *Alg. Ned. Tijds. voor Wijsbeg. en Psych.*, **46** (1953/54), 253-264.

lytic—although it would seem that this hypothetical judgment merely makes explicit something that is implicit in the relational concept
longer than; it surely does not state any geographical information.
Similarly, truth-functional tautologies, which are today often presented as a paradigm for analytic propositions, are either hypothetical or disjunctive in form and therefore do not fall within
the scope of the concept for Kant. The valid formulae of modern
symbol'c logic would no doubt be ruled out on this ground too;
but it is likely that such formulae would in any case be excluded
from the range of Kant's distinction between the analytic and the
synthetic on the ground that they do not express judgments.[7] Such
exclusions are much to be regretted but they do seem to be implied
by Kant.

We conclude, then, that certain judgments—though not the
ones Robinson supposed—and certain other formulae, which
we today might wish to count as propositions, do not fall within
the scope of Kant's distinction between analytic and synthetic judgments. The distinction does apply unrestrictedly, however, to categorical propositions.[8]

2. *Kant's Various Explanations*

Kant first says that in an analytic judgment "the predicate B
belongs to the subject A, as something which is (covertly) contained

---

[7] In the *Critique* Kant consistently speaks of "principles of logic" rather than
of "judgments of logic" or "truths of logic." Kant's term for 'principles' is
'Sätze', which can also be rendered by 'proposition' or 'sentence'. The important
point is that he used 'Urteile' in formulating his distinction between the analytic and the synthetic, but *not* in speaking about logical principles.

Kant does not observe the same terminological distinction in his *Logik*, for
in sections 36 and 37 he speaks of "analytische Sätze"; but he characterizes logical formulae in a way that makes it doubtful that they are to be regarded as
"Sätze": "F o r m e l n.—Dieses sind Regeln, deren Ausdruck zum Muster der
Nachahmung dient. Sie sind übrigens ungemein nützlich zur Erleichterung bei
verwickelten Sätzen und der erleuchtetste Kopf sucht daher dergleichen zu
erfinden" (Einleitung ix = Weischedel III.507).

[8] My conclusion seems to be close to that of Marc-Wogau, although he does
not draw out the consequences of it: "Als Gegenstand der Einteilung der Urteile
in analytische und synthetische betrachtet Kant . . . *kategorische assertorische
Subjekt-Prädikat Sätze die keinen Widerspruch in sich enthalten*" (*op. cit.* 142).

in this subject A" (B 10). Either a judgment is analytic in this manner or "B lies outside the concept A, although it does indeed stand in connection with it" (B 10). We are all perfectly familiar with the idea that something may be contained in something else, where the alternative is that the first thing lies outside the second. For example, if I put a wastebasket at the far end of my room and try throwing crumpled pieces of discarded manuscript into it, the result will most likely be that some of the paper balls will be contained in the basket and some will lie outside it. Tht difficulty which we have in understanding Kant's first explanation of analyticity is the difficulty of applying this familiar concept of containment in an unfamiliar context.

We know that in the case of physical objects there are limits to the application of the idea. If one of the crumpled pieces of discarded manuscript gets hooked on the top edge of the basket, or lies at the top of the heap above the plane of the brim of the basket, there is no saying whether it is contained in the basket or lies outside of it. In general the concept of containment loses its clear dichotomous character whenever the putative container either lacks sharp boundaries or has boundaries that an object can straddle. It follows that Kant must have assumed that concepts all have "sharp boundaries," so that one can always say definitively whether one concept is "contained in" another or not, if containment is to serve as a definitive criterion of analyticity.

Concepts, whether sharp or not, are not literally contained in one another in the same basic sense in which paper balls may be contained in or lie outside of a basket. If we look at the matter with this familiar sense of 'contain' in mind, we shall have to say that Kant was speaking metaphorically. This metaphor, like any other, may have valuable rhetorical force and may even be instructive; but we cannot understand exactly what the explanation is meant to convey until we can put it in nonmetaphorical terms. Presumably Kant's recognition of this need is one of the reasons why he offered further explanations of analyticity.

Kant next presents the explanation in terms of identity: "Analytic judgments (affirmative) are therefore those in which the connection of the predicate with the subject is thought through identity" (B 10).⁹ Again, it is necessary to be generous with Kant. The expression 'thought through identity' is not an expression which our ordinary familiarity with the language enables us to understand: there is no ordinary idiom according to which we speak of thinking something "through" something else.¹⁰ What then does Kant mean by saying that 'all bodies are extended' is thought through identity?

Kant's odd phrase makes it clear that an analytic proposition is not the same as an identical proposition, although there is a very intimate connection between the two. Some years later, in his essay on the progress of metaphysics since the time of Leibniz and Wolff,¹¹ Kant explicitly commented:

> A judgment is *analytic* if its predicate only sets forth clearly (*explicite*) what was already thought, albeit obscurely (*implicite*), in the concept of the subject. For example, that every body is extended. If one wished to call such a judgment "identical," one would invite confusion; for judgments of that sort contribute nothing to the elucidation of concepts, which must be the aim of all judgment, and hence are said to be empty. For example, that every body is a bodily (in another word, material) substance. Analytic judgments are indeed *based* on identity and can be resolved into it; but they cannot *be* identical, since they require analysis and there-

---

⁹ See also B 622: "If, in an identical proposition, I reject the predicate while retaining the subject, contradiction results; and I therefore say that the former belongs necessarily to the latter." And also B 135.

¹⁰ The German is no clearer and the idiom no more familiar: Analytische Urteile sind also diejenigen in welchen die Verknüpfung des Prädikats mit dem Subjekt durch Identität . . . gedacht wird. The expression is used in what appears to be a slightly different sense at B 74.

¹¹ "Preisschrift über die Fortschritte der Metaphysik," *Kants gesammelte Schriften*, Prussian Academy edition, Volume XX, pp. 253-332. Originally published with the title "Über die von der Königlichen Akademie der Wissenschaften zu Berlin für das Jahr 1791 ausgesetzte Preisfrage: Welches sind die wirklichen Fortschritte, die die Metaphysik seit Wolf's und Leibnitzens Zeiten in Deutschland gemacht hat?" (ed. D. F. T. Rink, Königsberg 1804). Rink's edition has been republished with the original pagination by Weischedel in Kant: *Werke*, Volume III (Wiesbaden, 1958). This essay will henceforth be cited as "*Fortschritte*," with references given first to the Academy edition and then to the original edition—e.g. (*Fortschritte* XX.265 = R 23).

by contribute to the clarification of concepts, which would not be done at all if they were identical *idem per idem*.[12]

But it is still obscure exactly how an analytic judgment is to be resolved into an identical proposition.

When Kant says that the judgment that all bodies are extended is "thought through identity," a part of what he means might be expressed by saying that this judgment is one which depends upon our acknowledging that the concept of a body is identical with the conceptual combination of a number of elements, one of which is the concept of being extended. To put it symbolically, in a symbolism suggested both by Parkinson (*op. cit.*) and by Beck,[13] we can say that analytic propositions are not of the form

All A are B

but of the form

All A = BX are B,

where X is a concept or a set of concepts which joins with B in a conceptual complex identical with A.

These symbolic representations of Kant's idea are doubly useful. In the first place they show how a judgment's being analytic depends upon its being "thought through identity": the subject-concept must be conceived as identical with a conceptual complex of which the predicate is one component. In the second place we can see in these symbolic representations the connection of which Parkinson speaks between the containment criterion and the identity criterion: the predicate must be "contained in" the conceptual complex with which the subject is conceived to be identical. Thus these two criteria go hand in glove, and separately they are simply aspects of one and the same idea.

Nevertheless there are still difficulties. One problem centers

---

12 Urteile sind nämlich a n a l y t i s c h, wenn ihr Prädikat nur dasjenige klar (explicite) vorstellt, was in dem Begriffe des Subjekts, obzwar dunkel (implicite), gedacht war; z.B. ein jeder Körper ist ausgedehnt. Wenn man solche Urteile identische nennen wollte, so würde man Verwirrung anrichten; denn dergleichen Urteile tragen nicht zur Deutlichkeit des Begriffs bei, wozu doch alles Urteilen abzwecken muss, und heissen daher leer; z.B. ein jeder Körper ist ein körperliches (mit einem andern Wort, materielles) Wesen. Analytische Urteile g r ü n d e n sich zwar auf der Identität, und können darin aufgelöset werden, aber sie s i n d nicht identisch, denn sie bedürfen Zergliederung und dienen dadurch zur Erklärung des Begriffs; da hingegen durch identische idem per idem, also gar nicht erklärt werden würde. (*Fortschritte* XX.322 = R 174-175).

13 L. W. Beck, *Studies in the Philosophy of Kant* (New York, 1965), pp. 74ff. Hereinafter cited as SPK.

around the way concepts are "combined" in "conceptual complexes." Leibniz held, reasonably enough, that the predicate of every true proposition must be a part of the subject (Gerhardt, ii. 52). Since this dictum applies to synthetic as well as to analytic propositions—or at any rate to propositions Kant regards as synthetic and which Leibniz would acknowledge to be contingent—, the manner in which concepts are "combined" in a Leibnizian subject must be different from the manner in which they are "combined" in the subject of one of Kant's judgments. Where the proposition involved is a contingent or synthetic one, let us call the first manner of combination 'Leibnizian combination', as opposed to 'Kantian combination'. The dilemma arises when we ask how one can tell, in a case where concepts are 'combined', whether the combination is Leibnizian or Kantian. The obvious answer is that the combination is Kantian if the judgment that might be framed from it is analytic. But this answer is not available to Kant, since it entails that we must know whether a proposition is analytic *before* we can apply the identity criterion or the containment criterion, and hence would make Kant's first two explanations of analyticity grossly circular.

Even if we knew the nature of this conceptual combination, the identity criterion would remain mysterious. *If* I conceive A as identical with BX, the judgment that all A are B is analytic. But how am I to know whether I *rightly* conceive A as identical with BX—that is, whether A *is* identical with BX? Such conceptual identity is by no means easy to understand, and nothing of Kant's which we have as yet examined throws any light upon the problem. The passage quoted above from *Fortschritte* throws this problem into even sharper relief; for Kant's insistence on the difference of analytic propositions from identical ones makes it perfectly plain that one can never have an adequate explanation of analyticity *just* in terms of identity, and hence that the heart of the problem is what the identity sign stands for in the symbolic representations, and how to tell whether or not a judgment can be "resolved into identity."

The third criterion of analyticity which we find in Kant is, or appears to be, a psychological one, in that whether a proposition is analytic or not depends upon how we think it.[14] We can already see a hint of this in the way in which Kant articulates the identity criterion, which emphasizes the way in which we think or conceive of the proposition, and Kant subsequently remarks that an analytic judgment is one in which "the subject is only divided into constituent concepts which were always conceived [thought] as existing within it, although confusedly" (B 11). This way of speaking surely makes it appear that whether a judgment is analytic or not depends upon the perspective or intention of the person making the judgment, and it would follow that a proposition might be analytic for one person and synthetic for another person.

One special obstacle to understanding these remarks is that Kant has elsewhere insisted (rightly) that general logic and psychology must be kept firmly separate, and in particular that matters of empirical psychology cannot bear upon matters of logic:

> There are therefore two rules which logicians must always bear in mind, in dealing with pure general logic:
>
> 1. As general logic, it . . . deals with nothing but the mere form of thought.
> 2. As pure logic, it has nothing to do with empirical principles, and does not, as has sometimes been supposed, borrow anything from psychology, which therefore has no influence whatever on the canon of the understanding (B 78).[15]

Hence what appears to be a psychological criterion for a general logical concept must simply be a manner of speaking.[16] As a manner of speaking this seeming psychology can no doubt be harmonized with the other criteria for the general logical distinction between analytic and synthetic propositions. But there is a suspicious ambiguity about the remarks, and in any case we are left without any satisfactory explanation of the term 'analytic'.

A fourth way in which Kant presents the distinction has to do

---

[14] Beck, SPK, 77ff., calls it "phenomenological."

[15] A point similar to that quoted from the *Critique* is made in the *Logik* (Einleitung i = Weischedel III.435).

[16] Or it could be a matter of transcendental logic rather than general logic, a possibility which it would be rewarding to explore but which I must pass by without further comment at this time. See, for instance, A 154.

with the manner in which one comes to know the proposition in question. "It would be absurd to found an analytic judgment on experience" (B 11). In framing an analytic proposition I do not need to "go outside" the subject-concept itself, according to Kant, for "I have already in the concept . . . all the conditions required for my judgment" (B 12). But in the case of a synthetic proposition I must go outside the subject-concept, either to experience or to "the unknown = X," in order to know that the predicate is connected with it. In the example which Kant gives, the proposition 'all bodies have weight', what one refers to beyond the concept of *body* is empirical evidence to the effect that there is a constant connection between the cases where the concept *body* is applicable and the applicability of the concept *weight* or of some scale of weights.

It should be noted that this explanation suffers from the same sort of ambiguity as the previous one: the question can be treated either psychologically or logically. If it is treated psychologically, one makes an empirical study of how it is that certain people arrive at certain beliefs, taking into account their experiences and other beliefs which they had at the beginning of the period in question. If one discusses the matter logically, the question of how the person has arrived at a belief is left aside, and the discussion centers instead on the question whether the belief is justified and what principles are required to make such justification explicit. Kant's statement of this epistemological criterion should certainly be read as logical rather than psychological and hence as equivalent to the familiar dictum that an analytic judgment must be justified a priori.

Still the matter is not easy to understand. If we admit that Kant's epistemological criterion has to do with justification rather than with the psychological side of knowing, we must then ask how in practice such justification is going to be given. Kant says (B 12) that the proposition that all bodies are impenetrable is analytic, whereas the proposition that all bodies have weight is synthetic. It is difficult to grasp and hold on to any firm difference in the way of knowing these two propositions; and some philosophers, among whom British idealists and contemporary American philosophers are prominent, maintain that the reason for the difficulty is that in the last analysis there is no difference to be grasped.[17] It would, for example, be plausible for someone to maintain that he didn't have to go beyond the concept of a body to know that all bodies have weight; he might insist that if some visual object could not be weighed, then it must be an illusion rather than a physical body. By refusing to apply the concept *body* where there was not an ability to assign some weight, even an indefinite one, he would be treating the judgment 'all bodies have weight', which Kant regards as synthetic, as analytic. On the other hand, it is also conceivable that a person should regard the concept of a body as requiring only that there be a certain figure, volume, and mass, and holding in addition that the fact that such physical bodies are often resistant to touch or to the intrusion of other physical bodies is a mere accident, for which we have a large amount of empirical evidence. Such a person would be treating this judgment, which Kant takes to be analytic, as synthetic. Nothing that Kant says makes it clear why these alternative perspectives are not legitimate. If they are legitimate, their legitimacy raises again the prospect that a proposition which is analytic for one person may not be analytic for another person.

Kant presents his fifth account of analyticity when he says that in order to determine whether a certain predicate is contained in the subject concept, "I have only to extract from it, in accordance with the principle of contradiction, the required predicate" (B 12). This reference to the principle of contradiction is very casual indeed, and is wholly omitted from the earlier version of this sec-

---

17 Edward Caird, for example, says that "all judgments are synthetic in the making and analytic when made" (*The Critical Philosophy of Kant* (Glasgow, 1889) Vol. 1, p. 269). N. Kemp Smith, in his *Commentary to Kant's "Critique of Pure Reason"* (London, 1918), argues:

There is little difficulty in detecting the synthetic character of the proposition: all bodies are heavy. Yet the reader has first been required to admit the analytic character of the proposition: all bodies are extended. The two propositions are really identical in logical character. Neither can be recognized as true save in terms of a comprehensive theory of physical existence [pp. 38-39].

Recent American work has tended to echo British Idealism on this point. See Morton G. White: "The Analytic and the Synthetic: An Untenable Dualism," in Sidney Hook (ed.), *John Dewey: Philosopher of Science and Freedom* (New York, 1950), pp. 316-330, reprinted in L. Linsky (ed.), *Semantics and the Philosophy of Language* (Urbana, 1952); and W. V. Quine: "Two Dogmas of Empiricism," *Philosophical Review* 40 (1951); reprinted in *From A Logical Point of View* (Cambridge, Mass. 1953), pp. 20-46.

tion (A 7-8). Nevertheless Kant explicitly says later on that the principle of contradiction is the "highest principle of all analytic judgments," and "the universal and completely sufficient *principle of all analytic knowledge*" (B 189-191).

One might be tempted to conjecture that Kant, in this later section, is putting forward a thesis about analytic propositions rather than explaining what they are, and that he refrained from putting any emphasis on the principle of contradiction in the earlier passage so as to ensure that his thesis would not be vacuous. Certainly it would be neater and more convincing to have the meaning of 'analytic' firmly tied down, in terms other than 'contradiction', before entering upon a discussion of the highest principle of analytic judgments. But Kant does not proceed in this manner. Instead he reformulates the principle of contradiction— "the proposition that no predicate contradictory of a thing (*Ding*) can belong to it" (B 190) —specially "in order that the nature of an analytic proposition be clearly expressed through it" (B 193). We are justified, then, in taking what Kant says in this regard as an elucidation of the meaning of 'analytic'.[18]

Explaining analyticity in terms of contradiction raises the hope, especially in the mind of a student trained in modern logic, that the idea will now become precise and clear. We might, for example, say that the epistemological criterion is to be applied in conjunction with the criterion based upon contradiction as follows: if I can know that the proposition 'all S is P' is true by showing that 'some S is not P' can be reduced to a substitution instance

---

[18] R. Robinson chastises Kant for *not* explaining the distinction between analytic and synthetic propositions in terms of contradiction: "This was the obvious way for Kant to explain his distinction between analytic and synthetic statements, because it would have shown where he stood with Leibniz, it would have been a clear and sharp distinction, and it would have been true" (*op. cit.*, 296). But Robinson's comment ignores the limited availability of Leibniz's logical doctrines and Kant's special reformulation of the principal of contradiction, as well as the fact that Kant did give *one* of his explanations in terms of contradiction.

H. W. Cassirer goes to the other extreme, suggesting that Kant does the whole job in terms of the principle of contradiction: "In Kant's opinion, analytic judgments exhibit one characteristic in virtue of which they are differentiated from every other kind of judgment, namely that the denial of their truth results in self-contradiction." *Kant's First Critique* (London, 1954), p. 110.

of the form 'P and not-p', the proposition is analytic; otherwise it is synthetic. Unfortunately such an interpretation does not fit Kant at all. Kant's formulation of the principle of contradiction— "that no predicate contradictory of a thing can belong to it" (B 190) —is itself a howler from a modern point of view, since it assumes contradiction to be a relation between things and predicates rather than a relation holding between propositions. Nor does the interpretation fit Kant's examples: following such a line it is very difficult to see how the judgment that all bodies have weight, or even the judgment that all bodies have volume, could ever be known to be analytic unless a definition were first supplied; whereas Kant, as Beck has pointed out (SPK 61-73), regards analytic judgments as more basic than definitions and prior to them. In view of the examples Kant gives of analytic and synthetic judgments, he must have in mind some notion of "conceptual contradiction," rather than one wholly based upon formal logic. Hence the explanation that analyticity is based upon the principle of contradiction does not remove the obscurity which surrounds Kant's concept.

There is a final explication of analyticity which can be constructed out of Kant's discussion of the role or function of the judgment in question. Kant says that an analytic judgment is illustrative or explicative, while a synthetic judgment is ampliative and therefore expresses a genuine bit of knowledge (B 11, 13-14; *Prolegomena* 2). In discourse, explication is often required in order to make clear what we mean: we must sharpen our linguistic tools so as to be able to work more efficiently at building a body of science. The propositions in which we set out such explications are analytic propositions. The object of our inquiry, however, will always be some matter of substance rather than mere explication of terms; and the matter of substance must be expressed in a proposition which is not explicative but ampliative. We may then distinguish between analytic and synthetic propositions according as the propositions enter into an inquiry simply to elucidate or stipulate how some term is to be used, or what some concept is to be regarded as "including." Propositions which do not have this explicative function, but which do enter into the inquiry in some other important way, will be synthetic rather than analytic.

But in spite of its plausibility this sixth explanation of Kant's conception of analyticity is very puzzling. The proposition that analytic propositions are explicative would seem on its face to be a thesis about analytic propositions—i.e. to be ampliative. But Kant does not seem to regard it as ampliative, since he does not give any reasons or evidence for it. Instead he assumes that any proposition we can call "analytic" will, as a matter of course, have an explicative function. Sometimes what is presented as obvious is a fact so commonplace that it would be merely tedious to elaborate or defend it; but in this case what is at issue is surprising rather than commonplace, for form and function rarely go hand-in-glove so neatly in linguistic matters. So the explicative function of analytic judgments must be obvious for Kant because having such a function is part of his conception of an analytic judgment. But, on the other hand, it is precisely because form and function are so different that it is hard to credit Kant with the view that having a certain function in discourse forms part of the same conception as that for which containment of the predicate in the subject is the chief criterion, since containment seems to be a matter of logical form.

3. Interpreting What Kant Said

We now have to try to understand what Kant meant. We have before us six alternative formulations of the distinction between analytic and synthetic judgments, as this distinction is presented to us by Kant. They are based respectively on: 1. containment, 2. identity, 3. psychology, 4. epistemology, 5. contradiction, 6. explication. There is no indication in what Kant has laid before us that he regards these alternative formulations as diverging in any way from one another; but we can hardly accept without careful consideration his apparent view that all six formulations are equivalent. Beck, for example, in his article in Kantstudien (op. cit.), has argued that "we have to suspect here a fundamental failure on Kant's part to distinguish the logical from the phenomenological aspects of thought" (171). He says further that "we can discern two criteria for analytic judgment" and that "Kant, in apparent disregard of their differences, uses first one and then the other as it suits his purpose" (171).

I shall follow Beck in regarding the six formulations of the distinction between the analytic and the synthetic as various verbalizations of two competing criteria of analyticity. I have already noted ambiguities in Kant's presentation, and it will be convenient now to make explicit the radically divergent aspects of his notion of analyticity. Beck sees the contrast as one between the logical and the phenomenological aspects of thought, but one might also see it as one between the form of a judgment and its function. Roughly, the first, second, and fifth of Kant's formulations of the idea of an analytic judgment seem to be based on the logical form of the judgment in question. The third, fourth, and sixth formulations, on the other hand, seem to be based on the way in which the judgment is related to the human beings who make it, or who may make it. The distinction intended is between those features of a judgment or statement which might be set out schematically by a logician, without consideration of the circumstances in which the judgment was made; and those features of a judgment or statement which require consideration of the intent or purpose of the speaker, and of the surrounding circumstances and the verbal context to the extent that they throw light on the purpose served (the intent expressed, or the role played) by the judgment or statement.

Starting from this recognition of two competing strains in Kant's notion of the analytic, two ways to interpret Kant suggest themselves. One might, on the one hand, suppose that Kant was proposing a formal, logical concept, and then explain Kant by offering a clear, precise formal definition, emphasizing the first, second, and fifth of Kant's explanations. On the other hand one might suppose that Kant's conception of the analytic was essentially phenomenological or functional, and that the formalism has to do merely with symbolizing analytic statements, not with their essential character. I want to propose an interpretation along the latter line, but I shall first consider the attempt to give a formal, logical defintion of 'analytic'.

Frege faced the lack of clarity and precision in Kant's discussion, and in order "to state accurately what earlier writers, Kant in particular, have meant" (GA 3n) [19] by the terms 'analytic' and 'synthetic', he offers the following definition:

---

[19] Citations beginning with 'GA' are to Frege's *Die Grundlagen der Arithmetik*, with a parallel English translation by J. L. Austin (Oxford, 1950).

The problem becomes, in fact, that of finding the proof of the proposition, and of following it up right back to the primitive truths. If, in carrying out this process, we come only on general logical laws and on definitions, then the truth is an analytic one, bearing in mind that we must take account also of all propositions upon which the admissibility of any of the definitions depends. If, however, it is impossible to give the proof without making use of truths which are not of a general logical nature, but belong to the sphere of some special science, then the proposition is a synthetic one [GA 4].

This defintion is admirable for its conciseness, its clarity, its continuity with Kant, and its harmony with recent advances in logic.

In Frege's discussion there is no question whether the epistemological considerations are a matter of psychology or a matter of logic. Frege has insisted that "we should separate the problem of how we arrive at the content of a judgment from the problem of how its assertion is to be justified" (GA 3), and his definition makes it clear that in determining whether a proposition is analytic it is only the logical question that counts. Thus he avoids one of the most troublesome ambiguities in Kant's discussion.

The expression 'general logical laws', upon which Frege's definition turns, does not occur in Kant's discussion of analytic judgments, and the connection between the two may not be immediately apparent. The thread which ties the two together is Kant's mention of the principle of contradiction as a criterion for determining whether a judgment is analytic (B 12). He also insists that the principle of contradiction "belongs only to logic" (B 190), and "must be recognized as being the universal and completely sufficient *principle of all analytic knowledge*" (B 191). It seems reasonable, therefore, to suppose that Kant would either regard the principle of contradiction as the only "general logical law," or else maintain that all "general logical laws" can be deduced from the principle of contradiction. Such a view belongs to a more traditional theory of logic from which Frege had broken away: Frege's propositional and functional logic is a form of modern symbolic logic in which the "principle of contradiction" no longer has a preeminent position. In modern symbolic logic all valid formulae can conveniently be regarded as having the same status; although certain "laws" are primitive in some systems, they may be derived in others, and thus their ultimate status cannot be different or more fundamental than that of other "general logical laws." The most obvious way for Frege to render Kant's distinction between the analytic and the synthetic serviceable within the framework of symbolic logic was to speak of "general logical laws" where Kant had spoken of "the principle of contradiction." And this is just what he did.

Frege's definition of 'analytic' provides a sharp and challenging presentation of the view that Kant's distinction is a matter of form. Its principal connection with Kant is via Kant's reference to the principle of contradiction, which belongs to the group of Kantian criteria which suggest a formal interpretation. General logical laws are based upon form alone, independent of any consideration of content or application; and by regarding a truth as analytic if it has a proof comprising only general logical laws and a limited sort of definitions, Frege has clarified and emphasized the formal aspect of Kant's distinction. It is also possible to account for some of Kant's more phenomenological remarks within the framework of Frege's interpretation. Logical proof is a matter of form, but it is also a way of knowing—that is, a way of ascertaining the cognitive acceptability of a string of symbols. Kant's epistemological criterion of analyticity can therefore be assimilated into Frege's interpretation, and the same may be true for Kant's other ways of explaining analytic judgments.

In spite of the clarity of Frege's definition of 'analytic', and the enormous influence it continues to exert through such philosophers as Russell, Carnap, Bergmann, and Richard Martin, there are sound reasons for not accepting it as an accurate account of what Kant meant. Two of these considerations are particularly powerful. The first is that Frege's definition of 'analytic' applies paradigmatically to logical formulae and tautologies, whereas Kant did not include formulae within the range of his notion and regarded tautologies as of marginal significance.[20] The second is that no Fregean conception of the analytic can have application to discourse in a natural language without relying on definitions, whereas Kant held that the relation between analytic truth and definition was quite the reverse, analytic truth being more fundamental

---

[20] See Section 1 above, and note 6.

than definition and prior to it.[21] A third point has to do with a radical divergence not in the framing of the notion of the analytic but in its application: all those who have espoused a Fregean definition of 'analytic' have held that laws of arithmetic are analytic, and some (e.g. Bergmann) have explicitly framed their definition in order to be able to hold this; whereas Kant maintained that mathematics, including arithmetic, provides the clearest example of synthetic a priori truth (B 14-17). A final tangential point is that Quine and White have shown the Fregean view of analytic truth to be seriously deficient,[22] and hence it would not do justice to Kant to interpret him as having intended it. I conclude, therefore, that the admirably clear concept of analytic truth put forward by Frege and refined by his successors, according to which 'analytic' is defined in terms of general laws of logic, is radically different from Kant's,[23] and I shall say no more about it.

A phenomenological or functional interpretation of Kant's conception of the distinction between the analytic and the synthetic— i.e. an interpretation which sees the distinction as turning on the job done in discourse by the judgment or statement in question, or on the role played by it—must begin by taking seriously what Frege left out of account, namely Kant's third, fourth, and sixth explanations of what an analytic judgment is. These explanations are based on phenomenological considerations and on whether the statement made is explicative or ampliative. Two paths of reinterpretation therefore suggest themselves, and both have been trod. The one lies in defining analyticity in terms of how the relation of concepts is conceived, or how a statement is intended, and is exemplified in C. I. Lewis' explanation of analytic truth in

---

21 See Beck's article cited in note 13.

22 See the articles cited in note 16.

23 The same conclusion is stated more sharply by Beth, albeit on somewhat different grounds:

Eine geradezu entgegengesetzte Haltung ist kennzeichend für diejenigen Philosophen [a note cites Bolzano, Frege, Heymans, Couturat, Schlick, Carnap, von Aster, and Scholz.—N.G.], welche Kants Lehren und namentlich seinen Ansichten über die Grundlagen der Mathematik kritisch gegenüberstehen. Dieser Denker geben Begriffsbestimmungen, welche die von Frege gegebene typische repräsentiert werden. . . . Diese Bergriffsbestimmung hat jedenfalls den Vorzug der Schärfe, sie hat jedoch . . . mit Kants Absichten nichts gemein und liefert daher auch keine Grundlagen für eine Deutung und Wertung Kants Ansichten [op. cit., p. 254].

terms of experiments in the mind.[24] Lewis' work is familiar, commanding, and has many merits as a contemporary restatement of Kant's idea of analytic truth. I wish to turn my attention to the other path, which lies in explaining analytic statements in terms of the role or function those statements play in discourse. Wittgenstein referred to such a distinguishable use of expressions as a "language-game" (PI, I. 23).[25] I propose to assume that making analytic statements is one such language-game and to inquire what the characteristics of this language-game are, other than the central one that statements used in this way are explicative. I shall also argue that what Kant calls an analytic judgment is the same thing as what Wittgenstein calls a grammatical proposition. This comparison is suggested by the fact that in an important passage where Wittgenstein introduces the idea of a grammatical proposition (PI, I. 247-252) he raises a question about the standing of Kant's paradigm, that a body is extended. The deeper reasons for proposing that grammar and analyticity are the same will become apparent as we consider what it means to say that analytic judgments are explicative.

4. *The Explicative Function of Analytic Statements*

We can, unfortunately, get only the barest hints from Kant himself about the explicative function of analytic judgments. He says that analytic judgments may be called explicative because they "add nothing through the predicate to the concept of the subject, but merely break it up into those constituent concepts that have all along been thought in it" (B 11), and that such judgments "are very important, and indeed necessary, but only for obtaining that clearness in the concepts which is requisite for such a sure and wide synthesis as will lead to a genuinely new addition to all previous knowledge" (B 13f). Meager though it is, we shall have to follow the lead that is given in these brief remarks. Analytic judgments serve primarily for obtaining clarity in concepts, and for this purpose Kant says that they are "very important, and indeed neces-

---

24 C. I. Lewis: *An Analysis of Knowledge and Valuation* (La Salle, 1946), p. 251; see also Book I, *passim.*

25 L. Wittgenstein: *Philosophical Investigations* (Oxford, 1953). Parenthetical citations indicate Part I or Part II and the section within each part.

sary" (B 13) . It seems reasonable to ask what this clarity consists in, and why and for whom it is important and necessary.

Whom might such a clarification serve, and in what circumstances? In answer to the first part of the question, Kant suggests in the first edition that "the concept which I already have is . . . made intelligible to me" (A 8) , and in connection with the second part he says that the time for analytic judgments is when we wish to prepare the way for a "genuinely new addition to all previous knowledge" (B 14) . Both these points deserve examination.

If I have a firm grasp on the concept *body*—that is, if I know all the rules of language pertaining to the word 'body'—, then I am in a position to know that the judgment *all bodies are extended* is analytic. Kant says that then "the concept which I already have is . . . made intelligible to me" (A 8) , but it is difficult to see how this could happen. If I have the concept, it must *already* be intelligible to me, and cannot be *made* intelligible by the analytic judgment. A concept can only be made intelligible to me by an analytic proposition if I have at most a vague understanding of it and am in particular uncertain about that aspect of the concept which is made explicit in the analytic proposition. But if I have such a vague and uncertain understanding of the concept, I can hardly be in a position to warrant the proffered judgment as truly analytic. Thus, on the view Kant suggests, analytic judgments are useless when they are possible and impossible when they are useful. Perhaps Kant himself saw this absurdity, for he dropped the passage at hand from the second edition of the *Critique*.

An analytic judgment which I make might conceivably be useful me personally, but a more typical case would be one where an analytic proposition is "important and indeed necessary" to some *other* person. This might be the case where you and I are discussing a problem and it becomes clear, either through my own admission or through my making clumsy or absurd remarks, that I have at best only a vague understanding of some expression you use. You may then make one or more analytic statements in order to clarify the expression for me. It is in this manner that an analytic proposition typically serves to convey to an uncertain reader or listener the clear understanding which the writer or speaker has of a concept.

When Kant said that analytic judgments help prepare the way

for "a genuinely new addition to all previous knowledge" (B 14), he must have had a scientific context in mind; for it is only in science that we can be sure of having a genuine addition to knowledge. Analytic propositions are important and necessary in such contexts because they enable scientists to explain to one another how they understand the concepts and terms which they use. For example, one might use the sentence 'An acid is a proton donor' to make an analytic statement, and thereby explain the term 'acid'—at the same time (what is the same thing) conveying that proton donation is to be regarded as an *essential* property, or *Merkmal*, of acids. There is no reason to doubt that such elucidatory remarks occur in conversations among scientists; but they must be far more important, and indeed indispensable, in the education of scientists, where young apprentices are initiated into the 'language' and vocabulary of the discipline.

It cannot be, however, that only scientists take advantage of this useful device. It would have been reasonable for Kant to be thinking primarily in terms of the advance of science when he propounded the distinction between the analytic and the synthetic, since he was then writing a book on the theory of knowledge. But many categorical judgments are made outside of any scientific context, and they too must fall under Kant's distinction. I can see no reason why analytic judgments should not be made "for obtaining that clearness in the concepts" which is requisite for an accurate moral appraisal, or a sensitive aesthetic evaluation, or a sound legal decision—in general, a reliable judgment in any walk of life. It seems likely that analytic propositions, grammatical remarks, have a special importance in moral discourse because of the common tendency to lose sight of the logic of moral concepts in the press of a difficult or dangerous predicament (cf. the opening third of Plato's *Crito*). And in all these other fields of endeavor, as in science, a large part of the employ for analytic propositions will be found in explaining technicalities and subtleties of the special "language" to laymen, and in training apprentices in the "language game" of the discipline.

These thoughts about whom an analytic judgment might serve, and in what circumstances it might do so, help to reinforce the suggestion that an analytic judgment is basically "grammatical" in Wittgenstein's sense, and this suggestion is reinforced when we examine the character of the clarification that is achieved through an analytic statement.

According to Kant the proposition *All bodies are extended* is analytic. The concepts involved in this proposition are those of *body* and *extension,* but it is clear from Kant's discussion he is primarily concerned with the concept *body,* for he refers to extension as a "character" [Merkmal] of the concept *body,* and he mentions in the same breath that figure and impenetrability are also characters of the concept *body* and bear the same sort of analytic relationship to it (B 12). In this case, therefore, it is the concept of a body which is clarified by the analytic judgment.

What is the nature of such clarification? One feature of it is that it relates the concept being clarified to another concept, namely that of being extended.[26] Another feature is that it presents us with, or makes clear, a rule pertaining to the use of the word 'body'—namely that if anything is to be called a 'body' it must be extended; or, that if it can be called a 'body' then it can also be called 'extended'. A third feature is that this rule about the use of the word 'body' has to do with the inference possibilities pertaining to that word, and not with its morphological and syntactic possibilities. A fourth and most important feature is that the inference possibilities presented in an analytic judgment, unlike those which may be construed in a synthetic judgment, require no justification: they can neither be confirmed by experience nor deduced from primitive truths, and hence may be called 'immediate'. Kant is explicit about this last feature when he says about analytic judgments generally that "in framing the judgment I must not go outside my concept" (B 11). We may then summarize briefly by saying that the clarification achieved through analytic propositions consists in presenting immediate inference possibilities pertaining to some word which expresses the concept that is being clarified.

It is worth reflecting on the fourth feature, that the analytic judgment requires no justification. If someone were to demand justification for my statement that all bodies are extended, I could

---

26 I follow Paton's note on characters, such as being extended, which takes the view that they are themselves concepts: "*'Merkmale'*. These may be taken as 'partial' concepts which together constitute the whole concept" (KME 84).

only say that that is the way the word 'body' is used, or (if he still protested) that that is the sense in which I should like to use the word. Such a response does not meet the demand for justification, but rather rejects it as an illegitimate demand. This rejection is accomplished by shifting the focus of the discussion: the original judgment is about bodies; whereas my response is not about bodies but about the word 'body', or the concept *body*. But the response is an apt one, even though it does not meet the demand for justification; for it not only fails to meet the demand but also indicates why the demand for justification cannot be met. Indeed, the very fact that such a response is apt shows that, when a statement is warranted just by the way we use its constituent words (or just by what its subject concept "contains") , it is inappropriate to ask that the statement construed as a statement about bodies be justified. We may, of course, be able to give some sort of justification for the remark we make about 'body', even though we cannot do so for our statement about bodies; but even here it is important to note that we need not be able to. As Wittgenstein puts it:

> If I have exhausted the justifications I have reached bedrock, and my spade is turned. Then I am inclined to say: "This is simply what I do" [PI, I. 217].
> When I obey a rule, I do not choose. I obey the rule *blindly* [PI, I. 219].

Though this is important, it should not be surprising: since the clarification achieved by an analytic proposition consists in presenting inference rules pertaining to the concept or the term in question, it is entirely reasonable that the only warrant required for such propositions should be how the concept or word is in fact employed.

Since the analytic proposition *All bodies are extended* serves to clarify the concept *body* by presenting a certain rule pertaining to the use of the word 'body', and since the only relevant warrant for it *qua* analytic proposition is the actual or stipulated use of the word 'body', we may say that *in this sense* this analytic proposition is not "really" about physical bodies but about the concept *body* or the word 'body'. But there is no sharp dichotomy between judgments "about bodies themselves" and remarks about the concept *body* or about the use of the word 'body'. A statement that is "about bodies themselves" will presumably set forth some *essential* characteristic of bodies, rather than a contingent or accidental feature. If this characteristic is really essential, there must be an associated rule pertaining to the use of the word 'body' which prohibits this characteristic being denied even implicitly of anything that is called a 'body'. If this rule were known and could be accurately stated, its statement would presumably settle the same doubts as the original statement 'about bodies themselves'. *"Essence,"* says Wittgenstein, "is expressed by grammar" (PI, I. 371), and hence facts "about bodies themselves" can be expressed in terms of the "logical grammar" of the word 'body'. But there is also the correlative point that "Grammar tells us what kind of object anything is" (PI I. 373); and hence certain "grammatical" remarks about the word 'body' can tell us something "about bodies themselves."

If analytic propositions are about words and present a certain sort of rule pertaining to the use of those words, it is reasonable to say that an analytic proposition is a kind of grammatical remark, and that the clarification it achieves explains a part of the grammar of the language.[27] Grammar is a descriptive discipline (PI I. 496), the aim of which is to characterize a language by stating rules for the use of various sorts of linguistic expressions, the empirical accuracy of such a description being determined by whether a person would have to follow such rules in practice in order to speak the language competently. In a narrow sense only rules of morphology and syntax count as rules of grammar, but in the broader sense intended here rules pertaining to phonology and to entailments and incompatibilities may be included too, since following them in practice is obviously necessary for having a command of the language. Analytic truths express rules of this last sort, just as do what Wittgenstein called "grammatical" remarks. Wittgenstein can therefore be read as representing in a new way what Kant rather cryptically referred to as the explicative role of analytic judgments.

---

[27] Compare H. Wang, "Notes on the Analytic-Synthetic Distinction," *Theoria* **21** (1955), 158-178; and J. M. E. Moravcsik, "The Analytic and the Nonempirical," *Journal of Philosophy* **42** (1965), 415-429. Both consider favorably the suggestion that a strong linguistic conception of grammar may suffice to give an account of at least some analytic statements.

I have so far based my interpretation of Kant on the last of the six accounts of the analytic-synthetic distinction which we earlier identified, and have tried to characterize making analytic statements as a particular language-game. It is impossible to deny that Kant's remarks on this subject are thoroughly ambiguous, in that they lend themselves to alternative interpretations; and hence that Frege's formal reconstruction of what Kant meant has a certain plausibility, and so has Lewis' way of explaining analyticity. At the same time one may insist that the view that making analytic remarks constitutes a distinctive language-game is easily compatible with all that Kant has said about the analytic and the synthetic. Indeed, at least one of his accounts becomes more readily intelligible on this interpretation.

Kant gave one exposition which appeared to be psychological, in that "the connection of the subject to the predicate is thought through identity" (B 10) and the predicate was "always conceived as existing within [the subject], although confusedly" (B 11). The two difficulties we had with these passages were that the idioms Kant uses are unfamiliar in both German and English, and that Kant has elsewhere (e.g. B 78) insisted that empirical psychology has nothing to do with general logic. But on the view that an analytic judgment functions as a kind of grammatical remark, in that it sets forth some inference possibilities pertaining to a word or phrase, these passages cease to be embarrassing. The connection between the subject and the predicate that is under consideration is not the result of the association of ideas, nor of any other empirical law, but is rather "thought all along" in the sense it depends upon and is required by certain rules for using the subject expression. And prior to the articulation or the acceptance of the analytic proposition, the connection may be thought "confusedly" in that the relevant rules are followed in practice without ever being formulated. Thus it is not empirical psychology which bears upon general logic, but some special sort of grammar.

Thinking along these same lines, it is easy to see that the famous containment criterion of analyticity lends itself to functional interpretation, for the predicate will be "contained in" the subject whenever it is "always conceived as existing within it" because of some rule, recognized in practice, for using the subject term. The account based on containment is one of those which has lent

weight to a formal interpretation of Kant's conception of an analytic judgment, and the association of this account with those based
on identity and contradiction shows that there will be no difficulty
applying what we said to these accounts. Indeed, we are now able
to make better sense of Kant's special and puzzling formulation of
the principle of contradiction, "that no predicate contradictory
of a thing can belong to it" (B 190). Following out the lines of our
interpretation of Kant's notion, a predicate may be said to be "contradictory of a thing" when it is a logical contrary or the logical
contradictory of a *Merkmal* of the thing, i.e. of a predicate attributed to the thing by a judgment which serves merely to clarify our
concept of the thing (cf. B 190f). Since such a judgment is the
very sort that Kant calls "analytic," this special formulation of the
principle of contradiction, however untidy it may be from the
standpoint of modern formal logic, does appear particularly congenial to Kant's conception of analytic judgment. Kant's remaining
account of analytic judgment, based on how we know, offers no
special difficulties, since it merely expresses that every analytic truth
is a priori.

5. *Some Consequences*

It remains to inquire how an interpretation such as I have been
urging affects the application of Kant's concept. I shall limit myself
to three points: that a proposition can no longer be assigned a definitive status as either analytic or synthetic, that the attacks of
White and Quine (*op. cit.*) cannot be effective against such a conception of the analytic, and that mathematics is synthetic.

Rules of language undergo change, and therefore a statement
that, at one time, is warranted simply by virtue of rules of language
may admit of empirical evidence at an earlier or a later time. There
are two reasons for this. The first is that grammar differs from logic
in that it is descriptive rather than normative (PI I. 81-124, 496),
and hence it lacks logic's ability to guarantee in advance that there
will not be changes in its rules and relevant changes are particularly apparent in the case of scientific terms (cf. PI I. 79). In addition to such changes in rules of grammar there are also variations
in the assumptions and guidelines that govern different moments
of discourse, and these variations are reflected in a fluctuation in

what counts as explicative: a statement which is explicative to one person may be ampliative to a second and gibberish to a third. Hence the view that analytic statements are explicative or grammatical entails that analyticity is relative to certain conditions and circumtances and that there may be a fluctuation between the analytic and the synthetic.

A conception of the analytic which makes analyticity relative and variable helps to stem the attacks of White and Quine on the analytic-synthetic distinction, but White argues against a variable distinction as well as a static one. Immunity from their attacks depends rather on the fact that analytic statements, as I have explained them, are not truth-claims at all but explications. What they attack is the thesis that there is a fundamental cleavage in the realm of truth-claims rather than a cleavage between truth-claims and explicative remarks. Quine, for example, says that what he rejects is "a belief in some fundamental cleavage between truths which are *analytic,* or grounded in meanings independently of matters of fact, and truths which are *synthetic,* or grounded in fact" (20). But what Kant was proposing, if I am right, was not a "fundamental distinction between truths." It was a distinction relative to context rather than an absolute one, and one between language-games rather than truths. The shoe, therefore, does not fit—and the reading I have given to Kant in fact seems quite congenial to the pragmatism Quine espouses in his essay. Similarly, White's attack is against a "dualism" in the realm of truths, and no such dualism follows from Kant's doctrine if we interpret him as distinguishing two roles which statements can play in discourse and reasoning.

There remains the matter of mathematics. Kant discusses the importance for his own philosophy of his distinction between analytic and synthetic judgment in *Fortschritte,* where he says that it constitutes the first step forward in metaphysics since the time of Leibniz and Wolff (XX. 265 = R 23). Its importance lay in the fact that it permitted Kant to ask for the first time how there can be synthetic a priori judgments, which question led to Kant's transcendental philosophy (XX. 265f, 323 = R 22ff, 177f). Mathematics provided Kant the most obvious case of synthetic a priori knowledge (B 14-17), and it seems reasonable, therefore, that an account of analytic judgments which claims faithfulness to Kant should preserve Kant's findings that all mathematical judgments are synthetic. We have noted that a Fregean conception of the analytic is invariably associated with the thesis that arithmetic is analytic, and in this way departs radically from Kant on a crucial point.[28] My functional account of the analytic, on the other hand, preserves the force and plausibility of Kant's insistence that mathematics is synthetic. In mathematics, as in any other discipline, there is a difference between definitions and explicative remarks on the one hand and axioms and results on the other—and this is true not only in arithmetic and geometry but in newer forms of algebra such as mathematical logic. Analytic propositions occur in mathematics, for it is necessary to clarify concepts and explain operations, and to do so carefully and exactly, if these concepts and operations are to be employed in investigating mathematical problems. But mathematical judgments themselves are, on a functional account, synthetic rather than analytic: they report results that are obtained by using mathematical concepts and operations. If a mathematician has understood the problem or question he has posed himself, he is not in need of any further clarifications or explicative remarks: what he is looking for is not an explanation of the question but an answer to the question. This is a very simple and obvious fact about mathematical research, and one that is independent of the question whether anything other than general logical laws are needed to prove mathematical truths. If, therefore, Kant intended his distinction between analytic and synthetic judgments to be based on the function or role a judgment serves in a conversation or in the course of an investigation, he was clearly justified in asserting confidently that all mathematical judgments are synthetic.[29]

---

28 In Frege's case one may note a suspicion that his difference with Kant may have been terminological:

[T]he more fruitful type of definition is a matter of drawing boundary lines that were not previously given at all. What we shall be able to infer from it, cannot be inspected in advance; here we are not simply taking out of the box what we have just put into it. The conclusions we draw from it extend our knowledge, and ought, therefore, on Kant's view, to be synthetic; and yet they can be proved by purely logical means, and thus analytic [GA 100f].

29 Compare Jaakko Hintikka, "Are Logical Truths Analytic?," *Philosophical Review* 74 (1965), 178-203, and Erik Stenius, "Are True Numerical Statements Analytic or Synthetic?," *ibid.*, 357-372. Both Hintikka and Stenius agree that some

6. *Summary*

Some sort of functional interpretation of Kant's distinction thus appears to be viable. The crux of such a view is that the distinction to be drawn is between different ways in which statements or propositions function in discourse, rather than between different logical forms which propositions may exemplify; and that the function of an analytic judgment is to explicate its subject concept by presenting certain linguistic rules. Because of their function, analytic propositions might be called 'grammatical', although there may be some stretching of the term in doing so.[30] According to this interpretation of Kant's famous distinction, the criterion of analyticity lies in the way in which the judgment is related to the human beings who make it, or who may make it. More specifically, what an analytic remark does is to clarify a concept by presenting immediate inference possibilities pertaining to some word or phrase which expresses the concept that is being clarified. Because an analytic statement presents a rule governing the use of some word or phrase, analytic judgments are a matter of grammar, and they are equally about words and about things themselves. Although much remains to be clarified about the nature of grammar and of rules of language, to look upon making analytic statements as a distinctive language-game, and upon analytic statements as different from synthetic statements in the same way that explications differ from truth-claims, helps to appreciate the soundness of some of Kant's puzzling or unappreciated remarks. There certainly are other concepts of analyticity than Kant's, but his is more relevant to contemporary discussions than one might have thought.

STATE UNIVERSITY OF NEW YORK AT BUFFALO

NEWTON GARVER

---

arithmetical and numerical truths are synthetic in some sense and both defend Kant's intuitions on this point. But their explications differ not only from mine but also from one another, and they both further argue that there is also a sense in which these (same?) truths are analytic.

[30] It might even be advisable to say that the propositions distinguished by having an explicative function are grammatical, since the other distinction, based on logical form, is admirably clear, clearly different from Kant's, and widely referred to as the distinction between the analytic and the synthetic; but it does not seem worthwhile to dispute about which concept is most deserving of being called that of 'analytic' propositions.

APPEARING AND APPEARANCES IN KANT

In recent writing on the theory of knowledge a distinction has been drawn between 'the language of appearing' and 'the sense-datum language' (or 'the language of appearances', as we may more loosely call it). The aim of this paper is to suggest that consideration of that distinction and of what Kant's attitude toward it would have been can shed light on two otherwise-puzzling aspects of his doctrine in the *Critique of Pure Reason*: his adamant conviction that there are things-in-themselves, and his confidence that the Antinomies are resolved once we admit the transcendental ideality of space and time.

I

In describing perceptual situations, a group of verbs are used including 'perceive', 'sense', 'intuit', 'see', 'hear', and many others. If there are different and conflicting ways in which this family of verbs are used in philosophical writing or in normal talk, that fact could be of philosophical significance, and consideration of it might well help to clarify some philosophical discussions, especially in cases in the history of philosophy where little explicit attention has been paid to such distinctions. Now, some recent philosophers, especially Ayer[1] and Chisholm,[2] have urged that there is a philosophically noteworthy distinction to be drawn between two different and conflicting ways in which this group of verbs are used. One way of speaking has been called the language of appearing (or, less felicitously, the terminology of appearing), and the other may be called the language of appearances (or of sense data). Let us review this distinction, not in order to evaluate its validity or

---

[1] A. J. Ayer, *The Foundations of Empirical Knowledge* (London, 1940), Chap. I, sec. 3.

[2] Roderick M. Chisholm, "The Theory of Appearing," *Philosophical Analysis*, ed. Max Black (Englewood Cliffs, N. J., 1950).

significance for contemporary philosophy, but only with a view to seeing whether it can illuminate Kant's way of thinking. For this purpose, it is not necessary to express the distinction with perfect clarity, even if that be possible; it will suffice to explain it in a way that would have seemed plausible to philosophers of the past.

According to the first of these two ways of speaking about perceptual situations, that someone perceives or sees a thing entails that the thing exists and is not merely in his mind. It would be self-contradictory, if we are using perceptual verbs in this first way, to speak of perceiving or seeing what does not exist outside the mind. For example, saying in this sense that a man perceives or sees a green oasis would involve claiming that there exists a non-mental oasis that he is aware of. A man who encounters what is merely a mirage may perhaps think that he is perceiving a green oasis, but he will be mistaken if he thinks so; since what he thinks he is perceiving does not exist, he does not perceive an oasis, according to this way of speaking. Instead, his situation can be described by saying that what he perceives (perhaps it is part of the sky) *appears* to him to be an oasis. If we want to give a description of what a man in such a situation is entitled to feel sure of, it would not be that he is perceiving an oasis, but rather that what he perceives appears to him to be an oasis. Because the notion of appearing plays this central role in it, this whole way of speaking may conveniently be called the language of appearing.

According to this language of appearing, when perceptual situations are being truly described, perceptual verbs that have grammatical direct objects always must have as direct objects words referring to things that exist outside the mind. Thus the terminology of appearing is apt for expressing the view that in perception we are "directly acquainted" with things outside our minds; that is, that such things are what we perceive, sense, see, hear, and feel; and that they are what is given to us and what appear to us.

If we wish to extend further our characterization of the language of appearing, we may also take account of descriptions of perceptual situations where perceptual verbs are followed by 'that'-clauses, as when we say a man perceives or sees that an oasis is green. According to the language of appearing, the man can perceive or see that the oasis is green only if it is green. And in general someone can perceive, sense, see, etc., that S is P only if S is P.

But the oasis can appear to someone to be green even when it is not; and even if there is no oasis, something can appear to someone to be an oasis and to be green. So again the notion of appearing can be used if we wish to express what it is that someone in such a perceptual situation is entitled to be sure of.

In contrast with this language of appearing, there is another way of using perceptual verbs. According to this second usage, to say that someone perceives a certain kind of thing is not to say that outside his mind there exists such a thing. Instead, it is only to say something about what goes on inside the mind. According to this way of speaking, someone perceives or sees an oasis whenever he has perceptual experience which to him is as of an oasis. Encountering a mirage which looks like an oasis can involve such an experience, so a person who encounters what is merely a mirage may, in this second sense, perceive or see an oasis. To establish that there was no oasis then is not to refute the claim that an oasis was perceived, when the claim is understood in this sense. Moreover, someone might in this second sense perceive or see that an oasis was green even though there was no oasis that was green; one can perceive that S is P even when it is not the case that there is an S that is P. The statement about what he perceived or saw thus merely describes his experience from the inside, as it were.

According to this second way of speaking, when perceptual situations are being truly described, perceptual verbs that have direct objects may have for their objects words referring to mental entities such as perceptions, sensations, ideas, impressions, sense data, appearances, or representations. If we ask what was seen by the man who encountered a mere mirage, it may seem awkward to answer "Nothing," for we do want to say that he was seeing, in this second sense—and where there is seeing one feels a tendency to expect that something must be seen. The answer to the question, if there is an answer, will be that he saw something mental in his own mind: a green-oasis appearance, or a green-oasis sense datum. Thus, this way of speaking is apt for expressing the view that we are not 'directly acquainted' with nonmental things, and that it is appearances or sense data with which we are directly acquainted: that these are what we perceive and what are given to us.

To what extent are these two languages equivalent? It is clear that over a wide range of ordinary perceptual situations, most of the descriptions that we might want to give using one of these ways of speaking could equally well be expressed in terms of the other way of speaking. When a man encounters a mirage, we can describe his perceptual situation either by saying in the language of appearing that he perceives something (say, part of the sky) which appears to him to be an oasis, though it is not; or by saying in the language of appearances that though what he perceives is an oasis-appearance, it is merely an appearance in his mind and corresponds to no oasis outside his mind. Either description will do, and for many ordinary cases there seems to be nothing to choose between the two ways of speaking. And because it thus seems easy in many ordinary cases to translate back and forth between the two ways of speaking, one may well be tempted to conclude that there is essentially nothing to choose between them. If this is so, then there is no reason why one should not feel free to speak whichever way one pleases, and even to speak sometimes in one way and sometimes in the other.

This idea of the equal legitimacy of the two languages and of their complete intertranslatability is an attractive idea. Its attractiveness is attested to by the fact that Ayer embraced the idea. He professed to find that the terminology of appearing and the terminology of sense data (as he called them) are on an equal footing, simply two alternative languages, and that it is not meaningful to ask which is more correct.[3] He himself elected to use the sense-datum terminology, holding that in some respects it is more convenient. But he maintained that this was merely an arbitrary verbal decision on his part.[4]

However, in philosophical discussions of perception it becomes more dubious that there is this intertranslatability of the two ways of speaking. Perhaps one can imagine a philosopher using these two languages in a carefully coordinated way, so that whenever he said anything about perception using the language of appearing he made clear how it was equivalent for him to something that could be said in the language of appearances, and whenever he said anything about perception using the language of ap-

---

[3] *Loc. cit.*

[4] This claim, along with much else in Ayer's account, has been subjected to trenchant criticism by J. L. Austin in his *Sense and Sensibilia* (Oxford, 1962).

pearances he made clear how it was equivalent for him to something that could be said using the language of appearing. Presumably Ayer thought that he was doing this in his *Foundations of Empirical Knowledge,* though after his first chapter he makes little or no effort to indicate how such translations could proceed. But in any case it certainly is no foregone conclusion that everything philosophers have said about perception using one of these languages can readily and clearly be translated into the other language. Indeed, most philosophers seem to have felt that one of these ways of speaking was more correct than the other.

Some philosophers have believed that what we strictly speaking perceive, see, sense, etc., are always things independent of the mind, rather than appearances of such things or sense data they engender in us. They would hold that the language of appearing is therefore the fundamentally correct way of speaking about perceptual situations. The language of appearances, from their point of view, if permissable at all is so only insofar as it is translatable into the language of appearing. This philosophical viewpoint may be called the theory of appearing. To use the language of appearing is not necessarily to commit oneself to the theory of appearing; but to embrace the theory of appearing is to commit oneself to the language of appearing.

Some other philosophers have believed that what we strictly speaking perceive, see, sense, etc., are never things independent of the mind but always are appearances of them in our minds or sense data in our minds engendered by them. These philosophers would hold that the language of appearances (or of sense data, or of ideas, etc.) is the fundamentally correct way of speaking about perceptual situations. From their point of view, the language of appearing, if permissable at all, is so only insofar as it is translatable into the terminology of appearances. This philosophical viewpoint may be called the theory of appearances. To use the language of appearances is not necessarily to commit oneself to the theory of appearances; but to embrace the theory of appearances is to commit oneself to the language of appearances.

Philosophers who embrace the theory of appearing are not likely to feel that solipsism presents any serious challenge to their position. We are not cognitively confined to a private mental world, from which escape is next to impossible, and solipsism is no threat, according to the theory of appearing. For according to it, what we are directly aware of are mind-independent things. To have perceptual experience is to be in cognitive contact with an external world. Doubtless things do not always appear to us as they really are, but at any rate there can be no room for doubt that things do appear to us. Thus solipsism can immediately be refuted, according to this viewpoint.

The theory of appearances embodies a sharp contrast, a bifurcation, between the mental appearances, with which alone one is supposed to be directly acquainted, and the things outside one's mind, with which one is supposed never to be directly acquainted. The theory is that the latter things are not perceived, sensed, seen, etc., and this of course makes it difficult to explain how anything definite can be known about them, even that they exist. Philosophers holding to this theory must maintain that if one knows anything definite about the nature or existence of things outside the mind, this knowledge must be inferential. Some sort of argument by analogy is required, reasoning from premises about the observed character of what is within the mind to a conjectural conclusion about what is outside it. However, any such inference is logically questionable, so the theory is haunted by the specter of solipsism.

Someone who wanted to hold, as Ayer did, that the language of appearing and the language of appearances are perfectly intertranslatable, would have to maintain that there is no real conflict between the theory of appearing and the theory of appearances. But now, what is such a person to say of the question whether solipsism is easy or difficult to refute? Should he say that the theory of appearances confronts itself with a mere pseudo-problem, on the ground that we have only to translate our remarks into the language of appearing in order easily to refute solipsism? Or should he say that the theory of appearing carelessly overlooks a real problem, for we have only to translate our remarks into the language of appearances in order to see that solipsism is difficult to refute? Neither way of looking at the matter is plausible. The claim that the two languages are fully intertranslatable is not compatible with there being a problem stateable in one language but not in the other. The claim that the two languages are fully intertranslatable is based on consideration of many ordinary descriptions that are given of perceptual situations, and one can feel the attractiveness of this claim. But if we take into consideration the kind of things that philosophers have been especially interested in saying about perceptual situations, then the claim of intertranslatability breaks down.

II

Let us turn now to the philosophy of Kant and consider where he stood on this matter. Did Kant embrace the theory of appearing or the theory of appearances? If Kant held the theory of appearing, then we should expect to find him saying that we sense things-in-themselves; that they are what we intuit, perceive, experience, etc.; that they are given to us. We should expect to find him saying that although we are aware of and know about things-in-themselves only as they appear to us and not as they are in themselves, nevertheless it is things-in-themselves that we are aware of and know about. On the other hand, if Kant held to the theory of appearances, then we should expect to find him saying that we sense appearances or representations, not things-in-themselves. We should expect to find him saying that appearances are what we intuit, perceive, and experience; that they are given to us.

Kant does often speak in the language of appearances. He says that appearances are given to us,[5] that they are given to us in intuition,[6] that what is first given to us is appearance,[7] and that "What the objects may be in themselves would never become known to us even through the most enlightened knowledge of that which is alone given to us, namely their appearance."[8] Also, he speaks of appearances as objects of perception.[9] All these remarks embody the language of appearances.

Yet also Kant often speaks in ways that do not jibe with the language of appearances. He says that our sense representation

---

[5] *Prolegomena*, Academy edition, Vol. IV, p. 290.

[6] *Critique of Pure Reason*, A 90.

[7] A 120.

[8] A 43.

[9] B 207.

is the way things-in-themselves appear to us.[10] He says that "the things which we intuit are not in themselves what we intuit them as being . . . we know nothing but our mode of perceiving them."[11] He says that intuition takes place only insofar as the object—here surely the thing-in-itself—is given and the mind affected by it.[12] And he says that in inner sense the mind intuits itself—meaning surely that what is intuited is a thing-in-itself.[13] These remarks embody the language of appearing.

The wealth of quotations that can be cited to illustrate Kant's use of each of these two languages shows that Kant speaks both these languages and does not distinguish between them. Indeed, sometimes we find both ways of speaking side by side in a single one of his sentences. Thus he says that things as objects of our senses existing outside us are given, but we know only their appearances, that is, the representations which they cause in us.[14] And he says that space can be ascribed to things only insofar as they appear to us, that is, only to objects of sensibility.[15] In both these sentences of Kant's the language of appearing and the language of appearance are used side by side, clearly indicating that Kant did not recognize any need to distinguish them. As Prichard put it, Kant makes "a transition from 'things as appearing' to 'appearances' . . . it is clear that Kant is not aware of the transition, but considers the expressions equivalent, or, in other words, fails to distinguish them."[16]

Kant's alternating so freely between these two ways of speaking strongly suggests that he did not embrace either the theory of appearing or the theory of appearances; at least, that he did not embrace either to the exclusion of the other, and they are by definition mutually exclusive. Consciously or unconsciously, he would seem to have agreed with Ayer's professed view that there is essentially nothing to choose between the two languages, and with its

---

10 *Prolegomena*, p. 287.

11 A 42.

12 A 19.

13 B 37.

14 *Prolegomena*, p. 289.

15 A 27.

16 H. A. Prichard, *Kant's Theory of Knowledge* (Oxford, 1909), p. 74.

implied corollary that both the theory of appearing and the theory of appearances are misguided in opposing one another.

Yet even if both these ways of speaking are present in Kant's writing, could it perhaps be held that one of them is more deeply and truly his? A philosopher might embrace the theory of appearing and yet still use both the language of appearing and the language of appearances, since use of the language of appearances does not need to commit him to the theory of appearances. Might it be the best interpretation of Kant to suppose that he did this? Some commentators have thought so. H. J. Paton, for example, regards Kant's doctrine as being definitely that "Things as they are in themselves are the very same things that appear to us, although they appear to us . . . as different from what they are in themselves."[17] Also he says that "the thing-in-itself is the reality which appears."[18] Paton concedes that Kant's way of speaking sometimes falls away from this and misleadingly suggests the other view; but Paton's position is that the theory of appearing is Kant's real position, and that Kant's use of the language of appearances is to be explained away.

Now, to hold that the theory of appearing is Kant's view is to claim that in principle whatever Kant says using the language of appearances—apart from slips that are to be neglected—can be translated into something expressible in the language of appearing. If the theory of appearing is Kant's view, then all the essential doctrines of his philosophy must in principle be stateable without using the language of appearances. Paton does not even try to show that this can be done. Indeed, even in his own commentary he freely uses locutions of his own that are not clearly translatable into the language of appearing, as when he says that appearances are ideas.[19]

There is much in Kant's teaching that cannot be expressed in the language of appearing, or that would suffer grave change of meaning if it were so expressed. Kant regularly speaks of appearances as due to the influence of things-in-themselves, and he speaks of things-in-themselves as affecting us, or affecting our sensibility and so pro-

---

17 H. J. Paton, *Kant's Metaphysic of Experience* (London, 1936), Vol. I, p. 61.
18 *Ibid.*, Vol. I, p. 62 note.
19 *Ibid.*, Vol. II, p. 442.

ducing in us appearances.[20] These theses cannot be dismissed as accidental or unimportant slips on Kant's part. They bulk large in his philosophy. The very formulation of his transcendental idealism employs the language of appearances, as when he says "By *transcendental idealism* I mean the doctrine that appearances are to be regarded as being, one and all, representations only, not things in themselves."[21] To this he adds that "The transcendental idealist . . . may admit . . . matter without going outside his mere self-consciousness . . . Matter is with him, therefore, only a species of representations."[22] This thesis, often reiterated by Kant, certainly is a rather essential part of his philosophy, and cannot be dismissed as inessential or as a mere lapse. It is highly doubtful that this thesis could be translated into the language of appearing, without suffering considerable change of meaning.

It seems proper to conclude that Kant decisively embraced neither the theory of appearing nor the theory of appearances, but oscillated between them without recognizing any need for making a choice. And the likeliest explanation of why he did so is that he regarded the language of appearing and the language of appearances as fully intertranslatable. Like Ayer, he must have noticed that in many ordinary cases, perceptual situations can be described legitimately according to either way of speaking, and this would have encouraged him to think, as Ayer thought, that there is nothing to choose between the two languages. The presence of both these ways of speaking and the resultant tension between them should then be regarded as fundamental to Kant's philosophy. If we tried to improve Kant's teaching by insisting that for the sake of consistency either the theory of appearing or the theory of appearances must be employed throughout, then the result would be an overall philosophy of knowledge essentially unlike Kant's.

III

Kant's refusal to choose between the theory of appearing and the theory of appearances can help to shed light on various aspects

---

[20] Paton grants this, *op. cit.*, Vol. I, p. 62.

[21] A 369.

[22] A 370.

of the *Critique of Pure Reason,* two of which will now be briefly examined. The first of these has to do with whether there are
things-in-themselves. Now, Kant declares again and again that
all our theoretical knowledge is of appearances only and that we
can have no theoretical knowledge of things-in-themselves, not even
of the self as a thing-in-itself. It is a cardinal tenet of his philosophy that no theoretical metaphysics can be legitimate which
pretends to offer information about matters that transcend appearances. Yet at the same time Kant himself continually speaks of
things-in-themselves as underlying appearances. He never shows
any willingness to countenance the slightest doubt that there are
things-in-themselves distinct from appearances. This is puzzling.
Since he insists that we can know nothing about things-in-themselves, how is it that he thinks we can know that there are such
things? Would it not have been more consistent with his rejection
of transcendent metaphysics for him to have said instead that
we cannot even tell whether there are things-in-themselves? What
is puzzling here is that it is difficult to see what could have led
Kant to feel so sure that there are things-in-themselves.

It might be suggested in reply that this is not really puzzling
and that the explanation is that Kant simply failed to recognize
the conflict between his rejection of transcendent metaphysics and
his retention of the thing-in-itself, because he failed to see that one
could doubt the latter. According to this suggestion, he inherited
from the dogmatic metaphysics of his predecessors the uncriticized
preconception that there could not be a world consisting only of
appearances, that such a world would lack the power to be by
itself. In line with this suggested explanation, Royce, for example, called the doctrine that there are things-in-themselves a
"personal presupposition" of Kant's.[23] This is to suggest that
it was not because of any argument that Kant held the doctrine. This suggested explanation is not a very satisfying one,
however. It amounts to saying that Kant had no to-him-compelling reason except mental inertia for his strong belief that there
are things-in-themselves, and this is difficult to credit. It would be
surprising if such a prominent feature of his philosophy were

---

23 Josiah Royce, *Lectures on Modern Idealism* (New Haven, 1919), p. 40.
Royce does not regard this as the whole story, however.

nothing but an unquestioningly inherited dogma. Surely it would be more plausible to suppose that he had some line of thought of his own that impelled him to this as a conclusion.

Another suggestion for removing the puzzle would be to say that Kant did have a to-him-compelling reason for affirming that there are things-in-themselves, but that this reason is supplied only by his ethical philosophy. In his ethical philosophy Kant holds that one's inexpugnable consciousness of the demands of morality requires one to believe that one possesses free will. And he holds freedom to be impossible in the sphere of appearances, where nothing can occur except according to deterministic laws. Thus the demands of morality, he thinks, require one to believe that one's self in its true nature is not just appearance but is something in itself. This line of thought does afford a practical (though not a theoretical) basis for affirming that there is a thing-in-itself (and also that there are other things-in-themselves, insofar as morality requires one to impute moral responsibility to others). However, important though this is to Kant, it is a line of thought that does not satisfactorily answer the puzzle about why Kant was so confident that there are things-in-themselves. Kant's affirmations that there are things-in-themselves occur from the beginning of the first *Critique,* whereas his practical postulate of freedom is enunciated only much later. Such being the case, it is implausible to suppose that he himself regarded his moral philosophy as providing the main basis for saying that there are things-in-themselves. Moreover, Kant never says that our knowledge that there are things-in-themselves is practical rather than theoretical knowledge, and one would have expected him to say this if he had believed it, for elsewhere he meticulously emphasizes the contrast between the theoretical and the practical. Kant's affirmations that there are things-in-themselves are unqualified and firm in tone; they convey none of that suggestion of unverifiable conjecture that is present in his discussion of the practical postulate of freedom. Thus we cannot suppose him to have thought that our right to say there are things-in-themselves is based mainly on the practical postulate of freedom.

This leaves us then with a puzzle. How are we to explain why Kant felt so confident that there are things-in-themselves distinct from appearances? Surely it is likely that he was moved by some kind of argument on this point that seemed compelling to him. It probably must have been a quite simple one which seemed too obvious to need emphasis. What might that argument have been?

An answer may be found in the language of appearing, as he used it. His statements in this language seem immediately to entail that there are things-in-themselves. In one well-known passage he himself comes close to saying this, for he speaks of "the absurd conclusion that there can be appearance without anything that appears."[24] Possibly one could read this sentence as expressing just the uncriticized dogma that a world constructed merely of ideas could not by itself possess the power to be. However, a more plausible interpretation of the sentence is obtained if we read it as expressing the theory of appearing. In the language of appearing, one cannot speak of appearings without implying that there is something which is independently real and which appears to us. This whole way of speaking seems by its very grammar to afford an immediate proof that there are things in themselves. If we may suppose that Kant oscillated between the theory of appearing and the theory of appearances, then we may suppose that this argument depending on the theory of appearing would have seemed compelling to him.

IV

A second puzzle concerns one line of Kant's thought in his resolution of the Antinomies of Pure Reason. Suppose we express the first two Antinomies in abbreviated form:

1st. The world is either finite or infinite in size and age.
Thesis: It cannot be infinite, so it is finite.
Antithesis: It cannot be finite, so it must be infinite.

2nd. The world either consists of atoms or its every part is divisible.

---

24 B xxvi-B xxvii.

Thesis: The parts cannot all be divisible, so the world consists of atoms.
Antithesis: Atoms are impossible, so each part is divisible.

Kant's view is that in each Antinomy the proof of the thesis and
the proof of the antithesis would be rigorously sound, provided
the initial disjunctive premise could be assumed true.

We may compare these antinomies with a more modern one,
Russell's antinomy in set theory. Russell showed that a contradiction ensues if we suppose that the set of all sets not members
of themselves must either be a member of itself or not a member
of itself. For if it is, then it cannot be, and if it is not, then it
must be. One way of escaping this antinomy is by rejecting the
assumption that the set of all sets not members of themselves
must either be a member of itself or not be a member of itself.
How could this assumption fail to be true? The most straightforward way of rejecting the assumption is by denying that there
is any such set as the one supposedly mentioned. That is, one
can reject the idea that the singular term 'the set of all sets not
members of themselves' names a set. If there is no such set, then
it neither is true that it belongs to itself nor true that it does not.

One line of thought in Kant's resolution of his Antinomies
is exactly parallel to this. In his Antinomies the singular term
'the world', meaning the spatio-temporal world of our experience, is used in the Theses and Antitheses as though it really
referred to something. If it does, then what it refers to must
possess one or the other out of every possible pair of contra-
dictorily opposed predicates (this follows from the Transcendental Principle of Complete Determination).[25] In particular,
being spatio-temporal, it must be either finite or infinite in
size and age, composed of atoms or having each part always further divisible, etc. But this would yield what Kant regards as
insoluble contradictions. The only way out, he feels, is in effect to
deny that there is any such thing as the spatio-temporal world:
"So long as we obstinately persist in assuming that there is an
actual object corresponding to the idea, the problem, thus viewed,

---

[25] A 572.

allows of no solution."[26] If the term 'the world' does not refer
to anything, then we can reject the proposition that it consists
of atoms *and* reject the proposition that its parts are always further divisible; and so on for all four Antinomies. The Antinomies
can be resolved only in this way, Kant thinks, and this seems to
him to constitute a striking indirect argument in favor of
Transcendental Idealism.[27] To suppose that things really are
spatio-temporal leads to unavoidable contradiction, so we must
conclude that nothing is spatio-temporal, and that space and time
are no more than "forms of our sensibility," ways things appear
to us.

To be sure, Kant's discussion of the resolution of the Antinomies certainly does contain other lines of thought besides this
one. But this is a central line of thought that is present in his
discussion, and it is a puzzling one. The puzzling feature of this
is that Kant is holding that nothing can be spatio-temporal,
yet also is holding that appearances are spatio-temporal—
for he affirms that the empirical world of our experience with all
that it contains is so. If there are appearances, and if these
are spatio-temporal, how can they escape the contradictions of
the Antinomies? By saying that there are spatio-temporal appearances, Kant seems to be abandoning the ground upon which his
resolution of the Antinomies supposedly rests. This criticism has
most forcefully been urged by G. E. Moore.[28]

Some readers of Kant would object that this criticism is crude
and unfair, for it leaves out Kant's notion of the world-whole
as existing only in potentiality; his notion of the spatio-
temporal world as a construction project, never completed, which
always may be carried further by the work of thought.[29] Of
course this notion of the merely potential existence of the
spatio-temporal world as a whole is present in Kant's discussion
of the resolution of the Antinomies, and his attempt to use
this notion to help resolve the Antinomies is an important line

26 A 482.

27 A 506.

28 G. E. Moore, *Some Main Problems of Philosophy* (London, 1953), chap. 9.

29 Such a response is offered by T. D. Weldon in *Kant's Critique of Pure Reason* (Oxford, 1958), 2nd ed., p. 207.

of thought there in addition to the line of thought already mentioned. However, the above criticism is not to be dismissed as unfair merely because it omits consideration of this notion, for this notion of potential existence wholly fails to yield a consistent Kantian answer to the criticism. This is seen as follows. To say that the world actually exists as a whole must be to say that each phenomenon that is part of it actually exists. What does it mean for Kant to say of a particular phenomenon that it actually exists in the world? He tells us that this means it can be found in the "empirical advance of experience," i.e., that if certain experiences were to occur then certain others would occur. To say this is to define the actual existence of phenomena in terms of the potential existence of experiences. But in terms of this definition of the actual existence of phenomena, certainly the spatio-temporal world as a whole does actually exist, since each phenomenon in it can be encountered in the "empirical advance." So Kant's notion of the merely potential existence of the world-whole, suggestive and valuable though it may be, does not protect him against the above criticism.[30]

Our puzzle, then, is to see what could have led Kant to suppose both that he could resolve the Antinomies through denying that anything is spatio-temporal and yet continue to affirm that appearances or phenomena are so. The answer again would seem to lie in Kant's nonchalant attitude toward the theories of appearing and of appearances. In his resolution of the Antinomies, Kant employs the theory of appearing, and says that though things appear to be spatio-temporal, nothing is so. But because he feels, as Ayer did, that there is nothing to choose between the language of appearing and the language of appearances, Kant allows himself to continue speaking in the language of appearances, and he says that appearances are spatio-temporal. Recognizing no transition between the one way of speaking and the other, he cannot feel the force of the contradiction into which his views have drifted.

S. F. BARKER

THE JOHNS HOPKINS UNIVERSITY

---

[30] This point is briefly made by Prichard, *op. cit.*, p. 102. He attributes it to J. Cook Wilson.

KANT'S SCHEMATA AS SEMANTICAL RULES*

In this paper I will sketch briefly a model for understanding the connection, in Kant's system, between categories, principles of the understanding, schemata, and the empirical instances to which the categorial framework is supposed to apply. I hope that the model will illuminate the general features of Kant's entire epistemological enterprise, although in the present context I am mainly interested in providing a way of removing the notorious obscurities of the Schematism passage in the *Critique of Pure Reason*.

Wilfrid Sellars is unqestionably right in pointing out that the main thrust of Kant's system is in the direction of providing us with an account of *judging*.[1] At the very outset of his discussion of conceptual knowledge Kant introduces the forms of judgment, and his main effort in what follows is to lay bare the detailed structure of what is involved in judging via concepts (subsuming empirical particulars under concepts) . Thus the first *Critique* provides us with what might be called the 'epistemological formalism of judging'. And the emphasis, I will insist, must be put on the reference to *form*. Kant is not doing the empirical psychology of judging; rather, like any good epistemologist, he is endeavouring to explicate the formal (epistemological, *not* logical in the narrow sense) requirements of empirical knowledge, knowledge that, for Kant, can only be generated by means of judgments.

First, then, a word about Kant's view of the categories. Elsewhere, I suggested that the categories supply the epistemological grammar for any system that is to make truth claims about matters

*A preliminary version of this paper was read at the 14th International Congress of Philosophy, Vienna, Sept., 1968. I am indebted to Professor Lewis W. Beck for valuable suggestions that have resulted in important revisions of the paper.

1 Wilfrid Sellars, "Some Remarks on Kant's Theory of Experience," *Journal of Philosophy*, 64, No. 20 (Oct. 26, 1967) , 634.

of fact.[2] Sellars is again right in pointing out that the categories specify both the narrowly syntactical features of the system (after all, the logical form of sentences expressing judgments is dictated by just these categories), and the broadly logical (epistemological) presuppositions of empirical knowledge.[3] So far so good, but, as has been pointed out by everyone including Kant himself, such general forms appear to be only logical shells when considered by themselves. But this admission should not occasion any confusion, as it has for some. The epistemological category-word 'cause' signifies a grammatical component in judgments of certain types in exactly the same sense in which the syntactical category-word 'noun' signifies grammatical components of some English sentences. 'Cause' does not collect causes any more than 'noun' collects nouns. Both category-words help to detail something about the form that some judgments or sentences can take in endeavouring to make true claims about the world or to assert syntactically well-formed sentences in English.

Kant's categories, then, are not so philosophically poverty stricken as some have assumed. However, a grammar, even an epistemological grammar, needs to be supplemented by some detailed rules of formation that make judgings or meaningful sentence-assertings possible. In large part this role is played by the principles of the understanding. On Kant's scheme, the categories will apply to specific experiences of objects and events in space and time. The point of the grammar, moreover, is to make more than merely immediate knowledge by acquaintance possible—the point is to make *generalizations* about experiences possible. When we talk about the principles of experience, we are talking about the a priori conditions of those generalizations that are candidates for the status of natural laws. As Kant says,

> . . . The laws of nature . . . without exception, stand under higher principles of understanding. They simply apply the latter to special cases in the field of appearance. These principles alone supply the concept which contains the condition, and as it were the exponent, of a rule in general. What experience gives is the instance which stands under the rule [A159 = B198].

---

2 Robert E. Butts, "Hypothesis and Explanation in Kant's Philosophy of Science," *Archiv für Geschichte der Philosophie,* 43, No. 2 (1961), 167.

3 Sellars, *op. cit.,* p. 641.

The principles, in other words, provide rules that specify the conditions that laws of nature must satisfy. But again, given that the principles provide this specification a priori, the specification can only account for the *form* that all possible natural laws must obey. The causal principle, for example, dictates that the form of all laws describing events be causal. The principle of the permanence of substance is equivalent to the claim that it is possible for us to write down any natural laws at all, for all laws must refer to *something* in experience that is more than transitory. Likewise the other principles tell us the forms that our laws must take. The 'must', of course, is not the logical 'must'; it is the 'must' of presupposition.

But the a priori machinery provided by the categories and the principles tells us nothing about the detailed experiences themselves. All that we know of these a priori within the system of presuppositions is that as experiences they will all and always occur within the boundary conditions of space and time. The categories and the principles give us only rules for constructing a system of a certain kind; experience itself must supply the detailed content. (Of course the conceptual system must obey one more fundamental condition, namely that any single judging (asserting something about matters of fact) must take place in a single unified consciousness. Judgings, just like the judgment-sentences that express them, require an identity condition. Leaving aside the obscure psychologistic talk, appeal to an identity condition that must be satisfied by all judgments seems to me to be what the transcendental unity of apperception comes to.) Kant's system of categories and a priori construction rules is, so to speak, an *uninterpreted* epistemic formalism. Inevitably, the question of the *application* of this formalism to empirical instances must arise. It arises, for Kant, at exactly that point where the notorious schemata are introduced.

Let me obviate one possible objection to Kant's view by simply agreeing with it. The objection is: given that Kant's system of categories and principles specifies what it is to be an object of experience, how can an account of the applicability of the categories be other than circular? Of course, the account, in a sense, *must* be circular; if there is a system by means of which we understand matters of fact (whether it be Kant's or not), we cannot be said to know, via *that* system, anything at all about the facts to which it applies, except by means of that system. The insistence in Kant that we are dealing always and only with phenomena, that we can have no independent (metaphysical) knowledge of the nature of fact, is all part of the same story. Nevertheless, even if every conceptual system generates its own observation language,[4] we must still know something about what that very language picks out as observable. And the *formalism* of the system cannot do that job.

Kant's schemata, it seems to me, do exactly the job of specifying the kinds of observables that are relevant to deciding the applicability of a category. They function, as it were, like semantical rules linking categories and observation predicates. Bennett is right in supposing that "Kant wants his schematism theory . . . to explain how we are able to recognize, classify, describe."[5] But he is wrong in thinking that one can so easily dispose of what Körner calls "referential rules."[6] Kant's schemata can indeed be understood as referential rules of a sort. Of course, as Bennett urges, one cannot have referential rules that directly link concepts to perceptions; rules of this sort always link concepts with concepts.[7] But that is just what semantical rules are ordinarily thought to do. What would it mean, after all, for a concept to be linked to a perception by means of a rule, when, on Kant's own account, what it means to be a conceptualizable perception is specified beforehand *by* the rules?

Retreat, for a moment, back to Kant's text. The usually-noted lines are the following:

> This representation of a universal procedure [rule] of imagination in providing an image for a concept, I entitle the schema of this concept [A140 = B180].
>
> The schemata are thus nothing but *a priori* determinations of time in accordance with rules [A145 = B184].

Unnecessarily restrictive attention to these and similar sentences focuses our attention upon two features of Kant's theory. First, we

---

[4] A position like this is developed at length by P. K. Feyerabend. See, for example, "Problems of Empiricism," in *Beyond the Edge of Certainty*, R. G. Colodny, ed. (Englewood Cliffs, N.J., 1965), pp. 145-260.

[5] Jonathan Bennett, *Kant's Analytic* (Cambridge, 1966), p. 143.

[6] S. Körner, *Kant* (Penguin Books, 1955), pp. 71-72.

[7] Bennett, *op. cit.*, p. 145.

become overly concerned with understanding Kant's psychology of the imagination, which teaches that imagination originates the schemata that we use to produce images with which given perceptions will be compared. Second, literal attention to these sentences yields the Kantian platitude that categories, to be applicable, must be subjected to temporal conditions; the objects to which the categories apply must be objects that occur in time. But I suggest that we suspend thought about Kant's treatment of universals in the context of imagination-originated schemata; and that we recognize that we knew all along that particulars of observation to which the categories apply must be construed as particulars occurring in time. If we agree to these two restrictions, we can then begin to look with infant delight upon two sentences in the schematism passage that are *not* usually noted and appreciated.

The two sentences are:

> The schemata of the pure concepts of understanding [categories] are thus the true and sole conditions under which these concepts obtain relation to objects and so possess *significance* [A146 = B185].
> The schema is, properly, only the phenomenon, or sensible concept, of an object in agreement with the category [A146 = B186].

The first of the sentences appears conclusive as evidence for my claim that the schemata are semantical rules. Categories are grammatical forms; to supply meanings that will take these forms something else is required, namely rules that tell us to what the form shall be applied. Thus, for example, the general pure concept of quantity will be interpreted to apply to *magnitudes,* that is, to objects *numerable in time,* which means, simply, to objects that are measurable by means of the successive addition of units in time. Similarly, the category of quality will licence predicates ascribing specific degrees of intensity to all empirical sensings. More briefly: an allowable observation predicate will be one that picks out measurable features of things. Thus '3 inches in length' is a permitted observation predicate under the category of quantity, '10° centigrade' is an observation predicate associated with the category of quality. If space permitted, one could give just this detailed account of the allowable observation predicates that fall under each category. But the general point will have to suffice. That point is simply that the schemata specify in general terms what kinds of observation predicates are permitted given the epistemic form of the system;

they settle the matter of applicability; they also foster, given the precise observables that specific experiences yield, the formulation of decision procedures by means of which the truth or falsity of a given well-formed judgment can be ascertained.

The second statement from the text appears to be obscure. It would seem that a schema cannot be both a rule for the selection of observation predicates and a sensible concept.[8] However, for Kant a concept is, or as he says, 'signifies', [A141 = B180] a rule. In general, for Kant, the following would seem to be true. We can take any concept, pure or empirical, and unpack it as a rule or set of rules for the production of something. If we take an empirical concept, say the concept of dog, then its *meaning* is *schematically* represented as a set of procedures. For example, to apply the concept of dog, I must be able to find ways of comparing it favourably with the sensible concept of four-footed animal; to apply the concept of dog, I must be able to find ways of comparing it favourably with the phenomenon of barking things; and so on. The same is true of the categories. Here the rules permit of quite general (and still a priori) determination. Thus I can say, "to apply the pure concepts of quantity and quality, I must be able to find ways of determining an empirical occurrence's place in space and its position on some scale of degrees of intensity."[9] In both cases, the sensible concept, or rule, that applies the higher-order concept, is just that which enables me to pick out, compare, describe; in general, observe, and hence to confirm or refute a judgment having the content interpreted by this rule. And if application, or schematization, is not that which permits relevant observation, then it is difficult to see how any conceptual system could be about anything at all.

Confusion will arise if we do not keep strictly in mind Kant's distinction between the schema of an empirical concept and the schema of a category [A142 = B181]. The schema of an empirical concept is a rule in accordance with which we produce an image corresponding to a certain concept. The concept is apparently applied to an actual empirical instance via the image, which is that

---

[8] I assume throughout that what Kant calls "sensible concepts" would all be expressible as observation predicates.

[9] In all these examples, the 'must' has merely legal or regulative force.

with which we compare the sensation. Clearly there are difficulties in this notion of the application of sensible concepts. Unless the notion is developed with great care (a task that Kant did not himself undertake to carry out) we can become quickly lost in the notorious problem of the general image that represents all individuals of a certain type. Kant appreciated this problem, and so thought of the schema of a sensible concept as a *procedure* for producing an image, a procedure that would allow the imagination to delineate a figure without making a specific image. But it is impossible to compare an actual sensation with a *procedure,* though it might be comparable with an image or with another experience. So the general image seems to have to re-appear, and with it the problem of the application of empirical concepts to sensations.

In addition, there is the tricky question whether an empirical concept can be fitted to an instance by the application of *any* rules. As I pointed out above, rules can be given for linking concepts to concepts, but none appear to be available for directly fitting concepts to experiences. To what rules do I turn when I want to know that the concept 'red' applies in a specific case to some given sensation? It would seem that when we are dealing with those sensible concepts that operate at the level closest to sensation (color and taste concepts, for example) no rules will be forthcoming that will decide the question of application. It is as if all we had at our disposal were names (like 'red', 'bitter', and the like) that could be pinned on the sensory givens at various times. Of course in the "Aesthetic" Kant does seem sometimes to suggest just this point. Against this view, however, is his continuing insistence that we do not have *any* concepts that are concepts of primary and unanalyzable givens—*every* concept introduces a form or rule for *interpreting* sensory givens. The program of the "Analytic," as I read it, is to show just how we can move from immediate intuited knowledge in the form 'this x seems red', to conceptual (objective) knowledge in the form 'this x is red'. The difficulty is compounded, however, when we realize that even in 'this x seems red', a concept is involved, and so the problem of application—which might be easily solved in the case of putatively objective knowledge claims—arises in a form that seems insoluble. This may be why Kant's last pronouncement on the problem of the application of sensible concepts to sensations amounts in effect to a conceding of defeat, and to a relinquishing of any possibility of discovering rules that will apply empirical concepts directly to instances.[10]

If Kant himself seems thus willing to concede defeat on the problem of linking sensible concepts to instances, it seems best to drop that problem altogether. And for the strongest of reasons: Kant's own system offers a solution of the *general* problem of the applicability of concepts to experiences, but only within the context of his full conceptual framework that works out the details of how it is possible to make objective knowledge claims. We must turn to Kant's view that when we are dealing with the schemata of categories, rather than of sensible concepts, no images, and no procedures for producing images, are involved. We shift to the problem of specifying rules that will link categories to sensible concepts; that will, in other words, shape the concepts operating close to the surface of experience in such a way that decisive observations can be made, if any decisive observations *can be made at all*. We see at once that there are not *two* problems of application, one of applying categories to experiences, the other of applying sensible concepts to experience; there is only one problem of application, namely, the problem of producing conceptual systems that will, *in toto,* be fitted to making truth claims about experience.

This is why Kant calls the schemata of categories sensible concepts, or bearers of the significance of the conceptual system. In addition to the epistemological grammar supplied by the categories, and in addition to the formalism of laws supplied by the principles of the understanding, there must be rules (the schemata) that determine the *formal content* of observation predicates that meet the other formal requirements of the system. The idea of formal content might seen unacceptable on general logical grounds. But it has a straightforward meaning. The schemata of the categories cannot tell us what the details of experience will be *as details,* but they can, and must, tell us what *kinds* of details we are to look for in constructing sciences.

In general, Kant will insist that the rules enable us to *mathematize* experience, i.e., the semantical rules will introduce observa-

---

10 Kant writes: "This schematism of our understanding, in its application to appearances and their mere form, is an art concealed in the depths of the human soul, whose real modes of activity nature is hardly likely ever to allow us to discover, and to have open to our gaze" [A 141 = B 180-181].

tion predicates that, if instanced, will yield numbers resulting from measurements of various kinds. But the semantical specification of predicate contents will be general. It will give us the semantics, as it were, of the general system of knowledge that will have to be applied in special cases given special sciences. Thus the schemata as semantical rules give the general form of observation predicates *within* the conceptual system of the categories and the principles, within the most general epistemological system that is possible. This system, of course, will in turn make possible the introduction of any number of particular scientific systems with their own (more narrowly conceived) categories, law forms, semantical rules, and observation predicates. The *specific* observables to be permitted in these lower-order scientific systems will result from *choices* of ranges of entities germane to those particular sciences.[11] But the general form of *any* observation predicates allowable in *any* science will be given by the schemata as the semantical rules operating in the epistemological formalism.[12]

---

[11] I may be criticized at this point for trying to turn Kant into a pragmatist. My reply is that Kant made himself into a kind of pragmatist, and I am only trying to be faithful to the insight resulting from recognizing that he did so. If we are to employ principles *regulatively* (and thus to employ schematized categories regulatively also) in the construction of sciences, we are quite at liberty to specify the range of entities that a given science will take as values of its variables. It is precisely because this is so that we can now abandon the vexatious problem of the application of concepts to experiences, where the concepts are empirical concepts ingredient in the observation language of a science. Briefly: just insofar as we use rules for selecting permitted observation predicates, and just insofar as we choose the range of entities which semantically interprets a formalism, we *are* applying the system, and in the only manner that makes epistemological sense. There is no question remaining that requires for its solution the introduction of curious ontological or psychological entities that mediate between sensation and conception. If space permitted I would also argue that this view of Kant's pragmatism regarding regulative employment of principles is vastly more faithful to the major features of his system than is the facile *als ob* theory.

[12] The matter cannot be discussed in detail here, but consideration should be given to the evidence for my interpretation that comes from Kant's discussion of mechanism as one preferred regulative scheme to be used in the study of biological phenomena. (Too often, Kant's philosophy of biology gets left out of discussions of his general philosophy of science, which discussions normally—and unjustifiably—stress the physical sciences.) In the *Critique of Judgment* (J. C. Meredith trans. Oxford, 1928), 2nd pt., Sec. 17) he insists that mechanical forms of explanation must be pursued to their utmost limits in the study of organisms. Why? I would

I will summarize Kant's complex concept of categorial subsumption (application of categories to objects) ,[13] by means of an example. Let the task be the application of the category of quantity. Kant construes quantity as magnitude (quantum). The associated principle is, 'all intuitions are extensive magnitudes', meaning that all empirical objects (viewed as events in time) are intuited as either space or time aggregates, complexes of previously given parts. This principle allows us to introduce laws formally regarded as obeying the rule that all empirical objects are aggregates, because it offers the a priori guarantee that all future experiences will be of objects having this form. At this point we link the vague general notion of magnitude with the observation language by specifying (via the schema of quantity) that all quantities be expressed as numbers, i.e., be measurable. We thus get observation predicates in numerical terms, and these make possible decisive observations of objects that either instance or fail to instance the predicates. The whole machinery, except for the specific observations themselves, is thus determined a priori.

A more formal analysis may clarify the model. The principle of quantity might be expressed as

(1) For all x, if x is an intuition (object of experience) , x is an extensive magnitude.

Interpreted as a rule, (1) licences (but does not logically entail) law forms as follows:

(2) This x_1 has extensive magnitude y_1.

(2′) All x_1s have extensive magnitude y_1.
The schema of quantity is the rule

---

suggest that the answer is given by my account above: if the general epistemological framework dictates categories, law forms, and a preferred general semantics, then the mathematization of experience must be realized in *every* science, i.e., in every conceptual sub-system legalized by the general epistemological system. Mechanical forms of explanation are paradigms of mathematical explanation; therefore, mechanical forms of explanation must at least be attempted (the 'must' is again regulative) in all sciences, including biology.

13 Butts, *op. cit.*, pp. 166-167. Though I think that 'categorical subsumption' is still a pretty fair term for expressing what is involved in applying categories to instances, my account of this procedure in the earlier paper is imperfect and partly wrong. I hope to make good these defects in the present account.

(3) Construe all ys as observation predicates which are numbers in measurement sets (e.g., '3 inches long by standardized measurements in yardstick space', 'lasted 10 minutes by standard clock time'.)

The observables generated by (3) are points on lines, positions of clock hands, and the like, encountered in normal experimental or observational contexts. Suppose that y_1 is 'lasted 10 minutes by standard clock time', and x_1 is 'the period of total eclipse of the moon'. The empirical instance of this claim is then got by counting up the times during which the eclipse was observable (a process normally gone through by the clock itself, thus only requiring the observer to note the position of the clock hands).

It would be odd to claim that a certain observed clock reading is, in the normal sense, conceptually subsumed by the category of quantity. Categorial subsumption, or the application of a category, involves the *production of,* or the *systematic demand for,* observations of a certain kind. It is precisely in this sense that Kant's claim that the categories specify what it means to be an object of experience is to be understood. But the categories cannot do the job alone; the schemata as semantical rules inject the empirical sense into the observation language. It is only thus that the categorial framework can come to be correctly regarded as the set of conceptual presuppositions of all possible empirical knowledge claims.

ROBERT E. BUTTS

UNIVERSITY OF WESTERN ONTARIO

'POSSIBLE EXPERIENCE' AND RECENT INTERPRETATIONS OF KANT

In an attempt to extract a coherent and still relevant structure of thought from its obsolete encumbrances, some of the recent interpretations of Kant have been needlessly hampered by neglect of the important concept of 'possible experience'. Failure to make the full use of this concept that Kant himself made has inevitably been damaging to the Kantian doctrine of phenomenal objectivity; and any version of Kant that is so damaged falls drastically short of the original. I should like, therefore, after making the problem a little clearer, to examine the concept of possible experience as Kant presents it; to attempt a clarification of difficulties in his presentation that may have contributed to the tendency to neglect the concept; and finally to indicate briefly the unfortunate consequences of this neglect in some recent instances.

In referring to phenomenal objectivity, I do not mean to raise the question of 'phenomenalism' (a term so diversely employed in Kant criticism as to be rendered useless in this context), but rather to consider what Kant means by the objectivity of the empirical world, the world of 'phenomena' as he understands the term. His problem is that of explaining how things as known (rather than 'in themselves') are nevertheless not merely identical with our perceptions of them; how we can conceive "an appearance itself which yet is nothing in itself"; how "appearance, in contradistinction to the representations of apprehension, can be represented as an object distinct from them. . ." It is the problem that Kant solves by attributing to objects a conceptual structure, a "rule which . . . necessitates some one particular mode of connection of the manifold." The rule determines, for instance, whether or not it is possible to see the house from top to bottom, even though I actually see it from bottom to top; whether or not it is possible still to see the ship upstream after I have seen it successively farther and farther downstream.[1]

Thus an objective thing is a system of determinate possibilities, and an objective event (i.e., an 'alteration' in the thing) is a substitution of possibilities, eliminating some and adding others. And when we try to understand just how we know —or, indeed, what constitutes—possibilities in this sense, we find ourselves immediately involved in the analysis of Kant's complex interrelation of the sensory and the conceptual at one of its focal points.

The 'manifold' that is connected in terms of an object, then, is not reducible to a set of actual sense perceptions because it includes also a set of possible ones; and it is the latter set, determined in accordance with categories which define an objective world, that provide Kant's answer to Hume's difficulties about unobserved objects. It is helpful to call to mind, here, the very clear elaboration of this point by C. I. Lewis, who in fact uses Kant's example of the parts of a house in this connection.[2]

> That for us there exist things which are now given in experience and now not, and which when given are still thicker than our experience of them—having, for example, another side—is correlative with our sense of something verifiable though unverified . . . the experientially possible but not experientially now actual.[3]

And Lewis makes the point, as applicable to Kant's view as to his own and for the same reason, that the kind of 'possible' required in this context is determinate and counterfactual. The thing that we see is *now* more than our perception of it, because it is *now* perceivable in other ways as well. To believe in "facts which obtain independently of being experienced," we must "believe that if something *were* tested, at times when it is in fact *not* tested, certain specifiable results *would* accrue

---

[1] *Critique of Pure Reason,* A 191-192 = B 236-238. Quotations from the *Critique* are from Norman Kemp Smith (trans.) , *Immanuel Kant's Critique of Pure Reason* (London: Macmillan and Co., Ltd., 1953) .

[2] Clarence Irving Lewis, *An Analysis of Knowledge and Valuation* (LaSalle, Ill.: The Open Court Publishing Co., 1946) , p. 20. Hereinafter cited as AKV.

[3] AKV, p. 17.

and not others."[4] Thus a rule providing mere predictions, to be realized within one's own actual experience in the future, would not serve the same purpose of determining the object as more than our experience of it; although the same rule may perform this function also.

We may wonder, then, why so indispensable a concept is so little emphasized by interpreters of Kant. Vleeschauwer, for one, flatly states that Kant himself, in his second edition, "did away with possible experience as an operative medium."[5] This view, however, seems to have no basis in the text, and is understandable only as a too eager anticipation of Kant's later development toward an ontological idealism. For most interpreters, the reason for failure to attribute any special importance to the concept of possible experience seems, rather, to be the belief that there is no real difference indicated between possible and actual experience—that Kant either does[6] or on his own premises should[7] regard the possible, the actual, and the necessary as identical. Indeed, the problem is explicitly identified and stated in these terms by Wolff, who sees that it concerns counterfactuals, ties it in with the problem of "substantial co-existence," and finds that "The plausibility . . . of the *Critique,* depends to a considerable degree on the possibility of solving the problem," but nevertheless minimizes the possibility of a solution by accepting at face value those of Kant's arguments that indicate the coexistensiveness of the possible, the actual, and the necessary.[8] I think, however, that acceptance of this conclusion is avoidable when Kant's uses of the modal terms are clearly distinguished and the relevant use kept in mind.

The present discussion, therefore, will have to analyze Kant's

---

[4] AKV, pp. 215-216.

[5] H. J. de Vleeschauwer, *The Development of Kantian Thought,* trans. A. R. C. Duncan (London and New York: Thomas Nelson & Sons Ltd., 1962), p. 109.

[6] T. D. Weldon, *Kant's* Critique of Pure Reason (2nd ed.; Oxford: Clarendon Press, 1958), p. 189.

[7] Norman Kemp Smith, *A Commentary to Kant's 'Critique of Pure Reason'* (2nd ed.; New York: Humanities Press, 1950), pp. 392-394. Hereinafter cited as *Commentary.*

[8] Robert Paul Wolff, *Kant's Theory of Mental Activity* (Cambridge: Harvard University Press, 1963), pp. 289-292, 298. Hereinafter cited as **KTMA.**

concept of possible experience, especially in terms of 'the possible' as explicated in the Postulates of Empirical Thought; then consider the crucial questions raised by this concept—first, whether the realms of the three modalities completely coincide, and second, how (if at all) counterfactual possibilities can fit in; and, finally, assess the effects on interpretation of Kant.

"That which agrees with the formal conditions of experience, that is, with the conditions of intuition and of concepts, is *possible*." Kant is here concerned, as he takes pains to indicate, not with the "purely logical significance" of modal distinctions but with their significance as "the possibility, actuality, and necessity of *things*." And things, by which Kant means empirical things, objects of experience, are possible only if they meet the conditions, already set forth by Kant, which determine the nature of "possible experience and its synthetic unity, in which alone objects of knowledge can be given."[9] In other words, to be logically possible is to be self-consistent and thus conceivable, while to be possible as an object of experience is to be consistent also with the requirements of the human capacity to experience (the forms of intuition and the categories) and thus to be experience-able (i.e., both perceivable and understandable). As Schnee-berger has pointed out, possibility, for Kant, always means consistency or agreement with something; different kinds of possibility differ as to the kinds of conditions with which consistency is required.[10]

The possibility that Kant defines in the first Postulate, then, is precisely the sort that has been the main concern of the Transcendental Deduction—that "possibility of experience," its conditions set by the structure of human consciousness, which is also "the possibility of the objects of experience."[11] When he speaks of "a possible experience" in this sense, he means "a possible experience in general,"[12] i.e., *any* possible experience, a possible *kind* of experience. Similarly, when he wants "to show

---

[9] A 218-219 = B 265-267.

[10] Guido Schneeberger, *Kants Konzeption der Modalbegriffe* (Basel: Verlag für Recht und Gesellschaft AG, 1952), p. 5. Hereinafter cited as KKM.

[11] A 158 = B 197; cf. A 111 and B 161.

[12] A 111.

the far-reaching utility" of the first Postulate, he demonstrates its use as a criterion for determining whether various conceivable kinds of things are eligible to be objects of experience.[13]

When we proceed to the second and third Postulates, however, we find that Kant's definitions of the actual and the necessary involve a different sort of possibility from the one just set forth; and it is this new version that has the significance with which this discussion is primarily concerned. "That which is bound up with the material conditions of experience, that is, with sensation, is *actual*."[14] The sensory content of experience, being given in consciousness, is of course actual in a very obvious sense. Kant, however, also includes as actual anything "bound up with . . . sensation"; and this seems to mean *inferable* from some sensation (or sensations) with the aid of "the analogies of experience, which define all real connection in an experience in general."[15] Thus, since the Analogies define rules for connecting one sense perception with another, what we infer must be another perception; and since it need not be one that we actually have, it must be one that we could have under conditions specifiable in empirical terms—i.e., a possible perception. What Kant wishes to classify as actual, in this context, is the object that we should regard such a perception as a perception *of*.

The actual object, then, may or may not be an object of actual experience; but it must be at least an object of possible experience.

> That there may be inhabitants in the moon, although no one has ever perceived them . . . only means that in the possible advance of experience we may encounter them. . . Nothing is really given us save perception and the empirical advance from this to other possible perceptions.[16]

It is very improbable that Kant expected anyone ever to pay an actual visit to the moon. Yet, when he speaks here of "the possible advance of experience" or "possible perceptions," the term

---

[13] A 221-223 = B 268-270.

[14] A 218 = B 266.

[15] A 225 = B 272.

[16] A 493 = B 521.

'possible' is clearly used in a stronger sense than that of the first Postulate. It does not mean—or does not mean only—a possible kind of experience, a kind that is generically compatible with our perceptual and conceptual ability to have experience. Such possibility of experience would be equivalent, as we have seen, to the possibility of its objects, not to their actuality. What Kant has in mind at this point is a determinate possibility of a particular, specifiable experience, one that would in fact occur under specifiable empirical conditions.

Thus, in the sense in which the first Postulate defines possibility, it is possible to perceive a mermaid, for example (because a mermaid would be sense-perceptible if there were one), though not other people's thoughts. In the sense implied by the second Postulate, however, it is possible to perceive the house next door, or even the center of the earth (because they are there), but not a mermaid. If the first concept is that of real as distinguished from logical possibility, it is tempting to call the second concept that of 'really real possibility'. Perhaps 'determinate' or 'specific possibility' would convey what is intended—no longer consistency of a kind of experience or object with the conditions of 'experience in general', but inferability of a particular (though hypothetical) experience as one that would occur under hypothetical conditions, from particular actual sense perceptions interpreted as experience of actual objects.

The second of these concepts of real possibility is the one that is both crucial and elusive. Kemp Smith distinguishes two separate meanings of possibility in the first Postulate and Kant's discussion of it, but his distinction is not the present one. He interprets agreement with "the formal conditions of experience" as not including sensory perceivability, and makes this a second meaning, still in terms of a general rather than a specific possibility.[17]

A distinction that is much more to the point is drawn by Schneeberger, whose full scale analysis of Kant's modal concepts is supported by detailed documentation from the *Nachlass* and to a lesser extent from the lectures on logic and on metaphysics, with some references to other works of Kant also. Schnee-

---

17 *Commentary*, p. 392.

berger emphasizes the fact that conformity to the general conditions for the possibility of everything still does not make possible the existence of individual things in their variety; for this
we need a different set of conditions for each thing.[18] Thus real
possibility as designated by the category is formal, a possibility
only of the general form of all changes but not of the concrete
content of any individual, particular change (*"einzelne besondere
Veränderung* in concreto").[19]

Yet, in contrasting the two kinds of real possibility primarily
as incomplete and complete possibility, in conceiving the second
kind exclusively in terms of conformity to the *entire* set of
conditions for a particular thing, Schneeberger identifies particular possibility with the possibility of the actual.[20] Thus, when
he explains the possible but not actual as that which is possible in some respects but not in all,[21] it is never quite clear
that this 'possible but not actual' may include not only formally
possible experience in general but also particular hypothetical
experiences. These, however, are just what we must explain, if
we want to understand possible experience of actual objects.

It is perhaps trivial to note that the hypothetical experience
must be possible in the general sense also, as must the hypothetical conditions under which it would be actual. It is perhaps less trivial—and certainly essential to Kant's analysis—that
the laws by which the inferences are made, although empirical
in content and derivation, are determined as to their form (and
thus invested with the necessity that laws have) by the same 'conditions' that determine possibility in the first sense. While Kant,
as we have noted, singles out the Analogies of Experience
for explicit mention in this connection, thus indicating that the
laws will be about substances and will be causal, he might equally
well have referred to all the other principles also. Indeed, if we
keep in mind that 'experience' in Kant's usage means objective
experience, we can see that the principles are conditions of 'the
possibility of experience' in the first sense precisely because they

---

18 KKM, p. 7.
19 KKM, pp. 18-19.
20 KKM, p. 9.
21 KKM, pp. 9, 68.

enable us to infer specific possible experiences in the second sense. This makes it all too easy for Kant to use the expression 'possible experience' ambiguously, not making clear which of the two senses he has in mind. Sometimes he may even have both senses in mind at once, as he probably does in speaking of "the existence of the thing" as "bound up with our perceptions in a possible experience."[22]

Moreover, since to be "bound up with . . . sensation" is to have a necessary connection with it, and since such a connection is necessary (for objective experience) only by virtue of the categories which define objective experience, the second Postulate is, as everyone notes, translatable into the third. "That which in its connection with the actual is determined in accordance with universal conditions of experience, is (that is, exists as) *necessary*."[23]

At this point, then, we are confronted by the obvious question, raised in many discussions of the Postulates beginning with Kant's own, whether the possible, the actual, and the necessary completely coincide. Kant's treatment of the problem,[24] unfortunately, is ambiguous and irrelevant. His failure to make clear whether 'the possible' under discussion is possible kinds of experience or possible particular experiences is here far from harmless; for although at one point he claims to rule out "extending the number of possible things beyond that of the actual,"[25] the entire supporting discussion concerns the question whether any kinds of objects are possible that we are not able to experience at all. What we want to know, of course, is whether particular, specifiable experiences are possible other than those that are also actual and necessary.

Kant does not always make clear, either, whether 'the actual' under discussion is actual experience or actual objects; and this distinction is important, because actual objects may be objects of merely possible experience. He does create a vague impression,

---

[22] A 225 = B 273.
[23] A 218 = B 266.
[24] A 230-232 = B 282-285.
[25] A 231 = B 284.

later made explicit,[26] that he is talking about actual objects; but it is easy to lose sight of this fact.

Finally, Kant is sidetracked into a rather ambiguous denial that anything is "added to the possible to constitute the actual."[27] Presumably he means to deny that any property is added to the concept of the possible thing to constitute the concept of the actual thing; the assertion of actuality does not, as he says later, "enlarge the concept."[28] (In other Kantian words, existence is not a predicate.) But possibility and necessity are not predicates either; *all* modal terms, as Kant has explained in introducing the group of Postulates, "only express the relation of the concept to the faculty of knowledge."[29] And since the structure of our faculty of knowledge, in Kant's view, is precisely what determines the structure of the world as object of knowledge, the question whether that structure has a place for anything possible but not actual is still significant and still not answered.

Kant's discussion, then, not only contains ambiguities but fails to focus on the significant aspects of the problem. Since the actual and the necessary, as we have seen, clearly coincide by Kant's definitions of them, the only question left open concerns the feasibility of differentiating them from the possible. On the other hand, the possible in the formal or general sense—every kind of experience compatible with the general conditions determining what kind of experience we are able to have—obviously includes much more than the actual, because the conditions require no relation to the existence of anything and are insufficient (as Schneeberger emphasizes) to make any particular actuality completely possible.

This, of course, is the very problem that comes to a head in connection with the reversibility of sequences of sense perceptions implied in the concept of a real, objective thing. As Wolff points out, once we have had a series of perceptions, we certainly cannot reverse the order of that series; what Kant really means

---

[26] A 234 = B 286.

[27] A 234 = B 286.

[28] A 233 = B 286.

[29] A 219 = B 266.

is that we could have proceeded in the reverse order instead.[30]
Nor is it sufficient that we can afterward proceed in the reverse
order; if it were, the ship that has moved downstream might
simply back up again, and there would be no distinction between
its movements and the permanence of the house viewed first from
top to bottom and then from bottom to top. The real point of
the matter is that the house can be seen in either order because
any part can be seen at any time; in other words, all the parts
are there at the same time. It is the existence of simultaneous
alternative possibilities, all but one of which are counterfactual
when that one is an actual experience, that constitutes the
existence of an actual object; and a change in our actual experience of the object is a change in the object itself only when it is
also a change in our possible experience of it—i.e., in the set of
simultaneous relevant possibilities.

The difficulty, then, is in the concept of simultaneous possibilities. If everything actual is necessary, it seems to follow
that no contrary alternative is possible. Does it make sense to
say that the house could have been seen in reverse order, or
could now be seen from the other side, when no observer could
have observed otherwise than he did, or could now be anywhere
except where he in fact is? But if not, how are we to distinguish between a subjective and an objective time order, and what
is an objective order the order of? In other words, how can a
deterministic system of necessary causal connections accomodate
alternative possibilities?

We must note, first of all, that without necessary connections
there could be no determinate possibilities either (as distinguished from the indeterminate possibility of just anything). Possibility, indeed, is itself a connection—a relation, as Schneeberger
observes, to conditions which make something possible.[31] Possible perceptions which are not actual, i.e., not known by being
given, can be known only by inference from actual perceptions
to those "bound up with" them; and the same laws that make
actual perceptions necessary under actual conditions are those
that make other perceptions possible (i.e., necessary under pos-

30 KTMA, p. 290.
31 KKM, p. 5.

sible conditions). The possible conditions, ordinarily having to do with an observer, are in turn possible because they would be necessary under other possible conditions; and so the difficulty moves on. How are *any* of the possible conditions possible, when contrary conditions are actual (i.e., necessary under actual conditions)?

A partial basis for alternative possibilities is suggested indirectly when Kant calls attention, in his "General Note on the System of Principles," to the fact that not only intuitions, but 'outer', or spatial, intuitions are required for the categories to be applicable.[32] Kant here argues primarily that the application of categories requires something permanent as well as something successive; and that the permanent is intuitively given through the spatial character of our sense perceptions, as the persistence of one space through a series of times. Another feature of space, however, is at least equally evident and important—the existence of many locations in space at one time, and thus the availability of many possible observation points for the perception of one object at one time, whether or not all of them are actually occupied. This feature of a spatially perceived world, although Kant does not call attention to it, fits very precisely into his general framework; the subjective order of sense perceptions requires only time, which is therefore fundamental in the Transcendental Deduction, while an objective order different from the subjective requires space in which to be different from it while still including it.

The relation between space and the concept of present counterfactual possibilities has been clearly noted by Victor Lowe, who points out that experience contrary to the actual can be imagined as happening not only at a different time but also at the same time at a different place, and that the latter possibility is the indispensable and distinctive basis of a realistic epistemology.[33] And indeed it is rather tempting to suppose that our

---

[32] B 291-293.

[33] Victor Lowe, "Belief in Unobserved Contemporary Reality: a Realistic Experiential Analysis," *The Journal of Philosophy*, 50, No. 18 (Aug. 27, 1953), 547. Hereinafter cited as "Reality." Lowe's paper, making a strong case for the meaningful role of present counterfactuals in the concept of an objective world, is formulated largely as a criticism of Lewis for alleged failure, inherent

problem is now solved; that, if we substitute the actual spatial existence of observation points for the possible presence of an observer, we can regard the relation between the location of an object and any point in space as theoretically determining a group of sense perceptions, and then interpret Kant's 'possible experience' as referring to these. The modal distinction in terms of "the relation of the concept to the faculty of knowledge"[34] and therefore to an observer, i.e., the distinction between the actual and the possible, is superseded by a distinction in terms of the relation of the object to points in space, some occupied and some unoccupied but all equally actual.

This solution, however, is not quite adequate, because in Kant's world, however 'objective', we cannot dispense with consideration of an observer, or rather a knower. The objective world is the world as object of knowledge, and actual objects are objects of knowledge. Without some observer of something, there is nothing actual, because no sensation for anything to be "bound up with." (Presumably there are things in themselves, but this fact is irrelevant to what Kant means by actuality.) Since perception is spatial, a variety of simultaneous perceptions of one object requires a plurality of observation points; but this condition, although necessary, is not sufficient for objectivity. Only if we can conceive that some of these points could be *occupied*, although actually they are not, can we think of them as part of the determining conditions of an objective order of experience, or an order of objects of experience. And however many observation points may be available, no observer can observe from more than one place at a time, and there are causes which necessitate each one's presence just where he is and not elsewhere.

I think that the answer, although Kant is not explicit about it because he so badly muddles the question itself, is one that

---

in his pragmatism, to recognize that present (rather than merely future) counterfactuals are required. I believe, however, that Lewis's views on this matter are the same as Lowe's own, although they do indeed come into conflict with some of the more typically pragmatist doctrines that Lewis also adopts. It is not feasible to present here the basis for this interpretation of Lewis, but I have previously tried to do so in "Lewis and the Theory of Truth," *The Journal of Philosophy*, 53, No. 19 (Sept. 13, 1956) .

[34] A 219 = B 266.

proceeds quite precisely along standard Kantian lines. It may be found in the distinction between the modalities in their 'absolute' sense and the same modalities as 'postulates of empirical thought', or conditions of experience. By 'absolute', in such a context, Kant means independent of all conditions, self-validating, in a real, existential sense rather than a merely logical sense. An absolutely or unconditionally necessary being is the God of the ontological argument, who is also the only absolutely or unconditionally possible being (having the "original" possibility from which the possibility of all other possible things is "derivative"). And such a being also "includes in itself all reality."[35] In such a being, possibility, actuality, and necessity would all be absolute and would clearly coincide. They would also coincide in everything determined by such a being, as indeed they do in Spinoza's universe, which is precisely of this kind. Kant, however, explicitly rules out knowledge of any such being or interpretation of the knowledge that we do have as knowledge of absolute reality.

The modalities as conditions of experience, on the other hand, mean merely that anything that we can experience, or even conceive as experience, must be understood in terms of modal relationships to further experience. Thus the possible, in terms of the Postulates, is "possible only under conditions which themselves are merely possible," not unconditionally possible.[36] It is also, we may note, necessary under those same conditions, though not actual because the conditions themselves are not actual; and this necessity is the only kind that the actual itself has. As Kant puts it, "everything which happens is hypothetically necessary," i.e., has "a conditioned and therefore intelligible necessity."[37] An event, in other words, is necessary through its connection with a cause and relatively to that cause; it is causally explicable. What is a necessary—i.e., necessarily actual—experience under one set of circumstances (the actual occurrence of the cause) is a possible experience under another set (the possibility but non-actuality of the cause); and the 'necessary connection' itself

---

[35] A 578 = B 606.

[36] A 232 = B 284.

[37] A 228 = B 280.

is the same in both cases, connecting the same conditions with the same experience.

Because the conditions that make something fully possible are thus also those that make it actual, Schneeberger infers that the specifically possible and the actual must be identical;[38] but this inference overlooks the difference that is made by a difference in the modal status of the conditions themselves. Lowe, on the other hand, realizes that the concept of the possible but not actual as that which is possible in some respects, though not in others, may be applied to specifiable empirical possibilities, and not merely (as Schneeberger applies it) to that which is formally but not specifically possible. Thus counterfactual possibilities are those for which some of the necessary factual conditions are fulfilled, while others are not;[39] although the unfulfilled conditions must be possible (Lowe says "imaginable") .[40]

To the modal status of the conditions in turn, of course, the same analysis applies. The conditions that make an actual experience necessary must in turn be the necessary effects of another actual cause; while the conditions determining a possible experience, or at least those conditions that are themselves possible but not actual, must have a further necessary connection with a further set of conditions including some that are possible but not actual; and so on. If the actual and possible experiences are mutually exclusive alternatives, e.g., seeing the roof and seeing the basement at a given time, then the same is true of at least some of the respective causal conditions of these experiences, e.g., looking up and looking down, and true also of the two entire series of causal conditions extending back into the past. This might seem to mean that the allegedly possible series never really had a chance, since it never got off to an actual start. Moreover, since the contrary series has been necessary at every point, is it not necessary as a whole, and the whole alternative series impossible?

But the answer, by now, is obvious. We must remember the antinomies. There is no whole series, or series as a whole, neces-

38 KKM, pp. 7, 9.

39 "Reality," p. 544.

40 "Reality," p. 552.

sary or possible, and neither of the two series ever got off to any sort of start, actual or not. Thus every modality is not only relative, but relative only to its immediate conditions, i.e., determined one step at a time; for knowledge of the real empirical world, unlike an abstract conceptual system, works outward in all directions in time and space from the point where we are. Thus "the real things of past time," Kant says, "are objects for me" in terms of "a regressive series of possible perceptions in accordance with empirical laws"[41]—not in terms of a series proceeding from a given logically and temporally prior starting point.

There is, however, one absolute involved in all this, and it must be taken into account. When Kant makes clear that both possibility and necessity in the empirical world are relative to empirical conditions, and thus hypothetical rather than absolute, he cannot do quite the same for actuality. The actuality of sense perceptions that actually occur, just *as* they occur, is, after all, unconditional. As Schneeberger points out, while we cannot know that something is actual by knowing that the entire series of conditions for its possibility is fulfilled (since we cannot complete such a series in knowledge), we can know that something is possible by knowing by means of experience that it is actual.[42] The actually given content of our experience, the ultimate concrete subject matter of our knowledge, might seem, therefore, to be an absolute starting point, determining which 'possible' series of conditional necessities is the actual one and thus *really* necessary, and ruling out any alternative as impossible.

It must be remembered, at this point, that in reference to a bare sensation, considered in isolation from experience as a whole, the concepts of possibility and necessity have no meaning. A sensation is simply given, just there—or it is nothing. In this sense, it may appropriately be regarded as actual; but then we are already contrasting it with the possible and the necessary, applying modal categories to it, dealing with it in terms of a conceptual structure. A given sensation as such, taken alone, makes nothing possible or impossible or necessary and determines no actuality except its own. It has necessary connections, inferences

---

41 A 495 = B 523.
42 KKM, pp. 20-21, 68.

can be drawn from it, only because it functions as a sense *perception*—because, in combination with other sense perceptions, it is interpreted in terms of a world of actual objects and objective events. The 'rules' for determining its necessary connections are themselves determined when we apply the concept of an object; and the particular concept of an object that we do apply can be so employed only as long as these connections hold empirically. For Kant is quite aware that no concept can make anything happen; it can merely determine necessary connections between events that do happen. If we look upstream and fail to see the ship that we saw there previously, we infer that the ship has moved on; and if we cannot find it anywhere, cannot find anyone who has ever seen it, cannot establish any necessary connections at all between our perception of it and any other empirical event, we have the kind of situation of which Kant says that we must "regard the succession as a merely subjective play of . . . fancy" or as "a mere dream."[43] Thus the actuality of objective things and objective events is a hypothetical, conditional actuality after all.

An actual causal series is of course distinguished from any alternative possible one by the fact that it contains the actual sense perceptions which make the whole structure empirically relevant. Yet we cannot trace it far in terms of actual sense perceptions alone; for we soon reach causal conditions which have not been perceived but could have been—the growth of the trees, for example, from which the lumber was cut to build the house and the ship. By starting with our actual perceptions of the house or ship and tracing 'necessary connections', we may infer that such trees actually did grow. This means, however, that it was possible to perceive them in the course of such a process, not that anyone did. Such a possibility is an objective, specifiable one, unlike the possibility of seeing a mermaid, because both its necessary occurrence under further possible conditions (concerning an observer) and the necessary series of effects of the perceivable but unperceived events, *up to the actually perceived house and ship,* depend on connections which are necessary if and only if the trees were there.

The absolute actuality that sensations may be said to possess

----

means that sensations must be included in any structure of knowledge that is to be existentially relevant; otherwise, even if we used empirical concepts, we should have an abstract conceptual construction in which "no mark of its existence is to be found."[44] But since nothing follows inferentially from sensations without concepts, their actuality in this absolute sense is not transferable. If we were to try to use the concept of absolute actuality in place of the modal concept of an actuality contingent upon the place of our perceptions in an understandable experience of an objective empirical world, we should have to say that the trees never grew and that there is no such world. This, however, is clearly not what Kant did.

Whether or not there is, as Wolff apparently believes, some special difficulty about counterfactual possibilities in connection with the principle of reciprocity[45] is difficult to determine, because of the special difficulties of Kant's entire discussion of the Third Analogy. The assertion that all coexistent substances "are in thoroughgoing reciprocity,"[46] that every substance has a relation of causal interdependence with *every* other substance contemporaneous with it, does seem to indicate a complete and absolute deterministic system much more explicitly than the assertion of the Second Analogy that every event has *some* prior event as its cause.

It is, of course, analytically true that any actual situation, at the time when it is actual, rules out any contrary situation at that same time as impossible; but this means merely that both cannot exist at once, not that the second could not under any circumstances exist instead of the first. And in the sense in which an actual sensation is simply what does in fact exist, an absolute starting point for determining what is actual or possible or necessary in the empirical world, we must come back to the fact that no mere sensation determines anything about any other, although it provides empirical content and existential relevance for the conceptual structure that does make the determinations. In cases of reciprocal causality as in those of one-way causality, the entities so related are not actual sensations but actual objects or objective events which happen to

---

44 A 225 = B 272.

45 KTMA, pp. 289-291.

46 B 256.

actual objects; and any such object *includes* a system of alternative possibilities.

Any of the language of the Third Analogy that may seem to imply more than this constitutes the kind of overstatement of his case into which Kant seems frequently to be led by his convictions as to the importance of meeting the presumed demands of Newtonian physics. Aside from such considerations, the entirely 'regulative' character of all three analogies is particularly evident in the case of reciprocity, when we recall that the organization of all experience into one system, appearing again in Kant's doctrine as the Ideal of Pure Reason, is there made the ideal limit of application of the entire system of categories, not the actually complete accomplishment of any one of them, or even an attainable accomplishment at all.

If in this way the inclusion of possible as well as actual experience in the actual objective world can be justified in terms of Kant's premises, the effectiveness of his analysis is immeasurably greater than it can otherwise be. If not, it is difficult to regard the actual object as quite satisfactorily objective.

The dissatisfaction is relatively mild on the part of Wolff, whose clear grasp of the problem includes a recognition that the criticism of Kant's view as scepticism is "extremely hard to meet" under these circumstances, but who tries to meet it nevertheless. If the demand for knowledge of "an independent universe of objects," "an ontologically independent object," is (as Kant has shown) a self-contradictory demand, Wolff argues, then we have no alternative but to accept Kant's great achievement—the substitution of "certain logical characteristics of judgments," i.e., universality and synthetic necessity, as constituting objectivity in the only meaningful sense.[47] But if this "synthetic necessity," as Wolff calls it, can be interpreted as including counterfactual necessity, and if the object of knowledge can thus be interpreted as including real particular possibilities not themselves experienced, there is a clear sense in which Kant's empirical world may very well be called "an independent universe of objects," even though it is not that "ontologically independent" universe that Wolff clearly recognizes to be ruled out as an object of knowledge.

---

47 KTMA, pp. 322-323.

When Strawson, on the other hand, speaks of Kant's "surrogate for awareness of the real, unknown object," the term 'surrogate' has a somewhat pejorative significance. It means to Strawson, as it would to those critics with whom Wolff contends in the passage just cited, that "*Really,* nothing comes within the scope of our experience but those subjective perceptions themselves."[48] According a high degree of importance and value to Kant's analysis of the conceptual structure of our knowledge of objects, but entirely overlooking the role that it assigns to determinately possible but non-actual experience, he recognizes no sense in which that structure may constitute an objective world in which perceptions are incorporated. Rather, he regards Kant as relegating the entire structure and all its contents to all-out subjectivity by refusing them the status of 'things in themselves'.

On the one hand, then, Strawson makes very clear and cogent Kant's argument that

> no one could be conscious of a temporally extended series of experiences as *his* unless he could be aware of them as yielding knowledge of a unified objective world, through which the series of experiences in question forms just one subjective or experiential route . . .

and that the permanent objective framework through which our temporal experience runs must be spatial. Yet, on the other hand, if such a world is not ontologically independent, it is not, for Strawson, genuinely objective after all; and the distinction between the subjective and objective time orders, although he greatly admires Kant's demonstration of its fundamental role, is itself a subjective distinction. This point of view is apparent when Strawson immediately goes on from this discussion to speak of the world so described as "spatial (or quasi-spatial) ."[49] Ironically, the function that Lewis has so clearly pointed out as fulfilled by that recognition of counterfactual possibilities which he finds in Kant is precisely that of establishing our own experience as "one subjective or experiential route" among many that are objectively possible.

Even Bird, for whom the concept of phenomenal objectivity is

---

48 P. F. Strawson, *The Bounds of Sense* (London: Methuen & Co., Ltd., 1966) , p. 91.

49 *The Bounds of Sense*, pp. 27-29.

of primary importance, runs into a certain amount of difficulty
with it by falling just short of recognition of the concept of possible experience in the specific sense. Arguing explicitly against
Prichard, whose views are paralleled in the relevant respects by
Strawson's, Bird sees that experience or appearance, in Kant's
view, is " 'of' something" that "could be experienced by other
people, or by the same person on different occasions, that is,
through different experiences." Yet the use of the word 'could' is
accidental here; Bird clearly means by it nothing explicitly different from 'can'. "Whatever is described in terms which can be applied to other particular experiences can be regarded as an object,"[50] he declares; and the "other particular experiences" are apparently assumed to be actual ones.

This comes very close to the mark nevertheless, but not quite
close enough when the role of causality is to be explained. There
is no way in which Bird can regard the objective time order as containing anything more than the subjective. It is the same events in
the same order, and differs only in being 'determinate' and thus
implying a 'determinant' or cause. (It must be conceded that Kant
himself sometimes gives this impression, but such passages are hardly
his most enlightening.) To differentiate the successive perceptions
of parts of the house from perception of an event, then, Bird must
argue that they do not imply a cause—that no "event can be inferred
from the description," although there are events (e.g., the movements of my eyes) in the "situation."[51] But it is not true that no
causal event can be inferred, if we take into account what we mean
by an objective house and what the role of the observer must be in
perceiving it; and if we do not take such factors into account, nothing can be inferred from any mere description. What we do infer is that the causal event is in the observer, not in the house;
but to recognize explicitly that there has been no change in the
house, we must recognize that all its parts have been simultaneously visible (i.e., it has been possible to perceive them) throughout
the time of the successive perceptions. The many merits of Bird's
interpretation generally tend to obscure inadequacies of this sort,
but they are there at the inevitable places.

---

50 Graham Bird, *Kant's Theory of Knowledge* (New York: Humanities Press,
1962) , pp. 132-133.

51 *Kant's Theory of Knowledge*, pp. 160-162.

All of these interpreters of Kant, it should be noted, make more or less frequent use of the expression 'possible experience' or 'the possibility of experience'. What they mean by it, however, is what Kant means by it in his first Postulate—the possibility of the kind of experience that we are equipped to have (the kind that is determined by space, time, and the categories) and the possibility of no other kind. Fundamental as this concept is in Kant's doctrine, however, it cannot fulfil the function of the concept of determinately possible (but not actual) specifiable experiences which Kant also calls 'possible experience' and which is indispensable for the understanding of his phenomenal world in its full objectivity.

BELLA K. MILMED

RUTGERS UNIVERSITY

KANT'S SECOND ANALOGY OF EXPERIENCE

I

That part of the *Critique of Pure Reason* entitled "Second Analogy (of Experience) ," which contains Kant's main treatment of causality, is of central importance in his system. After all, according to Kant, it was Hume's handling of causality which stimulated the "Critical" philosophy,[1] and it is the "transcendental deduction" of the principle of causality which Kant almost invariably cites as an example of that method.[2] Kant authorities as different as Adickes and Paton agree on its importance. The former calls it "truly the focus" of the whole work.[3] Paton writes that "it would be difficult to exaggerate the importance which Kant's proof" in the Second Analogy "has in the system of the Critical Philosophy"—"for Kant the real crux of his doctrine is to be found there."[4] Even some writers who consider that Kant's argumentation fails—like Jonathan Bennett in one of the most recent books on Kant—think that this section of the *Critique* is of major significance. Thus Bennett writes that the text of the first and second Analogies is "one of the great passages in modern philosophy."[5]

But despite this, and the immense literature on Kant, there is next to no measure of agreement about the correct appraisal of the argument in the Second Analogy, or even about what the argument is.[6] The main aim of the following paper is to answer both these

---

1 *Prolegomena*, trans. P. G. Lucas (Manchester, 1953) , p. 9.

2 *Critique of Pure Reason*, B 162-63, A 221 = B 268, A 542 = B 570, A 766 = B 794 (Kemp Smith's translation, pp. 172, 240, 496f., 610f.) .

3 *Immanuel Kants Kritik der reinen Vernunft*, ed. E. Adickes (Berlin, 1889) , p. 211 n.

4 H. J. Paton, *Kant's Metaphysic of Experience* (London, 1936) , Vol. II, p. 222 and n. (All further reference to Paton will be to this work.)

5 J. Bennett, *Kant's Analytic* (Cambridge, 1966) , p. 181.

6 Cf. L. W. Beck: "Once More Unto the Breach: Kant's Answer to Hume, Again" *Ratio*, 9 (1967) , 33: "It is a continuing scandal of philosophical scholarship that after nearly two centuries the question must still be debated:

questions. I shall not make any attempt to develop arguments which might be suggested by what Kant says, but which are more or less clearly not what he actually does say, though this is an important use to which the study of Kant may be put. I shall try as far as possible to take the Second Analogy as a self-contained piece of philosophical writing, and treat it in a way which presupposes as little as possible any detailed acquaintance with Kant.

Quotations from the *Critique of Pure Reason* will be in N. Kemp Smith's translation (2nd edition, 1933), page references to which are preceded by 'p', but the quotations are occasionally modified. As is customary, the first edition of the *Critique* is referred to as 'A' and the second edition as 'B'.

II

To begin with, I shall say something about the aim of the argumentation in the Second Analogy.

Without much doubt the goal is to prove that the principle of causality is a synthetic necessary statement.

What just has been called the principle of causality is referred to in A as the "Principle of Production (Erzeugung)" and formulated as: "Everything that happens, that is, begins to be, presupposes something upon which it follows according to a rule." This way of putting it is replaced in B by what is called the "Principle of Succession in Time, in accordance with the Law of Causality," which is formulated thus: "All alterations take place in conformity with the law of the connection of cause and effect." By way of gloss on this it may be remarked that Kant uses as synonyms 'alteration *(Veränderung)*', '*Geschehen*', '*Begebenheit*' (and cognates), which may be variously translated 'occurrence', 'happening',

---

What was Kant's answer to Hume? Until there is agreement about this, there is little reason to hope that the philosophical problem of the adequacy of a theory like Kant's to answer questions raised by a theory like Hume's can be solved." (I am indebted to Professor Beck for some critical comments on an earlier draft of this paper.) Beck's paper is, in part, a criticism of some recent contributions to this controversy, viz. E. W. Schipper, "Kant's Answer to Hume's Problem," *Kant-Studien*, 53 (1961), 68-74, M. E. Williams, "Kant's Reply to Hume", *Kant-Studien*, 55 (1965), 71-78, and R. P. Wolff, *Kant's Theory of Mental Activity* (Cambridge, Mass., 1963).

'event'. They all signify the coming to be or passing away of some 'determination' of a substance. Thus, the freezing of water is an event, for it is the coming to be of a state of the water, namely, solidity, which did not previously exist (the water having been in the liquid state) (B 162, p. 172) ; again, the movement of a ship drifting down stream, from one position to another relative to the banks, is an event (A 192=B 237, p. 221) .[7]

The principle of causality (as we may continue to call the above for short) is said to be synthetic, because the concept of cause is logically independent of the concept of an event.[8] This is comparatively uncontroversial. The real task is to show that the principle is also necessary, which amounts for Kant to its being knowable a priori as true.[9]

Besides this there seems to be a second strand running through the Second Analogy, namely the thesis that the causal relation is characterised by some non-empirical necessity, of the sort that Hume is generally taken[10] to have rejected. (That Kant held no other view of the modal status of causal laws is not absolutely definite.[11] But it is reasonably certain that it was his main view.) The tying together of the two theses comes out clearly enough, to cite just one example, where Kant contrasts the view that he is espousing with "all that has hitherto been taught in regard to the procedure of our understanding" (A 195-6 = B 240-1, pp. 223f.) . (It also emerges elsewhere, e.g., B 4-5, p. 44.) It is quite unclear

---

[7] Kant sometimes speaks of an event as a change of state of a substance (so, e.g. à propos the freezing of the water). But this is not appropriate for the description of his ship example, since, assuming that the motion of the ship is uniform and rectilinear, such a motion from one position to another is not, strictly, a change of the ship's state. Cf. Kant, A 207 = B 252, note a, p. 230.

[8] A 9 = B 13, A 301 = B 357, A 737 = B 765 (pp. 50 f., 302, 592) .

[9] E.g. B 4f., p. 44. See L. W. Beck, "The Second Analogy and the Principle of Indeterminacy" Kant-Studien, 57 (1966) , 199-205, for argument to the effect that the question of the viability of the Second Analogy is independent of any results, as regards indeterminism, of quantum physics.

[10] For queries regarding this standard view see W. A. Suchting, "Hume and Necessary Truth," Dialogue, 5 (1966) , 47-60.

[11] On the question of Kant's views regarding the logical status of scientific laws, and the relation of the latter to the general principle of causality see G. Buchdahl, "Causality, Causal Laws and Scientific Theory in the Philosophy of Kant," British Journal for the Philosophy of Science, 16 (1965) , 187-208.

whether Kant thought that 'Necessarily, every event has a cause' entails 'If A is a cause of B, then A and B are necessarily connected'. If he did, then he was wrong, for the two are logically independent of one another. It might be that necessarily every event has a cause, but that all particular causal relations are contingent; it might be that a cause is necessarily connected with its effect, but that not all events have causes, or, if they do, that this is only contingently the case. So that whether or not Kant succeeded in proving that the principle of causality is necessary in some sense, this has no direct bearing on the question of the modality of particular causal laws. It could be that Kant thought that the necessity of particular causal laws followed from this overarching thesis that the mind somehow stamps laws on the intrinsically formless given (whatever this may mean).[12] But whatever may be the case about this the thesis in question does not follow from the specific argumentation of the Second Analogy, with which we are concerned here. For these reasons I shall henceforth simply ignore this view about the modal character of laws as a thesis to be proved by the argument of the Second Analogy.

III

With regard to the actual argumentation of the Second Analogy, one of the only things that practically all writers on Kant agree on is that the presentation is unclear. However, very many of the commentators on this part of the *Critique* also agree that it contains more than one argument. Divergences arise rather about just how many different arguments there are, their interrelations, and so on.

But any account of the Second Analogy which finds more than one distinct argument must surely reckon with Kant's own assertion, almost at the end of the *Critique* (A 787-8 = B 815-6, p. 624), that "only *one* proof can be found for each transcendental proposition," and his citing precisely the deduction of the principle of causality as an instance of this. Of course, Kant may simply have been in error about the character of his own argument. Again, what he says here may be compatible with the existence of several

---

12 Cf. on this J. Bennett, *op. cit.*, pp. 156-9.

distinct arguments; perhaps he meant just that there was only one general line of argument. Nevertheless Kant's own words make it reasonable to say that an interpretation which makes just one basic argument out of what is said in the Second Analogy, and which is not subject to difficulties any worse than those which beset any other interpretation, is to be preferred on that ground alone.

In what follows I want to argue for such a univocal interpretation. Main attention will be focussed on three parts of the text. One is the second of the two paragraphs which Kant added in B at the beginning of the original A text. (The first of these two paragraphs simply recapitulates the First Analogy.) This may be taken to be Kant's final, summarising word on the argument, and, insofar, its importance for the interpretation of the argument is obvious. The second part of the text to be concentrated on is the first four paragraphs of A, or counting from the beginning of the B text, as is most convenient, paragraphs 3 to 6 (A 189-94 = B 234-9, pp. 219-22). A good many commentators take subsequent paragraphs in A to be, with one major exception, broadly speaking, different restatements of the line of argument enunciated here and the drawing of consequences from it. The exception is the argument of paragraph 13-15 (of the B text—A 199-201 = B 244-6, pp. 225f.), which has been generally taken to contain an argument quite different from anything else in this Analogy.[13] It is obvious that any attempt to find a single argument in the Second Analogy must pay special attention to this part of what Kant says, and so this will be the third of the main passages to be specially considered.

IV

A. To begin with, the following steps in Kant's argumentation may be distinguished, based on the first two of the above three passages.

---

[13] See here N. Kemp Smith's *Commentary on Kant's Critique of Pure Reason* (London, 1918), pp. 363, 375; A. C. Ewing, *Kant's Treatment of Causality* (London, 1924), p. 73, and his *Short Commentary on Kant's Critique of Pure Reason* (London, 2nd edition, 1950) p. 158. Paton notes this general opinion, p. 253.

(1) At least some of our perceptions of state of the same object are successive.

Kant himself asserts that all are; but this is both problematic and unnecessary for the purposes of the argument.

(2) Of these we take some to be simply successive perceptions of coexisting states, as when we stand fairly close to a large building and look at various portions one after another. Others we take to correspond to an objective succession of states, as when we watch a boat drifting downstream.

That we are conscious of an objective order in time is assumed as a result of the general 'transcendental deduction of the categories'.

Put otherwise, this premise asserts that succession in perception is not a sufficient condition for succession in what is perceived.

(3) Pure time, time in itself, cannot be perceived.

Therefore, which series of perceptions correspond to objective successions (events) and which do not cannot be determined by reference to time itself.

(4) We have no access to things, in the sense of entities statements about which cannot be translated into statements about actual and possible perceptions.

Therefore, which series of perceptions correspond to objective successions and which do not cannot be determined by reference to things. (We do not even know whether 'things' are temporal in nature. "How things may be in themselves, apart from the representations through which they may affect us, is entirely outside our sphere of knowledge." A 190 = B 235, p. 220.)

The phenomenalistic character of Kant's whole orientation, or at least, the idea that 'things', insofar as they exist, are not objects of knowledge, is worth remarking upon here, because it is very natural to read the Second Analogy from the point of view of a realistic framework. This is apparent in the locutions by which it is not unnatural to frame Kant's premises. Thus one speaks of perceptions *of* states, perceptions *corresponding to* events, and so on, its being thereby almost inevitably suggested that Kant thinks of the perception of the state (for example) as being different from the state. But such a reading is responsible for much puzzlement about Kant's meaning. For Kant the 'material' content of apprehension is always one and the same, namely, sense-impressions as they may be called. The different sorts of content are distinguished by the different relations of these sense-impressions to one another. Thus it would be less misleading, though intolerably awkward and prolix to speak not, for example, of perceptions of successive states, but rather of, say, successive-state-perception-series. But as long as this orientation is kept firmly in mind no great harm is done by using locutions with realistic overtones.

Assuming that there is no other avenue by which the requisite distinction might be sought, it is concluded that

(5) Which series of perceptions correspond to events must be determined by reference to characteristics of the series themselves. B. What then is the (relational) difference between series of perceptions which correspond to events, and those which correspond to coexisting states? I shall begin consideration of this point by citing what may be taken to be the relevent passages from each of the two parts of the argumentation of the Analogy to which attention has thus far been devoted.

Suppose the series of perceptions consists of just two perceptions, A and B; and suppose the first is the preceding. Then, Kant says,

> in an appearance which contains a happening . . . B can be apprehended only as following upon A . . . The order in which the perceptions succeed one another in apprehension is . . . determined (*bestimmt*) . . . In the series of . . . perceptions [of, for example, a house, there is] no determinate (*bestimmte*) order specifying at what point I must begin in order to connect the manifold empirically. But in the perceptions of an event there is always a rule that makes the order in which the perceptions (in the apprehension of this appearance) follow upon one another a *necessary* order . . . The objective succession will therefore consist in that order of the manifold of appearance according to which *in conformity with a rule,* the apprehension of that which happens follows upon the apprehension of that which precedes. . . . In conformity with such a rule there must lie in that which precedes an event the condition of a rule according to which this event invariably and necessarily follows. I cannot reverse this order, proceeding back from the event to determine (*bestimmen*) through apprehension that which precedes. For appearance never goes back from the succeeding to the preceding point of time, though it does indeed stand in relation to *some* preceding

point of time. The advance, on the other hand, from a given time to the determinate (bestimmte) time that follows is a necessary advance. Therefore, since there certainly is something that follows, I must refer it necessarily to something else which precedes it and upon which it follows in conformity with a rule, that is, of necessity. The event, as the conditioned, thus affords reliable evidence of some condition, and this condition is what determines (bestimmt) the event. (A 192 = B 237 — A 194 = B 239, pp. 221f.)

The corresponding passage in the introductory part of B runs:

In order that . . . the *objective relation* of appearances that follow upon one another . . . be known as determined (bestimmt) the relation between the two states must be so thought that it is thereby determined (bestimmt) as necessary which of them must be placed before, and which of them after, and that they cannot be placed in the reverse relation. But the concept which carries with it a necessity of synthetic unity can only be a pure concept that lies in the understanding, not in perception; and in this case it is the concept of the *relation of cause and effect,* the former of which determines (bestimmt) the latter in time, as its consequence . . . (B 234, p. 219)

C. These passages may be interpreted as containing the following premises:
(6) Necessarily, if A and B are the constituents of a certain event-perception, then the temporal order of perceptibility of A and B is what may be variously described as 'determined', 'determinate', 'in conformity with a rule', 'necessary'.

This is contrasted with the case of the temporal order of perceptibility of the constituents of a perception of coexistent states. In the latter case we can, in principle, go through the series in any order in time. In the stock example, we can begin with the top of the wall and move our eyes downward, or do the opposite, or undertake a number of other eye-movements. But if we choose to witness the event of a boat's floating downstream, then, given some standard physical circumstances, we can have a series of perceptions in only one order.
(7) Necessarily, if the temporal order of perceptibility of A and B is 'determined' (etc.), then A and B are causally related (directly or indirectly) .

The conclusion is that, necessarily, if A and B are constituents of a certain event-perception, then A and B are causally related (directly or indirectly) —which was to be demonstrated.

D. In his recent book, *Kant's Analytic* (Cambridge, 1966) Jonathan Bennett has concentrated his criticism of what he takes to be Kant's explicit argument in the Second Analogy on what is essentially premise (6) in the above formulation of the argument. A consideration of what I take to be the main point of Bennett's criticism may serve at least to illuminate Kant's argument here.

In brief, Bennett takes Kant to be saying that in the case of a given series of perceptions of coexisting states of an object—what Bennett usefully calls a 'survey'—I could have rearranged my visual states so that their order would have been different if I had behaved differently; but if, for example, I see a ship leave a harbour "no action of mine could have altered the order in which my visual states occurred." (*Op. cit.*, p. 222) Bennett objects that this cannot be a generally adequate basis for the distinction, because it is possible to construct examples in which the perception of what may be taken to be an event satisfies, not the condition just described, but rather the condition for a survey. For example,

> (a) I saw a long-boat being rowed out of the harbour; which, if Kant's analysis is right, entails not just that my visual states *did* occur in a certain order but that (b) *I could not have* had them in any other order. But since the coxswain of the boat was under orders from me, I *could have* secured for myself the spectacle of the boat being back-paddled, stern foremost into the harbour. So (a) is true and (b) false, and Kant's analysis of (a) is therefore wrong. (*Loc. cit.*)

But this ignores a crucial distinction between the two cases. Consider the event of the boat's moving from one part of the harbour outwards to another part. Kant may be taken to be saying that, given the situation as it was, I could not have had the perceptions making up *this* event in any order other than that which I had them. He could hardly have claimed that I could not have had similar perceptions in any other order, for, clearly, similar perceptions in the reverse order would have corresponded to the event of the boat's being paddled into the harbour sternwards. But this would have been a different event. And the difference between my bringing this about by orders to the coxswain and my bringing about a different order of perceptions of the parts of the wall is that in the former case I can bring about a different order of perceptions only by causally influencing the state of affairs itself, whilst in the case of the wall I can bring about the difference by causally influencing myself alone. The difference may be also brought out in the following way. If we suppose two people looking at the wall, then each can, at the same time, have a different series of perceptions of the wall. If we suppose two relevantly similar people looking at the boat leaving the harbour, then, given the same external causal conditions, each cannot but have the same series of perceptions. If we suppose that they look at the boat again, my having *this* time ordered the coxswain to row in backwards, then they will certainly now have a differently ordered set of perceptions; but each will have the same series as the other.

My conclusion is that Bennett's criticism does not invalidate Kant's argument at this point.

E. Let us now turn to an independent consideration of (6) and (7).

A matter of primary importance here is clearly the sense in which 'determined', 'necessary' (etc.) is to be taken in (6). Graham Bird in his generally very illuminating book *Kant's Theory of Knowledge* (London, 1962), takes it that the necessity which Kant speaks of in the passages quoted, and which is embodied in (6), is the logical necessity that to apprehend a certain event E is just to apprehend a certain fixed, determinate sequence of states, so that to apprehend any other sequence of these states would be, by definition, to apprehend an event other than E.

If this is the sense in which 'necessary' is to be taken in (6), then the latter is at the very least, very plausible indeed. But is the sense given (6) one which will also allow us to affirm (7), and so arrive at the desired conclusion? How is necessity in this sense linked with causality? Mr. Bird goes on to say, expounding Kant, and presumably, in the absence of any dissenting comment, agreeing with him:

> the idea of a determinate order between two states presupposes that of something which determines it; and this idea of a determinant or reason for such an order is that of a cause. (*Op. cit.*, p. 155)

But if this faithfully reproduces Kant's train of thought, then the argument at this crucial point rests simply on a pun. For without an equivocation how could one get from the proposition that events are *logically determinate*, in the sense that they are constituted by a determinately (i.e. definitely, specifically) ordered sequence of states, to the conclusion that this sequence is *causally determined*, i.e. such that the determinate order in question is due to some causal relation?[14] Not even the notion of 'presupposing' which has been asked to carry such a diversity and weight of philosophical burdens, is capable of sustaining this transition.

If such an error occurs, then it may be that Kant was misled by the very word '*bestimmt*' which he used, the latter being a common expression both for logically determinate as well as for causally determined. Or it could have been a fallacy of the following sort: to have inferred from (i) 'Necessarily, if A and B are the constituents of a certain event-perception, then the temporal order of A and B is necessary' that (ii) 'If A and B are the constituents of a certain event-perception, then necessarily, if A, then B', the latter conclusion's then being detached.

F. However, I do not think that Kant's argument is faithfully reproduced in this way, for I think that he has a specific argument in mind for the linking of that objective order of states in time, which constitutes an event, with causality, even though it involves a fallacy parallel to that just pointed out. This argument is only briefly indicated in that part of the passage already cited from A, which begins "I cannot reverse this order" and ends with the quotation. In this part Kant may be interpreted as putting forward a certain argument about the relation between the state-perceptions constituting an event, and the parts of the pure time in which they occur. I suggest that just this argument is spelled out in detail in the latter paragraphs 11-15, i.e. just those paragraphs which have been widely taken to be anomalous with respect to the other parts of the text of the Second Analogy and to contain a quite different

---

14 A confusion of this sort is pointed to by R. E. Hobart in his undeservedly forgotten paper "Hume Without Scepticism," *Mind*, 39 (1930), pp. 287-9. Cf. also P. F. Strawson, *The Bounds of Sense. An Essay on Kant's 'Critique of Pure Reason'* (London, 1966), pp. 28, 137f.

argument from the rest.[15] The main parts of this later passage are as follows:

> If . . . it is a . . . *formal condition* of all perceptions, that the preceding time necessarily determines (*bestimmt*) the succeeding (since I cannot advance to the succeeding time save through the preceding), it is also an indispensable law of *empirical representation* of the time-series that the appearances of past time determine all existences in the succeeding time, and that these latter, as events, can take place only in so far as the appearances of past time determine their existence in time, that is, determine them according to a rule . . . Understanding . . . [makes] the representation of an object possible at all . . . by carrying the time-order over into the appearances and their existence. For to each of them, [viewed] as (a) consequent, it assigns, through relation to the preceding experiences, a position determined *a priori* in time . . . absolute time is not an object of perception . . . On the contrary, the appearances must determine for one another this position in time, and make their time-order a necessary order. In other words, that which follows or happens must follow in conformity with a universal rule upon that which was contained in the preceding state . . . (A 199-200 = B 244-245, pp. 225f.)

If we adopt the interpretation suggested above, then Kant may be taken to be arguing the required connection between objective temporal succession and causality in the following way:

(a) Necessarily, if A and B are the constituents of an event-perception, then A and B occupy successive places in objective, pure time.

(b) Necessarily, the relation between A and B reproduces, empirically, the relation between the successive places in pure time that they occupy.

---

[15] Paton says in a note that the passage at A 194 = B 239 "bears a certain external resemblance to" the arguments at paragraphs 13-15 (p. 244 n.), and in another note (p. 253, n. 2) that "it seems . . . just possible that Kant may have regarded" the later passage "as an elaboration of what is obscurely hinted at" in the earlier. This caution is rather puzzling in view of Paton's tendency to stress the unity of Kantian arguments, and in particular his emphasis on the argument from the continuity of time to the necessity of causal connection (e.g. pp. 225, 256, n.l., 274, 292f.). The only other writer I have come across who emphasizes this strand of argument is Kuno Fischer in his *Immanuel Kant und seine Lehre* (Heidelberg, 5th edition, 1909), especially pp. 464f.

(c) Necessarily, successive parts of pure time are necessarily connected.

(d) Therefore, necessarily, the relation between A and B is the relation of necessary succession in time. But the latter is just the causal relation. Therefore, necessarily, if A and B are the constituents of an event-perception, then A and B are causally connected.

Before looking critically at this version of the argument, a couple of comments may be made about the grounds for taking this to be actually Kant's argument. It has already been suggested that a part of the first statement in A may be taken to be a highly compressed version of the later paragraphs 13-15. Nor is it impossible to find a connection with the passage already quoted from B. Such a connection may be discerned in the statement, right at the beginning of the part cited earlier to the effect that if the objective relation of states in time is to be "known as determined" it must be thought in accordance with the principle of causality. This may be read as suggesting that causal relations between states make possible the knowledge of the objective temporal relations which obtain between them and which obtain by virtue of their occupying successive parts of pure time. Again, the very closing sentences of the Second Analogy recapitulate just this argument.

> In the same manner . . . in which time contains the sensible *a priori* condition of the possibility of a continuous advance of the existing to what follows, the understanding, by virtue of the unity of apperception, is the *a priori* condition of the possibility of a continuous determination of all positions for the appearances of in this time, through the series of causes and effects, the former of which inevitably lead to the existence of the latter, and so render the empirical knowledge of the time-relation valid universally for all time, and therefore objectively valid. (A 210-11 = B 256, pp. 232f.)

(Compare also A 411 = B 438, p. 388.) Finally, the conjecture that the above is the essential line of the proof in the Second Analogy is supported by the central importance of this mode of argument in the First Analogy ("In all change of appearances substance is permanent."). In the A proof Kant writes, for example:

> the permanent is the *substratum* of the empirical representation of time itself . . . Permanence . . . expresses time in general . . .

In B he says:

time . . . is that in which . . . succession or coexistence can alone be represented. Now time cannot by itself be perceived. Consequently there must be found in the objects of perception . . . the substratum which represents time in general; and all change or coexistence must, in being apprehended, be perceived in this substratum, and through relation of the appearances to it. (B 225, p. 213)

G. At any rate, in what sense or senses, if any, do preceding parts of time 'in itself', 'pure' time (time considered in abstraction from changes in observable states of affairs) determine, necessarily, succeeding parts? And what is the relevance of this to the way in which one observable state of affairs may be said (causally) to determine another?

Kant says that "I cannot advance to the succeeding time save through the preceding." This may be construed as meaning that the past can be experienced only as before the future. But since, given some point of reference for the present, the past is, analytically, what comes before the future, this gets us no further. Suppose it be understood rather as saying that successive periods of time form a series in which no term can bear the same relation to that which precedes as to that which follows. But the only condition that this places on temporally qualified phenomena is that what is past with respect to something else cannot also be present or future with respect to it. But this is not equivalent to, nor does it entail that the same future must follow on the same past, i.e. that if a particular sequence has occurred once it must occur again whenever the relevant conditions are the same. Again, it might be understood as meaning that the limit of any period of time is fixed, on one side, by the time prior to it. Being a relation only, a period of pure time is wholly determined by external time-relations, for it is nothing but these. But when this period is considered concretely, as a qualitatively characterised series, its external time-relations constitute only one feature of it. Therefore, all that the argument would establish is that one aspect of the nature of time is determined by one of the relations it bears to other phenomena, i.e. the relation it bears to them as preceding or succeeding them in time. Furthermore, since the aspect thus determined is just its temporal relation to them as preceding or succeeding them in time, this is just a tautology. (This is also seen by considering the fact that a certain moment of time is determined not only by the preceding moment but also by the succeeding one.) The distinction between *events in* time and *moments of* time is just that an event is a particular which has characteristics other than its determinate temporal position, whereas a moment has only the latter (and any entailed relations). That t occurs before t+t′ entails that it is logically impossible that the latter should occur before the former, i.e. it is logically impossible that two moments of pure time should thus reverse their positions. Therefore it is simply analytic that two moments of time necessarily stand in the relative positions in which they do in fact stand.[16]

H. Finally, I want to consider a possible interpretation of the Kantian argument, the basis of which is not at all clear in the text of the Second Analogy itself, but might be read out of the argument of the Third Analogy.

The Third Analogy is concerned with judgements of objective coexistence, as the Second is concerned with judgements of objective succession. Kant repeats the point, already made in the Second Analogy, that if A and B are two coexistent states of a substance, then they can be perceived in either order. But he goes on to argue that the fact that they can be perceived in either order (as found by actual trial, for example) is not sufficient for objective coexistence. For suppose that whenever A is perceived, B temporarily vanishes, but reappears when attention is directed to where it was; and suppose A behaves similarly. Then, though A and B are perceivable in either order, they are not coexistent. In sum, the actual perceivability of A and B in either order is a necessary, but not sufficient condition for judging truly that A and B are objectively coexistent. Kant goes on to say that actual perceivability of A and B in either order is necessary and sufficient for judging truly that A and B are objectively coexistent, only relatively to the conditions that they are necessary conditions for the existence of each other. (A 211 = B 257, p. 234) That A and B are necessary

---

16 The criticisms advanced here have been made already by Ewing in his *Kant's Treatment of Causality* (London, 1924), pp. 74-6, and by C. D. Broad, "Kant's First and Second Analogies of Experience," *Proceedings of the Aristotelian Society,* **26** (1925-26), 208-10. For a defense of Kant here see Paton, especially pp. 254 n. 8, 255 n. 5, 256.

conditions for the existence of the other guarantees that whilst one is perceived the other is coexistent with it.

This line of argument may be applied to the case of judgements of objective succession. If A and B are two successive states of a substance, then they can be perceived in only one order. But that they can be perceived thus is not sufficient for objective successiveness. For suppose that whenever the first member is perceived it immediately passes out of sight (hearing, etc.) though it continues to exist. Then though A and B are perceivable in only one order they would be objectively coexistent and not successive. Thus, actual perceivability of A and B in only one order is a necessary, but not sufficient condition for judging truly that A and B are objectively successive. Kant might be taken to be arguing further that this is only necessary and sufficient relatively to the satisfaction of some condition that one does not exist until the other does. The requisite condition is, in the simplest case, that one state should be a causally necessary condition (in the circumstances) for the existence of the other. (In more complex cases it might be that one is simultaneous with a causal condition of the other, or that each is simultaneous with one of the two causally related states, and so on.) For, if in the simplest case, one is not a causally necessary condition for the existence of the other, it would always be possible that A and B should coexist.

H. But this argument would not show that there could not be an objective sequence that was not a causal sequence. It could be taken as suggesting an argument according to which the assumption of a causal relation between A and B is a necessary and sufficient condition for *reliably* judging them to stand in a relation of objective succession. Further filling in of the argument would be necessary here however in view of Kant's belief that "the great majority of efficient natural causes are simultaneous with their effects," (A 203 = B 248, p. 228). It might be that an independent argument can be worked out along these lines. But it would have a conclusion a great deal weaker than the official conclusion of the Second Analogy. Kant does indeed speak in the course of the latter of one's being "justified in asserting" that such and such a manifold is successive as dependent on that manifold's being subject to a rule. (A 193 = B 238, p. 222, and also A 195 = B 240, p. 223) But this can only be a manner of speaking, for the central thesis of the

Second Analogy relates to the impossibility of uncaused events, and not merely to the conditions, if there are any, under which certain sequences of perceptions may be justifiably or reliably judged to be event-perceptions.

In fact, it is very difficult to see how it would be possible validly to get from (6) to the conclusion in question. It is plausible to say, with regard to (6), that if A B constitute an event, then the order of apprehension is, given certain standard circumstances, independent of us. This is as much as to say that any similar person in just these circumstances would have the perceptions in this order. But it still does not follow from this that A and B must be causally related (even in contingent fashion). For it seems possible that, for example, A should have occurred in a causally determined way, but that the later B should have been causally undetermined. Then since B had not occurred when A occurred, the order of perceptibility is subject to the universal in question, but A and B are not causally related. (There may well be epistemic difficulties as to how it could be *known* that B *was* later, and not merely *noticed* later, but this does not affect the point being made.)

V

A final point concerning the interpretation of Kant's argument may be made. Kant has frequently been regarded as offering, in the tradition initiated by Leibniz, a causal theory of the nature of time, as suggesting that temporal relations are constituted by, or explicitly definable in terms of causal relations.[17] But, as has been seen, this is not the intent of Kant's argument at all. That Kant does not attempt to define temporal notions in terms of causal ones

[17] For a linking of Leibniz and Kant in this way, see, for example, H. Mehlberg, "Essai sur la théorie causale du temps" *Studia Philosophica*, 1 (1935), pp. 135f, 158, etc. H. Scholz, "Eine Topologie der Zeit im Kantischen Sinne," *Dialectica*, 9 (1955), p. 73, G. J. Whitrow, *The Natural Philosophy of Time* (London, 1961), p. 273 (but cf. p. 177), A. Grünbaum, *Philosophical Problems of Space and Time* (London, 1963), p. 179—Leibniz's path-breaking ideas in this direction are contained in his "Initia rerum mathematicarum metaphysica," written in 1716, but not published till 1863 in C. I. Gerhardt's edition of Leibniz's *Mathematische Schriften*, Vol. VII. See especially the passage on p. 18 (translated on p. 1083 of Vol. II of L. E. Loemker's edition of *Leibniz's Philosophical Papers and Letters*, Chicago, 1956).

is clear both from the general lines of his system and from specific passages in the *Critique of Pure Reason*. He uses the notion of something's following something else in time quite freely as a primitive notion, as is indeed proper, constitutive questions regarding time having already been dealt with in the *Aesthetic*. Again, Kant says very explicitly that the ordinary notion of cause makes essential reference to the notion of time. Thus:

> If I omit from the concept of cause the time in which something follows upon something else in conformity with a rule, I should find in the pure category nothing further than that there is something from which we can conclude to the existence of something else. In that case not only would we be unable to distinguish cause and effect from one another, but since the power to draw such inferences requires conditions of which I know nothing, the concept would yield no indication how it applies to any object. (A 243 = B 301, p. 262)

With regard to the distinction of cause and effect mentioned in this passage, Kant earlier noted in the Second Analogy that

> sequence in time is . . . the sole empirical criterion of an effect in its relation to the causality of the cause which precedes it. (A 203 = B 249, p. 228)

Hence, as Schopenhauer for one pointed out long ago,[18] Kant could not, non-circularly, say that A's being earlier than B is constituted by its being the cause of B (or simultaneous with a cause of B, etc.). Finally, any such project would have been thoroughly unKantian, since it involves the attempt to derive a form of sensibility (time) from a form of the understanding (causality). And Kant criticised precisely Leibniz's theory of space and time just on the ground that he had "intellectualised these forms of sensibility":[19]

---

[18] "Ueber die vierfache Wurzel des Prinzips des zureichenden Grundes," Section 23, *Sämtliche Werke*, edited by J. Frauentsädt and A. Hübscher (Wiesbaden, 1948), Vol. I, p. 91.

[19] E. Cassirer has argued that Kant's account of Leibniz's views in the following quotation is inaccurate. (*Leibniz's System in seinen wissenschaftlichen Grundlagen*, Marburg, 1902, pp. 264ff.). But whether this is so is clearly irrelevant to the point being made by means of this citation of Kant's view.

If I attempted, by the mere understanding, to represent to myself outer relations of things, this can only be done by means of a concept of their reciprocal action; and if I seek to connect two states of one and the same thing, this can only be in the order of grounds and consequences. Accordingly, Leibniz conceived space as a certain order in the community of substances, and time as the dynamical sequence of their states. That which space and time seem to possess as proper to themselves, in independence of things, he ascribed to the *confusion* in their concepts, which has led us to regard what is a mere form of dynamical relations as being a special intuition, self-subsistent and antecedent to the things themselves. (A 275-6 = B 331-2, pp. 285f.)

W. A. Suchting

University of Sydney

THE KANTIAN 'DYNAMIC OF REASON', WITH SPECIAL REFERENCE TO THE PLACE OF CAUSALITY IN KANT'S SYSTEM

I. *The Foundations of Theory*

One of the most fruitful approaches to Kant's central doctrines is a study of the manner in which the concept of causality is fitted into his conception of 'objectivity', or of 'nature in general',[1] and how from there it is linked with the conception of nature as subject to empirical laws,[2] and of these laws in turn being related as members of some theoretical system, forming what Kant calls 'a systematic unity',[3] which may also be taken as mirroring a 'unity in nature';[4] a unity which however possesses no more than postulational status, being labelled, in Kant's terminology, 'a mere idea'.[5]

This movement, from empirical fact to scientific law, and from law to theory, also works backward in an important way. For the system represented by a theory displays what Kant calls an 'order of nature';[6] e.g., the order displayed by a well-organised system of botanical or zoological classification, or again by some unified physical theory. Usually this order manifests itself as a system of particular empirical laws; laws which Kant affirms to have a necessitarian character, though they are at the same time 'contingent'

---

[1] I.e. 'nature' regarded as the 'sum of phenomena'. For this, cf. *Crit. of Pure Reason*, Kemp Smith trsl., p. 392 n. b [hereinafter cited as K.]; *Prolegomena*, trsl. P. G. Lucas, pp. 52-54 [hereinafter cited as P.].

[2] Cf. particularly *Critique of Judgement*, Introduction, sects. iv-v; trsl. J. H. Bernard, Hafner, New York, 1951, pp. 16-17, 19-21. [Hereinafter cited as J.].

[3] K. 563-66.

[4] K. 564.

[5] Cf. K. 544, 561, 566; J. 17.

[6] J. 21.

propositions since they are established on an empirical basis.[7] Now although if the laws did not possess this necessitarian character, 'they would not constitute an order of nature',[8] the latter is not 'given' but autonomously generated by the theoretical scientist's employment of a number of higher-level maxims of investigation, as well as a set of theoretical concepts.[9] We may thus say that the conception of lawlike necessity is to this extent defined by the character of the theoretical system, itself the resultant of 'the hypothetical employment of reason', in its 'regulative' function, which can do no more than 'project' the corresponding 'unity' into the world.[10]

Now, Kant expressly says, apart from such a projective process, all empirical laws, which have no more than an inductive foundation, are merely 'contingent' rules, each assigned to some particular thing or event regarded as cause; and the same goes for the system itself.[11] The necessitarian aspect is supplied only by our subjecting a given group of putative laws to this process of systematisation

---

[7] Kant mentions explicitly that we 'can never have any knowledge or special insight' into this necessity (*ibid.*), very much on the lines on which W. Kneale in our day has argued that although laws of nature constitute 'principles of necessitation', their necessity must always remain 'opaque to the intellect.' (Cf. *Probability and Induction*, Oxford, [1949], *passim*, for a defense of this view.) It will also be appreciated that for a particular law of nature to be both contingent and necessary is not the same thing as for a general principle of the understanding, e.g. the law of causation, to be both synthetic and *a priori*.

[8] *Ibid.*

[9] The maxims range from certain logical principles of classification to such methodological principles as the 'laws' of continuity, economy, and simplicity; cf. J. 18, 21; K. 535, 539-45. It should be noted that for Kant, they are however more than 'methodological', since we (or 'reason') read them as mirroring something corresponding in 'nature'; cf. K. 544.

[10] Cf. K. 535. Accordingly, it would not make sense to say that there exists such a unity—only that we operate with the corresponding concept.

[11] At J. 16, Kant writes expressly: 'These [laws], as empirical, may be contingent from the point of view of *our* understanding; and yet, if they are to be called laws (as the concept of nature requires), they must be regarded as necessary in virtue of a principle of the unity of the manifold, though it be unknown to us'. (For the sake of what follows, let me add that the 'manifold' here referred to is that of the system of empirical laws, and not that of individual perceptions which in the *transcendental* synthesis are likewise related through a 'unity of the manifold'.)

under the guidance of such methodological maxims, e.g. that 'nature takes the shortest way';[12] this teleological form explaining incidentally why Kant should have regarded these principles as 'principles of purposiveness'.[13]

II. *Empirical Laws and Causality*

So much for what I have called the movement from theory to law. What about the movement from law to contingent event, to the phenomena of nature *('Naturdinge')?*[14] Here, a result, important for the subsequent argument of this paper, must first be noted. The particular laws mentioned so far are established inductively, without there being made as much as a mention of any general principles of inductive justification. The only thing which may seem perhaps to correspond to such a justification, is the 'necessitarian' character of the laws. But that is *injected* in virtue of the regulative activity of reason; there is no question here of any general law of causation providing some putative inductive support for the empirical generalisations which on the contrary appear to

---

[12] J. 18; cf. J. 19-20 for the general point.

[13] J. 20. There are of course deeper and more pervasive reasons why Kant should have spoken here of 'purpose'. One of these lies in the special character of some of these systems, which unite laws that without a uniting principle would apparently seem to constitute a merely 'accidental' aggregate. For instance, that the laws of free-fall and of planetary motion form a system, is an expression of an underlying necessary unity, here of the force of gravity as well as the laws of motion. On the other hand, that such a very heterogeneous group of general laws as those of static equilibrium, collision, optics, should all be subject to a higher-order principle, i.e. the 'law of least action', is for Kant an indication of a 'purposive' adaptation of the parts of nature to one another. (Cf. *The only proof of the existence of God*, 1763, *Works, Akad. ed.*, ii, pp. 98-99. Kant's reference is to Maupertuis' *Essay de Cosmologie*, 1751, p. 21; cf. also *Histoire de l'académie royale des sciences et belles lettres*, 1746, pp. 268-94, under the title, "Les loix du movement et du repos déduites d'un principe métaphysique".) Kant is here operating in a peculiar way with the Platonic classification of 'necessity, chance and design', as employed, for instance, in the *Timaeus*. Although not mentioning Maupertuis by name, the whole point is repeated at J. 229-30 (§68). However, the direct suggestion of the coupling of minimum principles and teleology is no doubt due to Leibniz (cf. the latter's *Tentamen Anagogicum*.)

[14] J. 20.

receive such support solely through the systematisations of science. That, and that alone, can so far be meant by the expression that the world is subject to causal law, or shorter: subject to causality. Certainly this is not a causality without which we should not be able to formulate any cognitive judgements whatsoever; without which there would be 'no experience'—the kind of defense of general causality which we shall presently meet in the argument of the 'Analytic of Principles' of the first *Critique*. The only thing that notion gives us in connection with the present context is that without it there would be no *order of nature;* a condition which, as we noted, is also reversible.

To add confusion, it will be noted that the injection of causal necessity is undoubtedly an *a priori* matter, in the sense that this necessity is not *derived* from the inductive process of generalisation.[15] On the other hand, it is certainly not *a priori* in the sense which Kant made central in the 'Analytic', which is that of being a transcendental presupposition of experience. It follows, that the Kantian argument (to which I shall turn presently), that causality is a transcendental concept, can certainly not be regarded as relevant to the present aspect of nature viewed as an orderly system of laws. True, if we take our cue from both these fields, we may say summarily that causality is *a priori* as a transcendental presupposition for the possibility of contingent experience, as well as a generative source of the *causality of laws*. Nevertheless, it is vital to see that these are two altogether different contexts, however easily confused, and certainly interfused, in Kant's frequent descriptions of the place of causality in nature.

This brings me back once more to the matter whose consideration I deferred, the movement, as I called it, from law to contingent event. For if my sifting out of the complexities of Kant's presentation is correct, we may anticipate and say that one of the ways in which the causality which we have so far encountered at the level of 'reason' (i.e. systematic science) is going to make itself felt at the level of the 'understanding', is that the causality of *laws* is going to be used by Kant as a concept which defines the essential

---

15 There may be other senses. But Kant is usually silent on these; whether the causal concept has a psychological source, as the result of whose intimations it emerges into consciousness, is here irrelevant.

aspect (but now regarded as presupposition) of objective experience (*Erkenntnis*). Or, what comes to the same thing, that the
causality which we assert to govern the *order of nature*, is used as a
model through which we (i.e. the 'understanding') seek to 'generate' *nature* (or rather, its possibility) as the sum of physical objects
and processes. I think it is not implausible to suggest that Kant
treats one as a model for the other; the injection of causality into
empirical generalisations being regarded as something which is
analogous to the injection of causality into the empirical judgement concerning what Kant calls 'the succession [in time] of the
determinations of one and the same thing.[16]

This becomes clear if we look at some of Kant's examples. The
empirical generalisation that the pressure of air, when forced into a
smaller volume increases in inverse proportion to the volume,
acquires causal necessity, he claims, through 'subsumption . . .
under the concept of cause and effect';[17] and a similar subsumptive
procedure is required in order to convert the statement of regularity that when the sun shines, the stone grows warm, into the quite
different, causal statement, the sun warms the stone, regarded as an
instance of a causal law.[18] All these are cases, I wish to contend, of
what may be regarded as *models* for the quite different level of
transcendental argument to causation, and which Kant *illustrates*
by means of them. For his argument is supposed to show that the
concept of causation has to be added in order to 'generate experience';[19] and for this to have a sting, 'experience' must evidently be
regarded as a noncontroversial concept; being expressed by judge-

---

16 J. 19. Cf. 2nd Analogy, K. 218: 'Principle of Succession in Time, in
accordance with the Law of Causality'.

17 P. 60.

18 P. 60n.

19 I have chosen the language of the footnote at P. 64n, although there Kant
insinuates that the judgement of experience in question is the necessitarian
(i.e. causal) one, the sun warms the stone, where one 'follows from' the other
'necessarily'. But clearly, if Kant's argument depended on the assumption of
necessary propositions of experience, it would be weakened immeasurably, not
to say become circular. Unlike the *Prolegomena*, the *Critique* considers
contingent judgements of experience; the express generalisation to this case at
K. 159 makes this quite clear. However as later sections of this essay will
explain, there are additional reasons for such a 'confusion'.

ments concerning the sequence of states of a thing, or more generally, change in general.

III. *The Transcendental Structure of Phenomena*

Before asking how this isolation of levels affects Kant's general
contentions, in particular his claims against Hume, and other
related problems, we must first consider the transcendental argument, in order to see more precisely how we are to interpret Kant's
remark that the concept of cause has been added to perception in
order to generate experience.[20] To do this in detail would obviously involve us in a discussion of the whole *Critique of Pure Reason*,
which may seem unnecessary since it has been done so many times.
If nevertheless I make the attempt again it is because I need to give
the account in a language which will make my expression of the
later parts of the argument (employing similar locutions) more
meaningful; I shall do no more than sketch the core, as it relates to
the question of causation, hoping to bring out more clearly and
carefully just those ambiguities whose unravelling is the task of this
chapter.[21]

The central point is Kant's contention that the notion of
cognitive judgement (and of the related notions of experience and
knowledge, '*Erfahrung*' and '*Erkenntnis*') can only be defined relative to an 'object', or better: objective situation, e.g. an objective
sequence, which is regarded as 'appearance'. As an 'appearance',
the object is characterised from two sides. 1) It is something that is
set in an essential relation to the possibility of being experienced,
of being able to become an 'object' in a cognitive judgement. 2) On
the other side, this 'experience', like the object quâ 'appearance', is
exhibited (under transcendental analysis) as possessing a certain
'structure', constituted of three elements: i) its *a posteriori* constit-

---

20 I have tried this in a preliminary fashion in an earlier paper, which
however still contains some serious ambiguities and omissions. Cf. my 'Causality,
Causal Laws and Scientific Theory in the Philosophy of Kant', *Brit. J. Phil. Sc.*,
XVI (1965), 187-208.

21 Perhaps this may produce a certain degree of circularity. But it is not
possible to give 'an account' of the *Critique* without taking sides, and adding
interpretation. My interpretation is however intended not to repress the
ambiguities in Kant's approach, but if possible to bring out why they occur.

uent (what Kant also calls its 'matter', corresponding to sensation);[22] ii) the spatio-temporal framework; iii) the conceptual (categorial) apparatus, both of which are held to be *a priori*. The difference between the notion of the *a posteriori* and the *a priori*, in *this* instance[23] is as follows. Over the *a posteriori* we have no control; with respect to it, we are 'receptive' only. Furthermore, that with respect to which we are merely receptive, is not to be regarded as being given *with* its own spatio-temporal framework, at least, not at the particular transcendental level at which *it* 'is given'. Rather, space and time are to be regarded as the forms or manner or mode in which the *a posteriori* elements of sensation are viewed as *capable of being* ordered.[24] (I shall not in detail discuss Kant's reasons for this approach, except to note that it is partly a reflection of his rejection of both the Newtonian and the Leibnizian approach to space and time, and partly his technical interpretation of the need to avoid treating things as 'things-in-themselves'.) 'Ordering the manifold' involves a transitive grammar; and Kant correspondingly employs the model of 'spontaneity' (by contrast with that of 'receptivity') to indicate the difference between the elements of his transcendental structure. It is as though he said: it is we who effect the ordering, and we supply the framework in which the ordering takes place. In fact, what is operative here is simply our three-fold structure applied to a transcendental analysis of the concept of 'experience'. And space and time, as the second element of this structure, are thus regarded, not as forms *of* the *a posteriori* given, but as expressions of the mode in which the given is regarded as appearing to us, i.e. as forms of experience, or rather; those aspects of experience which correspond to the nonconceptual element in it; what Kant calls 'intuition' *('Anschauung')*. Finally, *that* these forms are an aspect of spontaneity (of a spontaneous

---

[22] K. 65; but *only* corresponding. Throughout his transcendental analysis Kant subtly transforms the philosophical key-terms of his predecessors into something which bears only an analogical resemblance to the former.

[23] Here, again, we meet with subtle transformations of received meanings.

[24] K. 66. Note that 'space and time as forms' only means that the sensory elements are *capable of being* ordered; not that they already *are* ordered. Kant himself misled his readers in the first edition by suggesting the latter reading, and altered it in the second edition, from 'geordnet angeschaut wird' to 'geordnet werden kann' (cf. K. 66n. 2) .

synthesis) ,[25] and that they are presupposed, rather than 'given', is the Kantian meaning of the *a priori*.[26]

There follows now a most important result from this analysis, as far as it has gone. For it implies that the *a posteriori* has not as yet anything in it which could supply us with the concept of an objective order, or of an object. Let us compare this with a philosophy like Locke's. Here there are two assumptions, both of which we shall find the Kantian analysis to reject. 1) The sensory elements, as they appear, passively received by the mind, can in some sense be taken to present us with the image of an object. (This is what Locke called 'an idea'). 2) There is always the question whether this ideal object *corresponds*[27] to the 'real object', of which the former is regarded the 'effect' (on the lines of the empirical scientific analogue, which describes brain states and sensations as produced by some physical causes, external to the *body*). Now the second assumption Kant meets through the denial that the concept of 'real object', in the sense here required, has as yet no meaning. This is not so much the argument against the 'thing-in-itself,' which belongs to another sphere (although no doubt echoing some of its difficulties also), but rather the contention that the concept of 'transcendental object' (which is here the shadow of Locke's 'real object'), is something of which we are likewise said to 'know nothing of what it is in itself'.[28] The question of 'correspondence' can thus not come up. More important, and more subtle, is however the rejection of Locke's first assumption.[29] This amounts to

---

25 Cf. K. 151.

26 This analysis restored for Kant the possibility of saying that appearances were given *in* space and time, which had created such difficulties previously, since space and time when regarded as 'containing entities' seemed, as Kant held, to be nothing at all. By making them transcendental forms of intuition, they could act as a framework in which everything appeared, without such perplexing consequences.

27 *Essay,* iv. 4.3 speaks of 'conforming'.

28 K. 271; cf. K. 268; and the contrast with the 'noumenon', K. 271; also K. 441, 467-68. On the other hand, at K. 269-70 Kant specifically mentions the temptation of construing an 'appearance', e.g. a Lockean idea, also to '*correspond*' to some 'object independent of sensibility', and this is indeed, he says, the 'concept of the noumenon'.

29 This assumption is also made by Locke's empiricist successors, Berkeley and Hume.

the contention, that the sensory elements, when regarded in Kant's manner as appearing *in* 'subjective' space and time, considered as mere forms of intuition, cannot even *begin* to contain anything objective. This point, often felt to be the most puzzling part perhaps of Kant's analysis of 'appearance', is easily grasped in the light of what has preceded if we understand it sufficiently abstractly. It simply means that the analysis of transcendental structure does not yield a concept of object, when we are considering only elements (1) and (2) of that structure; which is precisely what the procedure of Locke and his school implied. To use Lockean terminology, we might say that without the third element—an element which being *a priori*, it will be remembered, is not transcendentally speaking, 'given with' the sensory material (1), as moldable in (2), i.e. is not given with so far merely intuited 'perceptions' (Wahrnehmungen) —no *quasi-objective* 'idea' can even come up. More significantly, we may convert the Kantian denial into the positive point, that the notion of 'appearance' (the substrate of Locke's 'idea') must be viewed itself as so structured that it permits of the identification of 'objectivity' *within* itself. 'Objectivity' becomes as-it-were 'self-wrought'. As Kant once says, having failed to find a way of matching our concept with an object, we will invert the procedure, and bring the object to the concept.[29A]

To sum up: an *appearance* cannot become object, and hence not objective, until the third or conceptual element has been brought to bear upon intuition or perception *(Wahrnehmung)*. The corresponding contention, from the point of view of the perceptual subject, i.e. ourselves, which is that *experience* is not possible without the conceptual element, corresponding to the concept of the object, being injected at the intuitional level, is argued in the 'transcendental deduction of the categories'; this we shall not consider here, as not belonging into this chapter. Let us just remind ourselves, that the subjective mirror of the concept of the object is the so called 'transcendental unity of the synthesis of apperception', the mirror image of what Kant calls the 'concept of an object'.[30] It is this unity which enables us consciously to cognise the synthetically ordered intuitional manifold as an object; and its

---

[29A] K. 22.

[30] K. 156; also K. 134.

conceptual content turns out to be specified in the different categorial concepts each of which is a specific aspect of this 'unity'.
However, in this essay, we are primarily concerned with the thing,
or more specifically, changing states of a thing, regarded as 'appearance'.

IV. *Causality and Change*

We are now in a position to consider the way in which the
causal concept is injected into the transcendental structure as we
have defined it.[31] And here we note that Kant again employs
certain empirical analogues in order to explain his transcendental
contentions; contentions, if my assessment of his general philosophical position be accepted, should of course, like all the other
transcendental detail, be uncharacterisable in ordinary language.
Let us consider two successive states of a thing, A and B. What we
have to do now is to provide an analysis of the empirical contingent sequence A—B in line with the general analysis of 'possible
experience' and 'possible phenomenon' that has been given. Let us
then regard A, B first as mere 'perceptions', indicating this fact by
using primes, thus: A', B'.[32] Moreover, let us remember that in

---

[31] This is the account given primarily in the 'Second Analogy of Experience',
K. 218ff.

[32] It is vital to remember that perception ('Wahrnehmung') is a technical
term, whose meaning does not coincide with whatever present-day philosophical or non-philosophical literature may understand by it. Moreover, 'perception' in Kant occurs both in a plural and in a singular use. (At K. 208-9
both occur in the same sentence.) In the former use, they constitute the
components of an intuitional manifold; in the latter, the reference is to the
synthesis of the perceptions (plural use) regarded as some sort of pre-
experiential, quasi-conscious, function. In what follows, A', B', etc., always bear
the 'plural use'. It should be noted that Kant, especially in the *Prolegomena*,
employs the term 'judgement of perception' (singular use) which is there
contrasted with 'judgement of experience', as being 'subjective', and still
lacking the infusion of the categorial concepts. On this, one may take three
views: 1) that such a distinction is inconsistent with the main teaching of the
Critique; 2) that the conclusions of the *Critique* are not as tight-fitting as one
might have supposed; 3) that the notion of a *judgement* of perception is a
heuristic device, giving Kant a kind of metaphorical language in terms of
which to characterise the process of 'objectification'. Obviously, (3) is not
inconsistent with (1), and I shall adopt both in what follows.

virtue of element (2) of our transcendental structure, A′, B′ are capable of being ordered in time. Now we might perhaps want to describe the situation by saying, as Kant often does, that A′ and B′ occur successively. But this form of locution is already dangerous, and is only forced upon Kant because he *has* of course to use empirical (here: psychological) pictures in order to set out his account. For in a sense, he is now saying too much since he implies that this actually happens (even if only 'internally') ; whereas so far we have not yet got a concept corresponding to this 'actually happens'.[33] Let us remember that 'spatio-temporal form' expresses only the fact that A′, B′ are capable of being ordered. The actual ordering, as Kant also explains at length in the transcendental deduction, and repeats in the *Analogies,* involves a process of 'synthesis' of A′, B′.[34] Putting A′, B′ in *some order or other,* let alone, ordering them in accordance with some specific concept of time-order, presupposes holding them together in combination, as a unity or whole. But how am I to express the fact that, prior to the injection of the unity of this synthesis, or its corresponding concepts, there was as yet no 'objective order'? Clearly, it suggests itself, by describing the synthesis as so far 'purely subjective', though again being a matter of a transitive activity. The picture which Kant uses is that of our 'placing together' perceptions A′, B′, where however the order in which they are put together, is 'purely accidental.'[35]

It may perhaps be objected that this is entirely artificial, if not erroneous. Surely, so it will be said—and I think many people on first approaching Kant do say it—what appears in conscious awareness is just what comes up; surely we *are* just simply receptive; so how can a distinction between 'subjective' and 'objective' order be made at all? To attenuate such perplexity, many commentators thereupon supply further *empirical analogies.* (And in this Kant offers them a handle.) They contrast, namely, the order of our perceptions as they occur to us, or in us, with that order of the events as it happens in actual fact, without us; usually characteris-

---

[33] Let us be clear: We are not, throughout the Kantian analysis, concerned with what *does* actually happen, but only with the *concept* of 'actually happening'. *What* happens, belongs to the sensational content of the realm over which we have no control, i.e. (1) , the *a posteriori.*

[34] Cf. K. 209. Also K. 151-52; K. 131-38.

[35] K. 209.

ing the contrast as being between what *seems* to be the case, and what *is,* in reality. How indeed would you otherwise know, they say, whether for instance those states of consciousness, exemplified by the appearances of a house, which follow one another, do or do not *in reality* follow one another, rather than being simultaneous, as in fact they happen to be?[36]

In answer to this, I can only repeat what has already been pointed out. First, such an example is merely introduced as an *intimation* of the difference between stages (1) plus (2) and stage (3) of the analysis; between 'perception' (which takes place at a transcendental level, or below so to speak the 'transcendental surface') and the level of 'experience'; a concept which—as will have been realised—is likewise used by Kant in a highly technical sense, whilst at the same time intended also to retain its normal connotation! Clearly, if the example was not meant to be understood in this metaphorical way, the procedure would be question-begging. How indeed would we ever discover empirically whether a succession is 'subjective' or 'objective' in the sense of these terms required by Kant? And if we cannot discover this empirically, even less can we *discover* it by simply 'adding a concept'! So the most that Kant can be claiming is that the addition of the concept supplies us with the necessary *language* in terms of which we can claim that some given state of affairs is objective. Similarly, 'purely accidental order' will say only: prior to the addition of the concept. For we must remember the programme: which was, to introduce a 'structurification' into 'experience' (or 'appearance') itself, so that objectivity should be able to emerge *within* experience rather than being, as in Kant's non-critical predecessors, regarded as some form of hypothetical or postulated *correspondence* between a fully-fledged appearance (as 'idea') and an 'external object'.

With these cautions in mind let us now continue to consider carefully how the concept of causality gets into this transcendental structure. We have arrived at the stage of the synthesis of percepions A', B', and we 'do not know' (i.e. lack cognitive grasp of meaning or what Kant calls *Erkenntnis*), regarding the sequence A' —B', whether it is a sequence which is such as could be said to occur in actuality, as against being 'purely subjective', by virtue of its being the result of mere spontaneity. The question then is: what

---

36 Cf. K. 220.

has to be added, in order to convert the 'accidental sequence' A'—B' into an objective sequence, A—B?

Now remember, we have so far a merely 'accidental' time-order. Hence, it lies near to search for a concept which will give us the substratum of a time-order which is non-accidental; which, so to speak, 'ties down', or 'determines' the order of A', B', in an objective time, giving us A—B. The question is: which concept can we here use as supplying us with the required 'analogy'? What is required is a concept which shall say that it is A' which as such precedes B', and not vice versa (for that is what we mean by the notion of the objectivity of the time-sequence A—B); but it is the 'tying down' that is the essential point. Now the image which suggested itself to Kant (not surprisingly, of course) was that of causation. In a causal law, as we have seen, he regards the consequent, the effect, as being necessarily united to, and necessarily preceded by, its antecedent, the 'cause'.[37] If we now use this concept, it gives us a language in terms of which to describe those cases where A is said to precede B objectively, and not just accidentally, as was the case in the sequence A', B'. We simply imagine A', B' 'tied down'.[38]

Now we could imagine that A' was tied to B'. But it need not necessarily be A' that is here used. As Kant says in the Second Analogy: all that is necessary is that '*some* preceding state', and more-over, one that is quite 'indeterminate', be thought as preceding *necessarily* the one in question, here B'.[39]

We may then try to represent the whole process whereby a subjective sequence is converted into something objective through the following set of stages. Here—

---

[37] More specifically, Kant defines the concept of cause as a 'special kind of synthesis, whereby upon something, A, there is posited something quite different, B, according to a rule' (K. 124); the A being something 'such that something else, B, follows from it necessarily and in accordance with an absolutely universal rule' (K. 125).

[38] More strictly, the concept of causality is an analogy for the 'schema', which consists 'in the succession of the manifold, in so far as that succession is subject to a rule' (K. 185). It will be seen that what is operative here primarily is the concept of a rule. As an example, we might think of the rule which determines the succession of the members of the sequence 1, 2, 4, 8, 16 . . . etc. But Kant intends of course only the concept of rule in general.

[39] Cf. K. 225.

Let x′, y′, u′, v′, *mean* the indeterminate members of a schematised causal sequence, still using primes to remind ourselves that we are dealing with 'perceptions';

...   *mean* potential spatio-temporal order;

--   *mean* order of a subjective succession;

—   *mean* order of an objective succession;

➜   *mean* the relation of necessary connexions; in accordance with a rule

[ ]   *mean* the synthesis of perceptions.

The stages are:

(i)	A′, B′	The *a posteriori* component or 'content' of some given perceptions
(ii)	A′ ... B′	A′, B′ as members of some potential spatio-temporal order
(iii)	[A′ -- B′]	The 'subjective synthesis', whereby A′, B′ are placed in a subjective order of succession
(iv)	[x′ ➜ A′ ➜ y′; u′ ➜ B′ ➜ v′]	The representation of the concept of causality, A′ and B′ being regarded as placed in a determinate order, through integration in an *indeterminate* causal succession containing the variables x′, y′, etc.
(v)	A′ — B′	The objective sequence.
(v$_a$)	A — B	We may also write (v) as (v$_a$) in order to indicate that we are here abstracting from the condition that A and B should be regarded as perceptions. For through the objectivity of the time relation, the empirical judgement is now capable of referring us to *objective* happenings, which might be regarded as members of an event or process.
(vi)	A ➜ B	Represents an empirical causal law, whose instances would be given by A — B.

Here everything above the line, i.e. stages (i to iv) takes place beneath the transcendental surface, below the level of Kantian 'experience'. And let us note in passing that such a schema brings out graphically that what we are concerned with in Kant's transcendental treatment is not so much a 'proof' of what is 'presupposed' for the possibility of experience, but with an analysis of the concept of a public observation language. Such an analysis may seem at first sight relatively arbitrary. However, it is dominated by Kant's basic tenet that the aspect of intersubjective validity, or objectivity as such, should be located *within* the notion of 'experience', or the corresponding notion of 'appearance'. And it was for this reason that the definition of appearance as something 'not known as it is in itself' had to be so viewed that the element corresponding to the realm of the *a posteriori* is there deficient of those 'notes' that correspond to the implications of a public language. To a certain extent, such an analysis was conditioned historically. It begins with the critique of the ontological assumptions of a Locke and a Leibniz: from Locke it takes a sublimate of the notion of 'idea', under the guise of stage (i); from Leibniz it takes the notion of 'sufficient reason', as the sublimate of stage (iv); and from both it withdraws the uncritical operation with space and time, reformulating these notions in the way we have described. And even 'synthesis' has its counterpart in Locke's doctrine that all *complex* ideas are the result of the mind's activity of combination, except that again this notion is deprived—in the end, and specifically in the 2nd edition of the *Critique*—of most of its psychological trappings, and instead converted into a transcendental element of structure.

V. *Transcendental and Empirical Causality*

This representation of the way in which the concept of causal nexus enters the situation brings out the absolutely basic feature of the Kantian treatment, which is that it is the sole function of this concept (at least, at the level of the 'understanding') to 'generate experience',[40] i.e. to generate the possibility of cognitive judgements relative to objective happenings regarded as 'appearances'.

---

40 P. 64n.

Moreover, be it noted above all that the kind of judgement in question concerns matters that are empirical and hence contingent.[41] We may say that the 'justificational force' of the concept of causality is exhausted in the process of generating the possibility of contingent judgements of experience concerning a sequence of states. Any further relevance it may have, above all for empirical science regarded as a system of causal laws, must be a separate matter and does not seemingly concern the principle of causality regarded as providing something like inductive support. We must be careful therefore to read with this proviso in mind Kant-passages which appear to suggest this stronger interpretation. Whether Kant always sticks to the weaker interpretation is of course an open question.[42]

Confusion is for instance easily created by an expression like 'nature is subject to law'. Normally this denotes our belief in the universal prevalence of the realm of determinism; or, less sweeping, of the possibility (at least in principle) of everything being subject to natural laws. It is however quite clear that the argument of the Second Analogy does not support such conclusions. For according to this, the expression 'nature is subject to universal laws' refers to nature regarded as a collection of objective states of affairs, and only means that the possibility of each of these states presupposes the injection of the concept of an indeterminate causal nexus.[43]

---

[41] 'It holds good even if the judgment is itself empirical, and therefore contingent. . . . I do not here assert that these representations *necessarily* belong *to one another* in the empirical intuition, but that they belong to one another *in virtue of the necessary unity* of apperception in the synthesis of intuitions. . . .' (K. 159; italics in text).

[42] There is at least one case where the stronger interpretation at first sight appears clearly indicated, viz., in Kant's 'proofs' of the basic laws of Newtonian dynamics, as found in his *Metaphysical Foundations of Natural Science*. However, not only do these laws play a privileged part in the Kantian edifice, and must be distinguished from what he calls 'the particular empirical laws of nature', but it is still possible to argue that the transcendental principles of the Analytic are here *applied* ('borrowed', as Kant once puts it in his proof of Newton's third law) in the 'phenomenal' context of matter in motion.

[43] It should be noted that confusion is facilitated owing to Kant's habit of referring to the principles of causation, substance, and dynamic association as 'the universal laws of nature' (cf. P. 53), contrasting them with the 'particular empirical laws'.

However, such a situation might be quite compatible with the absence of a network of empirical laws, or of any laws whatsoever. The *argument* has certainly nothing to contribute (by way of basic *guarantees*) to this latter possibility, however much it may 'suggest' it.

Here it is important to note that this 'irrelevance' is graphically illustrated by the fact that the elements represented by the 'indeterminate' causal nexus are variables like x', y', etc. Now this may provoke a tempting suggestion: Why not say that the transcendental argument supplies us with the variables; and that observation and experiment give us the corresponding 'values', i.e. discovers the relevant substitution instances? Now this is precisely the answer which Kant seems to give quite frequently. Thus at K. 173, he points out that the special laws

> cannot in their specific character be *derived* from the categories, although they are one and all subject to them. To obtain any knowledge whatsoever of these special laws, we must resort to experience; but it is the *a priori* laws that alone can instruct us in regard to experience in general, and as to what it is that can be known as an object of experience.

This passage is of interest in two ways. The earlier part suggests that experience does in some way give us an *application* of the general principle of causality, and this more or less directly. The second part seems strongly to imply that the principle of causality provides us with a kind of *foundation* for this process. This is due to the vagueness of the term 'experience'.[44] However, it is equally possible that all this may be quite consistent with the 'weaker interpretation'; it would then simply tell us that the general principle is no more than a presupposition for the *possibility* of our experience of objects (regarded as contingent states of affairs).[45]

---

44 I have already noted this duplicity above, p. 354, in my comments on the footnote at P. 64n, which insinuates an interpretation of the judgement of experiences that makes it be concerned with a necessitarian state of affairs as such.

45 This is a case where the German original makes things immensely clearer; the last three lines of our passage read: 'Es muss Erfahrung dazu kommen, um die letztere überhaupt kennen zu lernen; von Erfahrung aber überhaupt und dem, was als ein Gegenstand derselben erkannt werden kann, geben allein jene Gesetze *a priori* die Belehrung.' Thus, the German puts the

Let us take a second passage in which the relation between the general principle and the particular laws is described. Kant writes:

> Even natural laws, viewed as principles of the empirical employment of understanding, carry with them an expression of necessity, and so contain at least the suggestion of a determination from grounds which are valid *a priori* and antecedently to all experience. The laws of nature, indeed, one and all, without exception, stand under higher principles of the understanding. They simply apply the latter to special cases [in the field] of appearance. These principles alone supply the concept which contains the condition, and as it were the exponent of a rule in general. What experience gives is the instance which stands under the rule.[46]

This passage, more forthrightly, looks in two directions at once, giving us both the strong and the weak interpretation. We are told that the particular empirical laws of nature stand under, and exemplify, as applications, the general principles, such as that of causation. On the other side, the latter govern the special laws,— and, so Kant *seems* to say, governs them *quâ laws*. But just drawing attention to this last point, at once shows that the weaker interpretation would work equally well.[46A] We would then have to say that the general principle of causation governs the laws only in the way in which it 'governs', let us say, their instantial sequences: i.e. through generating (together with the other 'higher' principles of the understanding) the *possibility* of the latter becoming objects of experience. As for 'application', we must then say that the laws do indeed constitute an application of the general principle, in the sense that a proposition like 'increase in pressure causes diminution of volume' *is a special instance* of the general proposition 'changes are due to the action of causes'. But although they are

---

emphasis definitely on 'object', bringing out more clearly what sort of 'experience' Kant has in mind, i.e. that of *specific particular*, and *not* of *lawlike* states of affairs. Again, the word 'überhaupt' is always a reference to 'the possibility' of something; Kemp Smith's 'in general' might cause us to overlook this.

[46] K. 195.

[46A] And it is almost certain that it *is* the interpretation intended, since Kant in the passage just cited says that the special laws are subject to *all* the 'higher principles of the understanding', and not just the general principle of causality.

special instances of the general rule, they are not *sanctioned* by the latter, since—as we have already seen—the logical force of that is expended in relation to particular contingent judgements.

Here, it is important to remember again how the 'general principle of causation' had got into the discussion. My table of the stages of the transcendental argument shows that the general concept of a causal nexus is required only on each and every occasion on which the notion of the *possibility* of a contingent judgement *as such* is to be made good.[47] But this is a completely *indeterminate* matter, as was represented in our schema by the variable letters x', y', etc. And in that representation, the variable-sign *exhausts* the logic of the situation. I.e. in so far as the concept of an object of experience is possible, so far the elementary constituents of such an object must be *thought* as members of some *indeterminate* causal sequence, such as the $x' \rightarrow A' \rightarrow y'$ in the schema on p. 354. The necessitarian nexus which operates below the transcendental surface is an indeterminate one, and must always remain so. For remember, I have to *think* A' as embedded in such a network, so that it shall be cognisable as a member, in the first instance, of a contingent empirical sequence. Anything taking place at the level of experience (above the transcendental surface), can exhibit only such contingency. So whilst I (which here means: the 'understanding') am constrained to *think* A' as a member of *some* general indeterminate causal nexus *below* the transcendental surface, I cannot be *compelled* to think it as a member of some *specific* nexus *above* that surface.[48] Put more graphically: it is the constituents (represented by the primed letters) *below* the transcendental surface that are 'necessarily' subject the causal connection regarded as an indeterminate schema, but it is the members of the corresponding empirical sequence (represented by the unprimed letters)

---

47 Kant repeats indeed endlessly that the category of causation, like all the other categories, is provable only as a condition of possible experience.

48 Let alone, to repeat, is it the case that A, quâ A, is necessarily connected with B. (Cf. passage from K. 159, quoted above, p. 24.) What is the case, is that A, regarded as 'perception', A', must be *thought* as 'time-determined' in accordance with an *indeterminate* concept which places it in a 'determinate' order, as though *governed* by a 'rule', which binds it down, on the analogy of the manner in which a mathematically formulated rule in physics binds the physical quantities which are its interpretation.

above the transcendental surface that are supposed to be causally connected in the *empirical* law. The causal concept, whilst sanctioning specific contingent experience (and hence, contingent objective succession) cannot at the same time *sanction* the possibility of specific causal sequences; it can only operate as a general formula. And this is precisely of course how one may understand the point towards the end of the passage quoted on p. 358: The general principles only *supply the concept* of a causal condition (quâ general notion, or 'exponent', of a rule). So it is wrong, or at least very misleading, to put this situation by saying that the Analogy has 'proved' that everything must have some causal antecedent or other, and that experience has only to 'discover' what this antecedent is.[49] What is true is that Kant has shown that the *concept* of causality does not just play the part of a *resultant* of our experience of regular sequences (as he took Hume to have held) but that it also functions as an '*a priori* ground', quâ presupposition, of possible experience. But this does *not* make it, as is so often suggested, an *a priori* foundation of the empirical laws of Newtonian science; and not even in the basic cases mentioned above, in footnote 42.

However, with such an interpretation, or indeed, because of it, we need not and cannot stop at this point. (And it is the very object of this interpretation to show why Kant cannot stop at 'nature in general' but must be driven to let 'reason' complete the task.) I, through my 'understanding', am obliged to *think* an element like A, quâ A', as a member of some as yet indeterminate causal law. It is clear, that such a locution suggests that I cannot rest, but must seek 'satisfaction'[50] of the 'suggestion' of the existence of a specific causal nexus (just as the logical grammar of empirical law carries in the reverse direction 'the suggestion' of an underlying transcendental necessity).[51] But the search for such a satisfaction,

---

[49] And we will charitably pass over the various conditions which nature would have to satisfy, just as in Mill, for 'experience' to discover such antecedents; my main point being that—unlike Mill—the principle of causation is not here a sanctioning ground but only a conceptual frame.

[50] For this locution, cf. below, pp. 370-71.

[51] As the last passage from K. 195 actually says.

indeed our insistence to find it, is not the same as providing a justifying quasi-inductive ground.

Let us test this against one more passage, this time from Kant's comments on the 'thesis' of the Third Antinomy.[51A] The concept of an objective sequence requires that we should regard its members, as perceptions, tied down in accordance with a rule, equivalent to the causal nexus. In the Antinomy passage Kant adds that we do not know, indeed, are not even 'able to comprehend how it can be possible that through one existence the existence of another is determined'; and he concludes that 'for this reason [we] must be guided by experience alone'.

The question now is: how and in what sense can experience 'guide' us towards the discovery of causal connections? The answer is: by observation, experimentation, theoretical and methodological processing, of the kind Mill first crudely sketched in his Canons. But it is part of such a method as Mill's that its inductive conclusions are said to presuppose the law of causation.[51B] We first must assume that it is in principle possible to discover lawlike uniformities, before setting out on our inductive process. That is however precisely *not* the task of the Kantian concept and corresponding principle of causality. For here I have to *think* the perceptions as united by this concept even where the sequence in question may be utterly contingent, certainly not an instance of a causal sequence, the kind we could discover by science. Nor should it be said that the concept and principle *potentially* at least give us those causal sequences which science uncovers; for clearly, if it *need* not give us such a sequence in a particular case, it can never be a justificative foundation for *any* case in general, taken at random. In other words, since I *have* to think causality in *every* such case, the Kantian argument, with respect to the laws of science, would *prove too much,* if it were regarded as a foundation for science in the sense of a lawlike network of nature, rather than being—as Kant

---

[51A] K. 413.

[51B] I omit here, as not relevant, the fact that this law is itself based by Mill on enumerative induction, whose validity is declared to be 'basic', not capable of further substantiation. In any case, this amounts substantially to the claim that nature can at least in principle be declared to be lawlike at the phenomenal level, and not only just 'beneath' that level, as in Kant.

has been found to state explicitly—only a foundation for nature in general, i.e. as "the sum of 'appearances'."

It follows that the Kantian concept can, with respect to science, do no more than *demand* that I should seek a cause, and a causal law, covering some particular sequence which it *has* to *think* in accordance with the indeterminate concept. And this is precisely what Kant often says, as we shall see in the next section: that science regarded as 'theoretical reason' can only try and 'satisfy' the 'requirements' of the understanding; and that it tries to satisfy these requirements, by subjecting itself to the *requirement* to search for causes. Clearly this is the price that has to be paid for the transcendental relocation of the concept of causality in the Kantian architectonic.

Anyway, this argument suggests that we might expect Kant to develop the notion of an 'activity' in which there will be found 'pressures' sufficiently great to yield the equivalent of the old 'inductive justification' or 'ground'. And this is precisely the function allotted to what Kant calls our 'reasoning faculty', and to its inherent 'dynamic'. To this point, which began this paper, I shall return presently. For the moment, we note the existence of a gap, which is smoothed over in Kant's writing partly by an ambiguity of the language in the presentation of his case, partly by his belief that the dynamic of reason, its search for something responding to the promptings of the understanding,[52] is an absolutely compelling force. If the need to define the possibility of experience as such requires causality in general, then the need to define the possibility of an empirical science of systematised groupings of particular laws will likewise generate the suggestion of particularised causal necessities.[53] The difference between the two cases consists only in this: whilst the possibility of a scientific 'architectonic' can never (as we shall see in the next section) rise above the status of a *problem* for the scientist, experience in general is more obviously something that is directly given, a 'constitutive', and not (as in the former

---

52 These, as we shall see below, are all expressions which Kant actually uses in his attempted characterisation of the relation between the two realms of understanding and reason.

53 This need is ultimately due to Kant's conception of God. I cannot enter into this matter in this essay.

case) a regulative element. Nevertheless, even here the difference is not as great as it seems, since this notion of experience moves only at the 'phenomenal level'; and to this extent there attaches to it the problematic nature of the concept of phenomenon, which must be at least as questionable as its 'limiting' opposite, the noumenon. (For Kant this is not a deficiency, for it reinforces the justification of reason as a necessary complement for the work of the understanding.) But we, as critics, of course realise that the whole argument only compels if it is granted that we adopt, in addition to the commonsense meaning of 'experience', also Kant's technical transcendental analysis of this concept. This illustrates, indeed, a very general feature of philosophical reasoning; the use of key concepts which *unite* both 'normal language' and technical meanings. For only through this, is what would otherwise be a purely deductive exercise, converted into something which offers intimations of the 'nature of reality'.

It will be evident from my reading of Kant that he cannot have intended the argument of the Second Analogy to provide a foundation for the putatively necessitarian character of the empirical laws of science. It is possible that some of his formulations lend themselves to such an interpretation, but the whole character of the relationship between understanding and reason which pervades the core of Kant's thinking would be falsified if a clear distinction between 'transcendental' and 'empirical' causality were not preserved.[54] The Second Analogy can be censured therefore *neither* on the ground that it fails to provide a justificational argument for empirical causality, *nor* that it fails but pretends to provide such an argument.

However, in a recent commentary on the *Critique of Pure Reason* P. Strawson has charged Kant on just these grounds. Unlike many other writers, Strawson at least makes it clear that the real import of the argument in the Second Analogy is to define the notion of an objective sequence, and that consequently any move from the transcendental to the phenomenal context involves a shift in the ' "application" of the word "necessary" ',[55] i.e. from what I

---

[54] For a study of this relationship cf. my "The Relation between 'Understanding' and 'Reason' in the Architectonic of Kant's Philosophy", in *Proc. Arist. Soc.*, Vol. 67, 1967, 209-226.

[55] *The Bounds of Sense*, London, 1966, p. 138.

have called 'transcendental' to 'empirical' causality. Unfortunately, he seems unaware of Kant's needs and intentions which require these two contexts of causality to be kept distinct, and in consequence he assumes that in the Second Analogy Kant must have meant to go beyond the latter's purely transcendental implications. It is claimed that Kant moved from the premise that *each member-event* of a sequence is 'tied down' in time by a 'tie' construed through the model of the causal relation, to the conclusion that the event, in the sense of *the whole sequence,* is itself necessitated, the sequence being necessarily conditioned by some indeterminate antecedent event; an imputation which—as will be shown in a moment—suffers itself from an unfortunate ambiguity in the use of the term 'event'. At any rate, Strawson claims that Kant does draw the above conclusion; a view of Kant's intentions which makes it easy for Strawson to charge Kant with 'a *non sequitur* of numbing grossness.[56]

In detail, Kant is made to argue that the fact of our having to conceive the perceptions A', B' as necessarily determined (in order to yield the notion of objective sequence) 'is equivalent to conceiving the transition of change from A to B as *itself* necessary'.[57] True, so even Strawson has to admit, we should not take Kant to mean that A causally necessitates B, but (Strawson claims) Kant does conceive 'the change from A to B as causally necessitated by *some* unspecified antecedent conditions'.[58] He concludes, summarily, that Kant must argue that

> any succession of perceptions is a perception of objective change only if the order of those perceptions is necessary; but the order of the perceptions can be necessary only if the change is necessary, i.e. causally determined.[59]

Now *prima facie* this reading is implausible on the quite general ground that if Kant had believed in this inference from the necessary determinations of the perceptions to the necessity of the sequence, there would have been no point in his invoking else-

---

56 *Op. cit.,* p. 137.

57 *Ibid.,* p. 138; italics in text.

58 *Ibid.;* italics in text.

59 *Ibid.*

where the complicated apparatus of hypothetical reason (in the third *Critique* called 'reflecting judgement') which in fact first supplies him with that 'principle of the unity of the manifold' of empirical uniformities, in virtue of which these latter may be 'called laws', and thus be 'thought of' as 'necessary'.[60] And the contention that reason (or judgement) *have* to supply the principle is for him, as we have seen, a matter of the utmost importance. This by itself seems to me already sufficient to rebut Strawson's interpretation but I will offer some additional evidence which seems to me to throw doubt on the contention that Kant was confused, and involved in a *non sequitur*.

To start with, it must be noted that if we adopt his interpretation, Kant is involved not only in a *non sequitur*, but in a contradiction. For he is made to say that it is a condition of our regarding a *contingent* sequence as objective that we regard it as necessary. Now it is true that Kant sometimes claims certain statements to be both contingent and necessary; this is for instance his view concerning the logical status of scientific laws.[61] But even in the case of these laws, contingency and necessity are located at different 'levels', the former belonging to the constitutive realm of the instantial basis of these laws, the latter being a function of the transcendental regulative employment of reason. Similarly, as Kant makes quite clear, the necessity that belongs to *all* contingent judgements of matter of fact (particular or general, and whether the latter be lawlike or not) refers to the level of the transcendental unity of apperception, a fact which we have noted before.[62] The categories have the prime function of replacing that framework of 'absolute time' which the very definition of anything called 'appearance' denies, and they do no more than serve as the logical equivalent for this 'absolute time', in the absence of which perceptions are related only in an 'accidental' order.[63] It does not therefore seem very likely that Kant would have accepted Strawson's characterisation of a position according to which the 'necessary order of perceptions' is *equivalent* to the necessity of the

---

[60] J. 16, 21; and above, p. 342, n. 11.

[61] Cf. above, pp. 341-342.

[62] Cf. above, p. 356 and n. 41.

[63] Cf. K. 226.

'objective change', i.e. of the sequence, a contrast which mixes transcendental and empirical necessity.

It should be noted that in the third *Critique* the contrast between these two contexts is drawn in specific terms. The principles of the understanding (or 'general laws of nature'), Kant there tells us, furnish only connections for each of those things taken singly, and whose 'sum' constitutes 'nature'; they do not relate specifically the *particular* beings of *nature;* for this we require reflecting judgement in order to yield an *a priori* principle which alone generates the notion of a system of laws, and thus an *order of nature.* Here Kant adds a for us most interesting proviso: the most we can say, he writes, is that the notion of such a system, which explicates the lawlikeness of nature, *is a 'necessary aim (a need)'* [*einer notwendingen Absicht (einem Bedürfnis)*] *of the understanding;* and it is precisely because we can grasp scientific uniformities only as something contingent, that we require reflecting judgement.[64]

Here it seems to me to be stated quite explicitly that *empirical* causality does not lie within the domain of transcendental presuppositions of the understanding; this is only one of its 'needs'—a need, which is not satisfied by a fallacious argument insinuated within the Second Analogy, but only by the regulative procedure of reason (or judgement).

There is however perhaps a specific explanation of Strawson's insistence that the Kantian *non sequitur* occurs within the Second Analogy, whereby Kant is supposed to move from the necessary determination of the members of a sequence to the necessitation of that sequence itself. For both the members of the sequence and the whole sequence may somewhat ambiguously be regarded as 'events'.

Now there is a similar ambiguity in Strawson's use of the term 'event', when he speaks of the 'event of change . . . as preceded by some causal condition . . .', where previously he had defined the sequence of the states A, B as 'a single event'.[65] This gives the impression that Kant has argued that the 'event' (*sc. succession*) A—B must be conceived as necessitated, since he does speak (as in the passage from K.225 cited below) of an 'event' (though here mean-

---

64 Cf. J. 20.

65 *Op. cit.,* p. 136.

ing 'member of succession') being placed in a determining relation with a preceding state.

Now actually, when Kant in the Second Analogy speaks of 'event' (for which he uses the German synonyms *Wirklichkeit, Begebenheit, Ereignis*[66]), he is invariably referring to states such as A, or B (quâ perceptions, i.e. A', B') separately. Thus, in the passage which Strawson seems to have in mind (since he speaks of '*some* unspecified antecedent conditions' which according to him Kant demands as necessitating 'the change from A to B'[67]), Kant says that in entertaining the notion of an objective sequence,

> there is created an order in our representations in which the present, so far as it has come to be, refers us to some preceding state or other as a correlate of the event [*Ereignis*] which is given; and though this correlate is, indeed, indeterminate, it none the less stands in a determining relation to the event as its consequence [*Folge*], connecting the event in necessary relation with itself [*sc.* the preceding state] in the time series.[68]

Here it is evidently the 'event' B, quâ B', which is determined, whether by A', or some 'indeterminate' x'; there can be no question of arguing that the 'event' A—B itself is claimed to be causally determined by some antecedent (or internal) condition x'! For if that had been Kant's intention, he would have spoken, as he indeed does in another context of the present Analogy, not of event, in the sense of '*Ereignis*', but of '*Begebenheit*', used to denote the sequence A—B, and which is very properly rendered by Kemp Smith through the term 'happening'.[69] Strawson's expressions 'transition of change' and 'event of change'[70] thus conceal an ambiguity, when properly in the argument as stated they should be used only to refer to a *member* of any succession (regarded as 'subjective' perception) and not to the succession itself. Kant is only arguing that *given* some such succession, the general concept of such a happening requires that we *think* each of its members when re-

---

[66] K. 221, 225.

[67] *Op. cit.*, p. 138, italics in text.

[68] K. 225.

[69] K. 221.

[70] Cf. above, pp. 364, 366, 34 E.

garded as 'perceptions' (whose order requires a transcendentally founded relation) as determined by some conditioning factor—a factor which (like the causal relation itself) must always be conceived in an entirely indeterminate fashion, and which *within* this argument, is never capable of concrete specification.

It is indeed an essential requirement for the preservation of the strength of Kant's transcendental argument that no question should arise concerning the putative existence of any causal determinations of the individual sequence A—B, understood to occur at the phenomenal level, and regarded as a contingent happening, since it is precisely this—in its contingent character assumed to be 'given'—which alone is strong enough to 'balance' the transcendental concept of causal necessity. Kant's transcendental arguments are never intended to furnish more than explications of what, on other grounds, he assumes as 'given', whether it be the synthetic *a priori* character of Euclidean geometry, the 'pure' laws of Newtonian dynamics, the contingent facts ('objects') of 'nature', or the empirical laws which supply that 'order of nature' which the scientist is driven to 'project' into nature. It would therefore have been peculiar if on just one occasion Kant had wanted to go beyond the general character of his philosophical procedure, and to mix, so to speak, the levels of his argument; and Strawson's suggestion of any explicit maneouvres on Kant's part in the case of causality (as distinct from his somewhat ambiguous language) must therefore be rejected. The rest of this essay will, I hope, give further support to my contention that Kant does in fact meticulously separate the domains of reason and understanding, and correspondingly of causality at the transcendental and at the empirical level.

VI. *Reason and Empirical Causality*

I have now tried to indicate the outlines of Kant's position vis-à-vis the place and function of causality in connection with an attempt to interpret two or three crucial passages to be found in the *Critique* and *Prolegomena*. We must now consider in more detail the place of 'reason' in the development of the 'suggestions' of the understanding.

The understanding, so we saw, has to *think* its intuitional elements, the 'perceptions', as determined in accordance with some indeterminate necessitarian or rule-like element, the analogy for which is the concept of causality. And we may interpret Kant as holding that this 'need" *spills over* from the situation as it exists in the understanding, into the realm of reason, taking its cue from the semantic content of the causal concept, which says: 'think the perceptions as governed by rule!', and going on from there to regard the resulting objective sequence as governed by some *particular* rule to be discovered by observation and experiment.[71] There are a number of passages in the *Dialectic,* especially the *Antinomy,* which clearly manifest this approach. The main burden of that argument[72] is as follows: Everything, quâ element of an appearance, is subject to causality. On the other hand, the actual search for concrete causes is a *separate* task.—Important here is the implication that the contention of there *existing* always such causes is essentially linked by Kant to the process of *searching,* of *attempting to fit* actual causal conditions to natural effects. For as he puts it: this 'regress in the series of the conditions of given appearances' is merely a 'rule'; the continuing search is merely 'set as a task';[73] we are for instance not to *anticipate* that this task can or can not come to an end. Such a principle which 'prescribes' the search for causes, Kant calls 'a regulative principle of reason'.[74] Now I am not so much here concerned with the question of the totality of conditions, as with the underlying view that the assumption of 'the

---

[71] Let us not forget the details of the situation as it exists at the level of the understanding. Referring back to p. 354, below the transcendental surface we have stage (iv). It does not follow from this, that there is a law, A→B, of which A—B are instances. A—B may be a *unique* contingent sequence. It is only quâ A', B', that these, as perceptions, have to be *thought* as members of a rule-like situation. That thereafter science ('reason') can seek a concrete rule or law is not thereby determined. Of course, I am not *suggesting* that Kant slides into saying that at the level of science we can discover laws which bind the elements A,B when *not* regarded as perceptions but as members of an objective sequence. For Kant knows full well that 'discovering' involves inductive logic. Any assumption to the contrary would correspond to a further slide, although it is one which is easily suggested by Kant's language.

[72] K. 450; 470-71.

[73] K. 449.

[74] By contrast with the corresponding 'constitutive principle' of reason which would postulate the completion of the regress as given.

existence of a cause' turns out to be essentially dependent upon the 'regulative task of reason' to *search* for such causes.[75]

The 'spilling over' process is even clearer in a later passage, where Kant wishes to argue that we can meaningfully speak of a 'causality that is not empirical but intelligible'.[76] Careful attention to the actual wording is necessary. First Kant notes that the principle of causality demands that there should not be an event (here regarded as cause) which begins to exist, with no other event preceding it. Thereupon, trying to contrast empirical or phenomenal with noumenal causality, he continues by saying

> that . . . for every effect in the [field of] appearance a connection with its cause in accordance with the laws of empirical causality is indeed *required*.[77]

We note here specifically that the fitting of causes is only 'required', a position consonant with Kant's general regulative approach.[78] But the relation between understanding and reason is brought out even more clearly in a passage which follows almost immediately.[79] Kant writes:

> The principle of the causal connection of appearances is *required* in order that we may be *able to search for and to formulate* [suchen und angeben] the natural conditions of natural events, that is to say, their causes in the [field of] appearance. If this principle be *admitted*, and be not weakened through any exception, the requirements of the understanding, which in its empirical employment sees in all happenings nothing but nature . . . are

---

75 This corresponds to the 'regulative employment of reason' in the search for the systematic interconnection of its laws, alluded to previously.

76 K. 471. The reference is to the problem of 'freedom'.

77 *Ibid.* My italics. The reference to 'empirical' denotes the particular empirical laws, not the general principles.

78 The search for causes can only be 'required' and not 'justified' at the level of reason, since—as Kant expressly remarks at K. 306—'that everything which happens has a cause, is not a principle known and prescribed by reason'. This is not to say that causality is not first found located in science, which is (as we have seen) generated by the activity of reason. But as already remarked, Kant is not concerned with the empirical or psychological source of the concept or law of causality.

79 Again the actual context of the argument is not relevant here. (The italics are mine.)

completely *satisfied;* and physical explanations may proceed on their own lines without interference.

So we see: whilst the principle of causal connections (a principle of the understanding) is a necessary transcendental presupposition for the possibility of experience of objective contingent events, it is only *'required'* by reason in its *search* for causes; this is a spontaneous matter, reason setting itself the task to engage on such a search, and in so doing it attempts to 'satisfy' the understanding, which *necessarily* employs this principle to generate experience; which is the purport of Kant's locution: the understanding sees in its empirical employment in all happenings nothing but 'nature'; nature being equivalent to 'objective happening'.—There is thus only a loosely fitting matching process between the fields of reason and understanding: Reason is *enjoined not to permit* exceptions, whereas the notion of the 'understanding' is so employed that general causality is entailed; there is no need to *enjoin it* to this! And the nature of the correspondence between the two processes is expressed as a 'satisfaction of the understanding'.[80]

The upshot of this demonstration is that whilst there is considerable 'looseness of fit' between the principles of the understanding and of reason, reason (in Kant's view at least) provides the necessary complement for the intimations of the understanding.

VII. *Causality and Determinism*

So far we have considered causality under the aspect of general principle of the understanding, and as a genus of which the particular empirical causal laws are the species. There are however two more cases to be considered which involve the notion of causality, and cast their shadow no doubt frequently upon the general discussion in the contexts so far considered. The first of these is a particular and tightened version of causal law, interpreted as yielding a rigid determinism, and which Kant believes to be a feature of all mechanical explanations in accordance with Newtonian physics. The second case concerns the basic laws of Newtonian physics itself, such as the laws of conservation of mass, the law of inertia, and the principle of action and reaction (con-

---

80 Cf., K. 471.

servation of momentum). These, as already remarked, are not for Kant instances of 'particular empirical laws', but on investigation turn out to be special interpretations (under the guidance of the Kantian connotation of the concept of matter) of the analogies of experience.[81] They are, in this sense, therefore metaphysical; a view which has re-emerged in our time as the acknowledgement that Newton's laws cannot behave like ordinary laws, being strictly speaking untestable, and instead function jointly somewhat like definitions, supplying the form of Newtonian technical language. In this essay we will consider the first of these cases, determinism.

It has sometimes been held that Kant has *smuggled* determinism into the *Critique* under the guise of the kind of causality which informs the 'understanding', or if not that, then the causality which is enjoined on us by 'reason'. On this, two comments are necessary. First, undoubtedly Kant's ambivalent language would make it possible to slide from any one position into another without making this explicit. On the other hand, secondly, it seems fairly clear that Kant did acknowledge a certain 'looseness of fit' between the two realms of reason and understanding, and that he normally claims no more than that one has suggestive implications for the other. One would therefore expect that the movement towards determinism is similarly imbued with a recognition that the two spheres in which causality reigns (and which we have so far considered), will cast a suggestive shadow (but no more!) on the third. If the result is often described by Kant as a sort of necessitarian fact, we need again not be too discouraged by these quirks of his style. Anyway, it is certain that if the subjection of nature to empirical laws does not—as I have argued—deductively follow from the requirements of the understanding, much less will there follow *necessarily* the *specific type* of laws which ought to be employed. Now I think that Kant does in fact pretty explicitly acknowledge that here also there is this looseness of fit, and the working of something like analogy.

The relevant discussion occurs in §70 of the *Critique of Judgement*,[82] where Kant argues that there is no contradiction in operating with *both* a maxim which says that all material things are

---

81 Cf. above, p. 356, n. 42.

82 J. 233-4.

organised entirely through the *efficient* causality of purely mechanical laws, *and* that some material things are not so produced, but
are to be judged through laws involving *final* causes. Now we are
not concerned with the details of Kant's resolution of this 'anti-
mony' but merely with the way he introduces it.[83] And here again,
Kant makes the point that although the 'universal laws of material
nature in general' are 'given . . . through the understanding', when
we turn to the 'particular laws', they 'can only be made known to
us through experience'. Moreover, the multitude of laws is such
that we require to unify them into a system, on the lines which the
first part of this essay has already explained. But now Kant adds
that to achieve such a 'contingent unity of particular laws', we
stand in need of a *further* 'guiding thread', if we are 'to hope for
connected empirical knowledge and understanding [*Erfahrungser-
kenntnis*] according to a thoroughgoing conformity of nature to
law'.[84] Now such a thread are the two maxims just mentioned, of
mechanism and of teleology. The way Kant in this text explains
the relation of the former to the understanding is vital for my
purpose: he explicitly says that the mechanistic principle is *a priori*
'suggested' [*an die Hand gegeben*] 'by the mere understanding';
and that the teleological maxim 'is *prompted* [*veranlasst*] by particular experiences' (e.g. of adaptive behaviour); these promptings
and suggestions bringing into play the expansionist activity of
reason.[85]

It is sometimes maintained that the apparatus of the *Critique of
Pure Reason* has as its main objective to secure the foundations of
Newtonian science; I think it will be seen that this is a somewhat
lopsided presentation which may indeed be very misleading.
Kant's attitude to science is rather more sanguine, and indeed more
in accord with our own present-day attitudes than might have been
expected. Having, I hope, now a better appreciation of the relations of the apparatus of the general principles of the understanding to the foundations of science in general, we are perhaps

---

[83] It should be understood that what in the *Critique of Judgement* is
labelled 'power of judgement' is equivalent to what in the first *Critique* we
encountered as 'the hypothetical employment of reason'.

[84] J. 233.

[85] *Ibid.*

liberated sufficiently from false presuppositions to accept the suggestion, which I introduced at the start, that Kant thinks of the lawlikeness of laws as a purely 'injected', or postulational feature, at best something which it is the task of synthetic reason to *seek*. The complementary side of this is an attitude of relative indifference towards inductive problems. Kant is quite aware of the existence of hypotheses in science, and appreciates their conjectural character.[86] And his general attitude is very well expressed when he writes, in the Antinomy, that unlike mathematics, where every conjecture (e.g. concerning the irrationality of π) must ultimately be resolvable into a clear Yes or No,[87] 'in natural science, on the other hand, there is endless conjecture, and certainty is not to be counted upon'.[88]

GERD BUCHDAHL

DARWIN COLLEGE
CAMBRIDGE, ENGLAND

---

[86] Cf. the remarks on inverse-deductive reasoning at K. 625-27.

[87] The proof of this irrationality was discovered and published by Lambert in 1768.

[88] K. 433.

KANT'S CONSTITUTIVE-REGULATIVE DISTINCTION

My purposes in this paper are to explain the constitutive-regulative distinction as set out by Kant in the Dialectic and Methodology, and to note its reappearance in contemporary philosophy.[1]

The constitutive-regulative distinction is of far greater importance than one would gather from reading the works of well-known Kant scholars. It is obvious that Kant himself regarded the distinction as being of some consequence, for he returns to it time and again. I wish to argue that this distinction is important historically, as it marks one of the first glimmerings of a problem which has been pivotal in much of contemporary philosophy, especially on the analytic side.

The problem to which I am referring is simply this: how are we to regard certain kinds of statements which are, one now sees, significantly different both from the ordinary observational statements that one encounters in the more mundane affairs of life, and from ordinary scientific statements? What are we to say of the sentence which contains words like 'substance', 'God', 'evil', or 'mind'? Are statements which contain such words all meaninglessly metaphysical? Or should one say, with the early Wittgenstein, "The correct method in philosophy would really be the following: to say nothing except what can be said, i.e. propositions of natural science—i.e. something that has nothing to do with philosophy— and then, whenever someone else wanted to say something metaphysical, to demonstrate to him that he had failed to give a meaning to certain signs in his propositions . . . What we cannot speak about we must pass over in silence"?[2]

The central problem for many contemporary philosophers has

---

[1] In the *Critique of Pure Reason*, Kant appears to have two usages for the constitutive-regulative distinction. One is to be found in the Analogies, and the other in the Dialectic and Methodology. In this paper I ignore the former usage.

[2] Ludwig Wittgenstein, *Tractatus Logico-Philosophicus*, trans. D. F. Pears & B. F. McGuinness (London: Routledge & Kegan Paul, 1963), 6.53 & 7.

been what stance to take with regard to claims which are couched in nondenotative language and which are, at the same time, unverifiable. It has seldom been remarked upon that Kant too felt this problem. This, I submit, is what the constitutive-regulative distinction is all about.

1. *Kant*

The writings of Kant are often confusing and sometimes confused. He employs a vocabulary that is not readily assimilated by the contemporary ear. Translated into one possible present-day idiom, Kant's constitutive-regulative distinction is as follows:

Language consists, in part at least, of terms and sentences or propositions. Some propositions apply directly to experience, some do not.[3] While we hold with certainty propositions belonging to both classes, there is a difference; and this difference has in part to do with evidence. Propositions belonging to the former class—the class of constitutive propositions—are in some sense verifiable. (B223)

A constitutive proposition describes the sensible world. A regulative proposition does not. A regulative proposition *prescribes*. It postulates what we ought to do, or how we ought to think. (A509-B537)

Regulative propositions cannot and do not tell us anything about objects. To regard unverifiable propositions as descriptive is always a mistake. (A510-B538)

Kant applies the constitutive-regulative distinction not only to propositions, but also to words and phrases. He says that such terms as 'virtue' and 'human wisdom' have practical power. They form the basis of the possible perfection of human actions. Such terms do not refer to objective reality, though they may be said to function as archetypes. (A569-B597)

The following two propositions are both regulative: (1) "There belongs to the world, either as its part or as its cause, a being that is absolutely necessary"; (2) "An absolutely necessary being nowhere exists in the world, nor does it exist outside the world as its cause."

---

3 Immanuel Kant, *Critique of Pure Reason,* trans. Norman Kemp Smith (Toronto: Macmillan, 1965), B359. Future references to this work will appear in the text itself.

(A453-B481) Both of these propositions are subjective, that is, neither concerns things in themselves as they might conceivably be known by an unfettered observer. These propositions prescribe only. They are unproved and incapable of proof. They serve only to guide or to reveal. They are *heuristic*. (A616-B644)

Likewise, the term 'God' or 'the supreme being' is merely regulative. Such a word directs us "to look upon all connection in the world *as if* it had originated from an all-sufficient necessary cause." It is, of course, Kant's view that humans cannot avoid the subreption or deliberate misrepresentation by which this term is used as constitutive, that is, is hypostatized. (A619-B647) While it is a mistake to employ such terms in a constitutive fashion, they do have "an indispensably necessary, regulative employment, namely, that of directing the understanding towards a certain goal . . . a *focus imaginarius*." (A644-B672)

Kant sometimes refers to regulative propositions as 'maxims'. While a maxim may seem to be an objective principle, it is derived "not from the constitution of an object, but from the *interest* of reason." (A666, italics mine) A maxim is a pragmatic device. Those who mistakenly regard maxims as constitutive will be led to believe that, where two maxims are in conflict—as in (1) and (2) above—there is a genuine case of factual disagreement. Once one comes to see, however, these maxims for what they are, one will realize that what one has here is, not a case of factual disagreement, but mere "differences in the *interest* of reason." This thinker, perhaps, "obtains satisfaction" from maxim (1), *that* person "obtains satisfaction" from maxim (2). Indeed, we may find that one and the same person sometimes and in one context puts forward (1), and at other times and in other contexts, lays claim to (2).

> When we observe intelligent people disputing in regard to the characteristic properties of man, animals, or plants—even of bodies in the mineral realm—some assuming, for instance, that there are certain special hereditary characteristics in each nation, certain well-defined inherited differences in families, races, etc., whereas others are bent upon maintaining that in all such cases nature has made precisely the same provision for all, and that it is solely to external accidental conditions that the differences are due, we have only to consider what sort of an object it is about which they are making these assertions, to realize that it lies too deeply hidden to allow

of their speaking from insight into its nature. The dispute is due
simply to the twofold interest of reason, the one party setting its
heart upon, or at least adopting, the one interest, and the other
party the other. The differences between the maxims of manifold-
ness and of unity in nature thus easily allow of reconciliation. So
long, however, as the maxims are taken as yielding objective insight, and until a way has been discovered of adjusting their conflicting claims, and of satisfying reason in that regard, they will not
only give rise to disputes but will be a positive hindrance and cause
long delays in the discovery of truth. (A667-B695, A668-B696)

It is important to notice that, according to Kant, these regulative terms and propositions contribute indirectly to the extension
of empirical knowledge. They do this without being in a position
to run counter to empirical knowledge. Thus we have Kant's

> transcendental deduction of all ideas of speculative reason . . .
> whereby this empirical knowledge is more adequately secured with-
> in its own limits and more effectively improved than would be pos-
> sible, in the absence of such ideas [regulative principles], through
> the employment merely of the principles of the understanding.
> (A671-B699)

For example:

> The method of looking for order in nature . . . and the maxim
> which prescribes that we regard such order—leaving, however, un-
> determined where and how far—as grounded in nature as such, is
> certainly a legitimate and excellent regulative principle of reason.
> In this regulative capacity it goes far beyond what experience or
> observation can verify; and though not itself determining anything,
> yet serves to mark out a path . . . (A668-B696)

Kant of course does not think of regulative concepts and propositions as a rough aggregate, any more than he thought the categories were such. Kant holds that there are logical reasons (see
the transcendental deduction) which make some regulative ideas
essential, and that a precise catalogue of them could be made. It is
not the case, then, that for Kant, every unverifiable proposition is
regulative. An idea or principle is not called 'regulative' because
it is unverifiable; it is called this because it directs the understanding, or regulates in some essential way. It is paradigmatic, not
because it is nondenotative or nonverifiable, but because it
regulates.

While it is the case that there are many nondenotative and nonverifiable propositions that Kant would not call 'regulative', it is nevertheless interesting and suggestive to notice that all of the (according to him) regulative principles *are* nondenotative and nonverifiable. And he does not dismiss such propositions—he does not, for example, call them meaningless—he says that they are useful and important; indeed, they are somehow necessary. Thus Kant has noticed that there are nondenotative, unverifiable propositions, and that some at least of these propositions can, nevertheless, have legitimate and important usages. These are 'discoveries' that one generally associates with the twentieth century.

The genericism-gradualism distinction, evolved in the context of discussions of the synthetic a priori, can also be applied here. Kant is clearly a genericist when it comes to saying which propositions are synthetic a priori, and he is also a genericist in the matter of regulative propositions. But it does not follow that the contemporary student should opt for genericism; nor does it follow that, in thinking about the notion of regulativity, genericism is closer to the truth. Might it not be interesting to extend Kant's use of 'regulative' to cover any proposition which, while being nondenotative and unverifiable, also has a legitimate and significant usage? Such propositions, whatever one calls them, have certainly acted as catalyst for a great many present-day philosophers.

In the sections that follow I hope to show that Kant and certain representative contemporary philosophers share a common concern for statements which are nondenotative, unverifiable, and in some sense useful.

2. *Mind*

Kant holds that some at least of the propositions involving talk about the mind are regulative propositions. Rejecting the view first expressed in modern philosophy by Descartes, Kant says that "we must proceed *as if* the mind were a simple substance which persists with personal identity (in this life at least)." (A672-B700) One would not, says Kant, be justified in assuming "thought-entities," because we cannot hope to extend our knowledge beyond the object of possible experience. (A674-B702)

According to Kant, when one sets out to investigate the 'I' itself, one must restrict oneself to experience. But experience reveals no such thing as a thinking substance or soul. Thus, talk of a simple, self-subsisting intelligence is nothing more than a maxim used to regard all mental phenomena as

> existing in a single subject, all powers, so far as possible, as derived from a single fundamental power, all change as belonging to the state of one and the same permanent being, and all *appearances* in space as completely different from the action of *thought*.

But we must remember that we are working on the regulative level only. "No windy hypotheses of generation, extinction, and palingenesis of souls will be permitted." (A682-B710, A683-B711)

It is noteworthy how much Ryle's basic approach reflects Kant's constitutive-regulative distinction. Like Kant, Ryle rejects the belief that minds are things, but different sorts of things from bodies. To think that the word 'mind' denotes a distinct entity (of whatever kind) is to make what Ryle calls "the Cartesian category-mistake." To make a category-mistake is to allocate a concept to a logical type to which it does not belong. The word 'mind' is not of the same logical type as those nouns that can be used ostensively. This is exactly the same point that Kant noticed, though Kant described his finding in quite different language. As Ryle puts the matter,

> 'Mind' is not the name of another person, working or frolicking behind an impenetrable screen; it is not the name of another place where the work is done or games are played; and it is not the name of another tool with which work is done, or another appliance with which games are played.[4]

I do not wish to exaggerate the similarity between Ryle and Kant. Ryle asserts dogmatically that the word 'mind' does not denote a separate entity; whereas Kant's claim is that, if 'mind' denotes a nonphysical substance, we do not *know* this. Nevertheless, both philosophers agree (Ryle reluctantly) that it is necessary or convenient at times to employ this term. In other words, these philosophers agree that propositions involving the term 'mind' are not constitutive. Ryle writes:

> Though it is not always convenient to avoid the practice, there is a considerable logical hazard in using the nouns 'mind' and 'minds'

---

4 Gilbert Ryle, *The Concept of Mind* (London: Hutchinson's, 1955) , p. 51. Hereinafter cited as CM.

at all. The idiom makes it too easy to construct logically improper conjunctions, disjunctions, and cause-effect propositions, such as 'so-and-so took place not in my body but in my mind', 'my mind made my hand write', and 'a person's body and mind interact upon each other' and so on.[5]

It is obvious that Ryle does not have the same pro-attitude that Kant does towards 'mind' in its regulative capacity. They are, nevertheless, in agreement that some at least of the propositions involving this term are no more than regulative.[6]

3. God

Bultmann, Bonhoeffer, Tillich, and the Suffragan Bishop of Woolwich—these men have, each in his own not always self-consistent way, reflected the Kantian claim that the central utterances of theology are merely regulative. The same is true, though in a less spectacular fashion, of theologians writing in the analytic tradition, for example, R. B. Braithwaite.

According to Kant, God is a "mere something in idea, of which, as it may be *in itself,* we have no concept." We "can never form the slightest concept of it." (A697-B707) The existence of a supreme being is postulated so that we may view the things of this world *"as if* they had their ground in such a being." "We misapprehend the meaning of this idea if we regard it as the assertion, or even as the assumption of a real thing . . ." (A681-B709)

One gardener says: "Look at the way these are arranged. There is purpose and a feeling for beauty here. I believe that someone comes, someone invisible to mortal eyes. I believe that the more carefully we look the more we shall find confirmation of this." The other gardener says: "I don't."[7] Of John Wisdom's gardeners, Kant says: "Each believes that his judgment has been arrived at through insight into the object, whereas it really rests entirely on the greater or lesser attachment to one of the two principles."

---

[5] Ryle, CM, p. 168.

[6] Perhaps one should note in passing that in Ryle the closest counterparts to Kant's notion of regulativity are decisions about the logical or grammatical geography of a set of terms.

[7] John Wisdom, "Gods," *Philosophy and Psycho-Analysis* (Oxford: Blackwell, 1957), p. 155.

(A667-B695) To Wisdom's first gardener, Kant would say, the things of the world must be viewed *"as if* they had received their existence from a highest intelligence," but this is "a heuristic not an ostensive concept." (A671-B699)

Kant sees talk about God as merely regulative, and he applies the same analysis to other religious notions. The devil:

> So it is not surprising that an Apostle represents this *invisible* enemy, who is known only through his operations upon us and who destroys basic principles, as being outside us and, indeed, as an evil spirit . . . This is an expression which seems to have been used not to extend our knowledge beyond the world of sense, but only to make clear *for practical use* the conception of what is for us un-fathomable.[8]

The fact that we have to hypostatize religious ideas and sometimes conceive them "in human guise" is a "limitation of human reason." Religious maxims are a product of having to "resort to some analogy to natural existences"; but to regard these maxims as extensions of our knowledge "is *anthropomorphism,* which has, from the moral point of view (in religion), most injurious consequences."[9]

Kant even discusses the idea of the virgin birth. He points out that the story is understandable from a practical or moral point of view, as it allows us to conceive the possibility of a person free from the propensity to evil. On the other hand, he says in understatement, "the idea is not without difficulty in theory." He concludes: "Yet of what use is all this theory pro and con when it suffices for practical purposes to place before us as a pattern this idea taken as a symbol . . ."[10]

According to the Bishop of Woolwich, questions such as whether the tomb was empty or not, the virgin birth, the Ascension, and so on, these are "secondary questions."

> Or take the Christmas story—the skies open up, the angels come, and the star lights the Wise Men to the stable and then halts above

---

8 Immanuel Kant, *Religion Within The Limits of Reason Alone,* trans. Greene and Hudson (2d. ed.: La Salle, Ill.: Open Court, 1960), p. 52. Hereinafter cited as RWLR.

9 Kant, RWLR, p. 58n.

10 Kant, RWLR, p. 74n.

it. This is contrary to all we know about the stars . . . There is, of course, a core of history in Christianity, and that Christ was born in Bethlehem is a historical statement. But there's a difference between historical and theological statements. That Christ was the Son of God is a theological statement, and the way the Gospel writers used it was their expression—their representation—of the life of Jesus.[11]

Tillich:

Symbols are representations. Bread is something to eat; it's not the body of Christ. It's a symbol of His sacrifice. Grape is something I suck, and wine is something I drink; it isn't the blood of Christ literally. All statements in the New Testament are symbolic in the sense that they are analogues, parables, and we have to interpret them in an existential way. By 'existential way' I mean that people's lives are different at different times and the Bible has to be re-interpreted each time according to the situation in which people find themselves.[12]

Bonhoeffer's religionless Christianity:

There is no longer any need for God as a working hypothesis, whether in morals, politics, or science. Nor is there any need for such a God in religion or philosophy (Feuerbach). In the name of intellectual honesty these working hypotheses should be dropped or dispensed with as far as possible.

This sounds, of course, as though Bonhoeffer had departed altogether from Kant. But he has not. In spite of many passages like the above, Bonhoeffer, in his writing, continues to employ what can only be regarded as regulative propositions involving 'God'. Man must

plunge himself into the life of a godless world, without attempting to gloss over its ungodliness with a veneer of religion or trying to transfigure it. He must live a 'worldly' life and so participate in the suffering of God . . . Just one more point for today. When we speak of God in a non-religious way, we must not gloss over the ungodliness of the world, but expose it in a new light. Now that it has

---

11 Ved Mehta, "The New Theologian," *The New Yorker* (November 20, 1965), p. 99f. Hereinafter cited as "New Theol."

12 Mehta, "New Theol." (November 13, 1965), p. 127.

come of age, the world is more godless, and perhaps it is for that very reason nearer to God than ever before.[13]

Braithwaite, like the writers mentioned above, starts from the premise established by Kant, namely, that important theological utterances are not constitutive. Like Kant, Braithwaite is, by explicit declaration, an empiricist. Like Kant, Braithwaite recognizes the impossibility of regarding religious and moral statements as verifiable propositions. It is Braithwaite's view that the "typical" use of religious assertions is—not factual or descriptive, but—"to announce allegiance to a set of moral principles."[14]

To make a religious assertion is (a) to express an intention to act in accordance with the specified policy of behavior of (say) Christianity, if one is a Christian; and (b) to refer, directly or indirectly, to a story (what many recent writers have called myth).

> The reference to the story is not an assertion of the story taken as a matter of empirical fact . . . to assert the whole set of assertions of the Christian religion is both to tell the Christian doctrinal story and to confess allegiance to the Christian way of life.[15]

Braithwaite makes it clear, it should be said, that he regards his view as holding true of other religions as well as Christianity.

> Educated Christians of the present day who attach importance to the doctrine of the Atonement certainly do not believe an empirically testable story . . . What I am calling a *story* Matthew Arnold called a *parable* and a *fairy tale*. Other terms which might be used are *allegory, fable, tale, myth* . . . Stories about the beginning of the world and of the Last Judgment as facts of past or of future history are believed by many unsophisticated Christians. But my contention is that belief in the truth of the Christian stories is not the proper criterion for deciding whether or not an assertion is a Christian one. A man is not, I think, a professing Christian unless he both proposes to live according to Christian moral principles and associates his intention with thinking of Christian stories; but

---

13 Mehta, "New Theol." (November 27, 1965) , p. 136f.

14 R. B. Braithwaite, "An Empiricist's View of the Nature of Religious Belief," in Hick's *Readings In The Philosophy of Religion* (Englewood Cliffs: Prentice-Hall, 1964) , p. 433. Hereinafter cited as "Empir. View."

15 Braithwaite, "Empir. View," p. 435.

he need not believe that the empirical propositions presented by
the stories correspond to empirical fact.[16]

4. *Ethics*

The entire development of twentieth-century Anglo-American
moral philosophy can be viewed rewardingly from the point of view
of Kant's constitutive-regulative distinction. Most traditional moral
philosophers from Plato and Aristotle through St. Thomas and
Spinoza to Bentham and Mill have proceeded on the assumption
that ethical propositions are *mutatis mutandis* constitutive. Most
have held that only if ethical terms are given a meaning by reference to entities and properties that are discoverable in experience
of one sort or another, can we deal with moral issues efficiently.

G. E. Moore, realizing with Kant that moral judgments are not
constitutive in any empirical way, nevertheless felt that moral
terms *must* refer to *some sort* of entities or properties. Thus, he
concluded that 'good' denotes some non-natural property. Even
G. E. Moore, then, could not bring himself to see ethical language
as merely regulative. The same is true of the other intuitionists,
Ross and Ewing.

The now fairly widely accepted belief that moral propositions
are regulative in the extended sense of this term can be seen to
have originated, in this century, with such philosophers as Ayer,
Carnap and Stevenson. Ayer pictured an ethical expression as primarily an ejaculation, or a venting of the emotion of the speaker.
The presence of an ethical term, such as 'right', in a sentence, adds
nothing to the factual content of the sentence. To say, 'It was
right of you to keep your promise', simply means, 'You kept your
promise. Hurrah!' Nor is it legitimate to think of ethical propositions as describing the feelings of the speaker. If they did, they
would be constitutive. They do not describe the feelings of the
speaker, they *express* the feelings of the speaker. And they can
also be used to arouse feeling in a hearer.

The emotive position of Ayer (and others) was given its most
elaborate development by C. L. Stevenson. He provides us with a
subtler (than Ayer, or Kant) analysis of the regulative functioning
of ethical language. It is Stevenson's view that there are roughly

---

[16] Braithwaite, "Empir. View," p. 436f.

two kinds of disagreement. The one is concerned with how matters are truthfully to be described and explained—disagreement involving constitutive propositions. The second is concerned with how matters are to be favored or disfavored. Such disagreements primarily involve differences of attitude, rather than factual belief. In Kant's language, such disagreements will be seen to evince regulative language.

> It is by no means the case that every argument represents one sort of disagreement to the exclusion of the other. There is often disagreement of both sorts. This is to say little more than that our beliefs and attitudes must not be compartmentalized. Our attitudes, as many have pointed out, often affect our beliefs, not only by causing us to indulge in wishful thinking, but also by leading us to develop and check such beliefs as point out the means of getting what we want. And conversely, our beliefs often affect our attitudes; for we may alter our form of approval of something when we change our beliefs about its nature.[17]

After Stevenson, and after the publication of Wittgenstein's *Philosophical Investigations,* a host of English-speaking moral philosophers turn to the analysis of what, in this context, I have been referring to as regulative language. Foremost amongst these are perhaps Hare and Nowell-Smith. What these philosophers have done is reveal to us an immense variety of kinds of regulative utterance. As he begins his task of analysis, Nowell-Smith, like the other philosophers already mentioned, writes a passage reminiscent of Kant.

> We must now begin to . . . try to understand the role of practical discourse by studying the purposes for which it is used rather than by trying to discover (or invent) entities to which the words used in it refer . . . To say that something is good, we are now told, is not to make a statement about it or to describe it, but to express a desire for or an attitude towards it, to express approval of it, to grade it, to praise it, to commend it, and so on.[18]

---

17 C. L. Stevenson, *Ethics and Language* (New Haven: Yale University Press, 1953) , p. 5.

18 P. H. Nowell-Smith, *Ethics* (Harmondsworth: Penguin, 1959) , p. 95.

5. Wittgenstein and Austin

Many of the philosophers whom I have mentioned, though by no means all, owe a debt not only to Kant, but also to Wittgenstein. While the debt to Kant, so far as I know, has seldom been acknowledged (hence the rationale for this paper), most writers do acknowledge the contribution of Wittgenstein. What the later Wittgenstein did was to free people from the assumption that language, in order to be meaningful, must denote entities existing in one realm or another. According to Wittgenstein, the word 'meaning' is being used illicitly if it is used to signify a thing that in one way or another is said to correspond to the word. The meaning(s) of a word is not a denoted object, but the way(s) the word is used in the language.[19] I think that it would perhaps not be too much to claim that with his constitutive-regulative distinction Kant came more than halfway toward this truth noticed by Wittgenstein.

Up to the present, no philosopher has done more to throw light on the regulative than Austin. In fact, it is tempting to regard Austin's constative-performative distinction as being the exact parallel of the Kantian distinction here under discussion. I think that it would perhaps be true to say that the class of statements referred to by Kant as constitutive and the class of statements referred to by Austin as constative would, to a large extent, overlap. According to Austin, a constative is, amongst other things, a straightforward statement of fact, either true or false. "To issue a constative utterance (i.e. to utter it with a historical reference) is to make a statement."[20] Nevertheless, statements are only typical or paradigm cases of constatives. There are, Austin claims, many qualifications to be made.

The distinction between performative and constative is the distinction between doing and saying.[21] To issue a performative utterance is, for example, to make a promise, or a bet.

---

[19] Ludwig Wittgenstein, *Philosophical Investigations*, trans. G.E.M. Anscombe (Oxford: Blackwell, 1953), #40 and #43.

[20] J. L. Austin, *How To Do Things With Words* (New York: Oxford University Press, 1965), p. 6n. Hereinafter cited as HTDT.

[21] Austin, HTDT, p. 47.

The uttering of the words, is, indeed, usually a, or even *the*, leading incident in the performance of the act (of betting or whatnot), the performance of which is also the object of the utterance, but it is far from being usually, even if it is ever, the *sole* thing necessary if the act is to be deemed to have been performed.[22]

Austin introduces another set of categories for his analysis of speech acts. To perform a "locutionary act" is to utter "a certain sentence with a certain sense and reference." Then there are "illocutionary acts," "such as informing, ordering, warning, undertaking, etc., i.e., utterances which may have a certain (conventional) force." A "perlocutionary act" is "what we bring about or achieve *by* saying something, such as convincing, persuading, deterring."[23] Here again it is tempting to make an equation where it would not be legitimate to do so. It is tempting to regard the class of constatives as being the same as the class of locutionary acts, and the class of performatives as being the same as (say) the class of illocutionary acts. But, in fact, as Austin points out, stating and describing are two of the many illocutionary acts.[24]

The fact of the matter is that one of the aims of Austin's work is "to play Old Harry with two fetishes which I admit to an inclination to play Old Harry with, viz. (1) the true/false fetish, (2) the value/fact fetish."[25] Thus it seems that while some at least of Austin's distinctions are *similar* to Kant's constitutive-regulative distinction, Austin's aim is to undo the work of Kant and others.

What are the apparent similarities beween Kant and Austin? As has been said, the constitutive and the constative may be roughly coextensive. It would be a mistake to equate the regulative with the performative. While these categories are not entirely dissimilar, Kant did not notice the performative aspect of language as such, i.e. he did not see certain utterances as the doing of an act. Again, to make a constitutive statement may be to perform a locutionary act and possibly an illocutionary act; and Austin's description of perlocutionary acts bears a certain interesting resemblance to Kant's

---

22 Austin, HTDT, p. 8.

23 Austin, HTDT, p. 108.

24 Austin, HTDT, p. 147f.

25 Austin, HTDT, p. 150.

descriptive of regulative statements. But I do not find an iso-morphism anywhere here.

Nevertheless, it may be felt that if Austin is successful in dis-crediting the fact/value and true/false "fetishes," Kant's distinction will be seriously undermined. Austin sets out to find some precise way in which to distinguish the performative from the constative utterance. Austin looks for a criterion or criteria of grammar. He finds that there is

> no one absolute criterion of this kind: and that very probably it is not possible to lay down even a list of all possible criteria; more-over, they certainly would not distinguish performatives from con-statives as very commonly the *same* sentence is used on different occasions of utterance in *both* ways, performative and constative. The thing seems hopeless from the start, if we are to leave utter-ances *as they stand* and seek for a criterion.[26]

This, of course, is an important point to notice. Austin is carrying out a descriptive study of how sentences are used. His claim is that, from a mere study of actual use, we cannot say of any given sentence that we somehow *know* that its primary or primitive use is state-mental or constative.[27]

Austin "plays Old Harry" with the fact/value fetish and the true/false fetish on the basis of a descriptive look at the way in which sentences are used. His claim is that any given constative can be seen to have a performative side. The same flexibility of use is true of performatives. Does this mean that Austin has shown Kant's constitutive-regulative distinction to be wrong-headed? I think not.

Kant was perfectly well aware that regulative propositions (including here some at least of the sentences that Austin would call performative) *are* used by most people in a constitutive way. Kant's claim was that amongst the propositions that are ordinarily used in a constitutive way, some ought not to be so used. Those that ought not to be used as constitutives are those which are unverifiable. Thus, if I understand Austin correctly, he is saying that ethical propositions, for example, or propositions about (say)

---

26 Austin, HTDT, p. 67.

27 Austin, HTDT, p. 72, and p. 91.

God, are used in a constative way (which is perfectly true), and this is all right. Kant says that this practice is not all right.

Again, it would seem as though we have an important disagreement between Kant and Austin. Once again, I am not convinced that this is the case. Take any proposition 'P' that has important uses in the human vocabulary, but which is not in any way verifiable. If 'P' is in his catalogue of regulative propositions, Kant says that 'P' is merely regulative. Austin says, no, it is used as a constative. But both philosophers agree that 'P' is unverifiable, and that it lacks reference. Both philosophers, indeed, agree that 'P' is ordinarily used as a constative.

If both philosophers agree that 'P' is unverifiable, and if, furthermore, both philosophers agree that 'P' has important non-referential uses, have we not then reduced this apparent conflict to a merely verbal dispute? Kant says: "Regulative!" Austin says: "Constative!"

I do not mean to belittle the work of Austin. He, after all, provides a much more minute analysis of language than Kant. Austin notices many things about language that Kant did not. What I am suggesting is that in (say) the analysis of moral language it is neither the case that Kant and Austin were saying exactly the same thing, nor is it the case that their disagreements were important ones.

Finally, it is interesting to ask what it was that Kant thought of himself as doing. Austin, as everyone knows, saw himself as giving "as full, clear, and accurate account as possible of the expression (words, idioms, sentences, grammatical forms) of some language, or variety of language,"[28] in the hope of solving or at least resolving certain (not necessarily all) traditional philosophical problems.

> Austin, for his part, thought that he had developed a technique for tackling certain problems that particularly interested him, problems about the nature of language. He did not imagine that he had first formulated the problems and he did not imagine that he had discovered the only method of tackling them.[29]

---

28 J. O. Urmson, "J. L. Austin," *The Journal of Philosophy* (October, 1965), p. 500.

29 *Ibid.*, p. 499.

It goes without saying that Austin did not see himself as some sort of quasi-scientist or super-scientist, discovering truths about the nature of things. This view of the philosopher's task is no longer *de rigueur* amongst Anglo-American philosophers. It is my view that in this area, as in others mentioned above, Kant was not so far removed from twentieth-century insights as has ordinarily been imagined. What Kant says, in the context of talking about the constitutive-regulative distinction, is this: "We are not here asking questions in regard to the nature of things, but only such questions as arise from the very nature of reason . . ." (A695-B723) This disclaimer is, of course, ambiguous. Some would say that Kant saw himself as "discussing parts of the occult life-story of persons."[30] This view of Kant is at least open to question. Kant, after all, denies that one can say anything constitutive about such "occult" entities as mind.

My own view is that Kant, though he did not always express himself in a felicitous fashion, saw himself as making observations about the ways in which we think, and the ways in which we express ourselves. What he was trying to do was not altogether different from what Austin and others like him have been trying to do in the twentieth century. Whether or not I am correct in thinking this, I think it extremely important to notice how germane is Kant's constitutive-regulative distinction to so much that is of value in twentieth-century philosophy.

STANLEY G. FRENCH

SIR GEORGE WILLIAMS UNIVERSITY

---

30 Ryle, CM, p. 318.

KANT ON COSMOLOGICAL ARGUMENTS

It seems that every so often in philosophy some argument widely accepted as conclusive is challenged, and those who have accepted it as well as he who originated it are alleged to have committed serious errors. Of late this sort of challenge has been levelled against Kant's criticism of cosmological arguments, and has taken two forms. In its first form it is the claim that Kant's criticism is irrelevant to those cosmological arguments of which Aquinas's "third way" is paradigmatic. In its second form this challenge is the claim that Kant's criticism of such arguments is vitiated by a logical error. The first two things to be shown in this essay are that these two claims are mistaken. The re-examination of Kant's argument involved here is important not merely because it returns Kant's criticism to its accustomed status. It is also important because it shows two further things. One of these is not too surprising; this is that Kant's criticism extends to attempts to prove the existence of God which do not involve the use of a scholastic or rationalist philosophical terminology. The other, however, may be fairly surprising to many; this is that Kant's criticism equally extends to attempts to prove the existence of any ultimate source of things, no matter how un-Platonic or non-Aristotelian or "scientific" that source may be. Thus this essay shows that what Kant has given us is not merely a successful criticism of cosmological arguments to prove the existence of God, but a successful criticism of cosmological arguments. Every such argument includes an ontological one and thereby either fails or begs the question. This in turn sheds some light on why metaphysical systems and religious positions must be presented for consideration rather than proved beyond objection.

I. *The Alleged Irrelevance of Kant's Criticism*

The challenge concerning the relevance of Kant's criticism has been raised with specific reference to Aquinas's "proof from possibility and necessity," but it clearly applies also to every other such supposed proof. Less clearly, perhaps, but no less seriously, it can be extended to any cosmological argument. But first let us consider it in its original form with its original intent. This challenge is made by P. Brown in a recent discussion of Aquinas's views of necessary being.[1] Referring to Kant's claim that:

> ... the concept of the *ens realissimum* is a concept, and indeed the only concept, which is appropriate and adequate to necessary existence ...[2]

Brown maintains that this cannot have been Aquinas's view, for Aquinas did not hold that created necessary beings are perfect. Therefore, Brown alleges, "Kant's celebrated refutation is completely off the mark."[3]

It is quite true that Aquinas held that there are created necessary beings. This is part and parcel of his "third way," and appears in several other places in his works as well. It is equally true that he distinguished things which are necessary through another from things which are necessary *per se*, holding the former to be hypothetically necessary, the latter absolutely necesssary.[4] Further, at least so far as existence is concerned, only God on Aquinas's view has absolute necessity. But none of this is peculiar to Aquinas; many others, including G. W. Leibniz, C. Wolff, and A. G. Baumgarten, have held the same views.[5]

---

[1] P. Brown, "St. Thomas' Doctrine of Necessary Being," *The Philosophical Review*, 73 (1964), 76-90; n.b. p. 80.

[2] I. Kant, *Critique of Pure Reason*, N. K. Smith trans. (2nd corrected impression; London: The Macmillan Co., Ltd., 1933), A 607 / B 635. This is quoted by Brown, *op. cit.*, p. 80.

[3] Brown, *loc. cit.*

[4] St. Thomas Aquinas, *Summa theologiae*, I, q. 2, a. 3; I, q. 19, a. 3, in: *S. Thomae Aquinatis Opera Omnia*, iussu Leonis xiii edita (Romae: ex Typographia polyglotta, 1888), T. 4. Cf. the citations under '*necessarium absolute seu simpliciter*' in R. J. Deferrari *et al.*, *A Lexicon of St. Thomas Aquinas*, Fascicle iv (Washington, D. C.: Catholic University of America Press, 1949), p. 727. References below to 'Aquinas, ST', are to the former work here.

[5] Cf.: G. W. Leibniz, "Leibniz an Coste," *Die Philosophischen Schriften von Gottfried Wilhelm Leibniz*, herausgegeben von C. J. Gerhardt, Dritter Band (Leipzig: Alfred Lorentz Buchhandlung, 1931), S. 400; *Nouveaux essais sur l'entendement*, in *Schriften*, Fünfter Band (Berlin: Weidmannsche Buchhandlung, 1882), Sn. 415-424; *Essais de théodicée*, in *Schriften*, Sechster Band (Leipzig: Alfred

This challenge raises two questions. One is whether or not Kant knew the distinction between the two kinds of necessity; the other is whether or not he kept it in mind while criticizing cosmological arguments. Given his philosophical ancestry one would expect that Kant knew the distinction. Nor is such an expectation mistaken; Baumgarten stated the distinction in its standard form in § 102 of his *Metaphysica:*

> That whose opposite is impossible in itself is *necessary in itself.* . . . That whose opposite is but extrinsically impossible is *hypothetically necessary.* . . . Therefore necessity is either *absolute . .,* or *hypothetical . .,* the former as something is in and through itself, the latter as something is but hypothetically, necessary.[6]

But, then, did Kant keep the distinction in mind while criticizing cosmological arguments? Again given his philosophical ancestry it would be difficult to suppose he did not, and there are many citations of his own works which might be brought to support the answer that he did.[7] But incontrovertible evidence here is provided by his own summation of cosmological arguments in the *Kritik:*

> If something exists, then an absolutely necessary being must also exist. Now I myself, at least, exist; therefore an absolutely necessary being exists. [A 604 / B 632][8]

Lorentz Buchhandlung, 1932), paras. 7, 37, 53. C. Wolff, *Philosophia prima sive ontologia,* in *Gesammelte Werke,* herausgegeben von J. Ecole, Band 3 (Hildesheim: Georg Olms Verlagsbuchhandlung, 1962), §§ 301, 309, 318-320, 322, 327. A. G. Baumgarten, *Metaphysica,* editio iiii, 1757, in *Kants gesammelte Schriften,* herausgegeben von der Preussischen Akademie der Wissenschaften, Band xvii (Berlin und Leipzig: Walter de Gruyter & Co., 1926), Sn. 48, 94, 107, 166.

6 Baumgarten, *Metaphysica,* § 102, S. 48, my translation.

7 Cf. not only the entire discussion of cosmological arguments in the *Kritik,* but also A 324-328 / B 380-385, and Kant's *Der einzig mögliche Beweisgrund zu einer Demonstration des Daseins Gottes,* in *Schriften,* Band ii (Berlin: Druck und Verlag von Georg Reimer, 1912), Sn. 157-158. It is interesting to note that this latter, which presents what is basically the *Kritik* criticism of cosmological arguments, was first published in 1763.

8 I. Kant, *Kritik der reinen Vernunft,* herausgegeben von R. Schmidt (Hamburg: Felix Meiner Verlag, 1956, nach der zweiten durchgesehenen Auflage von 1930). The bracketed page indications refer to the 1781 and 1787 editions of the *Kritik,*

If, *per impossibile,* further evidence is needed, then perhaps Kant's use of 'absolutely necessary' or some cognate at least twenty-five times in the twelve pages of the original editions of the *Kritik* containing his criticisms of cosmological arguments [A 603-614 / B 631-642] will serve.

Should there be any doubt as to the relevance of this to Aquinas's "third way," these two passages from his *Summa theologiae* may help:

> . . . something is said to be necessary in two ways, namely absolutely and from supposition. Something is judged absolutely necessary from the relations of terms, either inasmuch as the predicate is in the definition of the subject, as it is necessary that man be animal; or inasmuch as the subject is of the essence of the predicate, as it is in this way necessary that number be even or odd. Thus, moreover, it is not necessary that Socrates sit. But though this is not absolutely necessary, it can be said to be necessary from a supposition; supposing, for instance, that he sits, it is necessary that he sit while he is sitting.[9]

> For we discover among things those which have the possibility to be and not be; . . . . If, therefore, all have the possibility not to be, at some time nothing would be in things. But if this be true, even now nothing would be; . . . which is patently false. Therefore not all entities are possible, but it is required that there be something necesary in things. All which is necessary, however, either has a cause of its necessity in another, or does not. It is, moreover, not possible to proceed to infinity among necessary entities which have causes of their necessity, . . . Therefore it is necessary to posit something which is necessary of itself, . . . which all call God.[10]

The recognition that Kant's criticism of cosmological arguments is relevant to those for which Aquinas's "third way" is a paradigm is not, however, a recognition of two points of importance given the aims of this paper. It is firstly not a recognition that the criticism is successful against these. It is secondly not a recognition that

---

of course, and will be used in brackets in the text for subsequent citations and quotations. This and all subsequent quotations from the *Kritik* are my translations from Schmidt's edition.

9 Aquinas, ST, I, q. 19, a. 3, my translation.

10 *Ibid.,* I, q. 2, a. 3, my translation.

either the criticism or its alleged irrelevance have any bearing upon cosmological arguments for which Aquinas' is not a paradigm. These points are best taken up in the order of their listing.

II. *The Alleged Logical Mistake in Kant's Criticism*

This challenge to Kant's criticism holds that he made logical errors in his handling of 'all absolutely necessary beings are most real' and its converse, and that these make his attack unsuccessful. One variant of this challenge has been advanced by Fr. T. Johnston; it is the claim that Kant supposed that in a cosmological argument the existence of an absolutely necessary being *is* inferred from 'all absolutely necessary beings are most real' or its converse. Kant is held mistaken here since on his own assumption the initial part of a cosmological argument is supposed to establish this.[11] The other variant of this challenge has been advanced by, among others, J. J. C. Smart. It is the claim that the conversion of 'every absolutely necessary being is a most real one' to 'every most real being is an absolutely necessary one' presupposes a proof that there is an absolutely necessary being. Thus, it is held, Kant's thesis that the initial part of a cosmological argument, the appeal to experience, is otiose is a mistake.[12]

Satisfactory response to these two variants of the 'logical' challenge to Kant's criticism requires that we be quite clear as to exactly what this criticism is. One element of importance in attaining this clarity is the recognition that there are, on Kant's grounds, two distinct points at which cosmological arguments are open to attack. One of these is that part of the argument which proceeds from the claim that something exists to the interim conclusion that an

---

11 T. A. Johnston, S. J., "A Note on Kant's Criticism of the Arguments for the Existence of God," *Australasian Journal of Philosophy* [then: '*of Psychology and Philosophy*'], 21 (1943), 10-16, n.b. p. 15.

12 J. J. C. Smart, "The Existence of God," in *New Essays in Philosophical Theology*, eds. A. Flew and A. MacIntyre (London: SCM Press, Ltd., 1955), pp. 28-46, n.b. pp. 36-37. Hereinafter cited as "Exist. God." For a similar criticism, see G. H. Joyce, S. J., *Principles of Natural Theology* (London: Longmans, Green, & Co., 1923), pp. 221-224. See also A. Donagan's review of Fr. D. Hawkins' *Essentials of Theism* in the *Australasian Journal of Philosophy*, 28 (1950), p. 129, where Donagan, though accepting the claim that Kant did indeed blunder here, holds that Kant's criticism of 'necessary being', like Hume's, remains satisfactory.

absolutely necessary being exists. There are at least five distinct objections which can be brought against this inference on the basis of the *Kritik*. Firstly, it involves a misuse of the transcendental principle that empirically contingent things have causes, since this principle does not legitimate inference to a nonempirical cause. Secondly, it commits a mistake in the claim that the impossibility of an infinite series of causes requires a first cause, as the dynamical antinomies show. Thirdly, it commits another mistake in supposing that we have completed the concept of a series of conditioned things because we have removed all the conditions requisite to a concept of hypothetical necessity. Fourthly, it confuses the logical with the transcendental concept of the unity of all reality. Lastly, it involves an inadmissible hypostatization of necessity as a material condition of existence. [cf. A 609-610, 616 / B 637-638, 644] These attacks, however, are not as effective as might be desired, since it may require considerable argument to show that a given cosmological argument in fact makes the mistake it is alleged to make. This is so for at least two reasons. For one, such an argument may utilize language different from Kant's. For another, it may be embedded in a metaphysical system which tends to camouflage these errors and appears impervious to the arguments of the *Kritik*.

The second point at which cosmological arguments are open to attack, however, is one which involves none of the foregoing mistakes, and offers opportunity for a simpler criticism. This is the point which Kant selected for his criticism, arguing roughly as follows: Let us neglect the above-mentioned difficulties and grant, for the sake of further investigation, that the first part of a cosmological argument establishes that there is an absolutely necessary being. As traditionally conceived, the second part of this argument remains, for it supposedly proves the existence of God. Hence it must be shown that this absolutely necessary being is the most real being. This identity, however, cannot be established by appeal to experience; were that in order, no proof would be. But if what is involved in the 'conceptual' establishment of this identity is noted carefully, it will be seen that this is an ontological argument. To establish this identity is to establish that there is a most real being, whether this latter result is sought or not.

The first variant of the 'logical' challenge to Kant's criticism fails here. This variant supposes that Kant wished to insist that

only an ontological argument could be used to establish the existence of an absolutely necessary being. In fact Kant did not so wish.
What he intended to show was that that part of the cosmological
argument which supposedly depends upon experience is otiose,
since it does not remove the necessity of constructing an ontological
argument. This being so, and ontological arguments being unsatisfactory, so are cosmological ones.

The second variant of the 'logical' challenge to this criticism,
however, is not so simply rebutted. The question it raises is whether
or not Kant succeeded in showing that the first part of a cosmological argument is otiose. It cannot be simply held that there is no
basis for supposing Kant mistaken here. In his discussion of the
interrelations of the 'concept' of an absolutely necessary being and
that of a most real one, he certainly asserted that 'all absolutely
necessary beings are most real' is convertible *per accidens* to 'some
most real beings are absolutely necessary' [A 608 / B 636]. He then
did go on to hold that, there being no difference between one most
real being and the next (on the supposition that there is more
than one), the proposition can be converted *simpliciter*. On the
grounds that conversion *per accidens* requires that there be something of the sort named in the subject term of the universal affirmative proposition involved, those who advance this second variant
of the 'logical' challenge hold that the first part of a cosmological
argument is required for the construction of the second. If this be
so, then a cosmological argument does not involve an ontological
one, and the appeal to experience in a cosmological argument is
not otiose.

But Kant's position here is not as poor as the challengers have
suggested. This is so due to two things; one is the surrounding
discussion of cosmological arguments in the *Kritik;* the other is his
discussion of the conversion of universal affirmative propositions
in his lectures on logic. In his *Logik* Kant held that a universal
affirmative proposition can be converted simply in those cases where
the subject and predicate concepts are identical. There is no
indication that such conversion need be by way of the subalternate
of the proposition in question.[13] The oddity of this way of ap-

---

13 Kant, *Logik,* in *Schriften,* Band ix (Berlin und Leipzig: Walter de Gruyter &
Co., 1923), § 53, Sn. 118-119.

proaching the problem disappears when it is remembered that
Kant was working with what was left of classical 'aristotelian'
logic by the eighteenth century. There such unrestricted convertibility plays the role which material or logical equivalence, as the
case may require, plays in contemporary symbolic logic. In the
general discussion of cosmological arguments Kant unquestionably
maintained that the two 'concepts' involved in the proposition at
issue must be taken as thus equivalent. Patently the cosmological
argument requires that all absolutely necessary beings be most real.
Kant held it equally requires the converse, since one of the things
such an argument is supposed to establish is that there is at most
one most real being:

> But yet through this complete possession of all reality the con-
> cept of a *thing in itself* as entirely determined is presented, and
> the concept of an *ens realissimum* is the concept of a single being,
> . . . [A 576 / B 604][14]

This limitation suffices to justify the conversion at issue in the
following way. What must be established to meet the requirements of the cosmological argument is that there is at most one
most real being, and that any absolutely necessary being is *that*
most real being. But here the only way in which the converse
could be false while the original proposition is true is for there to
be no absolutely necessary beings at all, and this condition is
incompatible with the intent of any cosmological argument. To put
this another way, given that no assumptions which would prevent
a cosmological argument are to be introduced, and given that there
is at most one most real being, it follows that 'all absolutely necessary beings are most real' is equivalent to, simply convertible with,
'all most real beings are absolutely necessary'.

Those who have made the second variant of the 'logical' challenge would, however, retort here that their challenge has not been
rebutted. The foregoing, interesting though it may be, has not
reached the *nervus probandi,* to steal a phrase, of this challenge.
This is not the problematic convertibility just discussed, but is
rather the common contemporary interpretation of universal affirmative propositions. On this interpretation such propositions are

---

14 See also A 568 / B 604, and his *Beweisgrund,* Sn. 158, 83-84.

merely universally quantified conditionals. Consequently, the two propositions of interest here seemingly should be phrased as 'anything, if it is an absolutely necessary being, is identical with the most real being' and 'anything, if it is identical with the most real being, is an absolutely necessary being'. In symbolic notation these would be:

1. $(x) : Nx \supset .x = (^1y) Ry$ 2. $(x) : x = (^1y) Ry . \supset Nx$

and conjoined would yield:

3. $(x) : Nx \equiv .x = (^1y) Ry$

It would then appear that, e.g., 3. should be read as saying that anything is an absolutely necessary being *if and only if* it is identical with the most real being. The emphasis upon the connective here suggests that this is just another biconditional, and similarly that 1. and 2. are just two more conditionals. So viewed, none of these three asserts the existence of anything, and if this be so the allegedly otiose part of a cosmological argument is needed after all. It is from that part that the existence of something is clearly inferrable and must here be derived, for although 2. might be thought to be the principle of an ontological argument, it by itself merely shows the bankruptcy of such.

Kant, however, despite the limitations consequent upon his non-acquaintance with *Principia Mathematica*, has noted something here which his challengers have not. This is the peculiarity of the predicate terms in 1., 2., and 3. To think of an absolutely necessary being which does not exist is to think of an absolutely necessary being which is not even necessary, much less absolutely so. To think of a most real being which does not exist is to think of a most real being which is not even real, much less most so. Hence, if the symbolic expressions are to show the entirety of what is being asserted, they should be formulated this way:

1a. $(x) : Nx \supset .x = (^1y) Ry :. (\exists x) : Nx . x = (^1y) Ry$
2a. $(x) : x = (^1y) Ry . \supset Nx :. (\exists x) : x = (^1y) Ry . Nx$
3a. $(x) : Nx \equiv .x = (^1y) Ry :. (\exists x) : Nx . x = (^1y) Ry$

Each one of these entails both 4. and 5.:

4. $E! (^1y) Ry$ 5. $(\exists x) Nx$

Further, proof that the denial of 2. or 2a. is inconsistent with 1a. is simple indeed. Thus Kant was and is quite correct in holding that any cosmological argument involves an ontological one as an essential part. To recognize the truth of 'all absolutely necessary beings are most real', as such an argument requires, is to understand that there is an absolutely necessary being, that the most real being exists. Kant insists upon pointing out that recognition of the truth of this is a recognition which entails 'any most real being is absolutely necessary' since that is the usual basic formulation of an ontological argument. After all, the essence of such an argument is that the understanding of *what* a thing is is *eo ipso* an understanding *that* it is.

There are two further consequences of this re-presentation and validation of Kant's criticism of cosmological arguments that are worth noting prior to taking up those cosmological arguments for which Aquinas's "third way" is not a paradigm. One concerns Aquinas's other supposed proofs and his refusal to utilize an ontological argument; the other concerns Smart's lack of concern with the alleged error in Kant's criticism.

Aquinas's four other supposed proofs, although they do not explicitly involve the phrase 'absolutely necessary being', are hardly free from the Kantian criticism. One way to see this is to note that all five of his arguments are supposed to prove the existence of the same being, so that it must be possible to construct a series of identities connecting their conclusions. But this would be a series of identities involving the 'concept' of an absolutely necessary being. Another way to see this is to note that for Aquinas God is the most perfect being, and this is the same as Kant's most real being. Yet a third way of seeing this is to note that Aquinas's first two arguments are supposed to establish the existence of a first actuality, that the fourth is supposed to establish the existence of something which is most being, and that the fifth is supposed to establish the existence of a first intelligence which must be pure act. A first actuality which does not exist is not an actuality; a most being which is not is not even a being, and a non-existent intelligence is not a first one, much less one which is pure actuality.[15]

---

[15] See Aquinas, ST, I, q. 2, a. 3 for the best-known formulation of the other proofs; see also his *Summa contra gentiles* I, c. 13, and III, c. 64, in *Opera*. T. 13 (Romae: Typis Riccardi Garroni, 1918), and 14 (Romae: Typis Riccardi Garroni,

Thus in each of these "ways," as in the "third way," to understand
a crucial premiss is to accept an ontological argument.

Perhaps the major obstacle, however, to the recognition of the
effectiveness of Kant's criticism against Aquinas's position and those
for which this is a paradigm is Aquinas's refusal to utilize an ontological argument. It is important to note that this is a refusal, not
a rejection of such argumentation as *per se* inadmissible, and
hence not the same as Kant's criticism of ontological arguments.[16]
Aquinas's central basis for this refusal is his view that man does not
know the essence of God (at least in this life), and consequently is
not in a position to begin an ontological inference. But the problem
this sets for Aquinas's own position is this: the lack of knowledge
of God involved, if there be such, is also a lack of knowledge of
those identities essential to the construction of a cosmological argument. It is helpful here to distinguish attempts to prove the existence of God from attempts to establish the existence of other
things. In regard to the latter one can understand what is being
talked about without any understanding that there is something of
that sort, since, as Aquinas himself might phrase it, their essences
do not include their existence. But if God's essence is, as Aquinas
held, to be, and if, as Aquinas also held, there are no accidents in
God, then the only way in which one can know what is being argued
in any argument to prove the existence of God is to know God's
essence, i.e., that He exists. In short, as has often been held,
Aquinas contradicted his own position in rejecting ontological
arguments.[16]

Turning, then, to Smart's ease in holding that Kant did err in
his criticism of cosmological arguments, it is necessary to look again

---

1926), respectively. For Aquinas's view on God as the most perfect being, see his
ST, I, q. 4, and his SCG I, c. 28. For Kant's view, see A 573-576 / B 601-604. It is,
perhaps, well to note that Aquinas's proofs of the various properties of God depend
upon the identification of God as the most perfect being and also upon the several
identifications among the "five ways." Consequently, it is not possible, despite the
claim of Fr. F. Copleston (in his *A History of Philosophy*, vol. 2, ch. 34 § 7 [West-
minster, Maryland: The Newman Press, 1950]), to evade the Kantian criticism by
holding that these identities are dispensable because replaceable by the various
proofs for the properties of God, e.g., in ST, I, qq. 3 ff. These identification problems were first pointed out to me by Prof. A. Campbell Garnett.

16 For Aquinas's rejection of this argument, see ST, I, q. 2, a. 1, and SCG I, c. 11.

at the term 'necessary', or more precisely 'absolutely necessary'. Smart sees no problem in supposing Kant to have erred since he takes 'absolutely necessary being' to mean 'logically necessary being' and can then argue quite successfully that this latter phrase is self-contradictory. As against Thomist-type cosmological arguments, this is a successful move; it is evident from the above quotation of Aquinas on absolute necessity (p. 395) that he did so understand this phrase. But as Kant well knew, one can develop a sense of 'absolute necessity' which does not involve logical necessity, and should such a sense be used in the construction of a cosmological argument, Smart's criticism fails. On the other hand, Kant's criticism, though related to Smart's, does not fail in such an eventuality since it is not tied to any particular sense of 'absolutely necessary'. On this point Kant's argument in effect comes down to this: It makes no difference what sense is given to 'absolutely necessary'; all that is important is that the notion of an absolutely necessary being is a notion which includes the existence of that being. This gives Kant's approach an important general applicability, as the next section shows.[17]

III. *The Extent of Kant's Criticism*

It is hardly difficult to suppose that Kant's criticism of cosmological arguments has a relatively limited application. On Kant's own view, it is aimed at attempts to prove the existence of God. As a result of the terminology in which it is couched, it appears applicable only to such proofs when they are presented by means of this terminology. Thus there is at least a superficial basis for supposing that cosmological arguments not formulated by means of this traditional terminology may well evade his attack. There is also at least as strong a basis, to put it moderately, for supposing that cosmological arguments intended to establish that something other than God is the source of all that exists are entirely unaffected by Kant's criticism. These bases, however, are only apparent, and it is the intent of this section to make this clear.

It might, of course, be supposed that any effort to show that the central criticism of cosmological arguments applies to such nonstandard versions is a work of supererogation at best. In a sense,

---

[17] Cf. Kant, *Beweisgrund*, Sn. 81-83, and Smart, "Exist. God," pp. 37-39.

this is correct; these attempts at cosmological argument are no more free from the other criticisms which can be levelled at such argument than is any such which takes Aquinas's "third way" as a paradigm (cf. pp. 395 f.). But here, as there, these other criticisms may not be the most cogent, and there is also the problem that these criticisms may be supposed too closely linked to the 'positive' teachings of the *Kritik*. That is, it may well be supposed that these other criticisms are somehow so tied to the development of the schematized categories and all that that the criticisms are successful only if Kant's 'metaphysic of experience' is acceptable. If it is then held that the latter has certain deficiencies, there is no problem in rejecting the criticism. This view of the structure of the critical philosophy has just enough truth or near-truth in it to make its rebuttal a long and complicated affair. Thus, as in the classical case, there is good reason for utilizing the more direct and simpler criticism of cosmological arguments.

To set aside criticism of the initial portions of a cosmological argument here is, as in the classical case, to select for the point of criticism virtually the last step in such an inference. That portion of the argument which is accepted for the sake of developing this criticism is the establishment that there is some sort of originating and ultimate cause or source of the universe. The point of criticism is the attempted identification of this with whatever is supposed, according to the intent of the proponent of the argument, to be that cause. In some approaches this latter entity will be some sort of deity; in others, it will be some sort of 'naturalistic' thing, perhaps hydrogen from nowhere, perhaps a big bang, perhaps some sort of life force. But what this latter entity is supposed to be is nowhere as important here as is the attempt to identify it as an originating and ultimate cause or source of everything else. To say that something is such an originating cause or source is to say that while it is the source of everything else, it does not itself have a source, that while it provides the last step in the explanation of all else, it does not itself require or indeed permit explanation by anything else. In this sense it might be said to be its own cause or to be self-explanatory. If no more than this is noted, the situation would appear to be not at all extraordinary; the Newtonian concept of inertia, for example, provides such an ultimate explanation of unaccelerated motion. What makes the situation extraordinary with regard to cosmological arguments is the respect, if it may be called that, in which such an originating cause or source is its own cause or its own explanation. This 'respect' is its existence, for it is the existence of things, not their particular characteristics, which a cosmological argument is primarily supposed to explain. Thus, to speak here of an originating cause or source, of something which is self-explanatory or self-caused, is to speak of something which carries its existence with itself. It is once more to speak of something which carries its existence with itself. It is once more to speak of something such that understanding what it is is *eo ipso* understanding that it is. This being so, any non-classical cosmological argument, just as any classical one, includes as an essential element an ontological argument. Thus the appeal to experience remains otiose, and unless ontological arguments are acceptable, cosmological ones are not.

There are certain aspects of this clarification of the full sweep of the Kantian criticism of cosmological arguments which merit further comment. The most important of these is the relation between the notion of an absolutely necessary being and that of a self-caused or self-explanatory ultimate and originating cause. As was pointed out in the previous section of this paper, Kant's criticism of cosmological arguments does not rest upon any particular sense of 'absolutely necessary'. His position might be paraphrased in this way: to say that something is absolutely necessary is to say that it must be as it is in and of itself. Thus to say that something is an absolutely necessary being is to say that it must be, i.e., exist, in and of itself. The only difference between this and the notion of an ultimate and originating cause of everything which is its own explanation is the way the words are spelled. It is also important to note in this connection that if a cosmological argument is to be carried through at all, that ultimate source which it purports to establish must be so conceived as to exclude even the possibility of explanation by anything else. If it is not, it will make perfectly good sense to ask what its source is, and so long as this sort of question is in order, one is not dealing with an *ultimate* source. Nor will it do to suppose that this ultimate source "just happens," or "just is." If these phrases are taken in their obvious senses, they are equally applicable to everything else, and if this be so, then it will not be possible even to begin a cosmological argument. On the other hand, if these phrases are taken in some nonobvious sense, they will serve to assign a peculiar status to this ultimate source. Given that the ultimate source must be one whose existence *cannot* be explained by appeal to something else, this peculiar status will, no matter how disguised, be no more and no less than the self-guaranteeing one already noted.

The other aspect of this clarification of the sweep of Kant's criticism which is worth further comment is the relation of the notion of a most real being to the notion of whatever it is which is supposed by the proponent of a cosmological argument to be this ultimate source of things. Those offering nonstandard cosmological arguments might object to the foregoing extension of Kant's criticism to their efforts in the following way: That criticism involves as an essential element the concept of a most real being. Kant gave this a standard interpretation which amounts to holding that it is the sum of all perfections, and no such view is advanced in these nonstandard arguments. [cf. A 576 / B 604] The response to this attempted evasion of Kant's criticism is very much like that given to the previous attempted evasion: the words may be different, but the sense is the same. The ultimate source of things, no matter what it be labelled, is their ultimate source, and is thereby

> . . . a transcendental *ideal* which lies at the basis of the thorough-going determination which necessarily is to be found in everything that exists, and constitutes the highest and complete material condition of their possibility, to which all thought of objects in general concerning their content must be led back. [A 576 / B 604]

Every characteristic of everything else must be derived from this ultimate source, and such will not, as *derived* characteristics, be the characteristics which, to reinterpret a phrase, "belong to being absolutely" [cf. A 576 / B 604]. All and only those characteristics which this ultimate source has will thus belong to being; only these will be (at least according to the view at issue) the "really real" characteristics of things. But all this is hardly surprising, for it is not at all at variance with the traditional view of the sum of all perfections. On this view, whatever is held to be the sum of all perfections can be said to possess many a characteristic only in the sense that it is able to cause that characteristic in other things—compare Aquinas, Descartes, and everybody else.

IV. *Some Consequences*

The foregoing three sections have shown that Kant's criticism of cosmological arguments not only remains successful against the traditional formulations of such but also is successful against any other formulation of a cosmological argument. All such arguments attempt to conclude by identifying as the first cause or source of everything that exists something which is such that *what* it is guarantees *that* it is. This has some consequences for cosmological schemes, metaphysical systems, and religious positions which are at least worth mention before this paper closes. A lesser consequence is that Kant's criticism of cosmological arguments makes room for faith in two ways, not just one. That is, it not only removes the threat to faith posed by alleged proofs of the existence of God; it also removes the threat posed by alleged proofs that the universe has some other source. (Need it be noted that this is hardly a justification of faith, religious or otherwise?) A greater consequence is this: Kant's criticism clearly shows the impossibility of arguing for a cosmological scheme, metaphysical system, or religious position wherever such a scheme, system, or position includes an attempt at a complete explanation of things.[18] Because such an argument will invariably include an ontological argument, those to whom the argument is advanced can reject it by rejecting the definition of that ultimate entity which is the key entity in the scheme, system, or position. This being so, the best that the proponent of such a scheme, etc., can do is to present his position for the consideration of others. At this point a last consequence of Kant's criticism appears. Since the key entity in such a system, etc., is such that the understanding of what it is is an understanding that it is, it is hardly surprising that those who adopt and advocate such a system should find it impossible to believe that those who do not adopt it understand it or have given it serious consideration. It is also not surprising that debates about metaphysical positions so often seem to be jousting matches where the contestants appear in separate arenas and charge madly past one another but make

---

[18] For an interesting presentation of another way in which others of Kant's arguments have a similar result, see G. Bird, *Kant's Theory of Knowledge* (London: Routledge and Kegan Paul, 1962), pp. 189-204.

no contact. All this is so since, in a sense which needs more attention than it has usually received, one cannot discuss such a position without adopting it. This is the reverse side of the phenomenon that ontological arguments only convince those who need no convincing, the non-theistic form of the sting in Anselm's explanation of why the fool says that there is no God.[19]

WILLIAM H. BAUMER

STATE UNIVERSITY OF
NEW YORK AT BUFFALO

---

[19] St. Anselm of Canterbury, *Proslogion*, in *Fides quaerens intellectum* . . ., ed. par A. Koyré (Paris: J. Vrin, 1954), c. 4. Those who suppose that the arguments of this paper might be undermined by contemporary efforts at ontological argument might consult my "Ontological Arguments Still Fail," *The Monist*, 50 (1966), 130-144.

A KANTIAN CRITIQUE OF THE GOD-IS-DEAD THEME

In discussions of Kant's contemporary relevance, the term 'Kantian' is usually used in three ways. First, it signifies the effort to make a fresh analysis of the text of Kant himself, in order to bring out its meaning and problems with more accuracy and penetration. Next, it is employed in a broader sense to cover the philosophical work being done by someone who belongs, however vaguely, to the Kantian tradition itself and who is seeking to prolong its method into present-day issues. But there is a third meaning for the term, when it designates an independent treatment of a problem, in the course of which special attention is paid to the leads suggested by Kant for its resolution. The present paper can be called Kantian in this third sense. It does not attempt an exegesis of some texts in Kant himself, and neither does it work within the framework of a Kantian school of thought. But it does seek to show that one contemporary question receives considerable illumination, when the resources of Kant are brought to bear upon it.

The particular matter for study is the currently central God-is-dead topic. It is being thematized in many registers: popular and technical, literary and religious, theological and philosophical. In trying to find my way through this jungle of thought and emotion, I constantly find myself asking about what sense Kant would make of it and what evaluation of it would seem most pertinent to him. Clearly, this is a comparative question which must be handled on my own responsibility, and not treated as though Kant were supplying fully determinate answers from behind the curtain. To prevent the latter illusion from flourishing, the direct historical order of exposition will not be followed here. Many expositors of the God-is-dead theme refer somewhat vaguely to Kant as supplying the background of the whole movement. There is, of course, a legitimate but highly indeterminate sense in which Kant's parentage can be invoked for almost every major trend in the philosophical thought of the past century and a half. But the precise nature of the Kantian filiation and the countervailing influence of more recent factors quickly become the points at issue, rendering the general reference to Kant's role too indefinite to be useful. One must either work out the philosophical thinking on God's death in full historical detail or else be prepared to make a reverse time-journey. It is this latter path which will be followed in the present approach.

There are four significant stages in this reverse time-journey. A beginning can be made with the most articulate proponents today of the message that God is dead. Their own testimony concerning historical influences will next lead us to a consideration of some aspects in Nietzsche's contribution to the topic. The third step will bring us to the interplay between Hegel and the Hegelians of the Left, out of which still other elements in the main theme are drawn. And finally, we will be back on Kant's own terrain for a concluding appraisal of the entire movement of thought. But at every stage of the journey, the main concern will be to make an independent use of Kant's reflections insofar as they further the general plan of gaining a philosophical orientation toward the God-is-dead doctrine.

1. Sorting Out the Arguments

As the evangel that God is dead is presently being heralded by such theologians as Thomas Altizer and William Hamilton, it enjoys the unity of a warmly held and propounded human attitude.[1] This attitude is then made the subject of investigation in the philosophy of religion. Since there is no single privileged method to use in philosophy of religion, several approaches are actually being made to the subject. One of these is the phenomenological study of the complex intentional acts which become embodied in the theme of God's death. Here, a controlling influence is exerted by the unity of the attitude itself, which nourishes the view that ours is the age

---

[1] T. J. J. Altizer, *The Gospel of Christian Atheism* (Philadelphia: Westminster Press, 1966); T. J. J. Altizer and W. Hamilton, *Radical Theology and the Death of God* (Indianapolis: Bobbs-Merrill, 1966); G. Vahanian, *The Death of God* (new ed.; New York: Braziller, 1966). See also, T. J. J. Altizer (ed.), *Toward a New Christianity: Readings in the Death of God Theology* (New York: Harcourt, Brace and World, 1967).

of the eclipse of the sense of the divine presence among men. Many of the intending components in this interpretative attitude are found, however, to contain or imply arguments of various kinds and levels. This gives an opportunity for raising some methodological questions concerning the supporting arguments, and it is at this point that Kant's critical philosophy has something to contribute.

Insofar as the pronouncements about God-is-dead convey some argumentation and not merely express a thanatos-syndrome, they can find a place within the university setting of investigation. Here, however, they must submit to questioning similar to that advanced in Kant's work on *The Strife of the Faculties.* If the scholars who make the pronouncements are acting precisely in their capacity as theologians, then they have an integrity of method within which to operate and back up their statements. As reflective students meditating on the word of God, they can engage in the work of explication of that word in its Biblical form. This is not an entirely paradoxical situation, in which the word of God is interpreted as telling us about the death of God. The situation is tolerable, since its import may be that the divine message contains a commandment against idolatry, and that our ordinary conception of God is the greatest among the idols to be overturned and abandoned. On this reading, the God-is-dead proclamation is made within a properly theological setting and has, as its main intent, the endless purification of any finite, human notions about God. The peculiar intensity surrounding the message is then understandable as an instance of the reforming zeal with which men of God always seek to distinguish the divine reality from everything else, including our most exalted ideas about that reality.

The drawback with this restricted interpretation of the God-is-dead attitude, however, is that the limitation holds good only for those who share the theological standpoint and hence can view the message as a domestic purification of the house of the Lord. Two facts tell against such a theological restriction of intent: the theme of God's death is proposed by many men who are neither religious witnesses nor professional theologians; and even its theological exponents appeal to a broad range of considerations extending far beyond the direct analysis of the Biblical word and the church traditions. Only through the conjunction of these two circumstances does the theologian gain some common ground of discussion with others, so that the topic loses its narrow professional cast and becomes a matter of general intellectual discussion.

It is also at this point of common argumentation that Kant's insistence upon a *philosophical* clarification of such issues reaches home.[2] One cannot simply heap up arguments drawn from every quarter, and then expect to achieve a disciplined control over the interpretation and practical outcome of the mass of statements. In the degree that all participants in the discussion bring forward evidence addressed to human intelligence and will, the theme of God's death comes within range of philosophical analysis and judgment. It ceases to function solely as a component within religious witness or as a subject regulated ultimately by the method and presuppositions of theology. The philosopher is now charged with the task of sorting out the types of evidence, the underlying methods, and the relative validity of the reasoning. Advocates of the theme may indeed refuse to accept some particular philosophical evaluation, but they cannot refuse all such evaluations in principle, without at the same time withdrawing credibility from the entire contention. Once the God-is-dead topic enters the public forum, it ceases to be the private possession of one hermeneutic circle and submits to the common processes of philosophical criticism.

Today, one of the favorite modes of alliance for developing the topic is that between theology and sociology. On this view, the main evidence backing up the God-is-dead conclusion comes from a study of modern society. There is a massive withdrawal of interest in God throughout all levels of society, in all countries of the world. Men live their entire lives in accord with categories, and in pursuit of values, which exclude God from their compass. This effective theoretical and practical formation of the human spirit quite apart from any theistic ordination, or other acknowledgment of a divine principle, is the real operational meaning of the statement that God is dead. Belief in the divine is no longer a living principle shaping our social patterns and goals. To the sociological findings

---

[2] The demand that philosophy must raise the truth question and put to the test of critique every historical, theoretical, and esthetic statement made in theology and the other academic disciplines, is the core of Part I of Kant's *Der Streit der Fakultäten*, ed. K. Reich (Hamburg: Meiner, 1959), especially pp. 20-30.

on this matter can be joined the witness of an entire series of modern poets and novelists. From Blake to Camus and Albee, these searchers of the human heart testify that the thought of God no longer enlivens the imagination, that human passion looks elsewhere for values and guidance, and that the religious pieties have decamped from the modern city.

This is a good instance where Kant's insistence upon maintaining methodological boundaries can be helpful. The sociological reports on the recession from traditional beliefs and religious values are impressive; the literary evocation of the same process is moving. But how restricted or how radically definitive are these testimonies, insofar as they bear upon the divine reality itself? They do not carry along with them the intrinsically limiting provision that, while they confirm the theological estimate of the present condition of religious *faith,* they decide nothing about the *reality* or unreality of God Himself. There is one definite strand in the God-is-dead tradition which has always contended that the only locus for the divine actuality is found in our human convictions and practical attitudes. On this premise, the widespread decline of belief in God and of humanly inspiring conceptions of God means nothing less than a decline and near disappearance of the *only* hold upon actuality which can legitimately be claimed for a divine principle. This inference cannot be shaken merely by reiterating the discrepancy between the divine consuming fire and our feeble efforts to capture its warmth in human creed and rite and community service, since a philosophical challenge has been made of the validity of making the distinction upon which the pastoral judgment of discrepancy rests.

The unspoken question behind these clashing interpretations concerns how far the history and phenomenology of religious attitudes, whether studied in terms of Biblical or sociological or literary categories, entitles us to conclude anything about the divine reality. In his own century, Kant was faced with a somewhat similar difficulty in respect to divine providence and human moral progress. Can the truth about these conceptions be established exclusively from an examination of the course of history, granted that most parties in the inquiry concur in the theodicy-is-dead proposition, thus ruling out any old-style rationalistic justification of God and man? Cultural history can be written from three standpoints. The oscillatory view regards our social action as milling around a good deal, but as getting nowhere; the optimistic position sees the bright road of progress stretching out there, and enthusiastically urges us to march along it; and the terroristic approach predicts (whether with satisfaction or dismay) the dissolution of our religious and moral values, and then cultivates the fascinating sense of doom guaranteed to confirm the prediction. Proponents of all these theories may be supposed to be in full possession of the data, and even to be empathetically aware of the attractive points in each other's positions.

As long as one restricts the analysis to the framework of cultural history, Kant sees no route open for resolving the dispute. It cannot be settled by labeling a portion of the data as a salvational history, if the move means that faith in such a salvational plan becomes a stipulated condition for accepting a particular interpretation. This move would only lead to a split among the inquirers, and thus would spell the end of any joint investigation. The only way in which the circle of inquiry can be widened, without segregating the participants, is by showing the relevance of some evidence that is grounded in human experience, but that cannot be confined to the categories of cultural history. In a word, some critical considerations must be brought forward, within the field of humanly ascertainable evidence, to determine our conception of reality and human values more closely than is possible within the limits of cultural history.

Kant's suggestion is that human freedom and moral action require us to take a wider perspective. They come within the range of human experience and philosophical analysis, without requiring a special act of assent to revealed doctrine as the condition for reaching true conclusions about them. And yet these factors are not wholly determined by the discernible trends in cultural history. The latter provides a sustaining basis for our free moral action, but it does not exhaustively specify the meanings and possibilities open to the moral agent. Thus the philosopher must learn to include the *cultural* history of mankind, along with all theoretical constructions about human agency and the actualities with which it becomes engaged, within the more inclusive context of our *moral* history and its implications.[3] And since Kant regards the philosophical theory of religion as a prolongation of moral philosophy, all questions involving the reality of the God of religious acknowledgment must also become responsive to this broadened framework of inquiry. There is a built-in epistemological inconclusiveness about any judgments concerning the divine reality that depend solely upon inferences drawn from the moods and attitudes in cultural history.

In practice, most of the contemporary proponents of the God-is-dead outlook concede that their central contention cannot be fully sustained, on the sole basis of descriptive reports on the waxing and waning of social beliefs. Quite apart from any transfer of the discussion to the theological context of a loyal religious purification of our thoughts about God, there is a strong element of philosophical interpretation already at work in deciding what can be inferred, and what cannot be inferred, from sociological and literary analyses of modern religious attitudes. The philosophical mind is never satisfied to be a supine echo of such analyses, but employs them as content and illustration for argumentation shaped by its own principles. That is why the remaining stages in our time-journey are imposed upon us by the very constitution of the present discussion of God's death.

Nietzsche and the others are brought into the forum, not simply as cultural reporters about religious values in a past era, but above all as philosophers who contribute the added requirement of a theoretical basis for judging about the cultural phenomenon of a waning in religious theism. Hence these sources cannot be cited merely as descriptive authorities or as specially gifted voices for expressing a pervasive cultural theme. Their expressive work is never divorced from their metaphysical and epistemological judgment upon the data of the religious problem. It is illusory to make a patchwork use of such historical sources. One cannot merely quote them as witnesses and fillers of an anthology, because they

---

[3] This distinction regulates the treatment of the question of progress in Part II of *Der Streit der Fakultäten*, translated in the collection of Kant's essays *On History*, ed. L. W. Beck (Indianapolis: Bobbs-Merrill, 1963), p. 137. Cf. also pp. 51, 60-62, and 75 on the analysis of man as a biological, cultural and moral species or social reality.

demand of their exploiters that some philosophical position be taken on the argumentation underlying their interpretation of the human attitudes on God and the religious bond.

2. *Nietzsche as Educator*

What Nietzsche once said about Schopenhauer, that the latter educated him in the radical style of thinking about man and the world quite apart from God, can justly be affirmed about Nietzsche himself. He is the primary schoolmaster for the present generation of proclaimers of the God-is-dead gospel. It is mainly from him that they derive the emotional tonality with which they suffuse their communication of this good news. It has a liberating and humanly dignifying quality about it which was lacking in every previous announcement of some variant of atheism. Nietzsche has educated them to regard the announcement of God's death, not just as a bold paradox, but as the very condition for securing man's worth and the sacredness of the entire universe. If some of his readers would like to add that, in some ultimate way, they are also defending the honor of the divine and perhaps preparing for a new presence of God among His people, then they must search in the Nietzschean texts for hints of religious longing on the part of the master source as well.

This pedagogue-role of Nietzsche can be looked at from two sides. From the perspective of present developers of the God-is-dead topic, Nietzsche appears as a prophetic mind, as a writer of immense prescient power, because of his ability to anticipate their own mood and position. What was to him only a lonely bell, tinkling out the news of God's death to an unheeding world, has now become a sonorous tocsin that fills the intellectual and emotional atmosphere. Viewed in terms of a progressive return to the historical sources, however, the pedagogical relationship indicates the presence of a considerable lag between the original philosophical reflection and its theological popularization at all levels today.

Nietzsche did his creative work on the issue during the eighteen-seventies and -eighties, and in the course of it he pointed back to the Schopenhauer-Hegel-Kant tradition as the line of speculation that he was bringing to its bitter fruition. He also looked forward to a race of men who would have the courage to accept his message and work out its consequences in the valuational and institutional orders. But to remain true to his own spirit, they would also have to do their own philosophizing and win their own hold upon God's disruption of human truths and values. The existentialist philosophers of the first half of the twentieth century did wrestle independently with Nietzsche's suggestions, and in consequence arrived at quite distinctive and divergent positions of their own. The question about the current religious acceptance of the theme of God's death is whether it has the philosophical quality of being a new reflection, using all the resources of methodology and epistemology, metaphysics and theory of man, or whether it is simply a lagging and transposed echo of the creative work done under past conditions.

To maintain the philosophical character of the theme in Nietzsche, more attention has to be paid to his particular arguments than to the conclusion as such. One of them merits close inspection for the light it throws upon Kant's involvement in the tangled development of the God-is-dead thinking. It concerns the transformation in our scientific view of nature and its resonance upon the religious conception of the cosmos.

We must weigh the precise reasons given by Nietzsche's madman (in *The Gay Science*), as he conveys to the ironic crowd that the God he seeks has not gone on a journey, but has been murdered by modern men.

> All of us are his murderers. But how have we done this? How were we able to drink up the sea? Who gave us the sponge to wipe away the entire horizon? What did we do when we unchained this earth from its sun? Whither is it moving now? Whither are we moving now? Away from all suns? Are we not plunging continually? Backward, sideward, forward, in all directions? Is there any up or down left? Are we not straying as through an infinite nothing? Do we not feel the breath of empty space? Has it not become colder? . . .God is dead. God remains dead. And we have killed him. How shall we, the murderers of all murderers, comfort ourselves?[4]

---

[4] *The Gay Science*, 125; trans. W. Kaufmann, *The Portable Nietzsche* (New York: Viking Press, 1954) , p. 95. On the transformation of the seventeenth-century outlook, see E. J. Dijksterhuis, *The Mechanization of the World Picture* (Oxford:

This series of questions is not just a rhetorical device, but is an interrogative mode of calling attention to the precise meaning here of God's death and of the manner in which we men have accomplished it. To say that God is dead is somewhat misleading, since it seems to state a static fact whereas, in reality, it heralds an aggressive deed of man. Hence it is more accurate to speak of the God-has-been-*murdered*-by-man theme. The accent is being placed by Nietzsche upon certain actions of modern man, the outcome of which involves the breakup of a world view with which European thinking about God had been customarily associated. What has been murdered is "the old God," the meaning of the divine associated with a certain conception of the cosmos which has been rendered anachronistic by some human actions.

What are the mortiferous deeds in question? They consist of the great intellectual and emotive efforts required to call into question the pre-Copernican picture of the world and to achieve the mechanization of our view of the universe. Men have had to do violence to their customary imagery in order to break away from a fixed and absolute horizon, from a physics involving the natural place and movement of bodies in opposition to an unnatural or violent movement, from a cosy finite universe with its single sun and an easily imaginable set of dimensions in space and time. Dislodgment from the old house of the universe brings with it a feeling of vertigo, of loss of the old sureties and pieties. And Nietzsche is there to encourage us to live through this giddiness, to become aware of the full consequences of being in a desacralized universe, and then to enjoy the new tide of innocence with which we can henceforth set our own course on the open sea of human experience.

The God whom we have killed is that portion of our meaning of the divine which is perfectly proportioned to the older image of the universe. In calling attention to this mutual adaptation and to its undercutting by the modern scientific revolution, Nietzsche may be regarded as the last cardinal sitting on Galileo's inquisitional board. What he shared in common with the other board members was a great sensitivity for the integral unity and interdependence

Clarendon Press, 1961), part IV. For the religious significance of the passage from a mechanistic to an evolutionary universe, see W. J. Ong, *In the Human Grain* (New York: Macmillan, 1967), pp. 156-159.

of all components in the older world image, and hence for the religious revolution implicit in the scientific one. All the board members refused to consider whether theism has any reserves of meaning that were *not* being actualized in correlation with the pre-Copernican outlook, and that required precisely the dissolution of this imagery for their effective realization. But whereas the majority of the board felt that the solidarity of religious theism with the crumbling world picture warranted their announcement of condemnation for Galileo, Nietzsche felt justified in announcing the murder of God by modern men: not only by researchers but also by all who accept the new image as their daily frame of reference. Both verdicts outstripped the evidence in the case, but in both instances we have to live through the consequences of their proclamation and cannot expect speedy relief.

Nietzsche remarks that Kant's joke is to try to defend popular opinion against the tide of learning, and yet to express his defense in highly technical terms and not in a popularly accessible style. There is an insight here, but it is just as much abused by simplification as is Mendelssohn's view of Kant as the smasher of all things. The complexity of Kant's position comes out in his treatment of the argument from design in the universe to God as the designer. Nietzsche focuses upon the encomia with which the analysis of this proof is prefaced (it is easy to grasp, is in accord with the scientific interest in our world, and is suited to our sense of a divine order), whereas Mendelssohn's gaze is directed toward the critical assessment (the proof reaches at most to a finite shaper; it becomes infected with the logical deficiencies of the other proofs as soon as it seeks to arrive at the infinite being; and in any case, the religious value of a knowledge-claim about God is dubious). But Kant will not allow himself to be dissected into now a conspirer for the defense of everyday theism who unfortunately cannot use everyday language, and now a conspirer against the common man's belief who fortunately protects his real intent by means of an impenetrable jargon. His treatment of the design argument does not consist of a mismated preface and conclusion: it is a complex, continuous analysis which is very closely knitted into the general purposes of his philosophy. The strands whereby it is interwoven with these general purposes enable us to notice its bearing upon the God-is-dead theme, as proposed in the text quoted above from Nietzsche.

Kant questions the probative force and foundationally religious significance of the design argument.[5] In doing so, he performs the same service for the religious mind of the later eighteenth century as Descartes, Pascal, and Leibniz had performed for that of the previous century. During this entire period, believers were undergoing the crisis of learning to live and affirm their faith in God within a world of transition, where all the adaptive coherence was gone (as John Donne put it) from the pre-Galilean picture of God-and-the-world and where some new reaches of theistic meaning had to be painfully forged. One reason why Descartes and Leibniz proposed metaphysical arguments based upon the self, and why Pascal appealed directly to man's religious faith, was in order to make people more lucid about that aspect of their meaning of God which can never be neatly proportioned to any reigning scientific view of the universe. In moving from the finite universe of diverse kinds of matter, natural place and movement, and a homely qualitative environment, to the universe of scientific mechanism, religious minds had experienced a severe wrench. They did not have to wait for Nietzsche's madman to proclaim what was happening to their traditional conceptions about God. But they also learned from Descartes and the others that the scientific shift was an opportunity to explore other facets in the meaning of God that had remained dormant in the previous outlook, as well as to recognize more effectively the transcendent nature of religious faith itself.

But there is in every age an almost overwhelming tendency to achieve perfectly rounded coherence and adaptation among all components in the dominant world imagery. It is Kant's critical office to unsettle the new harmonization proposed between religious faith, theism, and the Newtonian mechanistic universe. There are good reasons why the meaning of God cannot be bound down to the proportions recommended in this harmonization. For one thing, a perfectly domesticated religious faith loses sight of its own

---

[5] That this is the ultimate thrust of his critique comes out clearly in Kant's summarizing remark that "physico-theology is therefore unable to give any determinate concept of the supreme cause of the world, and cannot therefore serve as the foundation of a theology which is itself in turn to form the basis of religion. . . . The only theology of reason which is possible is that which is based upon moral laws or seeks guidance from them." A 628 = B 656, A 636 = B 664; *Critique of Pure Reason*, trans. N. K. Smith (New York: St. Martin's Press, 1965), pp. 523, 528.

foundation and of how it is actually related with the going scientific account of things. It tends to obscure the crucial distinction between a faith that *comes to* the work of making a religious interpretation of the scientific findings, while nevertheless retaining its distinctive revelational basis, and a faith that *founds itself upon* the inference from these findings. Only in the former sense of a previously disposed mind does religious faith find traces of the holy God of worship in the scientifically described universe. But to this extent, the religious use of scientific materials does not function as a philosophical proof of God.

As far as Kant's philosophically developed theism is concerned, there is another basic confusion involved in design argumentation. What is the source of evidence for the moral traits attributed to the divine maker of the world? As far as *subjective motivation* on the part of users of the design argument is concerned, it stems from the need to establish the morally responsible use of power, so that acknowledgment of the orderer of things can have some religious significance. But Kant probes into the obscurity surrounding the *evidential basis* of the moral attributes found in such thinking. It cannot lie in our ordinary experience of the natural course of events. For every affirmation of moral order from such pre-scientific experience is countervailed by some move taken in the skeptical development of the problem of evil, from Bayle to Hume. Nor can that evidential source be found in the scientific notion of nature. As a dynamic way of viewing the laws and interconnections among physical phenomena, this notion is thoroughly nonmoral in its own constitution.

Kant resists any direct moralization of the meaning of nature, as depending on either our ordinary experience or our scientific analysis of the physical order in the world. We cannot read off any moral attributes of the divine maker, from the evidence intrinsically furnished by a conception of nature so established. It is out of frustration over trying to bring the evidential basis in line with their religious motivation that the partisans of design-based theism are eventually forced into the web of ontological reasoning. But even this support is futile, since the kind of goodness deduced from an ontologically conceived infinity does not carry the connotation of moral concern for which the religious inquirer is searching.

Seen in this perspective of critical sifting of the religious significance of the ever changing scientific frame for a modern outlook, Nietzsche belongs in the main tradition of philosopher-educators. In the century of evolutionism, his announcement of the murder of God is a particularly intense way of renewing the philosophical theme of the travail which man brings creatively upon himself, when he modifies some major element in his world picture and must then follow through with a radical rethinking of all the other elements in his interpretation of existence. Kant's refusal to moralize the intrinsic concept of nature finds its counterpart, under different historical conditions, in Nietzsche's celebration of the innocence of becoming and the feel for the open sea of nature. What these educators of our awareness encourage us to do is to refuse to confine the search for God to the categories that recommend themselves, as fitting in perfectly with the prevailing view of the universe. To shake off this conformism is the condition, in the time since Galileo and Darwin, for every deliberate effort to achieve a living religious relationship.

3. *The Resurrection and New Death of the Ontological Argument*

Nietzsche continues to be our educator with his remark that "he who said, 'God is a spirit,' took the biggest step and leap to disbelief that anybody has yet taken on earth: such a saying can hardly be redressed on earth."[6] Our time-journey is thereby pointed back toward the proclamation of Hegel's doctrine that God is spirit, and toward the correction attempted by Feuerbach and Marx. And this intertwining can be better understood by bearing in mind the relationship which the entire passage from Hegel to Marx has with Kant's critique of natural theology.

The God-is-dead theologians make frequent mention of Hegel's citation of the great chorale in Luther on God's dying on the cross. In addition, they point to Hegel's criticism of Christianity as the established religion of the modern state, as well as to his graphic remarks on the parlous condition of natural theology even in the

---

[6] *Thus spoke Zarathustra*, IV; W. Kaufmann trans., in *The Portable Nietzsche*, p. 426. Nietzsche places this remark ironically into the mouth of "the last pope," who justifies his participation in the ass festival by noting that men are driven away from the alienating thought of absolute spirit and into all sorts of foolish, but humanly understandable, religious symbolisms.

seminaries. All these data indicate the emotive strength and cultural inclusiveness of Hegel's experience of the dying away of all previously effective intellectual pathways to God. He does not terminate in this experience, however, as the last word to be said about God. Instead, Hegel uses his descriptive account dialectically, as a means of determining the initial point with which his philosophical reconstruction of religious consciousness must begin. Even the most moving and exquisitely detailed description of the God-is-dead situation can become inconsequential, unless it is linked with some rigorous philosophical speculation.

In the Hegelian analysis, it is not quite accurate to say that God is dead. The more adequate appraisal is that human experience is the bearer (in all its shapes, including the religious and theological) of a meaning for the divine which can no longer be contained within the older credal and philosophical forms. The kernel of the truth that the absolute is a process of spiritual self-becoming cannot be kept within the husk of theism, and our experience of growing pains here is the actual content of the conviction about God's death. What the traditional religions and philosophies have conveyed to us under the rubric of 'God', must now be recognized as a particular phase in our human exploration of absolute spirit. The old thinking about God must go under, insofar as it is treated as terminal, and must then be transformed into a now surpassed stage in our reflection on spirit. Thus the cultural mood set by the God-is-dead theme is a presentiment of the imperious need of spiritual actuality to widen its horizons beyond the dualism of man and God, created universe and God.

When Hegel affirms that God *is* spirit, he does not mean that the predicate of 'spirit' must be added as a determination of the meaning of God, but much more radically that the entire truth and actuality formerly denominated by 'God', must now be recognized as preliminary formulations of the truth and actuality of absolute spirit. The death of God signifies the transition in our awareness from the former to the latter interpretation. It is a transition from the primacy of the theistic God to that of Hegel's spiritual absolute, of which the entire history of theism is regarded as the necessary prologue and as yet unfolded content. And as far as the history of philosophical theism goes, the transit is marked precisely by the move from Kant's critique of natural theology to

Hegel's defense of absolute spirit. Out of the death sentence passed by Kant upon speculative knowledge of God comes the Hegelian resurrection of the underlying theory concerning the spiritual totality.

That is why Hegel returns constantly, throughout his writings, to the problem of proofs of God's existence. Whether his context is phenomenology or logico-metaphysics or theory of religion, he is concerned with showing operationally what we do in trying to prove God's existence.[7] His use of Kant is the negative one of exhibiting, in the supreme instance, what we really do *not* do in such an employment of our mind. We do not make a one-way passage from the finite world to God or from our abstract idea of God to His existence. Kant shows the invalidity of attempting to proceed in this fashion, but Hegel will not accept the conclusion that therefore we can have no speculative knowledge of God. What follows from the Kantian critique is only an assurance of the wrongheadedness of the ordinary theistic interpretation of what transpires in seeking proof of God's existence. We do not try fruitlessly to throw a bridge across the chasm separating us from a transcendent creator. This account remains captured within theistic categories, but the conviction about God's death means that we realize the need to burst out of such categories in our search for spiritual truth and life.

Hegel seeks to transcend the theistic straightjacket precisely at that point to which Kant reduces all speculative reasoning about God: the ontological argument. Anthologists today are fascinated by the recurrence of this argument from one age to the next. Yet each of its major historical revivers is careful to remark that the older versions are being transcended in his own presentation, and Hegel is no exception to this rule. He does not try to draw the truth of God's existence out of the exigencies of a purely human conception of the meaning of God. Instead, he uses all his logico-metaphysical resources to show that such a conception is

---

7 Hegel gives a mature unification of his several treatments of this issue in his *Lectures on the Proofs of the Existence of God*, included in the Speirs-Sanderson translation of his *Lectures on the Philosophy of Religion* (3 vols., London: Routledge and Kegan Paul, 1962), III, pp. 155-327.

itself an expression of the internally developing actuality of spirit, and hence that it is already fraught with spiritual being.

The so-called proofs of God's existence are, in Hegel's view, reducible to a twofold operation of the human spirit: a metaphysical act and a religious one. The *metaphysical* act consists in our reflective realization that we are internal pulsations in the developing life of absolute spirit. We come to see that our thought about God is a preliminary image of the truth about self-developing absolute spirit, and hence that to prove God's existence means to clarify one's mind about this relationship of inclusion between the spiritual totality and our finite determination of its meaning. The *religious* act consists in raising up all our experience of nature, history, and thought toward the spiritual absolute, but viewed under the distancing perspective of the man-God relationship. A primacy of truth must be accorded to the metaphysical reformation of theistic religion. The metaphysical act constitutes the only genuine ontological proof, and yet what it proves is not precisely the existence of God but the actuality of infinite-finite spirit. As for the theistic proofs criticized by Kant, they can function as expressions of our religious aspiration, as long as they submit to reinterpretation in terms of the spiritual absolute. For their truth value lies in their susceptibility to a process of detheization.

Thus every statement of Hegel about revivifying the theory of God is regulated by his twofold systematic reference to the metaphysical and the religious acts underlying all talk about God. This essential qualification means that the death of the primacy of the theistic God is a condition for the Hegelian rehabilitation of the vocabulary of the divine, the spiritual, and the religious. During the first generation after Hegel's death, the Left Hegelians took skillful advantage of the ambiguity inherent in this use of terminology. They spoke about God and religion in two accents: with professional philosophical exactitude, in which case theism and the religious attitude were being treated as surpassed standpoints within the Hegelian world of absolute spirit; and with popular overtones, whose connotation was broad enough to embrace any forms of theistic thought, worship, and action which might still be resisting reconstruction into the Hegelian totality. Thus the humanistic drawbacks that Feuerbach and Marx found in a spiritual totalizing of all modes of existence were also attributed to all forms of belief in God and religious practice. The argument was that these latter forms are (at least in principle) ordained toward the Hegelian organic unity of spirit, and hence share implicitly in its insensitivity to man's natural condition and values.

As it gets orchestrated in this historical context, the God-is-dead motif shares in the fundamental ambiguity of the post-Hegelian criticism of the doctrine of spirit.[8] Feuerbach and Marx set up a dilemma for the adherents of this doctrine. Either they must accept the irreconcilability of the spiritual totality with the value of man and the earth or else they must reinterpret every statement about spirit to refer exclusively to the thought and action of men, joined together in social efforts to penetrate and control the natural world. And on the premise that every other theory of religion and the man-God relationship is subsumed under the Hegelian arche-type, this dilemma is proposed without alteration for theistic thinkers and for all varieties of religion. Either confess your anti-humane and antinatural position or submit to reconstitution on the terms set by a purely immanent, naturalistic humanism. On either choice, the death of God is a predictable result. If belief in God is not voluntarily dissolved by accepting a naturalistic reconstitution of spiritual meaning, then it will wither away as a practical attitude from which no more practical values can be expected under im-proved social conditions. Hence Feuerbach proclaims anthropology to be the secret meaning, not only of spirit, but also of God.

Perhaps it is only after the Hegelian postulate of spirit has worked out its consequences to this extent that Kant's function in the whole discussion can be appreciated. In terms of his critique of natural theology, what happens in the movement from Hegel to Marx is an attempted resurrection of the ontological argument in a new key, along with a new death for that argument as soon as the price we are expected to pay in human values for reviving it is

---

[8] The general lines of this development are established in Karl Löwith's *From Hegel to Nietzsche: The Revolution in Nineteenth-century Thought* (New York: Holt, 1964), and in his collected essays: *Nature, History, and Existentialism* (Evanston: Northwestern University Press, 1966). The source materials are found in Ludwig Feuerbach, *Lectures on the Essence of Religion* (New York: Harper and Row, 1967), and in *Writings of the Young Marx on Philosophy and Society* (New York: Doubleday Anchor, 1967), ed. L. D. Easton and K. H. Guddat.

weighed. As long as there is something analogous to the Kantian critical inquiry operative in the examination of theism and the modalities of religious existence, there is also operative there a principle in the human order which resists incorporation into the spiritual totality of Hegel and into Marx's comprehensive totality of social man working in nature. Kant does not permit Hegel's epistemological hierarchization of reason over understanding to shake him loose from his initial criticism of the ontological argument. As far as we men are concerned, the starting point is made with human experience of the world and a human conception of the meaning of God. It is not possible to convert these premises into self-expressions of the absolute spirit, as the resurrected ontological argument would require, without dissolving the distinctive reality of man, the experienced world, and values and conceptions concerning them.

Where Kant and Marx would differ in their appraisal of the Hegelian theory of spirit is over the precise moment when human values become endangered. Marx would become alarmed, at the relatively delayed moment when the consequences of the renewed ontological argument are being spelled out for the aims and ordering of human society. But Kant would take his stand much earlier in the process, at the very outset of the reasoning which sets the ontological argument in motion. Natural human values are being threatened by the initial ontological effort to transform human thoughts about God into self-expressions of the developing spiritual totality. Hence Kant would be forced to insert quotation marks around all talk by Hegel and the Hegelian Left about "God's death." The insertion would signify that the entire Hegelian discussion about the succumbing of God to absolute spirit, and then the succumbing of God-as-modality-of-absolute-spirit to Marxian humanity at work in nature, occurs within a premise that is not conceded in the Kantian critique of the ontological argument. Not everyone who cries "God is dead," must be acknowledged as a harmonizing voice in one coherent pattern of human witness and philosophical argument. Here as elsewhere, there is a sharp diversity of conflicting meanings for a phrase used in common.

4. Kant's Terrain

Finally, I will try to determine briefly the sense in which the theme of God's death is present in Kant's own philosophy. As far as human statements about God and religion are concerned, they secure their Kantian note of authenticity in the degree that they can show some connection with the requirements of our moral life. It is not only a matter of being able to bring out such a connection, however, but also of respecting the right order of evidence in our development of a theory of God and religion. The ultimately decisive grounds for any theistic and religious assent (the two are not identical, but they function together in Kant's milieu) must be *drawn from* the nature of our moral situation, and not merely be *brought to bear upon* that situation from some other basis. Given the centrality of morally based evidence and principles, there are at least three kinds of departure from this standard that would qualify as sources for the God-is-dead theme. They comprise respectively the speculative, the moralistic, and the religious sources for this theme.

(a) *The speculative root.* This source is already implicit in our earlier discussion of the design argument and the ontological argument. What fundamentally vitiates these reasonings is that they try to reach the God of moral and religious significance from starting points which are treated as being bereft of such significance. The artificial procedure is attempted of giving an isolated independence to the speculative view of the world and of human thought, and then of treating the conclusion of the proofs in natural theology as a divine entity, from whose speculatively determined attributes some moral and religious ones can then be inferred. But neither the artisan of the world attained through the design argument nor the infinitely perfect being at which the ontological argument terminates enjoys any basic moral quality. For the power and perfection affirmed in a purely speculative fashion remain morally indeterminate.

To glide over this defect and interpret divine power and perfection in a morally and religiously significant way constitutes the speculative illusion in this sphere of thought. Men cannot live by their illusions forever. The disillusioning process begins with skepticism about the specific arguments, deepens into a question about our ability to determine any well founded meaning concerning our relationship with God, and concludes with a pervasive sense of the unreality of all talk about God. Thus for Kant, the uncritical claims made for speculative proofs of God are a major source of the God-is-dead conviction.

(b) *The moralistic root.* There are various ways in which men can install themselves at the moral viewpoint. Although Kant defends the autonomy of moral motivation, he does not identify such autonomy with an isolation of the moral agent from the world. Moralism consists in this confusion of action done out of respect for the moral law as such with a cutting off of human action from its consequences in this world. Such a confusion is often fostered by the notion that God and religious holiness are found only in an inwardness that permits no concern for the repercussions of moral attitudes and decisions upon the disposition of goods and power in the natural world. Hence it is little wonder that the connivance and nihilism generated by this break of moralism with worldly connections should be traced back to the reinforcement received from belief in the inward God and an incognito holiness. The connection is deadly, in the literal sense, for any conscientious person's belief in a good God, as Kierkegaard also testifies.

To prevent this moralistic inwardism from having such support, Kant locates the morally decisive evidence for assent to God nowhere else than in the situation furnished by the moral agent's involvement in nature and society. The God whom we encounter in the moral order is neither a withdrawn diety, who bids us withdraw from the natural context in our turn, nor an extrinsic adjuster of the weights of virtue and the measures of happiness. We reach a perspective for accepting the divine reality only at that locus where we also recognize the unconditionally demanding duty to act morally in this world and to embody moral purposes in the natural course of events.[9] The natural setting for human moral endeavor is viewed by Kant, not as grounds for eliminating all talk about God, but precisely as grounds for specifying the assent to God and all religious service in terms of our active responsibilities in this world. The death-of-God motif purifies the moral man of the temptation toward moralistic inwardism, but in

---

[9] That the Kantian assent to God is entailed by the moral law of altering nature and social history in a morally significant manner, is brought out by George Schrader, "Basic Problems of Philosophical Ethics," *Archiv für Geschichte der Philosophie,* 46 (1964), 102-117.

turn it must lead to an acknowledgment of God as practically relevant to man working in the realm of nature.

(c) *The religious root.* Kant's *Religion Within the Limits of Reason Alone* is a prolonged struggle against the efforts of religious assent to break away from the central hub of man's moral life. To treat religious creed and ritual as a means of making ourselves well pleasing to God, entirely apart from transforming our lives in a morally upright direction, is the essence of religious self-illusion. The hypocrisy and social irresponsibility to which this autonomization of the religious attitude leads furnish another potent source of the God-is-dead sentiment. When religious conviction does not make a noticeable difference in the sphere of moral attitude and social use of power, it has a deathly rather than an enlivening influence upon the human person and the community. A person imbued with this religious illusion

> proffers everything to God, from lip-offerings, which cost him the least, to the donation of earthly goods, which might better be used for the advantage of mankind, yes, even to the immolation of his own person, becoming lost to the world (as a hermit, fakir, or monk) —everything except his moral disposition. And when he says that he also gives his heart to God, he means by this not the disposition to a course of life well-pleasing to Him but the heart-felt wish that those sacrifices may be accepted in lieu of that disposition.[10]

A religious attitude thus structured is so alienated from our moral springs of action and responsibility that it elicits an act of disgusted turning away from a God who would accept it as praiseworthy.

Kant appreciates the depth of the repudiation and the search for a new meaning of life which become incorporated into the God-is-dead position, as a consequence of encountering a religious attitude sundered from moral purpose. Yet he also points out that such an attitude is illusory, not only if it pretends to satisfy the aims of human action, but also if it claims to realize the meaning of

---

10 *Religion Within the Limits of Reason Alone*, T. M. Greene and H. H. Hudson trans. (La Salle, Ill.: Open Court Publishing Co., 1934; reprinted New York: Harper Torchbook, 1960), p. 160, modified. For Kant, the deepest springs of the God-is-dead tendency lie within the religious order itself, insofar as some believers invert the human relationship between morality and religious service, making the latter a substitute for moral rectitude rather than its prolongation.

man's religious relationship with God. The name he gives to the object of offerings made in this spirit is: not God, but *a fetish* (in agreement with Hume and the Enlightenment discussion of deviations in religious life). Hence the attitude cannot properly claim to be a theistic religious one. A religious relationship genuinely involves God, only when we can show that it rests upon man's full acceptance of his moral situation and the use of freedom for the transformation of himself and the world.

Whatever the roots of the God-is-dead theme, Kant would not regard them as amounting to a sheer fatality, which lies entirely beyond the critical inspection of philosophy and the transforming power of our freedom. To treat the theme in this way is to indulge in a counterpart of the speculative, moralistic, and religious misreadings of human experience from which it takes its origin. Kant holds out the reasonable hope that we can assimilate the theme of God's death, along with its sources of provocation, and in consequence enrich our grasp of the complex religious relationship between man, nature, and the philosophically determinable meaning of the living God.[11]

JAMES COLLINS

SAINT LOUIS UNIVERSITY

[11] The God-is dead theme is situated within the classical modern philosophies of religion by James Collins, *The Emergence of Philosophy of Religion* (New Haven: Yale University Press, 1967), pp. 262-67, 341, 421.

KANT AND THE POSSIBILITY OF A SCIENCE OF PSYCHOLOGY*

I

Kant claims that "empirical psychology (empirische Seelen-lehre) must always remain outside the rank of a natural science properly so called."[1] What led him to this conclusion? Kant first points out that if we take nature to be the totality of things insofar as they can be objects of our senses, then the doctrine of nature will contain two parts corresponding to the two forms of our sensibility: a doctrine of body and a doctrine of mind. But an "historical doctrine of nature comprising nothing but systematically ordered facts" (i.e., classificatory and descriptive natural history) must be distinguished from natural science properly so called. For "only that can properly be called science whose certainty is apodictic; cognitions which can only have empirical certainty are only improperly called science" (MAN, p. 468). Since the chemistry of his day consisted of "mere laws of experience," Kant held that it was not really a science; the explanations it gives in terms of such laws leave us "unsatisfied because no *a priori* grounds can be given for these accidental laws which mere experience has taught" (MAN, pp. 468-69). There can be no proper natural science, so Kant argues, without "a pure part on which the apodictic certainty, which reason seeks in it, can be based" (MAN, p. 469). This metaphysical foundation of science is transcendental insofar as it is concerned with the concept of nature in general. If we specify it further by introducing the empirical concept of body, or of mind, the a priori cognitions which can then be established will

---

* Parts of this paper were read at the meetings of the American Philosophical Association, in Philadelphia, December, 1966.

1 *Metaphysische Anfangsgründe der Naturwissenschaft*, [1786] (Akademie edition, Berlin, 1910-   ), Vol. 4, p. 471. Hereinafter cited as MAN. I am responsible for all translations from the Akademie edition which appear in the text. I have used the Kemp Smith translation of the *Critique of Pure Reason* (New York, 1950) and all references which appear in the text without any other indication are to this work.

constitute a pure (metaphysical) part of physics, or of psychology, "in which transcendental principles are applied to the two types of objects of our senses" (MAN, p. 470).

The Principles of the *Critique* are the presuppositions of scientific thought as such, regardless of what subject matter is being investigated. When they are applied to the concept of body, we get the a priori foundations of physics. Since this is the task to which the *Metaphysical Foundations of Natural Science* is devoted, Kant has to justify his use of that title. The justification he gives is that physics is the only science, properly so called, because it is the only mathematical science and "in any particular doctrine of nature one can find only as much genuine science as one can find mathematics" (MAN, p. 470). Kant explains this by saying that science presupposes a priori cognitions

> but the possibility of a determinate natural thing cannot be cognized from mere concepts; from these the possibility of the thought (that it is not self-contradictory) can, indeed, be cognized, but not that of the object as a natural thing which can be given (as existent) outside of thought. Consequently, what is required for the possibility of a determinate natural thing, and hence for its *a priori* cognition, is that the intuition corresponding to the concept be given *a priori*, i.e., that the concept be constructed. But cognition of reason through the construction of concepts is mathematical . . . a pure doctrine of nature concerning determinate natural things (doctrine of body and doctrine of mind) is possible only by means of mathematics. And since in any doctrine of nature one can only find as much science proper as one can find *a priori* cognition, a doctrine of nature will contain science proper only to the extent to which mathematics can be applied in it [MAN, p. 470].

The point is that since pure concepts are mere forms of thought, while our faculty of apprehension is sensuous, the a priori cognition of "determinate natural things"—i.e., of bodies, or minds "as existent," in contrast to their logical conceivability as objects of thought—must be mediated by their construction in pure intuition. Since the Aesthetic has shown that mathematics provides the rules for the construction of objects in pure intuition, Kant concludes that an a priori science, be it of body or of mind, is possible only insofar as the object of that science can be constructed according to the rules of mathematics. Since mathematics is applicable to the objects of outer sense, empirical physics is possible as a science properly so called. By applying transcendental principles to the concept of body (i.e., that which is extended, movable in space, etc.) Kant develops this pure science of body in the MAN, thus providing the metaphysical foundation for a science of physics.

Since the chemistry of Kant's day was largely a qualitative description of the properties of materials like iron, etc., aiming at practical recipes for their use, he called it "systematic art rather than science" (MAN, p. 468). But Kant admits that chemistry might become a proper science if, e.g., one could find "a law for the attraction or repulsion of parts [of chemical materials] according to which, perhaps in proportions to their density, etc., their movements and its consequences could be intuited and represented *a priori* in space" (MAN, p. 471). For if this could be done, then mathematics could be applied to chemical changes and they could be treated like movements in mechanics. The MAN would, in effect, also become the a priori foundation of chemistry, and chemistry would become a Newtonian science. But Kant explicitly denies the possibility of psychology's ever becoming such a science on the ground that

> mathematics is not applicable to the appearances of inner sense and its laws, unless one were to take into account the law of continuity in the flow of inner changes; but this would be an extension of knowledge related to that which mathematics provides for the doctrine of body in about the way in which the doctrine of the properties of the straight line is related to the totality of geometry. For the pure inner intuition, in which psychic appearances are to be constructed, is time which has only one dimension [MAN, p. 471].

Psychology could become a proper science only if it were possible to construct a pure, mathematical science that can do for the appearances of inner sense what the MAN does for the appearances of outer sense. But while the "movement" of inner states through consciousness might suggest the possibility of a mathematical treatment of such mental changes, this cannot take us very far because time has only one dimension. Indeed, things are even worse than that because time

> cannot be a determination of outer appearances, it has to do neither with shape nor position, but with the relation of representa-

tions in our inner state. And just because this inner intuition yields no shape, we endeavor to make up for this want by analogies. We represent the time sequence by a line . . . (B 50).

That is, we can understand time only in terms of space; to say that it has only one dimension is already to appeal to an analogy with space.

Time, unlike space, simply does not provide material from which the understanding can construct an a priori science. Kant makes this point explicitly when he says that the only nonempirical principle that could be used to explain "what happens in our mind" is the flow of mental states in time

> but practically nothing can be made out of this for the purpose of explanation because the general doctrine of time, unlike the pure doctrine of space (geometry), does not provide sufficient material for a whole science.[2]

In another passage Kant contrasts what can be done a priori with "the spatiality of the objects of physics" with how little can be done with "the time-form, the basis of intuition through inner sense." He argues that "the concepts of full and empty space, of movement and moving forces, can and must be brought to their principles *a priori* in a rational physics," but we cannot develop an analogous rational psychology from the concept of mind as something non-material, i.e., something that is not in space.[3]

In the *Critique* Kant showed that the pretension to knowledge from the " 'I think' [which] . . . is the sole text of rational psychology" (A 343) rests on a paralogism. Having demonstrated that we can learn nothing about the self from the purely formal unity of the 'I' which is the subject of any act of consciousness, Kant concluded that "nothing is left for us but to study our soul under the guide of experience" (A 382). But now it turns out that, since there can be no rational psychology in the way in which the MAN is a rational physics, this empirical study of the mind can never be more than a "merely random groping." Physics was able to enter "the secure path of a science" because it could approach nature

---

2 "Über Philosophie Überhaupt" (1794), Akademie ed., Vol. 20, p. 237.

3 "Über die Fortschritte der Metaphysik" (1791), Akademie ed., Vol. 20, pp. 285-86.

with a priori principles "according to which alone concordant appearances can be admitted as equivalent to laws" (B xiii-xiv) —i.e., because its concepts could be "brought to their principles *a priori* in a rational physics." This could be done because space makes possible a mathematical science for objects of outer sense (i.e., a pure science of body). But time, unlike space, does not make any a priori science possible. Since there can be no pure, mathematical science of mind for objects of inner sense, whose only form is time, we have no way of understanding why inner states must occur in the way they do. We can only describe the sort of inner states that are followed by others as a matter of brute, contingent fact. Empirical psychology can never enter "the secure path of a science."

It is not surprising that Kant reached this conclusion. Like his contemporaries, he saw Newton's physics as the model of all science. And he recognized, correctly, that Newton's laws were not merely generalizations ("accidental laws"), but were basic rules of the conceptual framework which scientists used to identify what needed explaining and what could count as an intelligible explanation. Facts could not falsify the laws of mechanics in any straightforward way because the facts being what they are was itself something to be explained in terms of these laws. The history of science supports Kant's view of scientific theorizing at least insofar as his point is that merely phenomenal regularities become part of the established body of a science—i.e., "concordant appearances can be admitted as equivalent to laws"—only when they can be made intelligible in terms of the conceptual framework accepted by the scientific community.[4] And the rules of Newtonian mechanics constituted that framework in Kant's time.

The difference between the "secure path" of a theoretical science like mechanics, in which investigators agree on the objective validity of fundamental principles, and the "random groping" of a merely empirical inquiry whose findings are constantly at the mercy of contrary facts, is seen by Kant as indicating that scientific laws have a priori grounds. He thinks we can show that e.g., the empirical regularities expressed in the law of inertia must have

---

4 For some arguments in support of this reading of the history of science, see my "Pragmatic Aspects of Explanation," *Philosophy of Science*, 33, No. 1, 1966.

the form they do have by applying the principle of causality (taken from transcendental metaphysics) to "matter [which], as mere object of outer sense, has no determinations other than external relations in space." This enables us to see, according to Kant, that a change of matter must here be a change of velocity, that this change must have a cause and that the cause must be an external one. It follows that "all change of matter must have an external cause," a statement which Kant takes to correspond to Newton's Second Law (MAN, p. 543). In this way Kant tries to make explicit, in the MAN, the a priori grounds of the science of mechanics "on which the apodictic certainty, which reason seeks in it, can be based." His view is that "mathematical physicists cannot do without metaphysical principles," for there could be no mathematical science of nature without them, even if "they prefer to postulate [natural laws] without inquiring into their *a priori* sources" (MAN, p. 472).

Looking back from our vantage point in history, it is easy to say that Kant mistook the framework of Newtonian mechanics for the only possible framework of science and so tried to anchor its principles in the human understanding as such. But it is important to remember that Kant's belief that mechanics must be the model for any inquiry that would enter "the secure path of science" was widely shared during most of the 18th and 19th centuries. During this period most students saw Newton's mathematical physics as the paradigm of all scientific theory, and other sciences looked to them like imperfect attempts at doing mechanics. It is very characteristic that Kant should think chemistry can become a proper science only if chemical changes can be treated like movements in mechanics. In thinking about the possibility of making psychology into a theoretical science, Kant calls attention to the "continuity in the flow of inner changes" which is, in some ways, like a movement. But since this flow is purely temporal and time "cannot be a determination of outer appearances," the succession of our inner states is not really a movement. So Kant sees no possibility of ever developing a mechanics of mental states and concludes that psychology can never become a science properly so-called.

II

But psychology is not only "Seelenlehre," it is also concerned with behavior as it appears to outer sense. What of the relation between inner (mental) states and outer (bodily) processes? Kant says that problems about this relation arise from the "mere delusion" of regarding matter as something that exists "in and by itself, apart from our senses." So understood, mind and matter are completely heterogeneous and their "communion" is inexplicable. But, argues Kant, matter

> does not mean a kind of substance quite distinct and heterogeneous from the object of inner sense (the soul), but only the distinctive nature of those appearances of objects—in themselves unknown to us—the representation of which we call outer as compared with those we count as belonging to inner sense, although like all other thoughts these outer representations belong only to the thinking subject [A 385].

Thus to ask how bodily motions can produce mental states is to make the mistake of "bringing to bear on our thinking subject the activities which they [objects of outer sense] exhibit as appearances in relation to each other" (A 386). What we have to recognize instead is that "neither bodies nor motions are anything outside us . . . it is not, therefore, the motion of matter that produces representations in us; the motion itself is representation only, as also is the matter which makes itself known in this way" (A 387).

Kant's point is that the extended table which I see is not a noumenon but a representation of outer sense which, as such, must be a mind-dependent appearance. Of course, this representation must be distinguished from my seeing of the table which, in a different sense, is a representation whose object is the extended table. My seeing of the table is subjective in the sense of being dependent on me, while the table which I see is independent, not of perception in general, but of my perception—it is part of an objective world order. But the central argument of the *Critique* is that this objective, phenomenal order is produced by the synthetic activity of the understanding; the ordering of the manifold in accordance with its principles gives us the objective world order which we properly distinguish from merely subjective experience. And when this critical insight about the relation of my perceptions to the objective world order replaces the account of the mind-body relation which "in its ordinary form . . . rests on a crude dualism" (A 392), then, so Kant argues, we are no longer faced with an insoluble mind-body problem. For if we accept the critical philosophy we cannot properly ask how the motion of matter produces mental representations in us; we can only ask how the representations of outer sense are related to those of inner sense.

Now space is the form of outer, time of inner, sense. But the appearances of outer sense, when considered from the point of view of the perceiving subject, are also in time so that "all appearances whatsoever, that is, all objects of the senses, are in time and necessarily stand in time relations" (B 51). All my ideas may be regarded as modifications of my mind and, if we leave aside emotional and volitional states which do not belong to the cognitive faculty while inner sense is part of that faculty,[5] then there are no contents for inner sense different from those of outer sense. Outer sense is constituted by the five senses with their organs (Anthro., p. 154), and "the representations of the *outer senses* constitute the proper material with which we occupy our mind" (B 67); it is from "things outside us" that "we derive the whole material of knowledge, even for our inner sense" (B xxxix, note). So the distinction between the extended table which is "outside us" and the perception which is "in the mind" must be a function of the way we identify an experience as outer and ascribe it to objects in space, and the way we identify an experience as inner and ascribe it to ourselves in time. As Kant puts it, an empirical, as opposed to transcendental, object is "called an external object if it is represented in *space*, and an *inner* object if it is represented only *in its time-relations*" (A 373). To speak of empirical things "outside us" is to speak of *"things which are to be found in space" (ibid.)*, and

> In order to arrive at the reality of outer objects I have just as little need to resort to inferences as I have in regard to the reality of the object of my inner sense, that is, in regard to the reality of my thoughts [A 371].

Far from allowing that outer objects are inferred from inner states, Kant argues against this "problematic idealism" of Descartes that

---

[5] See *Anthropologie in pragmatischer Hinsicht*, Akademie ed., Vol. 7, p. 153. Hereinafter cited as 'Anthro'.

outer experience is prior to inner experience (B 275-B 279). He
claims that we cannot exhibit the "objective reality" of the categories without intuitions (B 288) —i.e., without intuition there can
be no a priori cognition of "determinate natural things"—and it is,
says Kant, "a noteworthy fact" that to demonstrate the objective
reality of the categories

> we need, not merely intuitions, but intuitions that are in all cases
> *outer intuitions* . . . in order to exhibit *alteration* as the intuition
> corresponding to the concept of *casuality,* we must take as our ex-
> ample motion, that is alteration in space. . . . For in order that we
> may afterwards make inner alterations likewise thinkable, we must
> represent time (the form of inner sense) figuratively as a line, and
> the inner alteration through the drawing of this line (motion),
> and so in this manner by means of outer intuition make compre-
> hensible the successive existence of ourselves in different states. The
> reason for this is that all alteration, if it is to be perceived as altera-
> tion, presupposes something permanent in intuition, and that in
> inner sense no permanent intuition is to be met with [B 291-B 292].

Is Kant here saying that the categories (particularly the schemata of substance and cause) "can acquire a meaning only by reference to outer appearances"[6] but can subsequently be applied to
inner appearances also? Or is he saying that in order to make inner
alterations comprehensible we can appeal to an analogy with outer
changes—much as we can, according to Kant, use causality in an
"analogical meaning" to make the relation between noumena and
phenomena comprehensible (B 431-2) —but that since this is only
an analogy there can be no scientific knowledge, properly so called,
concerning inner changes? Kant's arguments against the possibility
of psychology as a science suggest the latter alternative. If the principles of the understanding are designed to explain how our knowledge of Newtonian objects is possible, then they won't fit mental
states, which are not Newtonian objects, and there will be trouble
when one tries to establish the possibility of psychological knowledge by means of them (See B 294). This interpretation is also
suggested by the claim that the Analogies of Experience are "regulative" principles "according to which a unity of experience may

---

6 This is N. Kemp Smith's interpretation. See his *Commentary on Kant's
Critique of Pure Reason* (New York, 1950), pp. 311-12.

arise from perception"; Kant contrasts the objects with which the Analogies are concerned both with "mere perceptions" and with transcendental objects (B 223-4). The implication is that the principles of the Analogies apply to extended objects rather than to mental states. Moreover, in the first Analogy Kant identifies substance with "quantity of matter." And the examples of causal connection in the Second Analogy are all physical. Indeed, the ordering of the manifold in accordance with the principle of causality is just what is used to make the distinction between an objective order of physical events and a merely subjective association of our perceptions. (See esp. B 239-40.)

On this interpretation the critical philosophy would rule out a "science of mind" in the sense in which the Hartley-Mill school tried to develop it—i.e., as an investigation of causal relations between mental and bodily states which is modeled on the physical sciences.[7] For on this interpretation mental states would not be phenomena, they would not be the sort of things that could cause or be caused. Of course, mental states are connected by association, and Kant argues in the Analytic that this is made possible only by causal connections between objective phenomena. But while the association of ideas, as a whole, depends on the order of phenomena, just as the whole phenomenal order depends on an unknowable order of noumena, in neither case is this dependence causal. Moreover, when Kant holds that

> a *judgment* . . . is a relation which is *objectively valid,* and so can be adequately distinguished from a relation of the same representations that would have only subjective validity—as when they are connected according to laws of association [B 142].

he is denying that statements about mere perceptions are judgments involving the categories (see also *Prolegomena,* Sect. 18, 22). The association of ideas has only "subjective validity" and therefore differs from the causal relations between bodies which can, according to Kant, be established in mechanics. The point is that space is just as essential a condition for the application of the categories as is time—"we cannot form the least conception of any

---

7 See my " 'Emotion' and 'Motivation' in the Development of English Psychology: Hartley, J. Mill, Bain," *Journal of the History of the Behaviorial Sciences,* **2,** No. 2, April, 1966.

other possible understanding . . . which is different in kind from that in space and time" (B 139) —and without it there can be no knowledge, properly so called. Causality, used strictly and not in an "analogical meaning," pertains to the mechanical interaction of extended bodies in Newtonian space and time, and we could never get a proper science out of the introspective examination of the succession of representations in our consciousness. We can describe and classify our inner states, thus producing a history of inner sense. But the laws of association are, at best, *de facto* regularities ("accidental laws which mere experience has taught") and not laws in the sense in which there are laws of mechanics.

Nor could we hope to find scientific laws connecting material processes with mental states—"it is not," says Kant, "the motion of matter that produces representations in us." Of course, 'X sees a table' describes what happens when X, an organism of a certain sort, is put in specifiable relations with an object of a certain sort. So what happens when X sees a table is a series of occurences given to outer sense; physicists and physiologists can establish causal connections among these phenomena. But X's perception of the table, as an appearance of inner sense, is not among these phenomena and so is not something that could be caused by the operations of bodies. Indeed, there would be no sense in looking for an external, causal relation between these inner and outer appearances since Kant's theory, in contrast to Descartes', relates the mental and the physical internally. To speak of experience, to say e.g., "X sees a table," makes sense only if we presuppose both an objective order, which is independent of any particular perceiver, and a subject who perceives it. We cannot elucidate the concept of a subject to whom inner experiences are ascribed except by reference to external objects; that is why Kant says that all the material for inner sense must come from "things outside us." And we cannot elucidate the concept of an object "outside us" except by reference to a possible subject; though Kant's empirical object is independent of any particular subject, it must be an object of possible experience for a subject. Inner and outer experiences are not two separate experiences, and when we distinguish the table which is "outside us"—i.e., the extended bodily object which we attribute to outer sense—from what is "in us"—i.e., the non-spatial, mental 'object' which we attribute to inner sense—we are distinguishing the object that is correlative to the subject in experience. Since the mental, as appearance of inner sense, and the physical, as appearance of outer sense, are thus internally related as subject and object, we cannot suppose an external, causal relationship between them.

III

While this interpretation is consonant with Kant's discussion of the mind-body relation and with his arguments against the possibility of a science of psychology, it seems to conflict with the fact that in his discussion of freedom Kant assumes that the empirical self is causally determined in much the same way as are empirical objects. Commentators regard this as "the most decisive consideration" in favor of the view that Kant thought the categories applicable to inner as well as outer appearances.[8] But it should be noted that on the interpretation I am supporting human behavior, *qua* appearance of outer sense, would be a phenomenon in space and time. So the question is not whether the critical philosophy sees empirical behavior as caused, but whether it allows the application of causality to mental states. Of course, "every action [viewed] as appearance, in so far as it gives rise to an event, is itself an event or happening, and presupposes another state wherein its cause is to be found" (A 543-B 571); this has been established by the Analytic and "allows of no exception" (A 536-B 564). But given Kant's Newtonian approach to science, one would expect him to assume that since the human body is composed entirely of physical particles its behavior must, in principle, be explicable in terms of laws concerning the behavior of these particles. In other words, outer occurrences—phenomena in the brain and nervous system—would be natural candidates for the causes of behavior as it appears to outer sense. Why then does Kant

---

8 A. C. Ewing, *Kant's Treatment of Causality* (London, 1924), p. 139. A number of other commentators favor a similar interpretation (e.g., N. Kemp Smith, *op. cit.*, pp. 311-12; H. J. Paton, *Kant's Metaphysics of Experience* (New York, 1951), 2, p. 423), but Ewing makes the strongest and most explicit argument for this interpretation.

sometimes speak of a "psychological causality" that can "produce actions by means of ideas?"[9]

The answer may be that the presumed physiological causes were in fact unknown, and Kant thinks that even if they were known they would be irrelevant to any practical concern with human conduct. He defends a pragmatic rather than physiological approach to anthropology on the ground that

> Whoever ponders over causes in nature, e.g., what might be the basis of the faculty of memory, can reason subtly back and forth (in the manner of Descartes) about traces of impressions remaining in the brain, left behind by sensations which are suffered; but he must still admit that he is a mere spectator in this play of his representations and must let nature do, since he neither knows the nerves and fibres of the brain nor understands how to manipulate them to his purpose, so that all theoretical logic chopping about this is a pure loss [Anthro., p. 119].

But a lot of practically relevant things were known about human desires. And the psychology of Kant's time talked about desires in quasi-causal language. Kant defines desire *(Begierde)* as "the self-determination of a subject, through the representation of something future, as an effect of the latter" (Anthro., p. 251), and also describes it as the faculty of a being to cause, through its representations, the reality of the object of these representations (Abbott, p. 94n.). A quasi-mechanical view of desire is also suggested when Kant speaks of *"Hang"* (propensity) as "the subjective possibility for the development of a certain desire, which precedes the representation of its object" (Anthro., p. 265), and the German words Kant uses in connection with desire—*Triebfeder* (usually translated as 'incentive', but literally 'driving spring'), *Antrieb* (impulse) and, when the desire has a settled character, *Neigung* (inclination) —all suggest a nonrational push or force.[10] It was,

---

[9] *Critique of Practical Reason,* trans. T. K. Abbott (London, 1954), p. 190. Hereinafter cited as Abbott.

[10] Anthro., pp. 251-52, *et passim*. Desire is always directed at what is expected to give pleasure, and "what drives me directly (through sense) to leave my condition (to get out of it) is unpleasant for me—it pains me; what, in the same way, drives me to maintain it (to remain in it) is pleasant for me, it gives me enjoyment." (Anthro., p. 231.)

therefore, easy to talk of desire as, for practical purposes, the cause of behavior. When, as agents engaged in practical life with other agents, we ask "What led *A* to do *X*?" the answer often makes reference to *A*'s desires and these may be said, rather casually, to 'cause' his action.

But it is not clear that Kant intends such talk to have the force of scientific (i.e., theoretical) claims about causal relations between phenomena. For, in the first place, he argues that maxims which guide conduct by reference to an object of desire cannot be laws because such maxims are merely "empirical." Kant's arguments here are: (A) If desire for the object is the ground for the determination of the will, this is really a desire for the pleasure expected from the object, and our knowledge that it will give pleasure is merely empirical and hence, at best, probable. So the maxim will be valid only under the empirical, and so uncertain, condition that the object will in fact give pleasure (i.e., satisfy the desire). And (B) "since susceptibility to a pleasure or pain can be known only empirically," such a maxim will be "wanting in objective necessity, which must be recognized *a priori*" and so cannot be a law.[11] The core of both arguments is that when a theoretical proposition referring to desire is made into a practical proposition the result cannot be a practical law because the theoretical proposition is not objectively (i.e., universally and necessarily) valid—i.e., it is not a theoretical law.[12] But if causality were applicable to mental states then theoretical laws of the requisite kind should, in principle, be possible. By applying the schematized category of causality to desires, pleasures, etc., one should be able to establish objective, universally valid laws concerning the sort of objects that must satisfy certain desires, or about the susceptibility to pleasure, or to certain desires, which people must have under specified circumstances, just as one can, according to Kant, establish such laws about physical phenomena. If Kant denies this possibility, may his reason

---

[11] Abbott, pp. 107-08. See also L. W. Beck, *Commentary on Kant's Critique of Practical Reason* (Chicago: University of Chicago Press, 1960), pp. 94-97.

[12] It may be suggested that maxims cannot be laws simply because they refer to some object of desire and their applicability is thus contingent upon the fact that the desire is present. But the inapplicability of a law to something to which is it simply irrelevant does not argue against the objectivity (i.e., necessary and universal validity) of the law.

not be that causal talk about desires, etc., has only "analogical meaning" and is not really like talking about forces causing a change of motion?

In the second place, but perhaps even more important, Kant explicitly defines affects and passions—the so-called "driving springs" of action—by reference to practical reason. Affects are temporary feelings, passions are settled desires (inclinations), but their common characteristic is that they are "blind" and "stupid" because they tend to exclude practical deliberation (Anthro., pp. 251-54, 260, 265). Since the way a billiard ball is moved by mechanical impulses cannot be described as either blind or farseeing, either stupid or smart, the way we are moved to act by passions cannot really be like the way in which billiard balls are moved. Kant explicitly recognizes this point when he says:

> Passion always presupposes a maxim of the subject to act according to a purpose prescribed to him by the inclination. Consequently it is always connected with his practical reason, and passions cannot be ascribed to mere animals, any more than [they can be ascribed] to purely rational beings (Anthro., p. 266).

Thus, in spite of the quasi-casual language, Kant links feelings and desires to actions, not as merely mechanical pushes, but through the will which is identified with practical reason. For Kant, "interest . . . signifies a motive of the will insofar as it is conceived by reason" (Abbott, p. 172); interests are formulated in rules, and "we say of rational beings only that they take an interest in a thing; irrational beings only feel sensual appetites" (Abbott, p. 80n.). So while "everything in nature works according to laws," only rational beings "have the faculty of acting according *to the conception* of laws" and, therefore, have a will (Abbott, p. 29). The will is a relation between the understanding and the faculty of desire and, says Kant, the "understanding (in this case called reason) is practical through the mere conception of a law" (Abbott, p. 145). For the will is not determined directly by an object, "but is a faculty of taking a rule of reason for the motive of an action" (Abbott, p. 151).

The crucial point here is the identification of willing with the capacity for acting on a rule or maxim. Nonrational beings, since they have no will, can only feel desires which impel them to move, so that there is a reasonable analogy here to the pushes which move a billiard ball. But rational beings can take an interest in something, can state that interest in rules, and can follow these rules—they can act from the "mere conception" of a rule. Reason is practical when it decides what *should* be done in light of the situation confronting the agent and the nature of all his inclinations, desires, etc., and willing, which is practical reason, is not a mental push that sets us in motion but is acting on a rule of reason—i.e., an action is willed when it is done intentionally, with some end in view and some knowledge of what one is doing and why. Since such actions can be guided by the agent's conception of rules, the conduct of rational beings, unlike the behavior of machines or (for Kant) animals, can be blind or farseeing, stupid or intelligent. Though Kant sometimes uses causal language in this context—e.g., "the will is a kind of causality belonging to living beings insofar as they are rational" (Abbott, p. 65; also pp. 80n., 94n., 120) —the kind of causality involved is one that operates only through the agent's "conception of rules." Surely Kant is here trying to work his way out of the quasi-causal psychology of his time, towards a very different conception of what it means to will an action. When he speaks of 'cause' here, this is not a Humean antecedent (mental) event, nor is it a category of the understanding which introduces theoretical order into the succession of events. If 'cause' is appropriate here, it is so only in the practical sense in which an agent can cause something to happen—i.e., can do it, merely through his conception of rules. Nor is it surprising that Kant should use 'cause' in this way since he gives that term a variety of meanings; he even speaks of a "causality" which "arises from freedom" (A 532 = B 560).

While Kant maintains that man's "will has an empirical character, which is the empirical cause of all his actions" (A 552 = B 580), he distinguishes sharply between a will which is "necessitated" by sensuous motives (*arbitrium brutum*) and "freedom in the practical sense [which] is the will's independence of coercion through sensuous impulses" (A 534 = B 562). In the former case, e.g., when we are overcome with rage or fear, we are not really acting. In the latter case (*arbitrium liberum*) our conduct is based on some rule; we are not "coerced" but act, more or less intelligently, according to some interest. Such "practical freedom can be proved through experience" (A 802 = B 830) in that we in fact seem to act and not be pushed—at the least, it seems to us that nothing makes us behave as we do when we act on some principle. And this is true even if the rule on which we act is an hypothetical imperative pertaining to the satisfaction of some desire. There is, for Kant, a fundamental difference between such rule-following behavior and cases where, like billiard balls, we seem to be acted upon instead of acting.

But since the psychology Kant inherited spoke of desires in quasi-causal terms, he still tends to see some analogy between the two cases when the rule we follow is an hypothetical imperative. Though *arbitrium liberum* differs from *arbitrium brutum* in that reason guides what would otherwise be blind impulse, the *"Trieb-feder"* which determines the will indirectly is still provided by "sensuous impulses [which] impel me to will" (A 548 = B 576). The will is free of direct, sensuous necessitation, but the choice of the maxim which guides it is a function of desire. Now if one is influenced by a quasi-causal psychology, then it will be easy to think of actions guided by an hypothetical imperative as indirectly goaded; it may even seem as if the only clear-cut case of acting is one where the rule on which I act is a law which I give to myself as a rational being—only then will the action be 'autonomous', something the agent really does without being in any way 'heteronomously' driven. When, in the context of his moral philosophy, Kant contrasts autonomy with heteronomy,[13] he often makes it sound as if in the latter case desire is, at least indirectly, something that really 'drives' us to act as we do. But the point is that even if one were to say e.g., that, regardless of how things may seem to me, my desire for money made me act a certain way, this would not be a denial of my agency provided that one conceives of the desire, not as a mental state which causes the movements of my body, but as a condition sufficient to determine my

---

[13] It is in the context of developing his moral theory that Kant characterizes *arbitrium liberum* as only "the freedom of a turnspit, which, when once it is wound up, accomplishes its motion of itself"—a freedom inadequate for morality as Kant conceives of it. And it is especially worth noting that it is here, in a context which leads him to tend to assimilate such freedom to mere "mechanism," that Kant speaks of a "psychological" causality which can "produce actions by means of ideas." See Abbott, pp. 190-91, 195.

acting on the hypothetical maxim on which I do, in fact, act. To see my behavior in this way would be to deny that I acted freely, but it would not be to deny that I acted. And this seems to be just how Kant conceives the situation in the case of *arbitrium liberum*. Whatever one may think of the claim, suggested to Kant by the psychology of his time, that desires are normally, or always, sufficient to determine a man's doing what he does, Kant at least recognizes that when a man does something because of what he desires he is really acting. For even if he acts on an hypothetical imperative pertaining to the satisfaction of desire, and even if, given his character and situation, he could not have done otherwise, the fact remains that he was not just like an object being pushed, but was guiding his conduct by his "conception of rules." So when Kant speaks of the "motive causes" of actions (A 550 = B 578), "cause" has only an "analogical meaning" because he recognizes, so I have argued, that one cannot really assimilate the explanation of actions in terms of 'ideas' (i.e., desire, pleasure, etc.) to the causal model of mechanics.

IV

This interpretation, like others, may not fit neatly everything Kant says.[14] What it brings out is that aspect of Kant's thought

---

[14] In particular, some of the things he says about inner sense in B 152-59 (see also Ewing, *op. cit.*, pp. 131 ff.). Kant is committed to the view that self-knowledge, like all other knowledge, must be phenomenal. So rational psychology had to be refuted, but then Kant still had to account for self-knowledge and it is in this context that he speaks of inner sense as providing knowledge of the empirical self in a way that seems to parallel knowledge of empirical objects through outer sense. Though some of the things he says in this context may suggest that the understanding produces a synthesis of the manifold of inner sense, on a parallel with outer sense, it is worth noting that commentators have found great difficulty in finding a consistent intrepretation of Kant's views on inner sense. Moreover, Kant is also committed to the view that mere experience is not a sufficient basis for (scientific) knowledge. Empirical physics is possible as a science because rational physics tells us what we can know a priori about any possible object of outer sense. But since rational psychology is impossible, empirical psychology, so Kant clearly and consistently holds, cannot be a proper science. Surely this suggests that when Kant speaks of self-knowledge in the former context he does not mean knowledge "properly so called." Commentators who think that the categories are intended to apply

which leads to his recognition that our actions, like our thoughts, are not just a series of passively caused happenings, and so cannot be adequately understood on the model of Newtonian mechanics. Many writers, before and after Kant, attempted to provide 'scientific' explanations of human behavior by treating external events, or situations, as causes of internal events which in turn cause bodily behavior. Explanations of human 'responses' were thus fitted to the model of the physical sciences by interpolating 'mental events' in the causal series that runs from the 'stimulus' situation to the behavior it elicits. As a result, the relation between agent and patient presupposed in our ordinary, teleological explanations of human actions was reversed. For if the stimulus situation is the efficient cause of the behavioral response, then it is really the 'agent' which produces the behavior and the person is passive, being merely caused to move by it. In contrast to this, the interpretation of Kant here supported holds that the relation between inner states and outer objects cannot be causal in the Humean sense; it cannot be a correlation between two separately identifiable events because the mental and the physical are logically connected aspects of one and the same experience. This interpretation also suggests that the explanation of human actions must differ in type from the causal explanations of the physical sciences.

In order to develop this suggestion further, I will ignore the faculty psychology which Kant accepts. What follows is, therefore, not so much an interpretation of Kant as an extrapolation of an important direction in his thinking about the nature of psychology.[15] With this qualification in mind, one can say that on a Kantian

to inner states, as such, have, I think, failed to explain why Kant should hold that psychology, unlike chemistry, cannot, in principle, ever become a proper science.

[15] I am not saying that this is the *only* way of reading Kant. Kant was, I think, trying to work his way out of the quasi-mechanical psychology of his time towards a radically different view. But since much of the content of his psychology comes from writers of his day who thought of mental states as causally related to bodily conditions, it will not be hard to find passages in Kant which seem to conflict with my reading. All I claim for what follows is that it is a possible way of looking at the direction in which Kant's thought was moving, and that by looking at Kant in this light we can connect his insights with issues in philosophical psychology which are currently under active discussion.

view when e.g., I unexpectedly come across a snake, the snake cannot be the external cause of such inner states as my fear, my desire to escape, etc. Rather, the distinction between the extended snake, which is 'ouside', and the fear, or desire to escape, which is 'in the mind', will be a function of the way in which we identify outer and inner experiences and ascribe the former to objects in space, the latter to ourselves in time. In other words, if we extend Kant's claim that "it is not the motion of matter that produces representations in us" to our affective and volitional states, then our emotions and desires will not be in the category of things that can be caused by outer occurrences. Changes in heart beat, respiration, etc.,—which occur without my doing anything—are external events which, no doubt, have causal antecedents in my brain, which in turn result from occurrences in my eyes produced by light coming from the snake, etc. But while this story lists a set of outer occurrences which are necessary conditions for my inner states—in their absence I would not be afraid—my fear, or my desire to escape, are not among these external occurrences and so cannot be caused by them. Rather, my fear is related to its object, the snake, much as my 'representation' of the snake is related to the extended snake I perceive; these are correlative aspects of one experience. Seen in this light, the direction of Kant's thought has considerable affinity to the view which A. I. Melden, A. Kenny, and others have persuasively argued in recent times—namely, that the connection between emotions, desires, etc., and their objects is more than contingent because the former cannot be characterized without reference to the latter, so that there is some sort of conceptual relation between emotions, or desires, and their objects.[16]

Similarly, when I say that I ran because I was afraid of the snake, or because I wanted to escape from it, these conditions will not, on this interpretation, be construed as internal events which can be Humean causes of such external behavior. Of course, I could not run if my legs were paralyzed, etc., so that there will be a set of outer occurrences which are necessary conditions for my move-

---

16 See A. I. Melden, *Free Action* (London: Routledge & Kegan Paul, 1961), and A. Kenny, *Action, Emotion and Will* (London: Routledge & Kegan Paul, 1963).

ments, just as the normal operation of various bodily mechanisms is a necessary condition for my seeing. But the volition, intention, or desire to run, will not be among these outer occurrences and so will not be in the category of things that can be causally related to outer occurrences. In other words, they will not be Cartesian mental happenings that can cause, or be caused, by bodily happenings. Instead, the mental and bodily aspects of my running—what I do when I move my legs (i.e., my moving them) and their movement—will be linked as correlative subject and object of experience. So when Kant speaks of the will as "a kind of causality belonging to living beings so far as they are rational" (Abbott, p. 65), 'causality' might better be read as 'agency'. For 'willing' is, on Kant's view, our faculty of "acting according to the conception of laws," so that he is at least very close to seeing that human beings are agents who can move their limbs directly without first doing something different—i.e., willing, intending, or desiring them to move. Since the latter cannot, on this interpretation, be regarded as logically independent of the corresponding actions, the Kantian approach can be seen as similar to that of psychologists who now speak of the "isomorphism of experience and action,"[17] and of the philosophers who argue that there is a conceptual connection between intentions, desires, or volitions, and actions—that we cannot make sense of the former as Humean causes of the latter but must instead "recover our sense that a human being is an agent."[18]

On this approach, explaining the conduct of men is a very different sort of enterprise from explaining the movements of billiard

---

[17] D. T. Campbell, "Social Attitudes and Other Acquired Behavorial Dispositions," in S. Koch, (ed.) *Psychology: A Study of a Science,* Vol. VI, New York: McGraw-Hill, 1963, pp. 130ff. Campbell takes this phrase from S. Asch's *Social Psychology* (p. 159) and "isomorphism" is clearly being used in a somewhat loose, nontechnical way. Similarly, G. Murphy speaks of "the unity of perception and action," *Personality* (New York: Harper, 1947), pp. 354ff., and M. Sherif speaks of "the unity of perception and behavior," *Outline of Social Psychology* (rev. ed.; New York: Harper & Row, 1956), p. 72.

[18] A. I. Melden, *op. cit.,* p. 133. Similar arguments have been advanced, among others, by R. S. Peters in *The Concept of Motivation,* by R. Taylor in *Action and Purpose,* and by G. A. N. Vesey in *The Embodied Mind* (London: Allen & Unwin, 1965). It should be noted that Vesey explicitly links his views to Kant (pp. 43 ff., and p. 109).

balls. For when we say e.g., that a man ran because he was afraid of a snake, or wanted to escape from it, we are not describing inner (mental) events which are causally antecedent to outer (bodily) events, but are saying something about the "conception of rules" in light of which the agent directed his conduct. Since rules specify what should be, not what is, they have no application to events, except in the secondary sense in which scientific laws or principles can be regarded as rules followed by the scientific community in the pursuit of its inquiries.[19] Only agents can follow rules, and even if a man's character and circumstances were sufficient to determine what he does, his behavior would be that of an agent if it makes sense to say that it was determined through his conception of rules. And to explain his conduct in terms of that conception we do not take the point of view of a theoretician who accounts for the occurrence of certain events by specifying antecedent events, be they physical or mental, which caused them. Instead, we take the point of view of an agent who makes the conduct of another agent intelligible by putting it into a practical, social context in a way that brings out the point of what was done, the purpose the agent had in doing it. That is, we explain the action in terms of what Kant calls the man's "character" construed as a "way of thinking" *(Denkungsart)*. For character, in this sense, is "that property of the will, according to which the subject binds himself to certain practical principles, which he has prescribed to himself irrevocably through his own reason" (Anthro., p. 292) . When we know a man's character we know what to expect of him "not because of his instinct, but because of his will" (Anthro., p. 285). That is, we know the principles on which he acts—whether these be valid or faulty is here irrelevant (Anthro., p. 292) —and on their basis can predict what he will do in various situations. And we can explain such human behavior teleologically, in terms of the agent's "conception of rules," by making clear why, given the rules on

---

19 When Kant speaks of causality as necessary succession "in accordance with a rule," the rule is not one followed by events, but one followed by us in the ordering of events. In this connection see also my article in *Philosophy of Science*, 1966.

which this person acts, he saw what he did as the "appropriate" thing to do in the situation as he envisaged it.[20]

Here it becomes significant that most of Kant's specifically psychological views are to be found in his *Anthropologie in Pragmatischer Hinsicht,* and that he characterizes this study as concerned with discovering, not "what nature makes out of man," but "what he, as a freely acting being makes, or can and should make, of himself" (Anthro., p. 119; also pp. 285, 292). What is relevant to the development of such a science is, according to Kant, travel, history, biography, novels, etc. (Anthro., pp. 120-21). Introspection of inner states, far from being stressed, is repeatedly held to be misleading (Anthro., pp. 133, 143, 161-162, *et passim*) and also dangerous because it leads to confusion and even insanity (Anthro., pp. 132-34). As Brett perceptively remarked, Kant's *Anthropology* "is the real beginning of 'psychology without a soul.' "[21] The reason for this is, I suggest, Kant's recognition that understanding human actions is not a matter of discovering introspectively the inner doings that are causally antecedent to outer movements, but is a matter of understanding the "conception of rules" in light of which an agent directs his conduct. And that understanding is not derived by turning inward and looking for private states, but depends primarily on turning outward to the public arena in which men, as practical beings, cope with their fellows in the affairs of the world. For it is in this public, social world that we learn to see the behavior of men, not as a complicated series of bodily movements, but as the actions of coming or going, buying or selling, reading or writing, etc. We can explain such actions 'pragmatically' in terms of men's understanding of rules, but such explanations differ in type from the 'theoretical' explanations of the natural sciences and are applicable only to agents, never to events.

I have suggested that in Kant's thought the Cartesian conception of the relation between the mental and the physical gives way to

---

[20] For some attempts to sketch the character of such explanations and to defend them against some possible objections see my articles in *Philosophy and Phenomenological Research,* 22, No. 4, 1963, *The Psychological Review,* 71, No. 3, 1964, and *Philosophy of Science,* 3, No. 1, 1966.

[21] *Brett's History of Psychology,* ed. R. S. Peters (London: Allen & Unwin, 1962), p. 538.

the view that they are internally related; and the attempt to construct Newtonian explanations of human behavior gives way to 'pragmatic' explanations of conduct in terms of the agent's conception of rules, explanations which account for what a man does as means to his goals. Since explanations of conduct, given in the purposive language of practical human affairs, are teleological and normative, psychology (in this sense) becomes for Kant an anthropological science. And the anthropological sciences are seen as fundamentally different from the natural sciences because conduct —what a man does, in contrast to what occurs when he acts—cannot be explained in terms of concepts appropriate to the natural sciences (i.e., the sciences dealing with 'body' as an object of outer sense) without mixing what belongs to different categories.

Such a reading links Kant to many of the key themes of contemporary philosophical psychology. Writers in this tradition have sometimes cited Aristotle in their support,[22] but Kant may be a more appropriate ancestor. For Aristotle thought that purposive explanations could appropriately be given in all cases, including even inanimate behavior. But the "mechanical philosophy" of the 17th century was fully justified in its attack on the teleological explanations of Aristotelean physics, though it does not follow that only mechanical explanations can be "scientific" and that "anthropomorphism" has no place in the anthropological sciences. The suggestion of an irreducible logical difference between the anthropological and the natural sciences is, I think, one of the most interesting implications of Kant for today.

THEODORE MISCHEL

STATE UNIVERSITY OF NEW YORK
AT BINGHAMTON

---

22 See e.g., D. W. Hamlyn, "Behavior," reprinted in Chappell (ed.), *Philosophy of Mind* (New York: Prentice Hall, 1962), and R S. Peters, *The Concept of Motivation* (London: Routledge & Kegan Paul, 1958), p. 157. The only contemporary writer of philosophical psychology who explicitly links his views to Kant is, as far as I know, G. A. M. Vesey (*op. cit.*), though Strawson (in *Individuals*) also seems to be influenced by Kant.

HEIDEGGER'S ONTOLOGY AND
THE COPERNICAN REVOLUTION

Concern with ontology is central to much of Heidegger's writing which raises anew for us the question of the nature of 'Being'. This new focus of discussion seems, at first, strangely discordant with the predominant tenor of contemporary thought. Yet, a reconsideration makes it apparent that Heidegger's insistence on concern with ontology, as the central concern of philosophic reflection, is deeply rooted in Kant's Copernican Revolution. If this thesis is validated it immediately asserts the direct pertinence of the Critical Philosophy to contemporary philosophic discussion.

The central issue for Kant was the Copernican Revolution. In it are focused the various strands of thought and the entire problematic which Kant had sought to resolve. Quite clearly Kant envisaged the task set forth by the Copernican Revolution to be one of metaphysical concern. As he had clearly said in the First Edition Preface of the First *Critique,* "In this enquiry . . . I venture to assert that there is not a single metaphysical problem which has not been solved, or for the solution of which the key has not been supplied."[1] Virtually the entire Second Edition Preface would support Heidegger's claim—in full awareness of the contrary tradition—that to ignore Kant's metaphysical problematic and the context of the *Critique* is to misinterpret the work from the outset.[2]

Kant's Copernican Revolution reversed the 'common sense' view of the relationship between the knowing subject and the object known. Just because it locates the ground of any knowledge of any object with*in* the knowing subject, Kant's Revolution represents, as Heidegger recognized, the first serious attack on the

---

[1] Kant, *Critique of Pure Reason,* trans. N. K. Smith (New York: The Humanities Press, 1950) , Axiii, p. 10; cf. Bxxxvi, p. 33; hereinafter cited as CPR.

[2] Cf. Heidegger, *Kant and the Problem of Metaphysics,* trans. J. S. Churchill (Bloomington: Indiana University Press, 1962) , p. 10, n.2; hereinafter cited as KPM.

traditional Plato-Aristotle approach to insight into the nature of things by focusing on that which is to be known.[3] For Kant, in contrast to the Aristotelian tradition, thought does *not* know the thing itself without any intermediary;[4] thought merely interprets what sense-intuition 'reports'. The concept is *not* "necessarily in conformity with its object;"[5] the Copernican Revolution proclaims the reverse: it is the object that, to be known, must conform to the knowing requirements of the knower. One need but review the opening chapters of Aristotle's *Metaphysics* to note the complete reversal of orientation. If one recognizes Thomism as a "continuation and amplification"[6] of Aristotelian realism, one can surely appreciate the force of Gilson's relevant insight: "Today our only choice is . . . Kant or Thomas Aquinas. All the other positions are but half-way houses. . ."[7]

Kant has thus brought us to the point where the ground of the presence or absence of an object in knowledge is to be seen within the nature of the knower; he thus opened that new philosophic gateway through which we may proceed to seeking a "metaphysics of the subject."[8] The *Critique* offers us the insight that for us to have any particular bit of knowledge we must employ the cognitive a priori concepts which, "prior to the object being given,"[9] define that knowledge as, indeed, possible. For something to be an object of our knowledge it must conform to the conditions of our knowledge which permit it to be cognized by us. For something to be regarded as an existent thing, the a priori constitution of our knowing processes—the transcendental laws governing the synthesizing

3 Cf. KPM, p. 16.

4 Cf. Etienne Gilson, *The Philosophy of St. Thomas Aquinas,* trans. Edward Bullough, G. A. Elrington ed. (Cambridge, Eng.: W. Heffer & Sons, Ltd., 1929) , p. 268; hereinafter cited as PTA.

5 Gilson, PTA, p. 272.

6 Gilson, PTA, p. 21.

7 Etienne Gilson, *God and Philosophy* (New Haven & London: Yale University Press, 1941), p. 114.

8 Pierre Thévenez, *What is Phenomenology?,* ed and introd. James M. Edie, trans. James M. Edie, Charles Courtney, Paul Brockelman (Chicago: Quadrangle Books, Inc., 1962), p. 149.

9 Cf. CPR, Bxvii, p. 23.

operation of our immediate apprehensions and our pure concepts or categories—must 'permit' it to be recognized as such.

To take an empirical perceptual example, our ears can only 'hear', i.e., have an immediate awareness of, sound waves of between 50 and 15,000 cycles per second. We have, by mediated inference, reasoned that there must be other 'sound waves' and we make simple dog whistles geared to the sound-reception capabilities of canines, but not of men, so that dogs can be summoned home without disturbing men. For the normal human, that sound which his dog can hear, he cannot. For the human who is concerned neither with his wandering dog nor with scientific sound-wave investigation, that sound which his dog hears cannot enter his immediate sound perception and thereby it cannot exist or be or have being *qua* heard-sound for him. For any sound-wave to be, as such, in the sense of *immediate* 'sensory intuition'—which both Kant and Heidegger have emphasized as necessary to the empiricism of experience—it must be within the range of our possible auditory perceptive capacity. Thus, if I say, "I hear a whistle," I am claiming that the sound of the whistle exists for me, that it has being in my present *immediate* experience; it may be presumed with certainty that the sound *is* within the range of human, if not canine, auditory capacity.

The being of any object within our experience thus justifies the presumption that it conforms to those cognitive conditions which render experience of it possible. It can be described as coming within the limitations of those characterizations which mark out the capacity for experience which we, as human beings, have. If objects must conform to our cognitive requirements to be known by us, their status as perceived or known is thereby, by definition, confined within the limitations *of what we can* perceive, of what we can know. To the extent that we can know an entity it must conform to the transcendental grounds of our cognizability.

The meaning of the Copernican Revolution, then, is this insight that all knowledge of the particular things in our field of cognitive vision, is dependent on the prerequisite for something to be, to be knowable, for us. For something to be an object for us, the way it 'appears', and if it 'appears' at all, is determined, "in advance" of that object's appearing, by the capacity of our cognitive 'faculties' to perceive it and the manner in which we are able to perceive it, become aware of it, cognize it.

What Kant had, in effect, asserted, Heidegger points out, was the necessity of passing beyond the constitution of the being of objects to the laws of human cognition which prescribe the conditions for appearing within our experience.[10] Before we can determine the being-status of particular things as they appear to us, we necessarily invoke the laws governing our cognition—governing and setting the conditions of the possibility of a thing to be, to be present, to come into being within our experiential realm. We necessarily invoke these cognitional laws in any cognition whether or not we are aware of them or of our utilization of them.

When we invoke these transcendental a priori laws of our possibility of how-and-what we can know, we are concerned with the condition and the nature of being, of the meaning that is intended in the verb 'to be'. We thus find ourselves entering into that branch of metaphysical thought which has been concerned with the meaning and nature of being as such and has generally been termed 'ontology'. Metaphysical concern with particular or special kinds of beings was traditionally divided into theology (concerning the being of the divine being), cosmology (concerned with the being-status of the entities within nature), and rational psychology (the concern with the state of being of the human soul). In each of these traditional areas of concern, attention was focused on the 'whether' and on the 'how' of the particular kind of being investigated. Each of these areas of 'special metaphysics' is clearly, and traditionally, delineated from the 'general metaphysics' which is concerned with the meaning of being-in-general, with ontology.

In coming to the portal of questions of 'ontology', Heidegger has suggested the import of the Copernican Revolution: instead of seeking to abstract the nature of being-in-general from a study of particular or special kinds of being, ontology or 'general metaphysics' is necessarily prior just because it is concerned with the general question of what it means to be, what it means for any object to have the status of being within the ken of human knowledge. It is only after the grounds which render it possible for an entity to appear to human awareness, for coming into the focus of

---

[10] Cf. CPR, Bxiii, p. 20 & KPM, p. 16.

human cognition, are determined, that we can legitimately discuss the particular being-status of the particular objects that meet our prime requirements for appearing to us.

For Kant, these conditions for something to have the possibility of existence within our circle of awareness, of becoming manifest to us, were the a priori transcendental constituents of our cognizing 'faculties'; these transcendental conditions are to be found in the synthetic unity of our 'pure' (pre-empirical) intuition and the 'pure' concepts of our understanding. These transcendental a priori conditions are, it will be remembered, not particulars, but general, universal and necessary. Failure to recognize the necessary priority of these a priori grounds for any cognition, Kant had suggested, was responsible for the failure of metaphysical inquiry.

Our knowledge of these pre-experiential grounds of cognitive experience is, in Kant's terminology, 'transcendental knowledge'. In Heidegger's reformulation, as a consequence of the reasoning just outlined, this 'transcendental knowledge' is translated into the term 'ontological knowledge', i.e., the knowledge of the non-experiential (or Kantian a priori transcendental) grounds for any particular thing to be capable of being known by us.

Similarly, just as Kant regarded any empirical knowledge as a particular bit of information, and any particular intuition as the particular immediate apprehension of a particular individual object, so Heidegger has rendered this experiential particularity by the word 'ontic'. An 'ontic' investigation, then, would be one concerning particular facts, actual specific occurrences and empirical generalizations from them. An 'ontological' investigation, on the other hand, as a Kantian transcendental investigation, would be directed toward the general, universal and necessary grounds upon which, or limits within which, any 'ontic', or empirical, experience can occur. The transcendental or ontological is thus logically prior to, and renders possible, empirical or ontic objects or events.

An 'ontic' discussion, then, deals with particular, individual, actual things or situations; it is directed toward the specific objects of empirical cognition. An 'ontological' discussion, in contrast, is concerned with what makes that particular experience itself possible—the general structures, pervasive conditions, limiting possibilities within which any actual experience is necessarily contained. It thus delimits those qualities or characterizations of any possible objects which may appear to us within the range of the transcendental modes of human cognition. By defining, in advance of any experience, what attributes it is possible for an object-in-our-experience to have, it is thus defining the possible ways in which an object can be for us in the knowledge of it which we are able to have.[11]

What Heidegger has seen Kant as having done in the Copernican Revolution, without necessarily being aware of it, was the demonstration of the possibility of real ontological knowledge. He cites Kant's own statement of the Copernican Revolution and focuses our attention on one passage: Conforming our objects to our knowledge "would agree better with what is desired, namely, that it should be possible to have knowledge of objects a priori, determining something in regard to them prior to their being given."[12]

The 'something in regard to them prior to their being given' is precisely what Kant had called the 'transcendental conditions of knowledge' and what Heidegger refers to when he discusses the object of ontological knowledge, viz., the constitutional prerequisites imposed by the human mind on any object as a condition for it to be known, i.e., to have the possibility of affirmative being—status within the horizon or limitation of human cognition.

The pure intuitions of space and time prescribing the 'forms' of any particular, or ontic, intuitions, and the schematized categories and their modes of synthesis—in the Kantian scheme of things combine to permit, or qualify, particular experiences to take place, to have reality, to be actual, for us. In Heidegger's vocabulary-transformation of Kant, this is to say that these 'transcendental conditions' of any particular possible experience are the ontological grounds of the possibility for any entity to be, to be actual, to have being for us. These 'transcendental conditions' are the ontological constituents of any particular object, of the possibility for being-status of any thing that is *in* our experience. If we follow this

---

[11] It is here, incidentally, that Heidegger's reversal of the traditional priority of 'actuality' over 'potency', a reversal inherently implicated by his conception of time, may be considered to be grounded.

[12] CPR, Bxiii, p. 20 (quoted, KPM, p. 15).

vocabulary-transformation it is apparent that Heidegger has given us a fair summary of Kantian doctrine when he says, "By this Kant means: not 'all' knowledge is ontic, and where such knowledge is given, it is possible only through ontological knowledge."[13] Just as for Kant any empirical knowledge is predicated on transcendental conditions, so for Heidegger any particular or ontic knowledge is predicated on ontological conditions or qualifications whether explicitly acknowledged or unconsciously presumed. When we seek to explicate these conditions for something to be for us, these necessary characterizations of things to appear to us, we are seeking 'ontological knowledge', i.e., knowledge of the transcendental grounds which are presupposed in particular ontic experiences.

The prime feature of the Copernican Revolution, then, was this insistence that for an object to exist for us, it must be conformed to the conditions requisite for knowing it.

> But this necessity expresses precisely the dependence of the empirical object with regard to ontological knowledge, and it is this dependence which will permit, in the empirical order, that the object and knowledge should conform to each other and be able to be gauged in accordance with each other.[14]

It is crucial to note that the 'transcendental' and 'ontological' conditions for any object to appear to human cognition are the same conditions. Looked at from the side of the perceiving subject, the conditions are 'transcendental'; from the side of the object they are 'ontological'. But, however regarded, their source is in us. Because the possibility of knowing the obects-that-are in our experience constitutes the being of these objects for us, the knowledge of these necessary characterizations of objects as known, in advance of any particular encounter, is a knowledge of their ontological characteristics, viz., 'ontological knowledge'. It is in this sense that the possibility of ontological knowledge, the knowledge of what it means 'to be', is rooted in human nature (as Kant would

---

13 KPM, p. 17.

14 Alphonse de Waelhens and Walter Bieml, "Introduction," in Heidegger, *Kant et le problem de la metaphysique,* (4th ed.; Paris: Galimard, 1953), pp. 9-59, esp. p. 16.

have put it) ; it is in this essentially Kantian sense, that ontology becomes Heidegger's central concern.

This is to say that the *Critique* is not to be regarded as primarily an epistemological treatise or as a theory of the natural sciences. Either interpretation would seem to reduce the *Critique* to merely one consequence of itself. The *Critique* provides for both epistemology and for science without being reducible to either. If, however, one persists in regarding it as an essentially epistemological study, then Heidegger would counter: it only can be justifiable to do so if it is regarded as a study of that 'ontological knowledge' which is presupposed by all ontic experiences (or, in Kant's terminology, the transcendental grounds of any possible empirical cognition) ; for, we require a (logically, not temporally) prior knowledge (even if preconceptual) of what it means for something to be for us before we can know that a thing *is* within our experience. For, by clarifying "the complete outline of a system of metaphysics,"[15] Kant had directed our attention, not to the particular things which we cognize but to the necessary conditions of the things that do appear to us for them to be able to appear to us.

Heidegger has thus given us a new perspective on the *Critique* as an ontological propaedeutic to 'every future metaphysics'. The emphasis and interpretation, as well as the implications to be drawn, are his own—but an ontological focus is neither that revolutionary or unique. Kemp Smith, for example, has insisted that "the ontological . . . aspect of consciousness . . . must be constantly borne in mind if the Critical standpoint is to be properly viewed;" and has found the root of the Hegelian misreading of Kant to arise from a reduction of Kant's doctrine to a part of itself: "To eliminate the ontological implications of his theory of consciousness is, by anticipation, to render many of his main conclusions entirely untenable."[16] Gottfried Martin has joined Heidegger in declaring that "Kant's final intention . . . is directed toward an ontology, a doctrine of being."[17] Actually they both go

---

15 CPR, Bxxiii, p. 15 (quoted, KPM, p. 21).

16 N. K. Smith, *A Commentary to Kant's 'Critique of Pure Reason.'* (2d ed.: New York: The Humanities Press, 1950), p. xlv.

17 G. Martin, *Kant's Metaphysics and Theory of Science*, trans. P. G. Lucas (Manchester: Manchester University Press, 1965), p. 133.

much further than Heidegger in regarding the *Critique,* not merely as the preparation of an ontology but, as already being and providing one.[18] Whatever question there might conceivably be concerning this kind of characterization, it would seem plain that it is in accord with the whole direction of development of Kant's thought; as de Vleeschauwer has pointed out,

> Considered materially, metaphysics corresponds to ontology or to the study of the whole domain of a priori knowledge without distinction of type, so that the distinction earlier established between it and transcendental philosophy disappears almost completely. This ontology can be applied primarily to determinate objects. . .[19]

Kant had defined 'transcendental knowledge' as that knowledge "which is occupied not so much with objects as with the mode of our knowledge of objects insofar as this mode of knowledge is to be possible a priori."[20] Heidegger has generally transformed the adjectival 'transcendental' into the noun 'transcendence *(Transzendenz)*'. Thus the capacity for 'transcendence', for going beyond particular sense-data, for invoking the transcendental grounds of knowledge, is necessarily prerequisite to any particular knowledge. This transcendence is requisite to, and provides the possibility for, any ontic knowledge regardless of whether it is unconsciously invoked, consciously presupposed or deliberately applied. When this transcendence, this capacity to invoke and utilize the transcendental grounds of knowledge, is itself examined we attain to 'transcendental knowledge', i.e., knowledge of the transcendental grounds of our ability to know things, knowledge of the ontological grounds of their appearing as such to us. The 'transcendental' and 'ontological' grounds are the same, be it remembered, the former from the side of the knower, the latter from the side of the thing that is known.

The confirmation of this parallelism is to be seen in what Kant had called "The Highest Principle of All Synthetic Judgments," and which Heidegger regards as not only summing up the core of

---

18 Cf. Martin, *op. cit.,* p. 134 & J. Royce, *Lectures on Modern Idealism* (New Haven: Yale University Press & London: Oxford University Press, 1919), p. 55.

19 H. J. de Vleeschauwer, *The Development of Kantian Thought,* trans. A. R. C. Duncan (London & New York: Thomas Nelson & Sons, Ltd., 1962), p. 154.

20 CPR. A12/B25, p. 59.

the Critical doctrine but as explicating the justification of his own explicitly ontological interpretation. If knowledge is to have objective reference and not consist in empty concepts, Kant had pointed out, the "object must be capable of being in some manner given."[21] Without objects of cognition, there would be no knowledge, no experience, and even our notions of space and time would be empty and thereby meaningless. The reality of our knowledge is dependent upon its prior possibility; it is defined by that possibility. What we do know is known because it accords with the transcendental grounds defining the possibility of our knowing. What we do know is further dependent upon the possibility of bringing concepts into unity with the objects represented as the content of our knowledge. It is, as Kant put it, "The *possibility of experience* . . . [that] gives objective reality to all our a priori modes of knowledge."[22] This possibility of experience derives from the principles which define our modes of synthesizing representations and concepts a priori; as exemplified in the Schematism these pure concepts are actually operative as time-related synthesizing and organizing principles of cognition.

Actual experience is formulated in empirical judgments deriving from the unification of the field or manifold in which our perceptions occur. This unification itself occurs within the limits set by a priori rules, within that experiential range defined as possible. It is from this prior possibility of a given experience that its objectivity derives. Thus, "The highest principle of all synthetic judgments is therefore this: every object stands under the necessary conditions of synthetic unity of the manifold of intuition in a possible experience."[23] Synthesizing a priori principles are possible when the formal pre-experiential conditions of a priori intuition, imaginative synthesis and apperceptive unity are related to a possible empirical field. Thus, "the conditions of the *possibility of experience* in general are likewise [at the same time: *zugleich*] conditions of the *possibility of the objects of experience* . . ."[24]

21 CPR, A155/B194, pp. 192-93.

22 CPR, A156/B195, p. 192.

23 CPR, A158/B197, p. 194.

24 CPR, A158/B197, p. 194; Smith translated 'zugleich' as 'likewise' and Churchill as 'at the same time'; the latter more literal translation is essential to Heidegger's point; cf. KPM, p. 123.

Kant's "highest principle," as Heidegger has rightly insisted, combines our capacity to understand the modes of our own cognition and our ability to attribute ontological characterizations to the objects we cognize. The parallelism between the transcendental grounds of knowledge and the ontological conditions for something to appear as such in that knowledge is, within Kantian terms, complete.

Our knowledge, then, of the necessary characterizations of the things-that-are for us is 'ontological knowledge'; the capacity for this knowledge is the basic root of the activation of our capacity to go from the given in experience to the conditions of its possibility, from the fact of experience to its constituent structure, within us. "Nothing in a priori knowledge," as Kant put it, "can be ascribed to objects save what the thinking subject derives from itself."[25] Ontological knowledge is the ground of the empirical or ontic; it is recognition of the limits of our possible experience and these limits arise from the limitations which we *qua* humans necessarily prescribe to it. Ontological knowledge, then, is concerned only with those universal principles of our mental operation and with their intrinsic self-imposed limitations. Ontological knowledge has thus been taken by Heidegger to denote that immanent structure of knowledge which the human mind projects as the prerequisite for any experiential content.

The philosophy of the *Critique* has thus been seen by Heidegger as a 'metaphysics of experience' in that it seeks to bring to light the fundamental structure necessarily present in any ontic experience. In the structural elements of human reason it has sought out the a priori conditions of the possibility for us to have knowledge of what is requisite for something to be for us. This is to say that the essential point to be extricated from the Critical doctrine is that ontology is the center of metaphysics and, in Kant's landmark work, "is provided with a foundation and, for the first time, revealed for what it is in itself."[26]

The central concern of the Critical inquiry has thus become for Heidegger that of the nature of our capacity to go from the given to its conditions of being cognized by us. It thus demands an

---

25 CPR, Bxxiii, p. 25.

26 KPM, p. 21.

examination of our capacity for transcendence, i.e., our capacity to achieve ontological knowledge, knowledge of the nature and of the conditions of the being-status of the things-that-are or can be in human experience. Empirical or ontic knowledge can only arise within the limitations of the transcendental (or ontological) limitations imposed by our cognitive processes. It is this concern which Kant had summed up in his quest for the possibility of synthetic a priori judgments. This, Heidegger agrees, is the key question for metaphysical inquiry. The goal of Heidegger's attempt to re-examine the Kantian effort is to seek out the source-ground of our capacity for a priori synthesis, the Kantian source of the possibility of our knowledge. For Heidegger, as for Kant, this synthesis is what constitutes the human ability to discover, within itself, its capacity for transcending raw given data. Insight into the nature of this synthesis enables us to understand the transcendental or ontological structure of our mode of cognition and thus of the possibility and essential structure of our particular empirical or ontic cognitions.

The focus of metaphysical inquiry is thus shifted from the specific things-that-are to the grounds of their being for us. Focusing on this 'immanent' ontology—what is to be termed in the early Heidegger 'fundamental ontology'—the task becomes that of systematic inquiry into the a priori grounds of possible human knowledge. Such inquiry elicits the justification, as Kant pointed out, of the existential assertions we can make with certainty.[27] Metaphysics, as ontological investigation, thereby defines the possibility, structure and possible extent of the actual specific experience we do or can, indeed, have. By defining and justifying the universal categorial limitations on what the content of our experience can be, it proposes the necessary determinations for the character requisite for any particular entity in order for it to enter into our experience. It thus defines the ontological characterizations of the objects which are manifest to us in terms of the transcendental grounds of our capacity to become aware of them.

For Kant, the possibility of metaphysics was to be found in the synthetic unity of the human 'faculties' of cognition. This, Heidegger has interpreted to mean that, for Kant as for himself, "the

---

27 Cf. CPR, Axv, p. 11.

question of the basis of metaphysics is equivalent to the question concerning the true nature of man or, more specifically, of human reason."[28] Our ability to comprehend the nature and the structure of our world is dependent on our understanding of the ways in which we can know it. Our ability to have knowledge of objects is dependent on the ways in which we can recognize them as such. The human mode of cognition is the key to what can be discerned as the content of cognition. The limitations of human cognition thus impose limitations on what can appear in that cognition. The manner in which human cognition functions determines how appearances can arise for it. The possibility of a metaphysical description of the structure of the world we know is thus dependent on the world we can recognize as existing or being *for us*. Metaphysics is then reducible to ontology, to an immanent or fundamental ontology which describes the ways in which the necessary structure of human cognition is able to recognize the things that are present to it, the ways in which it ascribes the status of being to what it takes as real.

Kant's avowed intent was the discovery of the ground upon which a rigorous metaphysics could be erected in the light of the Copernican Revolution. He pursued this goal by exploring the nature of, and the presuppositions found in, human knowledge. The characteristics necessarily possessed by any object in order for it to be within human experience were identified as those a priori constituents defining the possibility, extent and inherent operational limitations of human cognition itself. These transcendental grounds of human knowledge thus comprise the modes of being of any object insofar as it can be known. As such, they constitute the ontological determinations of any object within human experience.

Heidegger has thus accepted Kant's reduction of the whole of possible experience to its subjective grounding. Both are concerned to seek out the grounds of objective cognition within the framework provided by the transcendental enabling-and-limiting conditions of human knowledge. Both seem satisfied that this is not a new subjective idealism but an empirical realism; both presume the being of that which appears to us. As Heidegger has put it, the

---

28 W. H. Werkmeister, "An Introduction to Heidegger's 'Existential Philosophy'," *Philosophy and Phenomenological Research*, 2, no. 1, p. 83.

appearance *is* of the entity as it appears to human cognitional capabilities, the "Appearance takes place in and with [the thing that is] itself."[29]

Kant had focused, as Heidegger has seen it, on the ground for the ontological determination of the objects which appear in human knowledge. It is from this knowledge that we have obtained our knowledge of the transcendental conditions of that knowledge and of our own being as well. To talk about the nature of an object, or its being-status, to talk about ourselves as truly being, to discuss either or both meaningfully, we first have to determine just what it is that we mean by the infinitive verb 'to be' itself. This understanding is prior to any meaningful assertion that something 'is' or has an affirmative being-status. This is the *Seinsfrage,* the question of the nature of being as such. In human thought, this question is related to the nature of man's mode of knowing, man's mode of being, to the characteristics of the ways in which human finitude is manifested in any act of knowledge—just because man's finitude, and its own categorial limitations, is the essential mode of being we have.

Kant had, in facing the problem of objectivity provoked by the Copernican Revolution, tried to determine the range of the possibility and degree of unity in our knowledge of the things we encounter. In formulating his solution he postulated a dually segmented mind (intuition and pure concepts) and two strata of the real (phenomena and noumena). In Heidegger's reconstruction of the Kantian formulation he has consistently protested these bifurcations and has sought to transmute the Kantian dichotomies into a unified ground. In place of Kant's two strata of the real, in place of the two independent sources of knowledge within the knowing subject, Heidegger's aim has been the unification of man with the world as it appears to him, the unification of man's structure in order to account for the coherence of human experience. In pursuing this end, he has remained faithful to the Kantian problematic and insisted on 'pulling' all possible human experience out of any supersensible realm into the Kantian subjective ground of experience.

---

[29] M. Heidegger, *Introduction to Metaphysics,* trans. Ralph Manheim (New Haven: Yale University Press, 1959), p. 108.

From his initial insistence on the essential unity of all elements of cognition, Heidegger has shifted the direction of philosophic inquiry to the essential unity of man—to the nature of man as a totally unified and unifying being. In man's being, he is cognizing, acting and providing the possibility for the appearing of the things-that-are for him while depending on their appearing to him within his experiential horizon for the knowledge he is capable of having. From the Kantian investigation into the transcendental (ontological) grounding of finite human knowledge, Heidegger has shifted the inquiry to the transcendental (ontological) grounding of the human being in the world of his experiential possibility. The comprehension of human reason, itself, has been grounded in the necessity of an ontological investigation into the finitude of human nature as such; it is this being of human nature that finds part of its mode of expression, of its self-manifestation, in the use of that theoretical reason in the quest for knowledge which Kant had been concerned to justify and to explain.

If we are concerned with attaining a fuller comprehension of the nature of the being-characteristics of the objects we encounter, the 'appearances that appear' as real things for us, or of our own being for ourselves, Heidegger's thesis is that a further step is requisite. Implicitly, he urges that we proceed from Kant's examination of the requisites for some thing to be in our experience, as our point of departure, to what has become the consequent problematic, the meaning of the infinitive verb 'to be' itself as it is manifested in our modes of human experience.

The basic question, then, is this: 'what does it really mean to say that some thing has being, that some thing is, that some thing has the capability to be?' The pursuit of this question takes us from Kant to Heidegger, from epistemology and metaphysics to ontology; it takes us to an ontology that is rooted in the subjective structure of human knowing and being; in full recognition of the revolutionary import of the Critical edifice, it takes us from the Copernican Revolution, and by its light, to 'fundamental ontology'.

CHARLES M. SHEROVER

HUNTER COLLEGE
CITY UNIVERSITY OF NEW YORK.

KANT'S CONCEPT OF A RIGHT ACTION[1]

Introduction. For the most part, Kant's moral philosophy is no longer taught. What is taught instead is a parody of Kant's moral philosophy. His views, generally used as a foil for some other view like utilitarianism, are summed up in a few popular cliches which have achieved the status of interpretive dogma. Small wonder that undergraduates go away thinking that Kant is, at worst, a moral fanatic or, at best, a well-intentioned bungler who allowed his right-wing political views and Pietist upbringing to get in the way of his philosophical acumen.

My purpose in this essay is to oppose one of these popular interpretive dogmas: the view that, for Kant, an action has no moral worth at all unless performed from the proper motive; that Kant's conception of a right action (i.e. one demanded regardless of the agent's motive in performing it) is not moral at all but is, at most, a legal conception. I have chosen to attack this particular dogma for three main reasons: it is mistaken, it is extremely common,[2] and it is not held merely by philosophers whose acquaintance with Kant is secondhand or superficial. It is, indeed, held by no less a Kant scholar than H. J. Paton.

Right Actions. It can hardly be doubted that Kant has a philosophy of right. The best evidence for this is that he published an entire work with the title *Rechtslehre*—a work later to become part of his *Metaphysik der Sitten*. What has often been disputed, how-

---

[1] I wish to thank Professors Lewis W. Beck and Robert L. Holmes of the University of Rochester and Professor Gareth Matthews of the University of Minnesota for their helpful comments on an earlier draft of this paper. Whatever mistakes that remain are, of course, my own responsibility. For I have (no doubt to my regret) resisted their enlightenment at many points.

[2] The most recent attribution of this view to Kant that I know of occurs in H. L. A. Hart's *The Concept of Law* (Oxford: 1961, pp. 168, 252). Hart argues that morality for Kant can command only internal dispositions and that it is law that represents the sphere of externally right actions.

ever, is that he has a philosophy of *moral* right. The phrase in Kant's ethics most often translated as 'right action' is the German *eine pflichtmässige Handlung*. A more literal translation of the German is probably 'a due action'[3] or, to spell this out in more detail, 'an action in accordance with what duty demands."[4] If, for example, it is my duty to keep a promise, then in keeping the promise (for whatever reason) I have performed a *pflichtmässig* action. Kant contrasts such actions which are merely in accordance with duty with other actions which are, in addition to being in accordance with duty, done from a respect for duty. These are *pflichtvoll* actions or actions done *aus Pflicht*.[5] No one would deny that Kant takes these latter actions to be indisputably moral. What is a legitimate question, however, is whether or not he holds that the former kind of actions (actions merely *pflichtmässig*) are morally significant. The general interpretive consensus is that he does not. They simply represent the sphere of Law, and are indeed to be placed in striking contrast to actions in the sphere of Morality.

Now I believe that this interpretation of Kant is completely incorrect—that it arises from Kant's own carelessness in terminology and his perversity in not telling his reader what he is up to. Before arguing for this, however, I shall first consider in this section the question of what Kant means by a right action. I shall then, in the closing section of the essay, debate the issue of whether Kant takes the concept of a right action to be a moral concept.

It is essential that Kant have some notion of a right or due action independent of the agent's motive in performing the action. For Kant makes it a necessary and sufficient condition of a morally good will that it is a will which acts in accordance with duty for the sake of duty.[6] Indeed, Paton goes so far as to claim that the

---

[3] This translation is recommended by H. J. Paton, *The Categorical Imperative* (London: Hutchinson, 1963), p. 117, hereinafter cited as CI.

[4] Kant seldom bothers to keep clear the distinction between right actions, obligatory actions, and duties. For purposes of this discussion, we may regard 'right' as a generic term including all morally permissible actions.

[5] For a general discussion of this terminology, see Paton, CI, pp. 116 ff.

[6] *Grundlegung*, 390 and 397 ff. (Beck, 6 and 15 ff.). All references to Kant's works are to the edition issued by the Royal Prussian Academy in Berlin. In quoting from these works, I have placed the page number from the Academy

universal ethical command for Kant is "Act in accordance with duty for the sake of duty."[7] From this it is obvious that he must be able to give some sense to 'right' and 'duty' independent of motives or the good will. For unless 'duty' is independently describable, the rider 'for the sake of duty' will simply be redundant. Kant quite obviously thinks that it is *possible* to act in accordance with duty from an improper motive. Otherwise he would not so belabor the point that we *ought* to perform these acts from the motive of respect for duty. Thus it is imperative that Kant have some notion of objective rightness or duty (whether moral or not) if this is to determine the will and make for a morally valuable total action. Fortunately, he does have such a notion.

Even in Kant's precritical period, his writings on ethics reveal a desire to distinguish between the morality of actions and the morality of motives. In the *Lectures* of 1780, for example, he claims that

> We must distinguish between measuringrod and mainspring. The measuringrod is the principle of discrimination; the mainspring is the principle of the performance of our obligation. Confusion between these has led to complete falsity in the sphere of ethics. If we ask, "What is morally good and what is not?" it is the principle of discrimination which is in question, in terms of which I decide the goodness of the action. But if we ask, "What is it that moves

---

edition immediately following the title citation. This is followed by a set of parentheses containing the page numbers of the translation upon which I have relied for the quoted material. There are two exceptions to this general procedure. In quoting from the *Kritik der reinen Vernunft*, I follow the standard practice of citing the page numbers of both the first ("A") and second ("B") editions of that work. Also, in quoting from the *Vorlesung Kants über Ethik*, I have relied exclusively on the English translation by Louis Infield and all page references are to this translation. The volumes of the Academy edition which contain the works cited are as follows: *Grundlegung zur Metaphysik der Sitten*, Volume IV (trans. L. W. Beck (New York: Library of Liberal Arts, 1950); *Kritik der reinen Vernunft*, Volume III, trans. Norman Kemp Smith (London: St. Martin's Press, 1963) *Metaphysik der Sitten*, Volume VI, Part I, *Rechtslehre*, trans. W. Hastie (Edinburgh: T. Clark, 1887); Part II, *Tugendlehre*, trans. Mary Gregor (New York: Harper Torchbooks, 1964); *Religion innerhalb der Grenzen der blossen Vernunft*, Volume VI, trans. T. M. Greene and H. H. Hudson (La Salle, Illinois: Open Court, 1934, and New York: Harper Torchbooks, 1960). Infield's translation of *Lectures on Ethics* was published by Harper Torchbooks in 1963.

[7] CI, p. 117.

me to act in accordance with the laws of morality?" we have a question which concerns the principle of motive.[8]

Here, then, we have a foreshadowing of the distinction between *pflichtmässig* and *pflichtvoll*—between the objective rightness of the action and the moral motive which prompts the agent to do it because it is right. And, in the *Reflexionen*, we get the following distinction between a right action and a good action:

> What agrees with the private will is agreeable; a universally valid will is good. What contains the conditions through which it becomes possible that a will can agree with the others, is right; that by which it actually agrees is good.[9]

In some preanalytic sense, then, we can say that a right action is an action in accordance with what a given situation objectively requires—as the making of a promise requires the keeping of the promise. The morally good action, on the other hand, is the right action performed *because* it is the right action—I keep my promise because I respect the moral law that one always ought to keep one's promises. So far, then, we have at least this much: Kant requires that in moral evaluation we separate the question of *what* the agent did from the question of *why* the agent did it. We can at this point grant significance to such phrases as "doing the right thing for the wrong reason."

Unfortunately, it is here that our difficulties really begin. What sense are we to give to the phrase 'doing the right thing' independent of reason or motive? We begin to lament the absence in Kant of any carefully worked out philosophy of human action.[10] The notion of *doing* something is not nearly so clear as Kant often seems to have supposed, for it is by no means always clear how much we are to build into a given description of *the* action performed by an agent.[11] Sometimes it seems that reason or motive

---

8 *Lectures on Ethics*, p. 36.

9 Quoted by P. A. Schilpp in his *Kant's Pre-Critical Ethics* (Evanston: Northwestern University Press, 1960), p. 125.

10 See Paton CI, pp. 32 f. for a discussion of the weaknesses left in Kant's ethical theory because of the lack of any detailed philosophy of action.

11 Indeed, R. M. Hare thinks that it is so difficult to draw a line between motives, actions, and consequences that the traditional distinction between teleological and deontological ethical theories ought to be abandoned (*Language of Morals*, 1961, pp. 56 ff. and *Freedom and Reason*, 1963, p. 124, both from Oxford at the

or intention must form a part of the description of the agent's action. In the law, for example, the presence of a *mens rea* ('guilty mind') in an agent is often a deciding consideration in determining whether a particular homicide should be described as an act of murder. We simply cannot always draw sharp lines and come up with the simple trichotomy of motive-action-results. Nor do I imagine that Kant really thought that we could. But his refusal to give any detailed treatment to action as such leaves us in a bit of a quandary as to what he actually did think on the issue.[12]

The only help we find in Kant relevant to resolving the many problems involved in describing or characterizing human actions is in his doctrine of maxims. Though this doctrine is presented in an incredibly muddled and ambiguous fashion, the insights it contains are of sufficient worth to reward the trouble required to sort them out. What I intend to argue is that Kant uses the term 'maxim' to mean at least two distinct things. Failure to keep the two different meanings separate (as Kant himself often failed to keep them separate) can lead only to hopeless confusion with regard to the fundamental teachings of Kant's ethical theory.

Now 'maxim', as Kant uses the term, can mean either of the following:

(i) $maxim_1$ equals by definition *the principle of the agent's action—i.e. the type of action of which the agent's particular action is an instance;*

(ii) $maxim_2$ equals by definition *the principle of the agent's action plus his motive in performing the action.*

'To neglect natural talents' would be an example of a $maxim_1$. 'To neglect natural talents from laziness' would be an example of

---

Clarendon Press). I am inclined to think that Hare overestimates the difficulties. For though we may lack an adequate *analysis* which will provide a procedure for drawing the motive-action distinction in all cases, we can still all *recognize* particular cases where the distinction is involved. When attending to a performance of Eliot's *Murder in the Cathedral*, for example, we all understand Beckett's worry that he might "do the right thing for the wrong reason."

12 Kant's omission of a philosophy of action is not carelessness, but is intentional. See *Grundlegung*, 390 (Beck, 6).

a maxim$_2$. In the following paragraphs, I shall discuss each of these two senses of 'maxim' in more detail.[13]

When Kant defines 'maxim' in his *Metaphysik der Sitten*, it is fairly clear that he is using the term 'maxim' in the sense of maxim$_2$ above. For he defines it as follows: "The rule that the agent himself makes his principle on subjective grounds is called his *maxim*. Thus different men can have quite different maxims with regard to the same law."[14] The crucial phrase here is 'on subjective grounds'. The maxim$_2$ includes not only the principle (what I have called the maxim$_1$) but also the grounds of its adoption. Kant gives us an illustration of such a maxim$_2$ in the *Grundlegung*.

> A man who is reduced to despair by a series of evils feels a weariness with life but is still in possession of his reason sufficiently to ask whether it would not be contrary to his duty to himself to take his own life. Now he asks whether the maxim of his action could become a universal law of nature. His maxim, however, is: *For love of myself*, I make it my principle to shorten my life when by a longer duration it threatens more evil than satisfaction.[15]

Kant here clearly includes the agent's reason or motive (self-love) in his statement of the maxim, and thus we have an instance of a maxim$_2$. Many commentators take this to be Kant's fundamental (or even only) sense of the term 'maxim',[16] but I shall argue that this interpretation is incorrect.

To present a man's maxim$_2$, then, is to answer the question 'What did he do and why did he do it?' Thus the same human action could have had many different maxims$_2$. This is not the case with a maxim$_1$, however, for a maxim$_1$ defines the very character of the action itself. For it answers merely the question 'What did the agent do?' with no regard to the agent's motive in

---

13 For a detailed treatment of maxims, rules and principles in the Kantian ethical philosophy, see L. W. Beck's *A Commentary on Kant's Critique of Practical Reason* (Chicago: University of Chicago Press, 1960), Chapter VI.

14 *Metaphysik der Sitten*, 224 (Gregor, 24).

15 *Grundlegung*, 421-422 (Beck, 39-40), italics my own.

16 "My maxim, as it were, generalizes my action, including my motive. My maxim is the principle which is in fact the determining ground for my action," Paton, CI, p. 60

doing it.[17] Kant's example of such a maxim$_1$ in the *Grundlegung* is the following:

> A man finds in himself a talent which could, by means of some cultivation, make him in many respects a useful man. But he finds himself in comfortable circumstances and prefers indulgence in pleasure to troubling himself with broadening and improving his fortunate natural gifts. Now, however, let him ask whether his maxim of *neglecting his gifts,* besides agreeing with his propensity to idle amusement, agrees also with what is called duty.[18]

Here, in a maxim$_1$, no reference is made to motivational considerations. The maxim simply describes a proposed course of action (neglect of talents) and Kant's question is whether such a course of action could be regarded as a duty.

Though all of this may appear like idle hairsplitting, it is nonetheless central to my interpretation of Kant's philosophy of right. For I want to suggest that Kant has two possible answers to the question 'What was Jones' action?' depending upon in what sense we intend to judge its moral worth. If we are interested in judging whether or not the action was right, we are concerned only with its maxim$_1$. We want to know, in effect, of what type of action it was an instance. Thus, if we are seeking to determine the rightness of action X, we need only be told that it was (for example) an instance of 'the keeping of a promise'. Here we take no account of the agent's worth in judging the worth of the action. We may hold the agent responsible for the action independently of his worth in performing it. This, for Kant, is holding the agent *legally* responsible.[19] However, if we are interested in the worth of the agent in addition to the rightness or wrongness of the action, our

---

17 But questions of intention are relevant. If the agent's 'action' was performed completely unintentionally, then we should be hesitant to describe his behavior as a human action at all. A possible exception to this would be a case where the agent's unintentionally performing a given 'action' occurred in a situation where a reasonable man is expected to pay attention to what he is doing. It is by the doctrine of what the 'reasonable man' can be expected to do that law is able to give sense to the phrase 'act of negligence'. See H. L. A. Hart's "Negligence, *Mens Rea* and Criminal Responsibility" in *Oxford Essays in Jurisprudence,* ed. A. G. Guest (New York: Oxford University Press, 1961).

18 *Grundlegung*, 422 (Beck, 40), italics my own.

19 *Lectures on Ethics*, p. 58.

answer to the question 'What was his action?' must include, not only *what* he did, but *why* he did it—a maxim$_2$. We all, for example, generally agree that the killing of one's wife is a wrong action. But we also judge less harshly the man who does it to end her suffering from cancer than we do the man who does it to collect the insurance. I have made this brief digression so that the reader will see the point of what I am doing in this section of the essay. I shall return to these issues in detail in the final section of the essay. At present, however, I want to show how confusion between maxims$_1$ and maxims$_2$ can generate utter chaos at crucial points in Kant's argument.

There is probably no more famous passage in Kant's philosophy than the statement of the first formulation of the Categorical Imperative: "Act only according to that maxim by which you can at the same time will that it should become a universal law."[20] This is a critical principle which forms the very foundation of law and morals. But, unfortunately, the presence of the term 'maxim' in this principle introduces ambiguity at the very core of Kant's ethics. Does he man maxim$_1$ or maxim$_2$? I shall argue that he must mean maxim$_1$ if his doctrine is not to be utterly absurd.

We can see this by considering Kant's application of the first formulation of the Categorical Imperative in determining perfect duties to oneself. We consider the case of a man contemplating suicide. We have already noted what Kant takes to be the maxim of the proposed action: "His *maxim* . . . is: For love of myself, I make it my *principle* to shorten my life when by a longer duration it threatens more evil than satisfaction."[21] In distinguishing between 'maxim' and 'principle' in this statement, Kant is making the distinction I have called a distinction between maxims$_1$ and maxims$_2$. The 'principle' in this statement is a maxim$_1$. It is a type description of the proposed course of action—i.e. a case of suicide. 'Maxim' in this statement is a maxim$_2$, for it rationally connects an incentive (self-love) to the maxim$_1$ or 'principle'. Thus Kant is operating here with both concepts of 'maxim'.

However, in working with these concepts, Kant gets himself into a great deal of confusion. For, as Jonathan Harrison has

---

20 *Grundlegung*, 421 (Beck, 39).

21 *Grundlegung*, 422 (Beck, 39-40), italics my own.

pointed out,[22] the reference to self-love is totally out of place in terms of what Kant is trying to show in this example. What he seeks to show, as revealed in numerous other passages, is that no system of nature could obtain in which suicide were universally practiced—*whatever the reason for committing suicide*.[23] The relevant question is always 'Could a system of nature obtain in which X were universally practiced?' Thus Kant's famous dictum should read 'Act only according to that maxim$_1$ by which you can at the same time will that it should become a universal law'.

Indeed, to suggest that maxim$_2$ is meant here is to suggest an absurdity. We can see this by supposing that someone offered me the following command: 'Perform action X for reason Y'. I could not possibly carry out this command. For if I am *commanded* to do X for reason Y, then surely I am commanded *both* to do X *and* to have reason Y. Otherwise the rider 'for reason Y' would be superfluous. But (and this is the crucial point) it makes no sense to command me to have a certain reason or motive. The command could not possibly influence my future conduct, for the simple reason that it is not within my power to *decide* what reasons will move me, to *choose* my motives. Prior to action it makes sense to try to decide what course of action I am going to follow, and the Categorical Imperative could aid me in determining whether or not my proposed course of action (on the basis of its maxim$_1$) is morally permissible. However, it makes no sense, prior to action, to *decide*, not only what I am going to do, but *why* I am going to do it. Were someone to say to me "Decide not only whether or not you are going to kill your wife but decide also why you are going to do it—whether for the insurance or because she is ill" I would not know what to make of this command. I cannot contemplate the act of 'having a reason' because having a reason is not a human action at all. I do, of course, have my reasons in acting. But I cannot decide prior to action which one will move me. Yet if

---

[22] "Kant's Examples of the First Formulation of the Categorical Imperative," *Philosophical Quarterly*, 7, 1957, p. 53. Harrison states: "The phrase 'from self love I make it my principle' has nothing to do with my maxim, but only with the motives which cause me to adopt the maxim."

[23] See, for example, *Lectures on Ethics* (pp. 152-153) where Kant argues that Cato's suicide, though performed from a noble motive, was still a wrong action.

'maxim' in the Categorical Imperative is interpreted as $maxim_2$, such a decision is precisely what would be demanded of me. Thus I should like to suggest the following: When Kant speaks of the Categorical Imperative as a test for maxims, his word 'maxim' should be read as $maxim_1$ in the sense I have outlined above. If this is not the way Kant always used the term in fact, it is the way he should have used it—at least when attempting to apply the Categorical Imperative.

I should now like to pass to a detailed characterization of what, for Kant, constitutes a right action. Unfortunately, however, there is one hurdle which must be overcome before I can proceed to this. For I have reached a point that no student of Kant can enjoy— a fundamental disagreement with H. J. Paton. Paton believes that the Categorical Imperative commands, according to Kant, not only that we adopt certain $maxims_1$ but also that we adopt certain $maxims_2$. He believes that Kant's fundamental ethical command reduces to 'Do your duty because it is your duty.' It commands the adoption of certain motives or reasons for action in addition to the actions themselves.[24] I shall thus present Paton's arguments and attempt to counter them.

Paton has three reasons for believing that Kant's universal ethical command should be interpreted in this way. These are the following:

  (i) Kant himself expressly interprets it in this way in his *Metaphysik der Sitten*.
  (ii) There is no absurdity in being commanded to adopt a certain motive.
  (iii) If we have no duty to act morally (i.e. a duty to do the right thing for the right reason), then there is no point in making moral judgments.

I shall now consider each of these in more detail.

  (i) The passage upon which Paton bases his view occurs in the introduction to the *Tugendlehre* in the *Metaphysik der Sitten*. It is the following:

Another can demand by right that my actions conform with the law, but not that the law can be also a motive for my actions. The

---

24 Paton's argument occurs in his CI, pp. 116-119. See also L. W. Beck's *Studies in the Philosophy of Kant*, pp. 23 and 192 ff.

same holds true for the *universal ethical command: do your duty from the motive of duty.* To establish and quicken this attitude in oneself is, again, meritorious; for it goes beyond the law of duty for actions and makes the law in itself the motive also.[25]

Paton quotes only the section I have italicized,[26] but I have included the surrounding material also.

I have two comments on this passage. First, it is unique in Kant's writings on ethics. No formulation of the Categorical Imperative includes a command to have the motive of duty, and it is only in the *Tugendlehre* that the supreme command is expressed in this way. Its presence in the *Tugendlehre* should thus come as a shock to Kant's readers—not to be calmly accepted as a statement of his true doctrine all along. Second, the passage itself is not so clear in intent as Paton seems to suppose. For the sentence immediately following the command *Handle pflichtmässig aus Pflicht* describes such action as "meritorious." And Kant expressly uses the word 'meritorious' *(verdienstlich)* to characterize those actions which are *beyond* what duty demands.[27] Thus I think we should be at least sceptical about basing any very strong interpretations on this passage alone. What seems to me most plausible is that Kant's interest in the doing of duty from the motive of duty is a part, not of his philosophy of right, but of his attempt to characterize the sphere of personal virtue. I shall, however, delay any further consideration of the meaning of this textual passage until the final section of the paper where I shall explore Kant's distinction between *Tugend* and *Recht.* I mention it here simply to suggest that its meaning and importance are not obviously as Paton conceives them.

(ii) Paton attempts to defend Kant's holding of the view that the supreme ethical command demands that we act from a certain reason or motive by considering the kind of objection I raised above. This objection, briefly stated, runs as follows: It cannot be our duty to act on certain motives or for certain reasons, for we cannot summon up reasons or motives at will. Thus the com-

---

[25] *Metaphysik der Sitten,* 391 (Gregor, 50).

[26] CI, p. 117.

[27] *Metaphysik der Sitten,* 226 (Gregor, 27).

mand 'One ought to act from a motive of duty' violates Kant's famous principle that 'ought' implies 'can'. To this sort of objection, Paton offers the following reply:

> On this view motives are regarded as feelings, and it is true that we cannot summon up feelings of benevolence or affection, which are sometimes regarded as moral motives. Kant himself (in so far as he takes a motive to be a feeling) regards the feeling of reverence as the only moral motive in man, but for him it is a necessary emotional accompaniment or consequence of my recognition of duty. Hence it does not need to be "summoned up"; if it were absent, I should recognize no duties, and I should be neither moral nor immoral, a mere animal and not a man. As he himself says of moral feeling, "no man is wholly destitute of moral feeling; for if he were totally unsusceptible to this sensation, he would be morally dead."[28]

Now this fails miserably as an answer to the kind of argument I am making. For it embodies three distinct confusions. First, it is not because the moral motive is interpreted as a feeling that it is absurd to command that we act from it. The absurdity holds even if we take the moral motive to be a reason. Motivating reasons are not in my power to summon up at will any more than feelings are.

Second, if Paton's answer proves anything, it proves too much. For if the feeling of reverence is, as Paton claims, a *necessary* emotional accompaniment of my recognition of duty, then having it cannot be a duty for the same reason that seeking my happiness cannot be a duty. According to Kant, anything we must necessarily do cannot be our duty to do.[29] If 'ought' implies 'can', it also implies 'might not'.[30]

Third, Paton confuses two separate issues or claims in Kant's ethical theory—namely, claims about what is valuable and claims about what we are obligated to do. It may very well be the case

---

28 CI, pp. 117-118.

29 *Metaphysik der Sitten,* 385 (Gregor, 44).

30 Paton's answer also proves too much in another way. If a feeling of reverence is a necessary accompaniment of my recognition of duty, then no *pflichtmässig* action (provided the agent knew it was a *pflichtmässig* action) could ever be performed solely from inclination. Yet I see no reason to believe that this is so or that Kant thought it was so.

that a man who does his duty because it is his duty has a character which is more *valuable* than that of the man who does his duty because it happens to coincide with his self-interest. But showing this does not show that he is *obligated* to have such a character. Merely showing that X is valuable is not sufficient to show that we are under an obligation to promote or attain X.[31]

(iii) Paton's final defense of Kant rests on his belief that, unless we have a duty to act morally, particular moral duties are themselves impossible. "Our supreme duty is to act morally, and if this were not so, we should have no particular duties at all. If we cannot act for the sake of duty as such, why should we even ask what our duty is?"[32]

Paton claims that a denial of this view would be a complete paradox. Still, paradox or not, its denial represents the true account. For the very notion of duty makes sense only within a moral context. Thus, if we have a duty to act morally, this can only be because what we mean by 'acting morally' is really included as a part under some wider system of moral criticism. We can always ask 'Why ought I do X?' because we may legitimately assume that, if X is really a duty, there will be relevant moral reasons that can be brought to bear to show why it is one.[33] If it be claimed that I have a duty to act according to the demands of this wider morality, then we can see the start of an infinite regress. The notion that we have a duty to act morally is absurd in just the same way the question 'What moral reasons are there for being moral?' is absurd. For a moral reason can be relevant only for someone who is already prepared to accept moral reasons as im-

---

[31] For an elaboration of this point, see my "The Highest Good as Content for Kant's Ethical Formalism," *Kant-Studien* 56, Heft 1, 1965, pp. 102-110.

[32] CI, p. 119 and p. 118n.

[33] According to A. R. C. Duncan, Kant's great insight in ethics was in seeing that ought judgments are incorrigible. If an agent questions an ought judgment, "then the only answer that can be given which will not destroy the moral character of the situation is that he ought to do it because he ought to do it" *(Practical Reason and Morality* (London: Thomas Nelson, 1957), p. 123). Such a view is confused. If the agent's "why?" is a request for a motive, then Duncan is on the right track. If the agent is asking for a justificatory reason, however, Duncan's answer would be the answer of a moral fanatic.

portant—is already playing the moral game. Thus I do not think that Paton has managed to make his case on this particular issue.

Having clarified certain essential notions in Kant's thought, I am now in a position to state in outline Kant's philosophy of right. A right action, for Kant, is an action whose $maxim_1$ is qualified to be an objective practical law—i.e. its $maxim_1$ is universalizable in terms of the Categorical Imperative. A duty is an action whose $maxim_1$ is made practically necessary because its denial is inconsistent with the universalizability demand of the Categorical Imperative—i.e. the denial of its $maxim_1$ is not qualified to be an objective practical law. For example: Suppose that I am contemplating not paying Jones the five dollars that I owe him in circumstances which would render repayment inconvenient for me. Am I contemplating a right action? In attempting to answer this question, I must determine the $maxim_1$ or principle of the action, the general type of action of which my particular action would be an instance. No question of motive or $maxim_2$ need be raised. Upon examination, I see that the $maxim_1$ of my proposed action is the following: 'To choose personal convenience over the paying of a debt whenever these are in conflict'. If this $maxim_1$ is universalizable in terms of the Categorical Imperative, if it is qualified to be an objective practical law, then I am contemplating a right action. If the $maxim_1$ is not so qualified, I am contemplating a wrong action, one from which I have a duty to abstain. Judgments of rightness and duty, then, are judgments on the value of $maxims_1$.

At this point, it is necessary that I begin considering whether or not right actions (in Kant's sense) are of any moral significance. In doing this I shall focus upon a contrast between Kant's theory of virtue and his theory of right as expressed in the *Metaphysik der Sitten*. This contrast will aid me in showing that rightness is, for Kant, a moral concept.

Legality and Moral Right. It is unfortunate but true that Kant is often at his philosophical best when he is also at his stylistic worst. When drawing his myriad distinctions, he is almost always alert and aware of the point of what he is doing (even if he forgets it two paragraphs later). When he does occasionally indulge himself in the making of short, bald-faced assertions, however, he almost invariably misleads his reader. The reader, finding in such assertions perhaps the first immediately comprehensible remarks he has yet come across in Kant, is too apt to take these assertions as expressions of sound and complete Kantian doctrine. Consider, with this warning in mind, some of the remarks we often come across in the *Grundlegung zur Metaphysik der Sitten*.

> To be kind where one can is duty, and there are, moreover, many persons so sympathetically constituted that without any motive of vanity or selfishness they find an inner satisfaction in spreading joy, and rejoice in the contentment of others which they have made possible. But I say that, however amiable it may be, *that kind of action has no true moral worth.*
> When *moral worth* is in question, it *is not a matter of actions which one sees,* but of their inner principles which one does not see.
> Imitation has *no place* in moral matters, and examples serve only for encouragement.[34]

These are strong statements, and similar passages could be supplied to the point of utter tedium. If these statements are taken at face value, then they directly show that the notion of a right action as I have characterized it above (as an action whose maxim$_1$ is qualified to be a practical law) is not a moral concept for Kant at all. The notion of a *pflichtmässig* action, though important, is not a part of moral inquiry proper. Its only use in moral inquiry is by way of contrast to morally worthy actions—actions performed *aus Pflicht.* As Kant tells us so many times, *pflichtmässig* and *recht* are legal rather than moral notions. "For the distinction between moral and pragmatic laws is that in the former it is the disposition and in the latter the action which is required."[35]

First of all, I want to insist that this view, whether Kant held it or not, is exceptionally strange. To maintain that the keeping of a promise, or the returning of a loan, has *no* moral significance in itself does violence to the way we all ordinarily use the word 'moral' in making judgments on human conduct. When, for example, we debate the moral issues concerning the United States' political and military involvement in South Vietnam, we never ask ourselves whether or not President Johnson is motivated to do what he is doing by a sense of duty. We are interested in whether

---

[34] *Grundlegung*, 398, 407 and 409 (Beck, 14, 23 and 25), italics my own.
[35] *Lectures on Ethics*, p. 51.

or not what he is doing *as a policy* is the morally correct thing in the situation as we see it. If we believe that our policy makers are well-meaning fools, this may incline us to judge *them* less harshly —but not to judge less harshly the *actions* they are performing. Kant may, of course, be recommending a new and more restricted use for the term 'moral', but it is a use I see no grounds whatsoever to adopt. However, odd as this view is, it is offered as Kantian doctrine by no less a commentator than H. J. Paton. In his *The Categorical Imperative* he argues that

> Kant insists that the moral imperative bids us pay our debts for the sake of duty; that is, it enjoins not merely a kind of action, but the doing of this kind of action from the moral motive of duty. Indeed on his view this is what differentiates mere law—that is, State law—from morality. If we do an action of the kind enjoined but do it without the moral motive, we call it an action "done in accordance with duty" *(pflichtmässig)*. We have no precise adjective for this in English. . . . The word "right" is sometimes used for this but . . . . it is not without the suggestion of some kind of value, which ought here to be excluded.[36]

Now I am not at all happy to see such a view attributed to Kant. And, fortunately, there seem to me very good reasons for *not* attributing this view to him. Paton is here very uncritical in taking Kant's term *Recht* as essentially equivalent to 'state law'. As I shall argue, this is hasty and blurs some important distinctions in the Kantian doctrine. If the text leaves us no choice but to attribute an absurd position to Kant, then of course we must do it. However, I do not think that the text points unambiguously in that direction. Thus, in the remainder of the paper, I want to argue for the following points:

> (i) That the remarks quoted previously (claiming that actions not done from a motive of duty have no moral worth) can be matched by other passages which point the way toward an alternative interpretation. If the evidence of the *Grundlegung* is thus ambiguous on this issue, justification is given for seeking his real view elsewhere.

---

36 Pages 117 and 117n.

(ii) That the concept of law is and must be a moral concept for Kant. It is not to be read as merely equivalent to positive state law.

(i) Kant has a very bad habit of becoming overinvolved in the particular issue he is discussing to a degree that causes him to say things that *prima facie* undercut other aspects of his doctrine. Perhaps the most famous instance of this is his section on the schematism in the first *Kritik*. The purpose of this section, for which he argues intensely, is to show the reader that the Categories do apply to experience. But his zeal at this point makes the reader wonder about the purpose of the Transcendental Deduction—which was supposed to show exactly the same thing.

It seems to me at least plausible that a similar occurrence takes place in the *Grundlegung*. Here he becomes so involved in discussing one aspect of morality that he speaks as though this one aspect were all of morality and thus says things that (according to his other works) he could not possibly mean. As Duncan remarks about the *Grundlegung*, it is difficult to support any interpretation of right actions with its text

> for the very good reason that Kant has remarkably little to say about actions which are what he calls *pflichtmässig* as his main interest lies in actions which are done *aus Pflicht*, from a motive of duty, which is a very different thing.[37]

Kant is so caught up in his discussion of actions performed *aus Pflicht* that we would do well to take anything he says concerning *pflichtmässig* actions with the proverbial grain of salt. If we can find in his other writings good reasons for interpreting Kant's philosophy of right in a different and more satisfactory way, then we should not allow the *Grundlegung* to override the other texts. Indeed, there is some evidence that Kant's very conception of morality changed radically from the *Grundlegung* to the *Metaphysik der Sitten*, and the latter work should get at least an equal hearing with the earlier.[38]

---

37 *Practical Reason and Morality*, p. 10.

38 At the writing of the *Grundlegung*, Kant did not intend to include a discussion of jurisprudence in his *Metaphysik der Sitten*. See H. J. de Vleeschauwer's *La Deduction transcendentale dans l'oeuvre de Kant* (Antwerpen, 1934-1937), Tome troisième, p. 560.

Now the *Grundlegung* seems to me almost totally taken up by what I will call Kant's theory of personal virtue.[39] By this, I mean his theory of what counts as a morally good man. His leading interest is in the moral character or disposition that makes a man worthy to be happy. And, he quite rightly reminds his reader that a man's worth of character is not necessarily a direct function of the actions he actually performs. He provides the Categorical Imperative as a criterion for the rightness of actions and then points out that one may act on maxims$_1$ sanctioned by this criterion and still be a villain. His primary goal, especially in the earlier sections, is to present a characterization or definition of the morally worthy man. And this man is, according to Kant, not one who merely performs right actions but one who performs these actions because he knows that he ought to perform them. Kant is, in other words, giving us a philosophy not primarily of moral action, but of the moral disposition. Consider the following passages:

> The metaphysics of morals is meant to investigate the idea and principle of a possible pure will and not the actions and conditions of the human volition as such.
> The good will seems to constitute the indispensible condition even of worthiness to be happy.
> The good will is not good because of what it accomplishes or because of its adequacy to achieve some proposed end; it is good only because of its willing, i.e., it is good in itself.
> If nature has put little sympathy in the heart of a man, and if he, though an honest man, is by temperament cold and indifferent to the sufferings of others, perhaps because he is provided with special gifts of patience and fortitude, ... would he not find in himself a source from which *to give himself far higher worth* than he would have got by having a good-natured temperament? This is unquestionably true even though nature did not make him philanthropic, for it is just here that the *worth of character* is brought out, which is morally and incomparably the highest of all: he is beneficient not from inclination but from duty.[40]

---

[39] I use the term 'virtue' in what I take to be its more or less ordinary philosophical usage here. *Tugend* is a technical term for Kant, but a complete explication of its technical usage need not detain us at present.

[40] *Grundlegung,* 390, 393, 394 and 398-399 (Beck, 7, 9, 10 and 14-15), italics my own.

Such passages can be supplied in volume from Kant's other writings, particularly the *Lectures on Ethics*.[41]

We have, then, two sorts of passages to consider. Some passages assert that *actions* have no moral worth unless performed from the proper motive. Other passages assert that *agents* have no moral worth unless they act from a good motive. Which are we to take as the true Kantian doctrine? My own view is that since the former position is ethically untenable, we should not pin it on Kant unless the text forces us to do so. If the passages I have quoted just above do show (as I think they do) that one of Kant's primary interests in the *Grundlegung* was a description of virtuous character or the good will, then there are at least some grounds for the view that when Kant slips from talking about good character to talking about good actions he is simply being careless.

It seems to me that Kant's great mistake in the *Grundlegung* is that he makes dozens of complicated distinctions without first making a few elementary ones. If he had distinguished between his theory of virtue and his theory of right (as he does elsewhere[42]) and had distinguished between his theory of the good action and his theory of the right action (as he almost does elsewhere[43]), much confusion would have been avoided. Kant is positively perverse in his refusal to let us know precisely what he is up to. The *Grundlegung* will no doubt remain Kant's most widely read work, but I strongly suspect that we will never be absolutely sure as to what Kant himself took the purpose of that work to be.[44] All I want to suggest at this point is that there is some evidence that the passages upon which Paton depends are more suspect than he realizes. If we are going to pick passages from the *Grundlegung* to rep-

---

[41] See *Lectures on Ethics*, pages 34-36, 42, 51 and 69. See also *Religion innerhalb der Grenzen der blossen Vernunft*, 66-67 (Greene and Hudson, 60-61).

[42] *Metaphysik der Sitten*. See (ii) below.

[43] See note 9.

[44] See, for example, the recent debate between Duncan and Paton. Duncan argues that the *Grundlegung* is not a work in ethics at all but a brief critique of practical reason (*Practical Reason and Morality* (Edinburgh: 1957)). H. J. Paton takes issue with Duncan's views in his "The Aim and Structure of Kant's *Grundlegung*" (*Philosopical Quarterly*, 8, 1958, pp. 112-130). Until we can determine what Kant is trying to do, it would be well to suspend judgment about whether or not he has done it.

resent Kant's ethical theory, we might as well give him the benefit of the doubt and pick one like the following:

> We have then to develop the concept of a will which is to be esteemed as good in itself without regard to anything else. In the estimation of the *total worth* of our actions it always takes first place and is the condition of everything else.[45]

This sounds like at least a plausible doctrine. To say that an action has *more* moral worth if performed for the proper reason is not to say that the action, if not so performed, has *no* moral worth. Only this latter seems to me an untenable position.

My purpose thus far has been to show that the text of the *Grundlegung* is sufficiently ambiguous that we are not immediately compelled to accept Paton's interpretation that an action, to have moral worth, must be performed from a moral motive. I now want to show something stronger: that *pflichtmässig* actions are, for Kant, indisputably moral. I shall do this by developing some of the doctrines in Kant's *Metaphysik der Sitten*. In this work, we can see many of the terminological confusions of the *Grundlegung* ironed out. And, with these no longer around to bother us, we can see his real philosophy of right in a much clearer light.

(ii) In his *Metaphysik der Sitten,* Kant makes a very useful distinction between *Ethik,* on the one hand, and *Sitten* or *Moralität* on the other—between 'ethics' and 'morality'. Kant was forced to draw this distinction because, as he constantly laments, the German language does not, in its terms for morally relevant concepts, always draw the sorts of distinctions that might prove useful to the philosopher.

> The idea of virtue hardly suffices to express the nature of moral goodness. Virtue signifies strength in self-control and self-mastery in respect of the moral disposition. . . . The words *Sitten* and *Sittlichkeit* have been used to express the idea of morality. *Sitten,* however, is a comprehensive term for the proprieties. . . . A science of social ethics *(Sitten)* is not yet a theory of virtue; and virtue in turn is not yet morality. But because we have no other word to express the nature of morality, we confuse morality and social propriety *(Sittlichkeit);* virtue we cannot so substitute for morality.[46]

---

45 *Grundlegung,* 396-397 (Beck, 13) , italics my own.

46 *Lectures on Ethics,* p. 73.

It is thus necessary that the philosopher modify ordinary language somewhat and form some terminological distinctions of a technical nature. Kant does this in the *Metaphysik der Sitten*.

> In ancient times *"ethics"* meant *moral philosophy (philosophia moralis)* in general, which was also called the *doctrine of duties*. Later on it seemed better to reserve the name "ethics" for one part of moral philosophy, for the doctrine of those duties that do not come under external laws (in German, the name *doctrine of virtue* was thought appropriate for this). Accordingly the system of the doctrine of duties in general is now divided into the system of the *doctrine of law (ius)*, which deals with duties that can be enjoined by external laws, and the system of the *doctrine of virtue (ethica)*, which treats of duties that cannot be so prescribed; and this division may stand.[47]

Kant thus approves this usage to serve as his technical language in the *Metaphysik der Sitten*. The relevant distinction here for my purposes is that between 'morality' and 'ethics'. It is sufficient to show that an action has moral worth if it can be shown that, as an external performance, it satisfies the objective moral demands of a given situation. An action has ethical worth if, in addition to satisfying the demands of the situation, it is performed from the proper motive. Thus merely juridical actions have moral, but not ethical, worth.

With this distinction in mind, we can now make sense of some of the problematical passages in the *Grundlegung*—where the word 'moral' is *not* used as a technical term. When Kant says that actions which are merely *pflichtmässig* have no moral worth, I submit that what he means is that they have no *ethical* worth—i.e. they tell us nothing about the inner principle or motive of the agent, nothing about his personal virtue. *Pflichtmässig* actions are determined solely with reference to maxims$_1$, and we must know something about the agent's maxims$_2$ before we are justified in having an opinion about *his* moral worth. For, as Kant remarks, "ethics does not give laws for actions but only for the maxims of actions."[48] In spelling this out, it is pretty clear that by 'maxim' here he means maxim$_2$. For in addition to demanding that our

---

[47] *Metaphysik der Sitten*, 378 (Gregor, 36).

[48] *Metaphysik der Sitten*, 387 (Gregor, 48).

contemplated action have a maxim$_1$ which conforms to the conditions of universalizability, ethics (as part but not all of morality) further demands "that this principle is to be conceived as the law of *your own will* and not of will in general."[49]

The province of ethics, then, is one part of morality as a whole. It is that aspect of morality which is relevant to determining the moral character of a man—one who does not follow the demands of morality of necessity but who, if he is virtuous in character, can overcome the obstacles of inclination and do what he ought because he ought. God, for example, can never act ethically or with virtue, for He is never tempted to do what He ought not do. This is not to say, however, that His actions are not moral at all. "For finite holy beings (who can never be tempted to transgress duty) there is no doctrine of virtue but merely a doctrine of morality."[50] Ethics, or the doctrine of virtue, evaluates a man on the basis of his maxims$_2$—his doing of what he ought because (if he is virtuous) he ought. Morality, on the other hand, is broader and includes actions whose moral rightness is independent of motivation. In the *Kritik der reinen Vernunft*, Kant defines 'morality' as follows: "Morality is the only code of laws applying to our action which can be derived completely *a priori* from principles."[51]

Morality thus does include *pflichtmässig* actions, for they are completely derivable from a priori principles. Both juridical laws (laws determining *pflichtmässig* actions) and ethical laws are derivable from the Categorical Imperative,[52] and it should thus come as no surprise that a doctrine of law (a doctrine of *pflichtmässig* actions) should be included in a metaphysics of morals. What is surprising is that Kant seems to have forgotten this in the *Grundlegung*. Morality includes all laws of freedom, and thus *pflichtmässig* actions and actions performed *aus Pflicht* are moral in this sense. They differ only in that *pflichtmässig* actions may be executed and enforced externally whereas actions performed *aus*

---

49 *Metaphysik der Sitten*, 388 (Gregor, 48).

50 *Metaphysik der Sitten*, 382 (Gregor, 41).

51 A 841, B 869 (Kemp Smith, 659).

52 *Metaphysik der Sitten*, 217-221 (Gregor, 16-20).

Pflicht may not.[53] We may compel a man to do something, but we cannot compel him to do it from a certain motive.

> Laws of freedom (as distinguished from laws of nature) are called *moral*. In so far as they have to do only with mere external actions and their lawfulness they are called *juridical* laws; but if they also require that they themselves (the laws) be the ground determining choice to actions, then they are *ethical* laws.[54]

With this evidence from the *Metaphysik der Sitten,* I think that we can be fairly certain that Kant's remarks in the *Grundlegung* that *pflichtmässig* actions have *no* moral worth are simply careless and not representative of his mature doctrine. Such actions are not necessarily virtuous or ethical, but moral they indisputably are.

This point can, I think, be made most forcefully by a *reductio ad absurdum.* If Paton were correct in his interpretation, if *pflichtmässig* actions had no moral worth but were only "actions in accordance with mere state law," then Kant's supreme ethical command *(Handle pflichtmässig aus Pflicht)* would reduce to the following:

> *Do your duty from a motive of duty* equals by definition *Do what state law commands because state law commands it*

Now this is certainly an unenlightened view—worthy of not even the worst of thinkers, much less of a philosopher who is supposed to have been the finest of his age. If Kant really held such a view, he would simply be the absurd old Prussian that he is all too often parodied to be. Paton clearly does not want to interpret Kant in this way, and such an interpretation would not be worthy of

---

[53] Kant often speaks as though, if virtuous, we can compel *ourselves* to perform actions *aus Pflicht.* I have already argued that this position is indefensible.

[54] *Metaphysik der Sitten,* 213 (Gregor, 11). Hart, in his *The Concept of Law* (Oxford: 1961), pp. 168, 252, argues that morality for Kant can command only internal dispositions and that it is law which represents the sphere of externally right actions. But passages like this one from the *Metaphysik der Sitten* should put an end to such interpretation. Kant does not say that law and ethics cannot command similar courses of action, only that ethics also demands something in addition to law. See also *Metaphysik der Sitten,* 219 (Gregor, 18).

him. But he has failed to see that such a view is the consequence of interpreting *pflichtmässig* in the way he does.[55]

We can see that Kant does not come near holding such a conservative view by considering his discussion of conflicts between moral laws and state laws. In these discussions, we see clearly that *Recht* (as he uses that term in the *Metaphysik der Sitten*) is for him a moral concept. Indeed, it can be argued with great cogency that Kant is an exponent of natural law theory in jurisprudence— i.e. the view that state laws are dependent for their validity on being in accordance with moral laws for the objective right.[56]

> All positive laws are conditioned by the natural law, and they cannot, therefore, rightly contain anything which conflicts with it.[57]

> Obligatory laws that can be given in outer legislation are called *external* laws *(leges externae)* in general. If their power to obligate can be recognized *a priori* by reason, even apart from outer legislation, they are *natural* external laws. But if actual outer legislation is needed to make them obligatory (and so make them laws), they are called *positive* laws. We can therefore conceive an outer legislation which would contain only positive laws; but this would still presuppose a natural law establishing the authority of the legislator.[58]

From these remarks, it can easily be seen that it is a gross distortion to pin upon Kant the simple-minded view that *pflichtmässig* actions are simply actions in accord with state law. His views on the relationship between law and morals are a bit more sophisticated than that.

Conclusion. There are, of course, many interesting issues that could be raised in connection with Kant's philosophy of law. However, I think that I have now shown enough to make the case that I set for myself—namely, to show that Kant has a philosophy of moral right and to give a general characterization to that philosophy. My conclusions may be summarized as follows: (i) By *pflicht-*

---

[55] It may be objected that I am making to much of Paton's brief treatment of *pflichtmässig*. However, part of what I am trying to show is that this doctrine is central to Kant and is not to be passed over briefly in a few sentences.

[56] See Roger Hancock's "Kant and the Natural Right Theory," *Kant-Studien,* 52, 1960-61, pp. 440-447.

[57] *Lectures on Ethics,* p. 133.

[58] *Metaphysik der Sitten,* 223 (Gregor, 23-24) .

mässig or 'right' action, Kant means an action whose maxim$_1$ is qualified to be an objective practical law. This notion is moral, but is not ethical in the technical sense outlined in the *Metaphysik der Sitten*. (ii) By calling *pflichtmässig* actions 'legal' in character, Kant does not mean that they are merely in accord with state law. Rather he means that they accord with a possible objective practical law or natural law. His frequent contrast between legality and morality is really a contrast between legality and ethics—both of which fall under morality. Thus I hope to have laid rest to a popular but thoroughly mistaken interpretive cliche—that, for Kant, an action has no moral worth unless performed from the proper motive. This view is not only ethically untenable, but is untenable as an interpretation of Kant.

JEFFRIE G. MURPHY

UNIVERSITY OF ARIZONA

INDEX

INDEX